THINK
PSYCHOLOGY
Second Canadian Edition

THINK
PSYCHOLOGY
Second Canadian Edition

Abigail A. Baird
Vassar College

Anjanie McCarthy
Fanshawe College

PEARSON

Toronto

Vice-President, Editorial Director: Gary Bennett
Editor-in-Chief: Michelle Sartor
Acquisitions Editor: Matthew Christian
Marketing Manager: Lisa Gillis
Supervising Developmental Editor: Maurice Esses
Developmental Editor: Cindy Miller, Element LLC
Project Manager: Ashley Patterson
Production Editor: Kelly Keeler, Element LLC
Copy Editor: Kathy Pruno
Proofreader: Deborah Cooper-Bullock
Compositor: Element LLC
Permissions Researcher: Christina Beamish
Photo Researcher: Terri Rothman
Art Director: Julia Hall
Cover Designer: Anthony Leung
Cover Image: Ferran Traite Soler/GettyImages

Library and Archives Canada Cataloguing in Publication

Baird, Abigail A.
   Think psychology / Abigail A. Baird, Anjanie McCarthy.—2nd Canadian ed.

Includes bibliographical references and index.
ISBN 978-0-13-282590-0

   1. Psychology—Textbooks. I. McCarthy, Anjanie, 1976– II. Title.

BF75.B353 2013   150   C2012-905238-8

ISBN 978-0-13-282590-0

BRIEF CONTENTS

CONTENTS

06

HUMAN DEVELOPMENT I: PHYSICAL, COGNITIVE, AND LANGUAGE DEVELOPMENT 80

07

HUMAN DEVELOPMENT II: SOCIAL DEVELOPMENT 94

08

SEX AND GENDER 108

09

EMOTION AND MOTIVATION 120

10

CONSCIOUSNESS 134

11

LEARNING 150

12 MEMORY 166

13 COGNITION 180

14 SOCIAL PSYCHOLOGY 198

15 PERSONALITY AND INDIVIDUAL DIFFERENCES 216

16 PSYCHOPATHOLOGY 230

17 TREATMENT OF PSYCHOPATHOLOGY 248

18 HEALTH 264

ABOUT THE AUTHORS

ABIGAIL A. BAIRD is a Professor of Psychology at Vassar College. She earned her undergraduate degree from Vassar College and both a M.A. and Ph.D. from Harvard University. Following completion of her Ph.D., she was awarded a post-doctoral fellowship at the Center for Cognitive Neuroscience, at Dartmouth College. Her numerous articles and presentations have covered topics such as adolescent brain development, cognitive regulation of emotion, juvenile justice, and manifestations of racial bias in mind brain and behaviour.

Abigail's research has received awards from Harvard University, the Society for Research on Psychopathology, and in 2008 the Association for Psychological Science named Abigail a "Rising Star in Psychological Science." Her research has also led her to be elected to several scientific societies including the International Society for Behavioral Neuroscience and the Gruter Institute for Law and Behavioral Research. Abigail has been repeatedly recognized for her excellence in teaching. In 2000 she received Harvard's George Goethals Teaching Prize, and in 2004 was awarded the Class of 1962 Excellence in Teaching Fellowship by Dartmouth College. Her professional accomplishments also include serving as secretary of the Association for Psychological Science, Honorary Faculty Member for the Order of Omega National Honor Society, Invited Faculty to the New York State Judicial Institute, and Advisory Board member on the Campaign for Youth Justice.

ANJANIE MCCARTHY is a Professor of Psychology at Fanshawe College. She has an undergraduate degree from the University of Toronto, and both master's and doctorate degrees in psychology from Queen's University, Ontario. Anjanie completed a post-doctoral fellowship at the University of Toronto before accepting a position at Fanshawe College.

Anjanie's research interests include the development of non-verbal behaviours during interpersonal interactions. For example, Anjanie has published on the development of eye gaze displays in different social contexts and socio-cultural and cognitive factors that affect eye gaze and other non-verbal behaviours. Her current research focuses on non-verbal communication in the classroom and ways to enhance communication between teacher and student.

As an instructor, Anjanie enjoys developing courses based on her research interests, such as *The Truth about Lies*, *Unravelling Youth*, and *Foodonomics: Starving for the Truth*. Anjanie lives in London with her husband, three sons, pet dog, and cockatiel.

"for my children, Christopher and Phoebe,
whose lives inspire me"

—A. B.

"I dedicate this book to my three beautiful sons,
Garnett, Caelan, and Isaac. I treasure every loving,
sweet, and funny moment I have with you."

—A. M.

INTRODUCTION

<<< Unfortunately, the Holocaust that George Brady survived is far from the only historical example of genocide. Even today, the Sudanese region of Darfur is still engaged in a conflict that many governments have deemed to be genocidal in nature. Several other countries, such as Syria and Ethiopia, also have escalating violence that could progress to genocide. What can the study of psychology teach us about the causes and consequences of such violent behaviour? What can psychology reveal about the complexity of human behaviour?

WHAT IS PSYCHOLOGY AND WHY DOES IT FASCINATE US?
WHAT IS THE HISTORY OF PSYCHOLOGY?
WHAT MAJOR QUESTIONS DO PSYCHOLOGISTS SEEK TO ANSWER?
WHAT ARE SOME DIFFERENT SUBTYPES OF PSYCHOLOGY?

What

is your life story? Who and what has shaped the person you are today? Whether your life is filled with great positive experiences or seemingly insurmountable obstacles, 'we all have a story to tell. Some of these stories are especially inspirational. The story of George Brady is one such story.

George Brady and his sister, Hana, worked in their family's general store and enjoyed skiing, skating, and spending time with their family—until Hitler changed their world forever. In 1941, their parents, Karel and Marketa Brady, were arrested by Hitler's army and taken to concentration camps. A year later George, aged 14, and Hana, aged 11, were sent to the ghetto of Terezin and separated. In 1944, George was sent to Auschwitz and a year later he escaped from the Nazi concentration camp. At the age of 17, George was the only member of his immediate family to survive the Holocaust.

George eventually immigrated to Canada where he still lives. He and a fellow Holocaust survivor established a successful plumbing business, and after 40 years George retired but remained active in charity work. He married and had three sons and one daughter. George stands as an example of the resilience and strength that resides within human beings. What was it about George that allowed him to overcome the emotional, mental, and physical damage of the Holocaust and create a normal life for himself?

And what gave George the strength to recount his painful and horrific past so many years later? In 2000, George received a letter from Fumiko Ishioka, executive director of the Tokyo Holocaust Education Resource Centre, explaining that she came across

Hana's suitcase and artwork while researching the Holocaust. Fumiko had opened a successful educational exhibition entitled "The Holocaust Seen Through Children's Eyes," and Hana's artwork was among those of other children's that were displayed. While visiting George in Canada, Fumiko and George were interviewed by the Canadian Jewish News and the CBC. In 2002, Karen Levine, of the CBC, wrote "Hana's Suitcase," which was later translated into 40 languages, adapted for the stage, and led to a Gemini Award–winning documentary, and other award-winning docudramas based on Hana and George's stories. In 2009, George Brady received the Order of Ontario.

For George and other survivors, the Holocaust will always be a pivotal, critical influence in who they have become and an important element of their life's story. When we hear about stories such as George Brady's, questions abound: What gave George the mental strength not only to survive his experiences but also to become stronger as a result of them? Was it the character he was born with, or did something in his experience make him the great man he has become?

The study of psychology sheds light on our life stories. It examines the many influences on our lives, why we behave as we do, and the thoughts, beliefs, and emotions that make us who we are today. Psychology helps us understand the lives of others and gain insight into ourselves.

CHAPTER **01**

>>> **James Mark Baldwin** established the **first psychological laboratory** in North America at the **University of Toronto** in 1889. A supporter of William Wundt, Baldwin became a leader in experimental psychology.

What Is Psychology?

Psychology is the scientific study of behaviour—overt actions and reactions—and mental processes—covert internal activity in the mind. While philosophers might speculate on why people act as they do, psychologists use scientific methods to accurately describe, explain, predict, or control human and animal behaviour. The scientific method has only fairly recently been applied to psychology; until approximately 130 years ago, psychology was considered to be a branch of philosophy. Throughout this chapter, we will examine the development of psychology as a formal discipline in its own right.

WHY STUDY PSYCHOLOGY?

What motivated you to study psychology? Maybe you are hoping to solve the "nature versus nurture" debate and learn whether environmental factors can truly ever trump genetics. Perhaps you are looking for tips on how to improve your relationships with your friends and family members, or maybe you're more interested in learning about how you can reduce stress and anxiety in your daily life. If you polled your fellow students about their reasons for studying psychology, you would likely discover that everyone has something in common—a fundamental curiosity about themselves and the world they live in. Among other things, studying psychology reduces our uncertainty about our own experiences by providing knowledge about ourselves (Why do I remember some things and not others? How can I break my bad habits?), other people (Why do people suffer from mental disorders? Why do people have different personalities?), and the world (Do people from other countries perceive the world differently? How does culture affect how we express ourselves?).

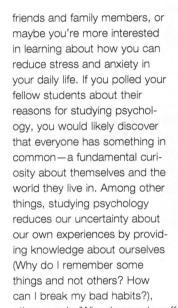

Psychology is the scientific study of behaviour and mental processes.

Dualism is the belief that the mind does not cease to exist when the body dies, and that thoughts and ideas can exist separately from the body.

Structuralism is a school of psychology concerned with the individual elements of consciousness and showing how they can be combined and integrated.

Functionalism is a school of psychology focused on how organisms use their learning and perceptual abilities to function in their environment.

Gestalt psychology is a school of psychology centred on the belief that people naturally seek out patterns, or wholes, in the sensory information available to them.

The History of Psychology

PRESCIENTIFIC PSYCHOLOGY

In the fifth century BC, Greek philosophers began to speculate about how the mind works and how it might affect behaviour. Socrates (470–399 BC) and Plato (428–347 BC) believed that the mind did not cease to exist when the body died, and that thoughts and ideas could exist separately from the body, a concept known as **dualism.** They theorized that knowledge is built within us and that we gain access to it through logical reasoning.

Although Socrates's and Plato's beliefs were developed nearly 2500 years ago, it was not until the Scientific Revolution of the late Renaissance period that French philosopher

René Descartes (1596–1650), a believer of Socrates's idea that mind is distinct from body, began to investigate how the two might be connected. By dissecting the brains of animals, Descartes concluded that the pineal gland at the base of the brain was the principal seat of the soul, where all thoughts were formed. He believed that the soul flowed through the body through hollow tubes and controlled muscle movement. Although anyone who still subscribes to Descartes's beliefs about the soul would probably fail a biology exam, the hollow tubes that Descartes noted were, among other things, important for controlling reflexes: We now know them as nerves.

Not all 17th century philosophers agreed with the theories of Socrates and Plato. British philosopher John Locke (1632–1704) believed that at birth, the human mind is a tabula rasa, a "blank slate," containing no innate knowledge. Locke proposed that people gain knowledge through their experiences by means of observation, laying the foundations for later studies in sensation and perception. His theory that knowledge is gained through careful external and internal observation planted the early seeds of empiricism and contributed to the development of the scientific method.

FOUNDATIONS OF SCIENTIFIC PSYCHOLOGY

Most psychologists agree that the birth of modern psychology occurred in a laboratory in Germany in 1879. The founder of the laboratory, William Wundt (1832–1920), argued that the mind could be examined both scientifically and objectively, and he invited students from around the world to learn how to study the structure of the human mind. This was the first time anyone had attempted to incorporate objectivity and measurement into the field of psychology, earning Wundt the moniker "father of psychology." His lectures gained popularity throughout the 1880s, and before long, the new science of psychology had evolved into two early schools of thought: structuralism and functionalism.

Structuralism and Functionalism

One of Wundt's students, Edward Titchener (1867–1927), believed that experiences could be broken down into individual emotions and sensations, much as a chemist or a physician might analyze matter in terms of molecules and atoms. His school of thought, which focused on identifying individual elements of consciousness and showing how they could be combined and integrated, became known as **structuralism.** Titchener's approach was to engage people in introspection, or "looking inward," training them to report various elements of their experiences as they patted a dog, thought about the colour blue, or smelled a flower. Introspection and structuralism were short-lived concepts, dying out in the early 1900s. Although they had little long-term effect on psychological science, the study of sensation and perception is still an important part of contemporary psychology (see Chapter 4).

Unlike Wundt and Titchener, American academic William James (1842–1910) believed that to break consciousness into individual elements was an act of impossibility. He saw consciousness as a continuing stream of ever-changing thoughts that could not be separated. Instead, James focused on how organisms use their learning and perceptual abilities to function in their environment, an approach that came to be known as **functionalism.** Influenced by Darwin's theories of evolution, James speculated that thinking developed because it is adaptive. He believed that useful behavioural traits (in addition to physical traits) could be passed from generation to generation.

Although functionalism is no longer a major perspective in psychology, elements of functionalist thought can still be seen in educational psychology and organizational psychology. For example, by emphasizing individual differences, functionalism influenced the theory that children should be taught at the level for which they, as individuals, are developmentally prepared.

Gestalt Psychology

In Germany, psychologists were also objecting to structuralism, albeit for different reasons. Max Wertheimer (1880–1943) believed that the acts of sensing and perceiving could not be broken into smaller elements and still be understood. When people look at a house, Wertheimer reasoned, they see a house, not a collection of doors, walls, and windows. Wertheimer and his colleagues believed that the act of perception entails more than just the sum of its parts. Their ideas developed into a school of thought known as **Gestalt psychology.** Roughly translated, gestalt

> "Wundt's lectures gained popularity throughout the 1880s, and before long, the new science of psychology had evolved into two early schools of thought: structuralism and functionalism."

means "whole" or "form." Gestalt psychologists believed that people naturally seek out patterns, or wholes, in the sensory information available to them. (See Chapter 4 for more information about Gestalt psychology.)

Psychodynamic Theory

If one of the hallmarks of fame is to have one's favourite terms and catchphrases become part of our everyday lexicon, then Sigmund Freud (1856–1939) has achieved the height of posthumous celebrity in the world of psychology. Have you ever described someone as anal, discussed the Oedipus complex, or accused someone of using humour as a **defence mechanism**? If so, you can thank Freud for these terms and the psychological theories behind them.

Freud was an Austrian medical doctor who specialized in disorders of the nervous system,

Psychosexual Stages are developmental stages during which the id's desire for pleasure focuses on many of the body's erogenous zones in turn.

Fixation is a focus on one particular erogenous zone of the body.

Defence mechanism is a mental process of self-deception that helps a person alleviate his or her worry or anxiety.

but his greatest contributions to psychology were his theory of **psychosexual development** and his conceptualization of the human psyche. According to Freud, human development progressed in stages, with each stage representing a significant developmental milestone. If an individual is unable to successfully accomplish the milestone, then they become "stuck" or fixated at that phase (see accompanying table). For example, in the anal stage of development, a child must develop the ability to control his or her bladder and bowels, thereby becoming "potty trained." If, however, during this stage the child is unable to successfully achieve this goal or if negative or traumatic events hinder his or her progression, then the child will carry these issues onward and not fully resolve the issues of this stage. This **fixation** at the anal stage of development has led to such terms as *anally retentive* to describe individuals who are overly controlling—perhaps to compensate for their lack of control during the anal stage of development.

Freud also believed that the human psyche was made up of three components: the id, ego, and superego. The id represents our unconsciousness. Freud believed that humans are motivated by primitive sexual drives, forbidden desires, and traumatic childhood memories that lay in our unconsciousness. According to Freud, these repressed urges constantly impinge upon the conscious mind, represented by the ego, and are expressed through dreams, slips of the tongue (now known as Freudian slips), or symptoms of psychological disorders. Finally, the third component of our psyche is the superego, which represents the moral or righteous aspect of humanity. According to Freud, there is conflict between the biological needs of the id (for sex, violence, food, etc.) and the superego, which dictates appropriate, civilized behaviours. The ego is caught in the middle, like a referee, and when the conflict becomes too great, the ego is in jeopardy of becoming damaged. Defence

Freud's Theory of Psychosexual Development

Stage of Psychosexual Development	General Age Range	Developmental Milestone To Be Accomplished
Oral stage	Infancy	Weaning
Anal stage	2–4 years	Toilet training
Phallic stage	4–7 years	Sexual identity Stage when we see Oedipal and Electra complex
Latent stage	7 years to the onset of puberty	No major conflict or task
Genital stage	Puberty onwards	Sexual behaviour, intimacy

mechanisms, such as denial, regression, and repression, protect the ego, which is essential because a damaged ego leads to psychological, physical, and behavioural problems.

Freud's theories, which formulated the **psychodynamic approach** to psychology, were highly controversial. Many of his Victorian contemporaries were shocked, both by his focus on sexuality and by the implication that people are not always in control of their actions. However, Freud's theories were held in high regard, inspired many well-known researchers, and formed the basis of modern psychotherapy, the development of which is discussed in Chapter 15.

Swiss psychologist Carl Jung expanded on Freud's ideas by focusing on dream analysis and the role of symbolism. His work not only led to key psychological concepts, such as the collective unconscious (a part of our unconsciousness that is universally shared

> "Freud's theories were held in high regard, inspired many well-known researchers, and formed the basis of modern psychotherapy."

by all living things), but also had a significant and broad influence on our understanding of society. For example, his influence is seen in discussions about the psychology of religion, the use of art as a form of therapy, and the concept of individuation, which is a key concept in analytical psychology.

The work of Anna Freud, Freud's daughter, expanded his theory of psychosexual development and helped to advance the field of psychoanalytic child psychology. Her work was among the first to examine the roles of stress and poor attachment on children and to address ways to improve their outcomes. Anna Freud's work became the foundation for "ego psychology."

Behaviourism

One disadvantage of psychoanalytic theory is that it is difficult to test it scientifically. For example, it is all but impossible to prove that a grown woman has relationship problems because she unconsciously resents her father for not being around when she was a child. The theories of structuralism and functionalism faced similar challenges because they both involved the study of consciousness—internal processes that could not be measured or validated. John B. Watson (1878–1958), however, wanted to make scientific inquiry a primary focus in psychology. In the 1900s, he developed the **behavioural approach** to psychology, which concentrates on observable behaviour that can be directly measured and recorded.

Watson's ideas were based on the work of Russian physiologist Ivan Pavlov, who showed that a reflex (an involuntary action) such as salivation could be trained (conditioned) to occur in response to a formerly unrelated stimulus, such as a ringing bell. Whereas Freud believed that behaviour stemmed from unconscious motivation, Watson used Pavlov's research to argue that behaviour can be learned. Watson and his colleague, Rosalie Rayner, famously proved that fear could be conditioned by teaching an 11-month-old child to fear a white rat. By repeatedly pairing the appearance of the rat with a loud, scary noise, the child eventually associated the rat with the noise and cried whenever he saw the creature (Watson & Rayner, 1920). Given the questionable ethics of this study, it is unlikely that Watson's experiment will ever be repeated, though similar results have been obtained using less damaging forms of conditioning. The ethical factors to consider when designing and carrying out an experiment are discussed in detail in Chapter 2.

Throughout the mid-20th century, behaviourism gained momentum through the work of B. F. Skinner, who supported Watson's idea of learning through conditioning. Skinner believed that behaviour could be altered through reinforcement—rewarding or punishing a learner when he or she engages in a particular behaviour. The ways in which Watson and Skinner influenced contemporary psychological approaches are discussed in Chapter 11.

Humanistic Psychology

In the first half of the 20th century, psychoanalysis and behaviourism were the two primary approaches to psychology. However, neither of them put forth the suggestion that individuals have significant control over their own destinies. Behaviourists maintained that people's actions were learned responses to various stimuli, while psychoanalysts claimed that people were influenced by their unconscious desires.

In the 1950s, a new psychological perspective emerged. This perspective emphasized the importance of self-esteem, self-expression, and reaching one's potential. Supporters of the **humanistic approach,** as it came to be known, believed that people have free will and are able to control their own destinies. Two founding theorists of the humanistic approach were Abraham Maslow (1908–1970), who studied motivation and emotion, and Carl Rogers (1902–1987), who made significant contributions to the study of personality and the practice of psychotherapy. Maslow believed that people

Psychodynamic approach is an approach to psychology based on the belief that behaviours are motivated by internal factors unavailable to the conscious mind.

Behavioural approach is an approach to psychology that concentrates on observable behaviour that can be directly measured and recorded.

Humanistic approach is an approach to psychology based on the belief that people have free will and are able to control their own destinies.

Cognitive psychology is a field of psychology focused on the workings of the human brain and seeking to understand how people process the information that they collect from their environments.

Evolutionary approach is an approach to psychology that explores ways in which patterns of human behaviour may be beneficial to people's survival.

Levels of analysis are various ways that psychologists can look at a psychological issue, such as from the level of the brain, the level of the person, and the level of the world.

should strive for self-actualization—the achievement of one's full potential.

Although the humanistic approach has had a pervasive effect in many disciplines, critics argue that it can come across as vague and naively optimistic. Chapter 15 provides an in-depth discussion of the facets of humanistic theory.

Cognitive Psychology

By the 1960s, developments in linguistics, neurobiology, and computer science were providing new insight into the workings of the human mind. The development of computers, in particular, stimulated an interest in studying thought processes. Pioneers in the field of **cognitive psychology** focused on the workings of the human brain and sought to understand how we process the information that we collect from our environments.

Focusing on memory, perception, learning, intelligence, language, and problem solving, cognitive psychologists expanded the definition of psychology to incorporate the study of specific mental processes into the more general concept of behaviour. Developments in brain-imaging techniques have enabled cognitive psychologists to examine neurological processes that previously mystified scientists, such as how we store memories or how damage to particular areas of the brain increases the likelihood of specific mental disorders. In a relatively short period of time, the cognitive perspective has become one of the most rapidly advancing perspectives in modern psychology.

Evolutionary Psychology

Why are people commonly afraid of snakes and spiders but not of cars or trains? It's generally believed that through the evolutionary process, our ancestors developed a healthy fear of things that might harm them (Seligman, 1971). Whereas fearless warriors who took on rattlesnakes with their bare hands probably didn't make it very far along the evolutionary ladder, those with more cautious approaches toward reptiles tended to survive, passing on their genes and eventually producing an entire population of people who naturally fear snakes. Since cars and trains have not been around for long enough to pass on a fear of crashes, we are not yet genetically predisposed to fear them.

Statistically, you are more likely to be killed in a **jumbo jet crash** than as a result of a **snake bite,** but our evolutionary instincts have yet to catch up with our natural phobias.

Based on Darwin's theory of natural selection, the **evolutionary approach** to psychology explores ways in which patterns of human behaviour may be beneficial to our survival. Evolutionary psychologists study issues such as parenting, sexual attraction, and violence among different species and cultures to explain how people might be genetically preprogrammed to behave in a certain way. For example, a recent study indicates that men with a gene variant called "allele 334" may find it more difficult to remain monogamous than men without the allele (Walum et al., 2008). Researchers have long speculated that the stereotype of the male philanderer developed as a result of gender differences between the sexes, and evolutionary psychologists might argue that while women require consistent, stable relationships because they spend more time nurturing children, it is evolutionarily ben-

eficial for men to father as many children as possible.

Over the years, the field of psychology has grown as scientists discover new and valuable ways of examining thoughts, actions, and behaviours. Today, psychologists use all of the approaches mentioned here—and more—to study the workings of the human mind. Some psychological perspectives may seem to contradict each other, and there's no consensus in the psychological community about which approach is the "right" approach. Rather, each of the many diverse approaches to psychology sheds new light on the fundamental questions of the field: Why do we act the way we do? What really goes on in our minds? Each perspective offers its own answers to questions like these, and each perspective, in turn, raises new questions of its own.

Levels of Analysis

Choose any question or issue in psychology, and you will be able to look at it from a number of different angles. Philosophers observed a long time ago that a single issue can be examined at multiple levels of analysis. For example, let's say you are studying the effects of the Holocaust on survivors such as George Brady. You might examine the survivors at the level of the brain (How do the biological mechanisms in Holocaust survivors compare to the biological mechanisms of other people?), at the level of the person (How have this person's beliefs and values changed as a result of his experiences?), or at the level of the world (How do Holocaust survivors interact with the people around them?). Psychologist Stephen Kosslyn identified these three categories as the major **levels of analysis,** although there are many more angles from which to approach a particular psychological issue.

Sometimes, psychological issues are ideally suited to a particular level of analysis. For example, if you are studying personality, it makes sense to focus your study at the level of the person. How do individuals react in stressful situations? What gives people a sense of achievement? How stable are individual

Nature describes inherited characteristics that influence personality, physical growth, intellectual growth, and social interactions.

Nurture describes environmental factors such as parental styles, physical surroundings, and economic issues.

Natural selection is a theory that states that organisms best adapted to their environment tend to survive and transmit their genetic characteristics to succeeding generations.

Nature vs. Nurture

Jeffrey was a happy, bubbly youngster who enjoyed riding his bike and playing with his pet dog, Frisky. Growing up in the 1960s, he had a stable family, with two loving parents and a younger brother. There was little in Jeffrey's upbringing to suggest that he should develop into anything other than a healthy, well-adjusted adult.

On July 22, 1991, Jeffrey Dahmer, one the world's most notorious serial killers, was arrested at his Milwaukee apartment. What police found inside was almost unspeakable. Gruesome photos of dismembered body parts, a severed head in the refrigerator, three more heads in the freezer—the list of atrocities went on and on. Further investigation revealed that Dahmer had killed 17 men and boys during a killing spree that went undetected for 13 years. Following a 160-page confession, Dahmer was sentenced to 15 consecutive life terms in prison. He was murdered in prison by a fellow inmate in 1994.

The story of Jeffrey Dahmer continues to underscore one of the biggest and most enduring issues faced by psychologists. Do our human traits develop through experience, or does a genetic blueprint determine who we will become? Are we primarily defined by nature—inherited characteristics that influence personality, physical growth, intellectual growth, and social interactions—or by nurture—environmental factors such as parental styles, physical surroundings, and economic issues? Although Dahmer was not subjected to the abuse or neglect that many serial killers experience during childhood, there were several incidents in his past that could have factored into his decline into sadism. A hernia operation at the age of six left him subdued and vulnerable, and he became increasingly isolated when his family moved to a new area. However, many people deal with far more traumatic childhood occurrences without resorting to murder. Was there

personalities? However, a comprehensive study should incorporate other levels of analysis. You might consider whether MRI scans have uncovered patterns that point to specific behavioural traits (the level of the brain), or you might study whether culture affects personality type (the level of the world). Many psychologists believe that it is only possible to understand events at one level of analysis if we take into account what is occurring at the other levels.

Levels of Analysis

Level of Analysis	Causal Process Studied	Category
Neural	Brain	Biological
Genetic	Genes	
Evolutionary	Natural selection	
Learning	Individual's prior experiences with the environment	Experiential
Cognitive	Individual's knowledge or beliefs	
Social	Influence of other people	
Cultural	Influence of the culture in which the individual develops	
Developmental	Age-related changes	

 There are many different **levels of analysis** from which to examine a psychological issue.

something inherent in Dahmer's biological makeup that made his sadistic killing spree inevitable?

HISTORY OF THE NATURE-NURTURE DEBATE

The nature-nurture debate has been raging at least since the time of the ancient Greeks. Plato's beliefs—that knowledge is built within us and that character and intelligence are largely inherited—placed Plato firmly in the "nature" camp. Flying the "nurture" flag was Plato's student, Aristotle, who disagreed with his teacher and claimed that people acquire knowledge by observing the physical world and passing information into the mind via the senses. In the 1600s, Locke and Descartes reignited the debate, with Locke arguing that the mind is a blank slate waiting to be filled by experience, and Descartes countering that some ideas are innate.

When Darwin sailed around the world in 1831, he collected evidence that would lend support to Descartes's views. Darwin's theory of **natural selection**, outlined in his 1859 book, *The Origin of Species*, explained variation within species as the result of evolution. Nature selects features that best enable an organism to adapt to its environment, and these features are passed on to future generations. Darwin's ideas (discussed in Chapter 5) remain the fundamental principles of biology, and the concept that traits may be heritable has strongly influenced contemporary psychology.

After many years of scientific debate and research, most psychologists agree that we become the people we are through a unique combination of hereditary and environmental factors. However, the debate continues with regard to just how influential each factor may be. For example, the subject of intelligence is still a hot-button issue. Canadian researcher J. Philippe Rushton (1991, 1992, 1997) believes that intelligence is 100% genetic. According to Rushton, certain racial groups are genetically or biologically more intelligent than other racial groups. However, University of Guelph researchers Michael Peters (1995, 1996) and Andrew Winston (1996, 2003, 2004) believe that Rushton is incorrect and that differences in intelligence are due to environmental factors, such as biased test questions, poverty, and education. Aspects of the nature-nurture debate may be addressed by considering multiple levels of analysis. For example, a psychologist studying intelligence levels might examine biological factors at the level of the brain by comparing MRI scans of the brains of people with different levels of intelligence. The psychologist may also examine environmental factors at the level of the person by investigating people's educational histories and childhood environments.

The nature-nurture debate raises interesting questions for contemporary psychologists. Are people with mental illnesses predisposed to suffer particular conditions, or do stressful life events or other environmental factors trigger mental disorders? How do children learn language—through repetition and education, or via a preprogrammed mechanism that stimulates the development of grammar? The answers to one question in particular may have fascinating social implications: Can people change? Is there hope of rehabilitation for men like Jeffrey Dahmer, or is a serial killer always a serial killer? Are men with the allele 334 gene variant destined to cheat on their wives, or can they overcome their natural urges? Could all Holocaust survivors have gone on to develop the mental fortitude and productivity displayed by George Brady, or did something in Brady's biological makeup awaken in him a sense of determination rather than one of hopelessness? The nature-nurture debate rages on.

Are **Olympic athletes** excellent competitors because of their **genes**, their **environments**, or both?

Types of Psychology

Based on the wide range of issues already mentioned in this chapter, you have probably figured out that the field of psychology is extremely diverse. The term *psychologist* describes everyone from the therapist listening to a client talking about his or her depression to the researcher measuring how violent video games affect children's behaviour to the scientist examining the structure of a rat's brain. Although these professions may seem unrelated, there is a glue that binds all psychologists together—an interest in human behaviours and the processes that influence them.

PSYCHOLOGICAL ORGANIZATIONS

Like most vocations, psychology has a number of professional bodies that promote specific interests and maintain standards within the industry. In 1892, psychologists, including James Mark Baldwin, founded the American Psychological Association (APA). The APA is now the largest psychological organization in the world, with nearly 150 000 members and 56 professional divisions. Many Canadian and international psychologists belong to the APA. The APA produces a number of books, research papers, and journals, including its official journal, *American Psychologist*. You may have written (or in the near future will write) papers using APA style, which is a formatting style commonly adopted in the social sciences.

Since the APA is primarily geared toward clinical psychology, several research-focused groups have formed their own organizations. In 1939, the Canadian Psychological Association (CPA) was founded, with the specific goals of improving the health and welfare of all Canadians and promoting psychological research, education, practice, and application of psychological knowledge. CPA publishes three journals: the *Canadian Journal of Behavioural Science*, the *Canadian Journal of Experimental Psychology*, and *Canadian Psychology*. CPA currently has 31 professional divisions, including Aboriginal psychology, clinical psychology, developmental psychology, international and cross-cultural psychology, extremism and terrorism, rural and northern psychology, and women and psychology.

Members of each division receive regular newsletters providing them with information about upcoming conferences and interesting developments within their field of expertise.

CAREERS IN PSYCHOLOGY

In 2006, 8% of all doctorate degrees earned in Canada were in psychology. Taking an average of six years to complete, a doctorate degree in psychology is both labour intensive and expensive (Statistics Canada, 2006). However, psychologists are in demand in Canada and throughout the world. But why do we need psychologists? Just look at the following facts and it is clear why psychologists are in demand. One in five Canadians will experience a mental disorder in their lifetime—depression and

> There is increasing demand for psychological services in schools, hospitals, social service agencies, and private companies. **The employment prospects for a psychology graduate are high.**

anxiety are most common. Canada loses $30 billion annually because of mental health problems and addiction. According to the World Health Organization, depression will be the second leading cause of disability (second to heart disease) by the year 2020 (CPA, 2010). In addition, there is increasing demand for psychological services in schools, hospitals, social service agencies, and private companies. The employment prospects for a psychology graduate are high.

Careers in psychology can be broadly divided into three main categories: clinical psychology, academic psychology, and applied psychology.

Clinical Psychology

Clinical psychologists diagnose and treat people with specific mental or behavioural problems, and the field of clinical psychology covers a wide variety of professions, ranging from mental health experts to family therapists. Clinical psychologists interview patients, give diagnostic tests, provide psychotherapy, and design and implement behavioural modification programs. Unlike psychiatrists, clinical psychologists are not medical doctors, and most do not have the ability to prescribe drugs. This is changing in some U.S. states; in 2002, specially trained and licensed psychologists in the state of New Mexico were granted the right to prescribe drugs, and psychologists in Louisiana are now permitted to write prescriptions after consulting with a psychiatrist. In Canada, however, clinical psychologists cannot prescribe drugs.

Areas of specialization within clinical psychology include neuropsychology (studying the relationship between the brain and behaviour), counselling (advising people on how to deal with problems of everyday living, such as career-related stress), social work (helping people resolve problems in their lives specifically related to poverty or oppression), psychiatric nursing (assessing mental health needs or diagnosing and treating people with mental disorders), and school psychology (addressing students' learning and behavioural problems). More psychology graduates

Projected Increase in Employment for Psychologists (2010–2020)

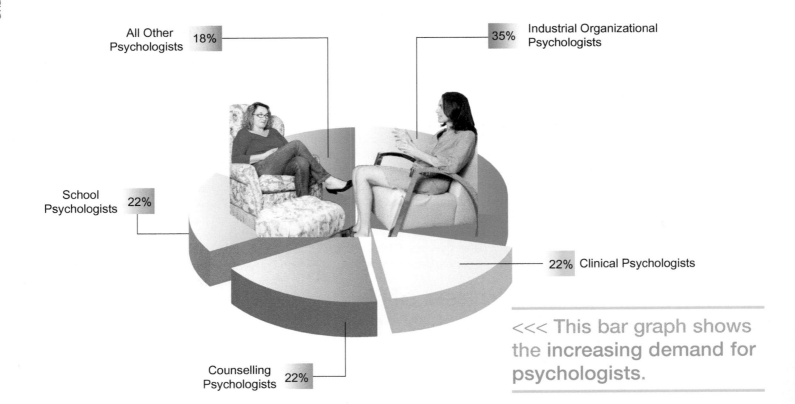

All Other Psychologists 18%

Industrial Organizational Psychologists 35%

School Psychologists 22%

Clinical Psychologists 22%

Counselling Psychologists 22%

<<< This bar graph shows the **increasing demand for** psychologists.

gain employment in the field of clinical psychology than in any other subdiscipline.

Clearly, there is a great need for clinical psychologists in Canada. However, clinical psychologists face challenges in treating clients. For example, it is estimated that only one-third of sufferers seek treatment for their mental illness and high demand can lead to long wait lists. In addition, not all psychological treatments are covered by public or provincial health insurance plans (ASHA, 2007; CPA, 2010).

Academic Psychology

Not all psychologists work directly with people who have mental or behavioural issues. If you talk to your psychology professors, you will probably learn that outside of the classroom, they each have specialty areas of interest in which they conduct research. **Academic psychologists** usually divide their time between supervising and teaching students, completing administrative tasks, and carrying out psychological research. The proportion of time that each psychologist devotes to each of these tasks depends on the nature of his or her academic institution; some academic psychologists spend the majority of their time teaching, whereas others, particularly at larger schools, devote more time to research. Teaching positions at universities are generally very competitive.

Some areas of academic expertise include developmental psychology (the study of the social and mental development of human beings), cognitive psychology (the study of internal mental processes), abnormal psychology (the study of mental disorders and other abnormal thoughts and behaviours), personality psychology (the study of patterns of thought, feeling, and behaviour that make a person unique), and social psychology (the study of group behaviour and the influence of social factors on the individual). Academic psychologists who specialize in these and other areas often aim to publish their research in approved journals related to their field of study.

Applied Psychology

The term *applied psychology* refers to the use of psychological theory and practice to tackle real-world problems. For example, rather than simply examining whether there is a link between high stress levels and coronary heart disease, a health psychologist may work with patients at risk of coronary heart disease to

reduce their stress levels. The field of **applied psychology** is not limited to any particular psychological discipline; it encompasses many different areas that share a common goal of using psychology in a practical form.

Imagine that you are an employer looking to select the best possible candidate for a position in your company. How can you guarantee that your interviewing strategies determine a person's true character? Once you have hired your new employee, how can you ensure that he or she thrives in a produc-

> "Not all psychologists work directly with people who have mental or behavioural issues. If you talk to your psychology professors, you will probably learn that outside of the classroom, they each have specialty areas of interest in which they conduct research.

tive, enjoyable working environment? Industrial and organizational psychology is a form of applied psychology in which psychologists study behaviour in the workplace and advise business owners based on their findings. An industrial/organizational (I/O) psychologist may conduct job analyses to determine candidates' suitability for a position, analyze fairness in employee compensation, use psychometric testing to assess employees' attitudes and morale, and train people to work more effectively in teams. Trends in the economic climate often play a vital part in determining the role of an I/O psychologist; in the current economic downturn, many are primarily involved with helping firms develop alternatives to employee downsizing or with managing layoffs in the most humane way possible.

Many businesses send their employees on annual team-building exercises to encourage bonding and teamwork in the office. Similar techniques are used in the rapidly growing field of sports psychology. If you were asked to name a film in which a new coach guides a poorly performing team to a seemingly impossible victory via a series of team-bonding exercises, you could probably rattle off several titles

without trying very hard. Sports psychologists believe that it is not enough for athletes to train their bodies; athletes also need to have a healthy mindset in order to succeed. Techniques to help athletes achieve this mindset include setting clear short-term goals, holding positive thoughts, using relaxation techniques, and visualizing a desired outcome, whether it be sinking a free throw or winning a race. If you're an athlete aiming for excellence, you might consider consulting a sports psychologist: Tiger Woods, perhaps the greatest golfer of all time, has been consulting one since age 13.

Although I/O psychology and sports psychology provide excellent examples of "real-world" psychology, applied psychology is useful in areas other than athletics and business, too. In fact, any subfield of psychology that has been mentioned in this chapter can be applied to real-world situations in some way. A personality psychologist may be consulted on the selection of a jury, for example, or an environmental psychologist might advise a town planning board. Contrary to the popular stereotype of a psychologist analyzing a patient on a couch, there are numerous industries to which psychologists can contribute their knowledge and insight.

Why might an **I/O psychologist** recommend that business employees participate in **team-building** activities together?

Chapter Summary

WHAT IS PSYCHOLOGY AND WHY DOES IT FASCINATE US? p.4

• Psychology is the scientific study of behaviour and mental processes.

• We study psychology in response to a fundamental curiosity about ourselves and our world.

WHAT IS THE HISTORY OF PSYCHOLOGY? p.4

• The Greek philosophers Socrates and Plato believed that knowledge is built within us, whereas John Locke believed that the human mind is a blank slate at birth.

• William Wundt, the "father of psychology," set up his laboratory in 1879. His student, Edward Titchener, founded structuralism. James Mark Baldwin established the first psychology laboratory in North America at the University of Toronto. William James proposed functionalism.

• Modern approaches to psychology include Gestalt psychology, Freud's psychodynamic theory, behaviourism, the humanistic approach, cognitive psychology, and evolutionary psychology.

WHAT MAJOR QUESTIONS DO PSYCHOLOGISTS SEEK TO ANSWER? p.8

• The question of whether our traits, behaviours, and mental processes are primarily the result of inherited characteristics (nature) or environmental factors (nurture) has been, and continues to be, a controversial topic in psychology.

• Most psychologists agree that humans are influenced by a unique combination of hereditary and environmental factors.

WHAT ARE SOME DIFFERENT SUBTYPES OF PSYCHOLOGY? p.9

• Clinical psychologists diagnose and treat people with mental or behavioural problems, whereas academic psychologists teach and carry out psychological research.

• Applied psychology refers to the use of psychological theory and practice to tackle real-world problems. Industrial/organizational psychologists and sports psychologists are examples of people who use applied psychology day-to-day.

Test Your Understanding

1. Psychology is
   a. the study of how we have evolved over time.
   b. the study of society.
   c. the scientific study of behaviour and mental processes.
   d. the scientific study of the role of genetics.

2. Why are some people interested in studying Psychology?
   a. To answer the nature vs. nurture debate.
   b. To improve reletionships.
   c. To learn how to reduce stress.
   d. All of the above are possible reasons for studying Psychology.

3. What is dualism?
   a. The belief that thoughts and ideas can exist separately from the body.
   b. The school of psychology that explains how elements of the consciousness can be combined and integrated.
   c. The school of Psychology that explains how we use our perceptual abilities to function in the environment.
   d. The belief that we gain knowledge only through experience.

4. Which of the following statements would Socrates and Plato most likely have agreed with?
   a. We can access innate knowledge through logic.
   b. The body and the mind are one.
   c. At birth, the human mind is a blank slate.
   d. People gain knowledge through experience.

5. Who is known as the "Father of Psychology"?
   a. Socrates.
   b. Wundt.
   c. Plato.
   d. Baldwin.

6. Mayu believes in structuralism; Jiaxun believes in functionalism. Which of the following statements best summarizes the differences between their concepts of the human mind?
   a. Mayu believes the mind is a sum of parts; Jiaxun believes the mind is a unified whole.
   b. Mayu believes the mind is best studied through empiricism; Jiaxun believes the mind is best studied through introspection.
   c. Mayu believes the mind is a unified whole; Jiaxun believes the mind is a sum of parts.
   d. Mayu believes the mind is best studied through Gestalt psychology; Jiaxun believes the mind is best studied through empiricism.

7. Who established the first psychological laboratory in North America at the University of Toronto?
   a. William Wundt
   b. James Mark Baldwin
   c. Edward Titchener
   d. William James

8. Which of the following influenced Watson's development of the behavioural approach?

   a. an interest in using past research to study psychology
   b. an interest in using direct measurement and observation to study psychology
   c. an interest in using introspection to study psychology
   d. an interest in using self-report data to study psychology

9. According the Freud our personality is composed of all of the following EXCEPT:

   a. ego
   b. superego
   c. id
   d. self-actualization

10. Which of the following is NOT an aspect of the humanistic approach to psychology?

   a. People should be encouraged to express themselves.
   b. People should strive to achieve their full potential.
   c. People should attempt to get in touch with their unconscious desires.
   d. People should understand the importance of free will and self-esteem.

11. The rapid rise of cognitive psychology can be largely attributed to:

   a. developments in brain-imaging technology
   b. the findings of Ivan Pavlov
   c. the development of the concept of self-actualization
   d. Darwin's theory of natural selection

12. Yuri is investigating the thought patterns of people afflicted with schizophrenia. Which of the following represents a question Yuri might ask at the level of the world?

   a. How do a schizophrenic patient's thought patterns vary over the course of the day?
   b. How are schizophrenic thought patterns reflected in brain activity?
   c. How do a patient's thought patterns vary in response to different stimuli?
   d. How do schizophrenic thought patterns vary across cultures?

13. Which of the following supports the "nature" side of the nature vs. nurture debate?

   a. Aristotle's ideas of self
   b. Darwin's theory of natural selection
   c. Locke's concept of a "tabula rasa"
   d. Skinner's behaviourist approach

14. Which of the following arguments is most likely based on ideas from the "nurture" side of the nature vs. nurture debate?

   a. Scientists should develop a method of genetic manipulation to create "designer babies."
   b. Programs that aim to rehabilitate criminals are a waste of time and money.
   c. A person who is predisposed to have a mental illness is virtually guaranteed to develop that illness.
   d. Children who perform poorly at failing schools will improve their performance if they are able to transfer to a more successful school.

15. The Canadian Psychological Association (CPA):

   a. aims to improve the health and welfare of all Canadians
   b. is the largest psychological organization in the world
   c. was founded by James Mark Baldwin
   d. publishes the journal American Psychologist

16. Which of the following statements regarding psychological treatment in Canada is true?

   a. Most people with a diagnosable mental disorder receive the treatment they need.
   b. All psychologists and psychological treatments are covered by public or provincial health insurance plans.
   c. Most people do not seek care for their mental disorder because of the stigma and cost associated with psychological treatment.
   d. There is no demand for clinical psychologists.

17. Neuropsychologists, counsellors, and social workers are specialists within the field of:

   a. academic psychology
   b. research psychology
   c. developmental psychology
   d. clinical psychology

18. Vivien, a professor of psychology, focuses much of her research on the patterns of thoughts, feelings, and behaviour that make a person unique. Vivien's academic specialty is:

   a. cognitive psychology
   b. personality psychology
   c. applied psychology
   d. clinical psychology

19. Which of the following is NOT an example of applied psychology?

   a. A health psychologist researches a potential link between depression and heart disease.
   b. A sports psychologist tells a soccer player to visualize herself kicking the ball into the goal.
   c. An I/O psychologist leads a group of office workers on a team-building scavenger hunt.
   d. A clinical psychologist teaches a patient to use breathing exercises to calm his anxiety.

20. Which of the following is true of clinical psychologists?

   a. They always work in hospitals.
   b. They tend to focus their research on cognitive psychology.
   c. They diagnose and treat people with specific mental or behavioural problems.
   d. They are medical doctors.

Remember to check www.thethinkspot.ca **for additional information, downloadable flashcards, and other helpful resources.**

Answers: 1) c; 2) d; 3)a; 4)a; 5)b; 6) a; 7)b; 8)b; 9)d 10) c; 11) a; 12) d; 13) b; 14) d; 15) a; 16) c; 17) d; 18) d; 19) b; 20) c

RESEARCH
METHODS

HOW IS THE SCIENTIFIC METHOD USED TO STUDY PSYCHOLOGY?

WHY ARE RESEARCH METHODS IMPORTANT TO THE STUDY OF PSYCHOLOGY?

WHAT ARE SOME TYPES OF RESEARCH STRATEGIES?

HOW CAN STATISTICAL METHODS HELP US GATHER AND ANALYZE DATA?

HOW CAN WE MINIMIZE BIAS?

WHAT ETHICAL ISSUES DO PSYCHOLOGISTS FACE?

Some people

experienced tingling sensations throughout their bodies and feelings of levitation. Others heard loud buzzing sounds and saw bright flashing lights. Most strikingly, people reported seeing strange figures hovering near their beds. What could possibly cause such bizarre phenomena? Convinced that something sinister had taken place, these people visited hypnotherapists to recover their "lost" memories. The resulting memories—of otherworldly visitations and worse—revealed the truth: These people had been abducted by aliens.

Or had they? Researchers from Harvard University believed that a more rational explanation was possible. While studying people's recovered memories of childhood sexual abuse, psychologist Susan Clancy and her colleagues faced a serious problem: They had no way of knowing whether the alleged victims' memories were real. Clancy wanted to determine whether people with recovered memories of traumatic events were particularly prone to false memory implantation, but because she couldn't figure out which of her subjects truly had false memories, she decided to focus her research on a slightly different group of subjects: self-professed alien abductees.

The abductees proved to be a useful comparison group: Like Clancy's previous subjects, many of them had recovered their alarming memories of abuse while in therapy. Most useful of all, however,

was the fact that while Clancy and her colleagues could not be sure whether the childhood abuse victims' memories were accurate or false, they were fairly certain that the alleged abductees had not actually been kidnapped by aliens. They used careful experimental research methods to support their hypothesis that supposed alien abductees were vulnerable to memory distortion. Clancy's team recruited three groups of people: a group who reported recovered memories of alien abductions, a group of individuals who believed they had been abducted but had no memories of the event, and a group who denied ever having contact with aliens. All three groups were asked to memorize lists of related words such as *candy, honey, soda, chocolate,* and *cake.* The researchers discovered that both people who had recovered memories and people who believed they had been abducted were more likely to falsely remember the word *sweet* as being on the list, even though it had been deliberately omitted from that list. This data led researchers to argue that people who claimed to have been abducted by aliens were more prone to developing false memories than were people with no alleged extraterrestrial experience.

Clancy knew that a smart experimental design is nothing to sneeze at. Innovative research methods can provide the key to unlocking even the trickiest mysteries of the human brain.

<<< The controversial Iranian missile tests in July 2008 made headline news all over the world. But was the photo of the four missiles doctored? Careful analysis of the picture revealed that some sections appeared to have been digitally altered. Just as newspaper editors have a responsibility to ensure that everything they print is factually accurate, so too do psychologists have a duty to use accurate and precise methodology to uncover the truth with minimal error and bias.

CHAPTER 02

Psychology and the Scientific Method

FOLK PSYCHOLOGY

You may have encountered some skepticism from people who do not believe that psychology is a science. This is a fairly common misconception, born out of the fact that much of what psychologists study may be personally experienced. For example, you may believe that men are more aggressive than women because you have two older brothers who are constantly engaged in fistfights and a younger sister who always takes on the role of family pacifist. Your individual experience has given you a false sense of actual scientific data that may or may not be true of the population as a whole.

This type of misconception is less common in the physical sciences. Few people would claim to have personal insight about the behaviour of accelerated electrons or the results of a chemical reaction between hydrogen and nitrogen. Before they state their theories as facts, physicists and chemists undergo careful scientific processes to prove or disprove their ideas. Although many people don't realize it, scientific processes are equally important in psychology. For example, the fact that you have personally encountered more aggressive males and less aggressive females does not necessarily indicate that everyone has had the same experiences. Maybe your family is atypical. Perhaps non-biological factors such as parental influence, social environment, or peer pressure have affected your siblings' behaviour. There are limits to what we can intuit about our own behaviour and the behaviour of others. We are limited not only by the boundaries of our own experiences, but also by the reliability of our memories and the dangers of our personal biases. To make generalized, objective, and well-supported statements about human nature, psychologists need to act as scientists rather than as casual observers.

Of course, casual observers are often on the right track: Many times, theories that seem like "common knowledge" are, in fact, supported by rigorous psychological research. (For example, several studies indicate that, in general, men are naturally more aggressive than women.) However, scientific psychological research also frequently disproves many of our culture's commonly held assumptions, highlighting the importance of critical, objective inquiry to the study of the human mind.

EMPIRICISM

Have you ever met someone for the first time and immediately made assumptions about him or her? Maybe you thought that because a stranger was wearing glasses, she must be intelligent, or maybe you connected a neighbour's playing music with violent lyrics to a violent worldview. When we make judgments like these, we rely on contextual assumptions and stereotypes to give us information about people, but more often than not, this information turns out to be at least slightly inaccurate. Like other scientists, psychologists aim to eliminate the effects of personal and cultural bias from their research. When psychologists draw conclusions about people, they do so through experimentation rather than through personalized judgments or stereotyping.

Most psychologists today believe in the importance of empiricism, or the view that knowledge originates through experience. In other words, information that you observe or collect yourself is more reliable than information that you can't observe or that you hear third-hand. As a result, psychologists who perform experiments use the scientific method, a process for conducting an objective inquiry through data collection and analysis.

1 **Identify a problem.** The first step in a scientific inquiry is to notice something that you would like to explain or investigate. It is important to choose a problem that you are able to study empirically. For example, there is no point in asking tempting philosophical questions such as "Why are we here?" or "What is morality?" Although the answers to these types of questions would provide valuable and fascinating insight into human behaviour and the human experience, they cannot be answered using the scientific method and thus do not fall into the psychological realm.

Once you have established a problem that can be studied empirically, you should ensure that there is only one factor, or variable, that changes throughout your experiment. Any other factors that might influence your results should be controlled. Let's say you are investigating how many times your siblings behave aggressively on an average day, so you observe them as they go about their daily business. Would this be a fair test? How would you make sure that all three siblings encounter the same potential stressors that might make them behave aggressively? How might factors such as traffic jams, disagreements with peers, and unpleasant chance encounters with strangers affect their behaviour? Before you begin your research, it is important to consider how you will collect and measure your data so that your results are as accurate and reliable as possible.

<<< Does playing violent video games make you violent? Scientific investigations both prove and disprove common assumptions.

The Scientific Method

2 **Conduct background research.** Has your question been studied before? If you are investigating a popular topic such as male and female aggression, there is probably already a great deal of research available that will give you further information about your topic of study. You can consult library and Internet resources to discover what research has already been done on your topic, how that research might be improved, and what areas might warrant further study.

3 **Formulate a hypothesis.** Based on your initial observations and your background research, you can make a hypothesis, or an educated guess about an explanation for your observations. Your hypothesis should be written as a statement that can either be proved or disproved. For example, you may have read several articles indicating that men are more likely to use aggressive actions than women, or that men are less patient than women when placed in stressful situations. Incorporating this research with your observations about your brothers and sister, you might hypothesize, "If a male is placed in a stressful situation, he will react more aggressively than a female who is placed in the same stressful situation."

4 **Test the hypothesis.** Psychologists use a variety of research methods, including surveys, case studies, and observations in laboratories or natural environments. However, the most conclusive way to test a hypothesis is to conduct an experiment. By manipulating a single characteristic, a researcher can study how this particular characteristic affects a specific outcome. Depending on the experiment, this outcome may involve the behaviour of a person, the behaviour of a group, or even the behaviour of the human brain. While undertaking this particular study, you would manipulate a particular situation and then examine the behaviour of several individuals within that situation. For example, you might select a group of men and a group of women of similar age, education level, and cultural background and individually place them in the same stressful situation—asking them to solve an impossible puzzle, for example, or exposing them to a loud, annoying noise for an extended period of time. You would then find some way of measuring the aggressive behaviour in each gender. You might, for instance, invite participants to take

out their frustrations on a punching bag, and then record how many times each person chooses to hit it. By controlling the environment in which the stressful situation takes place and creating the same stressful situation each time, you can ensure that you are only changing one variable in your experiment.

5 **Analyze your results.** Once you have completed your experiment, you can analyze your results to determine whether they support your hypothesis. Psychologists use statistical analysis to help them summarize their data and determine how likely it is that the results were due to chance. It is often helpful to repeat an experiment several times to dem-

Identify a problem.

Conduct background research.

Formulate a hypothesis.

Think critically and try again.

Test the hypothesis.

Analyze your results.

Results support the hypothesis.

Results do not support the hypothesis.

Report results.

onstrate that the first set of results was not due to chance.

If your results do not support your hypothesis, you should consider whether there is another possible explanation for your observations and construct a new hypothesis. Maybe your brothers' aggression results from playing a lot of contact sports. Maybe your sister is studying Buddhism and has adopted some of the religion's non-violent beliefs. Scientists continually refine their hypotheses until they are satisfied that their theories can be tested and proven.

6 **Report your results.** Whether or not the results of your experiment support your hypothesis, it is important to share your results by making them available to others. Other researchers may be able to use your findings to learn from your mistakes, refine your hypothesis, or attempt to replicate your experiment to add support to your research. Once a research paper has been established as credible, researchers may use it to predict behaviour based on the findings or use the results of the findings to modify or control behaviour. Published research also becomes the background information that is read by others who are formulating and refining their own hypotheses. Let's say that your research suggests that men do behave more aggressively than women in stressful situations. Other researchers may wonder whether this particular situation provokes a unique response in men and women, or whether other types of stress might have different effects.

The scientific method is not a hard and fast rulebook for every type of psychological study. For example, some studies collect data via observation rather than experimentation, and they follow different empirical procedures.

WHY DO WE NEED SCIENTIFIC METHODS?
Limitations of Empiricism

Empiricism does not guarantee that the information we acquire is completely accurate. Scientific studies are fallible and open to misinterpretation. Susan Clancy herself commented on the limitations of her research on alien abductees, noting that she had used a small sample of participants and that she had not screened her subjects for traumatic events other than alien kidnappings.

To reduce the possibility of errors while conducting empirical research, it is important to have a **method.** Methods are rules or techniques that provide a framework for our observations. They enable us to avoid the types of mistakes we might make through simply observing our subjects. When Clancy began to conduct her

∧
∧
∧ Was the devastation caused by **the explosions at the Fukushima nuclear plant in Japan** easily foreseeable, or is this an example of **hindsight bias?**

research, she first recruited three specific groups of participants. She then gave them all the same questionnaires to fill out and had them complete the same tests. Finally, she analyzed the test results carefully, using statistical data. These methods, designed to promote empiricism and minimize bias, ensured that Clancy's experiment contained as few errors as possible.

No matter how carefully we research our theory, or how closely we stick to our method, studying people is challenging. Why?

1 **People are complex.** We are not just a collection of cells that can be cultivated in a Petri dish and examined under a microscope. People have thoughts and feelings that affect their behaviour.

2 **People are different.** The extent to which we vary from our fellow humans makes it hard for psychologists to make generalizations about our behaviour.

3 **People react to situations differently.** We can't be pigeonholed into categories

easily because our reactions might change from one day to the next.

Finally, with every research finding comes the question, "What does this mean for me? How does this impact my life?" This desire for applicable research findings is one that scientists strive for at each step of the scientific process. However, not every research finding is immediately applicable to us, but even these findings are significant in terms of their benefits to science—they add to our understanding of phenomena and stimulate future investigation into key topics.

Hindsight Bias

Have you ever been described as a "Monday morning quarterback"? On Monday morning, it's easy to boast about how you would have played Sunday night's game differently. The other team's plays were so predictable that anyone should have been able to guess them easily! If you find yourself making this claim, you're probably experiencing **hindsight**

<<< If a study proved that running 10 kilometres everyday would extend your life by one year, but you had to run at 2 a.m. every morning, **would this research be of any practical use? How might scientists benefit from these research findings?**

bias, or the belief that you knew something all along. Canadian researchers Bernstein and colleagues (2011) examined the development of hindsight bias across the lifespan, from 3 to 95 years of age, and found that all age groups demonstrated hindsight bias. One reason for the early development of the hindsight bias and its persistence through life may be because the hindsight bias encourages us to see the world as more predictable than it actually is.

The hindsight bias, however, can lead to incorrect judgments. For example, some observations made in hindsight seem so obvious that they are often mistaken for common sense. The fact that engineers at the Fukushima nuclear plant did not anticipate the possible damage of an earthquake and subsequent tsunami seems like a grave and obvious failure, now in hindsight.

Even psychologists can be susceptible to hindsight bias, and their biased preconceptions or interpretations of results can seriously hinder their research. Luckily, the scientific method can minimize the effect of that bias.

False Consensus Effect

Another pitfall for psychologists (and other humans) is the **false consensus effect** (Ross et al., 1977; Wojcieszak, 2009; Dunn, Thomas, Swift, & Burns, 2011) or the tendency to overestimate the extent to which others share our beliefs and behaviours. Let's say you like to spend your free time chatting with like-minded friends on a political blog. It might seem to you and your fellow bloggers that your candidate of choice is practically guaranteed to win—after all, everyone supports him! Who wouldn't? Anyone with an ounce of common sense would agree with you that he's the best politician for the job. Or so it seems to you. However, it probably doesn't seem that way to your candidate's opponent or her supporters. In this case, your participation in the blogosphere, which in truth samples only a small portion of a self-selected population, has contributed to an occurrence of the false consensus effect. To minimize this type of problem—and avoid prejudice and bias—researchers try to gather a representative sample of people for their studies.

THE IMPORTANCE OF CRITICAL THINKING

It's important to approach scientific claims with an open but skeptical mind. "Where's the evidence?" is often the first question on the lips of someone adept at **critical thinking**—a way of processing information in which we examine assumptions, evaluate evidence, look for hidden agendas, and assess conclusions. Ask yourself whether the author had a motive for making a particular claim. Did he or she use reliable evidence to prove his or her theory? Might there be alternative explanations for the author's results? You may have personally experienced the same findings as the author of a particular paper (for example, a study claiming that the middle child in a family is more sociable than the eldest child may accurately reflect your own family), but it is important not to allow your personal experiences to increase the legitimacy of the results. A thorough examination of the author's use of the scientific process is required to determine whether the research is reliable.

Susan Clancy used statistical data to reach her conclusions. The ways in which she and her colleagues evaluated, questioned, and analyzed their findings illustrate their use of critical thinking skills. It's essential to think critically when carrying out scientific research. In other words, we need to examine our assumptions and challenge our gut instincts rather than relying solely on intuition and common sense, which are sometimes proved to be wrong. Good researchers do not blindly accept theories, no matter how obvious they might seem—they use scientific methods to question and examine those theories.

Critical inquiry also requires a degree of humility: Scientists need to be able to reject their own theories and open their minds to unlikely findings. Imagine if fellow scientists had persistently rejected Copernicus's heliocentric theory because it was common knowledge that Earth was the centre of the universe and the mere suggestion that things could be any other way was preposterous. The use of critical inquiry has convincingly discredited more recent assumptions, including the belief that we only use 10% of our brain (Lilienfeld & Arkowitz, 2008; Ezequiel, 2011) and that opposites attract (Holmes & Johnson, 2009; Morry, Kito, & Ortiz, 2011).

THE STORY OF CLEVER HANS

Clever Hans was an Arabian stallion purchased in 1888 by German math teacher Wilhelm von Osten. Von Osten believed that, given the proper education, horses had the potential to be as intelligent as humans. He began to tutor Hans in simple arithmetic. Hans

Do you believe everything you read? Critical thinkers evaluate and assess information with a degree of skepticism.

was taught to spell words by tapping his hooves to signify certain letters. He could also answer "yes or no" questions by moving his head up and down or back and forth. After four years of private tutoring, Hans could answer addition questions, figure out simple square root problems, and even tell time. Many professionals were astounded by Hans's apparent intelligence.

Hans's undoing came about as the result of an investigation by psychologist Oskar Pfungst. Pfungst believed that Hans was able to answer questions by responding to visual signals from his questioner. He began to test Hans by holding up numbered flashcards that Hans used for counting. First, von Osten was allowed to see the numbers on the flashcards before showing them to Hans. As usual, Hans tapped out the correct numbers with his hooves. Then, Pfungst asked von Osten to show Hans the cards without looking at them first. Hans was stumped. Pfungst began to study von Osten instead, and he noticed that von Osten made subtle unconscious gestures that cued Hans's correct responses. As Hans neared the correct number of hoof taps, von Osten would

FACT

Hans is correctly responding to basic arithmetic questions.

THEORY

Maybe Hans is taking clues from people around him.

FACT

Hans is unable to correctly respond to questions without visual aids.

Scientific Method

I predict that Hans will be unable to answer questions without visual aids.

HYPOTHESIS

I will take away visual clues from Hans to test his abilities.

STUDY

∧
∧ With results gleaned
∧ from earlier studies, scientists can formulate new **facts, theories, and hypotheses** and perpetuate the cycle of science.

change his posture without realizing it. Hans was certainly clever, but his math skills left something to be desired.

Facts, Theories, and Hypotheses

The story of Hans demonstrates how **facts, theories,** and **hypotheses** function in scientific research.

Facts are objective statements made using direct observations. Theories are ideas that help explain existing facts. Hypotheses, based on existing theories, are predictions about new facts.

Researchers use operational definitions of concepts to allow others to replicate their findings. In other words, they give a clear definition of their research methods so that other people can conduct the exact same experiment as precisely as possible. If many different researchers come up with the same results, those results are more likely to be reliable.

What Can We Learn from Hans?

Clever Hans may not have been a stellar mathematician, but his story illustrates three important lessons of scientific research:

1 **Be skeptical.** Consider alternative explanations for what you are observing. Not all popular claims are accurate—if they were, we'd be living on a flat planet surrounded by vicious sea monsters. It is important to try to disprove theories, including your own. As Aristotle once said, "It is the mark of an educated mind to be able to entertain a thought without accepting it."

2 **Observe carefully in controlled conditions.** Pay close attention during your study. Pfungst was the first professional to notice the unconscious signals von Osten was giving Hans. Less observant researchers were ready to sign the horse up for ninth-grade math. Researchers need to control conditions so that only one factor varies at a time. The only thing that changed between Hans's first counting session with Pfungst and his second was von Osten's knowledge of what was written on the flashcards. This level of control made it easy for Pfungst to pinpoint the source of Hans's cleverness.

3 **Be aware of observer-expectancy effects.** Watch out for researchers or observers who inadvertently communicate their expectations to participants and affect their behaviour as a result. Because she wanted to avoid the ramifications of this effect, Susan Clancy was very careful when she worded the newspaper notices recruiting participants for her alien abduction study. She tried not to give any non-essential or potentially biasing information.

As Aristotle once said, "It is the mark of an educated mind to be able to entertain a thought without accepting it."

Research Methods in Psychology

Because the study of psychology is scientific, it requires careful methods of observation and data collection. To answer questions about human behaviour, we need to collect and analyze data as systematically and objectively as possible. Before psychologists perform a research study, they must first ask themselves several questions:

WHAT **research strategies should I use to test my idea?**

HOW **can I guarantee that I obtain objective results?**

HOW **can I use statistics to analyze my results?**

HOW **can I ensure that people participating in my study are treated fairly?**

Types of Research Strategies

RESEARCH DESIGN: THE EXPERIMENT

Why do some people commit crimes? Why are teenagers often moody? Why do people sometimes become aggressive when they drink alcohol? Why do smart people sometimes do irrational things? The most conclusive way to test a hypothesis about human behaviour is to conduct an experiment. In an experiment, a researcher can manipulate one **variable**—a characteristic that can vary, such as age, weight, or height—while all other variables remain constant. This makes it possible to see how the variable that is manipulated affects an aspect of behaviour.

In 1956, Solomon Asch devised a series of simple experiments to test conformity among groups of people. He drew a standard line and asked his **participants** to determine which of three other lines it matched in length. Line C was clearly the correct response, but Asch wanted to see if people would give the correct answer under group pressure. He developed two conditions: In the first, he asked participants to answer the questions about line length alone. In the second, he put participants in groups with several **confederates,** people he'd previously instructed to give unanimous (and often incorrect) answers about the length of each line. The confederates served as the **independent variable,** or the variable that the

researcher can manipulate: Their presence was the one factor that differed between the two conditions. The **dependent variable,** or the measurable response to the independent variable, was the number of correct responses that the participants gave. Asch discovered that when asked to identify matching lines individually, participants gave the correct response nearly 100% of the time. However, when placed in a group of confederates who all swore that line C was the incorrect answer even though it was clearly correct, participants conformed to group pressure and gave incorrect responses more than one-third of the time.

Random Assignment

In some studies, each participant is exposed to all the independent variables in an experiment. These studies are called **within-subject experiments.** Other studies, known as **between-group experiments,** expose differ-

---

Facts are objective statements made using direct observations.

Theories are ideas that help explain existing facts.

Hypotheses are predictions about new facts, based on existing theories.

Variable is a characteristic that can vary, such as age, weight, or height.

Participant is a person who takes part in an experiment as a subject.

Confederate is a person who takes part in an experiment who is seemingly a subject but is really working with the researcher.

Independent variable is a variable that a researcher can manipulate in an experiment.

Dependent variable is a variable that is affected by the independent variable in an experiment.

Within-subject experiment describes a study in which each participant is exposed to all the independent variables in an experiment.

Between-group experiment describes a study in which different groups of participants are exposed to different independent variables.

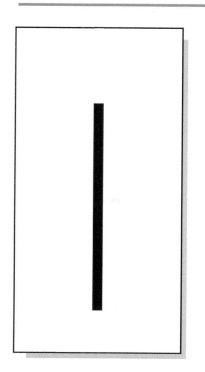

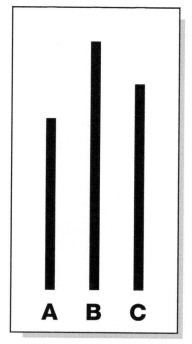

<<< **This image is an example of the stimuli used in Asch's conformity experiments. Participants were asked to match the length of the standard line on the left to the length of line A, B, or C on the right.**

A   B   C

Experimental group is a group of participants in an experiment who are subject to an independent variable.

Control group is a group of participants in an experiment who are either given no treatment or who are given treatment that should have no effect.

Random assignment is the process by which participants in an experiment are randomly placed into groups.

Matched sample is a group of participants in an experiment that is identical to at least one other group in terms of a particular variable or set of variables.

Matched pair is a set of participants in an experiment, one from one group and the other from another group, who are identical in terms of a particular variable or set of variables.

ent groups of participants to different independent variables. For example, many experiments feature an **experimental group,** which is subject to the independent variable, and a **control group,** which either gets no treatment or is given treatment that should have no effect (or a different effect than that caused by the independent variable). In a drug study, for example, the experimental group receives real medication while the control group might receive sugar pills. It's important to make sure that there are no major differences between these groups that may bias the results. This is achieved by **random assignment:** When participants are assigned randomly to one of two groups, it is likely that, given enough people, the two groups will be roughly equivalent in terms of the ages, genders, and other characteristics of their members. Any differences between groups are the result of chance, and researchers use statistics to take chance into account when they analyze the resulting data.

RESEARCH DESIGN: THE CORRELATIONAL STUDY

In a correlational study, a researcher does not manipulate variables, but instead observes whether there is a relationship between variables. Correlational

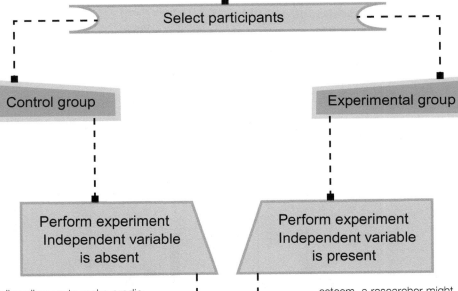

studies allow us to make predictions about one variable based on the knowledge of another. However, while good experimental studies can suggest cause-and-effect relationships, correlational studies do not usually indicate cause and effect: Correlation does not equal causation. For example, a correlational study might show a link between academic success and high self-esteem, but doing well in school may not necessarily cause high self-esteem. You might observe that increased

child mortality rates are related to increased ice cream consumption. So is ice cream deadly? Before you put down your ice cream cone, notice that both of these variables are also related to another factor—summer. In the summer, children eat more ice cream than they do during the rest of the year, and they are also more likely to get into accidents. Although both ice cream consumption and child mortality rise during the summer, neither of these variables causes the other to change. The third variable is, in fact, the actual cause of both events.

To prevent this so-called third variable problem, a researcher might choose research participants through the use of **matched samples** or **matched pairs.** Matched samples are two or more groups of people that are identical in terms of a third variable. For example, in a study to determine whether academic success is linked to high self-esteem, a researcher might want to reduce the effect of a third variable, age. It wouldn't make sense to compare third graders to college students, for example, because these two groups are at such different points in their lives that it would be hard for researchers to control all of the different variables in play. To reduce the effect of age, the researcher would create matched samples by ensuring that both sample groups are composed of similarly aged

> "When participants are assigned randomly to one of two groups, it is likely that, given enough people, the two groups will be roughly equivalent in terms of the ages, genders, and other characteristics of their members. **Any differences between groups are the result of chance, and researchers use statistics to take chance into account when they analyze the resulting data.**"

participants. Matched pairs take this principle to the next level—they ensure that each participant in one group is the same as a participant in another group in terms of a third variable. The self-esteem researcher might match a 15-year-old in one group with a 15-year-old in another group to create a matched pair.

RESEARCH DESIGN: THE DESCRIPTIVE STUDY

A descriptive study enables researchers to observe and describe behaviours without investigating the relationship between specific variables. Researchers may or may not use statistics to help them analyze their observations. Some descriptive studies have a narrow focus, such as observing how children react to a new environment or studying how adult males deal with confrontation. Other studies have a broader focus, such as observing the habits of animals in the wild. Descriptive studies may involve observing subjects (in either a natural habitat or a laboratory), using case studies, or conducting surveys.

Naturalistic Observation

Naturalistic observation is the study of people or animals in their own environment. It enables researchers to get a realistic picture of how their subjects behave. Canadian psychologists Debra Pepler and Wendy Craig study bullying using naturalistic observation. Using video cameras and remote microphones, they are able to observe naturally occurring peer interactions that happen on the playground, especially negative encounters that teachers may not witness. Natural observation is especially useful when studying bullying because children may alter their behaviour if they know someone is watching. Because the children do not know that they are being watched, they behave as they normally would, whether it is amicably playing with others or beating someone up.

One disadvantage of naturalistic observation is the possibility of **observer bias.** This occurs when the observer expects to see a particular behaviour and notices only actions that support that theory. One way to avoid observer bias is to use **blind observers,** or people who do not know what the research is about. It is also advisable to use

more than one observer, to enable them to compare notes. Another disadvantage to naturalistic observation is that because it takes place in real life, there is no possibility of repeating individual scenarios. This makes it difficult for psychologists to make generalizations based entirely on information from natural observations.

> ^^^ Why would researchers use naturalistic observation to study bullying? What might they learn?

Laboratory Observation

A **laboratory observation** enables a researcher to observe a person or an animal in a controlled setting. It is used when observing certain types of behaviour is not practical in a natural setting. For example, if a researcher wanted to test sleep patterns in college students, she would invite participants to take part in a sleep study. The participants would be fitted with electrodes and other devices, and the data would be displayed as waveforms and recorded onto a computer. This type of study would not be possible in a natural setting because of the vast amount of equipment required. But how do we know that the participants slept normally while not in their own beds? The disadvantage of laboratory observations is that participants' behaviour, and therefore the results of the study, might be artificial.

Naturalistic observation is the study of people or animals in their own environment.

Observer bias describes a situation in which an observer expects to see a particular behaviour and notices only actions that support that expectation.

Blind observers are observers who do not know what the research is about and are thus not subject to observer bias.

Laboratory observation is the study of people or animals in a controlled setting.

Case study is an in-depth study of one individual or a few individuals.

Case Studies

During a **case study,** researchers will study one individual or a few individuals in depth. They may use real-life observations, interviews, or tests to obtain information about their subjects. Developmental psychologist Jean Piaget (1896–1980) famously studied his own children as they grew. He was able to make powerful discoveries about cognitive development as a result of his observations.

Case studies are useful for providing information that would otherwise not be possible—or ethical—to obtain. For example, no one's likely to conduct—or line up to participate in—an experiment that requires participants to undergo severe brain damage. Enter the famous case study of Phineas Gage. Gage was a railway foreman who suffered severe brain trauma when an explosion propelled a metal spike through his skull—and the frontal lobes of his brain—in 1848. Amazingly, Gage recovered from his injuries, but he experienced drastic personality changes as a result of the accident. The case of Phineas Gage provided evidence that the frontal lobes play a role in personality and behaviour (Damasio et al., 1994).

Case studies can reveal fascinating information that we might not otherwise be able to obtain, but they do have their drawbacks. For example, since a case study provides only a single example of a phenomenon, that example may be atypical. It can be dangerous to make generalizations based on a case study without conducting further research.

Surveys

Have you ever gotten a phone call from a stranger who inquires, eagerly and persistently,

> **"Gage** was a railway foreman who suffered severe brain trauma when an explosion propelled a metal spike through his skull—and the frontal lobes of his brain—in 1848. Amazingly, Gage recovered from his injuries, but he experienced drastic personality changes as a result of the accident.**"**

about your opinion of everything from abortion to zero-emission engines? If so, you may have participated in a **survey.** To conduct a survey, a researcher will ask a series of questions about people's behaviour or opinions, in the form of a questionnaire or interview. Surveys can be useful because they have the potential to access private information from a large number of people relatively easily. Researchers commonly use surveys in both descriptive and correlational studies.

Researchers have to think long and hard about how they word their questions when they create a survey. Take a look at the following examples:

Do you approve of guest workers being given permission to remain in the country?
Do you believe that illegal immigrants are entitled to stay in the country?

Both of these questions have a similar meaning, yet using one instead of the other is likely to alter the outcome of the survey. The words *guest workers* and *permission* have more positive connotations than the words *illegal immigrants* and *entitled* do, and this difference in wording could impact the survey's results in an uncontrolled way. Researchers also need to be aware that people do not always answer surveys honestly, either through fear of being judged or by misremembering things.

Random sampling can help researchers make sure that their sample is representative of the general population. If you wanted to find out what people thought about gay marriage in Canada, you would get very different results if you interviewed only members of the gay community than if you surveyed only members of conservative religious groups. In any survey, it is important to question a cross-section of the entire group you're trying to learn about.

RESEARCH SETTINGS

All types of research can take place either in a laboratory or in the field. In a **laboratory study,** participants are taken to a location that has been specifically set up to facilitate collection of data and allow control over environmental conditions. A **field study,** on the other hand, is conducted in a setting other than a laboratory. Naturalistic observation is a type of field study because people or animals are observed in their natural environment rather than in a controlled setting. To overcome the disadvantages of both laboratory studies and field studies, researchers sometimes conduct both a laboratory study and a field study to investigate the same question. If researchers arrive at the same conclusion using both methods, they can be more confident about the reliability of their findings. For example, in 2008, researchers at Auburn University

asked participants to wear either sneakers or flip-flops as they walked on a special platform in a laboratory setting. After observing the flip-flop wearers' gaits, the researchers concluded that wearing flip-flops can cause injuries, specifically sore feet, ankles, and legs. But are flip-flops in the lab the same as flip-flops in the wild? If the researchers had performed a field study by observing flip-flop wearers in their natural environment, they would have been able to collect further data to determine whether flip-flops are less supportive than other shoes on everyday surfaces such as grass and asphalt.

The type of investigation usually determines the setting of the study. Experiments are often more effectively conducted in a laboratory because researchers have a higher level of control over the surroundings. Correlational and descriptive studies are usually performed in the field. However, the setting depends entirely on the individual investigation.

DATA COLLECTION METHODS

Self-report Methods

A **self-report method** is a form of data collection in which people are asked to rate or describe their own behaviour or mental state. Studies are usually in the form of **questionnaires** or **interviews.** You may have recently evaluated, with the invaluable help of a glossy magazine, your emotional neediness or your ideal celebrity match. Psychological questionnaires are similar in some ways to those magazine quizzes, but they have a stricter purpose and use careful controls such as precise wording, carefully constructed questions, and random sampling. A survey is one type of questionnaire.

In an interview, people provide oral descriptions of themselves to the interviewer. Interviews can be either strictly structured, with a set list of questions, or loosely structured and more conversational. In some structured interviews, interviewers use numerical methods to score people's responses to questions. This technique allows researchers to make precise generalizations from their results.

Observational Methods

When a researcher uses **observational methods,** he or she observes and records a subject's behaviour. Naturalistic observation is one example of an observational method. Another example is **testing.** By providing stimuli or problems for participants to respond to, researchers collect data about how participants complete a certain task. For example, if you participate in a research test, you might be asked to solve a logic puzzle or press a button every time you see a bulb light up.

Data Collection Pros and Cons

Frustratingly, no one method of data collection is perfect, and each has its advantages and disadvantages. Questionnaires and interviews are great for gathering private information, but there is no guarantee that people's responses are accurate. (Even those of us who are unfailingly honest don't have perfectly objective views of our own behaviour.) Naturalistic observations allow researchers to observe participants' natural behaviour first-hand, but it is difficult to observe behaviour without disrupting it, and analyzing observed results statistically can be tricky. Tests are convenient and easily scored, but they can be artificial: Your ability to solve a logic puzzle in 5.2 minutes may have no relationship to your ability to be logical in your everyday life. When researchers choose an experimental design, they have to make sure that their method of data collection will give them useful information about the theory they're studying.

Statistical Methods in Psychology

Once researchers have collected their data, they use statistics to analyze that data and to look for significant patterns. There are two types of statistics: **descriptive statistics,** which researchers use to summarize data sets (for example, height, weight, or grade point average), and **inferential statistics,** which use probability laws to help researchers decide how likely it is that their results are due to chance and, as a result, how likely it is that the observed results apply to a broader population.

DESCRIPTIVE STATISTICS
Measures of Central Tendency

If you had to find out what the average gas price in your province or territory was, or the average number of people who own hybrid cars in your community, what sorts of numbers would you be looking for? It all depends on your interpretation of the word *average*. There are three **measures of central tendency,** or most typical scores, in a set of data. The **mean** is the arithmetic average—the sum of all the scores divided by the number of scores. The **median** is the middle score in the data set: If all the scores were arranged in order from lowest to highest or highest to lowest, half of the scores would be above the median and half would be below it. The **mode** is the most frequently occurring score.

Observational methods are the processes of observing and recording a subject's behaviour.

Testing is a type of observational method in which participants are provided with stimuli or problems to respond to and researchers collect data about how the participants perform a certain task.

Descriptive statistics are statistics researchers use to summarize data sets.

Inferential statistics are statistics that use probability laws to help researchers decide how likely it is that their results are due to chance and, as a result, how likely it is that the observed results apply to a broader population.

Measures of central tendency are the three most typical scores in a set of data: mean, median, and mode.

Mean is the arithmetic average of the scores in a data set, or the sum of all the scores divided by the number of scores.

Median is the middle score in a data set.

Mode is the most frequently occurring score in a data set.

Variability is the degree to which the numbers in a set of data differ from one another and the mean.

Range is the difference between the highest and lowest values in a data set.

Standard deviation is a measure of the dispersion of a set of values using information from each individual score.

∧
∧ **Unlike most magazine quizzes, questionnaires**
∧ **used by psychologists are scientifically valid.**

Measures of Variability

The measure of **variability** is the degree to which the numbers in a set of data differ from one another and from the mean. The simplest measure of variability is the **range,** which is the difference between the highest and lowest values in a data set. If the unemployment rate was 15% in December but skyrocketed to 25% in June, the range of unemployment during that time period would be 10%. A range is not always an accurate estimate of variation because it does not take into account the extreme nature of some scores. For example, imagine that in the vast majority of Canadian provinces the unemployment rate was 10%. However, all the car manufacturing plants in Windsor were shut down, putting everyone out of work, and giving Ontario an unemployment rate of 22%. At the same time, in Alberta there is a hiring boom because of the increase in oil refineries, resulting in that province having an unemployment rate of 4%. These extreme changes in employment would create a deceptively high range in scores, even though the majority of scores are almost all the same.

A better measure of variation is **standard deviation.** Standard deviation takes into account the dispersion of a set of values by using information from each individual score. Each value is given a **deviation score,** which is the difference between the individual data point's actual value and the mean value of the whole data set. Calculating the standard deviation can give you a better idea of whether scores are closely packed together or spread out.

Frequency Distribution

Frequency distribution is a summary of how frequently each of the scores in a set of data occurs. To prepare a frequency distribution, researchers rank each data score from highest to lowest and group the data into intervals. They then create a frequency distribution table, putting the intervals in numerical order and identifying how many individual scores fall in each interval (or how many times each score appears in the data set). Finally, the researchers can create a graph to display the information. **Bar graphs** use vertical or horizontal bars that are proportional in length to the value they represent. A **histogram** is visually similar to a bar graph, but because it displays intervals

on the x-axis and frequency on the y-axis, it is particularly well suited for graphing frequency distribution.

INFERENTIAL STATISTICS

How can psychologists be sure that their results are valid, and not simply due to chance or coincidence? This is where statistical analyses come in.

Normal Distribution and Skewed Distribution

Once researchers have collected the data for their study, they must begin to make sense of that data. One of the first things that they may look at is how the data are distributed, or spread out. Data that are evenly distributed will form a bell shape if plotted on a graph. This is called a normal distribution and forms a **normal curve.** In a normal distribution the mean, median, and mode are the same, and the data tend to be greatest around the centre of the bell shape. If the data, however, are not evenly distributed, then they are said to be skewed—

the bell shape is off to one side. In a skewed distribution, the majority of data are clustered together on one end rather than in the middle. A **skewed distribution** will have a different mean, median, and mode. Although, most empirically collected data will not follow a normal distribution, we use the normal curve to determine whether the data show significant findings.

Statistical Significance

Let's say that you are interested in the nail-biting behaviour of individuals. You hypothesize that nail biting will increase when a person is under stress. You set up an experiment in which nail-biters participate and you record their nail-biting behaviour while they are at home watching TV and then while they are waiting in class to write their final exam. For these recordings, you count the number of times each participant bites his or her nails under the two conditions (home vs. exam). How can you determine whether your hypothesis is correct? You compare the average number of times participants bit their nails in the home (let's say 5 times) versus exam (let's say 25 times) conditions. If you find a large enough difference between these two conditions, then this difference has **statistical significance**—in other words, it's not simply due to chance. Most researchers say that a result is significant if there is less than a 5% chance that the result is due to chance. We use the letter p to represent the probability that a result is due to chance. So, in our nail-biting experiment, our results would be significant if $p < 0.05$, meaning that there was a less than 5% probability that the

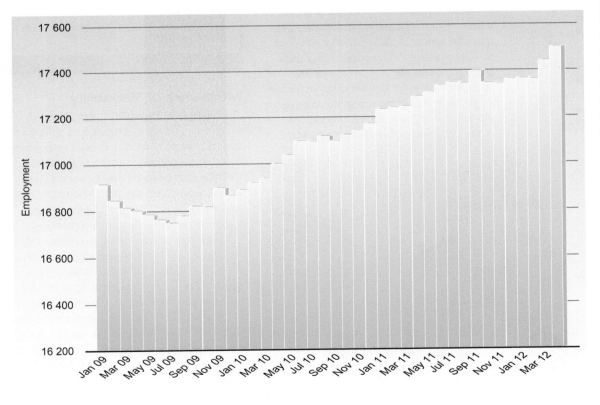

∧∧∧ Psychologists will often use **bar graphs** (like the one on the above), histograms, **and other graphical displays** when explaining their research findings. It is often **easier to see** changes in a data set when the data are displayed visually.

Normal Distribution

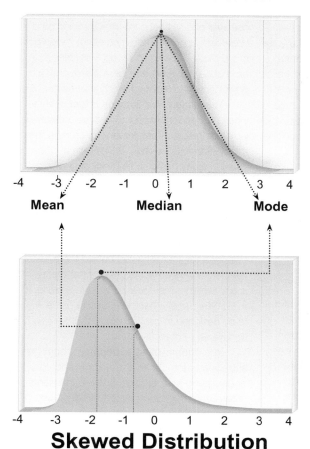

Skewed Distribution

differences we found in nail biting were due to chance. This means that there is a 95% probability that people bite their nails more when they are under stress, which supports your hypothesis.

When you determine a result's statistical significance, you'll need to take a few different factors into account: effect size, sample size, and how variable the data are within each group. An easy-to-remember rule is that if research produces a large observed effect, a large sample size, and little variability in data within groups, it's likely that the results of that research are statistically significant.

Minimizing Bias in Psychological Research

ERROR

Imagine that Susan Clancy inadvertently recruited a participant in her alien abduction study who lied in order to take part in the research. The results from that participant would introduce **error,** or random variability, into the results. Some degree of error is inevitable in psychological research

because as hard as we try, we can't control every variable that might influence the behaviour we're studying.

The presence of error doesn't necessarily mean that someone's made a mistake, and the consequences of error are relatively insignificant if the study is large enough. Researchers measure error by calculating the standard deviation of the relevant data. Then, they take this information into account when they perform a statistical analysis of the data.

BIAS

When Susan Clancy and her colleagues interacted with the participants in their experiment, they had to be careful to avoid **bias.** What would have happened if they'd treated everyone in the control group normally but treated those people who claimed to be alien abductees with scorn, ridicule, or condescension? It's possible that the researchers' results would have been affected as a result of this unequal, biased treatment. Bias is a serious problem in psychological research because it cannot be identified and corrected using statistical procedures. Whereas error only reduces the chance that results may be statistically significant, bias can lead researchers to draw false conclusions. To address this bias, scientists use multiple researchers in their experiments, and they follow careful training procedures to make sure that all researchers are following the same valid experimental techniques.

Bias is not only a problem from the researcher's perspective. **Demand characteristics** are aspects of a setting that can cause participants in a study to behave as they believe the researcher wants them to, potentially invalidating the results of the study in the process.

Avoiding Biased Samples

A sample is biased when the people in it are not representative of the larger population being studied. When participants are randomly assigned into groups, their individual differences are the result of error and can be taken into account during statistical analysis of the results. However, when participants are not randomly assigned into groups, there may be elements of both error and bias. Another potential problem is self-selection: Sometimes, participants in a study create bias merely by

choosing to take part in that study. For example, if a survey asks lots of personal questions, only people who feel comfortable answering personal questions will complete the survey. So what can we do to ensure an unbiased sample? The truth is that no matter how large a sample is, there will always be an element of bias. The trick is in keeping that bias as small and inconsequential as possible.

Avoiding Measurement Bias

A good researcher will check that his or her measurements are both reliable and valid. **Reliability** is the degree to which a measurement yields similar results every time it is used with a particular subject under particular conditions. A reliable measure may obtain different results from different participants, but if it is used with the same participant multiple times, it should get the same result every time. Checking that a measurement is reliable pertains to error rather than bias because it is a

Validity is the degree to which a measurement measures what it is intended to measure.

Face validity is the extent to which a study superficially measures what it is intended to measure.

Criterion validity is an indication of how closely a measurement correlates with another criterion of the characteristic being studied.

Predictive validity is a type of criterion validity in which you can use the results of a test to predict a person's score or performance in another area.

Construct validity is a type of validity that uses a specific procedure that measures or correlates with a theoretical or intangible concept.

Internal validity is a type of validity indicating that a researcher is able to control all extraneous values in a test so that the only variable influencing the results of the study is the independent variable.

External validity is a type of validity indicating that a test can be generalized to the rest of the population.

researcher's responsibility to make sure that he or she is consistent in his or her methods. If a measurement has a low degree of reliability, it is unlikely that a study based on that measurement will have any statistical significance.

The **validity** of a measurement is the degree to which it measures what it is intended to measure. This is a more critical issue than reliability, because a procedure may be reliable, but if it is not valid then nothing has been achieved. There are several different categories of validity:

1 Face validity. Face validity is the extent to which a study superficially measures what it is intended to measure. Imagine that you are a participant in an experiment designed to test intelligence, and the researcher asks you whether you like ice cream. This question has no face validity because it's not immediately apparent that ice cream preference has anything to do with intelligence. In this case, a measurement with face validity might take the form of a logical problem that you're asked to solve.

2 Criterion validity. You may score off the charts on an intelligence test, but how can the researcher be sure that the test is actually measuring intelligence? Ideally, the test has **criterion validity,** a term that refers to how closely a measurement correlates with another criterion of the characteristic being studied. To determine that an intelligence test is valid, a researcher might compare the results of the test with results of another measure correlated with intelligence. For example,

intelligence test scores are commonly compared with school achievement (Aiken & Groth-Marnat, 2005). If a large enough group of people who do well in school also perform well on an intelligence test, the test has criterion validity.

One type of criterion validity is **predictive validity.** If a test has predictive validity, you can use its results to predict a person's score or performance in another area. For instance, your career counsellor might give you a test with predictive validity to determine how likely you are to do well in certain professions.

3 Construct validity. If a test has **construct validity,** it uses a specific procedure that measures or correlates with a theoretical or intangible concept. You can't take out your intelligence and weigh it on a scale or wrap a measuring tape around it. However, an intelligence test that has construct validity will be able to produce concrete results that correlate with intelligence.

4 Internal validity. A test has **internal validity** if the researcher is able to control all extraneous variables so that the only variable influencing the results of his or her study is the independent variable. Internal validity enables the researcher to prove that there's a causal relationship between the dependent variable and the independent variable.

5 External validity. A test has **external validity** if it can be generalized to the rest of the population. If the researcher has used a representative sample in his or her study, the conclusions drawn should be applicable to any other group of people, and the study is likely to have external validity.

Avoiding Observer- and Subject-Expectancy Effects

Remember Clever Hans and his trainer? Researchers have desires or expectations during a study that they may inadvertently pass on to their participants, influencing the way participants behave. Wilhelm von Osten was providing Hans with subtle clues that biased the results of his "experiment." These expectations may also affect how the researcher perceives the participants' behaviour. If Oskar Pfungst had expected Hans

to be an equine Einstein, he wouldn't have been predisposed to notice von Osten's non-verbal cues. The **observer-expectancy effect,** or observer bias, is best overcome by using blind observers who are uninformed about the purpose of the study. In between-group experiments, a blind observer would also be unaware of which participants had received which treatments.

The **subject-expectancy effect** occurs when participants expect to behave a certain way as a result of their treatment, causing them to adjust their behaviour. This is best avoided by keeping study participants blind, or unaware of the treatment they are receiving. For example, Canadian psychologist Kang Lee studies children's lying behaviours. The children, however, think they are just playing a guessing game during which they are left alone and told not to peek at a toy that is placed behind them. Later the children are asked to guess what the toy is and whether they peeked at it while alone. If the children knew that the guessing game was really designed to catch them lying, they might behave very differently.

In a **double-blind experiment,** both the subject and the observer are kept blind. In double-blind drug studies, some participants receive the drug being tested, while others receive a **placebo** (an inactive substance that looks like the drug). Since neither the partici-

The placebo effect can be powerful. What does its existence tell us about the power of the mind? >>>

pants nor the observers know which is being taken, any differences in behaviour are more likely to be a result of the drug rather than a result of subject or observer expectations. This is how the now-famous impotency drug Viagra was tested. The results showed that 69% of attempts at intercourse while using Viagra were successful, while only 22% of men using the placebo were able to successfully have sexual intercourse (Goldstein et al., 1998).

The double-blind procedure is not completely immune to subject and observer expectations, however. The **placebo effect,** an extreme example of the power of suggestion, occurs when individuals taking a placebo react as if they were receiving treatment, simply because they believe that they are receiving treatment.

Ethical Issues in Psychological Research

In 1971, psychologist Philip Zimbardo from Stanford University recruited about 70 young men, mostly college students, to participate in a study of the psychological effects of prison life. After completing diagnostic tests, 24 volunteers were offered $15 a day to participate in the two-week experiment. The participants were arbitrarily divided into two groups with the toss of a coin. Half were told they were now prison guards, and half were assigned the role of prisoners. The "prisoners" were booked at a real jail, blindfolded, and taken to a campus building that had been turned into a realistic prison environment with the help of a former convict. Upon arriving at the prison, each prisoner was stripped naked, searched, deloused with a spray, and forced to wear a uniform.

On the second day of the experiment, the prisoners staged a revolt that was quashed by the guards. The guards became more aggressive, forcing the prisoners to perform humiliating tasks such as cleaning toilet bowls with their bare hands. Five prisoners had to be released early because they were so emotionally distressed that they became physically ill. The experiment was eventually cancelled on the fifth day (Zimbardo, 1971).

RESEARCH WITH HUMANS

Zimbardo certainly didn't set out to create an experiment that would harm its participants, but was the Stanford Prison Experiment ethical? When researchers conduct experiments on humans, they have to take three important issues into consideration:

1 **A person's right to privacy.** Researchers must obtain informed consent from each participant. Participants in a study must also be told that they do not need to share any information they are not comfortable sharing, and results must be kept anonymous.

2 **The possibility of discomfort or harm.** Zimbardo most likely wouldn't have gone ahead with his experiment if he had foreseen its outcome. Researchers have a responsibility to ensure that their participants are placed at minimal risk during a study and that any risk undertaken is outweighed by the potential human benefits. Participants must be aware that they are free to quit at any time (a questionable element of Zimbardo's study).

3 **The use of deception.** Some psychologists are opposed to any use of deception in a study because it undermines the concept of truly informed consent. Others believe that some processes cannot be studied without an element of deception involved. To avoid the use of deception, psychologists may **debrief** participants after the study by providing them with a verbal description of the true nature and purpose of the study.

> **When researchers conduct experiments on humans, they have to take three important issues into consideration: as person's right to privacy, the possibility of discomfort or harm, and the use of deception.**

RESEARCH WITH ANIMALS

Is it ethical to use animals in psychological research? Some people believe that procedures that cannot ethically be performed on humans may still be performed on animals. Many of the basic biological mechanisms underlying animal behaviour are similar to those underlying human behaviour, and animal research can provide valuable information (APA, 2012). Much of what we know about perception, sensation, drugs, and the way the brain functions was gleaned from animal research (Carroll & Overmier, 2001).

However, is it ethical to use animals in studies when they cannot give their consent?

Observer-expectancy effect see *observer bias*

Subject-expectancy effect is an occurrence where participants in a study expect to behave in a certain way as a result of their treatment, causing them to adjust their behaviour.

Double-blind experiment is an experiment in which both the subject and the observer are kept blind, thus negating the observer-expectancy effect and the subject-expectancy effect.

Placebo is a substance or procedure that resembles medical therapy but has no intrinsic therapeutic value.

Placebo effect is a phenomenon in which participants taking a placebo react as if they were receiving treatment, simply because they believe they are actually receiving treatment.

Debrief is to give a verbal description of the true nature and purpose of a study after the study occurs.

Canadian Psychological Association (CPA) is a scientific and professional organization that represents psychologists in Canada.

Institutional Review Board (IRB) is an ethics review panel established by a publicly funded research institution to evaluate all proposed research by that institution.

Any suffering that is caused must be weighed against the potential benefits of the study. Would we object to growing tumours on mice if doing so enabled us to find a cure for cancer? Who decides whether the consequences are justified? Some animal protection organizations propose that animals be studied in their natural environments rather than tested in laboratory experiments. These groups' opponents claim that following this proposal would prevent valuable research opportunities.

HOW CAN WE ENSURE ETHICAL RESEARCH?

The **Canadian Psychological Association (CPA)** has established a code of ethics for psychological research. Researchers must abide by these rules if they wish to publish their work in scientific journals. Furthermore, publicly funded research institutions are required by law to establish ethics review panels that evaluate all proposed research. These panels are commonly known as **Institutional Review Boards (IRBs).** As a result of these safeguards and guidelines, panels now routinely turn down studies that would have once been deemed acceptable, and some "classic" studies cited in this book—such as the Stanford Prison Experiment—would not be approved today.

02

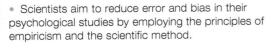

Summary

HOW IS THE SCIENTIFIC METHOD USED TO STUDY PSYCHOLOGY? p.16

- Scientists aim to reduce error and bias in their psychological studies by employing the principles of empiricism and the scientific method.
- The six steps of the scientific method that psychologists generally follow are identifying the problem, conducting background research, formulating a hypothesis, testing the hypothesis, analyzing the results, and reporting the results.

WHY ARE RESEARCH METHODS IMPORTANT TO THE STUDY OF PSYCHOLOGY? p.21

- Psychologists use scientific methods to carry out research, reducing the problems of hindsight bias and the false consensus effect.
- When carrying out empirical research, psychologists use existing facts and theories to come up with new hypotheses.

WHAT ARE SOME TYPES OF RESEARCH STRATEGIES? p.21

- Experiments, correlational studies, and descriptive studies (naturalistic observation, laboratory observation, case studies, and surveys) are used to conduct different types of research.
- Research can take place in a laboratory or in the field.
- Data collection may be self-reported or observational.

HOW CAN STATISTICAL METHODS HELP US GATHER AND ANALYZE DATA? p.25

- Descriptive statistics are used to summarize data sets and provide information about measures of central tendency, measures of variability, and frequency distribution.
- Inferential statistics are used to provide information about the statistical significance of data.

HOW CAN WE MINIMIZE BIAS? p.27

- A degree of error is inevitable in any psychological research and is taken into account during statistical analysis.
- Researchers can minimize bias by using representative samples, taking reliable measurements, and avoiding subject- and observer-expectancy effects.

WHAT ETHICAL ISSUES DO PSYCHOLOGISTS FACE? p.29

- When conducting a study, a psychologist needs to consider three issues: a person's right to privacy, the possibility of harm or discomfort, and the use of deception.
- Researchers must follow the Canadian Psychological Association's code of ethics if they wish to publish their work in scientific journals.

Test Your Understanding

1. Why are people's personal observations of human behaviour often unreliable?
   a. They are not empirical.
   b. They are not conducted in a laboratory setting.
   c. They are not conducted in an objective, scientific manner.
   d. They are not based on the principles of physics and chemistry.

2. Maria wants to use the principles of empiricism to investigate whether alcohol consumption affects people's sleeping patterns. Maria is most likely to:
   a. monitor people's alcohol consumption and then observe their brain activity during sleep
   b. interview sleep specialists about the effects of alcohol on sleeping patterns and then write an essay
   c. ask people to tell her about their personal experiences with alcohol and sleep
   d. read about the effects of alcohol on sleeping patterns in an approved psychology journal

3. Which of the following is NOT a method psychologists use to test their hypotheses?
   a. conducting case studies
   b. conducting experiments
   c. conducting surveys
   d. conducting background research

4. Without mentioning that he is researching a psychology project, Ben takes notes about his family members' behaviour while they are eating dinner. Ben is conducting:
   a. an experiment
   b. correlational research
   c. naturalistic observation
   d. a survey

5. Which of the following is an example of a self-report method?
   a. a questionnaire
   b. a hypothesis
   c. a proven fact
   d. a psychologist's notes

6. Yuan-Chun takes part in a study to test a new acne drug. Although she is part of the control group and has not been given the real drug, Yuan-Chun believes that her skin is significantly improving. Yuan-Chun is experiencing:

   a. the false consensus effect
   b. hindsight bias
   c. observer bias
   d. the placebo effect

7. Which of the following statements about case studies is true?

   a. Case studies are advantageous because they are cheaper and quicker than other methods.
   b. Case studies are more representative than other methods.
   c. Case studies are less subject to bias than other methods.
   d. Case studies can provide information that it would not be ethical to obtain using other methods.

8. Which of the following studies has face validity?

   a. a survey researching personality traits that asks a question about income level
   b. an experiment testing physical strength that involves lifting different objects
   c. a study of child development that includes a middle-aged man
   d. a sexual health questionnaire that includes a question about pets

9. Krishna conducts an experiment to prove that reduced levels of sleep cause memory deficits. For three days, he keeps his participants awake until 3 a.m. and wakes them up promptly at 7 a.m. He then gives his participants a memory test. What is the independent variable in Krishna's experiment?

   a. the participants' regular sleep patterns
   b. the results of the memory test
   c. the amount of sleep
   d. the attitude of the participants

10. Alexis researches the number of long-term relationships people have typically been in by the age of 30. Her results are: 2, 3, 2, 1, 0, 2, 3, 4, 5, 7, and 4. What is the mean number of relationships?

    a. 4   b. 3   c. 7   d. 2

11. Which of the following helps to control the effect of observer bias?

    a. blind observers
    b. random assignment
    c. using a placebo
    d. trained observers

12. To avoid potential bias in her study, Kim tells her participants that they will be taking part in an intelligence test. In actual fact, she is researching common interactions between strangers. What should Kim do to make sure that her experiment is ethical?

    a. She should promise participants that the study will not harm them.
    b. She should ask an IRB member to perform the study for her.
    c. She should pay participants appropriately for their time and effort.
    d. She should debrief the participants when they have completed the study.

13. Which of the following p-values is statistically significant?

    a. 0.7   b. 0.4   c. 0.6   d. 0.8

14. Which of the following is NOT true of surveys used to conduct research?

    a. They allow researchers to access private information from a large number of people.
    b. They should be used in conjunction with random sampling.
    c. They allow researchers to draw conclusions about cause-and-effect relationships.
    d. Their accuracy depends on participants' truthful responses.

15. While analyzing two sets of data, Jin notices that people who eat carrots more than twice a week live longer than people who rarely eat the vegetable. Jin writes an article for his college newspaper with the headline "Eating carrots increases longevity." What is wrong with Jin's article?

    a. A correlational link does not necessarily indicate cause and effect.
    b. The positive correlation is not strong enough to draw this conclusion.
    c. Jin should have referred to at least two other studies before printing his article.
    d. Jin did not credit the researchers of the data in his headline.

16. Adam measures the feet of five male classmates. His results are 29 centimetres, 30 centimetres, 27 centimetres, 30 centimetres, and 28 centimetres. What is the range of Adam's results?

    a. 3   b. 29   c. 27   d. 5

17. Malik makes sure that he uses a representative sample of the population for his study. Because of this, Malik's results will most likely have:

    a. external validity
    b. internal validity
    c. construct validity
    d. criterion validity

18. Researchers at a publicly funded institution who want to publish their work in a scientific journal must:

    a. abide by the CPA code of ethics and have their research proposal evaluated by an institutional review board
    b. abide by the CPA code of ethics and submit their research proposal to the CPA in writing
    c. have their research proposal evaluated by an institutional review board
    d. submit their research proposal to the CPA in writing

19. You frequently find yourself using the phrase, "I knew it all along." Which of the following does this phrase best illustrate?

    a. false consensus effect
    b. critical thinking
    c. hindsight bias
    d. dogmatism

20. Alisha needs to conduct a behavioural experiment in a laboratory. Which of the following is most important for Alisha to consider?

    a. She may not be able to draw conclusions regarding cause-and-effect relationships.
    b. Her experiment may not use a representative sample of the population.
    c. Her results may depend on participants' willingness to answer questions honestly.
    d. Participants' behaviour may be affected by the artificial setting.

Remember to check www.thethinkspot.ca for additional information, downloadable flashcards, and other helpful resources.

Answers: Answers: 1) c; 2) a; 3) d; 4) c; 5) a; 6) d; 7) d; 8) b; 9) c; 10) b; 11) a; 12) d; 13) b; 14) c; 15) a; 16) a; 17) a; 18) c; 19) c; 20) d

PSYCHOLOGICAL SCIENCE

Short Report

Becoming Friends by Chance

Mitja D. Back, Stefan C. Schmukle, and Boris Egloff

University of Leipzig

> When you read the introduction, you should be able to extract what the study is testing, any previous findings that are relevant to the study's research question, and a very general preview of how the research question will be approached.

May the development of friendship be due to chance? Since the days of the ancient Greek philosophers, friendship has been conceived of as an intentional choice based on common values and interests (cf. Blieszner & Adams, 1992). However, contemporary experimental psychological research has shown that many choices are not exclusively made on the basis of intentional and controllable processes, but are also influenced by superficial situational factors and automatic processes (e.g., Bargh & Chartrand, 1999; Dijksterhuis, Bos, Nordgren, & van Baaren, 2006; Pelham, Carvallo, & Jones, 2005). This might also hold true for the social choices that people make in everyday life. The famous actor Sir Peter Ustinov (1979) lent his support to this view when he stated, "Contrary to general belief, I do not believe that friends are necessarily the people you like best, they are merely the people who got there first" (p.93).

It has, in fact, been demonstrated that mere similarity of age, marital status, or ethnic background influences the development of friendships (e.g., AhYun, 2002; Newcomb, 1961). Moreover, mere proximity (e.g., living nearby—Festinger, Schachter, & Back, 1950; Latané, Liu, Nowak, Bonevento, & Zheng, 1995; Nahemow & Lawton, 1975), as well as mere assignment to the same group (e.g., being in the same work unit—Hogg & Tindale, 2001; Segal, 1974), increases the likelihood of becoming friends. Do these involuntary factors also have an influence when they are restricted to initial encounters, rather than persisting over a longer period of time? This study examined whether randomly determined physical proximity and group assignment during an initial encounter

Address correspondence to Mitja D. Back, Department of Psychology, University of Leipzig, Seeburgstrasse 14-20, 04103 Leipzig, Germany, e-mail: mback@uni-leipzig.de.

> This phrase marks the research question. How is the research question related to the researchers' hypothesis? (To review the definition of a hypothesis, turn to p.21.)

are each sufficient to influence the likelihood of a friendship developing in a real-life context.

METHOD

Subjects

We assessed a group of psychology freshmen ($N = 54$) when they encountered one another for the first time and again after their first year of study. Participants were 36 female and 18 male students from various places of origin in Germany. Their average age was 22.22 years ($SD = 4.57$).

Procedure

The first measurement occasion took place at the beginning of an introductory session for freshmen studying psychology. Students received a randomly assigned seat number when entering the room and took their assigned place. They were then requested to individually step forward, beginning on the right-hand side of each row, and briefly introduce themselves. These self-introductions ranged in length from 4.00 to 21.30 s ($M = 7.51, SD = 3.27$). Immediately after each introduction, the other freshmen rated the person (from 0 to 5) on two scales ("How likeable do you find this person?" and "Would you like to get to know this person?"). Following the evaluation, the students in that row all moved one seat to the right, and the evaluated participant took the empty seat at the far left-hand side of the row. This procedure was repeated, row by row, until all students had been rated. During the experiment, each dyad in the sample ($N = 54 \times 53/2 = 1431$) sat in neighboring seats (proximity), sat in the same row but not in neighboring seats (same group), or sat without any perceivable physical relation to one another (control).

One year later, we obtained friendship ratings in individual laboratory sessions. Participants were given photographs of their fellow students and asked to indicate the intensity of their friendship to each, using the following four items: "I like this person," "This person likes me," "I know this person well," and "I am friends with this person." Ratings were made on scales ranging from 0, *not at all*, to 5, *very much*.

Computation of Attraction and Friendship Measures

Aggregate measures of attraction and friendship intensity were computed by averaging the ratings made at

The Method section answers the question, "What was done?" It describes the people who participated (the "subjects" or "participants") and explains the steps that the participants followed (most often called the "procedure").

What is the independent variable in this study? What do you think the dependent variable will be? (Independent and dependent variables are discussed on p.21.)

Why do you think the researchers decided to seat students randomly? Review Chapter 2 (p.21) for more information about randomization in research studies.

R1-2 Reading

Measuring Friendship

In the Results section, the study's findings are catalogued and described in detail. Tables and graphs are also often used to visually present results.

the first and second measurement sessions, respectively. According to Kenny's (1994) social relations model, interpersonal perceptions (e.g., attraction) may be decomposed into three independent components (plus error): a perceiver effect (e.g., harshness of the perceiver), a target effect (e.g., popularity of the target), and a relationship effect (after controlling for perceiver and target effects; e.g., relational attraction to a person). Analyses of our round-robin data indicated that our aggregate measures of attraction and friendship intensity contained significant amounts of perceiver variance (16.44% and 14.94%, respectively), all $t(53)$s > 4.29, $ps < .01$; target variance (10.75% and 6.42%, respectively), all $t(53)$s > 4.28, $ps < .01$; and relationship variance (51.76% and 65.63%, respectively), all $t(53)$s > 27.09, $ps < .01$ (Bond & Lashley, 1996).

RESULTS AND DISCUSSION

We first tested whether proximity and group assignment influenced initial attraction ratings. To do this, we performed a multilevel analysis for dyadic data, using SAS proc mixed (Kenny, Kashy, & Cook, 2006). To examine effects on relational attraction, we included perceiver and target as random effects at Level 1. Sitting in neighboring seats and sitting in the same row were fixed-effects predictor variables at Level 2. Compared with dyads who had no perceivable physical seating relation ($M = 2.99$, $SD = 0.55$), those who sat in neighboring seats ($M = 3.87$, $SD = 0.65$) and those who sat in the same row ($M = 3.20$, $SD = 0.62$) had higher initial attraction scores, $F(1, 1378) = 75.69$, $p < .01$, and $F(1, 1379) = 11.97$, $p < .01$, respectively.

Might pure chance also influence the formation of friendships? To answer this question, we performed another multilevel analysis. Results are presented in Figure 1. Sitting in neighboring seats as a

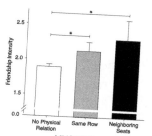

Fig.1 Mean friendship intensity as a function of randomly assigned seating at the first encounter a year earlier. Friendship intensity was rated on a scale from 0 to 5. Error bars represent standard errors of the means. Asterisks indicate significant differences between conditions, p < .05.

result of randomly assigned seat num-

P-values indicate the probability that the results are due to chance rather than to the experimental procedure. Since most of these results have p-values of less than 0.05, there is a less than 5% probability that these results are due to chance. This means the results are statistically significant. (See p.26 for more about p-values.)

bers, compared with sitting in seats with no perceivable physical relation, led to higher ratings of friendship intensity 1 year later, $F(1, 1380) = 5.06$, $p < .05$. Sitting in the same row also led to higher ratings of friendship intensity than did sitting in seats with no perceivable physical relation, $F(1, 1383) = 4.84$, $p < .05$. The effects of random seat assignment on friendship persisted in an additional analysis controlling for initial attraction at Level 1, $F(1, 1382) = 3.42$, $p = .06$, for sitting in neighboring seats and $F(1, 1370) = 4.20$, $p < .05$, for sitting in the same row.

To conclude, coincidentally being near another person or being in the same group with him or her during an initial encounter may promote the development of a friendship with that person. In a nutshell, people may become friends simply because they drew the right random number. Thus, becoming friends may indeed be due to chance.

Acknowledgments— We thank Steffen Nestler for inspiring discussions of this research.

REFERENCES

AhYun, K. (2002). Similarity and attraction. In M. Allen, R.W. Preiss, B.M. Gayle, & N.A. Burrell (Eds.), *Interpersonal communication research* (pp. 145–167). Mahwah, NJ: Erlbaum.

Bargh, J.A., & Chartrand, T.L. (1999). The unbearable automaticity of being. *American Psychologist, 54,* 462–479.

Blieszner, R., & Adams, R.G. (1992). *Adult friendship.* Newbury Park, CA: Sage.

Bond, C.F., Jr., & Lashley, B.R. (1996). Round-robin analyses of social interactions: Exact and estimated standard errors. *Psychometrika, 61,* 303–311.

Dijksterhuis, A., Bos, M.W., Nordgren, L.F., & van Baaren, R.B. (2006). On making the right choice: The deliberation-without-attention effect. *Science, 311,* 1005–1007.

Festinger, L., Schachter, S., & Back, K. (1950). *Social pressures in informal groups: A study of human factors in housing.* Stanford, CA: Stanford University Press.

Hogg, M.A., & Tindale, R.S. (Eds.). (2001). *Blackwell handbook of social psychology: Group processes.* Oxford, England: Blackwell.

Kenny, D.A. (1994). *Interpersonal perception: A social relations analysis.* New York: Guilford Press.

Kenny, D.A., Kashy, D.A., & Cook, W.L. (2006). *Dyadic data analysis.* New York: Guilford Press.

Latané, B., Liu, J.H., Nowak, A., Bonevento, M., & Zheng, L. (1995). Distance matters: Physical space and social impact. *Personality and Social Psychology Bulletin, 21,* 795–805.

Nahemow, L., & Lawton, M.P. (1975). Similarity and propinquity in friendship formation. *Journal of Personality and Social Psychology, 32,* 205–213.

Newcomb, T.M. (1961). *The acquaintance process.* New York: Holt, Rinehart, and Winston.

Pelham, B.W., Carvallo, M., & Jones, J.T. (2005). Implicit egotism. *Current Directions in Psychological Science, 14,* 106–110.

Segal, M.W. (1974). Alphabet and attraction: An unobtrusive measure of the effect of propinquity in a field setting. *Journal of Personality and Social Psychology, 30,* 654–657.

Ustinov, P. (1979). *Dear me.* New York: Penguin.

The Discussion section explains the research findings. It often concludes with a description of the study's limitations, and suggestions for future studies.

Remember, empirical studies using inferential statistics (p.25) do not prove things; they simply allow us to draw inferences about how the findings can be interpreted and generalized.

THE
HUMAN
BRAIN

WHAT CHARACTERISTICS DESCRIBE THE HUMAN BRAIN?

HOW IS THE NERVOUS SYSTEM ORGANIZED?

HOW DOES THE NERVOUS SYSTEM OPERATE AT THE CELLULAR LEVEL?

WHAT ARE THE DIFFERENT PARTS OF THE HUMAN BRAIN, AND WHAT ROLE DOES EACH PART PLAY?

This is your

brain. How much do you really know about it?

Tell me about your brain. What do you know about it? You may know that it is relatively small in size compared to the rest of your body, weighing in at only 1.4 kilograms. You may also know that it is responsible for everything we do; our thoughts, behaviours, and desires all originate in our brain. Yet despite the power of our brain

<<< *The human brain is creative, adaptable, sophisticated, and innovative. What other "super powers" does the human brain display?*

many of us do not really know how it works. Many misconceptions about the brain continue to exist. Perhaps the most persistent misconception is that we only use 10% of our brain at any given time. This simply is not true! Barry Gordon (deceased), from Simon Fraser University, first identified this as a "brainscam" in 1990, and researchers (e.g., McCutcheon, Apperson, Hanson, & Wynn, 1992; Lilienfeld, Lynn, Ruscio, & Beyerstein, 2010) have consistently shown that this belief is invalid. Research using brain imaging has failed to show an "inactive" region of the brain, and damage to any brain area will cause deficiencies in functioning. But, not all beliefs about the brain are false. For example, perhaps you have heard that some of us are left-brained while others are right-brained. These terms are used to describe individuals who are analytical and highly verbal compared to others who are artistic, creative, and have high spatial skills. Read this chapter to find out whether this belief and other common beliefs about the brain are valid.

CHAPTER **03**

The Brain in Context

WHY STUDY THE BRAIN?

To put it simply, the human brain enables behaviour. Exactly how it does this, however, remains a mystery to scientists. At present, we can't draw simple relationships between brain

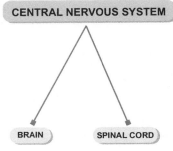
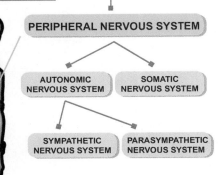

THE NERVOUS SYSTEM

CENTRAL NERVOUS SYSTEM → BRAIN, SPINAL CORD

PERIPHERAL NERVOUS SYSTEM → AUTONOMIC NERVOUS SYSTEM, SOMATIC NERVOUS SYSTEM

AUTONOMIC NERVOUS SYSTEM → SYMPATHETIC NERVOUS SYSTEM, PARASYMPATHETIC NERVOUS SYSTEM

Central nervous system (CNS) is the largest part of the nervous system; it includes the spinal cord and the brain.

Peripheral nervous system (PNS) is the part of the nervous system that serves the limbs and organs.

Somatic nervous system is the part of the peripheral nervous system that picks up stimuli from the outside world, coordinates movements, and performs other consciously controlled tasks.

Autonomic nervous system is the part of the peripheral nervous system that performs tasks that are not consciously controlled.

Sympathetic nervous system is the part of the autonomic nervous system that is always active and acts as an accelerator for organs.

Parasympathetic nervous system is the part of the autonomic nervous system that is responsible for functions that do not require immediate action and acts as a brake for organs.

Neurons are excitable cells that receive different types of stimulation; they are the building blocks of the nervous system.

Dendrites are relatively short, bushy, branch-like structures that emerge from the neuron's cell body and receive signals from adjoining neurons.

Soma is the cell body of a neuron.

Axon is a cable-like extension that transmits a signal away from a neuron's soma toward the target of communication.

Myelin is a fatty substance that coats and insulates axons.

Terminal buttons are structures at the ends of the branches that extend from axons.

Sensory neurons carry information from the sensory receptors to the brain as a coded signal.

Motor neurons carry information away from the central nervous system to operate muscles and glands.

Interneurons carry information between sensory neurons and motor neurons.

Glial cells (glia) are cells that support neurons by, among other things, keeping neurons in place, creating myelin, and providing nutrition and insulation.

Blood-brain barrier is a fatty envelope that filters substances trying to leave the bloodstream and reach the brain.

Network is a large community of neurons.

Nerve is a tight grouping of neurons.

---

events and human behaviour, but we can establish a number of consistent and predictable relationships between brain regions and classes of behaviour. Understanding how the human brain works is crucial to understanding why we do what we do.

Speaking generally, the human brain has three major characteristics:

1 **Integration.** The brain's structures are constantly competing and co-operating.

2 **Sophistication.** Even the most high-tech computers can't match the human brain in complexity of thought and behaviour.

3 **Adaptability.** The human brain is always working and constantly changing. The brain can adapt and function fully under very unusual circumstances.

THE BRAIN AND THE NERVOUS SYSTEM

The nervous system is subdivided into two parts, the **central nervous system (CNS)** and the **peripheral nervous system (PNS).** The central nervous system is the largest part of the nervous system and includes the spinal cord and the brain. The peripheral nervous system resides outside of the central nervous system and serves the limbs and organs.

The peripheral nervous system is further divided into the **somatic nervous system** and the **autonomic nervous system.** The somatic nervous system picks up stimuli from the outside world, coordinates our movements, and performs other tasks that we control consciously. The autonomic nervous system consists of the **sympathetic nervous system** and the **parasympathetic nervous system.** The sympathetic and parasympathetic nervous systems act in opposition to each other and affect the same organs. The sympathetic system acts as an accelerator for the organs, while the parasympathetic system

acts as a brake. The parasympathetic system is responsible for functions that do not require immediate action. The sympathetic system, in contrast, is always active and becomes significantly more active during stress.

The two systems have rhyming job descriptions: While the sympathetic system's job is "fight or flight," the parasympathetic system's priorities are "rest and digest."

Neurons: Their Anatomy and Function

Neurons are the building blocks of the nervous system. A neuron is an excitable cell that receives different types of stimulation, most often signals from other neurons. In response to a signal, a neuron can "fire" by passing the signal along to other neurons, but it can also hold its fire by not transmitting the signal. While neurons are binary in nature—they either fire or they don't—they can fire at various rates (from 100 to 1000 times a second) and thus pass on highly nuanced information to other neurons.

NEURON ANATOMY

Dendrites are relatively short, bushy, branch-like structures that emerge from the neuron's cell body and receive signals from adjoining neurons. A single neuron may have as many as 2000 connections to other neurons through its dendritic branches.

The neuron's cell body, the **soma,** contains the nucleus. All of the information collected by the dendrites converges in the soma, which processes this information. In effect, the soma calculates the sum of all incoming signals, and if the summed voltage is above a specific threshold, the neuron will fire and pass the signal along to the cells with which it connects.

When a neuron fires, the signal travels down the neuron's **axon,** a cable-like extension that transmits the signal away from the soma toward the target of communication. Axons "talk to" three different targets: muscles, glands, and dendrites of neighbouring neurons. Axon length varies quite a bit among neurons. Some axons are relatively short, while others can extend from the base of the brain to the tips of the toes.

Most, but not all, axons are covered by a **myelin** sheath. A fatty substance that acts a lot like the plastic coating on electrical wires, myelin insulates the axon, thereby improving the strength and speed of signals travelling down its length.

Axons pass their signals to neighbouring dendrites via **terminal buttons,** structures at the ends of the many branches that extend out from each axon. When they receive a signal, the terminal buttons release chemicals into the space between neurons and excite neighbouring dendrites.

Types of Neurons

Although all neurons are generally similar in structure, they come in a variety of shapes and sizes. All neurons, however, fall into three categories, depending on their location and function in the nervous system:

- **Sensory neurons** carry information toward the central nervous system from the sensory organs (eyes, ears, nose, tongue, and skin).
- **Motor neurons** carry information away from the central nervous system in order to operate muscles and glands.
- **Interneurons** send information between sensory neurons and motor neurons.

Interneurons are the most numerous type of neuron in the human nervous system: There are millions of sensory and motor neurons, but there are about 100 billion

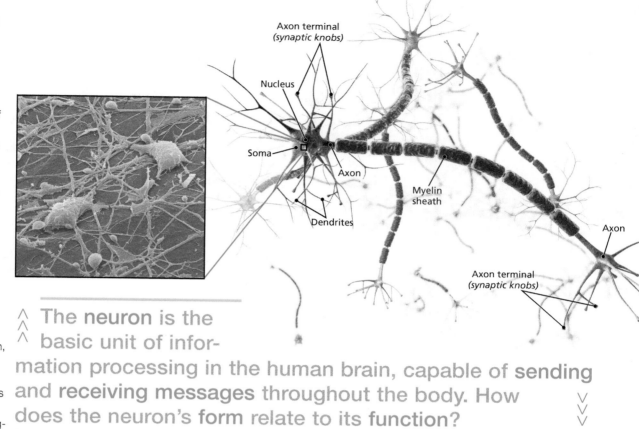

Axon terminal *(synaptic knobs)*
Nucleus
Soma
Axon
Dendrites
Myelin sheath
Axon
Axon terminal *(synaptic knobs)*

∧∧∧ The **neuron** is the basic unit of information processing in the human brain, capable of **sending** and **receiving messages** throughout the body. How does the neuron's **form** relate to its function? ∨∨∨

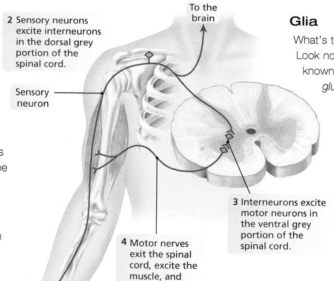

2 Sensory neurons excite interneurons in the dorsal grey portion of the spinal cord.

To the brain

Sensory neuron

3 Interneurons excite motor neurons in the ventral grey portion of the spinal cord.

4 Motor nerves exit the spinal cord, excite the muscle, and initiate a movement.

1 Flame stimulates pain receptors (sensory neurons).

interneurons. Located exclusively in the central nervous system, interneurons are capable of receiving and combining information from a variety of sources. As the workforce of the CNS, these cells are responsible for generating perception from sensation, creating our internal mental worlds, and organizing and initiating behavioural actions.

Glia

What's the glue that holds neurons together? Look no further than the **glial cells,** also known simply as **glia,** the Greek word for *glue*. There are about 10 glial cells for every neuron in the human brain. Glia support those neurons in many ways: Among other tasks, they keep neurons in place, create myelin, and provide nutrition and insulation.

Additionally, a specialized form of glial cells, called astrocytes, surrounds the brain's blood vessels and creates what is known as the **blood-brain barrier,** a fatty envelope that filters substances trying to leave the bloodstream and reach the brain. Since many toxins and poisons are not soluble in fat, they cannot penetrate the blood-brain barrier and harm the brain.

COMMUNICATION BETWEEN NEURONS
To Fire or Not to Fire

Neurons are very social creatures. They live in large communities called **networks** and cluster in tight groupings called **nerves.** Neurons depend on contact with one another for survival, and they work both as individuals and as part of larger groups.

Every neuron has a specific **threshold** that must be reached in order for it to fire. Whether the number of positive inputs exceeds the threshold by 1 millivolt or 100, the result is the same: If the threshold is crossed, the cell will fire. This is called the **all-or-none principle.** When you're standing on a diving board, you either jump or you don't; there is no "in between" state. The same is true for neurons.

When a neuron fires, the signal that the dendrites and cell body receive must travel down the axon to the terminal buttons at the opposite end of the neuronal cell. To accomplish this, the neuron creates an **action potential,** an electrochemical ripple that works its way from the cell body to the terminal buttons and terminates in the release of neurotransmitters that will stimulate the next neuron.

While at rest, a neuron's fluid interior contains an excess of negatively charged particles, while its external environment has a surplus of positively charged ions. This relatively negative state inside the neuron is called the **resting potential.** It's maintained by negatively charged protein molecules and chlorine atoms within the cell as well as by ion pumps in the cell membrane that keep more potassium ions inside the neuron and more sodium ions outside the neuron. Not surprisingly, potassium and sodium ions use different channels to enter and exit the cell.

When the neuron is stimulated, the axonal membrane closest to the cell body selectively changes the status of its ion channels. As a result, potassium channels close and sodium channels open. Consequently, the amount of positively charged sodium ions inside the cell increases. This influx of sodium ions changes the internal state of the axon from negative to positive and propagates the action potential to the next section of the axon's membrane. The movement of sodium ions into the neuron and potassium ions out of the neuron, as well as the pumping that puts the ions back where they came from, continues down the axon, creating a moving electrical signal. This signal moves down the axon in the same way that a human wave at a sporting event travels around a stadium.

The self-propagating action potential works its way down the membrane to the terminal buttons, where it causes the release of chemicals that excite the neighbouring neuron. Myelinated neurons are able to speed up this process. The myelin sheath that covers the axon is not continuous; rather, the glial cells that make up the myelin form insulated sections, leaving small bits of bare axon called

∧
∧ Unlike a game of "telephone"
∧ where distortions in the message can lead to harmless fun, **distortions in the messages passed on from one neuron to another can have very serious consequences.**

Neurons communicate in much the same way people do when they have a bit of interesting gossip. Imagine an eighth grader tearing down the hallway of her school to tell her closest friend the "latest." Her excitement is palpable. Upon reaching her friend, she whispers in her ear; the friend shrieks in excitement and is off to tell the next student. Of course, neurons transmit information via energy rather than whispers, but their basic pattern of communication might seem familiar to a teenage social butterfly.

Neurons fire only when they are stimulated by a source, such as another neuron or a sensory receptor that has been stimulated by heat, light, or pressure. Many different neighbouring cells can relay signals to a single neuron. Some cells instruct the neuron to fire—to transmit information to other neurons—while others tell the neuron not to fire (a process called **inhibition**). Faced with these conflicting messages, the neuron does something very social: It goes with the majority.

The Neuron at Rest
During the resting potential, the neuron is negatively charged inside and positively charged outside.

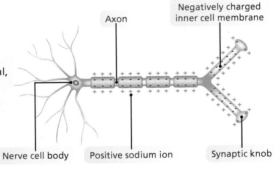

Axon

Negatively charged inner cell membrane

Nerve cell body   Positive sodium ion   Synaptic knob

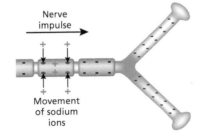

Nerve impulse →

Movement of sodium ions

The Neural Impulse
The action potential occurs when positive sodium ions enter into the cell, causing a reversal of the electrical charge from negative to positive.

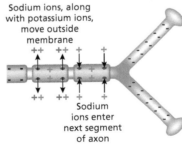

Sodium ions, along with potassium ions, move outside membrane

Sodium ions enter next segment of axon

The Neural Impulse Continues
As the action potential moves down the axon toward the axon terminals, the cell areas behind the action potential return to their resting state of a negative charge as the positive sodium ions are pumped to the outside of the cell, and the positive potassium ions rapidly leave.

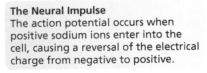

∧
∧ **The movement of negatively and positively**
∧ **charged particles allows an electrical signal to travel down the axon.**

the **nodes of Ranvier.** The action potential can jump from bare spot to bare spot. This jumping from node to node allows the signal to move down the axon with great speed.

The Synapse

Upon seeing **synapses** under his microscope, anatomist Santiago Ramón y Cajal (1937) nicknamed them "protoplasmic kisses." A synapse is a connection between two neurons through which information is transmitted. Often, the synapse is made up of a narrow space, or a **synaptic cleft,** between the transmitting neuron's terminal buttons and the receiving neuron's dendrites. The neuron that delivers the signal to the synapse is called the **pre-synaptic neuron,** and the neuron that receives the signal from the synapse is called the **post-synaptic neuron.** Synapses are also located between neurons and muscles as well as between neurons and gland cells.

Synapses convert the electric action potential that's travelled down the axon into a chemical message, called a **neurotransmitter.** When a neuron fires, its terminal buttons release neurotransmitters into the synaptic cleft. Some of those neurotransmitters then travel across the synapse and chemically stimulate the neighbouring neuron. That neuron, in turn, converts the chemical signal back to an electrical signal. Thus, communication within a neuron is electrical, while communication between neurons is chemical.

Neurotransmitters don't stay in the synaptic cleft for long: A process called **reuptake** moves many of the released neurotransmitters back to the pre-synaptic neuron. (Research has shown that glia also play a role in removing neurotransmitters from the synapses [Volterra & Steinhäuser, 2004].) If a neurotransmitter doesn't quickly attach to a receptor on a neighbouring neuron, it will fall victim to the reuptake process.

A specific class of drug designed to relieve symptoms of depression owes its effectiveness to this process: One theory of depression hypothesizes that a lack of a neurotransmitter

> Communication within a neuron is electrical, while communication between neurons is chemical.

called serotonin prevents cells from communicating the way they do in people without depression. Drugs called selective serotonin reuptake inhibitors, or SSRIs, block the reuptake of serotonin from the synaptic cleft. Because SSRIs prevent pre-synaptic neurons from rapidly reabsorbing serotonin, more neurotransmitters remain in the synaptic cleft longer, increasing the likelihood that they will stimulate the neighbouring cells' post-synaptic receptors.

Synaptic Plasticity

One impressive characteristic of the brain is its **plasticity,** or its ability to adapt and change. This plasticity is evident not only in the brain as a whole but also at the cellular level. In 1949, Canadian psychologist Donald Hebb first proposed the idea of synaptic plasticity as a theoretical model to account for how the brain learns and retains memories. Hebb theorized that the more cells talk to one another, the more plentiful their synaptic connections become. In addition to providing a compelling model for learning and memory, this phenomenon helps us understand how individuals recover from damage to areas of the brain. Since the brain cannot make new functional

Inhibition is a process in which a neuron is instructed not to transmit information to other neurons.

Threshold is the number of positive inputs a neuron must receive before it transmits information.

All-or-none principle states that once the threshold for a particular neuron is reached, it will transmit all of its information, no matter how many more positive inputs it receives over that threshold.

Action potential is an electrochemical ripple that works its way from the cell body to the terminal buttons and terminates in the release of neurotransmitters that will stimulate the next neuron.

Resting potential is a relatively negative state inside a neuron in which the neuron's fluid interior contains a surplus of negatively charged particles.

Nodes of Ranvier are parts of an axon that are not insulated by myelin.

Synapse is the area between neurons across which nerve impulses travel.

Synaptic cleft is a narrow space between a transmitting neuron's terminal buttons and a receiving neuron's dendrites.

Pre-synaptic neuron is a neuron that delivers a signal to a synapse.

Post-synaptic neuron is a neuron that receives a signal from a synapse.

Neurotransmitter is a chemical message created by a synapse from an electric message transmitted by terminal buttons.

Reuptake is a process in which neurotransmitters are released back to a pre-synaptic neuron.

Plasticity describes a flexible ability to grow and change.

>>> Drugs like **SSRIs** are designed to affect the reuptake process and alter signal transmission across synapses. What might be the benefits and drawbacks of these drugs?

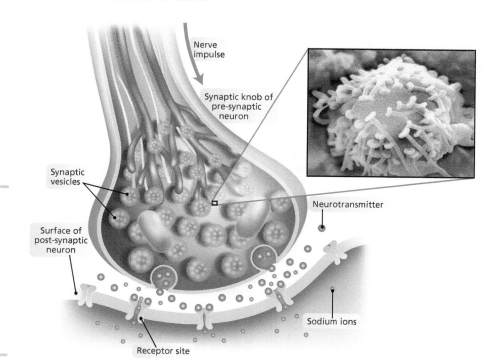

Nerve impulse

Synaptic knob of pre-synaptic neuron

Synaptic vesicles

Surface of post-synaptic neuron

Neurotransmitter

Sodium ions

Receptor site

neurons, it recruits and fortifies smaller, previously underutilized connections. Recent discoveries further support Hebb's theory of synaptic plasticity. In one study, London taxi drivers exhibited increased hippocampus volume compared to similarly aged adults who were not taxi drivers. (The hippocampus is a structure critical to spatial memory that will be discussed in more detail later in this chapter.) Scientists believe that the drivers' increased hippocampus volume results from increased synaptic density, stimulated by learning numerous complicated driving routes (Maguire, Spiers, Good, Hartley, Frackowiak, & Burgess, 2003).

The Central Nervous System: The Spinal Cord

The **spinal cord** connects the spinal nerves to the brain and organizes simple reflexes and rhythmic movements. It is organized in ascending and descending tracks: Ascending tracks carry sensory information from the body to the brain, while descending tracks deliver motor commands to the muscles from the brain.

THE JOB OF THE SPINAL CORD

Specifically designed to keep you alive, **reflexes** are rapid and automatic neuromuscular actions generated in response to a specific stimulus. Most often, the spinal cord organizes these automatic actions without the conscious participation of the brain. To produce a reflex, a sensory neuron must carry the stimulus to the spinal cord, where an interneuron enables connection to a motor neuron that produces a specific motor pattern. Consider the following example: You are walk-

>>> The **spinal cord** connects the brain to the **peripheral** nervous system.

ing barefoot on the beach when you begin to step on something sharp. The sensory neurons in your foot are immediately activated by the painful stimulus and send a signal to the interneurons in the spinal cord. Interneurons in turn answer this call by exciting the motor neurons leading to your foot. As a result, before you have time to really "think about it," your foot has jerked up off the sand, and you have avoided injury.

Have you ever felt like you don't have control over your body's movements? When it comes to reflexes, you don't have conscious control. It would be inefficient for a signal to travel all the way to the brain and back when only a simple movement is required. When there's the potential for harm, elaborate decision making becomes less important than getting away from the stimulus as fast as possible. Of course, if you step on something sharp, the pain signal will eventually reach your brain, though the signal travels more slowly than the spinal reflex does. When the signal arrives, you will consciously experience pain, followed by the awareness of your own rapidly moved foot. But reflexes and conscious awareness aren't really connected: Although people with spinal cord injuries exhibit spinal reflexes, they have no conscious or sensory awareness of doing so.

DAMAGE TO THE SPINAL CORD

Unlike a great deal of tissue in the human body, the spinal cord is not able to repair itself following injury. The overwhelming majority of spinal cord injuries involve motor vehicle accidents and people between the ages of 16 and 30. Most frequently, damage to the bones of the spinal column severs or chokes the spine itself.

Injuring the spine is like cutting a string of

Labels on diagram: Brain (CNS), Spinal cord (CNS), Nerves (PNS)

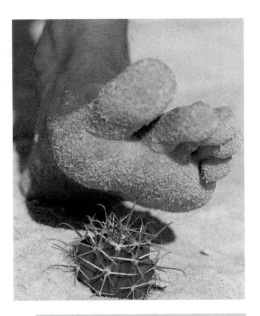

∧
∧ Reflexes keep us safe.
∧

Christmas lights: All the bulbs that follow the cut will no longer light up. Similarly, a person may lose all of the functions controlled by the area of the spine below the injury. For example, damage to the cervical vertebrae can cause the brain to be out of touch with the body. This injury would paralyze the chest and lungs (requiring patients to rely on a machine to breathe) as well as the trunk and both arms and legs. In contrast, injury to the lumbar, or lower spine area, may result in hip and leg paralysis. The spinal cord is rarely completely severed, so some patients manage to recover certain aspects of function; however, complete recovery is unlikely.

The Central Nervous System: The Human Brain

All cells or structures found in humans are also found in other animals. Why, then, are humans fundamentally different from the vast majority of the animal kingdom? What gives rise to uniquely human thoughts and emotions such as symbolic representation, empathy, and misanthropy? We don't really know the answers to these questions, but we do know that the structure of the human brain is not terribly unique. In fact, it shares a number of structures with the brains of animals farther down the evolutionary ladder. However, the ways in which these structures are used may be what makes the human brain truly unique.

>>> How does MacLean's model of the triune brain illustrate the brain's sophistication, integration, and adaptability?

Paul MacLean (1990) has written extensively about the "triune" brain. According to MacLean's model, the human brain is best understood within a socio-cognitive context by dividing it into three regions.

The primary and evolutionarily oldest part of the brain is the **brainstem,** which is responsible for survival-oriented functions such as breathing, cardiac function, and basic arousal. The second region, which emerged more recently in evolutionary terms, is the **limbic system.** Comprising a number of structures that control social and emotional behaviour, the limbic system also influences cognitive processes, most notably forms of memory. The evolutionarily newest part of the brain is the **neocortex,** specifically the **prefrontal cortex.** This advancement is credited with hurling humans up the evolutionary ladder by enabling symbolic representation, the cornerstone of most complex cognitive processes.

Following MacLean's model, we'll explore the human brain from the "bottom up," taking

Limbic System

Neocortex

Brainstem

a look at the most basic and rudimentary structures before working our way to the more complex or "evolved" portions of the brain.

THE BRAINSTEM AND SUBCORTICAL STRUCTURES

The brainstem is exactly what it sounds like: the "stem" or base of the brain. Connected to the spinal cord, the brainstem houses the

Spinal cord connects the spinal nerves to the brain and organizes simple reflexes and rhythmic movements.

Reflexes are rapid and automatic neuromuscular actions generated in response to a specific stimulus.

Brainstem is the base of the brain; responsible for survival-oriented functions such as breathing, cardiac function, and basic arousal.

Limbic system is a system in the brain made up of a number of structures that control social and emotional behaviour; it influences cognitive processes, most notably forms of memory.

Neocortex is the evolutionarily newest part of the brain; it enables symbolic representation.

Prefrontal cortex is the very front of the brain and part of the neocortex; it is responsible for the executive functions, such as mediating conflicting thoughts and making choices between right and wrong. It is essential for the cognitive experience of emotion.

Foramen magnum is the largest opening in the skull; it allows the spinal cord to connect to the brain.

Medulla is a part of the brain that regulates cardiac and respiratory function.

Pons is a part of the brain that is involved in sleep, dreaming, left-right body coordination, and arousal.

structures that control basic survival functions. Like the spinal cord, these structures are capable of reflexive action.

The brainstem has two main functions. First, it's a conduit for incoming sensory information and outgoing motor commands, much like the spinal cord. Second, it possesses integrative functions that are critical for cardiovascular system control, respiratory control, pain sensitivity control, alertness, and consciousness. Taking this information into consideration, it's easy to see why damage to the brainstem is often life threatening.

Unfortunately, the brainstem is vulnerable to both direct and indirect damage. The adult skull is made of very hard bone with few openings. The largest opening is the **foramen magnum** at the base of the skull, which connects the spinal cord to the brain via the brainstem. Most significant traumas to the brain result in swelling. Since the skull is a hardened sphere, the swollen brain has no place to expand other than through the large opening at the base of the skull. The "extra" volume of brain tissue creates a great deal of pressure at the base of the skull and can actually compress the brainstem enough to cause a coma. In the most dramatic case, swelling can disrupt the **medulla** and the **pons,** the centres that regulate cardiac and respiratory function, causing death. While we know that the brain is flexible and adaptable, it

Basal ganglia (a group of nuclei located in both hemispheres, on either side of the corpus callosum and thalamus)

Corpus callosum

Thalamus

Cerebellum

Brainstem

<<< The brainstem controls basic survival functions.

Thalamus is a part of the brain located just above the brainstem that receives sensory information, processes it, and sends it to the cerebral cortex; it helps to regulate the states of arousal, sleep and wakefulness, and consciousness.

Cerebral cortex is an outer part of the brain that is mainly involved in the coordination of sensory and motor information.

Cerebellum is a part of the brain that coordinates muscle movements and maintains equilibrium. It is involved in conditioning and forming procedural memories and habits related to movement.

Basal ganglia are a set of interconnected structures in the brain that help with motor control, cognition, different forms of learning, and emotional processing. They are involved in forming procedural memories and habits related to movement.

Caudate is a part of the basal ganglia; it is involved in the control of voluntary movement and is part of the brain's learning and memory system.

Putamen is a part of the basal ganglia; it is involved in reinforcement learning.

Globus pallidus is a part of the basal ganglia; it relays information from the caudate and putamen to the thalamus.

Amygdala is a part of the limbic system; it is involved in fear detection and conditioning and is essential for unconscious emotional responses such as the fight-or-flight response.

Hippocampus is a part of the brain involved in processing explicit memories, recognizing and recalling long-term memories, and conditioning.

Hypothalamus is a small structure in the brain that links the nervous system to the endocrine system.

Cingulate cortex is a part of the brain that is divided into four sections and is involved in various functions such as emotion, response selection, personal orientation, and memory formation and retrieval.

<<< The **cerebellum** helps athletes perform **rapid, complex movements.**

states of arousal, sleep and wakefulness, and consciousness.

The Cerebellum

The "little brain," or **cerebellum,** in many ways resembles a smaller version of the cerebral cortex (e.g., it contains two distinct hemispheres) and is located just behind and underneath it. The cerebellum works as an integrator, allowing us to control and process our perceptions and motor movements. Many neural pathways link the cerebellum with both the cerebral motor cortex and the spinal cord. The cerebellum smoothly integrates these pathways, receiving feedback about the body's position and using this information to direct our movements.

Because the cerebellum modifies motor movement rather than producing it, damage to the cerebellum causes movement-related difficulties rather than paralysis. These difficulties tend to be most obvious during rapid,

well-timed sequences of movements such as dialing a telephone, playing sports, or playing a musical instrument. Motor control isn't the cerebellum's only forte, however: The cerebellum also helps us pay attention to stimuli and process a variety of sensory information.

The Basal Ganglia

The **basal ganglia** are a set of interconnected structures (the **caudate, putamen,** and **globus pallidus**) next to the thalamus. The human basal ganglia are richly connected to the brainstem, thalamus, and cerebral cortex and are an essential participant in motor control, cognition, different forms of learning (particularly motor learning), and emotional processing. Illnesses that affect the basal ganglia, such as Huntington's disease, often cause patients to experience muscle spasms in the arms, legs, or face. Damage to the basal ganglia may also cause poor coordination.

THE LIMBIC SYSTEM

The limbic system, which has rich reciprocal connections with both the brainstem and the neocortex (Davis, 1992), is responsible for a number of survival-related behaviours. Simply, the limbic system is a series of neural structures that are critical for human emotion, motivation, and some forms of emotional and social learning. There is, however, some disagreement with regard to which specific structures are included in the limbic system. Given the purpose of the present discussion, description of the limbic system will be limited to structures involved in emotionally driven behaviour, including the **amygdala,** the **hippocampus,** the **hypothalamus,** and portions of the **cingulate cortex.**

isn't always able to use these qualities to ward off serious damage to the vulnerable, valuable brainstem.

The Thalamus

The **thalamus,** located just above the brainstem, has multiple critically important functions. It acts as a translator that receives sensory information directly from most of the sense organs and processes that information into a form that the **cerebral cortex,** or the outer part of the brain, can understand. It then sends that information to various parts of the cerebral cortex. Additionally, the thalamus helps to regulate our

Cingulate cortex

Hypothalamus

Hippocampus

Amygdala

<<< The structures of the limbic system are involved in motivation and emotion.

The Amygdala

The amygdala (from the Greek word for "*almond*," which describes its shape) is involved in fear detection and conditioning. Scientists describe this structure as "a neural system that evolved to detect danger and produce rapid protective responses without conscious participation" (LeDoux, 1994). Imagine that you awake in the middle of the night to hear banging against your window. Before you can understand what you are seeing or hearing, the amygdala has received a "rough copy" of this sensory information. If the amygdala appraises the information it receives as threatening, then it will initiate a physiological response called the **fight-or-flight response** that prepares your body for action. You may notice that your heart is racing and that you suddenly feel wide awake. Meanwhile, a second, more detailed, message travels from your eyes and ears to the appropriate sensory cortex for more extensive processing and conscious perception. The banging sound you heard is analyzed in detail, using information from many parts of the brain. Once your brain has decided whether the threat is real or imagined, a message to this effect is sent back to the amygdala. If a burglar is entering your bedroom, your amygdala has prepared your body to react. If the sound you heard was a branch tapping against your window, the fear circuit is switched off and you are able to go back to sleep (although it may take you a while to relax).

The Hippocampus

The hippocampus, which means *seahorse* in Greek, is named for its curved shape when seen in cross-section. It is essential for creating and storing new memories. The hippocampus can be thought of as a top-notch administrative assistant in a very busy office. It is responsible for creating and logically storing memory "files," knowing where those files are, and retrieving them when necessary. Like a good administrative assistant, the hippocampus knows where everything is, meaning that it plays a critical role in a variety of memory processes, including spatial memory (remember the London taxi drivers described earlier?). Individuals with hippocampus damage are

able to hold new information for a short time, but are unable to make enduring memories.

The Cingulate Cortex

The cingulate cortex lies along the midline of the brain in each hemisphere, just above the **corpus callosum.** The cingulate is functionally and anatomically segregated into four distinct regions (Vogt, Vogt, Farber, & Bush, 2005). The **anterior cingulate cortex,** closest to the forehead, has a primary role in emotion and in the integration of visceral and cognitive information. The **midcingulate cortex** lies just behind the anterior cingulate and is involved with response selection, particularly among competing stimuli. The **posterior cingulate cortex,** closest to the back of the head, is closely tied to personal orientation. It not only helps you determine where you are in space, but also allows you to gauge your personal involvement and relevance in social situations. The final—and least understood—region of the cingulate cortex is the **retrosplenial cortex,** which is believed to be closely involved in memory formation and retrieval.

The Hypothalamus

The hypothalamus is a relatively small but critically important structure that links the nervous system to the **endocrine system.** It regulates body temperature, hunger, thirst, fatigue, anger, and circadian cycles. Located underneath the thalamus (*hypo* is Greek for "underneath"), the hypothalamus is situated directly above the **pituitary gland,** which regulates a number of other glands in the body. It is through these connections that the hypothalamus is able to regulate a vast number of body processes. Receiving its directives from above, the hypothalamus translates these instructions into chemical messages that are then sent out by the pituitary gland.

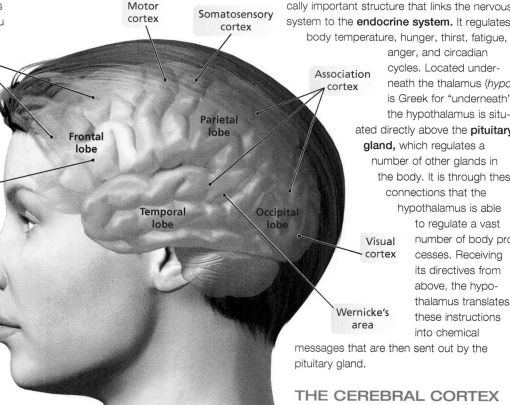

THE CEREBRAL CORTEX

The cerebral cortex is, evolutionarily speaking, the newest part of the human brain. Translated from Latin, *cerebral cortex* means "brain bark."

∧
∧ The cerebral cortex, the outermost portion of
∧ the brain, is packed full of neural connections.

Grey matter is a substance that makes up the cerebral cortex; it covers the cerebrum and cerebellum.

Gyri are bulges in the cerebral cortex.

Sulci are grooves in the cerebral cortex.

White matter consists of myelinated axons that form the connections within the brain.

Primary cortex is a part of the cerebral cortex that serves basic sensory and motor functions; one exists in each lobe of the cerebral cortex.

Association cortex is a part of the cerebral cortex that helps basic sensory and motor information from a specific lobe integrate with information from the rest of the brain; one exists in each lobe of the cerebral cortex.

Occipital lobes are parts of the brain involved in visual processing; it is the smallest of the four lobes in the human brain.

Primary visual cortex is a part of the brain that receives input from the eyes and translates that input into what people see.

Temporal lobes are parts of the brain involved in auditory processing.

Parietal lobes are parts of the brain primarily concerned with bodily sensations, including those of touch, taste, and temperature.

Primary auditory cortex is a part of the brain involved in auditory processing.

This is an apt name, as the cortex itself is actually made up of **grey matter,** which is 1.5 to 5 millimetres thick and covers the cerebrum and cerebellum like bark covers a tree. Like bark, too, the cerebral cortex is ridged and wrinkled

>>> **This homunculus illustrates the somatosensory cortex. Why doesn't our brain devote the same space to processing information about all our body parts?**

into bulges (called **gyri**) and grooves (called **sulci**). These folds aren't merely aesthetic: Because they increase the cortex's total surface area, they also increase its processing power. If you flattened out the entire cortex, it would cover approximately 0.23 square metres and would be much too large to fit in a human skull.

The human brain is somewhat like an orange in its construction. The grey matter is like a thick orange peel, making up about two-thirds of the brain's total volume. The grey matter of the cortex is made up mostly of cell bodies, which give it its pinkish grey colour. The interior of the cerebral cortex—where the blood supply meets the brain—contains the cell bodies that do the work of the brain. If you were to peel away the cortex (again, think of an orange), the remaining tissue would look white and shiny. You'd be looking at **white matter,** the myelinated axons that form the trillions of connections within the brain. It is these connections that enable the human brain to do some of the astounding things it does. Think of the grey matter as cities (where things are "happening") and the white matter as roads that connect the cities. Their functions are unique and equally vital.

The cerebral cortex is divided into two hemispheres, right and left. Each hemisphere is further divided into four lobes that have relatively specialized functions. The boundaries of the four lobes are created by particularly deep sulci on the brain surface. Each lobe contains an area of **primary cortex** (motor or sensory) that serves basic sensory and motor functions. Each lobe also contains an area of **association cortex** that helps basic sensory and motor information from

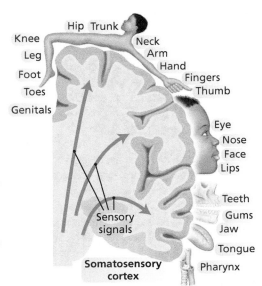

Hip Trunk
Knee   Neck
Leg   Arm
Foot   Hand
Toes   Fingers
                      Thumb
Genitals
                      Eye
                      Nose
                      Face
                      Lips
Sensory   Teeth
signals   Gums
                      Jaw
                      Tongue
Somatosensory   Pharynx
cortex

a specific lobe integrate with information from the rest of the brain.

The Occipital Lobes

Located at the rearmost portion of the skull, the **occipital lobes** are the smallest of the four lobes in the human brain. The occipital lobe is known for its visual processing prowess. The **primary visual cortex** receives input from the eyes and is able to translate that input into things we "see." The occipital lobe's association cortex integrates the colour, size, and movement of our visual perceptions so that visual stimuli become recognizable to us. The association cortex then shares this information with other regions of the brain. For example, it can send its results to the temporal lobe, which finds the stimulus's name, and to the parietal lobe, which determines where it's located in space.

The Temporal Lobes

The **temporal lobes** are located just in front of the occipital lobes and are primarily involved in auditory processing. They lie at the sides of the brain, beneath the **parietal lobes.** Seen in profile, the human brain looks something like a mitten. If you think of the brain this way, the temporal lobes are where you would expect the mitten's thumb to be.

The temporal lobe is home to the **primary auditory cortex.** The association cortex that surrounds the auditory cortex is devoted to the complicated task of understanding language. Because the temporal lobe's association areas are so involved with language, they often contribute to visual tasks (such as naming observed objects) and memory-related tasks (such as creating narrative contexts for the information we want to remember).

of the cortex that controls motor movements is directly adjacent to the somatosensory cortex and has a nearly identical homunculus. This makes sense since all movements require immediate sensory feedback in order to confirm their proper execution. One of the most important examples of the interaction between motion and sensory feedback is the process of human speech. A region within the frontal lobe, **Broca's area,** initiates the movements needed to produce speech, and it is the careful interplay

The Parietal Lobes

The parietal lobes are located above the occipital lobes, just behind the frontal lobes. The **primary somatosensory cortex,** which receives and interprets information about all of our bodily sensations, is located within the parietal lobe. Strange (and gruesome) as it may seem, we can think of this area of the cortex as a homunculus, or "little man." The homunculus is a distorted body map, with each part of the body sized according to how much space the brain gives to processing information about that body part (Jasper & Penfield, 1954). For example, because so many neurons process information from the hands and lips, the homunculus's hands and lips are remarkably oversized. The primary somatosensory cortex doesn't literally look like an outlandish person, but its regions correspond to the regions of the homunculus: A lot of space in the cortex is devoted to the hands, while the area devoted to the hips doesn't take up much room.

The Frontal Lobes

The **frontal lobes** are the part of your brain that is behind your forehead. Often referred to as the "executive" or "conductor" of the brain, the frontal lobe performs a variety of integration and management functions. At the very back of the frontal lobes lies the **primary motor cortex,** which is responsible for generating the neural impulses that control the execution of movements. This is an extremely important function, as no behaviour can "get out" of the human brain without some sort of action. The related association cortex is devoted to helping integrate and orchestrate movement. For example, the frontal lobe must work closely with the parietal lobe to make sure that movements are performed correctly within space and that visual information is translated into the appropriate movements. The portion

Left visual field
Right visual field
Optic nerves
Speech
Optic chiasm
Visual area of left hemisphere
Corpus callosum (split)
Visual area of right hemisphere

of the motor and sensory cortices that keeps you from mispronouncing words.

The foremost portion of the frontal cortex is the brain's taskmaster. Providing the brain bases for overt attention and working memory, it makes sure the task at hand is attended to and completed. It also coordinates a vast amount of complicated information and supports such processes as reasoning, problem solving, and a variety of complex social behaviours.

THE DIVIDED BRAIN
Symmetry in the Brain

The brain is divided into two hemispheres that are connected by an enormous band of axons called the corpus callosum. A great number of brain functions, such as primary sensory and motor areas, are located in both the right and left cerebral hemispheres. What is interesting about this symmetry, however, is the fact that the brain and body are criss-crossed: For example, the motor cortex in the right hemisphere controls the movement of the left side of the body. This kind of connectivity can be described as **contralateral.** While the majority of brain-body connections are contralateral, there are also **ipsilateral** connections that link one side of the brain to the same side of the body. This division of labour may seem fairly straightforward, but in some areas of the brain, the relationship between mind and body gets infinitely more complicated.

The corpus callosum is the largest band of axons in the human brain. What would happen if the corpus callosum were severed?

Language and the Brain

The most ubiquitous and well-studied functional asymmetry in the human brain is language. Language is most commonly found in the left hemisphere, particularly among right-handed males. Left-handed people are more likely to have some language functioning in the right hemisphere, and women are more likely to have some language function in each hemisphere. However, it is nearly impossible to find a human who does not have some language function in his or her left hemisphere. People who have suffered damage to the left hemisphere almost always

" Speaking very generally, the left hemisphere is critical for language, while the right is critical for spatial relationships. "

have difficulty understanding or producing language as a result of the injury. Damage to comparable areas in the right hemisphere produces deficits in the performance of such tasks as reading maps, drawing shapes, and

recognizing faces, all of which rely on perceiving and integrating the spatial relationships of stimuli. Speaking very generally, the left hemisphere is critical for language, while the right is critical for spatial relationships.

The Developing Brain

The way in which functions are distributed in the brain is largely a product of human development. Early in life, a great deal of the cortex is very flexible with regard to the types of functions

Picturing the Brain:

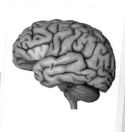

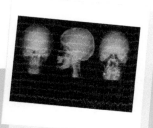

1861
French surgeon Paul Broca identified the speech centre in the brain through autopsies.

1911
Santiago Ramon y Cajal's drawings and staining methods advanced those of Camillo Golgi for visualizing neurons, dendrites, and axons. Cajal promoted the "neuron theory," the fundamental principle of modern neuroscience, which holds that neurons are the basic unit of the central nervous system. More important, Cajal realized that neurons communicate across a small gap, or synapse.

1929
Electroence-phalograms (EEGs), which measure and record minute wave-like electrical signals produced by neurons as they "fire," are introduced.

1973
The first computed tomography (CT) camera is created. This camera produces a composite image of the brain with a scanner that revolves around the skull, taking thousands of X-rays.

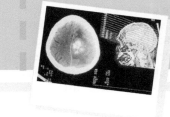

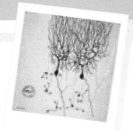

Source: Adapted from *The Dana Sourcebook of Brain Science*, 3rd Ed.

it can perform. As a result, a significant number of developmental influences such as sex, gender, experiences, and culture—to name only a few—are capable of having a profound influence on the way the brain is organized. These developmental influences make it hard for us to generalize about brain functions other than those that have been very well studied.

Of Two Minds?

Few have contributed as much to our understanding of the brain's asymmetries as Michael Gazzaniga and his colleagues. During the 1960s, doctors treated a group of patients with intractable epilepsy by cutting the corpus callosum to prevent seizures from spreading between the hemispheres. This surgery gave patients great relief from their epilepsy and did not seem to have much of an impact on their day-to-day living. Gazzaniga, however, was able to devise a series of tests that demonstrated two different minds, each with different abilities, in these patients. When common objects were presented to the left hemisphere of split-brain patients, the patients had no trouble telling the experimenter what they saw. This was not the case when objects were presented to the right hemisphere. Patients claimed that they had not seen anything, or they guessed randomly. Gazzaniga then had subjects use their right or left hands to identify the object (remember that the sensory cortex for each hand is contralateral). The startling result was that when patients were unable to use speech to identify the object they were seeing, they were able to select the same object using their left hand (right hemisphere). Gazzaniga interpreted this to mean that the right hemisphere can function well independently, but has no discernible access to language.

A Brain Imaging Timeline

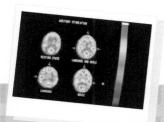

1975
The first positron emission tomography (PET) camera is unveiled. The PET camera uses the principle that blood is rushed to busy areas of the brain to deliver oxygen and nutrients to the neurons. Patients are injected with radioactive glucose, then scanned for the rays emitted as the solution metabolizes, highlighting neuronal activity.

1977
The first magnetic resonance imaging (MRI) camera produces images by subjecting the patient's head to a strong magnetic field, followed by several pulses of radio waves, producing three-dimensional computer-generated images.

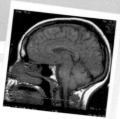

1992
Functional magnetic resonance imaging (fMRI) is introduced. fMRI is used to map brain activity by detecting variations in the response of hydrogen atoms when oxygen is present in the blood.

2009
Toronto researchers Tom Chau and Sheena Luu use infrared light brain imaging to determine people's preferences. Their research could one day lead to portable devices that could be used by individuals who cannot speak or move. Other researchers are using infrared light to examine other mental activities, such as telling lies.

2010
The Clinical Magnetoencephalography (MEG) Lab opens in Halifax, Nova Scotia, making Canada a leader in brain imaging. This new lab offers earlier diagnoses and better treatments for neurological conditions and attracts the world's best researchers.

Review

Summary

WHAT CHARACTERISTICS DESCRIBE THE HUMAN BRAIN? p.38

- The human brain has three major characteristics: integration, sophistication, and adaptability.

HOW IS THE NERVOUS SYSTEM ORGANIZED? p.38

- The nervous system consists of the central nervous system (the brain and the spinal cord) and the peripheral nervous system (the neurons and nerves that serve every other part of the body).

- The peripheral nervous system is divided into the somatic nervous system, which registers stimuli and regulates conscious actions, and the autonomic nervous system, which controls involuntary actions.

- Within the autonomic nervous system, the sympathetic system stimulates organs and responds to stress, and the parasympathetic system calms the organs and maintains normal functioning.

HOW DOES THE NERVOUS SYSTEM OPERATE AT THE CELLULAR LEVEL? p.38

- The brain is made up of neurons and glial cells. Neurons are communication cells that receive, process, and pass on neural signals.

- Glia support and insulate neurons.

- Neuron signalling is an all-or-nothing event. When the number of positive inputs exceeds a certain threshold, the neuron fires an action potential—an electrochemical signal that travels down the axon. In the synapse, neurotransmitters pass on information to the next neuron or gland.

- Communication within neurons is electrical. Communication between neurons is chemical.

WHAT ARE THE DIFFERENT PARTS OF THE HUMAN BRAIN, AND WHAT ROLE DOES EACH PART PLAY? p.42

- The brainstem is connected to the spinal cord and houses the structures that maintain basic life functions.

- The limbic system regulates emotion, motivation, and social and emotional learning.

- The cerebral cortex performs most information processing. It has four lobes: The occipital lobe processes visual information; the temporal lobe handles auditory input and language; the parietal lobe interprets sensory information; and the frontal lobe coordinates memory, reasoning, problem solving, social behaviour, language, and movement.

- The brain is divided into two hemispheres that are connected by the corpus callosum. Language is most commonly processed in the left hemisphere. Spatial information is most commonly processed in the right hemisphere. Cutting the corpus callosum prevents communication between the right and left hemispheres.

Test Your Understanding

1. Remembering a family vacation would activate which lobe of the cerebral cortex?
   a. frontal lobe
   b. parietal lobe
   c. occipital lobe
   d. temporal lobe

2. Which part of the nervous system would enable you to coordinate a turn while salsa dancing?
   a. central nervous system
   b. parasympathetic system
   c. somatic nervous system
   d. sympathetic nervous system

3. Neurons indicate the strength of a stimulus by:
   a. changing firing frequency per second
   b. increasing or decreasing the number of dendrites
   c. calculating input differently in the soma
   d. sending signals faster or slower down the axon

4. When you smell freshly baked cookies, olfactory information is carried to the central nervous system via:
   a. interneurons
   b. motor neurons
   c. sensory neurons
   d. glial cells

5. Seeing the face of a friend or relative might activate the thalamus, limbic system, basal ganglia, occipital lobe, and frontal lobe. This demonstrates which characteristic of the human brain?
   a. plasticity
   b. ingenuity
   c. adaptability
   d. integration

6. A pitch thrown by a left-handed pitcher would be directed mostly by the pitcher's:
   a. left motor cortex
   b. right motor cortex

    c. left somatosensory cortex
    d. right somatosensory cortex

7. When you play the piano, the relay of information about hand movements occurs through:
    a. the occipital lobes
    b. the brainstem
    c. the limbic system
    d. the frontal lobes

8. Damage to the left hemisphere of the brain would most likely cause:
    a. deficits in map-reading tasks
    b. losses in memory
    c. difficulties producing language
    d. poor coordination

9. Neurotransmitters communicate messages between neurons:
    a. chemically
    b. electrically
    c. through a myelin sheath
    d. through the blood-brain barrier

10. Terminal buttons process:
    a. chemical signals into electrical ones
    b. electrical signals into chemical ones
    c. resting potentials into action potentials
    d. action potentials into resting potentials

11. If a neuron receives inhibitory signals, will it still fire?
    a. Yes, if it also receives positive inputs.
    b. No, any inhibitory signal prevents a neuron from firing.
    c. No, receiving conflicting messages causes a neuron to temporarily cease firing.
    d. Yes, if the total positive inputs exceed the neuron's threshold.

12. One function of glial cells is to:
    a. make myelin
    b. relay information
    c. help create new neurons
    d. fight potential pathogens

13. If sodium ions flow into a cell as potassium ions flow out, the cell's charge:
    a. alternates
    b. remains the same
    c. becomes more positive
    d. becomes more negative

14. Which of the following allows an action potential to move faster down the axon?
    a. terminal button
    b. synaptic cleft
    c. nodes of Ranvier
    d. interneurons

15. According to the theory of synaptic plasticity, learning a foreign language or a musical instrument might increase synaptic density by:
    a. increasing brain size
    b. creating new neurons
    c. increasing neurotransmitters
    d. fortifying neural connections

16. Hannah accidentally placed her hand on a hot stove and instantly jerked it away. Which part of Hannah's nervous system controlled her reflex action?
    a. the spinal cord
    b. the cerebellum
    c. the frontal lobe
    d. the parietal lobe

17. The decrease in respiration rate as you fall asleep is controlled by the:
    a. occipital lobe
    b. brainstem
    c. spinal cord
    d. hypothalamus

18. Feeling a tap on the shoulder while you are watching a horror film would most likely activate your:
    a. amygdala
    b. hypothalamus
    c. globus pallidus
    d. cingulate cortex

19. Trying to remember what you need at the grocery store without using a grocery list engages which brain structure?
    a. the caudate
    b. the putamen
    c. the thalamus
    d. the hippocampus

20. Damage to which brain structure would most likely result in death?
    a. cerebellum
    b. medulla
    c. basal ganglia
    d. hippocampus

Remember to check www.thethinkspot.ca for additional information, downloadable flashcards, and other helpful resources.

Answers: 1) a; 2) c; 3) a; 4) c; 5) d; 6) b; 7) d; 8) c; 9) a; 10) b; 11) d; 12) a; 13) c; 14) c; 15) d; 16) a; 17) b; 18) a; 19) d; 20) b

THINK READINGS

BOOK REVIEW

Your Creative Brain: Seven Steps to Maximize Imagination, Productivity, and Innovation in Your Life

Shelley Carson
Harvard Health Publications, Boston, MA

> **How is your brain creative?**

> **What parts of our brain do you think would be involved in creativity? Review the parts of the brain and their functions discussed in Chapter 3.**

The products of our creative brain are evident everywhere we look. Not only do we see them in the amazing feats of artists and scientists that enrich our personal and collective lives, but also in the many novel and useful ideas we generate that enable us to navigate our daily lives. Then how is it that despite its ubiquity, creativity has proven such a hard nut to crack? In this wonderfully written book, Shelley Carson argues that the riddle of creativity can be solved by peering into its neurological origins. Specifically, neural function (rather than structure) holds the key to creative cognition. In turn, stimulating creativity becomes a matter of engaging in behaviors that target its very source—brain function.

There are three main principles that lay the foundation for this book. First, people who exhibit creativity are distinguished from those who do not based on their brain activation patterns while they are being creative. In other words, creativity is the cognitive and behavioral manifestation of brain states. Second, there is no singular roadmap to creativity. Rather, creativity emerges from the interplay of a series of brain states—what Carson calls brainsets—that facilitate it. A brainset can be viewed as the biological analogue of a mindset. This idea gels very nicely with modern notions in neuroscience according to which higher-order mental functions such as creativity and reasoning are built on component processes and corresponding neural systems (Goel, 2007). Third, to the extent that each brainset can be trained, one should expect to observe enhancements in creativity. This last point holds the most value for practitioners of creativity.

The book is divided into three parts. In Part 1 the reader is introduced to the CREATES brainsets model, a set of seven brain activation states that comprise the creative process: Connect, Reason, Envision, Absorb, Transform, Evaluate, and Stream. Accessing each brainset functions as a portal to a specific mental state, which in turn contributes to creativity. Although most of us would be familiar with all seven brainsets, we also have what Carson refers to as our own "mental comfort zone." This is the brain state we prefer to be in. For example, a brainset which should have instant caché for creative persons but perhaps not be everyone's cup of tea is the Absorb brainset, which involves opening the mind to new experiences. To explore our individual differences in mental comfort zones, Part 1 includes a series of exercises which we can determine our own preferred brainset. This is followed by a brief tour of neuroanatomy, and a concise description of pathways of arriving at creative solutions. In essence, Part 1 provides the reader with the layout of the major nodes (i.e., brainsets) in CREATES, and sufficient neuroanatomical detail to rec-

PSYCHOLOGY OF AESTHETICS, Creativity, and the Arts 2011, Vol. 5, No. 4, 389–390

> **What higher order mental functions are predominately found in the left and right hemispheres of the brain?**

ognize the key brain landmarks that embody them.

Part 2 is the heart of the book. In it, a separate chapter is devoted to each brainset of the CREATES model. In each chapter, Carson moves from a description of each brainset to specific ways of training it, and outlines the neural systems in the brain wherein the training would be realized. This feat is achieved by drawing on a remarkable body of knowledge from neuroimaging experiments, brain injury and neuropsychological case studies, interviews of creative persons, experimental results from the assessments of participants on tests of creative cognition, and studies of the biographies of bona fide geniuses. Yet, despite this multilayered approach, the arguments are clearly laid out and the suggestions for training ring true. Of course some readers may disagree with the effectiveness of some of the training recommendations or the inclusion of specific brain structures in some of the brainsets, although that would be to miss the point. Specifically, the discussed neural systems are not meant to represent the final word on the topic. Rather, as our understanding of brain function advances, one would hope to see continued refinements of the neural systems that are linked to each brainset, which should in turn impact the recommended training regimens.

Part 3 offers concrete recommendations for implementing the CREATES model in one's daily life. For example, because no two brainsets are the same and they all contribute to the creative process, the exhibition of creativity depends on the ability to move flexibly in and out of brainsets as a function of task demands (see Martindale, 1999). This insight—that flexibility to navigate between mental states is key to creativity— captures a critical and trainable ability. Another concrete and important recommendation is to engage in continued learning. Unfortunately, this simple idea has been lost in most recent thinking about creativity, and its resurrection here has much to commend it. Given the 10-year rule for gaining expertise in a field, and the exponential rate of information increase, it is all the more important to add to one's depth of knowledge in a given area while also increasing one's breadth of knowledge in other areas. This takes time!

Although most of the book is devoted to coverage of the CREATES model, Carson also manages to touch on some important and potentially controversial issues along the way. I found most interesting her updating of Freud's ideas of primary process and secondary process thinking. Briefly, whereas secondary process thinking is abstract, rational, and realistic, primary process thinking is concrete, dreamlike, and fantasy-driven. Freud believed that creative people can switch flexibly between these two modes of thinking such that creative thoughts originate in unconscious primary process thinking, but are refined by conscious secondary process thinking. Data from the neurosci-

ences have shown that creative people slip into more relaxed modes of cognition when generating ideas, but return to more focused and deliberate modes of cognition (that require executive function) when evaluating those ideas—the latter itself is a hallmark of the reason brainset. It appears that Freud's hunch about the workings of the brain during creativity may have been right after all, and it's great to see Carson touch on it here.

If you're looking for a book that will provide you with concrete recommendations for flexing your creative muscle, this is the book for you. Along the way you'll learn about the neuroscience of creativity, and the amazing ability of the human brain to construct solutions to difficult problems under less than ideal conditions (see Montague, 2007). It will also remind you of Richard Feynman's idea that demystifying nature need not reduce any of its splendor. In fact, it can have the opposite effect.

Reviewed by Oshin Vartanian, University of Toronto DOI: 10.1037/a0023486

REFERENCES

Goel, V. (2007). Anatomy of deductive reasoning. *Trends in Cognitive Sciences, 11,* 435–441.

Martindale, C. (1999). Biological bases of creativity. In R. J. Sternberg (Ed.), *Handbook of creativity* (pp. 137–152). New York: Cambridge University Press.

Montague, R. (2007). *Your brain is (almost) perfect: How we make decisions.* New York: Plume.

What types of neuroimaging techniques could be used to study creativity?

What are some commonly believed ways for us to improve creativity and brain power overall?

What did you learn about Freud's theories from Chapter 3?

SENSATION AND PERCEPTION

WHAT ARE SENSORY THRESHOLDS?

HOW DO WE PROCESS STIMULI FROM THE OUTSIDE WORLD?

WHY ARE WE ABLE TO EXPERIENCE ONLY ONE PERCEPTION AT A TIME?

WHAT ARE SOME MAJOR THEORIES OF PERCEPTION?

IS PERCEPTION DEVELOPED BY NATURE OR NURTURE?

Can you see

with your ears?

Ben Underwood enjoys cycling. He plays basketball with his friends and excels at video games. He seems like a typical 16-year-old boy. But to watch Ben sink a basket or ride a bike is to witness some of the most extraordinary uses of the human senses ever seen. Ben, who lost his eyes to retinal cancer at the age of three, is completely blind. He "sees" using sound.

Brian Borowski, a 56-year-old man from Southwestern Ontario, has been blind since birth and also uses sound to navigate the world around him. Brian is helping researchers at the Brain and Mind Institute at Western University gain insight into our senses and the ways in which we can compensate if we damage or lose the ability to use them.

What makes Ben and Brian so interesting to researchers is that they are among the very few people in the world who use echolocation to navigate their way around. They locate objects by making clicking noises with their tongue and listening for the echoes that bounce back to them.

Echolocation allows Brian and Ben to locate a basketball net, avoid an oncoming car, or determine how quickly a line is moving at Tim Hortons (Hutchinson, 2012). They are using the same highly developed system that dolphins and bats use to navigate and find food.

People once believed that the visual cortex becomes useless in the brains of blind people, but scientists have discovered that this is not the case. Mel Goodale, director of the Brain and Mind Institute, and colleagues are studying echolocators, such as Brian and Ben, and have discovered that the visual cortex is activated during echolocation. It appears that the brains of Brian and Ben have adapted to enable them to "see" objects using echolocation.

What do the stories of Brian and Ben tell us about how we experience the world? Even though most of us don't use echolocation, we all constantly use our senses to collect information about the world around us, and we all use our brains to give that information meaning. Like Brain and Ben, we rely on sensations and perceptions to help us navigate through our lives. What do their stories tell us about our brain's ability to adapt to damage or loss of a sensation?

<<< *Dolphins and bats use echolocation to navigate their surroundings. Blind individuals, such as Brian Borowski and Ben Underwood, also use echolocation to "see" the world around them. What does this tell us about the adaptability of the human senses?*

CHAPTER 04

Sensation

Sensory systems, the parts of the nervous system responsible for processing sensory information, allow people and animals to interpret stimuli from the outside world. These systems are essential for survival and reproduction. Imagine if our ancestors were unable to hear the snap of a twig to warn them of approaching danger. The human race would not have lasted long! Sensory systems are need-specific. In other words, each species has a unique sensory system according to its behaviour and environment. For example, bats hunt in the dark of night, so they cannot rely on their eyesight. Instead, their hearing is so finely attuned that they can use echolocation to track down prey the size of a mosquito.

Sensation is the process through which we detect physical energy from the environment and code that energy as neural signals. The way we select, organize, and interpret this sensory information is the process of **perception.** Sensation and perception work together to enable us to receive and interpret stimuli from the outside world.

Sensory Thresholds

PSYCHOPHYSICS

We are unable to detect much of the physical energy around us. For example, sound waves that have very low or very high frequencies are out of the human range of hearing. Every species has a different sensory threshold. This is why blowing a dog whistle has little effect on a person, but produces an instant response from any dog in the area. **Psychophysics** is the study of the relationship between physical characteristics of stimuli and the sensory experiences that accompany them. It helps us know how much sensory stimulation is needed to see a candle in the distance, or to hear a mouse scamper across a kitchen floor.

Absolute Thresholds

An **absolute threshold** is the smallest amount of energy needed for a person to detect a stimulus (light, sound, pressure, taste, or odour) 50% of the time. Psychologists can establish an absolute threshold by presenting a stimulus at different intensities and asking people whether they sense anything. Adults generally have a higher absolute threshold than children, but all of us are remarkably sensitive to changes in the world around us. For example, a human being can smell a single drop of perfume in a three-room apartment (Galanter, 1962).

Signal Detection Theory

People are not always consistently able to detect stimuli. Awareness can depend on whether the individual is feeling tired or alert, whether the stimulus is expected, or the potential consequences of the stimulus. If you were told that your failure to detect the sound of a footstep would cause an explosion, you would probably be considerably more alert than usual. Psychologists using **signal detection theory** attempt to understand the differences between people's responses to different stimuli and how they vary depending on the circumstances. Signal detection theorists measure how often a person observes a weak stimulus by counting the number of successful detections compared to the number of false alarms.

> **People are not always consistently able to detect stimuli. Awareness can depend on whether the individual is feeling tired or alert, whether the stimulus is expected, or the potential consequences of the stimulus.**

Difference Thresholds

The **difference threshold,** or **just noticeable difference (jnd),** is the minimum difference between two stimuli needed to detect the difference 50% of the time. This threshold

Sensory system is the part of the nervous system responsible for processing sensory information.

Sensation describes the process through which we detect physical energy from the environment and code that energy as neural signals.

Perception describes the way a person selects, organizes, and interprets sensory information.

Psychophysics is the study of the relationship between physical characteristics of stimuli and the sensory experiences that accompany them.

Absolute threshold is the smallest amount of energy needed for a person to detect a stimulus 50% of the time.

Signal detection theory predicts how and when we detect the presence of a faint stimulus amid background stimulation.

Difference threshold or just noticeable difference (jnd) is the minimum difference between two stimuli needed to detect the difference 50% of the time.

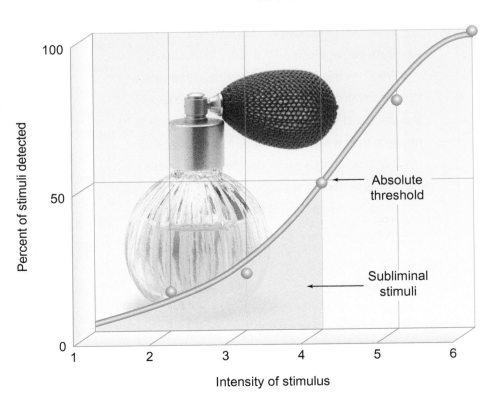

	Respond "Absent"	Respond "Present"
Stimulus Present	Miss	Hit
Stimulus Absent	Correct rejection	False alarm

∧
∧
∧ A psychologist asks a man to nod every time he hears a beeping noise. Based on the man's response and the presence or absence of the noise, the psychologist will mark the man's response as a miss, a hit, a correct rejection, or a false alarm.

Weber's Law states that regardless of size, two stimuli must differ by a constant proportion for the difference to be noticeable.

Receptor cell is a specialized cell that responds to a particular type of energy.

Sensory neuron is a neuron that carries information from the sensory receptors to the brain as a coded signal.

Transduction is a process through which physical energy such as light or sound is converted into an electrical charge.

Sensory adaptation is a process in which sensory receptor cells become less responsive to an unchanging stimulus.

increases with the size of one of the stimuli. For example, if you add a spoonful of sugar to a cup of tea, you will probably notice that it tastes sweeter. However, if you add a spoonful of sugar to an industrial-sized tea urn, you will probably not be able to tell the difference.

Ernst Weber (1795–1878) noticed that regardless of size, two stimuli must differ by a constant proportion for the difference to be noticeable. His principle became known as **Weber's Law.**

Sensory Processes

Psychologists are interested in analyzing the relationships between physical stimuli, our physiological responses to those stimuli, and the sensory experiences that result.

If someone asked you how many senses the human body possesses, you would probably think it was a trick question. But which sense tells the body when it is balanced? Or lets us know where our hands are in relation to our feet? We actually have many more senses than the traditionally studied five.

Sensation occurs when a **receptor cell** in one of the sense organs is stimulated by energy. When the energy level exceeds the absolute threshold, the receptor cell fires neural impulses. **Sensory neurons** carry information from the sensory receptors to the brain as a coded signal.

The process through which physical energy such as light or sound is converted into an electrical charge is known as **transduction.** The strength of the stimuli will affect how rapidly the sensory neurons fire. For example, a bright light may rapidly fire a set of sensory neurons, while a faint glow would set off a slower rate of neuronal firing. Each receptor cell is sensitive to a specific form of energy. Thus, receptor cells in the eye will respond only to light waves, while receptor cells in the ear will respond only to sound waves.

Think about the smell you encounter when you first walk into a barn or drive past a chemical factory. At first, an unpleasant smell can be overpowering, but after a

few minutes, we no longer notice it. This is because our sensory receptor cells become less responsive to an unchanging stimulus, a process called **sensory adaptation.** Sensory adaptation enables us to focus on changes in our environment. Without it, we would be constantly aware of the pressure of the ground under our feet or the humming of the air conditioner in the office.

Three factors control sensory adaptation: the number of receptor cells, the rate at which they fire, and the corresponding sensory cortex in your brain.

Is a **soldier** more likely to detect weak stimuli in **wartime** or **peacetime?** >>>

Visual accommodation is a process in which the lens adjusts in shape from thick to thin to enable a person to focus on objects that are close by or far away.

Retina is a multi-layered tissue at the back of the eye that is responsible for visual transduction.

Rod is a photoreceptor cell in the retina that responds to varying degrees of light and dark.

Fovea is a depressed spot in the retina that occupies the centre of a person's visual field.

Cones are photoreceptor cells in the retina that enable a person to see colour.

Acuity refers to sharpness of vision.

Ganglion cell is one of several neurons that connect the bipolar neurons in the eyes to the brain.

Optic nerve is a bundle of axons of ganglion cells that carries neural messages from each eye to the brain.

Optic chasm is the point near the base of the brain where some fibres in the optic nerve from each eye cross to the opposite side of the brain.

Feature detector is a specialized brain cell that only responds to particular elements in the visual field.

Simple cell is a feature detector that only responds to a single feature of a stimulus.

VISION

Which of your senses do you value the most? When faced with this question, many people choose vision. Even though Ben Underwood has become a master at navigating his sightless world, adapting to vision loss effectively is a challenge. Vision is a key sense—but how does it work?

The Structure of the Eye

Focus your attention on an object within reach. Now look out of the window and focus on something in the distance. How is it possible that you can see both equally well? The lens adjusts in shape from thick to thin to enable us to focus on objects that are close by or far away. This process is called visual accommodation. Ask an elderly relative to try the same thing (without glasses!) and he or she will probably have difficulty with the task. As we grow older, the lens hardens and we are unable to accommodate for distance, a process known as presbyopia.

The retina is the multi-layered tissue at the back of the eye that is responsible for visual transduction. Because of the size and structure of the eye's lens, images are projected onto the retina upside-down, which could lead to much confusion. Fortunately, receptor cells in the retina convert light energy into neural impulses, which are sent to the brain for processing. Here, they are constructed into an upright-seeming image, enabling us to see the world the right way around.

There are two types of photoreceptor cells in the retina: rods and cones. Named for their characteristic shapes, rods and cones each have specific parts to play in the visual process.

Rods respond to varying degrees of light and dark. They are found everywhere outside the fovea—a depressed spot in the retina that occupies the centre of your visual field. Have you ever tried staring at a star at night, only to have it disappear before your eyes? Try shifting your gaze to the side. Since rods are able to function in dim light, we are able to see objects in dim light clearer when the light hits just outside the fovea. This happens when we do not focus directly on the object, but instead look slightly off to the side.

Cones enable us to see colour. They are primarily found in the fovea. Cones work best in bright light, which is why we cannot see colours in the dark. Cones are specialized for acuity, or sharpness of vision, and colour perception. When you want to examine something carefully, do you move it into bright light, or turn the light off? Since cones are specialized for acuity and colour perception, we need to use bright light in order to see things in detail.

VISUAL INFORMATION PROCESSING

The retina is actually an extension of the brain—during fetal development it moves from the brain to the eye. When we process an image, light waves hit the retina and are transmitted to the ganglion cells, whose axons make up the optic nerve. Light from the left side of each eye's retina translates into a neural message that travels along the optic nerve to the left visual cortex. Information from the right eye crosses to the left hemisphere at the optic chasm. Similarly, messages from the right side of each eye's retina travel along the optic nerve to the right visual cortex. Information from the left eye crosses to the right hemisphere at the optic chasm. The visual cortex at the back of the brain then processes this information.

Feature Detection

Canadian David Hubel and American Torsten Wiesel received the Nobel Prize in 1981 for showing that the primary visual cortex has feature detector neurons that respond to specific types of features. They found that simple cells respond to a single feature, such as a vertical

Physiological response

Physical stimulus

Sensory experience

∧
∧ Our sensory systems work in a
∧ three-step process. What would happen if one or more of these steps were impaired?

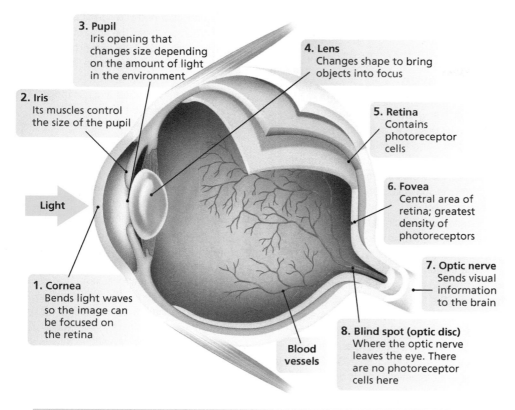

3. Pupil
Iris opening that changes size depending on the amount of light in the environment

4. Lens
Changes shape to bring objects into focus

2. Iris
Its muscles control the size of the pupil

5. Retina
Contains photoreceptor cells

Light

6. Fovea
Central area of retina; greatest density of photoreceptors

1. Cornea
Bends light waves so the image can be focused on the retina

7. Optic nerve
Sends visual information to the brain

Blood vessels

8. Blind spot (optic disc)
Where the optic nerve leaves the eye. There are no photoreceptor cells here

∧∧∧ Light rays enter the eye through the **cornea** and the **pupil**. The light travels through the eye and is focused onto the **retina** by the **lens**. Visual information is then sent to the brain via the **optic nerve**.

Complex cell is a feature detector that only responds to two features of a stimulus.

Hypercomplex cell is a feature detector that responds to multiple features of a stimulus.

Fusiform face area is an area of the visual cortex that specifically responds to and recognizes faces.

Parallel processing describes the process of doing several things at the same time.

Blindsight is a condition in which a person experiences blindness in part of his or her field of vision.

line, while **complex cells** respond to two features of a stimulus, such as a vertical line that moves in a horizontal direction. **Hypercomplex cells** respond to multiple features of a stimulus, for example, a vertical line moving in a horizontal direction that is a particular length. When many neuron systems work together, we are able to perceive whole objects. Some areas of the brain are very good at perceiving specific types of objects. For example, one area of the visual cortex, just behind the right and left ears, specifically responds to and recognizes faces. This is known as the **fusiform face area.** This brain area is significantly more active on fMRI scans when pictures of faces are viewed.

Parallel Processing

Unlike a machine that works using a step-by-step process, our brains are able to do several things at once. In other words, the brain has a talent for **parallel processing.** When we view a painting, different areas of the brain process its colour, depth, motion, and form (Livingstone & Hubel, 1988). Amazingly, we're able to reconstruct the image in our minds by pulling all of this information together in a

fraction of a second. It's like putting together a jigsaw puzzle at record-breaking speed.

The concept of parallel processing explains why brain damage can cause some unusual visual disabilities. Take Patient M, who suffered stroke damage near the rear of both sides of her brain, resulting in a loss of her ability to perceive movement. Pouring a cup of tea became more than a little tricky because the liquid appeared to be frozen in mid-air (Hoffman, 1998).

Brain damage (to the primary visual cortex) may also cause people to experience blindness in part of their field of vision, a concept known as **blindsight.** Despite having blind spots in which no stimuli can be consciously seen, patients are still able to maintain a high degree of accuracy when asked to guess about features of stimuli shown in their blind spots. For example, patients may not be able to see an object such as a rod in their blind field, but when asked about whether the rod is

For a **visual experience** to occur, **messages** must travel from the **eyes** to the **visual cortex**. Do you remember what happens to visual experiences if the corpus callosum is cut? >>>

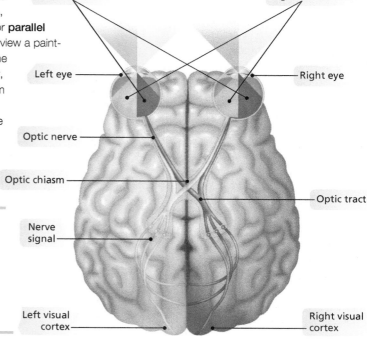

Left visual field

Right visual field

Left eye

Right eye

Optic nerve

Optic chiasm

Optic tract

Nerve signal

Left visual cortex

Right visual cortex

vertical or horizontal, these patients will nearly always make the correct determination.

COLOUR VISION

Why is the sky blue? In a technical sense, the sky is every colour but blue, because it reflects blue wavelengths. Light rays themselves are not coloured; we create the experience of colour in our brains. The human brain is able to distinguish 7 million different colour variations (Geldard, 1972).

The wavelength of the light that reaches our eyes creates a particular colour, or **hue.** The intensity, or purity, of the colour is called its **saturation.** The intensity of the light waves affects the **brightness** of the colour.

Our experience of colour depends on context. We perceive familiar objects as having consistent colour, despite lighting and wavelengths constantly changing. This phenomenon is known as **colour constancy.**

Try wearing a pair of tinted sunglasses. Does everything still look brown after a couple of seconds, or are you able to distinguish the green grass from the blue water and the grey buildings? Our perception of an object's colour is not an isolated phenomenon; it depends on the colour of surrounding objects.

HEARING (AUDITION)

The average person may not be able to use echolocation like Ben Underwood, but our sense of hearing is still pretty amazing. With the help of our brains and

ears, we gracefully convert **sound waves**—caused by the vibration of air—into meaningful noises.

Sound Waves

If you travelled into deep space, you wouldn't hear a single sound. Why? A sound wave is a change in air pressure caused by molecules of air or fluid colliding and moving apart. In deep space, there are no molecules to collide with each other. Sound cannot exist in a vacuum (the next time you watch *Star Wars*, look out for inconsistencies!).

Sound can be represented as sine waves. Like light waves, sound waves have wavelength, amplitude, and purity.

The **frequency,** or pitch, of a sound wave is measured in cycles per second, or hertz (Hz). The first wave on the diagram might represent a trombone, or a tuba, while the third wave might show the high-pitched sound of a flute. The human ear is able to hear sounds that range from 20 to 20 000 Hz. This makes us practically pitch deaf compared to dolphins, who can hear up to an astonishing 200 000 Hz.

The **amplitude,** or height, of a sound wave is interpreted as its

volume—how loud or soft a sound is. Volume is measured in decibels. The absolute threshold for hearing is 0 decibels, and prolonged exposure to anything above 85 decibels can produce hearing loss. Some rock bands play at a whopping 140 decibels at close range, making it pretty amazing that they (and their die-hard fans) are able to hear at all.

Have you ever covered your ears in horror while listening to early Canadian Idol auditions? The disillusioned contestants probably need to work on their **timbre,** or the quality and purity of their tone. A good musician will be able to judge the sound quality or resonance of a note. A poor musician will be labelled tone deaf and unceremoniously asked to leave the stage.

The inner ear is responsible for the transduction of sound energy. Sound waves move through the ear and are translated into neural signals by the receptor cells in the basilar membrane. The volume of a sound affects the number of hair cells that are activated. The brain can interpret the loudness of a sound from the number of activated hair cells. Too much noise can permanently damage hair cells by withering or fusing them.

Subtractive colour mixing

Additive colour mixing

∧ **Subtractive colour mixing** with paint results in a brown/
∧ black colour because each colour's **wavelength** is
absorbed by the others. **Additive colour mixing** with light
creates white light because **wavelengths** from each light
reach the eye.

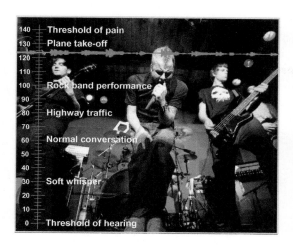

140	Threshold of pain
130	Plane take-off
120	
110	
100	Rock band performance
90	
80	Highway traffic
70	
60	Normal conversation
50	
40	
30	Soft whisper
20	
10	
0	Threshold of hearing

if you are breathing in the scent of rose petals on a summer's day, but you might want to hold your breath the next time you drive past a sewage treatment plant.

Have you ever left the gas on by accident? Your sense of smell is an early warning system that helps you detect danger. The chemical senses are also used to attract partners, a concept that is persistently exploited by the multi-billion-dollar-a-year perfume industry. Our sense of smell is not as acute as our eyesight or hearing, and it's downright embarrassing compared

Tonotopic pertains to the way in which the primary auditory cortex is organized so that neurons that respond to particular frequencies are grouped together.

Sound shadow is an area of reduced sound intensity around the ear farther away from where a sound originates.

Echolocation is a process in which sound waves are emitted and the environment is analyzed by listening to the frequency of the waves that are reflected back.

∧ ∧ ∧ How much **stress** do you put on your **ears** every day?

The primary auditory cortex is organized in a **tonotopic** arrangement. This means that particular neurons respond to specific frequencies, and are grouped together according to their preferred frequencies.

Locating Sounds

Have you ever wondered why our ears are on either side of our head, rather than at the front or back? It isn't just more aesthetically pleasing—the location of our ears enables us to hear stereophonically. When a dog to our left starts barking, the sound reaches our left ear a bit sooner and slightly more intensely than our right ear. Our heads cast a **sound shadow,** meaning that a sound has to go through or around the head to reach the other ear. As it travels, the sound weakens, providing an extra clue as to where the sound came from.

Few people can claim to be experts in sound location. However, if, like Brian Borowski and Ben Underwood, we could teach ourselves **echolocation,** we'd be able to navigate by using sound. Animals with this talent include bats and dolphins. They send out sound signals to analyze and locate objects in their environment by listening to the frequency of the waves that reflect back to them.

SMELL (OLFACTION)

Like taste, smell is a chemical sense. Molecules of a substance are carried through the air to the receptor cells at the top of our nasal cavities, meaning that we effectively inhale part of everything we smell. Not so bad

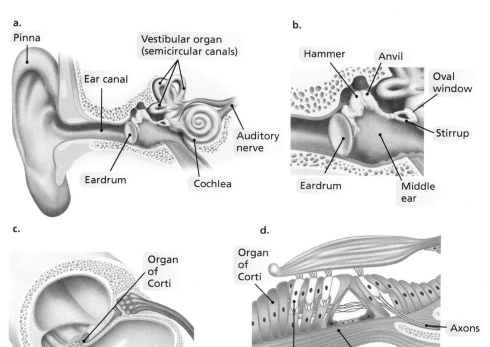

∧ ∧ The **process of hearing: a.** The **outer ear** acts as a funnel for **sound waves,** which travel to the **eardrum,** causing it to **vibrate. b.** The **hammer, anvil, and stirrup** strike each other, carrying the vibrations to the **oval window** and on to the **cochlea** in the **inner ear. c.** The **fluid** in the cochlea is moving, which causes ripples in the **basilar membrane. d.** The **basilar membrane** is lined with **hair cells.** Cilia on the tips of the hair cells stimulate the **receptor cell axons** to send messages via the **auditory nerve** to the temporal lobe's **auditory cortex.**

to the smelling abilities of dogs, which each possess at least 125 million scent receptors (compared to a paltry 5 million per human). However, human beings are still pretty impressive when it comes to smell: We're able to distinguish 10 000 different odours (Malnic, Hirono, Sato, & Buck, 1999).

As molecules travel to the top of our nasal cavity, they reach olfactory receptor sites—large protein molecules on the olfactory neurons that bind to specific odorants. We have 400 types of sensory neurons that work in a similar fashion to a lock and key. When a particular odour is encountered, it fits like a key into the receptor that is sensitive to that individual smell. Since we do not have a distinct receptor for each of the 10 000 smells we encounter, it is likely that each odour triggers combinations of receptors.

Have you ever caught a whiff of a particular fragrance and been reminded of a happy occasion? Maybe the scent of laundry detergent loses you in the reverie of your first kiss, which happened to take place in the laundromat. The area of the brain that receives information from receptor cells in the nasal cavities is closely linked to the limbic system associated with memory and emotion. Furthermore, smell signals don't have to travel through the thalamus; they have direct links to the brain's emotion and memory centres like the amygdala and the hippocampus. Thus, odours have the ability to evoke memories and feelings. Whether these memories are happy or sad depends on our earliest experiences with the particular smell (Herz, 2001).

> Have you ever left the gas on by accident? Your sense of smell is an early warning system that helps you detect danger.

You have probably heard people with a cold complaining that everything tastes like cardboard. Our senses of smell and taste are inextricably linked because the back of the mouth cavity is connected to the nasal cavity. Pinch your nostrils, close your eyes, and have a friend feed you chunks of apple and raw potato. Can you tell the difference?

Age and Sex Differences

Are you male? Over the age of 49? A smoker? If you answered "yes" to all three questions, you are unlikely to be hired as a perfumer. Our ability to identify scents peaks in early adulthood. Women generally have a more acute sense of smell than men do, and their ability to identify odours increases with repeated exposure more than men's (Dalton, Doolittle, & Breslin, 2002). Our sense of smell is also negatively affected by smoking, alcoholism, Alzheimer's disease, and Parkinson's disease (Doty, 2001).

Communication and Pheromones

Pheromones are a chemical substance released by an animal to trigger sexual arousal, aggression, or territorial behaviour in other members of that species. Companies sell human pheromone spray with the claim that it will increase our sex appeal. But there is more to pheromones then just sex appeal! University of Toronto professor Joel Levine genetically modified fruit flies so that they no longer produced pheromones (Billeter, Atallah, Krupp, Millar, & Levine, 2009). These "pheromone free" flies were irresistible to other fly species, suggesting that pheromones are necessary to ensure that we mate only within our own species. They "turn on" our own species but "turn off" others. In addition, pheromones are good for our brains. Scientists from the University of Calgary found that pheromones secreted by male mice sparked new brain cells in their female partners and could help repair injured brains (Mak et al., 2007).

a.
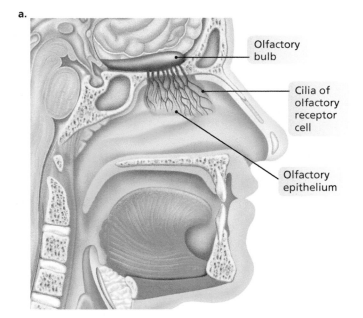

b.
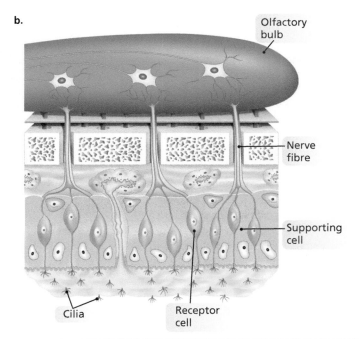

∧ **The olfactory system receptor cells** in the **nasal cavity send messages to the** ∧ **brain's olfactory bulb.**

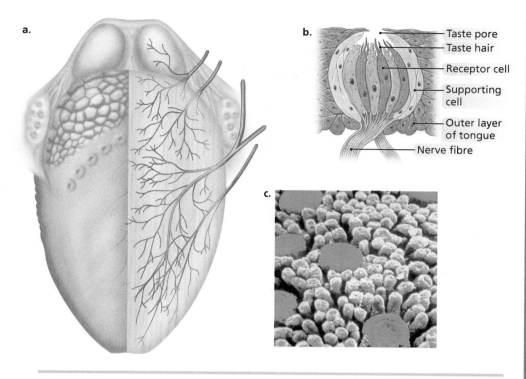

a.

b.
- Taste pore
- Taste hair
- Receptor cell
- Supporting cell
- Outer layer of tongue
- Nerve fibre

c.

Pheromones are a chemical substance released by an animal to trigger sexual arousal, aggression, or territorial behaviour in other members of that species.

Taste bud is a structure on the tongue that contains the receptor cells for taste.

Papilla is a bump on the tongue in which taste buds are embedded.

Microvillus is a tiny hair at the tip of a taste receptor cell.

Skin senses are the senses relating to pressure, touch, and pain.

Kinesthetic sense is the sense relating to how a person's body parts interact with one another.

Vestibular sense is the sense relating to movement and body position.

Nociceptive pain is a negative feeling caused by an external stimulus.

Neuropathic pain is a negative feeling caused by a malfunction in the central nervous system.

Referred pain is a negative feeling that occurs when sensory information from internal and external areas converges on the same nerve cells in the spinal cord.

∧ Figure a shows the **nerves** in the **tongue**. Figure b
∧ shows the anatomy of a **taste bud**. Figure c shows
∧ a microphotograph of the **surface** of the tongue.

TASTE (GUSTATION)

If our ancestors had enjoyed the taste of milkweed, we might not be around today. Fortunately, our natural inclination to avoid bitter-tasting foods developed as a result of the natural defence mechanism of many poisonous plants to produce a bitter-tasting substance. Chemical companies introduce bitter-tasting chemicals into cleaning products to discourage people from ingesting them. Our sense of taste warns us when food may be unsafe to eat.

Taste receptor cells are located in the **taste buds,** which are embedded in the tongue's **papillae**—the bumps that you can see on your tongue. **Microvilli**—tiny hairs at the tips of the taste receptor cells—generate a nerve impulse, interpreted in the brain as a particular taste. When we eat, saliva dissolves the chemical substances in food, which slip between the papillae in order to reach the taste buds. Taste signals are passed to the limbic system and the cerebral cortex.

Psychologists now recognize five basic tastes: sweet, salty, sour, bitter, and umami (a Japanese word that describes the taste of foods such as soup, chicken, cheese, and anything containing monosodium glutamate). Receptor cells for each taste are located on distinct regions of the tongue.

Our emotional responses to taste are hard-wired. If you place a bitter substance on a newborn baby's tongue, the baby will react with a disgusted expression similar to one an adult might make (Bartoshuk, 1993).

BODY (SOMESTHETIC) AND SKIN (CUTANEOUS) SENSES

Our fifth sense is commonly known as touch, but it's actually a combination of several senses: the **skin senses,** which relate to pressure, touch, and pain; the **kinesthetic sense,** which relates to how our body parts interact with one another; and the **vestibular senses,** which relate to movement and body position.

Pain

Feeling pain is necessary for survival, and an inability to feel pain would eventually prove fatal. Pain is your body's way of telling you that placing your hand on a hot oven or running into a brick wall is a bad idea. It encourages us not to try those things again, which prolongs our survival. People who have rare genetic disorders that prevent them from detecting pain often die before they reach adulthood.

There are actually several different kinds of pain. **Nociceptive pain** is a negative feeling caused by an external stimulus. If you sprain your ankle, bruise your arm, or burn yourself on a hot stove, you are feeling nociceptive pain. This type of pain is usually time limited; when the injury heals, the pain fades.

Neuropathic pain derives from a malfunction in the central nervous system. It may be triggered by an injury or through diseases such as cancer that disturb cellular functioning. Phantom limb pain is also an example of neuropathic pain—amputees sometimes feel pain or movement in nonexistent limbs (Melzack, 1992). This is treated with drugs and therapies, but problems are often not fully reversible. Canadian researchers (Ware et al., 2010) have found higher potency marijuana to be an effective pain reliever for neuropathic pain.

Referred pain occurs when sensory information from internal and external areas converges on the same nerve cells in the spinal cord. In other words, pain is experienced in a different part of the body than the location of the injury. The most common example of this is when heart attack victims experience pain in their shoulders or left arms.

Why do some people seem to feel pain more acutely than others? The best current explanation for the way we feel pain is the gate-control theory (Melzack, 1980; Melzack & Katz, 2004). Pain signals pass through a "gate" in the spinal cord that either blocks the signals or allows them to pass to the brain. When pain signals reach the brain, they activate cells in the thalamus, somatosensory cortex, and limbic system. The brain interprets the messages and sends signals that either open the gate further, causing greater pain, or close it, preventing us from feeling further pain.

You have probably heard of an athlete managing to finish a race with a broken leg, or a football player completing a game with a broken collarbone, and wondered why they weren't crumpled on the ground in a world of pain. **Endorphins,** the body's answer to morphine, inhibit the transmission of pain signals to the brain, enabling us to perform seemingly superhuman feats when we are under stress.

Touch

Did you know that you have about 2 square metres of skin on your body? That's a lot of receptor cells! We have several types of cells in layers of skin that process pain, pressure, and temperature.

Imagine a world in which you couldn't hold

hands with a partner, kiss your parents hello, or console a friend with a hug. If it sounds like a terrible place to live, that's because it is—touch is necessary for our development and well-being. Infant rats deprived of maternal grooming produce less growth hormone and have a lower metabolic rate than their contemporaries (Schanberg & Field, 1988). Infant monkeys not allowed to touch their mothers become desperately unhappy, while monkeys that are separated from their mothers by a screen that allows touching are far more content (Harlow, Dodsworth, & Harlow 1965).

Body Position and Movement

Our kinesthetic sense provides information to our brains about the positions and movements of our muscles and joints. Without it, we would be unable to walk in a straight line, raise a glass to our lips, or bend down to pick up a pencil. Signals from specialized nerve endings, or **proprioceptors,** provide a constant stream of information from our muscles

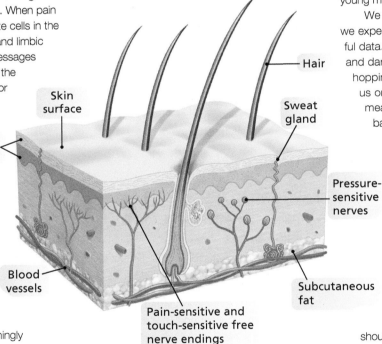

Skin surface

Skin layers

Hair

Sweat gland

Pressure-sensitive nerves

Blood vessels

Subcutaneous fat

Pain-sensitive and touch-sensitive free nerve endings

∧∧∧ Skin has several layers. Some receptor cells are wrapped around the ends of the hairs on the dermis, some are located near the surface of the epidermis, and some are found under the top layer of tissue. The subcutaneous layer stores fats and lipids.

through our spinal cords and on to the cortex of the parietal lobe.

The vestibular sense monitors the body's position in space. It originates in the inner ear, which is why you sometimes lose your sense of balance when you have an ear infection. Hair cells in the **semicircular canals** send messages to the brain as they move back and forth. Movement also stimulates tiny crystals in the **vestibular sacs,** which connect the canals to the cochlea. The receptors send messages to the cerebellum, enabling it to maintain the body's sense of balance.

Perception

Perception is the way we organize and interpret sensory information from the outside world to give it meaning. No two people perceive the world the same way. Take the tattooed skinhead sitting at a bus stop. Some of us might hurriedly cross the road in an effort to avoid the brutal thug, while others may compliment the creative young man on his body art.

We perceive when we take the sensations we experience and interpret them as meaningful data. Rather than seeing patterns of light and darkness, we are able to perceive a frog hopping into a pond or a car whizzing past us on the freeway. But how do we create meaning from the sensory data that bombards us every day?

Attention and Perception

Our conscious attention is selective—we are able to focus on only one perception at any given time, even though we know that alternative interpretations are possible. Try it yourself by staring at a Necker cube. You should find that your mind switches back and forth between images, never allowing you to see both interpretations at the same time.

Sometimes our attention is **endogenous,** or directed by our internal decisions. We make explicit choices to pay attention to particular stimuli. You might be making a conscious effort to pay attention to this book, rather than focusing on the new CD you are playing in the background.

At other times our attention is **exogenous,** or directed by external stimuli. If a plane crashes loudly outside your bedroom window, your attention will automatically

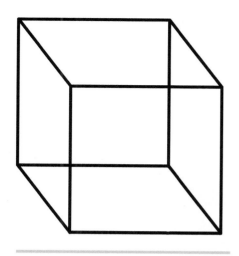

∧
∧ Which way is the
∧ cube facing?

be drawn to it, no matter how fascinating the information in your textbook might be.

> Stimuli that are important or interesting to us are called pop-out stimuli— they "pop out" at us and keep our attention.

UNATTENDED STIMULI AND POP-OUT STIMULI

Since we are constantly being bombarded with stimuli, we are able to select just a few to process at any one time. This is why driving while talking on a cellphone is an extremely bad idea—if we are concentrating on last night's gossip, we are missing important traffic signals that would otherwise be the main focus of our attention. Our failure to perceive a given stimulus is known as **inattentional blindness.**

Would you notice if the person you were giving directions to suddenly changed his or her appearance? We like to think that we are observant, but most of us are subject to **change blindness,** or failure to detect drastic visual changes in a scene. In a 1998 study by Simons and Levin, an experimenter who was dressed as a construction worker stopped a person in the street and asked for directions. Workers carrying a door passed between the experimenter and the person giving directions, enabling another experimenter dressed as a construction worker to take the place of the first. In two-thirds of cases, the person continued to give directions

without noticing that the construction worker had changed in appearance.

Change blindness can also have a negative impact on our ability to accurately remember past events. Researchers Kelly Nelson and colleagues (2011) examined the role of change blindness on eyewitness testimony. In their study, over 700 participants viewed videotapes in which a crime was committed. Participants who viewed videos in which the perpetrator of the crime was replaced with an innocent actor were more likely to falsely identify the innocent actor as the guilty party, compared with the control group. In fact, 95% or participants did not notice that the perpetrator had been replaced by another person; they thought they were the same person.

Similar examples of inattentional blindness can be observed with **change deafness**—the failure to detect drastic auditory changes—and **choice blindness**—the failure to detect alterations to choices we have made. For example, participants in a study were shown pairs of cards with photos of female faces on them and asked to pick which face they found more attractive. Once the participants chose a particular card, the experimenter handed them the other photo in a sleight of hand manoeuvre. The participants were then asked to justify their choice, even though the card they had been given was not the card they chose. Not only did most subjects fail to notice the switch, they also justified their "choice" using features of the non-preferred face (Johansson, Hall, & Sikström, 2005).

How are we able to carry out a conversation in a crowded room? The **cocktail party effect** is a good example of how selective attention allows us to concentrate on one voice and ignore many others. Stimuli that are important or interesting to us are called **pop-out stimuli**—they "pop out" at us and keep our attention.

PREATTENTIVE PROCESSING

If you glance at an image for a fraction of a second, you will probably not be able to describe it in any great detail. However, you might know more about it than you think. **Preattentive processing** is the complex processing of information that occurs without our conscious awareness. If we are shown an image of a red dot in a grid of blue dots, even for a split second, we are likely to remember the red dot.

Preattentive processing enables us to analyze the images we see using a guided search process. We are able to quickly filter images through our brains by looking for particular features, such as colour or shape.

Inattentional blindness describes the failure to perceive a given stimulus.

Change blindness describes the failure to detect drastic visual changes in a scene.

Change deafness describes the failure to detect drastic auditory changes.

Choice blindness describes the failure to detect alterations to choices a person has made.

Cocktail party effect is a phenomenon in which selective attention allows a person to concentrate on one voice and ignore many others.

Pop-out stimulus is a stimulus that is important or interesting to a person.

Preattentive processing is a complex processing of information that occurs without a person's conscious awareness.

Multi-tasking is the act of juggling independent sensory inputs.

Top-down processing refers to our use of beliefs, experiences, expectations, and other concepts to shape our view of the world.

MULTI-TASKING

While you are reading this textbook, you might be listening to the radio or flicking between TV channels. You might have tried to read a page while having a phone conversation with your friend or making a cup of tea. When you juggle independent sensory inputs, you are **multi-tasking**—a skill many people in today's fast-paced society pride themselves on. But are we really able to do more than one thing at a time?

Brain scan studies conducted on a particular form of sensory information, such as auditory, have demonstrated that when we focus on a noise, areas in the brain specialized for auditory processing increase in activity, while areas for other forms of sensory information, such as visual recognition, decrease.

These studies indicate that directing resources to one form of sensory information can drain resources from another, because there is a limited amount of blood circulating in the brain. So, brainpower actually decreases when we try to multi-task, even when different parts of the brain are used for different tasks. This explains why talking on a cellphone inhibits our driving ability (Strayer & Johnston, 2001).

Theories of Perception

TOP-DOWN PROCESSING

The way we perceive the world is affected by our beliefs, experiences, and expectations—a concept psychologists call **top-down processing.**

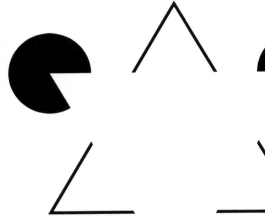

Why do we perceive a white triangle in the centre of this image when it is not really there?

Unconscious inference is a phenomenon in which a person's visual systems use sensory information to draw conclusions about what he or she sees.

Illusory contour is a visual illusion in which lines are perceived without actually being present.

Perceptual set is a mental disposition based on previous experiences and expectations that influences the way a person perceives things.

German physiologist Hermann von Helmholtz (1821–1894) argued that our conscious perceptions are determined by **unconscious inferences,** in which our visual systems use sensory information to draw conclusions about what we see. For example, when we hold a finger in front of the moon, how do we know that the finger and the moon are not the same size? Helmholtz argued that we learn how to interpret spatial concepts through experience.

Our brains have a natural desire to create logic and order. Often, we create the perception of contours and borders to construct a logical form, even if it is not really there. An **illusory contour** is a visual illusion in which lines are perceived without actually being present. Researchers have discovered that illusory contour images activate specific regions in the visual cortex. Cells in these areas respond as though the contours were formed by real lines or edges (Von der Heydt, Peterhans, & Baumgartner, 1984).

In White's illusion (shown at the top of p.67), the grey rectangles on the left appear darker than the rectangles on the right. In actual fact, they are identical. Our perception of brightness depends on the context of a stimulus. The rectangles on the right are mostly surrounded by white, while the rectangles on the left are mostly surrounded by black. Our brains assess the relative reflection of light compared with surrounding objects.

Perceptual Sets

Our previous experiences and expectations give us a mental predisposition, or **perceptual set,** that influences the way we perceive things. For example, if a child hands you a page scrawled with scattered squiggles in brown crayon and tells you he has drawn a picture of a horse, you will be more likely to perceive the messy brown scribble as a horse. Top-down processing enables us to use pre-existing knowledge to create a coherent image in our brains.

Perceptual sets are not just restricted to vision. Have you ever misheard something one of your friends said because you were expecting her to say something else? Our perceptual set is determined by our previous experiences, through which we form schemas, or internal representations of an object. This can be influenced by culture. For example, Europeans and North Americans are likely to perceive diagrams differently than people in Native cultures. We can find evidence of this with a diagram commonly known as the "devil's trident." Europeans and North Americans have a natural desire to interpret it as a three-dimensional object, yet people in Native cultures are able to view the diagram as two-dimensional—just a series of lines and circles (Deregowski, 1969).

GESTALT PRINCIPLES

The German word *gestalt* means "form" or "whole." In psychological terms, it refers to the way in which we naturally group objects together and perceive whole shapes, rather than a number of individual parts. For

<<< Based on previous experiences, we assume that the **two people** are standing in a **normal room,** the **same distance** away from us. As a result, our **brains** perceive the person on the **right** to be much **larger** than the person on the left.

∧∧∧ Which **rectangles** are **darker**?

shapes that form around their centre—the law of **symmetry.** When we see two unconnected but symmetrical shapes, we automatically perceive them as one object.

Common Fate. The **law of common fate** dictates that if the parts of a stimulus are all moving in the same direction, we perceive them as parts of a whole. If you see four people standing together at a party, and two of them walk toward the kitchen, while the other two head for the living room, you will no longer perceive them as a group of four, but rather as two pairs.

Law of pragnanz is a law that states that a person organizes a stimulus into the simplest possible form.

Proximity is the tendency to perceive objects that are close to one another as part of the same group.

Similarity is the tendency to perceive objects that are the same shape, size, or colour as part of a pattern.

Closure is the tendency to perceive images as complete objects and overlook incompleteness.

Continuity is the tendency to view intersecting lines as part of a continuous pattern.

Symmetry is the tendency to perceive two unconnected but symmetrical shapes as one object.

Law of common fate states that if the parts of a stimulus are all moving in the same direction, they are perceived as parts of a whole.

Figure is the object on which a person is focusing.

Ground is the environment surrounding the object of focus, or the figure.

Reversible figure refers to an illusion in which staring at an image long enough causes the figure and ground to reverse.

View-dependent pertains to the idea that previously seen objects are stored as a template that is compared to a viewed shape in the retinal image.

View-independent pertains to the idea that the visual system recognizes objects as a combination of their visual parts.

example, a Necker cube is really a series of converging lines, yet when we look at it, we see a three-dimensional object. Gestalt psychology developed in Germany at the beginning of the 20th century, partly as a reaction to the introspective methods used in structuralism.

Grouping

The main concept of Gestalt psychology is the **law of pragnanz** (German for *conciseness*), which says that we organize a stimulus into the simplest possible form. Six-month-old infants are already able to follow certain rules for grouping stimuli together (Quinn, Bhatt, Brush, Grimes, & Sharpnack, 2002).

Proximity. We tend to perceive objects that are close to one another as part of the same group—a principle known as **proximity.**

Similarity. **Similarity** is the tendency to perceive objects that are the same shape, size, or colour as part of a pattern. For example, members of a police force all wear the same uniform so that they are instantly recognizable as part of a group.

Closure. **Closure** is the tendency to perceive images as complete objects and overlook incompleteness. When shown a series of disconnected curved lines in a circular pattern, we will invariably describe it as a circle.

Continuity. **Continuity** is a tendency to view intersecting lines as part of a continuous pattern, rather than as a series of separate lines. A cross is usually perceived as two intersecting lines, rather than four lines that meet at a central point.

Symmetry. Our perceptual systems tend to organize objects in terms of symmetrical

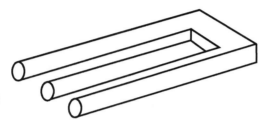

∧∧∧ How do you perceive the **devil's trident**?

Figure-Ground Relationships

An important part of the perceptual process is being able to distinguish the object we are focusing on—the **figure**—from its surroundings—the **ground.** The figure-ground relationship relates to all of the senses, not just vision. For example, we might hear our name being called amid a cacophony of voices during a sports match or be able to distinguish the smell of freshly baked bread among an array of scents we encounter on the street.

Sometimes it is tricky to distinguish the figure from the ground, as seen in **reversible figure** illusions such as the Rubin vase. When you first look at the image, you perceive the figure and the ground one way, but if you stare at the

image long enough, your perception changes, reversing figure and ground. You'll find that it's not possible to perceive both at once.

OBJECT RECOGNITION

There are two main theories about how we recognize objects. According to supporters of **view-dependent** theories, previously seen objects are stored as a template, or mental representation, that is compared to a viewed shape in the retinal image. In contrast, proponents of **view-independent** theories propose that the visual system recognizes

Gestalt principles of perceptual organization ∨∨∨

    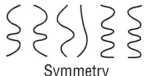

| Similarity | Proximity | Continuity | Closure | Symmetry |

Distal stimulus is a stimulus from an object that exists in the surrounding environment.

Proximal stimulus is a pattern of physical energy created by the distal stimulus that stimulates a person's receptors.

Feature integration theory suggests that people organize stimuli based on knowledge of how their features should be combined.

Illusory conjunction results from mistakenly combining features of two different stimuli.

Geon is a simple three-dimensional shape that, with other geons, makes up all other objects.

Recognition-by-components theory is a theory that states that a person recognizes an unfamiliar object by piecing together the cylinder, cone, wedge, and brick shapes of which it is composed.

Critical period is the optimal time period shortly after birth during which normal sensory and perceptual development takes place.

objects as a combination of their individual parts.

When we hear a dog barking or see a bird sitting on a tree branch, we are using information from the **distal stimulus**—the barking of the dog or the actual bird—to interpret the physical energy. The **proximal stimulus**—the barking sound stimulating our auditory receptors or the retinal image of the bird—recreates the distal stimuli in our minds.

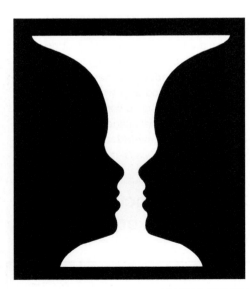

∧
∧ Do you see the
∧ silhouettes of two
faces or a goblet?

Feature Integration Theory

How do we recognize a car even if we have never seen that particular model before? Psychologist Anne Treisman proposed the **feature integration theory**—that every stimulus can be broken down into primitive features, or simple parts that make up an object, and combined using a two-step process (Treisman & Gelade, 1980). According to Treisman, we first use parallel processing to detect visual features—our brains rapidly and preattentively scan an object for pop-out stimuli (such as the red dot in the grid of blue dots). Serial processing then takes place in which we combine features to form objects, often using our stored knowledge to help us determine what we are seeing.

Treisman's theory is supported by the fact that when we are not focusing our attention, and have no stored knowledge about an object, errors in feature combinations can occur to produce **illusory conjunctions.** Even though we have detected all the individual features, we combine them incorrectly during the serial processing stage. The result is to perceive a blue C and a red A when you have actually been shown a red C and a blue A.

Components Theory

Irving Biederman proposed that all objects are composed of simplistic three-dimensional shapes called **geons.** According to his **recognition-by-components theory,** we recognize an unfamiliar object by piecing together the cylinder, cone, wedge, and brick shapes of which it is composed (Biederman, 1987). Biederman's theory is supported by the fact that our ability to identify an object quickly depends on the clarity of its external edges, rather than features such as colour or inner line detail.

Context and Motion

As you can see from the images above, it is much easier to identify parts of an object in context. Motion can also assist our perception. In 1973, psychologist Gunnar Johansson attached small lights to the major joints and head of a person who was filmed walking in the dark. When stationary, it was not possible to distinguish the person as a coherent form. However, while the person was moving, she could easily be recognized as a person walking, proving that we do not need to see a complete image as long as the unconnected points are

1. Can you guess what this is? 2. How about now?

∨
∨
∨

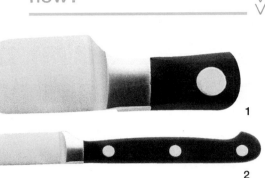

1

2

moving in a recognizable manner (Johansson, 1973). We're also good at recognizing unique motions: If you've ever recognized a friend across the street by her distinctive walk, you're well aware that people's movements can be crucial clues to their identities.

Perceptual Interpretation

Do we learn how to perceive the world through experience, or are we born with an innate ability to interpret our surroundings? Proving the answer to this question would make you an instant millionaire; it has been debated by philosophers for centuries. German philosopher Immanuel Kant (1724–1804) argued that perceptual knowledge exists at birth, while British philosopher John Locke (1632–1704) insisted that we learn through our experiences. The nature versus nurture debate still rages on today, influencing everything from crime prevention techniques to educational theory.

Are people who are born blind ever truly able to see, or does early sensory deprivation cause permanent damage? Studies suggest that there is a **critical period,** or optimal time period shortly after birth, during which normal sensory and perceptual development takes place. For example, adults who were born blind but later regained vision after having cataracts removed never enjoyed full sight. They were able to distinguish figure from ground and could perceive brightness and colour, but were unable to recognize objects (von Senden, 1932). Similar perceptual limitations are found with deprivation in other senses.

∧
∧ How might our **cultural background** affect the
∧ way we perceive the world around us?

Perceptual adaptation is a process in which a person adjusts to changes in the environment by adjusting sensory input.

Synaesthesia is a condition in which signals from the sensory organs are processed in the wrong cortical areas of the brain.

Letter/digit colour synaesthesia is a condition in which seeing, hearing, or even thinking about a letter or digit creates a visual experience of a specific colour.

Associator is a person who associates colours with letters; he or she does not actually see the colour.

Projector is a person who actually sees letters as being certain colours, even though he or she knows what colour the type actually is.

Time-space synaesthesia is a condition in which a person experiences time units as occupying specific spatial locations.

Number-form synaesthesia is a condition in which a person experiences numbers in complex spatial arrangements.

PERCEPTUAL ADAPTATION

While sensory adaptation allows us to adjust to changes in our environment, **perceptual adaptation** helps us adjust to changes in the way we experience the environment. Have you ever tried on a friend's glasses? At first, the world seems blurry, but if you kept the glasses on for a day or two, your eyesight would adjust (although your friend might not be happy!).

Perceptual adaptation enables us to adjust sensory input so that the world seems normal again. This is true even for radically altered visual fields. In a month-long study, Japanese psychologist Kaoru Sekiyama (2000) asked four students to wear prism glasses that reversed their left-right vision. While they were initially disoriented, within a few weeks the students were able to carry out tasks requiring complex coordination skills, such as riding a bicycle. At the end of the experiment, the students quickly readapted to normal vision.

SYNAESTHESIA

Imagine being able to taste the words you speak or hear a piece of music as a rainbow of different colours. People who interpret sense information as more than one sensation have a condition called **synaesthesia**, in which signals from the sensory organs are processed in the wrong cortical areas of the brain. According to the

Synaesthesia Research Group at the University of Waterloo, the most common type of synaesthesia is **letter/digit colour synaesthesia**, in which seeing, hearing, or even thinking about a letter or digit creates a visual experience of a highly specific colour, for example, thinking of the letter *A* as red. Some synaesthetes are **associators**—they might associate the letter *A* as being red, but they do not actually see the colour red. A small number of people with the disorder are **projectors**—they actually view the letter *A* as red, even though they know that the type they are reading is black.

Other types of synaesthesia include **time-space synaesthesia**, in which a person experiences time units (e.g., minutes in an hour, months of a year) as occupying specific spatial locations (e.g., January is located 30° to the left of midline), and **number-form synaesthesia**, in which a person experiences numbers in complex spatial arrangements. For example, University of Waterloo researchers studied individuals who

experience the numbers 1 through 10 running vertically from bottom to top, 10 to 20 horizontally from left to right, and 21 to 40 from right to left. (Jarick et al., 2009a, 2009b).

It is estimated that one out of every 2000 people experiences some form of synaesthesia. Canadian researchers (Mann, Korzenko, Carriere, & Dixon, 2009) found that synaesthetes may have a cognitive advantage over non-synaesthetes. Many artists who have synaesthesia use their abilities to create unique paintings or musical compositions.

Hip-hop artist Pharell Williams used **synaesthesia** as the basis for N.E.R.D album *Seeing Sounds.* >>>

04

Summary

WHAT ARE SENSORY THRESHOLDS? p.56

• An absolute threshold is the smallest amount of energy needed to detect a stimulus such as light, sound, or pressure 50% of the time.

• A difference threshold is the minimum difference between two stimuli needed to detect the difference 50% of the time.

HOW DO WE PROCESS STIMULI FROM THE OUTSIDE WORLD? p.57

• Sensation occurs when a receptor cell in one of the sense organs is stimulated by energy. Transduction is the process of converting physical energy into electrochemical codes.

• Light enters the eye through the cornea and pupil and is focused by the lens on the retina. Light waves are transmitted to the ganglion cells that make up the optic nerve. Neural messages travel along the optic nerve to the visual cortex.

• Sound waves cause the eardrum to vibrate. Vibrations are carried to the cochlea, causing ripples in the basilar membrane. Hair cells in the basilar membrane stimulate receptor cells to send messages to the auditory cortex.

• Airborne molecules stimulate receptor cells at the top of the nasal cavity, sending messages to the brain's olfactory bulb.

• Microvilli at the tips of receptor cells in the taste buds send messages to the limbic system and cerebral cortex. The five basic taste qualities are sweet, sour, salty, bitter, and umami.

• Receptor cells in skin process pain, pressure, and temperature. Pain is currently explained by the gate-control theory.

• The kinesthetic senses provide information about muscle movement and changes in posture. The vestibular senses provide information about the body's position in space.

WHY ARE WE ABLE TO EXPERIENCE ONLY ONE PERCEPTION AT A TIME? p.64

• Perception is the brain's process of organizing and making sense of sensory information.

• Conscious attention is selective—we can only experience one perception at a time. Failure to perceive a stimulus is known as inattentional blindness.

WHAT ARE SOME MAJOR THEORIES OF PERCEPTION? p.65

• Gestalt psychologists point out that we group stimuli together when the objects are near each other; are similar sizes, colours, and shapes; or complete a pattern.

• Treisman's feature integration theory proposes that we use parallel processing to detect visual features, then serial processing to combine them.

IS PERCEPTION DEVELOPED BY NATURE OR NURTURE? p.68

• Normal sensory and perceptual development takes place during a critical period shortly after we are born.

• Perceptual adaptation enables us to adjust to changes in the way we perceive the environment.

• People who interpret sense information as more than one sensation have a condition called synaesthesia, in which signals from the sensory organs are processed in the wrong cortical areas of the brain.

Test Your Understanding

1. Shameka conducts an experiment in which she plays a series of recorded noises at different frequencies and asks participants to indicate when they hear a sound. Shameka's experiment is based on:
   a. the cocktail party effect
   b. signal detection theory
   c. top-down processing
   d. recognition-by-components theory

2. As Mike drives along a coastal road, he catches a whiff of fresh, salty air that reminds him of a family beach vacation when he was seven. What is happening in Mike's brain?
   a. Smell signals are travelling directly to the amygdala and hippocampus.
   b. Smell signals are bypassing the amygdala and hippocampus.
   c. Smell signals are travelling directly to the thalamus.
   d. Smell signals are bypassing the thalamus, amygdala, and hippocampus.

3. A person who trips over a rock and cuts his or her knee is suffering from:
   a. neuropathic pain
   b. referred pain
   c. nociceptive pain
   d. chronic pain

4. Jamal and his grandmother are trying to read a road sign in the distance. Jamal can easily make out the words, but his grandmother struggles to do so. This is likely because:
   a. as we age, the lens hardens
   b. as we age, the iris weakens
   c. as we age, the cornea and pupil let in less light
   d. as we age, the retina becomes more sensitive

5. When Yoko points out a cloud and says she thinks it looks like a dragon chasing its tail, her friend Gwen agrees that the cloud

does bear a striking resemblance to the mythical beast. Gwen has most likely been influenced by:

a. visual accommodation
b. a perceptual set
c. the law of pragnanz
d. an illusory conjunction

6. Which of the following may be affected if we have an inner ear infection?

a. proprioceptors
b. endorphin levels
c. cutaneous senses
d. vestibular sense

7. On what does a reversible figure such as the Rubin vase rely to create an optical illusion?

a. the principle of proximity
b. the principle of symmetry
c. recognition-by-components theory
d. the figure-ground relationship

8. A person with a genetic disorder that prevents him from feeling pain is most likely to:

a. suffer from other sensory losses
b. experience thickening of the somatosensory cortex
c. die before he or she reaches adulthood
d. produce more endorphins than other people

9. Kwame is shown a series of pictures for a fraction of a second each. Although he cannot describe the pictures in detail, he is able to recall whether each one contained a large black rectangle in the centre. Kwame is using:

a. preattentive processing
b. top-down processing
c. inattentional blindness
d. perceptual adaptation

10. William takes his coffee with one sugar. Jessica likes one and a half sugars, while Ed takes four. When William accidentally takes a sip of Jessica's coffee, he doesn't notice, yet when he drinks from Ed's mug he recoils in disgust. Why is this?

a. The amount of sugar in Jessica's coffee does not reach the absolute threshold.
b. The amount of sugar in Ed's coffee exceeds the difference threshold.
c. William is unable to establish an absolute threshold.
d. William is unable to establish a difference threshold.

11. Which of the following statements about taste is true?

a. The bumps that you can see on your tongue are called taste buds.
b. Receptor cells for the five basic tastes are located on different regions of the tongue.
c. Taste signals are passed to the amygdala and the cerebral cortex.
d. Papillae generate a nerve impulse that is interpreted in the brain as a particular taste.

12. Which of the following is an example of endogenous attention?

a. noticing smoke billowing out of an oven
b. hearing a friend shouting your name
c. seeing a streak of lightning
d. studying for an exam

13. Alkira sees a man and a woman standing close together at a bus stop. Although they are not speaking, she perceives them to be a couple. Which Gestalt principle is Alkira employing?

a. similarity
b. proximity
c. closure
d. continuity

14. Which of the following does not influence sensory adaptation?

a. the number of sensory receptor cells
b. the sensory cortex in the brain
c. the rate at which the receptor cells fire
d. the strength of the stimulus

15. Poor hearing will most likely result from repeated exposure to which of the following?

a. sound waves with a low frequency
b. sound waves with a poor timbre
c. sound waves with a high amplitude
d. sound waves with a high frequency

16. A person who processes sensory information in the wrong cortical areas of the brain is most likely suffering from:

a. synaesthesia
b. blindsight
c. neuropathic pain
d. choice blindness

17. If you want to see an object in dim light, what should you do?

a. Focus directly on the object, using the cones in the fovea.
b. Look to the side of the object, using the rods outside the fovea.
c. Focus directly on the object, using the rods in the fovea.
d. Look to the side of the object, using the cones outside the fovea.

18. Which of the following lends support to Treisman's feature integration theory?

a. the critical period of sensory development
b. the process of perceptual adaptation
c. the phenomenon of illusory conjunctions
d. the existence of perceptual sets

19. Which two senses are inextricably linked?

a. vision and smell
b. hearing and smell
c. touch and taste
d. smell and taste

20. Tyler sees a sheep eating grass in a field. Which of the following represents the distal stimulus?

a. the retinal image of the sheep
b. the neural message along the optic nerve
c. the light waves in the ganglion cells
d. the sheep itself

Remember to check www.thethinkspot.ca for additional information, downloadable flashcards, and other helpful resources.

Answers: 1) b; 2) a; 3) c; 4) a; 5) b; 6) d; 7) d; 8) c; 9) a; 10) b; 11) b; 12) d; 13) b; 14) d; 15) c; 16) a; 17) b; 18) c; 19) d; 20) d

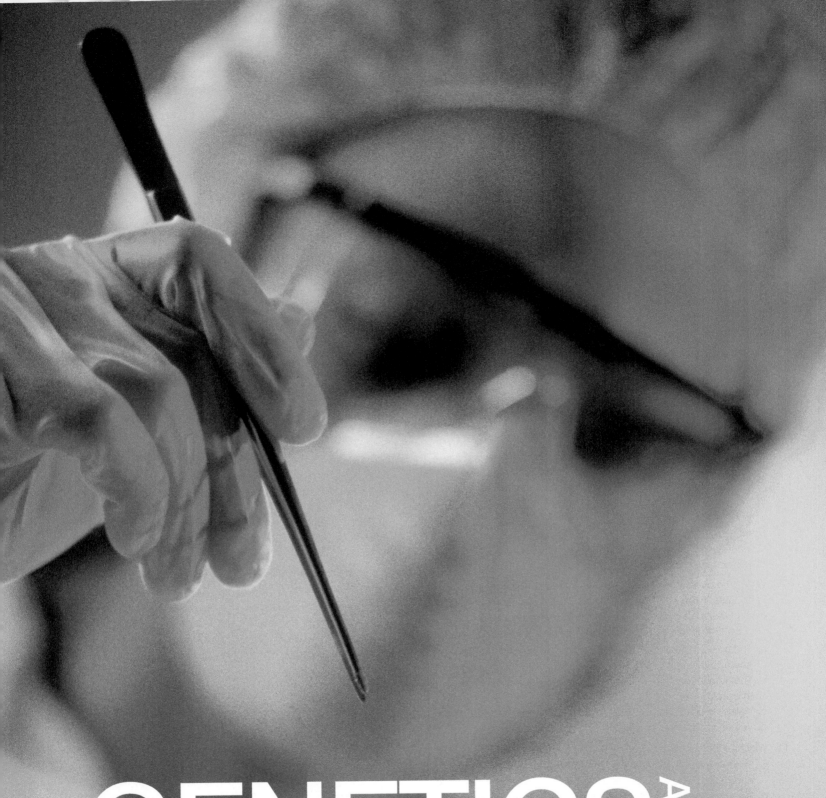

GENETICS AND EVOLUTION

ARE THE GENETIC MECHANISMS OF TRAIT INHERITANCE?

IN WHAT WAY DO GENES AND ENVIRONMENT INTERACT TO MAKE US WHO WE ARE?

HOW HAS THE IDEA OF EVOLUTION BY NATURAL SELECTION INFLUENCED THE STUDY OF HUMAN BEHAVIOUR?

WHAT ARE THE TYPICAL MATING PATTERNS OF DIFFERENT SPECIES?

Brian

slowly rocks back and forth, flapping his arms rhythmically as if trying to fly. He prefers to spend time alone or with a few trusted objects rather than with people. He never speaks. Brian is 4 years old and he has autism.

Autism, from the Greek word for self, is the name for an incurable brain disorder that impairs a person's ability to communicate and relate to others. Symptoms may include repetitive behaviours such as headbanging, avoidance of physical or eye contact with others, and communication through gestures instead of words. About 40 percent of children with autism do not talk.

Autism is believed to have a strong genetic basis but the actual cause is still unknown. Some 200,000 Canadians are living with autism, which occurs in all racial, ethnic and social groups.

And the incidence of autism is on the rise. In fact, the number of children diagnosed as autistic climbed by 400 percent in the last decade alone. We do not know whether the increase is due to better diagnostic tools or environmental factors.

Today, 1 in every 500 children in North America is diagnosed with autism. It is more common than pediatric cancer, juvenile diabetes and HIV-AIDS combined.

Unfortunately, by the time autism is diagnosed—usually around the age of 3—the best time for treating it has already passed. According to Dr. Steve Scherer of the Hospital for Sick Children and the University of Toronto, it's a classic Catch-22: to be most effective, intervention should take place before age 3 but it's very difficult to diagnose autism before that age.

Dr. Scherer heads a team of the country's leading geneticists, developmental pediatricians and genome scientists taking part in a 10-nation project studying autism. With funding from Genome Canada, the team is working on isolating genes that may make some-

one susceptible to autism. Once those genes have been identified, physicians will be able to diagnose the condition much earlier and treat it more effectively.

This groundbreaking work will extend our knowledge of the biological nature of autism and could lead to drugs for treating the disorder. "The implications of this research are profound," says Dr. Scherer, "most importantly for these children and their families, but also for the Canadian health care system, which spends billions on autism every year."

Current treatment consists of concentrated behavioural therapies, often requiring nearly round-the-clock involvement by trained specialists—an expensive and labour-intensive approach. According to Dr. Scherer, if treatment starts early enough, many children may not need special services by the time they enter school, resulting in greater independence and lower costs.

What's more, with an understanding of the genetic basis, it will be possible to predict whether autism is likely to recur in a family. This would significantly lessen the anxiety of prospective parents. It would also facilitate early diagnosis.

The research has already attracted interest from some of the world's largest pharmaceutical companies, including Schering and GlaxoSmithKline. They see genomics discoveries and profiling as potential first steps toward developing effective drug therapies. This means opportunities for licensing agreements and two patent applications have already been filed.

For Brian and the millions of other children like him, however, cracking the medical mystery that is autism means even more: the chance for a better life.

Source: Genome Canada (2012). Cracking the Mystery of Autism. http://www.genomecanada.ca/en/info/human/autism.aspx

<<< *Genome Canada researchers are exploring the genetic causes of autism and other disorders, such as diabetes, macular degeneration, and bipolar disorder.*

CHAPTER **05**

Natural Selection

In the mid-19th century, evolution was already the controversial topic it continues to be today. When Charles Darwin began publishing his research in this area, he carefully avoided using the term *evolution* when drawing conclusions about the origins of humans. Despite these efforts, the public mocked what they assumed were his "man from monkey" ideas.

While controversy still surrounds these ideas, the concept of **natural selection** that Darwin introduced in his 1859 book *The Origin of Species* has become the guiding principle of biology and psychology. Darwin theorized that organisms with features best adapted to their environments were more likely to survive and reproduce. In other words, strong organisms are naturally selected for survival. As this process occurred, distinct species could evolve in response to different environmental pressures but would still resemble each other if they shared common ancestry. Humans share 99% of our genetic information with chimpanzees.

Genetic Mechanisms

CHROMOSOMES, GENES, AND DNA

If Darwin had only known about genetic mechanisms such as chromosomes, genes, and DNA, people may have taken him more seriously. Twentieth-century discoveries not only

Chromosomes are made up of long **strands of DNA**. **Genes** are sections of the **DNA molecule**, which has a **double helix spiral** form.

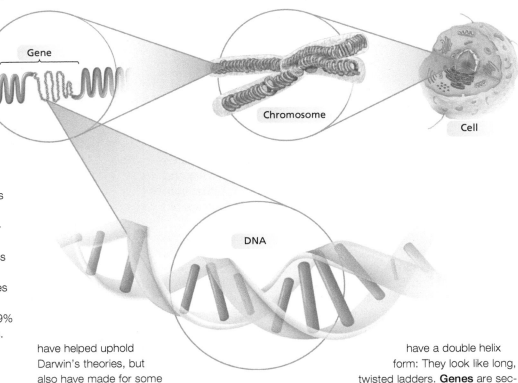

Gene

Chromosome

Cell

DNA

have helped uphold Darwin's theories, but also have made for some high-tech drama in TV shows such as *Cold Case* and *CSI*.

Chromosomes

To help solve crimes, investigators on TV and in real life analyze **chromosomes**, long strands of genetic material found in the nuclei of all cells. They are like biological blueprints that contain all the genetic information required to create each organism. Scientists study chromosomes to find out how closely different species are related, or in the case of a chimera, to determine how closely family members are related.

Normal human cells have 23 pairs of chromosomes, 46 in total. In addition to 22 true pairs, each cell also has an XX or XY pair that makes the individual female or male. Generally, chromosomes are spread throughout the nucleus and cannot be seen, but they become visible just before cell division. When chromosomes duplicate themselves, they form an X-like structure comprising two sister **chromatids**, the two strings of chromosomes, joined by a **centromere**, a place where the two strings meet.

Genes and DNA

The building blocks of chromosomes are **DNA**, or deoxyribonucleic acid. DNA molecules

have a double helix form: They look like long, twisted ladders. **Genes** are sections of the DNA that contain specific recipes to make thousands of different proteins in the body. Because genes control the types of proteins in the nervous, sensory, and motor systems of an organism, they affect the individual's traits and behaviour.

In organisms that reproduce sexually, the egg and sperm cells contain only half the number of chromosomes of all the other cells. During fertilization, the chromosomes of the mother pair up with those of the father to create a full set. As the fertilized egg divides, the DNA is replicated so that all cells contain the complete genetic information of that organism.

The Human Genome

Despite the observable cultural and physical differences between human beings, our common human **genome**—the complete instructions for making an organism—makes us very similar, behaviourally and biologically. No more than 5% of genetic differences arise from average population, racial, or ethnic group differences.

Since the discovery of chromosomes and DNA, scientists have been on a quest to map all the genes in the human body or human genome. Through the development of Genome

---

Natural selection is a theory that states that organisms best adapted to their environment tend to survive and transmit their genetic characteristics to succeeding generations.

Chromosomes are long strands of genetic material found in the nuclei of all cells.

Chromatids are pairs of duplicated chromosomes.

Centromere is the place where two chromatids meet.

DNA is a complex molecule that is the main ingredient of chromosomes; it forms the code for all genetic information.

Genes are sections of DNA that contain specific recipes to make proteins in the body.

Genome is the complete set of instructions for making an organism.

Canada, Canada has become a leader in genetics research. What our researchers discover could forever change the way disorders and diseases are described, categorized, and treated.

In 2000, Genome Canada was established with the purpose of developing and implementing projects in the field of genetics. For example, the International HapMap Project examines genetic variations that could explain the development of disease and how certain environmental factors influence our DNA. To date, this project has already yielded several groundbreaking discoveries: Researchers have identified genes involved in type 2 diabetes and ovarian and colon cancer, and researchers around the world have used HapMap to identify common genetic variations for diseases, including macular degeneration (the leading cause of blindness in seniors), tuberculosis, coronary heart disease, type 1 diabetes, rheumatoid arthritis, Crohn's disease and ulcerative colitis, and bipolar disorder. In addition, Dr. Stephen Scherer and his team made headlines in 2010 when they reported their findings from the Autism Genome Project (Ghahramani Seno et al., 2010). Their project, involving 120 scientists from more than 50 institutions in 12 countries, compared the DNA of 1000 people with autism spectrum disorder with that of 1300 people without it (Genome Canada, 2012). Scherer and his team identified over 100 autism-related genes, which helps to explain why different people show different symptoms (Genome Canada, 2012). The results of this study will ultimately improve autism treatments for people like Brian.

Genes and Environment

Recently, researchers have been working to identify the genetic roots of conditions as diverse as schizophrenia and obesity. But genes are not constant and unchanging; they work with the environment, self-regulate, and react by switching on and off, depending on the individual's environment. Environment includes everything around the organism and its surroundings, including an individual's life in utero.

Events and conditions in the individual's environment activate the genes that create proteins, which affect the individual's traits and behaviour. The **external environment** includes what happens in the individual's outside world—the wealth or poverty of a nation, a loving or unloving family, a calm or stressful life. What happens inside the organism makes up the **chemical environment**. In a study of mice and nurturing, researchers found that mice who had not given birth normally avoided newborns, but would eventually begin to care for them after prolonged exposure. Their external environment activated a cluster

> No more than 5% of genetic differences arise from average population, racial, or ethnic group differences.

External environment consists of events and conditions in the outside world.

Chemical environment consists of events and conditions inside an organism.

Genotype is the entire set of genes inherited by an organism.

Phenotype is the observable property that comes from a genotype.

Mendelian heredity refers to the idea that units of heredity come in pairs and one pair can dominate another.

Alleles are pairs of genes located in the same position on the pair of chromosomes in a unit of heredity.

of brain cells known to influence motivation to attend to young, showing that learning involves activation of genes (Johnston & Edwards, 2002).

Genotype and Phenotype

The entire set of genes inherited by an organism is its **genotype;** the observable properties that come from these genetics are **phenotypes.** Even if individuals have the same genotype, they can display different phenotypic characteristics or behaviours, depending on the environmental conditions they experience. The mice in the nurturance study who shared the same genotype would exhibit different observable behaviours depending on whether they had given birth or experienced prolonged exposure to newborns. These environmental factors changed the behaviour of the rodents so that their genotype remained the same, but their phenotypes differed.

Mendelian Heredity

Have you ever wondered how traits pass from parents to children? Why do some people resemble their blood relatives more than others? In the mid-19th century, Gregor Mendel, an Austrian monk, crossbred strains of round-seeded garden peas with wrinkled-seeded ones. When the offspring had round seeds, he concluded that inherited traits came from two factors and that the round-seeded factor dominated the wrinkled-seeded one. According to the idea of **Mendelian heredity,** a unit of heredity comes in pairs, and one pair can dominate another. Today, we know that these factors are chromosomes. Genes located in the same position on the pair of chromosomes are called **alleles.** We also know that most genetic traits involve a more complicated interplay of multiple chromosomes.

Autism Affects Many Parts of the Brain

The **cerebellum** regulates motor skills (balance, gross and fine body movements, coordination, and muscles used in speaking) and is involved in our ability to shift our attention from one task to another.

The **cerebral cortex** is our "grey matter" and it is functionally separated into the frontal lobe, temporal lobe, parietal lobe, and occipital lobes. Autism affects

- the **frontal lobe**, which is responsible for planning, organizing, problem solving, and impulse control
- the **parietal lobe**, which is responsible for language processing (speaking, hearing, and understanding language)
- the **temporal lobe**, particularly the **amygdala**, which regulates emotional expression, including aggression

The **hippocampus** is involved in memory and learning.

Hypothalamus
Pineal gland
Cerebral ortex
Septum
Thalamus
Hippocampus
Olfactory bulb
Fomix
Pituitary gland
Midbrain
Medulla oblongata
Pons
Cerebellum
Spinal cord

Dominant and Recessive Genes

Identical pairs of alleles are **homozygous** and non-identical pairs are **heterozygous.** In heterozygous pairs, how does the body choose which gene to express? Like the round seeds of Mendel's pea plants, some genes are **dominant** and will always present themselves when paired with another gene that is **recessive.** For example, the widow's peak gene dominates other genes to produce a certain observable trait, or phenotype. If an individual's hairline has a widow's peak, he or she has at least one allele for the widow's peak. If paired heterozygously with a gene for a straight hairline, the widow's peak allele will ensure that the individual has a widow's peak.

Not all genes are either dominant or recessive. Some just blend with each other and combine the traits carried by both genes. For instance, crossing red-petal four-o'clocks with white-petal four-o'clocks will produce offspring with pink petals. Most traits come from a combination of multiple genes from one or more chromosomal pairs.

SEXUAL REPRODUCTION

Sexual reproduction combines the genetic information of one parent with that of the other to produce a new and unique combination of genes. Our reproductive cells—eggs and sperm—contain only half the genetic information of other cells in the body. When the sperm and egg successfully combine, they form a new cell called a **zygote.** The 23 pairs of chromosomes of one parent pair up with another set of 23 from the other parent, forming the necessary genetic component pairs that make a person uniquely who he or she is. The diversity of individuals created by this continual recombination of genes gives organisms that reproduce sexually a great evolutionary advantage. As genes rearrange themselves, new traits may arise that help the organism adapt to new environments.

Sibling and Twins

While gene recombination makes each person unique, family resemblances prove that human beings also share many inherited characteristics. You might share your high-pitched voice with your sister, your curly hair with your dad, or your short stature with your mom. People generally share only 50% of their genes with their siblings and, on average, 25% with each parent, so you still have many differences.

Identical, or **monozygotic,** twins are essentially individuals cloned by nature. After fertilization, the single zygote divides and separates into two zygotes that develop into separate fetuses with 100% identical genetic material. Fraternal, or **dizygotic,** twins come from two separate zygotes created from two different eggs that were fertilized by two different sperm cells around the same time. They are basically ordinary siblings born at the same time, so they share the same 50% of genetic material as any other set of siblings.

Cell Division

An organism's reproductive cells are called **gametes.** Sexually reproducing organisms produce gametes through a special process of cell division, known as **meiosis.** During meiosis, chromosomes duplicate themselves, and the cell divides to form two new cells. These two cells divide a second time, distributing

> " People generally share only 50% of their genes with their siblings and, on average, 25% with each parent, so you still have many differences. "

half the chromosomes to one cell and half to the other. The result is four new cells with half the number of chromosomes of the original.

∧∧∧ Modern paternity tests compare a baby's DNA profile to that of the suspected father's profile. What other **applications** have come from our increased knowledge about genetics?

Each of these cells is now an egg or sperm cell, which combines with the sexual partner's gametes during conception. However, not all cells are designed to be reproductive cells; in fact, the vast majority of cells in the body reproduce through a more typical method of cell division—**mitosis.** During mitosis, chromosomes duplicate themselves before the cell divides, creating two cells genetically identical to the original.

At first glance, the first phase of cell division in meiosis seems a lot like mitosis, but in fact the initial division differs in an important way that adds significantly to the genetic diversity of the sexually reproducing organism. During the first division (meiosis I), sections of the duplicated chromosomes cross over and recombine to form new chromosomes. When these two new cells divide in meiosis II, the four new gametes contain chromosomes unlike the original parent cell and also unlike the other gametes. Essentially, sexual reproduction shuffles the cards in the genetic deck twice, once during meiosis and once during fertilization. If for any reason the original parent cell mutates before meiosis, the mutation can also be passed on to the gametes, creating another opportunity for genetic variation. Hemophilia and colour blindness occur in individuals that inherit the mutated gene for these conditions. Mutations can also occur during meiosis if chromatids do not separate properly, leaving more genetic information in one cell than in another. For example, an extra copy of chromosome 21 in the cell nucleus causes Down syndrome. Mutations can have positive effects as well. People with sickle-cell anemia have a mutation that causes their red blood cells to have a sickle shape. While this mutation inhibits the ability of their blood to carry oxygen, causing pain and fatigue, it also makes them resistant to malaria.

Trait Inheritance: The Nature vs. Nurture Debate

SINGLE-GENE TRAITS

The theory of Mendelian heredity explains how single-gene traits pass from parents to offspring. Cystic fibrosis, a disease that affects lung and digestive function, originates in one specific gene. Mutations in a gene located on chromosome 7 leads to cystic fibrosis. The recessive cystic fibrosis gene must be present in both alleles for an individual to develop the disease.

POLYGENIC TRAITS

Most traits do not correspond to a single gene pair, so scientists look for **gene complexes,** a group of genes acting together. Hair colour, eye colour, and height are all examples of **polygenic** characteristics, or characteristics resulting from more than one gene. Pigmentation or colour traits such as skin, hair, and eye colour are known as **continuous traits** because they come not just in two colours but in a variety of shades along a spectrum.

Multiple genes also interact with the environment to produce certain characteristics. A person may have a genetic predisposition to grow to a certain height, but how tall that person actually becomes depends on growth hormones secreted by the pituitary glands and on the kind of nutrition received during childhood. Diseases with polygenic sources include heart disease and cancer. Multiple genes interact with environmental factors, such as diet and living conditions, to determine whether an individual will or will not develop the disease. As complex polygenic characteristics, intelligence and personality also vary widely in people. They do not appear in one single form or another, and they are influenced by environment.

Mitosis is the process of cell division in which chromosomes duplicate themselves before the cell divides, creating two cells genetically identical to the original.

Gene complex is a group of genes acting together.

Polygenic means "coming from the interaction of several genes."

Continuous traits such as height, weight, and skin colour have a range of possible values.

Sexual selection refers to the process by which a mate is chosen.

Selective breeding is the process by which pairs of organisms of the same species with desirable characteristics are mated in order to select for those characteristics.

SEXUAL SELECTION

Any experience with dating will tell you that individuals do not attract mates equally. In humans and in other sexually reproducing species, this process of **sexual selection** affects which traits pass on to subsequent generations. In species that emphasize mate selection, males often display distinctive and easily observable characteristics to attract females. Male birds with bright feathers can compete for females more effectively than their less colourful fellow birds. As a result, the genes for sexual characteristics, like colourful plumage or large antlers, continue into the next generation so that bigger antlers or brighter plumage may appear over the course of generations.

SELECTIVE BREEDING

Selection can also be done artificially through **selective breeding.** Varieties of dog breeds have all been produced by mating individuals with desired characteristics in order to select for those traits. Over time, dogs were bred specifically for hunting, following scents, or even for just being small and fluffy. In a famous 1940 study, Robert Tryon showed through selective breeding that genes can strongly influence behavioural traits. First Tryon identified two types

∧
∧ **Skin pigmentation** is one example
∧ of a **continuous trait.** Which of your
other traits are **continuous?**

of rats: those that made their way through a maze with few errors (maze bright) and those that made their way through with several errors (maze dull). Then Tryon mated rats that were maze bright with other maze bright rats, and he also mated maze-dull rats with other maze-dull rats. After more than 21 generations of breeding bright with bright and dull with dull, he created two genetically different types of rats. Almost all the bright rats made fewer errors than even the smartest dull rat, illustrating how traits develop over generations.

BEHAVIOUR GENETICS

Would it surprise you to discover that individuals with identical DNA could differ in their personalities and interests?

Researchers in **behaviour genetics** try to determine the relative effects of genes and environment on behaviour and mental processes. One way to examine the relative roles of genetics and environment is through the use of twin studies. Researchers compare identical twins raised together with identical twins raised separately. When twins raised separately show similar traits, researchers infer that these traits probably have genetic origins. When twins raised together show different traits, researchers infer that environmental factors may have affected these differences.

Twin Studies

When Elyse Schein went looking for her birth mother, she had no idea that she had a twin sister. The first time they met, Elyse and her sister, Paula Bernstein, noticed that they had many similarities. They shared similar speech rhythms, facial expressions, gestures, and medical conditions. Both Elyse and Paula had been the editors of their high school newspapers, and both had taken trips to Italy at the same age. They had both even studied film in New York. Like Elyse and Paula, identical twins raised apart have shown remarkable similarities in many areas such as career choice, food preferences, and gestures (Wolff, 2007). But identical twins raised apart have more dissimilar personalities than those raised in the same family (Pedersen, Plomin, McLearn, & Friberg, 1988).

Adoption Studies

In addition to twin studies, behaviour geneticists use adoption studies to distinguish the degree of influence of nature and nurture. To calculate how particular traits are inherited, researchers compare the degree to which an individual's traits resemble those of biological parents as opposed to adoptive parents. Interestingly, adoptees have been found to resemble their biological parents more than their adoptive ones in certain preferences, personality, and behaviour. Adoption studies have illustrated the genetic influence on conditions such as obesity and some forms of alcoholism (Cloninger, Bohman, & Sigvardsson, 1981).

Heritability

Heritability refers to the degree to which genetics explains the individual variations in observable traits. In similar environments, heritability is important in influencing individual differences. If environments vary or influence certain traits, heritability would explain individual differences to a lesser degree. A trait such as eye colour has a high heritability because differing genetics cause variations in eye colour without any environmental influence. In contrast, intelligence has a much lower heritability because environmental factors also influence intelligence differences among individuals. Heritability does not tell us the percentage to which a trait is caused by genetics but rather the percentage to which variation among individuals can be attributed to genetic influence.

A hundred years ago, people had much less access to food and burned more calories in their daily activities. Today, with food available everywhere and few calories burned through activity, North Americans as a group have become heavier and heavier. Since our genes have not changed, the environment must have a powerful impact even on traits with a strong genetic basis, such as weight. Even a temperament trait such as happiness has a genetic component, and some people are literally just naturally relatively happier people. Researchers found no concordance between dizygotic twins in their sense of happiness. But they found an 80% concordance rate in happiness ratings for monozygotic twins (Lykken & Tellegen, 1996). The heritability of schizophrenia has also been solidly established. If one identical twin has schizophrenia, the other twin has a 50% chance of developing the condition. If a fraternal twin has schizophrenia, the other twin has a 27% chance of developing the disorder (Cardo & Gottesman, 2000).

MOLECULAR GENETICS

Suffering from problems in the lungs and digestive system, people with cystic fibrosis go through life malnourished and often die by the age of 30. But the outlook for treatment of this hereditary disease dramatically improved in 1989, when researchers in **molecular genetics** found the exact location

Clearly, great advancements have been made in genetic research. Are all these advancements positive? Can you think of any negative or potential dangerous outcomes of these advancements? >>>

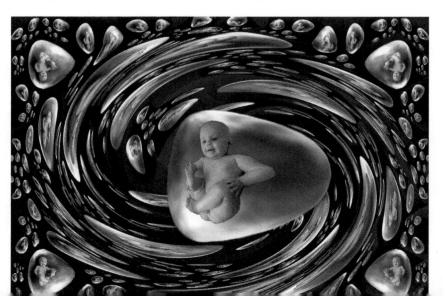

of the cystic fibrosis gene on chromosome 7 (Hillier et al., 2003). Molecular geneticists study the molecular structure and function of genes and try to identify the specific genes responsible for a certain disease, trait, or behaviour. Their work has led to genetic tests that can now predict which populations may be at risk for certain diseases. With advancing prenatal screening techniques, parents can receive an exact read-out of their child's genetic data, anomalies and all. While this new knowledge could lead to early treatment of certain diseases, it could also raise ethical issues in the distant future if parents are able to selectively abort fetuses to create "custom" babies with exactly the traits they prefer—a baby Mozart or a mini-Einstein.

Evolution by Natural Selection

EVOLUTIONARY PSYCHOLOGY

Like most people, you probably prefer eating sweet fruits to sucking on sour lemons and swallowing bitter medicines. Poisons often have a bitter taste, and food begins to taste sour as it spoils. Preferring sweet things to sour or bitter things probably helped our ancestors survive by avoiding foods that could make them sick. Those individuals without the ability to distinguish among these tastes probably didn't live long enough to reproduce. Therefore, all of us now share this taste preference. Researchers in **evolutionary psychology** explain the development of our mind and behaviour by studying how adaptive behaviours, such as certain taste preferences, helped our ancestors survive and reproduce.

Friendly Foxes: Man's New Best Friend?

One area of study that interests evolutionary psychologists is the domestication of wild animals. Russian researchers Belyaev and Trut set out to domesticate foxes and accomplished in a few decades behavioural changes that would naturally take thousands of years to develop. Over 30 generations of foxes, the scientists bred the tamest males with the tamest females. After 40 years, the wild and suspicious foxes had become a new breed of friendly, attention-loving foxes. The animals were so tame that the research institute even started selling them as house pets. By mating only the friendliest animals, the researchers

essentially gave an evolutionary advantage to this character trait (Trut, 1999).

Innate Traits

Just having a particular trait does not necessarily make that trait **adaptive**, but many of our traits do help us adjust and function in our environment. All human babies turn toward the cheek being stroked and suck objects put to their lips. Turning toward the touched cheek helps them make contact with the nipple, and automatic sucking ensures that babies will nurse and get the food they need to survive. Evolutionary psychologists study how innate traits such as **infant reflexes** evolved. They also consider whether common phobias have innate origins. Why do people fear spiders and snakes far more often than things more likely to harm them, like driving? Today, people in the developed world encounter more cars than spiders and snakes, but in our evolutionary past, spiders and snakes would have been the threat. In the past, the fear of snakes and spiders offered important protection, and its persistence is a good example of how long it takes for evolutionary processes to adjust our innate fears to new environments.

Issues with the Evolutionary Perspective

Critics of the evolutionary perspective claim that it starts with an effect or trait and works backward, so it cannot fail to explain a particular trait. To understand how a certain trait evolved, evolutionary psychologists must speculate about its cause, but they cannot prove that the explanation is correct. For example, some men may try to explain away their infidelity by claiming that it is an innate trait with an evolutionary advantage, but scientists have yet to identify a "cheater gene."

ACQUIRED CHARACTERISTICS: AN EARLY THEORY OF EVOLUTION

Before Darwin, a French biologist named Jean-Baptiste de Lamarck proposed a theory of evolution based on the inheritance of **acquired characteristics.** He argued that different species had common ancestry but evolved and changed into "higher" organisms by acquiring useful characteristics that they then passed on to their offspring. Giraffes that could stretch their necks would produce offspring with longer necks, and over generations, the necks of giraffes would get longer.

Evolutionary psychology is a branch of psychology involved with explaining the development of the human mind and behaviour by studying how adaptive behaviours helped human ancestors survive and reproduce.

Adaptive refers to the ability to adjust and function according to one's environment.

Infant reflexes are a set of innate traits in humans.

Acquired characteristics are useful traits acquired by an organism.

Artificial selection is a concept that contrasts with natural selection in that humans are involved in selecting the desired characteristics to pass on to an organism's offspring.

Lamarck's theories introduced the idea of evolution, but they did not adequately explain inheritance. An individual's use of a particular trait will not cause the trait to be passed on to offspring, just as its disuse won't prevent it. However, the utility of a trait could give the animal a better chance at survival and reproduction, and these are the ideas upon which Darwin expanded.

> Some men may try to explain away their infidelity by claiming that it is an innate trait with an evolutionary advantage, but scientists have yet to identify a "cheater gene."

DARWIN AND SELECTIVE BREEDING

Darwin went much further than Lamarck in explaining how evolution actually occurred. Darwin explained that just as people use **artificial selection** to selectively breed livestock and crops for desired characteristics, nature also conducts a selective breeding process—natural selection. Unlike Lamarck, Darwin believed that inheritance does not happen because certain traits are useful but because the usefulness of the traits helps the organism survive and reproduce and allows those traits to pass on to the next generation. Although Darwin did not know about genetic mechanisms, he knew that new traits develop by chance. Advances in genetics tell us that this diversity occurs because of genetic reshuffling during meiosis and fertilization and because of mutations that happen during DNA replication.

ENVIRONMENTAL CHANGE

Climate change, catastrophic events, and even minor events mean that environments change continually. These changes in the environment promote evolution by natural selection. More than 100 years after Darwin, Peter and Rosemary Grant (2002) studied the same species of birds on the Galapagos Islands to learn how environment affects natural selection. When a drought left only large seeds, only birds with large beaks could break and eat these seeds, so more of the larger birds survived. Heavy rains created the opposite effect. Because of the many small seeds available, the birds with smaller beaks survived and became more numerous. Their small size allowed them to grow to adulthood and reproduce more quickly, so their numbers increased more than those of the large-beaked birds.

Misconceptions About Evolution

Evolution happens in response to environmental change and does not have foresight or a predetermined end. Species do not change in order to prepare for environmental changes or to become more "highly evolved" organisms. Finches could not develop larger or smaller beaks in anticipation of a drought or abundant rainfall. Different

birds simply had different-sized beaks, and when conditions changed, those with the beaks most suited to that environment survived in the greatest numbers. Another misconception is that single-celled organisms such as amoebas are "less evolved" than human beings because of their lack of complexity. These single-celled organisms are equally well adapted to their environments, and therefore not any less evolved.

HUMAN EVOLUTION: BIPEDALISM, ENCEPHALIZATION, AND LANGUAGE

The 1% to 2% of human DNA that differs from that of chimps accounts for our exceptionally large brains, our ability to walk on two legs, and our capacity for language. Between five million and ten million years ago, our ancestors started walking on two legs instead of four. Between two million and three million years ago, our human genus, *Homo,* first started developing from our evolutionary family tree. **Bipedalism,** the ability to walk on two legs, let us use tools and manipulate our environment. **Encephalization,** the increase in our brain size, meant that we could better think, plan, and remember. Our unusual ability for abstract thought, which evolved in a way that is still unclear to scientists, allowed us to develop language. Being able to communicate through language meant that human beings could share knowledge with each other, co-operate, and pass on information to future generations.

Evolution of the Human Brain

In only tens of millions of years, an evolutionary blink of an eye, tremendous genetic changes produced our nervous system. Recent evidence has shown that the **phylogeny**—species development—of the human brain evolved far more quickly than the brains of other species. Specifically, the genes that design proteins in the nervous system evolved more quickly in our ancestral primates than in rodents and other animals. Scientists suspect our evolutionary speed may have something to do with an unusually large number of mutations in many genes and a selection for the mental abilities that these mutations allowed (Dorus et al., 2004).

Believe it or not, our species may be getting even smarter. Two separate genes that control brain size developed and spread as recently as 37 000 and 5800 years ago (Evans et al., 2005; Mekel-Bobrov et al., 2005). If we keep evolving at this rate, who knows where we'll be 100 000, or even 50 000 000 years from now. Just how big can our brains get before we have trouble holding up our heads or giving birth?

Species-Typical Behaviours

HUMAN BEHAVIOUR

Cats climb trees, dogs bark, and squirrels hoard acorns. But dogs do not climb trees, cats do not hoard acorns, and squirrels do not bark.

∧ Humans can identify the **emotions** behind a wide variety of **facial expressions.**
∧ What emotions do you think are conveyed in these photographs?

All animals have **species-typical behaviours,** instinctive or characteristic ways of behaving particular to a certain species. Smiling, talking, and walking on two legs are behaviours common to all human beings. Animals, including humans, communicate emotions through posture, movement, and facial expression. In *The Expression of the Emotions in Man and Animals* (1872), Darwin argued for the universality, and therefore genetic innateness, of facial expressions and the emotions they express.

Universality of Facial Expressions

In the 1960s, Paul Ekman and Wallace Friesen picked up on Darwin's idea and asserted that humans across cultures share common facial expressions that communicate specific emotions. The researchers compiled an "atlas of emotions" of the numerous human facial expressions and identified the six universally recognized emotions as surprise, fear, disgust, sadness, anger, and happiness. In one study, they asked non-literate people from New Guinea to look at photos of actors making certain facial expressions and to identify the emotions. As in the other 31 cultures the researchers studied, the New Guineans identified the emotions correctly. Conversely, the researchers videotaped members of the New Guinea tribe making certain expressions and asked American college students to identify the corresponding emotions. Again, the college students identified the emotions correctly (Ekman & Friesen, 1975; Ekman, 1982).

But the universality of emotions seems to have its limits. Although people around the world recognize common expressions, they have an easier time identifying those of members within their cultural groups (Elfenbein & Ambady 2002, 2003). Cultural variations in the way people express emotions give group members an "in-group advantage." Facial expressions may be universal because of genetic predisposition, common learned behaviour, or a combination of the two, but if people within a cultural group recognize each other's emotions more easily, learning probably does play some role.

Role of Learning

Many species-typical behaviours based on predispositions become expressed only as a result of learning. Human beings have a genetic predisposition to walk on two legs, but babies are not born ready to walk. They learn it over time, and before they do, they practise balancing and taking steps. Similarly,

humans also probably have a genetic predisposition to acquire language, but babies are not born speaking sentences or even articulating words; instead they come prepared to learn the language around them. They make nonsense sounds until they learn the phonemes (discrete sounds) of words in a specific language. Through learning, they start pronouncing words correctly and begin to develop the grammar and syntax of their native language.

Biological Preparedness

How does our biology control what we learn, as well as how and when? **Biological preparedness** refers to the extent to which biological features evolved to promote certain traits. Human beings are biologically prepared to walk on two legs. Physically, we have an upward tilted torso, strong hind limbs, and weak forelimbs. Our nervous system also prepares us to coordinate two-legged walking.

Through conditioning, animals can be trained to perform certain tricks or behaviours, as when four-legged animals walk on two legs, but they soon revert back to their original instinctive behaviours, a tendency known as **instinctual drift** (Breland & Breland, 1951, 1961). Raccoons taught to pick up a coin and drop it into a piggy bank would first rub the coins together, just as they would to remove shells from crayfish, before dropping it into the container. Pigs taught to do the same trick would drop the coins on the ground and root at them with their snouts, as they do to their food, before dropping the coins in the container. Despite conditioning, animals kept up these preliminary instinctual behaviours, and these tendencies even increased over time. Those behaviours that remained the longest were

> Male emperor penguins tend to incubation duties, and this species practises serial monogamy; they are faithful to a single mate for a year but won't necessarily wait around for the same partner when it's time to breed again the next year.

Bipedalism is the ability to walk on two legs.

Encephalization is an increase in brain size.

Phylogeny is the development of a species.

Species-typical behaviours are instinctive or characteristic ways of behaving particular to a certain species.

Biological preparedness is the extent to which biological features evolved to promote certain traits.

Instinctual drift is the tendency for an organism to revert to instinctive behaviours after being trained to have new behaviours.

Parental investment consists of the time, energy, and risk involved in producing and raising offspring.

the ones for which the animals were more biologically prepared and likely had a strong genetic basis.

Mating Patterns

DIFFERENTIAL PARENTAL INVESTMENT THEORY

A familiar cliché says that women want commitment with one person while men want sex with many people. In looking for an evolutionary explanation for age-old patterns, evolutionary psychologist Robert Trivers found that mating patterns depend on gender differences in the amount of **parental investment** (1972). Parental investment includes the time, energy, and risk involved in producing and raising offspring. Which gender gets to choose a mate and which gender must compete for a mate depends on the amount of parental investment. The more invested gender will be choosier in picking a mate, and the less invested gender will have to compete against other individuals for the right to mate. This idea confirms the stereotype that women want to seek commitment with "Mr. Perfect" while men are content to compete with each other in order to gain that title. Of course, in highly developed Western societies, the availability of alternatives, such as artificial insemination and adoption and the presence of women in the workforce who can support themselves, moves us in the direction of making this point moot.

POLYGYNY: ONE MALE WITH MULTIPLE FEMALES

Most mammalian species are polygynous because females invest a great deal of time

∧
∧ In 2011, the British Columbia Supreme Court upheld Canada's law against
∧ polygamy. Should this law also apply to polyandry?

and effort in pregnancy and child care, whereas the work of males tends to be over after they impregnate the female. Long gestation and lactation periods limit the number of offspring females can produce. To maximize the genetic potential of their children, females have to choose the preferred mates with whom to combine their genes. On the other hand, males don't need to put much time or effort into raising children, so they can mate with as many females as they can. Increasing the number of offspring they produce means that more of those offspring may survive and the male's genes are passed on. Generally, the more polygynous a species, the greater the size difference between males and females. Large size makes a difference when males compete with each other over the right to mate, and not all males will win that right. For humans, it's important to keep in mind that our highly evolved brains override the pressure for males to be polygynous.

Polygamy is illegal in Canada, but in 2009, the British Columbia Supreme Court threw out polygamy charges against two rival polygamy leaders from Bountiful, B.C. Canadian researcher John Graham and his colleagues report that polygamy leads to increased psychological distress and phobia for women and impairs children's psychological and social functioning (Al-Krenawi & Graham, 2006; Al-Krenawi & Slonim-Nevo, 2008).

POLYANDRY: ONE FEMALE WITH MULTIPLE MALES

Less common than polygyny, polyandry happens when females have less parental investment, as in some egg-laying fish and birds. Because the female has a short pregnancy and does not nurse, less of the reproductive cycle depends on her body. Once she lays the eggs, either parent can take care of the offspring. In these species, females have evolved to be larger, stronger, and often more brightly coloured. Not surprisingly,

they actively and aggressively court males. The female Northern Jacana bird keeps a large territory in which multiple males have smaller territories. She mates with each of the males and, within a few days, lays eggs that hatch into offspring that males raise (Ehrlich, Dobkin, & Wheye, 1988).

MONOGAMY: ONE MALE WITH ONE FEMALE

When individuals of both genders make an equal parental investment, a species tends to be monogamous. More than 90% of bird species are monogamous because offspring need the care of both parents. Although males and females pair up in family units and practise "social monogamy," sexual fidelity has not been known to be a part of any species' repertoire. In one study, female blackbirds whose mates had vasectomies still managed to produce hatchlings (Bray, Kennelly, & Guarino, 1975). Male emperor penguins tend to incubation duties, and this species practises serial monogamy; they are faithful to a single mate for a year but won't necessarily wait around for the same partner when it's time to breed again the next year. In mammals, monogamy tends to happen in species such as foxes and coyotes that must provide their young with food other than milk. The offspring of certain species, particularly rodents such as the prairie vole, also need the male parent to protect them from predators.

POLYGYNANDRY: MULTIPLE MALES WITH MULTIPLE FEMALES

Polygynandry characterizes species such as chimps and bonobo apes that live in large groups of two to three dozen individuals and share a communal parental investment. When females ovulate, they develop prominent pink swellings on their rumps, and they typically mate with all the males in the group. Unlike gorillas, male chimps and bonobos must compete less against each other for mating privileges, promoting harmony (De Waal, 1995). By preventing infanticide, paternity confusion also benefits the group as a whole. Conversely, male lions, like males of other species that put a premium on paternity, will kill the offspring of rival males (Packer & Pusey, 1983).

HUMAN MATING PATTERNS

Since males are slightly larger than females, it follows that humans tend to be primarily monogamous and slightly polygynous. While human mating patterns vary with culture, all cultures have some form of long-term mating bonds, often through socially recognized marriage contracts, and no human culture is as promiscuous as our closest relatives, chimps and bonobos. Western culture has made polygyny illegal, but cultures with less Western influence tend to practise a mixture of monogamy and polygyny. However, many European cultures have an unspoken acceptance of extramarital relationships.

> Although we sometimes think of "survival of the fittest" as the very definition of natural selection, Darwin did not originate this idea. Instead, philosopher Herbert Spencer coined the phrase to explain his belief that society and culture evolved toward higher forms.

Monogamy makes sense for humans because human children, more than any other primate, need extended care. Across cultures, mothers provide most of the direct physical care for children, whereas fathers indirectly provide food, shelter, and other provisions. But taking both direct and indirect care into account, male parental involvement lags behind female involvement. Romantic love and sexual jealousy, the biological preparedness for mating bonds, make human beings more similar to birds than chimps in their mating behaviour. But biological preparedness also predisposes humans to seek sex outside the pair bond. Across different groups and cultures, 2% to 10% of children in socially monogamous families have not been fathered by the husband (Marlowe, 2000).

Fallacies

By the late 19th century, Darwin's ideas had made such a great impact that philosophers and political thinkers tried to apply the idea of evolution to government, society, and all human relations. Often, they misunderstood

Social Darwinism is a theory that states that society and culture evolved toward higher forms through the process of individuals adapting to hardship by either adapting and surviving or falling by the wayside.

Naturalistic fallacy is the claim that whatever is natural is good or right.

Deterministic fallacy is the claim that traits and behaviours can be explained entirely through genetics.

Darwin's ideas or interpreted them in a way that suited their purposes. Although we sometimes think of "survival of the fittest" as the very definition of natural selection, Darwin did not originate this idea. Instead, philosopher Herbert Spencer coined the phrase to explain his belief that society and culture evolved toward higher forms. According to his theory of **social Darwinism**, individuals either adapted and survived or fell by the wayside, which supported his belief that governments should not aid those struggling with poverty or other social problems. Philosopher G. E. Moore later argued that Spencer had committed the **naturalistic fallacy** by equating the "natural" with the "good" or "right." Moore criticized Spencer for applying a natural explanation to the non-natural phenomena of society and government and also for presenting his personal ethical opinions as facts. At this point, we do not know if individualism and competition will be beneficial to the species in the long run.

With new genes being mapped continually and knowledge of genetics increasing dramatically, people sometimes make the **deterministic fallacy** and try to explain traits and behaviours entirely through genes. Genetics work with the environment to build or change the biological structures that then interact with the environment to produce behaviour. While we know that genes are necessary, they are not sufficient to fully account for traits and behaviours. Genes may influence us, but they are not able to dictate who we are because, ultimately, humans can and do control their own behaviour.

Summary

WHAT ARE THE GENETIC MECHANISMS OF TRAIT INHERITANCE? p.68

• Made up of DNA, chromosomes inside cell nuclei contain all the genetic information needed to make an organism.
• Human cells contain 23 pairs of chromosomes, including an XX or XY pair that determines whether an individual is male or female.
• Egg and sperm cells contain half the genetic information of other cells. They combine during fertilization, passing on parents' genetic information in a new permutation.

IN WHAT WAY DO GENES AND ENVIRONMENT INTERACT TO MAKE US WHO WE ARE? p.69

• Traits are carried on genes. Genes can be recessive or dominant.
• Dominant genes suppress the expression of the other gene in a pair of alleles.
• Recessive genes are suppressed by the dominant gene in a pair of alleles.
• Some traits, such as eye colour, depend entirely on genetics. Others, such as height and weight, can be influenced by the environment.
• While genetics might predispose an individual to a certain trait, how that trait is expressed can depend on environmental factors.
• An environment may be external or chemical.

• Behavioural genetics examines the relative contributions of genetics and the environment on who we are, through the use of twin and adoption studies.
• The study of genetics has led to many advancements in our understanding of illness, diseases, and disorders. These advancements continue to have a great impact on the diagnosis, classification, and treatment of autism, cancers, diabetes, and so on.

HOW HAS THE IDEA OF EVOLUTION BY NATURAL SELECTION INFLUENCED THE STUDY OF HUMAN BEHAVIOUR? p.68, 70, & 72

• According to the theory of natural selection, organisms with features that best adapted to their environment are more likely to survive and reproduce.
• Some genes are dominant or recessive, affecting the likelihood that a particular trait will be passed on.
• Research in behaviour genetics, molecular genetics, and evolutionary psychology has developed from the idea of natural selection.

WHAT ARE THE TYPICAL MATING PATTERNS OF DIFFERENT SPECIES? p.76

• Mating patterns depend on gender differences in parental investment.
• There are four types of mating patterns: polygyny, polyandry, monogamy, and polygynandry.

Test Your Understanding

1. Which of the following is an example of Mendelian heredity?
   a. Adoni enjoys cycling, but his brother prefers running.
   b. Both Katie and her mother have freckles.
   c. Marco is unable to remain in a monogamous relationship.
   d. Ashley is the first person in her immediate family to develop lung cancer.

2. Which of the following statements about genetics is true?
   a. Phenotype refers to the entire set of genes inherited by an organism.
   b. Genotype refers to the observable property that comes from a phenotype.
   c. Genes are consistent and are not influenced by environmental factors.
   d. Research from Genome Canada has led to groundbreaking discoveries.

3. Chromosomes act as the blueprints for an organism because they:
   a. are found in cell nuclei

   b. can mutate during meiosis
   c. provide genetic information
   d. recombine during fertilization

4. Genes make us uniquely who we are because they:
   a. control our behaviour
   b. create specific proteins
   c. come in analogous pairs
   d. are inherited from our parents

5. Meiosis increases genetic diversity by:
   a. duplicating chromosomes
   b. recombining chromosomes
   c. combining chromosome pairs
   d. passing on an X or Y chromosome

6. If Xavier's genotype predisposes him to be tall, what will be his most likely phenotype?
   a. He will be tall if both of his parents were tall.
   b. He will be tall only if provided with the right nutrition.

c. He will be tall, regardless of his environment.

d. He will probably be tall, given the right nutrition.

7. Which of the following statements about polygamy is true?

a. Polygamy can lead to increased psychological stress and phobia for women.

b. There are no polygamist communities in Canada.

c. In 2009, the British Columbia Supreme Court convicted two rival polygamy leaders on charges of polygamy and sexual abuse.

d. Polygamy has no effect on children.

8. Yorkshire terriers, originally bred for hunting rats, most likely had ancestors that were:

a. loud

b. fluffy

c. friendly

d. persistent

9. The fact that identical twins share so many characteristics proves that:

a. twins share the same environment

b. twins raised apart will still be similar

c. many traits have a genetic component

d. genetics count more than environment

10. Eye colour has a high degree of heritability, which means that your eye colour:

a. is determined 50% by genetics and 50% by environment

b. is almost completely determined by genetics

c. depends primarily on environment

d. depends primarily on your father's eye colour

11. Why was Lamarck's theory of acquired characteristics important?

a. It expanded on Darwin's theory of evolution.

b. It showed how using a trait causes it to be inherited.

c. It introduced the idea of evolution through adaptation.

d. It correctly explained how organisms evolve into higher forms.

12. According to Darwin, what role does chance play in inheritance?

a. Adaptive traits are always passed on, so chance is irrelevant.

b. Chance determines whether organisms inherit adaptive traits.

c. Through mutation and recombination, new traits develop by chance.

d. Since traits pass on if the organism survives, chance plays a minor role.

13. If global warming continues, which equatorial animals might be more likely to survive?

a. those that can hunt alone

b. those that require less water

c. those that can reproduce faster

d. those that forage for food in groups

14. Gina wants to help identify genes that cause particular diseases. Which field of research is likely to interest Gina?

a. behavioural genetics

b. molecular genetics

c. evolutionary psychology

d. social psychology

15. According to evolutionary psychologists, which of the following phobias most likely results from an innate, preconditioned fear?

a. fear of dogs

b. fear of horses

c. fear of cars

d. fear of heights

16. A bird building a nest is an example of:

a. monogamy

b. instinctual drift

c. parental investment

d. species-typical behaviour

17. Which of the following demonstrates biological preparedness?

a. A previously tame bear cub suddenly attacks its keeper.

b. A monkey uses its long tail to swing across tree branches.

c. The human brain continues to evolve in size.

d. Identical twins share similar characteristics.

18. The universality of facial expression suggests that:

a. global communication has brought us all closer

b. facial expressions have a strong genetic component

c. human beings have a limited repertoire of emotions

d. culture has no effect on emotional expression

19. According to the theory of differential parental investment, wolves are monogamous because:

a. both parents care for the offspring

b. the entire pack cares for the offspring

c. only an alpha male and female reproduce

d. they live in a pack and compete for mates

20. Why is polyandry uncommon in animals?

a. females are smaller than males

b. males tend to dominate females

c. males are naturally less nurturing

d. females have long pregnancies and nurse

Remember to check www.thethinkspot.ca **for additional information, downloadable flashcards, and other helpful resources.**

Answers: 1) b; 2) d; 3) c; 4) b; 5) b; 6) d; 7) a; 8) d; 9) c; 10) b; 11) c; 12) c; 13) b; 14) b; 15) d; 16) d; 17) b; 18) b; 19) a; 20) d

THINK READINGS

The Normative Implications of Biological Research

Peter K. Hatemi and Rose McDermott
University of Sydney, Brown University

In Chapter 8 we examine some of the common stereotypes that exist for males and females. What stereotypes do you have about the sexes?

How might the research conducted by Genome Canada researchers achieve these goals?

What misconceptions about evolution were discussed in this chapter?

If an identical twin has schizophrenia, there is a 50% chance that the other twin will develop the disorder. In Chapter 16 you will read more about schizophrenia.

One of the concerns that has plagued research on the biological and genetic underpinnings of social behaviors and individual differences is the fear that such information can be used for ill. This fear rests on a foundation of good reason. Early abuses involving the use of selective phrenology and other purportedly "scientific" methods to establish moral hierarchies among races or between sexes have exerted profound and lasting damage on society, as well as on later attempts to more productively examine the biological bases of individual difference. Eugenics unquestionably constitutes a moral stain on the history of scientific efforts to provide systematic explanations for individual variance, but many other policies focusing exclusively on social factors have created great pain and suffering too, although these approaches have rarely received as much direct criticism. Some of the best examples of this kind of damaging research are the models that suggested that bad mothering was responsible for the development of schizophrenia and autism, diseases that we now know rest on some combination of genetic vulnerability and in-utero development.

Interestingly, the ways in which biology and genetics can be used for good ends are rarely discussed in the social sciences; instead, the focus of this field is often directed toward how these areas of study could potentiate sexism, racism, and other social ills. But psychiatric genetics, for example, has maintained a focus on leveraging biological analysis to attack diseases and alleviate suffering, while at the same time striving to dispel social myths that wrongfully assign blame to victims and primary caregivers, or otherwise oversimplify behavior. We argue here for a similarly positive valuation of such an approach in political and social research.

Similar debates have occurred in the past. Darwin's early attempts to categorize humans as having evolved from species of related primates, such as great apes and chimpanzees, only served to aggravate the tendency for people to view science as hostile to humanity by implying an implicit hierarchy in evolutionary processes and categorizing humans as the highest form of life. Yet while clearly reflecting some of the particular cultural and racial biases of his time, Darwin did not deserve to be forever identified with some of the worst abuses of "social Darwinism." Indeed, he was careful to assert in *The Descent of Man* that no clear distinction exists among racial groups. Darwin himself fought for notions of equality, although his ideas were unfortunately widely and incorrectly associated with the phrase "survival of the fittest," which Herbert Spencer coined in 1864.

Later tendencies to attribute racist categorizations to Darwin's ideas of natural selection and evolution are actually primarily attached to eugenicist notions first perpetuated by Sir Francis Galton. Galton's story remains instructive as a warning for the pitfalls and challenges that can arise at the intersection of scholarly and policy debates. Largely viewed as the father of eugenics, Galton published his book *Hereditary Genetics* in 1869.... By studying the family histories of famous men and searching for patterns, Galton came to believe that intellectual and other valuable qualities, like physical characteristics, had to be heritable. He argued that with careful marriage, human qualities could be improved through selective breeding, much like farm animals. His desire to create a

Reproduced with permission of the copyright owner. Further reproduction prohibited without permission.

What evidence from this chapter supports the idea that we can pass on certain traits through selective breeding (see "Friendly Foxes: Man's New Best Friend").

regulated marriage market to strengthen human skills and abilities became known as positive eugenics. Galton's ideas of using science to measure and improve desirable human characteristics reached its perverse climax with the Nazis' attempt to eradicate Jews based on the outrageous claim that Jewish people somehow constituted a "lesser" race....

This perversion of science achieved additional notoriety with the rise of phrenology, or the study of the size of human skulls, and its later instantiations in measurements of brain volume. Samuel Morton, an early-nineteenth-century physical anthropologist, collected perhaps the largest group of human skulls from various racial groups. Based on his reading of skull size, Morton wrongly argued for the existence of significant racial differences in intelligence, with larger skull size translating into greater intelligence. This work received a great deal of criticism on methodological and theoretical grounds; indeed, there are no a priori scientific reasons why head size should be correlated with intelligence (Gould 1996).

More recent attempts to measure brain volume similarly find a small but significant relationship between the size of some brain structures and overall IQ, although none of these differences are correlated with racial differences. Some sex differences in patterns of relationships between brain size and IQ exist that are likely based on body size to weight correlation differ-ences, but these differences do not correlate with overall levels of IQ (Andreasen et al. 1993). Rather, prenatal nutrition appears to be an important independent variable that influences head circumference (Ivanovic et al. 2004).

... Many people have openly voiced concerns that such work might be used to perpetuate future abuses similar to those wrongs committed in the past. But such anxiety can be applied to all scientific fields and methods. Aspects of almost all economic, social, psychological, and physical approaches can be and have been used for nefarious purposes. This reality will likely never change. However, far less discussion occurs about how biology and genetics might be used to further positive ends; instead, the focus, particularly in the social sciences, almost always remains on how these fields potentiate the possibility for sexism, racism, and other social ills. In this article, we seek to offer some balance to these arguments and argue that genetics can prove a liberating as much as constraining field of study. After all, genetics has been able to demonstrate, among other things, that most racial differences in social behaviors are not "genetic" after all.

The irony of the automatic associations among biology, genetics, and the potential for misuse lies in the equally egregious abuses that can be laid at the feet of socialization models. Indeed, policies that focus exclusively on social factors have created as much pain and suffering as genetically focused policies. Perhaps the most obvious, if not the worst, example of such an abuse derives from early work on the origins of schizophrenia and autism. Although a deduction of biological or genetic causes for these disorders might have seemed obvious, given that the disease appeared to run in families and manifested a universal base rate across cultures of about 1%, scholars instead argued that the fault for schizophrenia could be laid at the feet of bad mothers. Specifically, it was claimed that refrigerator[1] mothers or mothers who placed their children in so-called "double bind" psychological situations were most likely to produce schizophrenic or autistic children (Bateson 1960). In reality, schizophrenia and autism are diseases that we now know derive from genetic vulnerability, epigenetic processes, and environmental conditions and are apparently unrelated to postnatal mothering. Similarly, until recently, homosexuality was considered a psychological disorder, and many etiological models implicated domineering and/or over-enmeshed mothers in combination with distant or emotionally detached fathers as the putative cause. This connection was, of course, far from true. Homosexuality is not a disorder, nor does its etiology have anything to do with parenting, although it does appear to be related to genetics, gene expression, hormones introduced in the womb, and other neurobiological factors (Kaminsky et al. 2009; Wilson and Rahman 2005).

Sexual orientation is discussed further in Chapter 8.

In Chapter 13 you will read about the relationship between brain size and intelligence.

In Chapter 9 you will learn why many people have room for dessert even when they are full after a meal.

What ethical considerations must a researcher consider (see Chapter 2)?

You will read more about the effects of drugs and their addictive qualities in Chapter 10.

In what ways might innovations such as this benefit society? Are there any drawbacks?

In these cases and many others, differences were considered forms of psychological illness, and these "abnormal" behaviors were attributed to dysfunctional processes of socialization within the family. This social blame approach caused untold agony and guilt among numerous parents who believed that they had helped create their progeny's suffering. Now, genetic and neurobiological analyses have shown that, at least with regard to schizophrenia, autism, and sexuality, nothing could be further from the truth…. Biological analysis has thus provided liberation in areas in which models of socialization had created turmoil and ignorance.

The point here is not that models of socialization are always misguided or that biological models are always helpful; indeed, when placed in the wrong hands or used for malign purposes, or when poor research is conducted, each approach can prove disastrous or exploitative. Rather, we suggest that in the case of genetics and biology, ignorance does not constitute bliss. Choosing to not uncover the genetic or biological knowledge that it may be possible to learn puts scholars at a decided disadvantage over their industry, government, and other counterparts who systematically use this knowledge to serve their own designs and intentions. Indeed, a clear identification of the sources and expression of individual differences can help people to more properly see the ways in which they

can be or are being manipulated by others, such as media elites, public policy leaders, and political decisionmakers.

…

The tobacco industry provides perhaps the best illustration of this phenomenon, although the mechanisms or processes of manipulation can just as easily be applied to insurance companies, political campaign managers, or pharmaceutical corporations that seek to sell policies or drugs for profit…. In the case of the tobacco industry, many individuals worked long and hard to uncover the biological processes that enhance and maintain addiction in order to keep and expand their markets and sales (Glantz et al. 1995; Carpenter, Wayne, and Connolly 2005; World Health Organization 2008). By examining the human brain, tobacco companies were able to create a more addictive product that users would have difficulty foregoing. A class-action suit brought by 46 states against four of the major tobacco companies that was settled in 1998 and is referred to as the Master Settlement Agreement demonstrated the malicious and conscious manipulation of consumers at a huge cost to public health care systems.[2] The complainants were able to show that companies were exploiting biological factors for the express purpose of increasing demand and profit, thereby demonstrating the tobacco companies' clear intent to manipulate the public to its detriment.

Similarly, fast-food restaurants have conducted extensive research to find the most addictive combination of fat and salt for their recipes, particularly for French fries, to keep customers coming back for more (Schlosser 2001). Part of what makes these manipulations so challenging to overcome is that those who fall prey to their power are often unaware of them. Because the desire for sweet or salty food is at least partially innate (Birch 1999), agricultural groups that capitalize on this desire can profit at the expense of victims, who may attribute their subsequent weight problems and associated negative health outcomes solely to their own lack of willpower and not their unconscious exploitation by financially motivated capitalists. Already, some firms such as Neurofocus have begun to use biological information to improve neuromarketing, an attempt to improve marketing through an investigation of attention, memory, and emotion to anticipate consumer preferences. Through proper recognition of the underlying scientific processes involved, scholars of the biological and genetic bases of preferences and behavior can help consumers become more aware of the ways in which others may try to manipulate them for their own gain without the consumers' conscious awareness or participation.

Understanding the manifestation of these individual differences more fully can help create equality instead of fostering and perpetuating existing inequalities. Rather than adopt a one-size-fits-all approach to important policy issues, we can create more tailored programs designed to produce more effective results in more cost-efficient ways. Just as it would not be appropriate to prescribe one drug for every person suffering from a given condition, certain social interventions may not be suited for every population or individual....

We offer a couple of examples of how such targeted interventions might improve cost and efficiency. First, not every student approaches education in the same way. In particular, recent research suggests that boys learn in ways that are manifestly different than girls. Specifically, physical activity and interaction remain integral elements of many aspects of male social learning (Gurian and Stevens 2007; James 2007). Thus, budget cutbacks that threaten recess, for example, exert an unintentional sex bias in effect, making it more difficult for boys than girls to learn in the absence of the regular outlet provided by physical activity. In less clear-cut categories, some individuals learn better by hearing information, while others process information more accurately with visual cues, and multimodal stimuli appear to speed learning (Seitz, Kim, and Shams 2006). Allowing parents and children to select into the categories that work best for them can not only enhance the depth and quality of learn-

ing, but also reduce rates of truancy and absenteeism and perhaps even improve graduation rates.

Second, important health interventions work differently for individuals with the same diagnosed condition. For example, many people with diabetes need to lose weight. The conundrum confronting doctors and other health care providers concerns the best way to encourage patients to do so. Research indicates that all diets may work well initially, but that most people regain weight over time; similarly, certain diets work well for some people but not others. People can be divided according to the way in which their bodies process blood sugar, and thus can be assigned a more appropriate diet for their body type. Some individuals suffer from a "sugar addiction"; once this addiction is identified and the neurobiological elements of the addiction categorized, health care providers can develop an individually based program that may, for example, avoid carbohydrates and other simple sugars. Some individuals with this addiction tend to have success with the Atkins diets, on which, despite the high fat intake, they lose weight rapidly without hunger and with no ill effect to their cholesterol levels (Shai et al. 2008). Conversely, other individuals tend to suffer from more behavioral challenges, since they need to eat every few hours to keep their blood sugar steady. Such individuals also need to consume moder-

ate amounts of carbohydrates to stave off hunger and lose weight and thus respond well to diets such as South Beach. However, if a doctor put such an individual on an Atkins diet, this person's cholesterol would likely skyrocket, leading to a failure to lose weight and a lack of subsequent motivation. Thus, awareness of individual differences can improve the specificity of targeted interventions in ways that can improve outcomes and reduce discomfort.

Examining the biological and genetic underpinnings of social and political behavior can enhance the prospects for social good as much as ill in the same way that models of socialization can be used to help or hurt those people who embrace them. It is crucial to recognize that regardless of scholars' attempts to ignore or reject biology because of past misuses, such factors will continue to be investigated and employed by people and groups seeking to manipulate the public for profit or other advantage. In these cases, knowledge constitutes the best defense, and conscious education can facilitate more cost-effective and beneficial social policies for everyone.

Because such information can and has been used for malign purposes in the past, we argue that we must use fire to fight fire. Those in the academy are positioned to balance the power and resources of private corporations or government agencies that might use such information for purposes inspired by greed or a need for

This is called "physical dependence" and is discussed in Chapter 10.

The behavioural aspect of addiction is referred to as "psychological dependence" and is discussed further in Chapter 10.

endless supplies of fresh manpower to perpetuate conflict. The value of this research goes beyond simply understanding trait variation for its own sake, but its findings and implications can be used to protect the public, particularly by increasing awareness of the myriad ways in which such technology is being used for malign intent, and by generating remedies.

We have moved into an age of rich technological growth, speed, and sophistication in which a massive amount of information is being linked up without public knowledge. These interconnections are not being forged as they were in the past, when the public was aware of the need for confidentiality and laws ensuring privacy. In this new environment of ever-increasing technological interconnection and sophistication and instant global propagation of information, we need to build legal protections regarding the links being made to transmit personal information of which we are not aware. Certainly, corporations will use whatever means necessary to achieve decisive economic advantage, including the use of any and all biological information they can garner to determine influences on key behaviors of interest, such as those related to purchasing, website activity, e-mails, insurance claims, medical records, and pharmaceutical purposes. Every swipe of your supermarket rewards card, every pharmaceutical purchase, every website visited is recorded and used to build a profile. The

analysis of such information occurs in every major industry in the private sector, and few groups outside of the academy are in a position to balance these forces by pursuing independent research and releasing their own results to the public. If scholars do not undertake biological research, this work will not take place in a rigorous and scientific manner. However, the research will still proceed, but will only be conducted by individuals or groups interested solely in profit or personal advantage; thus, private industries may use such information without the knowledge or willingness of the public, and few people will be able to provide an objective, unbiased, and scientifically rigorous counter to this influence. We believe that making this kind of biological and genetic research available to the public is an ethical obligation, which will allow the public and policymakers to decide how to use that information. The alternative to such a strategy will not prevent such information from existing; rather, information will continue to be used without our knowledge by those with intentions and purposes of which we are unaware and with which we may not agree.

. . .The discovery of biological and genetic influences on political factors has tremendous policy implications for issues such as the kinds of legal protections mentioned previously. In addition, widespread recognition of such factors can influence how policy is made and might even

influence the nature of political campaigns. For example, just as the Supreme Court decision in *Schenck v. United States* does not allow a person to falsely yell "fire" in a crowded theater because of the chaos that might ensue, we might consider whether it should be illegal to create political advertisements that are designed solely for the purpose of inciting public fear in order to gain partisan political advantage. Should candidates be allowed to use subliminal measures and fear-based strategies to incite particular reactions without public knowledge? Should public figures be protected from campaigns that hint at assassination or portray candidates in gun sights? Should political advertisements come with warnings, much like those that appear on cigarette cartons (e.g., "this commercial is intended to elicit an adrenaline release, thereby altering your behavior")?. . . .

The questions that political science can help answer can also advance public debate on a wide range of topics, including such salient challenges as post traumatic stress disorder, the high rate of suicide in the military, and health care reform. We are attempting to go beyond the kind of bioethical questions involved in challenging research programs such as stem cell research. We are focusing here not on the ethics of conducting this research, but rather on the ethical need for this research to be conducted. We believe that it is time to change the discourse

Do you feel that your privacy is endangered by today's technology?

There are many forms of manipulation and coercion. You will learn about the factors that affect obedience, conformity, and compliance in Chapter 14.

These topics are discussed further in Chapter 16 and 17.

from a focus on what is bad about biological research or how it might have been used for reprehensible purposes to concentrate on how to carry out this kind of research in as ethical a manner as we can, with the goal of protecting the public. Let us work to be sure of the long and short-term implications of our work and how such research can be used and misused by various people, organizations, and governments for their own purposes. We must be self-conscious as we conduct this work, realizing that the path is difficult.

We may encounter dangerous shores to navigate. But just as Galton's warped attempt to improve the human species was further perverted by Nazis who wanted to destroy those groups that they deemed less fit, the recognition of such evil was necessary in order to halt its advance. …Work on the genetic and biological bases of political behavior is still ongoing, and if the academy moves to prevent scholars from producing and publicizing such knowledge independently, only the private sector is left to exploit such information. As a result, we deem it our ethical responsibility to make such knowledge available to the public, fully realizing that all research enterprises are flawed, but also believing in the value of accumulating knowledge over time. We remain optimistic about the value of the scientific enterprise to continue to discover information that can be used to help alleviate human suffering.

. . . ▪

NOTES

1. The term "refrigerator mothers" was coined by Leo Kanner and promoted by Bruno Bettelheim in *The Empty Fortress: Infantile Autism and the Birth of the Self* (1972) to describe a style of cold parenting, lacking in any genuine kind of maternal warmth. He described children as "left neatly in refrigerators which did not defrost." Parents of autistic children were discussed as those who "just happen to defrost enough to produce a child."
2. This document can be found at http://www.ag.ca.gov/tobacco/pdf/1msa.pdf.

REFERENCES

Andre as en, Nancy, M. Flaum, V. Swayze II, D. S. O'Leary, R. Alliger, G. Cohen, J. Ehrhardt, and W. T. Yuh. 1993. "Intelligence and Brain Structure in Normal Individuals." *American Journal of Psychiatry* 150: 130–34.

Bateson, Gregory. 1960. "Minimal Requirements for a Theory of Schizophrenia." *Archives of General Psychiatry* 2: 477–91.

Bettelheim, Bruno. 1972. *The Empty Fortress: Infantile Autism and the Birth of the Self.* New York: Free Press.

Birch, Leann. 1999. "Development of Food Preferences." *Annual Review of Nutrition* 19: 41–62.

Carpenter, Carrie, Geoffrey Wayne, and Goeffrey Connolly. 2005. "Designing Cigarettes for Women." *Addiction* 100: 837–51.

Galton, C. J., and D. J. Galton. 1998. "Francis Galton and Eugenics Today." *Journal of Medical Ethics* 24: 99–105.

Galton, D. J. 2005. "Eugenics: Some Lessons from the Past." *Reproductive BioMedicine Online* 10 (suppl. 1): 133–36.

Glantz, Stanton, Deborah Barnes, Lisa Bero, Peter Hanauer, and John Slade. 1995. "Looking through a Keyhole at the Tobacco Industry: The Brown and Williamson Documents." *JAMA: Journal of the American Medical Association* 274 (3): 219–24. http://www.tobacco.neu.edu/litigation/cases/mn_trial/TE18983.pdf.

Gould, Stephen Jay. 1996. *Mismeasure of Man.* New York: Norton.

Gurian, Michael, and Kathy Stevens. 2007. *The Minds of Boys: Saving Our Sons from Falling behind in School and Life.* New York: Wiley.

Ivanovic, Daniza, Boris P. Leiva, Hernán T. Pérez, Manuel G. Olivares, Nora S. Díaz, María Soledad C. Urrutia, Atilio F. Almagià, et al. 2004. "Head Size and Intelligence, Learning, Nutritional Status and Brain Development: Head, IQ, Learning, Nutrition and Brain." *Neuropsychologica* 42 (8): 11,118–131.

James, Abigail. 2007. *Teaching the Male Brain: How Boys Think, Feel, and Learn in School.* New York: Corwin.

Kaminsky, Z. A., T. Tang, S. C.Wang, C. Ptak, G. H. Oh, A. H.Wong, L. A. Feldcamp, et al. 2009. "DNA Methylation Profiles in Monozygotic and Dizygotic Twins." *Nature Genetics* 41: 240–45.

Schlosser, Eric. 2001. *Fast Food Nation.* New York: Penguin.

Schulze, Thomas, Heiner Fangeraub, and Peter Propping. 2004. "From Degeneration to Genetic Susceptibility, from Eugenics to Genetics, from Bezugsziffer to LOD Score: the History of Psychiatric Genetics." *International Review of Psychiatry* 16 (4): 246–59.

Seitz, Aaron, Robyn Kim, and Ladan Shams. 2006. "Sound Facilitates Visual Learning." *Current Biology* 16 (14): 1,422–27.

Shai, Iris, Dan Schwarzfuchs, Yaakov Henkin, Danit R. Shahar, Shula Witkow, Ilana Greenberg, Rachel Golan, et al. 2008. "Weight Loss with a Low-Carbohydrate, Mediterranean, or Low-Fat Diet." *New England Journal of Medicine* 359: 229–41.

Wilson, G., and Q. Rahman. 2005. *Born Gay: The Psychobiology of Sex Orientation.* London: Peter Owen.

World Health Organization. 2008. *Evolution of the Tobacco Industry Positions on Addiction to Nicotine.* Geneva: World Health Organization. http://www.who.int/ tobacco/publications/IndustIntr_web-ready_FINAL_9789241597265.pdf.

What ethical considerations do you think biological researchers should consider to ensure that their work is conducted ethically?

In what ways has science influenced politics, technology, media, and business?

HUMAN DEVELOPMENT I
Physical, Cognitive,
and Language Development

HOW DO OUR BIOLOGY AND OUR ENV
MENTS INFLUENCE OUR DEVELOPMEN
WHAT UNIVERSAL CHANGES DO WE E
IENCE AT DIFFERENT STAGES IN OUR L
WHAT ARE SOME OF THE LANDMARKS
PHYSICAL, COGNITIVE, AND LANGUAGE
DEVELOPMENT?
HOW DO PSYCHOLOGISTS STUDY HUM
DEVELOPMENT, AND WHAT QUESTIONS
YET TO BE ANSWERED?

Do you

remember learning how to tie your shoelaces? Remember labouring over the laces, your fingers fumbling with what you hoped would somehow turn into a bow? Remember the frustration, the knots, and finally giving your shoe over to an adult? Now, imagine that you had to learn to tie your shoelaces with your left hand and someone else's right hand. Imagine typing an e-mail, but relying on someone else's hand to control half the keyboard. Imagine learning to walk and trying to run with your left leg and someone else's right leg. Sounds pretty impossible, right? Not for Abigail and Brittany Hensel.

Now in their 20s, the Hensel twins are one of only three or four documented cases of dicephalic twins—twins who have two heads but share a two-armed, two-legged body. They share most of their organs from the waist down, including reproductive organs and a bladder, but they each have their own stomach, heart, and brain. In a marvellous example of the human body's capacity to adapt, the two girls are able to coordinate their movements to clap, run, drive, and type e-mails, even though each of their brains thinks independently and controls a separate side of the body they share.

Doctors can't really explain how two separate brains can work in such perfect synchronicity to allow them to complete complicated movements without the girls conferring with each other. In most other ways, the girls have developed just as others do. They have separate personalities, tastes, and goals for the future: Abby is girly, likes orange juice at breakfast, and wants to be a dentist, while Brittany is spunky, likes milk for breakfast, and wants to be a pilot. At school, they take tests individually and get different grades. They both want to eventually get married and have children.

Abby and Brittany's coordination, as well as their unique qualities, are of interest to psychologists, who often explore the question of biological and environmental differences as we develop into who we are. As identical twins, Abby and Brittany have identical genes, and as dicephalic twins, they have also had identical environments. To better understand the case of the Hensel twins, we first need to understand how lifespan development typically occurs (Chang, 1996; Wallis, 1996; Weathers, 2006).

<<< *Dicephalic twins Abigail and Brittany Hensel share two arms and two legs, as well as most of their organs from the waist down. They have identical genes and grew up in an identical environment, yet their personalities are very different. The Hensel twins' unique situation is of great interest to developmental psychologists, who examine how we are influenced by genetics and by life experiences.*

What Is Developmental Psychology?

Somewhere in the back of the family vault you may find photo albums, films, and baby books that preserve important moments throughout your life so far: that first tentative step, your first lost baby tooth, a traumatic first day of school, that regrettable fourth-grade haircut. Just as parents sometimes track their children's progress, **developmental psychologists** study the physical, cognitive, and social changes that we experience throughout our lifespans. While you might look back at your own development and wonder why your family dressed you in silly outfits when you were a baby, developmental psychologists frame their questions around three major issues:

- **Stability/Change:** What aspects of you are present throughout your life, and what aspects have changed across your development?

- **Nature/Nurture:** How do both your genetics and your life experiences influence your development?

- **Continuity/Stages:** Is development a continual, gradual process, or do we develop in a series of stages?

RESEARCH METHODS

To answer these questions, developmental psychologists conduct research that documents developmental changes in two ways: **Age changes** track how individuals change as they age, while **age differences** consider how people of varying ages differ from one another. However, age is only one element to consider; differences in experience play an even more important role. Researchers use **normative investigations** to determine the landmarks of development—characteristics present at certain ages or stages of development. By identifying norms, or standard development patterns, researchers can differentiate between **chronological age**—the amount of time someone has spent alive—and **developmental age**—the point at which someone falls among developmental stages. Developmental psychologists tend to rely on two types of studies to frame their research questions. **Cross-sectional studies** observe different individuals at different ages to track age differences. While these studies are relatively quick,

inexpensive, and easy to conduct, they can't control for differences among age groups being studied. **Longitudinal studies** observe the same individuals over a period of time to track age changes. While they often provide very valuable insights, longitudinal studies require a great deal of time, money, and effort.

Conception – 2 Weeks

Starting at conception, your zygote—the cell resulting from sperm and egg fusion—entered the germinal stage, a two-week period of rapid cell division during which your cells differentiated into structural and functional specializations. At 10 days, you attached to Mom's uterine wall, forming the placenta, through which she passed you nourishment. If you were an identical twin, your zygote would have split in half during this period.

CONCEPTION

2 Weeks – 8 Weeks

During your six weeks in the embryonic stage, your organs began to form and function, and your heart began to beat. At the end of this stage, you were a whopping 2.5 centimetres long.

8 Weeks – Birth

The fetal stage lasts from eight weeks until birth. During this time, you were responsive to sound: You could hear your mother's muffled voice (Ecklund-Flores, 1992) and kick in response. At six months, your organs were fully developed, and you would have had a chance at survival if born prematurely. From that point until birth, you grew rapidly in size and developed an insulating layer of fat beneath your skin. Maturation of the respiratory and digestive systems, as well as sensitive brain development, also occurred.

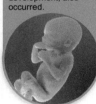

BIRTH

GERMINAL STAGE

EMBRYONIC STAGE

FETAL STAGE

Physical Development

PRENATAL DEVELOPMENT

We may not like to think about it, but for most of us, our development began during inter-

course. Long before you were even a twinkle in her eye, your mother was born with all the immature eggs, or **ova,** she will ever have. Of these ova, only one in 5000 are ever released from the ovaries. Mom's eggs are 85 000 times the size of one of Dad's sperm, but he beats her in quantity: Starting at puberty, he produces sperm cells 24 hours a day for the rest of his life, and he releases an average of 200 million sperm during a single act of intercourse. Only a few make it to the egg, and they begin eating at its protective coating. As soon as one sperm penetrates, the egg blocks the others out and uses fingerlike projections to pull the lucky guy in. In less than half a day, Dad's sperm and Mom's egg have fused into a single zygote: you.

Stress and Harm

How much impact can a mother's lifestyle have on her unborn child? A pregnant woman's experiences are often shared with the developing life inside her. While the placenta blocks some harmful agents from passing from the mother to the embryo or fetus, other **teratogens** such as chemicals and viruses can infiltrate the womb and cause birth defects. Sounds like a good time to give up alcohol!

When a pregnant woman drinks alcohol she puts her unborn child at risk for developing **Fetal Alcohol Spectrum Disorder (FASD)**. FASD is the leading cause of preventable birth defects, mental retardation, and developmental disabilities in Canada. It causes physical, cognitive, behavioural, and learning disabilities. FASD is 100% irreversible! But it is also 100% preventable! Researchers do not know when in pregnancy alcohol exposure will lead to FASD, and there is also no known "safe" amount of alcohol for a pregnant woman (Braun, 1996; Ikonomidou et al., 2000). FASD includes **Fetal Alcohol Syndrome (FAS)**, a more serious condition, and **Fetal Alcohol Effects (FAE)**, a milder condition. In Canada, the incidence of FAS is greater than the incidence of either Down syndrome or spina bifida. The incidence of FAE is five to ten times higher than the incidence of FAS. Between 123 and 740 babies are born with FAS each year in Canada, and around 1000 babies are born with FAE (based on 370 000 births per year) (Health Canada, 2012).

A mother's psychological state and stress level are also believed to affect the fetus. Pregnant women with low self-esteem and high levels of pessimism, stress, and anxiety may be more likely to have premature births or babies with low birth weight (Rini, Dunkel-Schetter, Wadhwa, & Sandman, 1999).

Infant Reflexes

Even before you had much time to adjust to the world outside Mom's amniotic sac, you were hard-wired to interact with it. At birth, your body began breathing air, regulating its temperature, and crying when hungry. You also entered the world with a set of reflexes to help you survive. For example, the rooting reflex is an instinctual response aimed at ensuring successful feeding. When your cheek was stroked you turned your head in the direction of the touch and opened your mouth for feeding. When you were an infant, doctors checked your reflexes to evaluate your growth and development.

INFANCY AND CHILDHOOD
Neural Development

You were born with almost all of the brain cells you have today. While in the womb, your body formed nearly a quarter of a million nerve cells a minute, while your brain cortex peaked in its production of neurons at 28 weeks, subsiding to a mere 23 billion cells when you were born.

Although your brain might have reached its full capacity of cells as a newborn, your nervous system was still immature. As you interacted more with the world around you, the neural networks that allowed you to walk, talk, and remember underwent a major growth spurt. From ages three to six years, your brain experienced the greatest growth spurt in the frontal lobes—the area of the brain associated with higher mental functions, such as personality and complex decision making—which continue to develop throughout your lifespan. Among the last areas of the cortex to develop are those associated with thinking, memory, and language.

When will I be able to sit, crawl, and walk like my big brother?

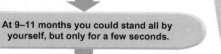

At 4 months you were able to turn from your stomach to your side.

↓

By 6–7 months you were able to turn from your stomach to your back.

↓

At 7 months you could sit up all by yourself.

↓

At 8–10 months you could crawl.

↓

At 8–10 months you could stand, but only if you held on tight!

↓

At 9–11 months you could stand all by yourself, but only for a few seconds.

↓

By 12–15 months there was no stopping you! You could walk all by yourself and were now a toddler.

Motor Development

As your muscles and nervous system developed, so too did your physical coordination.

Motor development—the emergent ability to execute physical actions—tends to occur in the universal sequence shown to the left. This sequence tends to be true for visually impaired children as well, suggesting that these behaviours do not merely reflect imitation.

Two general rules govern the development of motor skills. The cephalocaudal rule is the tendency for motor skills to emerge in sequence from top to bottom. Recall the rooting reflex, which causes the baby to move her head, open her mouth, and search for a nipple; as a baby, your head had very capable motor skills long before your legs would allow

∧
∧ Why do you think our motor development pro-
∧ ceeds in this way? Is there any evolutionary
advantage to the order of these milestones?

Proximodistal rule is the tendency for motor skills to emerge in sequence from inside to outside.

Adolescence is the period of transition from childhood to adulthood.

Puberty is the period in which a person's body goes through the changes that allow him or her to reproduce.

Primary sex characteristics are sexual organs present at birth and directly involved in human reproduction.

Secondary sex characteristics are sexual organs and traits that develop at puberty and are not directly involved in reproduction.

Menarche refers to a girl's first menstruation.

Spermarche refers to a boy's first ejaculation.

Menopause is the end of the menstrual cycle and ability to bear children.

Andropause describes gradual sexual changes in men as they age that include declines in sperm count, testosterone level, and speed of erection and ejaculation.

you to walk. The **proximodistal rule** is the tendency for motor skills to emerge in sequence from inside to outside. As a child, the centre of your body possessed motor skills before the periphery. Do you remember learning to write? You probably started out by holding the pencil far from the tip because you initially used your shoulder to make the pencil move. The source of movement then worked its way down to your elbow, and finally to your fingers and thumb (Payne & Isaacs, 1987).

While the sequence of motor skill development is generally universal, the timing can vary based on biological and environmental factors. Researchers from Montreal and British Columbia (Kennedy, Majnemer, Farmer, Barr, & Platt, 2009) found that infant motor development was positively correlated with "tummy time" (prone position). However, delayed motor development is twice as likely to occur in overweight infants compared to non-overweight infants (Slining, Adair, Goldman, Borja, & Bentley, 2010). But experience can do little to rush motor skills before adequate muscular and neural maturity have been reached. Most babies are ready to walk at around one year, when the cerebellum has developed enough to enable physical coordination. A parent could try to beg or cajole a six-month-old infant into walking earlier than his peers, but it will have little positive impact. Other physical skills, such as bowel and bladder control, are also resistant to being hurried along.

ADOLESCENCE
Puberty

After a period in childhood during which we grow and refine our skills, the onset of **adolescence**—the period of transition from childhood to adulthood—is marked by one of the most awkward periods of our lives: **puberty.** During this period, our bodies go through the physical changes that allow us to reproduce. These include growth spurts in height, changes in body shapes, and development of **primary sex characteristics**—reproductive organs and external genitalia—and **secondary sex characteristics**—nonreproductive traits, such as breasts and hips in girls, facial hair and deeper voices in boys, and pubic and underarm hair for both. As you may well remember, the landmarks of puberty are **menarche**—a girl's first menstruation—and **spermarche**—a boy's first ejaculation.

In North America, the average age for the onset of puberty is 10 for girls and 12 for boys. In pre-industrial cultures, the growth spurt starts about four years later, consistent with North American trends 125 years ago. A similar trend is evident with menarche, which tends to occur between ages 12 and 13 in North America today and, consistent with 19th-century onset, between ages 16 and 17 in some pre-industrial cultures. Factors such as increased food intake and decreased incidence of disease are believed to contribute to the relatively early onset of puberty in North America.

Brain Development

If the awkwardness of puberty isn't enough of an explanation as to why adolescents are characteristically moody, emotionally immature, and all-around difficult, a look at what's going on with the brain during this period should provide more insight. Up until puberty, brain cells are increasing their connections, but during adolescence, the brain adopts a "use it or lose it" policy and selectively prunes neurons and connections that aren't being used (Durston et al., 2001).

Adolescents are also dealing with different rates of development in their brains. The maturation of the limbic system, which controls emotions, occurs more quickly than the maturation of the frontal lobe. Teens may feel like adults, but they lack the ability to make sensible, well-thought-out decisions (Baird & Fugelsang, 2004). Couple this with surging hormones and you have

^ ^ Why do **children** grasp **writing tools** with their **whole fist?** When we **learn to**
^ ^ **write,** our distal **motor skills** still need some **fine-tuning.**

a perfect storm, resulting in the impulsive and risky behaviours for which adolescents are infamous. Teenage immaturity can lead to significant consequences if adolescents go so far as to break the law. However, both the Canadian and American legal systems recognize a biological deficiency in adolescent judgment. As the frontal lobes become more fully developed in the later teenage years and early 20s, most will experience a marked improvement in judgment, impulse control, and the ability to plan for the future (Bennett & Baird, 2006).

EARLY ADULTHOOD

If we manage to make it through the travails of adolescence, we are rewarded with the peak physical abilities of early adulthood. As with the onset of puberty, women tend to peak earlier than men. In our mid-20s, our muscles are strong, our reaction times are quick, and most of us barely notice the early signs of physical decline, such as wrinkles around the eyes and neck.

MIDDLE ADULTHOOD

As we move into middle adulthood, physical vigour becomes less to do with age and more to do with our health and exercise habits. No longer can we party until the early hours, eat pizza for breakfast three times a week, and still feel fit enough to run a marathon. Smokers, heavy drinkers, and sunbathers are more likely to look and feel older than those who avoid unhealthy behaviours, pay attention to nutrition, exercise, and reduce stress. However, there is generally little we can do to fully combat the inevitable declines in hearing, vision, metabolism, physical strength, and fertility.

Depending on how we perceive the aging process, physical changes can bring about varying psychological responses. Western cultures tend to view aging negatively—a perception that often causes the stereotypical mid-life crisis. The term *mid-life crisis* was first coined by Canadian psychologist Elliott Jaques in 1965. He used the term to describe a period in development when adults realized their mortality. Today, the term is used to describe a middle-aged person's vain attempts to regain his or her youth. Ever seen a middle-aged man with hair plugs driving a convertible sports car? How about a woman whose breasts seem unnaturally perky for her age? They are likely experiencing a fear of aging. While research suggests that only 10% reported experiencing a mid-life crisis (Brim, 1999), an overall obsession with age is evident on TV, in the movies,

in advertisements, and in Western cultural beliefs. Still, others embrace aging for the wisdom and stability that often accompany it. In some Eastern cultures, with aging comes great respect and power.

Decline in Fertility

Tick-tock. Tick-tock. Despite advancements in gender equality and science, women in middle (and sometimes even early) adulthood have a hard time shutting out the sound of the ticking biological clock counting down their fertile years. For women between the ages of 35 and 39, a single act of intercourse is half as likely to result in pregnancy than it would be for a 19- to 26-year-old (Dunson, Colombo, & Baird, 2002). However, despite this decrease in fertility, the average age of Canadian women at the time of the birth of their children was 29.3 years in 2008, and 49.6% of all births were to

> Teenage immaturity can lead to significant consequences if adolescents go so far as to break the law. However, both the Canadian and American legal systems recognize a biological deficiency in adolescent judgment.

mothers who were 30 years of age or older (Statistics Canada, 2012).

Within a few years of age 50, most women begin **menopause**—the end of the menstrual cycle and ability to bear children, accompanied by a reduction in estrogen, which can have uncomfortable effects, such as hot flashes. As with aging in general, a woman's psychological response to menopause will depend on her attitude toward it. One study of postmenopausal women found that most of them recalled feeling "only relief" when their periods ceased, and only 2% felt "only regret" (Goode, 1999). Some women may lose a sense of their femininity and experience a decreased interest in sex, while others may celebrate that they no longer have to bother with feminine hygiene products and birth control methods.

Aging men experience more gradual sexual changes than women. What some call **andropause** (Carruthers, 2001) includes decline in sperm count, testosterone level, and speed of erection and ejaculation. If

testosterone levels decline too rapidly, men may experience depression, irritability, insomnia, impotence, or weakness—effects that can be treated with testosterone replacement therapy. For men, psychological reactions to a perceived decrease in virility may be tempered by the relatively long-term and subtle onset of these changes.

LATER ADULTHOOD
Life Expectancy

In July 2010, the Canadian population was just over 34.1 million with an average growth rate of only 1.1% between 2000 and 2010 (Statistics Canada, 2012). Canadians have a life expectancy of almost 81 years, and we are undergoing a shift in our demographic. In 2010, the median age of Canadians was 39.7 years, with an estimated 4.8 million Canadians aged 65 years or older. The number of older Canadians is projected to double in the next 25 years to reach 10.4 million seniors by 2036. By 2051, about one in four Canadians is expected to be 65 or over (Statistics Canada, 2012). A similar trend is being seen throughout most of the world. For example, by the year 2050, approximately 35% of the European population will be over age 60 (Population Division of the Department of Economic and Social Affairs of the United Nations Secretariat, 2006).

The world's aging population is such a potential economic, social, medical, and cultural crisis that Canadian researcher Parminder Raina of McMaster University and his colleagues have undertaken the Canadian Longitudinal Study on Aging (CLSA). This study will follow approximately 50 000 Canadian men and women between the ages of 45 and 85 for at least 20 years. The researchers will collect information on the biological, medical, psychological, social, and economic changes that occur as we age. This information will give us invaluable information about the factors that lead to healthy aging; the symptoms, causes, and prognosis of diseases, such as Alzheimer's; and how best to use financial, medical, and social resources to assist our aging population.

Despite increases in life expectancy, few people live to be 100—in fact, if you are lucky enough to reach your centennial year in the U.K., you will receive a telegram from the Queen. However, the honour may come with a pretty steep price. The decline in our vision, muscle strength, reaction time, stamina, hearing, distance perception, and sense of smell make daily living rather challenging.

The aging body is also vulnerable to many things it could have easily handled in youth, such as hot weather and falling. Although older people are less likely to suffer common short-term ailments because of all the antibodies they have accumulated over a lifetime, their ability to fight off other diseases makes them susceptible to life-threatening ailments like cancer and pneumonia. Conjoined twins such as the Hensel sisters face even more challenges as they age, especially those who share important organs. The oldest known conjoined twins lived to age 63.

Even if these and other ailments didn't exist and no one died before age 50, we would probably only ever top out at an average life expectancy of 85 years (Barinaga, 1991). Evolutionary biologists propose that the reason we eventually decline relates to the survival of our species. We are best able to pass on our genes when we raise young, then stop consuming resources, so younger generations are more likely to have what they need to reach child-bearing age and reproduce.

Brain Development

Like the body, the brain also declines with aging. Neural processing slows, and older adults take more time than younger adults to react, solve perceptual puzzles, and remember names. Memory decline may be partly explained by the gradual loss of brain cells that begins in early adulthood and causes an approximately 5% reduction in brain weight by age 80. The region of greatest cell loss tends to occur in the frontal lobes, which handle memory storage and other higher mental functions. This decline is slower in women and active adults. Exercise, which causes increased oxygen and nutrient flow, not only enhances muscle strength, bone strength, and energy, as well as prevents obesity and heart disease, but also stimulates the development of brain cells and neural connections.

Cognitive Development

We now know the physical changes that the body experiences, from conception to old age. But how does our ability to develop thought materialize? When do we begin to remember our early experiences? How do we learn to communicate? Psychologists study **cognition,** the plethora of mental activities associated with sensation and perception, thinking, knowing, remembering, and communicating, to find answers.

INFANCY AND CHILDHOOD
Sensation and Perception

Although babies' sensory systems are fully functioning at birth, their vision is still immature, so research into this area of their cognitive development is challenging.

Researchers have developed investigative techniques, such as eye-tracking machines and electronically wired pacifiers, to capitalize on the baby's ability to gaze, suck, and turn the head. Findings show that babies turn their heads in the direction of human voices, look longer at images that look like faces than images that look like other patterns (Fantz, 1961), and prefer to look at objects that are 20 to 30 centimetres away, which is the approximate distance of the baby from the mother while nursing (Maurer & Maurer, 1988). These perceptual abilities develop rapidly; a few days after you were born, your neural networks had attuned to your mother's smell and voice. When placed between a gauze pad from the mother's bra and that of another nursing woman, a one-week-old nursing baby will turn toward that of its mother (MacFarlane, 1978). A three-week-old baby will suck on a pacifier more when recordings of his mother's voice are played than when those of a female stranger are played (Mills & Melhuish, 1974; Kisilevsky et al., 2003).

Stimuli Preferences

As with vision, speaking ability in infants is also immature, so they can't tell researchers why they do the things they do. Using several studies, researchers have inferred that babies have a preference for new stimuli and stimuli that they can control. The preference for new stimuli is associated with observed **habituation**—decreased responsiveness with repeated stimulation. Imagine that you came home from work to find a horse in your living room—you would probably react fairly strongly! But if the horse remained in your living room for several weeks, you would eventually get used to it being there when you came home and respond less dramatically. Infants who are repeatedly exposed to a familiar stimulus will begin looking

>>> **From aerobic exercise to Tai Chi, seniors** can experience a multitude of **health benefits** by adopting a **more active lifestyle** (Kuramoto, 2006; Martins et al., 2010).

away from it sooner than they previously did and are more likely to look longer at an unfamiliar stimulus than at a familiar stimulus when presented with the option. This tendency suggests that babies have memory for the familiar stimulus and that they seek to learn from things that are new to them.

The tendency for five- to six-month-old babies to examine—manipulate and explore objects by holding them in front of the eyes, turning them around, and passing them from hand to hand—also appears to be related to a desire to learn. Examining, which seems to be an innate behaviour that doesn't need to be learned and is present in every culture, also declines with an object's increased familiarity.

Interestingly, it seems we all start out with type-A tendencies: Babies display a particular interest in the parts of their environments that they can control. In one study, two-month-olds attended more to a mobile they controlled with

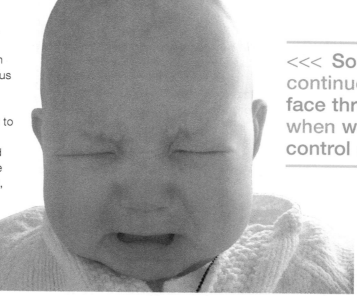

<<< **Some of us continue to make this face throughout our lives when we don't have control over situations.**

their own bodies than to a mobile they did not control (Watson & Ramey, 1972). They also learned to turn on a video and sound recording of the *Sesame Street* theme song by pulling a string attached to their wrists. When the device was disconnected and the babies could no longer control it, they showed facial expressions of anger. Follow-up research at four to five months revealed that babies showed the same facial expressions of anger and sadness when they couldn't control the video/sound recording even if it still came on (but was instead under the experimenter's control)

(Alessandri, Sullivan, & Lewis, 1990; Lewis, Alessandri, & Sullivan, 1990).

Piaget's Theory of Cognitive Development

Jean Piaget's early 20th-century observations led him to believe that children didn't simply know less than adults, but that they instead understood the world around them differently. His revolutionary ideas presented children's minds not as miniature adult minds but rather as minds that develop in a series of stages, driven by an intrinsic motivation to explore and understand.

Piaget's theory described two processes by which we adjust our **schemas**—concepts or frameworks around which we organize and interpret information. Using **assimilation**, we interpret new experiences in terms of existing schemas.

Memory is one cognitive process that develops and changes during childhood.

∨ ∨ ∨

	BIRTH–1	1–2	2–3	3–4	4–7	7–8	8–10	10–15	15–adulthood
Lasting Memories	We often retain no memories that took place before age 3. The average age of earliest conscious memory is 3.5 years (Bauer, 2002), around which time we start organizing memories differently. As the brain cortex matures, toddlers develop a sense of self, and long-term memory increases.			Only a small number of episodic memories from 3–4 years survive into adulthood.		Adults can remember detailed memories from after age 7.			
			Although we may not consciously remember things from a certain age, our nervous system does seem to remember. 10-year-olds who were shown pictures of preschool classmates that they hadn't seen since preschool recognized only 1 in 5. However, physiological responses (e.g., skin perspiration) were greater in response to former classmates whether or not they were consciously remembered (Newcombe et al., 2000).							
Working Memory	The amount of information we can hold in working memory increases with age and reaches adult levels at about age 15.								
Semantic Memory	The first indications of **semantic memories**—explicit memories for facts, beliefs, and word meanings—appear when babies start to correctly name objects at 10–12 months.								
Episodic Memory		Research suggests that to form **episodic memories**—explicit memories for events in one's life—children must first develop the ability to encode experiences into words. By 20–24 months, they begin developing the ability to talk about occurrences from earlier that day or the previous day.		By 3–4 years, children begin to reliably answer questions about past experiences.		By 7 years, children are highly capable of encoding and recalling experiences verbally.			

Under this process, a child with a pet cat might see a dog for the first time and say "cat" because both animals have four legs and fur. However, once the child learns the differences between dogs and cats, she will use **accommodation** to adjust and refine her schema for cat in order to incorporate the new information she has learned about the differences between cats and dogs. The main idea of Piaget's theory is that mental development derives from children's interactions with the world around them. This idea implies an educational approach that is interactive and hands-on and that encourages (even the very youngest) students to think for themselves.

Piaget described this cognitive development as occurring in four stages from infancy to adulthood. These stages focus more on sequencing than the age at which milestones are reached. They are summarized in the following table.

Reflections on Piaget's Theory

While Piaget's ideas about children learning through interacting with their environment have been widely adopted in the educational world, many researchers today understand cognitive development as more fluid and continuous

Piaget's Stages of Cognitive Development

STAGE	COGNITIVE DEVELOPMENT	EXAMPLE
Formal Operational (12 years – adulthood)	People begin to think logically about abstract concepts.	Teenagers may get involved in **hypothetical thinking**—imagining possibilities or impossibilities.
Concrete Operational (7–12 years)	Children gain the mental operations that allow them to think logically about concrete events.	Children understand **conservation**—the principle that properties such as mass, volume, and number remain the same despite the objects' changes in the form.
Preoperational (2–7 years)	Children learn to use language but do not yet possess the abilities to understand mental operations of concrete logic.	Children exhibit **egocentrism**—not intentional selfishness, but difficulty taking another's point of view. As they develop **theory of mind**—ideas about their own versus others' mental states—they can infer others' feelings; tease, empathize, and persuade; explain people's behaviours in terms of perceptions, emotions, and desires (2–3 years); understand that thoughts may cause feelings; and understand that spontaneous self-produced thoughts may create feelings (5–8 years).
Sensorimotor (birth–2 years)	Infants know the world mostly in terms of their sensory impressions and motor activities (i.e., looking, hearing, touching, mouthing, and grasping).	Young infants lack **object permanence**—awareness that objects continue to exist when they are no longer perceived. Infants under 5 months may fail simple object permanence tests due to difficulty planning the correct movement of the hidden object. By 8 months, infants exhibit memory for things that are not perceived.

than Piaget did. Many also believe that he may have underestimated children's cognitive abilities. While Piaget thought that babies couldn't think before age two, researchers have found that babies do possess some logic: They look longer at unexpected scenes, such as a car passing through a solid object (Baillargeon, 1995, 1998, 2004; Wellman & Gelman, 1992) or numerically impossible outcomes (Wynn, 1992, 2000). Researchers now disagree about whether the foundations of formal operational thinking emerge earlier than when children begin adolescence and whether Piaget may have underestimated the role of social interactions in cognitive development.

Vygotsky's Social Influence Theory

Leading the case for social influence on cognitive development was Russian psychologist Lev Vygotsky, who believed that development occurs on a social level before it occurs at the individual level. He considered the **zone of proximal development**—the difference between what a child can do alone versus what a child can do together with a more competent person. While learning in the zone of proximal development, dialogue can encourage critical thinking and revision and questioning of ideas so that they are either improved or discarded.

Unlike Piaget, who took the view of the child as a scientist with the goal of developing logic skills, Vygotsky believed the child was more like an apprentice with the goal of developing the ability to function effectively in adult society. According to Vygotsky, children want to participate in the activities that are central to their culture. As a result, the cognitive development of children is influenced by their specific cultural experiences—their homes, schools, and meeting places. While a child in an industrialized country may learn math in a formal school environment, a child in a non-industrialized country may learn arithmetic through interactions with others in the community.

We can see Vygotsky's theories

in practice when we watch babies using cues from adults to guide their behaviour. Canadian researchers found that six-month-olds mimic adults' actions on objects, and from six to 12 months, they engage in **joint visual attention**—they look at the adult's eyes, follow the gaze, and then direct their own gaze toward whatever the adult is looking at (Corkum & Moore, 1998). This tendency helps babies learn what is of most interest to adults and aids in language development. By the end of the first year, babies engage in social referencing—they look at the emotional expressions of caregivers for cues about what may be dangerous (Rosen, Adamson, & Bakeman, 1992).

Accommodation is a process in which a person adjusts and refines his or her schemas based on new information.

Zone of proximal development refers to the difference between what a child can do alone versus what a child can do together with a more competent person.

Joint visual attention describes a behaviour in which a baby looks at an adult's eyes, follows the adult's gaze, and then directs his or her own gaze toward whatever the adult is looking at.

Reason is the skill of organizing information and beliefs into a series of steps leading to a conclusion.

> You may have felt a new kind of social awareness and moral judgment during adolescence. It's no coincidence that adolescents begin to think about and criticize society and to have strong opinions about, well, pretty much everything. Early adolescence typically focuses reasoning on the self.

ADOLESCENCE
Reasoning

Teenagers are often stereotyped as moody and impulsive, and this stereotype isn't entirely unfair: While plenty of adolescents see themselves as completely grown up, our frontal lobes aren't fully developed until we reach our early 20s. As the frontal lobes develop, they enable us to **reason**—to organize information and beliefs into a series of steps leading to a conclusion. You may have felt a new kind of social awareness and moral judgment during adolescence. It's no coincidence that adolescents begin to

think about and criticize society and to have strong opinions about, well, pretty much everything. Early adolescence typically focuses reasoning on the self. If you ever yelled something like "You don't understand what I'm going through!" and stormed off to your room, slamming the door and turning up your music, then you understand that adolescents often feel as though their experiences are utterly unique and earth-shatteringly significant. This tendency may have been tempered in the case of the Hensel twins; although they each have individual senses of "self," neither really has the option of going through life without considering at least one other person.

Gradually, most adolescents reach the formal operational stage described earlier. As they become increasingly capable of abstract logic, they can reason hypothetically, reach conclusions, and identify flaws in others' opinions.

ADULTHOOD
Memory

As with physical vigour, some types of learning and remembering peak in early adulthood. While younger adults have higher recall than older adults (for example, being asked to

<<< "You don't understand what I'm going through!" Teenagers have a tendency to focus on the self.

Prospective memory is remembering to perform a specific action.

Cohorts are groups of people raised during the same time period.

Morphemes are the smallest meaningful units of language that represent the objects, events, ideas, characteristics, and relationships in that language's vocabulary.

Phonemes are elementary vowel and consonant sounds that combine to form morphemes.

Phonology refers to how phonemes may be arranged to produce morphemes.

Morphology refers to how morphemes may be arranged to form words.

Syntax refers to how words may be arranged to produce phrases and sentences.

Overextended describes the relatively broad use of common nouns.

Underextended describes the relatively narrow use of common nouns.

Content words are words that have meaning.

Grammatical words are words that provide structure.

Language acquisition device (LAD) is a theoretical mechanism that provides children with an inherent foundation for the principles of universal grammar.

Language-acquisition support system (LASS) is the social environment into which a baby is born.

remember a list of words in a memory test), they don't have higher recognition (for example, being shown a list of words and asked to point out which words were in the memory test). Moreover, unless adults are given caffeine, recognition is better earlier rather than later in the day (Schonfield & Robertson, 1966).

Additionally, older people tend to make more errors than younger people when trying to recall meaningless information, such as nonsense syllables and unimportant events (Gordon & Clark, 1974a). Although meaningful information is more easily remembered, older adults take longer than younger adults to produce their memories. **Prospective memory**—remembering to perform a specific action, such as calling someone back or bringing lunch to the office—remains strong if time-management and reminder cues are used. Time-based and habitual tasks, however, are challenging. The good news for older adults is that their ability to learn and remember skills declines less than their verbal recall ability.

Intelligence

Understanding intelligence in later adulthood has been challenging and controversial. David

Wechsler, who is perhaps best known for his intelligence scales, believed that deterioration of mental ability is an inherent part of aging. His cross-sectional study compared 70-year-olds and 30-year-olds from different eras, so his conclusions were based on confounded comparisons that failed to account for differences among **cohorts**—groups of people raised during the same time period.

Later longitudinal studies have brought down the myth of declining intelligence across the lifespan, with findings that intelligence remains stable and may even increase into later adulthood. However, these studies also have their pitfalls: It is possible that individuals who survived to the end of the studies were those with intelligence least likely to deteriorate.

But what exactly is intelligence? While generally conceived as the ability to learn from one's experiences, acquire knowledge, and use resources to adapt to new situations (Sternberg & Kaufman, 1998; Wechsler, 1975), intelligence is an imprecise catch-all term that describes many different traits, making intelligence studies extremely problematic.

> " Although there are thousands of different languages across the world, **several characteristics are common among them all.** "

Language Development

We might have an IQ of 130, but without the ability to talk our genius would likely remain undiscovered. Language allows us to think in words rather than pictures, communicate our thoughts and feelings to others, and learn by asking questions. It is obviously a vital skill, but how does our ability to use language develop?

UNIVERSAL ELEMENTS OF HUMAN LANGUAGE

Although there are thousands of different languages across the world, several characteristics are common among them all. These similarities may account for the observed cross-cultural similarities in language development among humans. Every language has the same structure of units.

Morphemes are the smallest meaningful units that represent the objects, events, ideas, characteristics, and relationships in a language's vocabulary. **Phonemes** are the elementary vowel and consonant sounds that combine to form morphemes. Grammar governs the appropriate ways to arrange units at each level with rules of **phonology**—how phonemes may be arranged to produce morphemes, **morphology**—how morphemes may be arranged to form words, and **syntax**—how words may be arranged to produce phrases and sentences.

LANGUAGE DEVELOPMENT PROCESS
Cooing and Babbling

When you were born, you already had the capacity to communicate. You cried to communicate hunger and made other sounds to communicate distress. At about two months, you developed the capacity to make pleasant cooing sounds—repeated and drawn-out vowel sounds—to communicate happiness. At about six months, your cooing progressed to babbling—repeated consonant and vowel sounds. Cooing and babbling helped you develop and strengthen the muscle movements necessary for speech.

These early sounds appear not to depend on the spoken sounds an infant hears. Babbling is as likely to contain sounds of a foreign language as of a native one. Prior to 12 months, Japanese babies differentiate *ra* and *la* sounds, which are not present in their native language (Werker, 1989). By eight months, hearing infants tend to babble in ways that mimic the language to which they are most exposed, and by 10 months their babbling resembles syllables and words of the native language. This change may result from parents reinforcing the babbling sounds that most mimic their adult language (Skinner, 1957). At 10 months, if hearing-impaired infants, who babble at the same time and in the same way as hearing infants, are exposed to sign language, they will begin "babbling" with their hands, repeating hand movements that resemble those of sign language (Petitto & Marentette, 1991).

Vocabulary Development

Before you could produce words, you were able to understand what some of them meant. By about nine months, you could respond to some common words by looking at the correct object that had been named and could follow simple commands (Balaban & Waxman, 1997; Benedict, 1979). Shortly thereafter, at around 10 to 12 months, you began producing your first recognizable words, and the rate of word acquisition accelerated from 15 to 20 months. At about 18 months, you went through a period of naming explosion during which you learned up to 45 new nouns each day to refer to the objects around you. Before you pat yourself on the back for your prolific rate of achievement, you probably hadn't yet perfected correct usage of all these words: You likely **overextended**—used common nouns more broadly than the adult language would—or **underextended**—used them more narrowly than the adult language would. Some research suggests that the latter is more common that the former (MacWhinney, 1998). How do these tendencies relate to Piaget's concepts of assimilation and accommodation?

Grammar

After a long period of one-word utterances, at about 18 to 24 months, you began to put together mostly **content words**—words that have meaning—as opposed to **grammatical words**, which provide structure. Your utterances probably contained mostly nouns and verbs along the lines of "kitty eat" and "doggy sleep." Before formal schooling began, you actively and unconsciously inferred grammatical rules from the language you heard. However, you probably overgeneralized the new rules you acquired, such as adding *-s* to pluralize. By age four, you had acquired much of the grammar necessary to carry on meaningful conversations. Rules of grammar are encoded in implicit memory (memories that aren't easily brought into conscious awareness and are necessary to perform tasks, skills, habits, and learned reflexes) rather than explicit memory (memories of events from the external world that are easily brought from long-term storage to short-term memory), and people can often correctly apply grammatical rules that they can't name or describe.

THEORIES OF LANGUAGE ACQUISITION
Chomsky's Language Acquisition Device

In contrast to B. F. Skinner's ideas that children learn language through reinforcement, linguist Noam Chomsky argued that children are born with a **language acquisition device (LAD)** that provides them an inherent foundation for the principles of universal grammar. In his book *Syntactic Structures,* he emphasized the hierarchical structure of sentences and argued that a person must have a meaningful representation of the sentence in mind before producing it and then must apply grammatical rules to that representation and fill out the lower levels of the hierarchy (Chomsky, 1957).

Critical Period

Similar to the way the senses must be used early on in life in order to function properly, language acquisition has a critical period—it is acquired most effectively in the years before puberty (Lenneberg, 1967). Therefore, children deprived of the opportunity to learn language during this time face major difficulties learning it later, and they never fully master the grammar.

People who learned their first language during the critical period are able to learn a second language reasonably well at

> At 10 months, if hearing-impaired infants, who babble at the same time and in the same way as hearing infants, are exposed to sign language, they will begin "babbling" with their hands, repeating hand movements that resemble those of sign language (Petitto & Marentette, 1991).

any point in life. However, a second language is better learned during one's early years, as those who learn one after they are 10 or 11 years old almost always speak with an accent and don't acquire grammatical rules as fully or easily as those who learned the language when they were younger.

Bilingualism in Canada

Canada has a long history of bilingualism that includes our adoption of both French and English as our official languages, as well as the many additional languages of our large immigrant population. Bilingualism brings many cognitive and economic benefits. For example, bilingual children focus their attention better than monolingual children (Bialystok & Martin, 2004; Carlson & Meltzoff, 2008), and native-English children who learn French develop a deeper understanding of the structure of English (Lambert, Genesee, Holobow, & Chartrand, 1993). In a recent study, French immersion children were found to outperform English-only students on the English Reading tests for the Education Quality and Accountability Office of

Ontario evaluations (EQAO) at both the grade three and grade six testing levels (Genesee & Jared, 2008). The benefits of bilingualism continue to be evident as we age. Employment rates and salaries are higher among bilingual individuals than monolingual individuals (Canadian Council on Learning, 2008), and bilingual individuals maintain higher cognitive capacities and less age-related cognitive decline compared to monolingual individuals (Bialystok, Craik, Klein, & Viswanathan, 2004). Do you speak a second language? Maybe we all should!

Social Environment

Psychologists widely agree that inborn mechanisms cannot fully account for language acquisition. Normal language development requires the **language-acquisition support system (LASS)**—the social environment into which the baby is born. To help children learn, adults often alter their speech into child-directed speech or "motherese," which features exaggerated, high-pitched intonation and may contain affective messages in order to grab infants' attention, keep them interested, provide support, and give warnings. Canadian researchers Nicholas Smith and Laurel Trainor (2008) found that mothers changed the pitch of their infant-directed speech based on feedback from their infant. Infant-directed speech is used in multiple cultures but specific speech patterns differ across cultures. For example, Western mothers use more information-oriented speech than Japanese mothers, who use more emotionally expressive speech (Barratt, Negayama, & Minami, 1993; Tamis-LeMonda, Bornstein, Cyphers, Toda, & Ogino, 1992). However, children around the world acquire language at about the same rate, despite great differences in the nature and degree of adult verbal interactions with children.

Summary

HOW DO OUR BIOLOGY AND OUR ENVIRONMENTS INFLUENCE OUR DEVELOPMENT? p.82

• During pregnancy, teratogens can pass through the placenta and cause irreparable harm to an embryo or fetus.
• Increased food intake and a decrease in disease may contribute to the earlier onset of puberty in industrialized countries.

WHAT UNIVERSAL CHANGES DO WE EXPERIENCE AT DIFFERENT STAGES IN OUR LIVES? p.83

• Newborn babies exhibit reflexes.
• Motor skills tend to develop in sequence from top to bottom and from inside to outside.
• During puberty, the body develops primary and secondary sex characteristics.
• The gradual loss of brain cells as we age leads to a decline in memory.

WHAT ARE SOME OF THE LANDMARKS OF PHYSICAL, COGNITIVE, AND LANGUAGE DEVELOPMENT? pp. 82, 87, & 90

• Physical landmarks include the germinal, embryonic, and fetal stages; newborn reflex actions; motor development; puberty; menopause and andropause; and the physical decline of old age.
• Piaget theorized that children use assimilation and accommodation to adjust their informational schemas. Vygotsky believed children's cognitive development is influenced by cultural experiences.
• Language development landmarks include cooing and babbling, producing vocabulary, and learning grammatical rules.

HOW DO PSYCHOLOGISTS STUDY HUMAN DEVELOPMENT, AND WHAT QUESTIONS HAVE YET TO BE ANSWERED? p.82

• Developmental psychologists study the physical, cognitive, and social changes we experience by examining three issues: stability/change, nature/nurture, and continuity/stages.
• Researchers perform both cross-sectional and longitudinal developmental studies.
• Normative investigations enable researchers to distinguish between chronological age and developmental age.

Test Your Understanding

1. During puberty, the adolescent brain:
   a. produces new cells and connections
   b. selectively prunes neurons that are not being used
   c. experiences the greatest growth spurt in the frontal lobes
   d. peaks in its production of neurons

2. Kerry studies the temperaments of three young children. Two years later, she returns to the same children to assess changes in their social development. She completes her research two years later with a final visit to the same three children. Kerry is conducting:
   a. a longitudinal study
   b. a cross-sectional study
   c. correlational research
   d. a biased experiment

3. Which of the following statements is true about the aging process?
   a. Older people make fewer memory errors than younger people.
   b. Exercise can stimulate brain cells and slow down memory decline.
   c. Intelligence declines as we age.
   d. Older people are more likely to suffer common short-term ailments than younger people.

4. According to the cephalocaudal rule of motor development:
   a. the upper part of the body develops motor skills before the lower part of the body
   b. the centre of the body develops motor skills before the periphery areas of the body
   c. the ability to execute physical actions occurs in a universal sequence
   d. the timing of motor skill development varies according to individual experience

5. At what age do infants typically begin to walk on their own?
   a. 4–6 months
   b. 8–10 months
   c. 12–15 months
   d. 18–24 months

6. Which of the following illustrates the existence of the zone of proximal development?
   a. Seven-year-old Mia is able to memorize the names of the planets using a mnemonic rhyme.
   b. Six-year-old Tim is unable to read his new school book by himself, but with the help of his teacher, he understands some of the more difficult words.

c. Eight-year-old Samson learns better when he is working in a group than when he is working individually.

d. Six-year-old Sara was at the bottom of her class last year but suddenly undergoes a rapid learning period and is now one of the top students.

7. During which early stage of development do the organs fully develop?

a. the fetal stage
b. the germinal stage
c. the embryonic stage
d. the neonatal stage

8. The observance of habituation indicates that babies:

a. prefer stimuli they can control
b. prefer colourful stimuli
c. prefer more complex stimuli
d. prefer new stimuli

9. Which of the following physical developments is a landmark of puberty in males?

a. spermarche
b. andropause
c. menopause
d. menarche

10. Which of the following statements about Fetal Alcohol Spectrum Disorder (FASD) is NOT true?

a. FASD is the leading cause of preventable birth defects, mental retardation, and developmental disabilities in Canada.
b. The rate of FASD is higher in communities where there is more alcohol consumption.
c. FASD includes Fetal Alcohol Syndrome (FAS), a more serious condition, and Fetal Alcohol Effects (FAE), a milder condition.
d. FASD is reversible.

11. Chiyo is conducting a study on working memory at different stages of life. She tests five people between ages 18 and 25, five people between ages 26 and 35, five people between ages 36 and 50, and five people above age 50. Chiyo is conducting:

a. a longitudinal study
b. a cross-sectional study
c. naturalistic observation
d. a survey

12. According to Piaget, a child who is able to think logically about abstract concepts has reached which stage of cognitive development?

a. preoperational
b. formal operational
c. sensorimotor
d. concrete operational

13. Andrea is a 55-year-old female who is trying to fight the aging process. Which of the following factors is Andrea able to control?

a. sensory decline
b. metabolism
c. fertility
d. physical vigour

14. Which of the following actions demonstrates prospective memory?

a. remembering the name of a former co-worker
b. remembering how to solve a quadratic equation
c. remembering to put the trash out every Friday
d. remembering a sentimental moment from high school

15. Two-year-old Khalil has learned to say "mama sing" and "dada play" and uses the words repeatedly. Khalil is:

a. developing content words
b. babbling
c. developing grammatical words
d. cooing

16. Which of the following statements is true about bilingualism in Canada?

a. Monolingual individuals make more money than bilingual individuals.
b. Bilingual adults experience more age-related cognitive declines compared to monolingual individuals.
c. Bilingual children focus their attention better than monolingual children.
d. French immersion students did poorly compared to English-only students on the EQAO tests.

17. Andrew, a 55-year-old male, experiences a rapid drop in testosterone levels. Andrew's likely side effects include:

a. joint and muscle pain
b. weakness and irritability
c. high blood pressure
d. frequent, severe headaches

18. A baby who is engaging in joint visual attention is most likely to:

a. maintain eye contact with an adult who is in the room
b. focus on moving stimuli rather than stationary stimuli
c. pay attention to objects that are unique or that haven't been seen before
d. follow an adult's gaze and direct his or her attention to what the adult is looking at

19. Lamar asked an 18-year-old woman and a 68-year-old woman to memorize a list of words. He then showed both women several words and asked them to identify which words were on the original list. Lamar is likely to find that:

a. both women are able to recognize the same number of words
b. the 18-year-old woman can recognize more words than the 68-year-old woman can
c. the 68-year-old woman can recognize more words than the 18-year-old woman can
d. the number of words recognized is higher if both women are asked later rather than earlier in the day

20. If there were no diseases or other ailments that commonly affect people in old age, experts believe that life expectancy would:

a. continue increasing indefinitely
b. remain about the same
c. increase to an average of 100 years
d. top out at an average of 85 years

Remember to check www.thethinkspot.ca **for additional information, downloadable flashcards, and other helpful resources.**

Answers: 1) b; 2) a; 3) b; 4) a; 5) c; 6) b; 7) a; 8) d; 9) a; 10) d; 11) b; 12) b; 13) d; 14) c; 15) a; 16) c; 17) b; 18) d; 19) a; 20) d

THINK READINGS

BRIEF REPORT

Happy as a Lark: Morning-Type Younger and Older Adults Are Higher in Positive Affect

Renée K. Biss and Lynn Hasher

University of Toronto and Rotman Research Institute, Toronto, Ontario, Canada

> You will learn more about circadian rhythms in Chapter 10.

> Do you classify yourself as a lark or an owl?

A literature on young adults reports that morning-type individuals, or "larks," report higher levels of positive affect compared with evening-type individuals, or "owls" (Clark, Watson, & Leeka, 1989; Hasler et al., 2010). Morning types are relatively rare among young adults but frequent among older adults (May & Hasher, 1998; Mecacci et al., 1986), and here we report on the association between chronotype and affect in a large sample of healthy younger and older adults. Overall, older adults reported higher levels of positive affect than younger adults, with both younger and older morning types reporting higher levels of positive affect and subjective health than age mates who scored lower on morningness. Morningness partially mediated the association between age and positive affect, suggesting that greater morningness tendencies among older adults may contribute to their improved well-being relative to younger adults.

There are substantial age and individual differences in chronotype, or patterns of sleep/wake activity and energy levels that are tied to time of day and governed by internal circadian and sleep drives (Horne & Ostberg, 1977; May & Hasher, 1998; Mongrain, Carrier, & Dumont, 2006; Roenneberg et al., 2007). Morning types, or "larks," wake up early, plan activities early in the day and tend to retire early in the evening. In contrast, evening types, or "owls," awake later and are often active until late at night. Of course, many individuals fall between these two extremes (Horne & Ostberg, 1977). Research on young adults suggests that larks and owls differ in terms of well-being and susceptibility to psychiatric illness. For example, morningness is associated with a more stable personality (DeYoung, Hasher, Djikic, Criger, & Peterson, 2007) and greater subjective well-being (Randler, 2008). In contrast, eveningness is associated with increased susceptibility to depression (Drennan, Klauber, Kripke, & Goyette, 1991; Kitamura et al., 2010) and increased alcohol and stimulant use (Wittmann, Dinich, Merrow, & Roenneberg, 2006). Evening types are also more likely to report being in fair or poor general health (Paine, Gander, & Travier, 2006).

Central to these differences in well-being and psychopathology may be variations in emotional state: Morningness among younger adults is associated with higher positive affect across the day (Clark et al., 1989; Hasler, Allen, Sbarra, Bootzin, & Bernert, 2010). Morning types also score higher on measures of energy-alertness and lower on tiredness compared with evening types (Froberg, 1977). In contrast, negative affect does not appear to vary with chronotype (Clark et al., 1989; Hasler et al., 2010). Thus, existing evidence suggests an association between chronotype and affect, with morning types reporting greater overall experience of emotions associated with positive activation, including excitement, cheerfulness, and alertness, compared with individuals with later time of day preferences.

This conclusion, however, is based solely on data from younger adults, and may

> In Chapter 16 you will learn about mental illnesses.

> You will read more about our emotions in Chapter 9.

be limited because the individuals in this age range show very different time of day preferences compared to individuals of other ages. While morning chronotypes are most common during childhood, there are more evening types in adolescence, reaching a peak at around age 19 in women and 21 in men (Kim, Dueker, Hasher, & Goldstein, 2002; Roenneberg et al., 2007). Thereafter, there are greater morningness tendencies in each subsequent age group, such that by age 60, a majority of individuals report feeling at their best in the morning (May & Hasher, 1998; Mecacci, Zani, Rocchetti, & Lucioli, 1986). These chronotype differences are thought to be linked to age-dependent changes in the concentration and timing of certain hormones, including cortisol and growth hormone, which influence the timing and quality of sleep (Roenneberg et al., 2007; Van Cauter, Leproult, & Plat, 2000). Although longitudinal evidence is lacking, retrospective self-assessments of chronotype for various stages in development support the pattern of cross-sectional differences (Roenneberg et al., 2007). Thus, older adults (ages 60–80) markedly differ from younger adults in terms of chronotype; their sleep–wake times are shifted earlier as is their preferred time for activities.

Given substantial age-related differences in chronotype patterns, it is unknown whether the relationship between morningness and emotional state observed in younger adults also holds for older adults. There is evidence that positive affect and subjective well-being are higher in older adulthood (Carstensen et al., 2011; Mroczek & Kolarz, 1998; Stone, Schwartz, Broderick, & Deaton, 2010). Considering the association

between morningness and age, this raises an intriguing possibility: Reports of age differences in positive affect may be tied to the greater proportion of morningtype individuals age 60 and above. In addition, given previous evidence that eveningtype individuals are more likely to report being in poorer health (Paine et al., 2006), it is also possible that chronotype may contribute to individual differences in older adults' subjective health ratings. Subjective health is an important component of well-being and is known to be a strong predictor of objective health outcomes and mortality in older people (Idler & Benyamini, 1997).

To address the question of whether the association between morningness and well-being exists in older adults, we obtained measures of chronotype, affect and subjective health in both younger (ages 17–38) and older adults (ages 59–79). Because older adults report both improved positive affect and a stronger tendency toward morningness, we also tested whether age differences in chronotype partially explain age-related differences in well-being.

METHOD

Participants

Four hundred thirty-five younger adults (ages 17–38 years, $M = 19.7$, $SD = 2.7$) and 297 older adults (ages 59–79 years, $M = 67.8$, $SD = 4.9$) participated in this study. Younger adults (153 men, 282 women) were undergraduate students at the University of Toronto who participated for course credit or monetary compensation. Older adults (125 men, 172 women) were healthy, community-dwelling volunteers who received monetary compensation. The majority of older adults were

retired. As is common in social and cognitive studies of aging, older adults had more years of education ($M = 16.6$, $SD = 3.7$) compared with younger adults ($M = 13.6$, $SD = 1.9$), $t(398) = 12.79$, $p < .001$, who were still enrolled in university.

Measures

Participants filled out pencil-and-paper questionnaires individually in a laboratory setting during the typical working day (9:00 a.m. to 6:00 p.m.) as part of several studies on cognition and aging.

Chronotype was determined using the Morningness-Eveningness Questionnaire (MEQ; Horne & Ostberg, 1976), a reliable and well-validated measure of chronotype. The MEQ includes 19 questions gauging an individual's preferred rising and sleep times, and optimal time for physically or intellectually demanding activities based on his or her own "feeling best rhythm" (e.g., "Considering your own" feeling best "rhythm, at what time would you get up if you were free to plan your day?", "How alert do you feel during the first half hour after having woken in the morning?", "At what time in the evening do you feel tired, and, as a result, in need of sleep?"; Horne & Ostberg, 1976). Questions are given scaled scores and summed to determine each individual's morningness-eveningness rating. Scores range from 16 to 86, and can be categorized as *definitely evening* (16–30), *moderately evening* (31–41), *neutral* (42–58), *moderately morning* (59–69), and *definitely morning* (70–86) chronotypes (Horne & Ostberg, 1976). Test–retest reliability for the MEQ is high (Kerkhof, 1984), and MEQ scores predict measures of circadian timing and sleep drive, including oral temperature,

---

Side annotation boxes:

In this chapter you read about the physical changes that happen from infancy to adulthood.

In Chapter 18 you will read about the factors that affect our health. What do you think are ways that we can improve our health?

What does cognition mean? You can find out in Chapter 13.

Based on what you learned in this chapter, do you agree with classifying 17- to 38-year-olds as younger adults? Do you think this age range is too narrow or too broad?

In this chapter you read that over 25% of the Canadian population will be 70 years of age or older by 2051. What are some of the challenges that we will face as the population ages?

Do you remember what "reliability" and "validity" mean (see Chapter 2)?

sleep/rising times, and patterns of alertness (Horne & Ostberg, 1977; Zavada, Gordijn, Beersma, Daan, & Roenneberg, 2005). The MEQ has been widely used with both younger and older adults and predicts variations in cognitive performance across the day in both age groups (e.g., May & Hasher, 1998).

Individual differences in affective state were measured using the Brief Mood Introspection scale (Mayer & Gaschke, 1988), which requires participants to rate the extent to which they currently feel each of 16 mood adjectives on a 7-point response scale. Scores were calculated on a positive-tired dimension (ranging from *active* and *peppy* to *tired* and *drowsy*) and a negative-relaxed dimension (ranging from *jittery* and *nervous* to *calm*), corresponding respectively to the positive and negative affect dimensions of emotion as theorized by Watson, Wiese, Vaidya, and Tellegen (1999). Both scales have good factor validity and reliability (Mayer & Gaschke, 1988). In our sample, internal consistency was acceptable for each scale in younger and older adults (Cronbach's alphas > .74).

Participants were also asked to judge their overall health on a scale from 1 (*poor*) to 10 (*excellent*). This measure is similar to other single-item subjective health indicators that have previously been shown to predict morbidity and mortality (Idler & Benyamini, 1997).

Results

The distribution of chronotypes for younger and older adults is shown in Table 1. Older adults mean MEQ score was 59.4 (*SD* = 10.4), a value in the moderately morning range. Younger adults mean MEQ score was 43.8 (*SD* = 10.0), a value close

to the evening side of the neutral category. Consistent with past research (May & Hasher, 1998; Mecacci et al., 1986), older adults showed a reliably greater tendency toward morningness, $t(730) = 20.37$, $p < .001$, $d = 1.53$.

Older adults reported better moods, with higher positive affect ($M = 20.8$, $SD = 7.1$) compared with younger adults ($M = 10.8$, $SD = 6.4$), $t(730) = 19.92$, $p < .001$, $d = 1.48$, and lower negative affect ($M = 4.0$, $SD = 5.9$) than their younger counterparts ($M = 8.4$, $SD = 5.9$), $t(730) = 9.92$, $p < .001$, $d = 0.75$. Older adults also rated their subjective health more highly ($M = 8.0$, $SD = 1.5$) compared with younger adults ($M = 7.7$, $SD = 1.3$), $t(552) = 2.69$, $p = .01$, $d = 0.21$.

Participants had choice about their appointment times, and there was a moderate association between MEQ score and time of measurement for younger adults ($r = -.18$, $p < .001$) and for older adults ($r = .13$, $p = .02$). Thus, we included time of measurement as a covariate in all analyses. The partial correlations for MEQ scores, affective ratings, subjective health, and age within younger and older adults are shown in Table 2. As can be seen, a greater tendency toward morningness was associated with higher positive affect for

both younger and older adults. Negative affect was not associated with morningness in either age group. Morningness was also associated with improved subjective health ratings in both groups. Among younger adults, age was associated with higher positive affect, but not chronotype, negative affect or subjective health. In the older adult group, age was not associated with chronotype, affect or health.

To test the hypothesis that age-related differences in chronotype contribute to well-being, we constructed a mediation model across all participants in which age in years predicted positive affect with morningness as a mediator. Following Baron and Kenny's (1986) criteria for mediation, age predicted positive affect (β = 0.207, $p < .001$), and age also predicted the mediator, morningness (β = 0.322, $p < .001$). Critically, morningness predicted positive affect when age was controlled (β = 0.149, $p < .001$). This mediation was partial, because the association between age and positive affect remained when morningness was added as a mediator (β = 0.159, $p < .001$). We also conducted formal significance testing of the indirect effect using the Sobel test of mediation and a bootstrap approach, as recommended by Preacher

Table 1

Distribution of Morningness-Eveningness Questionnaire (MEQ) Types and Means for Each Category for Younger and Older Adults

Type	Younger adults (*n* = 435)		Older adults (*n* = 297)	
	%	M	%	M
Definitely evening	9.2	26.9	1.0	27.7
Moderately evening	33.8	36.8	5.7	37.9
Neutral	49.7	48.7	36.0	52.4
Moderately morning	6.4	61.9	38.0	63.1
Definitely morning	0.9	74.5	19.2	73.1

Sidebar callouts:

What does the p-value tell us (see Chapter 2)?

What is a hypothesis (see Chapter 2)?

Learn about the leading causes of death in Canada in Chapter 18.

and Hayes (2004). Both procedures indicated that morningness partially mediated the relationship between age and positive affect β = (0.048, $p < .001$, 95% confidence interval [CI] = [0.033, 0.065]).

Discussion

Our results demonstrate that morningness is associated with higher positive affect among both younger and older adults, as has previously been shown in younger adults only (Clark et al., 1989; Froberg, 1977; Hasler et al., 2010). Negative affect was not associated with individual differences in chronotype in either age group (see also Clark et al., 1989; Hasler et al., 2010). These two findings are consistent with the theoretical position that positive, but not negative affect should be closely tied to an individual's internal biological clock (Watson et al., 1999), as positive affect is known to fluctuate according to a 24-hr cycle (Murray et al., 2009). Our study adds to evidence of a relationship between positive affect and chronotype by demonstrating that morningness is associated with greater positive but not negative affect in a similar manner in both younger and older adults. We note that this particular association with chronotype may not hold for all behaviors related to positive affect (e.g., see Soehner, Kennedy, & Monk, 2007).

Morningness was also associated with better subjective health, a relationship that is consistent with research suggesting that evening types are more likely to rate their health as fair or poor relative to morning types (Paine et al., 2006). This finding is particularly important in regards to older adults, because subjective health ratings in older age are a strong predictor of objective health outcomes and mortality (Idler & Benyamini, 1997). Morningness may be a protective factor associated with improved health in later life. Of course, it is also possible that declining health could lead to a movement away from morningness.

We also found an effect of age group on subjective health: Older adults gave higher subjective health ratings than younger adults. While at first glance this may seem surprising, previous work suggests that older adults sometimes show a positivity effect when rating their health, particularly when an age-comparative reference point is used (Suls, Marco, & Tobin, 1991). It is possible that younger and older adults tested here used different reference points when evaluating their health.

Our results show that older adults report higher levels of positive affect and lower levels of negative affect compared to younger adults, replicating previous evidence of differences in emotional state across the life span (Carstensen et al., 2011; Mroczek & Kolarz, 1998; Stone et al., 2010). The data reported here demonstrate that morningness at least partially accounts for age differences in positive affect, suggesting that circadian rhythm or sleep timing mechanisms may contribute to greater positive affect in the senior years. These processes may or may not be separate from other theorized mechanisms, such as age-related improvements in emotion regulation (Carstensen, Isaacowitz, & Charles, 1999; Urry & Gross, 2010). It is possible that morningness interacts with improved emotion regulation to boost older adults' positive affect: For example, if morning-type older adults more effectively regulate emotions in the morning, they may be in a more positive state for the rest of the day (i.e., by "starting the day off right"). Improved emotion regulation in the morning might be predicted from findings that cognitive control processes (such as those used to enhance positive information; Mather & Carstensen, 2005)

Table 2
Spearman Rank Order Correlation Coefficients for Chronotype, Well-Being, and Age

Measure	1	2	3	4	5
Younger adults					
1. MEQ	—				
2. Positive affect	.25**	—			
3. Negative affect	−.04	−.21**	—		
4. Subjective health	.12*	.19**	−.19**	—	
5. Age	.02	.13*	−.04	.09	—
Older adults					
1. MEQ	—				
2. Positive affect	.19**	—			
3. Negative affect	−.08	−.34**	—		
4. Subjective health	.18*	.33**	−.22**	—	
5. Age	.02	−.04	−.09	.03	—

Note. MEQ = Morningness-Eveningness Questionnaire. The effect of time of measurement is factored out as a covariate.

*$p < .01$.   **$p < .001$.

Why might the researchers have found this difference in subjective health ratings between younger and older adults?

From this suggestion, what recommendations could we make for older adults?

What do you think is involved in emotion regulation (Chapter 9)?

What other factors would influence a person's mood?

In Chapter 10 you will learn about the dangers of sleep deprivation.

What are the benefits and drawbacks of self-report methods (Chapter 2)?

What are the strengths and weaknesses of using a cross-sectional design to study developmental differences? (Hint: you read about this in this chapter.)

function optimally in the morning among morning-type older adults (May & Hasher, 1998).

Our findings suggest that there are positive emotional consequences tied to morningness tendencies that are common among older adults. However, a number of limitations to this study should be noted. First, all measures were self-report; use of more specific circadian or sleep timing data would be helpful. Also, participants rated their current affective state only; future research using a trait measure that asks how participants usually feel would provide a more stable measure of individual differences in affect. An additional limitation is the use of a cross-sectional design. Some authors (e.g., Lindenberger, von Oertzen, Ghisletta, & Hertzog, 2011) have identified concerns about the use of meditational analyses to examine age-related variance in cross-sectional designs. Future longitudinal work that includes middle aged adults is needed to establish whether there are age-related changes in chronotype and affect that occur in parallel. Both retired older adults and, to a lesser extent, undergraduate students, are relatively free to determine morning rising times, and it is unclear how this may have influenced the pattern of results. The inclusion of adults who are working full time, and therefore less able to wake at their preferred time, would help determine how employment status may influence this association.

Why might morningness be beneficial to positive affect and health? One possibility is that morning-type individuals benefit from the close correspondence between societal expectations and their preferred

times for activity. In contrast, normal school and work schedules that begin early in the day force evening-type individuals to wake earlier than their preferred time, a phenomenon dubbed "social jetlag" that can result in sleep loss and emotional distress (Wittmann et al., 2006). It is possible that older adults are less vulnerable to these social jetlag effects because they are more likely to be morning types and therefore have a preferred time of day in line with societal expectations. They may also be less affected by these expectations if they are retired (Wittmann et al., 2006). Some evidence also suggests that biological mechanisms related to circadian and homeostatic sleep drives may contribute to the association between chronotype and affect. For example, morning light exposure, which results in a phase advance of the sleep/wake cycle, improves depressive symptoms in seasonal affective disorder (Lewy et al., 1998). In addition, shifting sleep earlier by 6 hr successfully alleviates nonseasonal depression in some cases (Wirz-Justice & Van den Hoofdakker, 1999). These improvements suggest that early sleep/wake times may have positive emotional effects. It is possible that shifts toward morningness can improve one's levels of positive affect and subjective health, and do so in a similar manner across the life span. Waking up early may indeed make one happy as a lark.

REFERENCES

Baron, R. M., & Kenny, D. A. (1986). The moderator-mediator variable distinction in social psychological research: Conceptual, strategic, and statistical considerations. *Journal of Personality and Social Psychology, 51,* 1173–1182. doi:10.1037/0022-3514.51.6.1173

Carstensen, L. L., Isaacowitz, D. M., & Charles, S. T. (1999). Taking time seriously: A theory of socioemotional selectivity. *American Psychologist, 54,* 165–181. doi:10.1037/0003-066X.54.3.165

Carstensen, L. L., Turan, B., Scheibe, S., Ram, N., Ersner-Hershfield, H., Samanez-Larkin, G. R., . . . Nesselroade, J. R. (2011). Emotional experience improves with age: Evidence based on over 10 years of experience sampling. *Psychology and Aging, 26,* 21–33. doi:10.1037/a0021285

Clark, L. A., Watson, D., & Leeka, J. (1989). Diurnal variation in the positive affects. *Motivation and Emotion, 13,* 205–234. doi:10.1007/ BF00995536

DeYoung, C. G., Hasher, L., Djikic, M., Criger, B., & Peterson, J. B. (2007). Morning people are stable people: Circadian rhythm and the higher-order factors of the Big Five. *Personality and Individual Differences, 43,* 267–276. doi:10.1016/j.paid.2006.11.030

Drennan, M. D., Klauber, M. R., Kripke, D. F., & Goyette, L. M. (1991). The effects of depression and age on the Horne-Ostberg morningnesseveningness score. *Journal of Affective Disorders, 23,* 93–98. doi:10.1016/0165-0327(91)90096-B

Froberg, J. E. (1977). Twenty-four-hour patterns in human performance, subjective and physiological variables and differences between morning and evening active subjects. *Biological Psychology, 5,* 119–134. doi:10.1016/0301-0511(77)90008-4

Hasler, B. P., Allen, J. J. B., Sbarra, D. A., Bootzin, R. R., & Bernert, R. A. (2010). Morningness-eveningness and depression: Preliminary evidence for the role of the behavioral activation system and positive affect. *Psychiatry Research, 176,* 166 –173. doi:10.1016/j.psychres.2009.06.006

Horne, J. A., & Ostberg, O. (1976). A self-assessment questionnaire to determine morningness-eveningness in human circadian rhythms. *International Journal of Chronobiology, 4,* 97–110.

Horne, J. A., & Ostberg, O. (1977). Individual differences in human circadian rhythms. *Biological Psychology, 5,* 179–190. doi:10.1016/ 0301-0511(77)90001-1

In this chapter you read about the longitudinal design.

Idler, E. L., & Benyamini, Y. (1997). Self-rated health and mortality: A review of twenty-seven community studies. *Journal of Health and Social Behavior, 38,* 21–37. doi:10.2307/2955359

Kerkhof, G. A. (1984). A Dutch-language questionnaire for the selection of morning and evening type individuals. *Nederlands Tijdschrift voor di Psychologie, 39,* 281–294.

Kim, S., Dueker, G. L., Hasher, L., & Goldstein, D. (2002). Children's time of day preference: Age, gender and ethnic differences. *Personality and Individual Differences, 33,* 1083–1090. doi:10.1016/S0191-8869(01)00214-8

Kitamura, S., Hida, A., Watanabe, M., Enomoto, M., Aritake-Okada, S., Moriguchi, Y., . . . Mishima, K. (2010). Evening preference is related to the incidence of depressive states independent of sleep-wake conditions. *Chronobiology International, 27,* 1797–1812. doi:10.3109/07420528.2010.516705

Lewy, A. J., Bauer, V. K., Cutler, N. L., Sack, R. L., Ahmed, S., Thomas, K. H., . . . Jackson, J. M. (1998). Morning vs. evening light treatment of patients with winter depression. *Archives of General Psychiatry, 55,* 890–896. doi:10.1001/archpsyc.55.10.890

Lindenberger, U., von Oertzen, T., Ghisletta, P., & Hertzog, C. (2011). Cross-sectional age variance extraction: What's change got to do with it? *Psychology and Aging, 26,* 34–47. doi:10.1037/a0020525

Mather, M., & Carstensen, L. L. (2005). Aging and motivated cognition: The positivity effect in attention and memory. *Trends in Cognitive Sciences, 9,* 496–502. doi:10.1016/j.tics.2005.08.005

May, C. P., & Hasher, L. (1998). Synchrony effects in inhibitory control over thought and action. *Journal of Experimental Psychology: Human Perception and Performance, 24,* 363–379. doi:10.1037/0096-1523.24.2.363

Mayer, J. D., & Gaschke, Y. N. (1988). The experience and meta-experience of mood. *Journal of Personality and Social Psychology, 55,* 102–111. doi:10.1037/0022-3514.55.1.102

Mecacci, L., Zani, A., Rocchetti, G., & Lucioli, R. (1986). The relationships between morningness-eveningness, ageing and personality. *Personality and Individual Differences, 7,* 911–913. doi:10.1016/0191-8869(86)90094-2

Mongrain, V., Carrier, J., & Dumont, M. (2006). Circadian and homeostatic sleep regulation in morningness–eveningness. *Journal of Sleep Research, 15,* 162–166. doi:10.1111/j.1365-2869.2006.00532.x

Mroczek, D. K., & Kolarz, C. M. (1998). The effect of age on positive and negative affect: A developmental perspective on happiness. *Journal of Personality and Social Psychology, 75,* 1333–1349. doi:10.1037/0022-3514.75.5.1333

Murray, G., Nicholas, C. L., Kleiman, J., Dwyer, R., Carrington, M. J., Allen, N. B., & Trinder, J. (2009). Nature's clocks and human mood: The circadian system modulates reward motivation. *Emotion, 9,* 705–716. doi:10.1037/a0017080

Paine, S-J., Gander, P. H., & Travier, N. (2006). The epidemiology of morningness/eveningness: Influence of age, gender, ethnicity, and socioeconomic factors in adults (30–49 years). *Journal of Biological Rhythms, 21,* 68–76. doi:10.1177/0748730405283154

Preacher, K. J., & Hayes, A. F. (2004). SPSS and SAS procedures for estimating indirect effects in simple mediation models. *Behavior Research Methods, Instruments, & Computers, 36,* 717–731. doi:10.3758/BF03206553

Randler, C. (2008). Morningness–eveningness and satisfaction with life. *Social Indicators Research, 86,* 297–302. doi:10.1007/s11205-007-9139-x

Roenneberg, T., Kuehnle, T., Juda, M., Kantermann, T., Allebrandt, K., Gordijn, M., & Merrow, M. (2007). Epidemiology of the human circadian clock. *Sleep Medicine Reviews, 11,* 429–438. doi:10.1016/j.smrv.2007.07.005

Soehner, A. M., Kennedy, K. S., & Monk, T. H. (2007). Personality correlates with sleep-wake variables. *Chronobiology International, 24,* 889–903. doi:10.1080/07420520701648317

Stone, A. A., Schwartz, J. E., Broderick, J. E., & Deaton, A. (2010). A snapshot of the age distribution of psychological well-being in the United States. *Proceedings of the National Academy of Sciences, USA, 107,* 9985–9990. doi:10.1073/pnas.1003744107

Suls, J., Marco, C. A., & Tobin, S. (1991). The role of temporal comparison, social comparison, and direct appraisal in the elderly's self-evaluations of health. *Journal of Applied Social Psychology, 21,* 1125–1144. doi:10.1111/j.1559-1816.1991.tb00462.x

Urry, H. L., & Gross, J. J. (2010). Emotion regulation in older age. *Current Directions in Psychological Science, 19,* 352–357. doi:10.1177/0963721410388395

Van Cauter, E., Leproult, R., & Plat, L. (2000). Age-related changes in slow wave sleep and REM sleep and relationship with growth hormone and cortisol levels in healthy men. *Journal of the American Medical Association, 284,* 861–868. doi:10.1001/jama.284.7.861

Watson, D., Wiese, D., Vaidya, J., & Tellegen, A. (1999). The two general activation systems of affect: Structural findings, evolutionary considerations, and psychobiological evidence. *Journal of Personality and Social Psychology, 76,* 820–838. doi:10.1037/0022-3514.76.5.820

Wirz-Justice, A., & Van den Hoofdakker, R. H. (1999). Sleep deprivation in depression: What do we know, where do we go? *Biological Psychiatry, 46,* 445–453. doi:10.1016/S0006-3223(99)00125-0

Wittmann, M., Dinich, J., Merrow, M., & Roenneberg, T. (2006). Social jetlag: Misalignment of biological and social time. *Chronobiology International, 23,* 497–509. doi:10.1080/07420520500545979

Zavada, A., Gordijn, M., Beersma, D., Daan, S., & Roenneberg, T. (2005). Comparison of the Munich Chronotype Questionnaire with the Horne-Östberg's Morningness-Eveningness score. *Chronobiology International, 22,* 267–278. doi:10.1081/CBI-200053536

HUMAN
DEVELOPMENT II
Social Development

HOW DO WE FORM BONDS OF ATTACHMENT?
WHAT ROLES DO PEERS PLAY IN SOCIAL DEVELOPMENT?
HOW DO WE DEVELOP MORALITY?

New mothers

are often said to "light up" when they talk about their little bundles of joy. But research (Strathearn, Li, Fonagy, & Montague, 2008) has shown that when it comes to seeing their babies smile, the expression is more than just figurative. Specifically, the image of a newborn baby smiling activates the dopamine-associated reward centres of a mother's brain, causing the areas to "light up," or become more active, on MRI scans. In effect, when new mothers see their babies smiling, they get a "natural high."

In this study, researchers monitored the brain activity of 28 new mothers while they viewed photos of their own babies, as well as photos of unknown infants, aged between five and ten months. In some photos, the infants were smiling; in others, they had a neutral expression; and in the rest of the photos, the infants were crying.

The results of the study showed that when mothers viewed images of their own babies smiling, all of the reward-processing areas of the brain were activated, but this was not the case when they viewed an unknown baby's smiling face. Surprisingly, when the mothers viewed photos of a baby crying, it made no difference whether the mothers were looking at their own baby or an unknown baby—neurologically, the results were the same. It seems that new mothers are able to empathize with a distressed infant whether the child is related to them or not.

So what does this mean in terms of human relationships? The study is an important step in understanding the brain processes that strengthen the bond between mothers and babies. Further research could explain how a crying infant triggers an angry response in some mothers, or how maternal depression affects brain responses.

The bond between a mother and a baby is an intense emotional connection. But how does it develop, and why is it so important?

<<< One of the most powerful human relationships is the bond between a mother and her newborn baby. The emotional ties between a child and his or her caregiver are often studied by developmental psychologists. They are interested in learning how emotional attachment develops and how it affects individual people throughout their lives.

CHAPTER **07**

Attachment

As we develop, we become attuned to the behavioural norms within society. We may learn that getting a good education is a valuable asset, while being naked in public after the age of six or seven is a cultural no-no. This process of **socialization,** in which we shape our behavioural patterns according to the values of the society we live in, begins almost at birth. Our behaviour is influenced both by people—our parents, relatives, friends, and teachers—and by institutions—our schools, places of worship, and workplaces.

The emotional bond that newborns share with their caregivers is called **attachment,** a term developed by psychologist John Bowlby in the 1950s. Bowlby believed that emotional ties between a child and caregiver developed out of instinct (Bowlby, 1969). Babies will smile and coo when they are near their caregivers, and whimper when the caregivers go away. They recognize familiar faces and voices and show preferences for them. At about eight months of age, this preference becomes even stronger and develops into a fear of strangers, called **stranger anxiety.** If you have ever attempted to greet an infant sitting next to you in a restaurant and been met with loud, disapproving screams, you should not take it personally. Stranger anxiety is a survival strategy that enables babies to perceive unfamiliar faces as potentially threatening.

ORIGINS OF ATTACHMENT
Body Contact

Why do we bond with our caregivers? Psychologists initially believed that infants become attached to people who provide them with nourishment. However, a 1950s study by University of Wisconsin psychologist Harry Harlow showed otherwise.

Socialization is the process through which a person shapes his or her behavioural patterns according to the society he or she lives in.

Attachment is an emotional bond that newborns share with their caregivers.

Stranger anxiety is fear of strangers.

Critical period is the optimal time period shortly after birth during which normal sensory and perceptual development takes place.

Imprinting is a process of early attachment in which the first thing a newborn sees is considered its mother.

While working with infant monkeys that had been separated from their mothers, Harlow noticed that the infants became strongly attached to the cloth pads used to cover the floors of their cages. When the cloths were taken away from the young monkeys, they threw violent temper tantrums. Infant monkeys raised in bare wire-mesh cages without a cloth pad survived with difficulty, if at all. Although the cloths provided no nourishment, they seemed to be important to the monkeys' development.

To test his theory, Harlow created two artificial mothers. One was a bare wire cylinder, while the other was a wooden cylinder covered in sponge rubber and soft terry cloth. Both types of surrogate mothers were placed in the monkeys' cages, but only one type provided nourishment. Harlow discovered that whether or not the cloth mother provided nourishment, the infant monkeys invariably preferred it, spending a greater amount of time clinging to the cloth surrogate than the wire surrogate. His results indicated the importance of body contact from a comforting caregiver (Harlow, 1958).

Human infants similarly become attached to parents who are soft and warm and who provide gentle contact. Emotional communication through touch not only facilitates attachment, but also is a vital part of our development.

Familiarity

Familiarity is also vital to attachment. You may remember from Chapter 4 that adults who are born blind and have cataracts removed later in life never fully regain their sight. In many animals, there is a similar **critical period,** during which exposure to certain stimuli produces proper development. For example, the first moving object that a gosling, duckling, or chick sees after it hatches is usually its mother. From this point onward, the young bird will follow her and only her. This process of early attachment is called **imprinting.**

But what if the first thing that a duckling sees is a car, or a sheepdog, or a young child on a tricycle? Konrad Lorenz (1937) explored this concept by ensuring that he was the first moving creature seen by newly hatched

^ ^ ^ Wherever **Konrad Lorenz** went, his gaggle of **imprinted geese** would follow.

goslings. The result was an instant team of devoted followers. Similar studies have proved that although birds imprint best to their own species, they will imprint to any number of moving objects, forming a bond that is difficult to break.

While children do not imprint, they do become attached to what they are familiar with. Mere exposure to a particular person or object encourages attachment. Former babysitters may recall being asked to read the same bedtime story, perform the same card trick, or sing the same song to their charges for the hundredth time. For children, familiarity is a sign of safety and contentment.

DIFFERENCES IN ATTACHMENT

Does the behaviour of the main caregiver affect attachment? Psychologist Mary Ainsworth (1979), who studied at the University of Toronto, developed a "strange situation" test, in which one-year-old infants were briefly separated from their mothers and left to play in a new environment under a stranger's supervision. Watching how the infants responded to their mothers' return, Ainsworth noted several different types of attachment:

* **Secure:** The majority of infants that Ainsworth studied were labelled as secure. These

children were quite happy to play in their new environment while their mothers were present, became upset when she left, but were soon comforted by parental contact upon their mother's return.

- **Anxious-ambivalent:** Ambivalent infants were ill at ease to begin with, and became extremely distressed when their mothers left the room. They were difficult to soothe, even when their mothers returned. Infants often displayed a mixed reaction to their mothers' return, simultaneously demanding to be picked up and pushing or kicking their mothers away.
- **Anxious-avoidant:** Avoidant children did not appear to be particularly distressed when their mothers left the room. Upon the mothers' return, infants actively ignored their mothers and instead focused on a toy or other object in the room.

Subsequent researchers added a further category to Ainsworth's findings (Main & Hesse, 1990):

- **Disorganized-disoriented:** Infants who were labelled disorganized did not have a consistent response to their mother's return. They seemed unable to decide how they should react, suggesting a lack of a coherent coping pattern.

Ainsworth's results correlated with the behaviour of the infants' mothers. Mothers who were loving, warm, and sensitive to their child's needs had secure babies, while mothers who were unresponsive or insensitive had anxious, insecure children. Is it possible that the inattentive mothers' brain processes differed from their attentive counterparts? Further research may shed light on why some mothers do not bond as well with their children.

Limitations of the Strange Situation Test

Critics of Ainsworth's test have pointed out that placing young children in an unfamiliar situation may not capture the interaction between mother and child in less stressful circumstances. The temperament of the infant may also affect the mother's reaction. For example, a child with a high reactive, or generally anxious, temperament is naturally hard to soothe, no matter how attentive the mother. Some Japanese researchers believe that the test is not a valid measurement of attachment in their culture because Japanese infants are rarely separated from their mothers (Miyake, Chen, & Campos, 1985). Finally, researchers have noted that the behaviour of

children may differ when separated from their mother in a laboratory setting, thereby limiting the generalizability of the strange situation test (Kappenberg & Halpern, 2006).

Relationships Throughout the Lifespan

In most cultures, from the age of four or five onward, we spend more time with our peers than with our parents. Our relationships with the people we surround ourselves with play an important role in our social development.

> Remember how you used to play "Duck, Duck, Goose"? Or the time you dressed up as your favourite superhero and saved the world with your trusty sidekick? You were actually learning important socialization skills. Children play in every culture, and the way they interact is surprisingly universal.

THE ROLE OF PLAY

Remember how you used to play "Duck, Duck, Goose"? Or the time you dressed up as your favourite superhero and saved the world with your trusty sidekick? You were actually learning important socialization skills. Children play in every culture, and the way they interact is surprisingly universal.

Gender Segregation

Children develop gender awareness at a very young age, and they play in groups segregated by sex. By doing so, they develop the gender-specific skills and attitudes of their culture. If you walk into an elementary school playground, you will most likely see large groups of boys playing competitive, rough-and-tumble games, while the groups of girls are generally smaller and geared toward maintaining group cohesion. It's a division psychologist Eleanor Maccoby describes as "the two cultures of childhood" (Maccoby, 1998).

Human-Specific Skills

Play helps children develop the skills they need in later life. A simple game of tag encourages physical stamina and agility, while playing with dolls encourages a nurturing role. Both chase games and play nurturing are universal across cultures. Similarly, constructive play such as building brick towers or creating a play den out of boxes helps children develop skills in making things with their hands. Word play helps to develop language skills, while fantasy role-playing exercises children's imagination.

Cultural Skills and Values

If you study children playing in a particular culture, it is often possible to see how their play reflects the values and skills of the

Is the **behaviour of adults** in a society reflected through **children's play?**

∨∨∨

society they live in. Anthropologist Douglas Fry studied the behaviour of children ages three to eight in two Zapotec communities in Mexico. While the play methods in the two villages were very similar—boys played with toy plows and girls made pretend tortillas—the communities differed in one crucial aspect. Villagers in La Paz valued peacefulness and discouraged play fighting. Children rarely witnessed violence between their parents. In San Andrés, however, violence was common. Children witnessed adults fighting each other at parties and siblings beating each other with sticks. Play fighting was actively encouraged and took place three times more often than in La Paz. Fry concluded that aggression was the result of learned social behaviour, which begins in childhood (Fry, 1992; 2006; 2007).

Learning Social Rules

How do we learn acceptable forms of behaviour? Development psychologist Jean Piaget argued that unsupervised play with peers is critical to moral development (Piaget, 1932). It enables children to resolve their own conflicts and develop an understanding of social rules based on reasoning, rather than authority. In other words, little Jason learns to give the toy truck to little Tommy because he reasons that it is fair to take turns, not because his parents threaten to deny him his favourite TV show for three weeks if he doesn't comply. To further support Piaget's clams, psychologist Ann Kruger found that children's moral development is strengthened more when youngsters discuss social dilemmas with their peers than when they discuss them with their parents (Kruger, 1992).

Can playing by the rules develop our self-control? Russian psychologist Lev Vygotsky believed that children learn to control their natural impulses while playing by sticking to the rules of the game. For example, if a child imagines herself to be the mother and her doll to be the child, she will obey the rules of maternal behaviour (Vygotsky, 1978). Play allows children to practise self-discipline, a concept known as **self-regulation.** In support of this idea, researchers have found that young children put a lot of effort into planning and reinforcing the rules in fantasy role play. Good-humoured babysitters may have found themselves clad in capes and leotards while playing dress-up with children, only to be scornfully informed by their charges that "Superman doesn't run like that." Despite their occasional criticism of their babysitters' acting skills, these types of kids are more likely to grow up to be well-adjusted members of society: Positive correlations have been found between the amount of social fantasy role play children engage in and their subsequent levels of self-confidence and self-control (Elias & Berk, 2002).

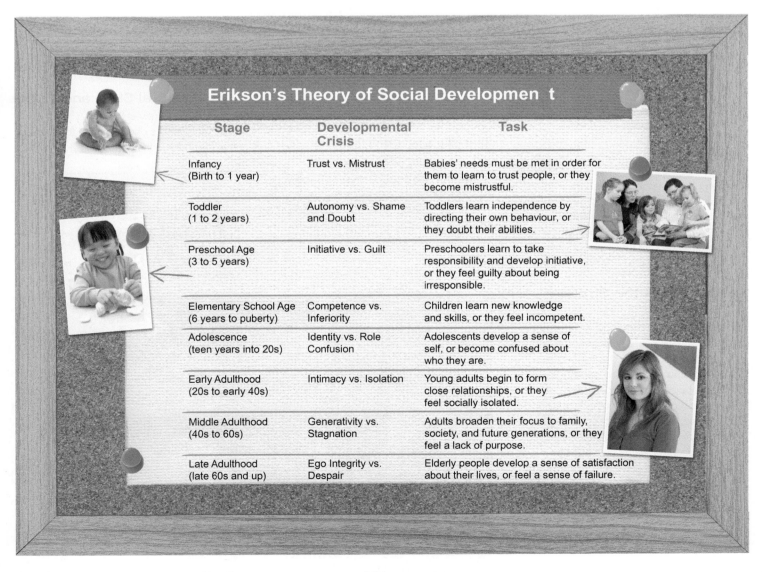

Erikson's Theory of Social Development

Stage	Developmental Crisis	Task
Infancy (Birth to 1 year)	Trust vs. Mistrust	Babies' needs must be met in order for them to learn to trust people, or they become mistrustful.
Toddler (1 to 2 years)	Autonomy vs. Shame and Doubt	Toddlers learn independence by directing their own behaviour, or they doubt their abilities.
Preschool Age (3 to 5 years)	Initiative vs. Guilt	Preschoolers learn to take responsibility and develop initiative, or they feel guilty about being irresponsible.
Elementary School Age (6 years to puberty)	Competence vs. Inferiority	Children learn new knowledge and skills, or they feel incompetent.
Adolescence (teen years into 20s)	Identity vs. Role Confusion	Adolescents develop a sense of self, or become confused about who they are.
Early Adulthood (20s to early 40s)	Intimacy vs. Isolation	Young adults begin to form close relationships, or they feel socially isolated.
Middle Adulthood (40s to 60s)	Generativity vs. Stagnation	Adults broaden their focus to family, society, and future generations, or they feel a lack of purpose.
Late Adulthood (late 60s and up)	Ego Integrity vs. Despair	Elderly people develop a sense of satisfaction about their lives, or feel a sense of failure.

Age-Mixed Play

Although the traditional, age- and grade-based educational system in the North America does not encourage age-mixed play, social interactions between younger and older children can have several advantages. Children of different ages tend to be less competitive with each other, and younger children are able to learn more advanced skills by watching their older peers (Brown & Palinscar, 1986). Conversely, older children learn how to nurture their younger counterparts by helping them, which promotes healthy social interaction (Ludeke & Hartup, 1983).

ADOLESCENCE

We've all been through it—one day everything makes sense and the next we're moody, we're confused, and our parents are threatening to put us up for adoption. Adolescence is the famously awkward period in life in which our **identity,** or our sense of self, becomes a critical part of our relationships with others. Psychologist Carl Jung believed that we do not establish a sense of self until we reach adolescence.

A Search for Identity

Do all teenagers go through an identity crisis? Theorist Erik Erikson (1963) believed that every stage of life has a crisis in need of a resolution and that the plight of the adolescent is to experience identity versus role confusion—establishing a sense of self by deciding on individual beliefs and value systems. Which political party should I support? What do I think about religion? Which career path should I choose? Adolescence is a time of transition and confusion.

To form an identity, most adolescents will find themselves trying out different roles— the diligent student at school, the clown among friends, the moody teenager at home. Eventually, as the adolescent develops a stronger sense of self, these roles fuse into one cohesive identity. However, Erikson noticed that some adolescents form their identities

Conforming to a particular peer group can help adolescents form a sense of identity. >>>

much earlier than others by taking on parents' values and expectations. Other adolescents adopt a negative identity that deliberately opposes their parents' views, while still others align themselves with a particular peer group, proving there is an element of truth to teen movies like *Mean Girls* that group together stereotypical goths, jocks, and geeks.

Erikson believed that once we have a clear and comfortable self, we are ready to develop intimacy—close relationships with others.

> 66 For many parents, the possibility of negative peer pressure luring their child into a world of alcohol, drugs, and casual sex is a constant source of worry. Research suggests that these fears are well founded— teenagers of the same friendship group usually indulge in similar risky behaviours, and teens who start smoking usually do so because one of their friends offered them cigarettes or made it look cool (Rose, Chassin, Presson, & Sherman, 1999). 99

Conflict in Adolescence

Adolescence can be a difficult time, but are teenagers really as rebellious and scornful as pop culture suggests? Not exactly: Studies frequently demonstrate that most teens admire their parents and support their religious and political beliefs. Conflicts usually arise over deceptively minor topics such as hairstyles and clothing, but

---

Self-regulation is the process of practising self-discipline.

Identity is a person's sense of self.

Clique is a small, same-sex group of three to nine members who share intimate secrets and see themselves as best friends.

---

these parent-child spats often boil down to a much more basic issue—control. Adolescents want to be treated as adults, while parents worry that allowing their teens too much freedom exposes them to alcohol, drugs, and other potential dangers. Intense conflict usually occurs during the early teen years. The battle for independence is usually resolved in the late teens, when many adolescents and their parents manage to establish some sort of balance between childhood dependence and self-sufficiency.

Peer Support

If you got your heart broken in high school, it's likely that the first person you called to help you through that traumatic, near-death experience was a friend rather than a parent. Adolescents increasingly turn to their peers for emotional support, enabling greater independence from their parents and a stronger sense of self.

Australian researcher Dexter Dunphy (1963) identified two kinds of peer groups: cliques and crowds. **Cliques** are small, same-sex groups of three to nine members who share intimate secrets and see themselves as best friends. However, even if you pinky swore to be

best friends forever with Tori and Lisa in seventh grade, you may have found that by tenth grade, your soul mates had become mere passing acquaintances. Cliques tend to break down by mid-adolescence, giving way to more loosely associated groups. **Crowds** are larger, mixed-sex groups who tend to get together socially on weekends, often for parties. Crowds of boys and girls interact, and the gender barriers that were so firmly established in childhood break down, increasing the number of opposite-sex peers in an adolescent's social network.

Peer Pressure

If you've ever been dumped by a former best friend or shunned in the cafeteria, you're well aware that social ostracism, especially among teens, can be vicious and painful. Being a social outcast as an adolescent is often seen as a fate worse than death, resulting in groups of teen clones all anxious to fit in by talking, dressing, and acting like their peers. For many parents, the possibility of negative peer pressure luring their child into a world of alcohol, drugs, and casual sex is a constant source of worry. Research suggests that these fears are well founded— teenagers of the same friendship group usually indulge in similar risky behaviours, and teens who start smoking usually do so because one of their friends offered them cigarettes or made it look cool (Rose et al., 1999). While the selection effect—choosing friends who have similar interests and behaviours—partly explains peer similarities, friends usually become increasingly similar to each other in terms of frequent smoking, drinking, or other risky behaviour.

Although peer pressure is usually seen in a negative light, it can have positive effects. For example, teens in China often meet to do homework together and encourage each other to do well academically. Parents and teachers in China view peer pressure as a positive influence.

Adolescent Sexuality

During elementary school, you probably viewed members of the opposite sex as the enemy, or at best ignored them completely. Then, all of a sudden, that red-haired guy in your art class started looking strangely attractive. While girls develop physically earlier than boys do, the onset of sexual interest occurs at the same time for both boys and girls. This suggests that **adrenal androgen,** the hormone that increases in production during puberty, plays an important role in the development of sexual interest.

Sexuality is a confusing issue for adolescents in industrialized cultures: Although teens have the ability to reproduce, they are not socially accepted as adults. While being bombarded with sexually suggestive advertisements, magazines, and television shows, teens are expected to abstain from sexual activity, and those who are sexually active are often associated with delinquency.

The United States has the highest teen pregnancy rate in the Western world. Every year, almost 750 000 adolescents between ages 15 and 19 become pregnant (Guttmacher Institute, 2006), and nearly one-third of the pregnancies end in abortion. Teen moms are less likely to graduate from high school, less likely to improve their economic status, and less likely to sustain long-term marriages (Coley & Chase-Lansdale, 1998).

While these statistics may seem alarming, the teen pregnancy rate in the United States is actually the lowest it's been in the past 30 years. In 2006, Canada had the lowest teen birth/abortion rate per 1000 women aged 15 to 19 (27.9) followed by Sweden (31.4), England/Wales (60.3), and the United States (61.2) (SIECCAN, 2010). In 2008, the rate of teen births in Canada continued to fall to 12.0 births per 1000 teenagers (Statistics Canada, 2012). According to Alexander McKay from the Sex Information and Education Council of Canada, sex education, easier access to birth control, and reducing socioeconomic inequality are key factors in preventing teen pregnancy (SIECCAN, 2010). In addition, parents' increased willingness to discuss sex openly with their children and teenagers appears to be convincing adolescents to practise safe sex.

> "What do you do with a B.A. in English? What is my life going to be? Four years of college and plenty of knowledge have earned me this useless degree. I can't pay the bills yet 'cause I have no skills yet. The world is a big scary place. But somehow I can't shake the feeling I might make a difference to the human race."
>
> —*Avenue Q,* Broadway musical

EMERGING ADULTHOOD

The term *quarter-life crisis* was coined to capture that unsettled period in life between adolescence and early adulthood. A generation or two ago, people were expected to reach sexual maturity, find a job, get married, and have children, all within the space of a couple of years. But increasing opportunities for higher education, combined with numerous career choices, has meant that, in industrialized cultures, adolescents are taking more time to finish college, fly the ever-comfortable nest, and establish their independence. In Canada, the average age for a first marriage has gradually increased over the past 20 years. In 1972, the average age was 24.9 years for men and 22.5 years for women, and in 2008, the average age was 31.1 years for men and 29.1 years for women (Statistics Canada, 2012).

It's not unusual for people in their 20s to ask their parents for a little help paying the rent, buying a car, or moving into a new apartment. Throughout this phase of life, which some have dubbed **emerging adulthood** (Arnett, 2000), it is all too tempting to return to the family home when an exam result is not what we expected or we are having difficulty settling into a new job. In fact, in 2006, 1.74 million Canadians between the ages of 20 and 29 lived with their parents, a 2.5% increase from 2001 (Statistics Canada, 2007; 2012). This period of uncertainty is usually resolved by the later 20s, when people tend to achieve total independence from parental support and develop the ability to empathize with others as fellow adults.

ADULTHOOD

At what age do people buy their first house? How old are first-time parents? When should we aim to retire? Whereas childhood and adolescence are punctuated by formal rites of passage that occur at roughly the same time, adulthood is less predictable. Behavioural scientist Bernice Neugarten emphasized the difference between **chronological age,** the amount of time that has passed since we were born, and **social age,** our maturity level based on life experiences (Neugarten, 1996). In today's society, not everyone enters the workplace at 18 and retires at 65. Some people transition from adolescence to adulthood much later than others, while many continue working well into their 80s.

What defines an adult? Erikson's lifespan theory proposes that the ability to establish intimate, caring relationships and find fulfillment are primary tasks of early and middle adulthood. Similarly, Freud (1935) defined emotional maturity as the capacity to both love and work.

Love and Marriage

People are often said to be "insanely in love," a phrase that implies that romance and sanity aren't altogether compatible. While being in love won't actually drive you crazy, it does cause specific brain activity. Remember how a picture of a baby's smile can activate the reward centres of the mother's brain? The neural and hormonal mechanisms of mating bonds between two adults are similar to the bonds between an infant and a caregiver. Partners feel most secure and confident when they are together, and they may even show physiological evidence of distress when they are separated. It is not uncommon for elderly couples to die within a few days of each other, apparently unable to bear life alone.

Just as infants form different types of attachments with their caregivers, adult relationships can be characterized by partners' behaviours. In a **secure relationship**, both partners provide each other with comfort and security. An **anxious relationship** is characterized by worry about love or a lack of love from a partner. In an **avoidant relationship**, there is little expression of intimacy, and partners may be ambivalent about commitment.

Studies have shown that people's descriptions of their adult romantic attachments are closely related to their recollections of early relationships with their parents. For example, those who were rated as having more positive, loving relationships with their mothers as children became more trusting adults. They were therefore more likely to seek comfort from their romantic partners and enjoy an honest, open relationship with them (Black & Schutte, 2006).

We usually consider marriages to be strong if they're based on emotional and material support, intimacy, and mutual shared interests, although long-term married couples may not necessarily share the same hobbies. Sometimes the strength of an emotional bond between partners is revealed only

after a divorce or the death of a partner, when the remaining partner may experience long periods of grief and depression.

So why do some marriages work and others fail? In Canada, roughly 40% of marriages ends in divorce. In 2006, unmarried Canadians outnumbered married Canadians—51.5% to 48.5%—for the first time in history (Statistics Canada, 2007; 2012). Statistically, marriage is most likely to last when couples marry after the age of 20 and are well educated. In interviews and on questionnaires, happily married couples also:

- consistently say they like each other
- use the term *we* rather than *I* when describing their activities
- value interdependence more than dependence
- discuss their individual commitments to the marriage
- argue as much as unhappily married couples, but do so constructively
- remain sensitive to the unspoken needs and feelings of their spouse

So how can we become part of a happily married couple? Many people think that testing a relationship by cohabiting before marriage is a good way to iron out any potential problems. Many couples happily cohabit, and those who do often get married, but studies have shown that couples who live together before marriage are more likely to divorce than non-cohabiting couples (Myers, 2000). Keep in mind that this finding is a correlation, not a causal link: Couples

who choose not to cohabit due to strong religious or moral beliefs may also be less likely to divorce based on those same beliefs, while couples who believe it's morally acceptable to cohabit may also find it easier to accept the idea of divorce if their marriages deteriorate.

What about having kids? While seeing a newborn baby may activate the pleasure centres in Mom's brain, research has shown that parents usually report a lower level of marital

Crowd is a large, mixed-sex group whose members get together socially.

Adrenal androgen is a hormone that increases in production during puberty.

Emerging adulthood is the period during a person's early 20s in which that person often still greatly depends on his or her parents for financial and emotional support.

Chronological age is the amount of time that has passed since a person was born.

Social age describes a person's maturity level based on his or her life experiences.

Secure relationship is an intimate relationship in which both partners provide each other with comfort and security.

Anxious relationship is an intimate relationship characterized by worry about love or lack of love from a partner.

Avoidant relationship is an intimate relationship in which there is ambivalence about commitment and little expression of intimacy.

>>> **Wedded bliss increases our levels of overall contentment.**

satisfaction than do non-parents, and that the more children a couple has, the less marital satisfaction they report. Employed women, who often find themselves overwhelmed with juggling their careers along with the bulk of household chores, are particularly likely to report marital discontent (Belsky, Lang, & Huston, 1986).

Despite the odds being stacked against newly married couples, the institution of marriage is showing no signs of collapse. Far from being threatened by gloomy divorce statistics, many gay couples are currently campaigning for the right to marry. In Western cultures, three in four adults who divorce will remarry, and their second marriage is likely to be pretty much as happy as an average first marriage (Vemer, Coleman, Ganang, & Cooper, 1989).

Marriage is a good general predictor of happiness, health, sexual satisfaction, and income level. Most Canadians report that they are very satisfied with their marriage. Married people report higher levels of life satisfaction and happiness, better mental and physical health, fewer suicides, and lower mortality rates compared to unmarried people. Men seem to benefit more from being married than women, and men report higher levels of martial satisfaction compared to women (Roberts et al., 2005). Lesbian couples also report being happier than single lesbian women (Wayment & Peplau, 1995). Canadian researchers Elizabeth Clearwater and Carol Harvey (2007) report that, among lower-income Canadians, the best predictors for marital satisfaction are companionship, money management, and husband's occupation. And if you live in a neighbourhood with a high

marriage rate, you are likely to benefit from a low crime rate, few delinquent teenagers, and low numbers of children with emotional disorders (Myers, 2000).

Employment

We spend about a third of our adult lives working, so it makes sense to choose a job that doesn't fill us with a growing sense of dread every Sunday evening at the thought of returning to work the next day. At its best, work has the same psychological benefits for adults as play does for children. It brings people into social contact with peers outside of their family, presents problems to be solved, and offers us a chance to improve our physical and intellectual skills.

Most Canadians report that they are satisfied with their jobs (Roberts et al., 2005). Work is perceived as enjoyable if it is complex rather than simple, varied rather than routine, and not closely supervised by another. Sociologist Melvin Kohn refers to these desired job characteristics as **occupational self-direction** (Kohn, 1977). Jobs with high occupational self-direction enable a worker to make many choices and decisions throughout the day. Surprisingly, despite the high demands that these jobs pose, most people find them less stressful than jobs in which workers make few decisions and are under close supervision.

Since it became socially acceptable in the 1960s for women to juggle a career and a family, the combination of raising children, completing housework, and holding down a paid job has become a fine balancing act. Although men are more involved in housework and child care than they were 30 years ago, the bulk of household chores usually falls to women. The most recent figures from the University of Wisconsin's National Survey of Families and Households show that the average wife does 31 hours of housework per week, while the average husband does just 14 hours' worth of household chores (Belkin, 2008). Despite the additional workload, most women report that having a paid job increases their self-esteem (Elliott, 1996), and most say that they would continue to work even if they didn't need the money (Schwartz, 1994).

GROWING OLDER

Baby boomers, those multitudes of North Americans born between the end of World War II and the early 1960s, are throwing sixtieth birthday celebrations across the country even as you read this. Life expectancies are increasing throughout most of the world. In Canada, for example, there will be over 14 000 individuals aged 100 years or older by 2031. Canada's

Why might **older people** report **more satisfaction** with their lives than **younger people** do?

aging population prompted the government to establish a Special Senate Committee on Aging (Aging, 2009) that recently put forward several recommendations aimed at promoting positive aging and inclusiveness among all Canadians.

Ageism, or prejudice against the elderly, often leads to negative stereotyping that can cause isolation and poor self-image among members of the older community. When reporter Pat Moore disguised herself as an 85-year-old woman and wandered the streets of more than 100 cities in the United States, she was ignored, treated rudely, and nearly beaten to death by a mugger, because she was seen as an easy target. Most people assumed she was hard of hearing and shouted at her, or pushed ahead of her in grocery store lines (Moore, 1985).

While aging does involve many losses—physical strength, agility, sensory acuity, and memory, as well as the loss of employability and other social roles—most elderly people report that old age isn't as bad as young people seem to think. Many assume that the years after age 65 are the worst time of life (Freedman, 1978); however, ratings of life satisfaction actually increase after middle age (Mroczek, 2001). In a surprising "paradox of aging," elderly people report greater enjoyment of life than do middle-aged people, who in turn report greater enjoyment of life than do young adults. While you might regard old age as a long, slow walk to death, when you get there, the stroll might not actually be so bad.

Theories of Aging

What motivates us when we no longer have to get up for work in the morning? How do we feel when our children suddenly stop needing parental support? According to the **disengagement theory of aging** (Cumming & Henry, 1961), elderly people gradually and willingly withdraw themselves from the world around them. In preparation for death, members of the older generation sever all social ties and become increasingly preoccupied with their own memories, thoughts, and feelings. Cumming and Henry theorized that this enabled a transfer of power from the older generation to the younger generation, making it possible for society to continue functioning after its individual members die.

In contrast, the **activity theory of aging** (Havinghurst, 1957) suggests that elderly people are happiest when they stay active and involved in the community. Contrary to

the view that the elderly willingly disengage themselves from the outside world, the activity theory proposes that disengagement takes place only when people are forced to retire or are no longer invited to social engagements.

Recent research has shifted from the question of whether elderly people prefer to

> "Age is an issue of mind over matter. If you don't mind, it doesn't matter."
> —Mark Twain, novelist (1835–1910)

be active to questions about the types of activities they choose and their reasons for choosing those activities. Laura Carstensen (1991) proposed the **socioemotional selectivity theory of aging,** suggesting that as people grow older and realize that the time they have left is limited, they focus on enjoying the present rather than looking to the future. Elderly people pay more attention to people with whom they have close emotional ties, and spend less time with casual acquaintances. Couples in long-term marriages become closer, marital satisfaction increases, and ties with children, grandchildren, and long-term friends are strengthened. Those who continue working into old age report a higher level of enjoyment than they had when they were younger because they are more interested in maintaining social relationships with colleagues than with career progression.

Memory and Mood

We might become more wrinkled and less inclined to go bungee jumping, but at least one good thing comes from aging—we begin to tune out bad memories. Carstensen and her colleagues conducted a series of experiments in which they showed young adults (age 18–29), middle adults (age 41–53), and elderly adults (age 65–80) pictures displaying positive, negative, and neutral scenes. Each group was then asked to recall and describe as many pictures from memory as possible. The results showed that older people recalled fewer scenes overall, indicating a decline in memory with age. However, whereas the younger group remembered both positive and negative scenes, the older group recalled more positive images than negative images, suggesting that as we age, we are able to pay selective attention to the positive (Munsey, 2007).

Neurological studies on the same topic show that although an older adult's amygdala, a centre of emotion in the brain, is likely to show less activity in reaction to negative events than a younger adult's amygdala does, both elderly and younger brains show the same responsiveness to positive occurrences (Mather et al., 2004). In other words, it appears that as we get older, we learn not to let negative emotions drag us down.

Why do we rarely see elderly adults jumping up and down with excitement? It's not just due to older bodies—as we age, our moods become less extreme but more enduring. Whereas adolescents deal with emotions that quickly range from elation to despair, the mood swings of older people are much less extreme. Although they feel fewer periods of intense excitement, they also suffer from fewer periods of extreme depression (Costa et al., 1987).

Moral Development

If you found $20 on the street, would you keep it? What if the money were inside an unmarked wallet with no identification? Now imagine that you saw the money fall from a stranger's jacket. Would you pocket the cash or hand it back? Developing character and learning to distinguish between right and wrong is an important part of adolescence. Developmental psychologist Lawrence Kohlberg (1981, 1984) built on Piaget's idea that children's moral judgment is based on their cognitive development. He assessed moral reasoning by presenting people with hypothetical scenarios and asking them how they thought the person in the scenario should act. Here is one of Kohlberg's scenarios called the "Heinz Dilemma":

> In Europe, a woman was near death from a special kind of cancer. There was one drug that the doctors thought might save her. It was a form of radium that a druggist in the same town had recently discovered. The drug was expensive to make, but the druggist was charging ten times what the drug cost him to make. He paid $200 for the radium and charged $2000 for a small dose of the drug. The sick woman's husband, Heinz, went to everyone he knew to borrow the money, but he could only get together about $1000, which is half

Kohlberg's Ladder of Moral Reasoning

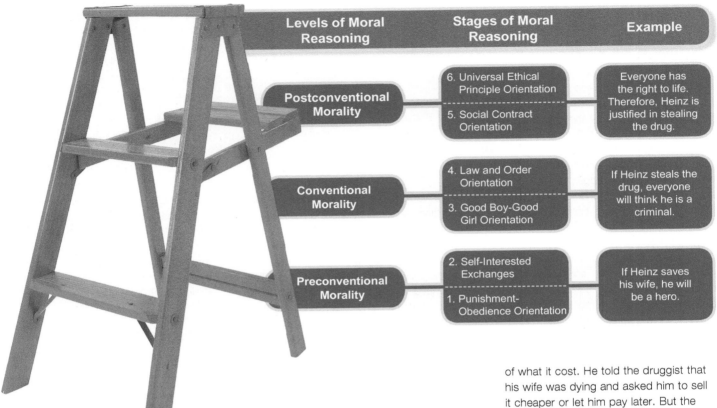

Levels of Moral Reasoning	Stages of Moral Reasoning	Example
Postconventional Morality	6. Universal Ethical Principle Orientation 5. Social Contract Orientation	Everyone has the right to life. Therefore, Heinz is justified in stealing the drug.
Conventional Morality	4. Law and Order Orientation 3. Good Boy-Good Girl Orientation	If Heinz steals the drug, everyone will think he is a criminal.
Preconventional Morality	2. Self-Interested Exchanges 1. Punishment-Obedience Orientation	If Heinz saves his wife, he will be a hero.

What motivates people to help others in their community?

of what it cost. He told the druggist that his wife was dying and asked him to sell it cheaper or let him pay later. But the druggist said: "No, I discovered the drug and I'm going to make money from it." So Heinz got desperate and broke into the man's store to steal the drug for his wife. (Kohlberg, 1969, p. 379)

Should Heinz have stolen the drug? Kohlberg was not interested in people's beliefs, but rather in how they reached their conclusions. He believed that moral reasoning developed through a series of six stages, progressing from simplistic and concrete to abstract and principled. To reach each stage, people had to progress through the stage before it. Kohlberg believed that not everyone reached the highest level of moral development, with most faltering at the fourth stage, and many not progressing beyond the second or third stage. While the stages of moral development were not linked to specific ages, Kohlberg proposed that adolescence and young adulthood were the most likely times in which a person may advance to higher levels.

Preconventional morality. Preadolescent children tend to view morality in terms of punishment and reward. Behaviour that is rewarded is right, while behaviour that is punished is wrong.

Conventional morality. By early adolescence, morality is defined by convention—caring for others and conforming to social laws is right simply because they are the rules within society.

Postconventional morality. The highest levels of moral reason are based on abstract principles such as justice, liberty, and equality. People who reach this level may not necessarily agree with societal norms, but follow their own personal set of ethics.

MORAL ACTION

If you are able to reason that handing a $20 bill back to a stranger is the right thing to do, does that necessarily make you a good person? Kohlberg recognized the differences between moral reasoning and moral action. It is often easy to theorize the correct moral choice, but it's not quite as simple in a real-world situation. How many Nazi concentration camp guards would have classified themselves as ordinary "moral" people before World War II? We all know that we should conserve natural resources, buy fair-trade products, and reduce our energy consumption, but how many of us actually live this way?

Today's character education programs focus on doing the right thing, as opposed to merely thinking in moral terms. For example, in co-operative learning schools, children are taught empathy for others' feelings, with the emphasis on group learning rather than competition. When group learning is of central importance, children become more socially responsible, academically successful, and accepting of other students (Leming, 1993). Many service learning programs engage students in community-spirited actions such as cleaning their neighbourhoods, assisting the elderly, or volunteering in homeless shelters. Schools that participate in character education programs and promote service learning tend to have lower drop-out rates and improved attendance (Greenberg et al., 2003).

Moral Feeling

How do adolescents' thoughts and experiences contribute to their moral development? Psychologist Daniel Hart and his colleague studied 15 New Jersey youths from a low-income, inner-city neighbourhood of Camden, who had been identified as morally exemplary by various community organizations. The teens had resisted involvement in criminal activities and spent much of their time volunteering in soup kitchens, shelters, counselling groups, and community gardens.

According to Kohlberg's theory, the teens should have been motivated by abstract thoughts of right and wrong, but Hart discovered that the volunteers were motivated simply by wanting to do what was right. Part of their self-image was tied up with a desire to set a good example to others. Hart also noted

> It is often easy to theorize the correct moral choice, but it's not quite as simple in a real-world situation. We all know that we should conserve natural resources, buy fair-trade products, and reduce our energy consumption, but how many of us actually live this way?

that the teens' self-ideals were much closer to those of their parents than a matched comparison sample of peers who did not participate in volunteer work (Hart & Fegley, 1995). This study suggests that social factors such as parental influence can contribute to moral development.

As members of industrialized countries, are we responsible for ensuring the basic rights of workers around the world? According to Jonathan Haidt's **social intuitionist account of morality,** you instantly

Social intuitionist account of morality states that a person has an instant gut reaction to moral situations that precedes moral reasoning.

thought of a "yes" or "no" response to that question and then justified it with reasons. Haidt theorized that we have an instant gut reaction to moral situations, which precedes moral reasoning (Haidt, 2001). He believed that our moral reasoning convinces us of what we feel intuitively.

Take one of Haidt's less-than-salubrious examples: A brother and a sister are on vacation in France. They drink some wine, one thing leads to another, and they decide they want to have sex. They use two different kinds of contraception and enjoy it, but decide they won't do it again. Haidt presented this scenario to people and asked for their reactions. Invariably, people said it was morally wrong and when pushed for a reason, most pointed to the possibility of birth defects. Upon being reminded that the brother and sister used two forms of contraception, the interviewees were stumped, but still adamant that the scenario was immoral. Haidt referred to this phenomenon as "moral dumbfounding," supporting his theory that we have an initial gut reaction to moral situations. Why might this be? Acceptable reactions to socially prohibited concepts such as incest are drilled into us from a very young age. We hear the negative comments of friends and family members and read terms such as *deviant* and *twisted* in the media. Over time, our responses of disgust become automatic, so that when given Haidt's scenario, we produce an instant gut reaction. Similarly, children of parents who consistently reiterate the values of honesty and integrity are more likely to hand back a $20 bill they saw fall out of a stranger's pocket than children who have been given mixed moral messages from their parents.

07   • Review

Summary

HOW DO WE FORM BONDS OF ATTACHMENT? p.96

- Attachment is an emotional bond between a newborn and caregiver.
- Touch and familiarity are vital to attachment. Many animals have a critical period during which normal development takes place. In some species, this manifests through imprinting.
- According to Ainsworth's strange situation test, the behaviour of a caregiver can determine whether an infant forms secure or insecure bonds of attachment.

WHAT ROLES DO PEERS PLAY IN SOCIAL DEVELOPMENT? p.97

- Play is an important form of socialization for children. It is universally gender-specific, encourages skill development, and often reflects the values and skills of an individual culture.
- A sense of identity is established during adolescence. Adolescents form two kinds of peer groups: cliques and crowds.

Until they have a firm sense of self, teenagers are subject to peer pressure that can result in risky behaviour.

- Emotional ties with parents loosen during emerging adulthood. Adulthood is often characterized by the ability to establish intimate, caring relationships and find career fulfillment.
- According to the socioemotional selectivity theory of aging, as people get older, they focus on enjoying the present rather than looking to the future. They also pay closer attention to loved ones and less attention to casual acquaintances.

HOW DO WE DEVELOP MORALITY? p.104

- Morality develops in adolescence and young adulthood. According to Kohlberg, moral reasoning develops through six stages. Few people progress beyond level four.
- Modern character education programs stress the difference between moral reasoning and moral action, encouraging young people to practise sharing, empathy, and social responsibility.

Test Your Understanding

1. Kyaire reads a story about a gosling that follows a remote-control toy car everywhere it goes. What process may have caused this phenomenon?
   a. socialization
   b. imprinting
   c. stranger anxiety
   d. self-direction

2. Which of the following is believed to result from an increase in adrenal androgen?
   a. decreased energy
   b. decreased growth
   c. increased sexual interest
   d. increased longevity

3. Which of the following scenarios supports the disengagement theory of aging?
   a. Rose, a 78-year-old woman, quits her pottery class and spends all her time at home with her cat.
   b. Rose, a 78-year-old woman, joins a pottery class and decides to volunteer at a local school.
   c. Rose, a 78-year-old woman, decides to call off a visit with a passing acquaintance to spend more time with her husband.
   d. Rose, a 78-year-old woman, goes on a two-week vacation to visit relatives in Alberta.

4. A child who becomes distressed when his mother leaves the room and shows mixed reactions upon her return would be classified by Ainsworth as:
   a. secure
   b. anxious-ambivalent
   c. anxious-avoidant
   d. disorganized-disoriented

5. Five-year-old Mercedes is pretending to be a doctor. She wears a toy stethoscope, listens to her family's heartbeats, and gets upset when her brother doesn't act the way she thinks a medical patient should. Mercedes is practising:
   a. self-regulation
   b. role confusion
   c. age-mixed play
   d. familiarity

6. Which of the following best fits the definition of a clique?
   a. a pair of prepubescent boys
   b. a mixed-sex group of eight teens
   c. a group of five teenaged girls
   d. a class of 30 schoolchildren

7. Which of the following statements is true?
   a. Teens within the same friendship group usually indulge in similar risky behaviours.

b. Peer pressure is always a negative influence in adolescent lives.

c. Teenagers tend to choose friends who have interests that are dissimilar from their own.

d. Parents of teenagers usually worry unnecessarily about negative peer pressure.

8. According to Kohlberg, which level of morality have preadolescent children usually reached?

a. postconventional

b. conventional

c. preliminary

d. preconventional

9. Which of the following occurs as we age?

a. We pay selective attention to negative events.

b. Our memory sharpens.

c. Our beliefs become more extreme.

d. Our moods become more enduring.

10. According to Erikson, the primary task of early adulthood is to:

a. learn new skills

b. direct one's own behaviour

c. form close relationships

d. develop a sense of self

11. Fourteen-year-old Alex is shy and quiet in class. Among his friends, he is cocky and loud-mouthed. At home, he becomes sullen and angry. Alex is experiencing:

a. stagnation

b. isolation

c. generativity

d. role confusion

12. What is the most important factor to consider when determining a person's social age?

a. number of friends

b. date of birth

c. level of education

d. life experience

13. Which of the following jobs has a high level of occupational self-direction?

a. manager of a busy warehouse supervising 20 employees

b. trainee server at a fast-food restaurant

c. long-serving cashier at a grocery store

d. low-level administrative assistant with several bosses

14. Conflicts between parents and young adolescents tend to centre on the issue of:

a. politics

b. control

c. religion

d. clothing

15. Gina is engaged to be married, and she wants to make sure her marriage has the best possible chance of succeeding. Based on statistical evidence, Gina should:

a. cohabitate with her fiancé before marrying

b. date her fiancé for at least five years before marrying

c. wait until she graduates from college before marrying

d. have children as soon as possible after marrying

16. Latisha hears a story about a man whose pet dog was hit by a car and killed. When the man found his dog on the road, he took the dog home, cleaned it, and ate it for dinner. Latisha is horrified by this story, but she can't think of a moral argument to explain her disgust. Latisha is experiencing:

a. moral feeling

b. moral action

c. moral dumbfounding

d. moral development

17. According to Erikson, what crisis do infants experience?

a. initiative versus guilt

b. competence versus inferiority

c. identity versus role confusion

d. trust versus mistrust

18. Kyle polls a group of older couples on their levels of marital satisfaction over the years. Kyle's results are likely to indicate that marital satisfaction:

a. declines steadily over the years

b. rises steadily over the years

c. rises during the childrearing years, but then decreases

d. declines during the childrearing years, but then increases

19. During which stage of a child's life are the child and his or her parents most likely to experience conflict?

a. toddlerhood

b. early adolescence

c. mid to late adolescence

d. early adulthood

20. Which of these factors is NOT cited as a cause of the decline in teen pregnancy rate?

a. an increase in abstinence for religious reasons

b. an increase in the use of contraceptives

c. better sex education in schools

d. better communication between parents and children

Remember to check www.thethinkspot.ca for additional information, downloadable flashcards, and other helpful resources.

Answers: 1) b; 2) c; 3) a; 4) b; 5) a; 6) c; 7) a; 8) b; 9) d; 10) c; 11) d; 12) d; 13) a; 14) b; 15) c; 16) c; 17) d; 18) d; 19) b; 20) a

SEX AND
GENDER

WHAT ARE THE BIOLOGICAL AND S
INFLUENCES ON GENDER?
WHAT ARE THE TYPICAL AND ATYPIC
PROCESSES INVOLVED IN AN INDIVIDU
DEVELOPMENT OF A GENDER IDENTIT
WHAT SIMILARITIES AND DIFFERENCE
BETWEEN THE GENDERS HAVE BEEN
OBSERVED AND STUDIED?
WHAT DO WE KNOW ABOUT THE BIC
AND SOCIETAL INFLUENCES ON SEXU
ORIENTATION?

Like plenty

of married couples, Thomas and Nancy Beatie wanted another child. And like plenty of married couples, they faced a significant roadblock: Nancy, whose uterus had been removed, was unable to conceive. While plenty of married couples have turned to surrogate mothers or adoption agencies in situations like this one, the Beaties are not just any married couple. Thomas and Nancy were able to find a unique—and surprising—solution to their problem: Thomas became pregnant.

Man Is Pregnant! screamed the headlines. But how was it possible? Formerly a Miss Teen Hawaii U.S.A. finalist named Tracy, Thomas Beatie began taking testosterone 11 years ago, had his sex officially changed from female to male, and legally married his wife, Nancy. Although he had chest reconstruction surgery to remove his breasts and grows a well-groomed beard, Thomas kept his female reproductive organs intact so that he could one day experience the miracle of childbirth first-hand.

In preparation for carrying his child, Thomas stopped taking testosterone for about two years and needed no additional female hormone supplements before his body started having a regular menstrual cycle again. The couple conceived via artificial insemination with one of Thomas's eggs and donor sperm, which Nancy inserted into Thomas with a syringe-like device in the comfort of their own bedroom.

But the process wasn't wholly without difficulties. Thomas's first pregnancy resulted in ectopic triplets that didn't make it to term, and the couple has faced discrimination from several obstetricians who mocked them or even refused to see Thomas as a patient. The couple has also dealt with unfavourable public opinions about their lifestyle, although anyone who didn't know better could have easily mistaken Thomas for just another man with a beer belly.

The couple's efforts paid off on June 29, 2008, when Thomas endured 40 hours of labour to give birth to Susan Juliette. Thomas has said that "wanting to have a biological child is neither a male nor female desire but a human desire." He will surely feel this desire fulfilled the first time he hears the daughter he gave birth to call him "Dad." (Banerjee, 2008; Bone, 2008; Clark, 2008; Goldman, 2008).

Thomas Beatie and Jenna Talackova illustrate that gender and sex are not always clear-cut issues.

<<< At the 2012 Miss Universe Canada Pageant, Jenna Talackova, the first transsexual contestant, challenged common assumptions about what it means to be a "woman."

CHAPTER 08

Sex and Gender

To lots of people, the words *sex* and *gender* mean pretty much the same thing. When we're asked to identify our sex or gender on a standardized test, many of us fill in the bubble marked male or female without much thought. But, as Thomas Beatie can probably attest, sex and gender are far from synonymous.

Our **sex** is our biological classification as either male or female based on the sex chromosomes contained in our DNA. Females have two **X chromosomes,** one from each parent. Males have an X chromosome, from the mother, and a **Y chromosome,** from the father.

Gender, on the other hand, is the set of behaviours and characteristics that define individuals as boys and men or girls and women in society. In other words, while sex is a biological phenomenon, gender is psychological. Some have gone so far to say that a person's sex is located between their legs, while a person's gender is located between their ears. Identifying with a particular gender isn't usually as complicated for most of us as it was for Thomas, but the process does involve the influences of both biology and our

> Thanks to new advances in surgical techniques and hormone treatments, those people who, like Thomas, **face a conflict between sex and gender can modify their bodies to align with their genders, rather than the other way around.**

interactions with society. In the vast majority of cases, gender is aligned with biological sex: Someone born with two X chromosomes will come to identify herself as female, and someone born with one X chromosome and one Y chromosome will come to identify himself as male. However, Thomas's case shows us that it doesn't always work out that easily: Some people with two X chromosomes feel more like men than women, and some people who are genetically male feel more comfortable identifying as female. Gender is not merely a stark division between male and female, either: It can be experienced on a continuum, and it's possible for people to feel varying degrees of gender intensity. Thanks to new advances in surgical techniques and hormone treatments, those people who, like Thomas, face a conflict between sex and gender can modify their bodies to align with their genders, rather than the other way around.

The Nature of Gender

PRIMARY SEX CHARACTERISTICS

The process of identifying with a gender begins long before we are aware of it. As soon as we are born and our **primary sex characteristics**—the sexual organs present at birth and directly involved in human reproduction—are visible to doctors, nurses, and parents, they begin to treat us a certain way. The minute we are swaddled in a pink or blue hat and a onesie embroidered with dainty butterflies or big, tough fire trucks, we have not only a sex but a gender, too.

Primary sex characteristics, including gonads, internal sex organs, and external genitalia, emphasize the main ways in which males and females are different—their roles in reproduction. However, you might be surprised at just how similar male and female primary sex characteristics are for much of prenatal development.

Gonads and Internal Sex Organs

The first sex organs to develop are the **gonads,** which are identical in male and female fetuses for the first four weeks of prenatal development. Then, if a Y chromosome is present, it activates the enzyme that turns gonads into testes for males. If the Y chromosome is absent, however, the fetus is female, and it begins to develop ovaries.

Until the third month of pregnancy, the fetus, regardless of its sex chromosomes, has both the **Müllerian system**—the precursor of female sex organs—and the **Wolffian system**—the precursor of male sex organs. During the third month, a male's testes will secrete **androgens,** or male hormones, to make the Wolffian system develop. They'll also produce an anti-Müllerian hormone to stop development of the female sex organs. In the absence of these androgens, the Müllerian system will develop and the Wolffian system will wither away; in other words, the fetus will develop female sex organs.

External Genitalia

The development of **external genitalia**—the penis and scrotum in males and the labia, clitoris, and external vagina in females—also depends on the presence or absence of androgens. In rare cases in which the fetus's receptors for androgens fail to function, **androgen insensitivity syndrome** causes a genetic male to develop external female genitalia. Varying degrees of androgen insensitivity can cause males' testes to develop internally or cause boys to develop breasts during puberty.

SECONDARY SEX CHARACTERISTICS

When we reach reproductive age, our bodies change to prepare for reproduction and alert others that we're physically ready to reproduce. These changes involve the development of **secondary sex characteristics**—sexual organs and traits that develop at puberty and are not directly involved in reproduction. Both sexes begin to grow pubic hair and experience an

Sex is a person's biological classification as either male or female based on the sex chromosomes contained in his or her DNA.

X chromosomes are sex chromosomes that exist as a matched pair in females and as part of an unmatched pair in males (the other part being a Y chromosome).

Y chromosomes are sex chromosomes that exist in males as part of an unmatched pair (the other part being an X chromosome).

Gender is a set of behaviours and characteristics that define individuals as boys and men or girls and women in society.

Primary sex characteristics are sexual organs present at birth and directly involved in human reproduction.

Gonads are the first sex organs to develop; these are identical in male and female fetuses for the first four weeks of prenatal development.

Müllerian system is the precursor of female sex organs.

Wolffian system is the precursor of male sex organs.

Androgens are male hormones.

External genitalia consist of the penis and scrotum in males and the labia, clitoris, and external vagina in females.

Androgen insensitivity syndrome is a condition in which a genetically male fetus's receptors for androgens fail to function, resulting in the development of external female genitalia.

Secondary sex characteristics are sexual organs and traits that develop at puberty and are not directly involved in reproduction.

overall growth spurt. Females begin this development about two years before males do, which explains why most of the girls towered over most of the boys at your seventh-grade dance. Females grow breasts and their hips widen to prepare for childbirth, while males grow facial hair and chest hair. Both males and females develop lower, more adult voices; this change is particularly noticeable in boys, who sometimes seem to change from sopranos to basses with astonishing sped.

HORMONES

As you've probably already figured out, hormones play a significant role in the development of our sex characteristics. The androgen **testosterone** is the principal male hormone. The male's Y chromosome includes a single gene that triggers the testes to produce testosterone. In females the ovaries produce testosterone, but to a much lesser extent. Many studies have examined the impact of atypical concentrations of testosterone in genetic males and females on the development of **gender identity**—our sense of being a boy or girl, man or woman.

Evidence from several cases suggests that while excess androgens in female embryos may create more "masculine" girls, these male hormones don't cause girls to identify themselves as boys. If a female embryo exposed to excess androgens is born with male-looking genitals, doctors may surgically "correct" the genitals by making them appear female. Although these girls tend to be typical tomboys, act more physically aggressive than most girls, and play in ways more typical of boys than girls, their gender identification as girls is not altered by the excess male hormones (Berenbaum & Snyder, 1995; Money & Matthews, 1982; Money & Norman, 1987). Research into other species from rats to monkeys shows that female embryos that are exposed to male hormones go on to develop

a masculine appearance and act more aggressively than typical females of their species do (Brody, 1981).

Some genetic males with normal male hormones are born with penile deformity, causing some well-meaning parents to raise their sons as daughters. However, genetic males who are raised as females often come to reject their female gender identity. In the past, the medical community was quick to recommend sex reassignment surgery for genetic males born with deformed or very small penises. One study of 14 such cases found that six of these individuals later identified as men and five identified as women, while the remaining three had unclear gender identities (Reiner & Gearhart, 2004).

The case of David Reimer, whose story was told in *Rolling Stone* in 1997, convinced many readers of the biological basis of gender. David was born a normal genetic male with an identical twin, but his penis was destroyed in a botched circumcision. Doctors performed sexual reassignment surgery, and David was raised as a girl. Since David's twin provided a natural control, doctors followed the case for many years in an effort to prove that gender was entirely learned. Although David didn't learn of his history until age 14, and despite his parents' efforts to raise him as a girl, he always displayed typically masculine behaviours and preferences. When he did learn what had happened to him, he began to live as a man, but the experience took a tragic toll on David, and he eventually committed suicide (Colapinto, 1997, 2000; Walker, 2004). (Interestingly, David's twin brother had committed suicide two years prior.)

As researchers learn more about the biology of gender, sex reassignment surgery isn't taken

as lightly as it once was. The Intersex Society of North America advocates for the rights of **intersex** individuals—those born with non-standard male or female genitals—not to have surgical sex assignment forced upon them in infancy. As the medical community has come to understand more about the complexities of gender, doctors have become more willing to leave intersex individuals' genitalia intact and far less eager to surgically alter infants' anatomical features. Even when an individual chooses to have sex assignment (or reassignment) surgery performed as an adult, the process isn't undertaken hastily: Gender has such a powerful impact on our lives that people who choose to have this type of surgery must undergo extensive counselling to ensure that they are fully informed about—and comfortable with—their decision.

The Nurture of Gender

GENDER TYPING

It's hard to deny that we all have ideas about gender that go beyond just what nature determines. When we see a baby, we look for external clues about its gender so we know how we're supposed to act around it. If it's a girl, we're expected to gush over her beauty; if it's a boy, we're expected to marvel at how strong he looks. And if you've ever mistaken a baby girl for a baby boy, you know the wrath of the mother who corrects you while quickly searching for a way to clip a barrette to her baby daughter's hairless head. Gender ambiguity—whether a girl baby mistaken for a boy or a woman who becomes a man and gives

∧
∧ **It's not unusual for girls
∧ who are tomboys as
children to become more
feminine as women.**

>>> With his rugged **virility**, propensity for (often shirtless) **athleticism**, and Southern **charm**, **Matthew McConaughey** exhibits very masculine gender typing.

Gender typed refers to boys and men who show traditionally masculine traits and behaviours, and girls and women who show traditionally feminine traits and behaviours.

Androgynous people are neither specifically masculine nor feminine.

Gender identity disorder is a condition in which a person feels he or she was born with the body of the wrong sex.

Transsexual is a person who has had sex reassignment surgery.

are comfortable displaying whatever behaviours and traits are most appropriate in a given situation (Bem, 1975, 1981, 1993). Imagine that a woman gets a flat tire on her way to the fabric store (a typically feminine locale). If she ranks high on the feminine scale and low on the masculine scale of the BSRI, she might find herself stranded if the idea of trying to change the flat herself (a traditionally masculine task) doesn't cross her mind. If she is androgynous—that is, if she ranks about equally on both the feminine and masculine scales—she might be more likely to change her own tire and still make it to the fabric store before closing time.

was a biological error. The first widely known **transsexual**—a person who has had sex reassignment surgery and lives as a member of the "new" sex—was Christine Jorgensen, a former U.S. Army soldier who travelled to Denmark for her surgery in the early 1950s. Other transgender individuals—people who participate in any of a wide range of behaviours that in some way conform more to the opposite sex than the one they were born—may alternate between living dressed as men or women or, in the extreme, may dress as the opposite sex in order to perform in drag shows. Jenna Talackova and Thomas Beatie are recent and controversial examples of transsexual individuals who question traditional laws, rules, and perspectives about gender and sex.

birth—generally causes discomfort in a society in which gender is such a significant part of a person's identity.

Although it is clear that biology plays a part in our sense of gender identity, many of the behaviours and ideas associated with each gender are socially constructed. Women may be viewed as emotional, nurturing, and passive, while men may be viewed as rational, dominant, and aggressive. These associations are most apparent in people who are highly **gender typed**—boys and men who show traditionally masculine traits and behaviours, and girls and women who show traditionally feminine traits and behaviours.

> "Although it is clear that biology plays a part in our sense of gender identity, many of the behaviours and ideas associated with each gender are socially constructed. Women may be viewed as emotional, nurturing, and passive, while men may be viewed as rational, dominant, and aggressive."

ANDROGYNY

Although gender has traditionally been viewed as an either-or dichotomy, psychologist and gender studies researcher Sandra Bem developed a sex role inventory (known as the BSRI) to measure both the degree to which people are masculine and the degree to which they are feminine, rather than how far they lean in one direction or the other. Those who rate themselves equally on both masculine and feminine traits are **androgynous.** Bem and others believe that androgynous people are highly functioning and effective because, rather than limit themselves according to gender typing, they

GENDER IDENTITY DISORDER

Unlike androgyny, which involves a healthy combination of masculinity and femininity, **gender identity disorder** causes a person to feel that he or she was born with the body of the wrong sex. Gender identity disorder has nothing to do with sexual orientation; people with gender identity disorder believe that their gender does not match their body's anatomy, but this mismatch is not associated with sexual preference. These people, like Thomas Beatie, may seek sex reassignment surgery to "fix" what they feel

GENDER IN CHILDHOOD

The majority of people who deal with some sort of gender dissonance in adolescence or adulthood, including David Reimer and Christine Jorgensen, report having had such feelings since childhood. David's mother recalls him clawing at a dress the first time she dressed him in one, and his brother recalls David preferring the rough-and-tumble play of boys to dolls and tea parties (Colapinto, 1997). This early gender expression also suggests roots in both society and biology.

Babies are treated differently as soon as their sex is known. A father may talk to his son about cars while he's still in the womb, and a mother may read her in utero daughter stories about princesses. As infants, boys and girls are dressed and treated differently. Girls tend to be talked to more often and treated more gently than boys, who are played with more roughly (Maccoby, 1998). Children are given gendered toys to play with and may even be discouraged from playing with toys typical of the other gender. Recently, Disney Consumer Products created a pink, glitter-encrusted cash cow in the form of its best-selling Disney Princesses toys, which successfully play to the idea that all

<<< What **factors** might contribute to the **gender gap** in fields like **math and science?** What strategies might **teachers and parents** use **to close** this gap?

little girls love ball gowns, tiaras, and handsome princes. Disney's princess-based marketing plan clearly does not have boys in mind. Some researchers have found that male babies as young as one year show a preference for balls, guns, and trucks, while girls show a preference for dolls, stuffed animals, and cookware (Caldera, Huston, & O'Brien, 1989). Studies with non-human primates have revealed similar preferences (Alexander & Hines, 2002). While these findings may suggest some biological influence, we are still left to wonder what use a female monkey of any age would have for cookware.

Perhaps more detrimental are the different assumptions that adults have about the interests and abilities of school-age boys and girls. These assumptions can lead to unequal treatment: For example, adults tend to offer more help and comfort to girls, while they expect boys to solve problems on their own (Maccoby, 1998). Boys often receive more encouragement and instruction in math and science than do girls (Sadker, 2000), who tend to pursue careers in these fields less often than their male counterparts (O'Rand, 2004). Proponents of single-gender education claim that without classroom competition between genders, both boys and girls receive equal opportunities and encouragement (Hughes, 2007).

THEORIES OF GENDER

Psychologists consider not only what aspects of gender are learned, but also how that learning occurs. The **social learning theory** assumes that children learn gendered behaviour by observing and imitating adults and responding to rewards and punishments. The **gender schema theory**, however, combines the social learning theory with the element of cognition. According to the gender schema theory, the process of gender differentiation begins at

∧
∧
∧ Do you believe that gender equality exists in Canada today? Do you think gender equality is possible in all countries?

> **Adults** may not encourage girls to pursue math and science careers because of old assumptions or stereotypes that women will go on to raise children while their husbands serve as the breadwinners. **This arrangement may work fine for the women and men who want to fill those roles, but it's important to recognize that this formula of male and female roles may be nothing more than a holdover from another time—especially in the 21st century, it doesn't work for everyone.**

a very young age. Before age one, children learn to differentiate between male and female faces and voices (Martin, Schmidlin, & Williams, 2002). As children develop schemas for other things around them, they also begin to develop a schema for their gender and to adjust their behaviour to align with it. As they begin to learn language, children are forced to organize words based on gender, whether through male and female pronouns or through masculine and feminine classifications. Studies show that by age three, children prefer to play with members of their own sex; they generally reach the peak of gender rigidity at age five or six (Bem, 1993).

GENDER ROLES IN SOCIETY

Children may be treated differently according to the **gender roles**—expectations about the way women and men behave—that they are expected to fill. Adults may not encourage girls to pursue math and science careers because

of old assumptions or stereotypes that women will go on to raise children while their husbands serve as the breadwinners. This arrangement may work fine for the women and men who want to fill those roles, but it's important to recognize that this formula of male and female roles may be nothing more than a holdover from another time—especially in the 21st century, it doesn't work for everyone.

While those dissatisfied with limited gender roles may feel that it takes hundreds of years to change them, women's roles around the globe have changed vastly in just the last century. In the early 1900s, the only place where women had the right to vote was New Zealand, but by the end of the century, the only place where women didn't have the right to vote was Kuwait. In just 30 years, the percentage of Canadian women with university degrees rose from 3% in 1971 to 15% in 2001 (Statistics Canada, 2009). In less than a decade, the percentage of women who agreed that married women should be full-time homemakers dropped from about 45% in 1967 to 15% in 1972 (Glater, 2001).

Several examples of a third gender exist throughout the world. In 2005, India included a designation on passports for the Hijra, a distinct gender that is neither man nor woman. Hijra are typically born male or intersex, and they adopt a feminine dress but reject both the terms *man* and *woman*. The kathoeys of Thailand and the winkte of indigenous North American cultures are other examples of third genders living in the world today. When not all males are men and not all females are women, it becomes easier to see how sex and gender don't always go hand in hand.

STEREOTYPES AND SEXISM

A **gender stereotype** is a widely held concept about a person or group of people that is

> **Social learning theory** emphasizes the role of cognition in motivation and the importance of expectations in shaping behaviour.
>
> **Gender schema theory** states that the process of gender differentiation begins at a very young age; as children develop schemas for other things around them, they also develop a schema for their gender and adjust their behaviour to align with it.
>
> **Gender roles** are expectations about the way men and women behave.
>
> **Gender stereotype** is a widely held concept about a person or group of people that is based only on gender.

based only on gender. These stereotypes have both positive and negative characteristics. For example, in many cultures, women are commonly stereotyped as being nurturing and empathetic, but they are also stereotypically overly emotional and irrational. Stereotypes portray men as powerful and rational, but also as aggressive and inattentive.

These stereotypes often lead to **sexism**—prejudice and unfair treatment against men or women based on gender stereotypes. Schoolteachers who call on boys more often than girls in math and science classes may not even realize that their bias is a result of sexism. Sexism can be more blatant, too. During Hillary Clinton's run for the Democratic presidential nomination in 2008, the media and blogosphere were rife with sexist claims against the feasibility of a female president. Arguably more attention was paid to what Clinton wore than what she stood for. Ben Barres, a transgendered Stanford neurobiology professor who attended MIT as Barbara Barres, knows all about sexism. According to Barres, his colleagues' treatment of him has changed noticeably since he changed his gender, and this change in treatment has led Barres to believe that sexism in the scientific community is likely responsible for the relatively small number of women who hold tenured academic positions in the sciences. Barres describes one fellow scientist who mentioned to him that Barres's work was much better than that of his "sister," Barbara. Barres's academic ability hadn't changed at all, but his change in gender altered people's perceptions of his work.

Another type of sexism is more insidious. **Benevolent sexism** is the acceptance of positive stereotypes or favourable biased behaviour that propagates unfairness and inequalities based on gender (Glick & Fiske, 2001). Certain aspects of chivalry could be considered examples of benevolent sexism. When men open doors for women and insist on footing the bill for every romantic evening out, both the men who act "chivalrously" and the women who expect them to do so are perpetuating the sexist idea that women are helpless, weak, and unable to provide for themselves. Of course, holding the door for someone isn't inherently sexist, but in order to eliminate the effects of benevolent sexism, both men and women should be willing to hold open doors for people of any gender.

∧
∧ **Gender testing** occurred during the
∧ 2012 Olympic Games. Do you think athletes should be required to undergo this type of testing? What are the implications of this type of test? What does it say about our beliefs about being male or female?

Gender Similarities and Differences

Before the 2008 Beijing Olympics, organizers created a "gender determination lab" where female athletes could be given genetic tests to determine whether or not they were truly female. The decision to create this lab was most likely made in the spirit of fair play, based on the idea that men are generally physically stronger than women and would have an innate biological advantage if they posed as women and competed against female athletes. The mere fact that sporting events, including the Olympic Games, are almost always divided into men's competitions and women's competitions reinforces this generalization. But are men and women really so different? And what are the ethical implications of testing athletes' genders? How do transgender athletes, intersex athletes, and others who blur boundaries of sex and gender fit into the picture? Even at the "gender determination lab," the question of differences and similarities between genders persists.

While much effort has been made to emphasize the equality of men and women, several studies have found ways in which they are consistently different. As with gender itself, these differences are likely not rooted in biology alone. After all, 45 of our 46 chromosomes are unisex. The way that parents, siblings, peers, and society as a whole treat people differently according to gender certainly has an influence on the ways in which they are different. Often, our expectations about the ways we think people will act become a self-fulfilling prophecy. We should also remember that variation among individuals is much greater than generalized variation between genders.

PHYSICAL DIFFERENCES AND PSYCHOLOGICAL VULNERABILITIES

Some differences between men and women are more clear-cut than others. The average woman has 70% more fat and 40% less muscle and is 13 centimetres shorter than the average man. She also enters puberty two years sooner and dies five years later. These findings are fairly innocuous in that they are unlikely to lead us to draw stereotypical conclusions. Studies of male and female brain differences, however, are more complicated.

Many studies have supported the popular ideas that men excel at spatial puzzles, while women are better with words. Researchers have found that, consistent with these generalizations, the part of the parietal cortex associated with spatial perception is thicker in adult men than it is in adult women, who have a thicker part of the frontal lobes associated with verbal fluency than their male counterparts (Gur et al., 1999).

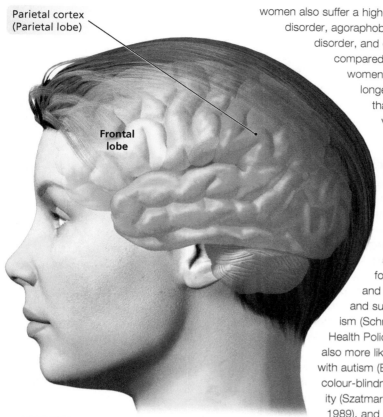

Parietal cortex (Parietal lobe)

Frontal lobe

women also suffer a higher incidence of panic disorder, agoraphobia, social anxiety disorder, and eating disorders compared to men. However, women in Canada have a longer life expectancy than males (83 years vs. 78 years) and are less likely to be overweight or heavy drinkers (Statistics Canada, 2012). Men, on the other hand, are four times as likely to commit suicide (Centers for Disease Control and Prevention, 2005) and suffer from alcoholism (Schneider Institute for Health Policy, 2001). They are also more likely to be diagnosed with autism (Baron-Cohen, 2002), colour-blindness, hyperactivity (Szatmari, Offord, & Boyle, 1989), and antisocial personality disorder (Torgersen, Kringlen, & Cramer, 2001). Again, notice that these are likelihoods of diagnosis and may not reflect actual prevalence. Remember, too, that the medical community is not immune from gender bias.

AGGRESSION AND POWER

Surveys, experiments, and observed cultural behaviours lend support to the idea that physical aggression is more prevalent in men than in women. One study found that men are more likely than women to administer what they believe are more painful shocks to another person (Bettencourt & Kernahan, 1997). Men also commit more violent crimes; the male-to-female arrest ratio is five to one in Canada (Statistics Canada, 2009) and nine to one in the United States (FBI, 2004). In 2004, women were charged with committing 17% of all crime in Canada. Women between the ages of 15 and 18 have much higher levels of criminal activity than adult women (Statistics Canada, 2009). Female adolescents are also more likely to engage in bullying behaviours that include indirect or verbal aggression, gossiping, and spreading rumours (Bjorkqvist, Lagerspetz, & Kaukiainen, 1992).

∧
∧ Part of the **parietal**
∧ **cortex** is thicker in **men** than in **women**, and part of the **frontal lobes** is thicker in **women** than in **men**. Why can't we draw **conclusions about causality** based on brain differences?

However, scientists still know very little about how our brains work, and it's just as likely that repeated practice with spatial puzzles thickens that area of the brain in men, who may have more exposure to these puzzles than women due to gender-targeted toys and education. In fact, a study conducted by Ian Spence and colleagues at the University of Toronto (2009) found that women could perform both basic and complex spatial tasks as well as men once they had participated in training tasks to develop their basic spatial abilities.

We also can't conclude much about causality based on the different vulnerabilities that are seen, on average, in men and women. In Canada, females make up the majority of the population with disabilities, and in general,

Canadian Women and Men in Managerial Positions in 2009

37% ■ Women ■ Men **63%**

Source: Statistics Canada, *The Daily* (2012). Women in Canada. http://www.statcan.gc.ca/daily-quotidien/060307/dq060307a-eng.htm

∧
∧ Last year in Canada, the employment rate for men
∧ was 66% compared to 58% for women. Canadian women earned only 75% of what men earned last year—a gap that has not changed substantially in the past decade (Statistics Canada, 2012).

Perhaps in line with their aggressive tendencies, men are also more socially dominant in most cultures. Men not only tend to be leaders in groups, such as juries and companies (Colarelli, Spranger, & Hechanova, 2006), but also held 84% of seats in the world's governing parliaments in 2005 (United Nations, 2005). Studies comparing male and female leaders have found that men tend to be more directive, autocratic, and opinionated and more likely to talk assertively, interrupt, initiate touching, and stare, and less likely to smile, while women tend to be more democratic, more welcoming of subordinates' participation in decision making, and more likely to express support (Eagly & Johnson, 1990; van Engen & Willemsen, 2004; Aries, 1987; Wood, 1987; Hall, 1987; Major, Schmidlin, & Williams, 1990).

SOCIAL CONNECTEDNESS

It seems to follow that if men are more aggressive and autocratic, then women are more affiliative and socially connected. Psychologist and feminist Carol Gilligan and her colleagues (1982, 1990) described the desire for social connectedness as largely female and the desire for a separate identity as largely male. Many studies show how this pattern begins in childhood and persists throughout adulthood.

Childhood

Gender segregation in childhood play reaches its peak at ages eight through 11. It is reinforced not only by adults but also by other children who ridicule any peers who don't seem to buy into the dominant "girls versus boys" mindset. The kinds of play seen in these separate groups are also distinct. Boys tend to play in large groups that focus on activity over discussion, while girls tend to play in smaller groups or pairs with little competitiveness and more focus on social relationships.

Adulthood

As the play of childhood gives way to the conversations of adulthood, men and women continue to show differences. Women are more receptive to feedback than men, many of whom suffer from a condition amusingly dubbed **male answer syndrome**: Men are more likely than women to guess at answers to difficult questions rather than

reveal their uncertainty (Campbell, 1992). Women are also more interdependent; they use conversation to explore social relationships (Tannen, 1990) and to cope with stress (Tamres, Janicki, & Helgeson, 2002; Taylor, 2002). Interestingly, both women and men report having more intimate, enjoyable, and nurturing friendships with women (Hall, 1984).

SEXUAL EAGERNESS

The gender double standard regarding sexual activities isn't news to anyone. We've all witnessed the guy who gets pats on the back when people hear of his sexual endeavours and the girl who is deemed what your grandmother might have called "loose" when people hear of hers. Encouraging boys to seek out and take pride in sexual adventures is a practice that seems to be true cross-culturally, not just in North America. This observation begs investigation into possible biological influences.

Many theories based on evolutionary principles speculate that men are encouraged to seek out sex more often and with more people than women because of men's and women's differing reproductive roles. This argument generally states that men are biologically driven to propagate their genes as much as possible, and by impregnating many women,

> "Perhaps in line with their aggressive tendencies, men are also more socially dominant in most cultures. **Men not only tend to be leaders in groups, such as juries and companies (Colarelli et al., 2006), but also held 84% of seats in the world's governing parliaments in 2005 (United Nations, 2005).**"

they are able to do just that. Men are also more likely to report being eager to have sex just for the sheer pleasure of it. Women, who take a more dominant role in raising children and are more likely to associate sex with love, prioritize finding one mate who will take care of his family (Gordon & Gilgun, 1987; Michael, Gagnon, Laumann, & Kolata, 1994). But are any of these evolutionary theories even relevant when the majority of today's sexual encounters involve doing everything possible to avoid pregnancy, not seek it out? Cross-cultural

studies reveal that male and female promiscuity occurs more frequently in cultures in which men devote little time to caring for offspring, while male and female sexual restraint is more likely in cultures in which men spend more time caring for their children (Marlowe, 1999).

Sexual Orientation

While a lot of the research into sex and gender is based on heterosexual relationships and norms, there has also been research into the causes of alternative sexual orientations. **Sexual orientation** refers to an enduring sexual attraction toward members of our own sex (homosexual), the other sex (heterosexual), or both (bisexual). Until 1973, homosexuality was listed as a mental illness by the American Psychiatric Association. This classification endured until 1993 at the World Health Organization, 1995 in China, and 2001 in Japan. While there are still groups out there claiming to "cure" homosexuality, psychologists now focus on conducting research to determine the environmental and biological factors related to a person's sexual orientation.

Early psychological research concluded that sexual orientation was entirely the result of one's upbringing: childhood sexual abuse or, according to Freud, unresolved pre-Oedipal conflicts, for example. However, more recent and reliable research has failed to identify any aspect of parenting that significantly impacts sexual orientation, and there is little support for the idea that early sexual encounters leave a lasting impact on a person's sexual preferences, either. Current research tends to focus on potential biological factors that may affect sexual orientation.

But biology may be only part of the story. Social psychologist Daryl J. Bem (1996) put forth his exotic-becomes-erotic theory, which posits that biology doesn't directly influence sexual orientation. Instead, our biology plays an indirect role by influencing our temperaments and determining the activities that we prefer. Children who follow behaviour patterns that are typical of other children of their sex come to see their own sex as familiar and the opposite sex as unfamiliar. Children who follow sex-atypical behaviour patterns, however, may see members of their own sex as unfamiliar. Bem's theory suggests that we're likely to feel romantically interested in the sex we view as more "exotic," or more different from ourselves. The exotic-becomes-erotic theory has come under fire from many critics who find it both insufficiently substantiated by scientific data and inaccurate in its explanation of homosexuality in both genders (Peplau, Garnets, Spalding, Conley, & Veniegas, 1998; Stein, 1999).

There is still much we don't know about the origins of sexual orientation, and even determining the percentage of homosexuals in a given population is challenging and unreliable. One study found that sexual orientation might even function differently in men and women. Women may experience **erotic plasticity**: Their sexuality tends to be less strongly felt and can be more fluid than men's (Baumeister, 2000). One generally accepted idea is that sexual orientation is neither wilfully chosen nor wilfully changed.

THE ROLE OF GENETICS

Studies involving twins and family members consistently suggest that genes play at least some role in determining a person's sexual orientation. Male and female homosexuals tend to have a larger proportion of homosexual siblings than heterosexuals do (Bailey & Bell, 1993). Other studies have found that 33 out of 40 homosexual brothers had the same genes in common in one area of the X chromosome even though other genes on that chromosome were different (Hu et al., 1995; Turner, 1995; Hamer, Hu, Magnuson, Hu, & Pattatucci, 1993). Since males get their X chromosomes from their mothers, these studies are consistent with those that have found homosexual men to have more homosexual relatives on their mother's side of the family than on their father's side (Camperio-Ciani, Corna, & Capiluppi, 2004).

There is an even more compelling finding for the influence of genetics on sexual orientation: In male identical twins (whose DNA is identical), if one of the twins is gay, the other has a 50% chance of also being gay, while the fraternal twin or non-twin sibling of a gay man has only a 15% chance of also being gay (Bailey et al., 2000; Dawood, Pillard, Horvath, Revelle, & Bailey, 2000). But those percentages mean that one identical twin can be homosexual and the other can be heterosexual, so we know for certain that there must be more to sexual orientation than genes.

Many researchers think that birth order can play a role in the determination of sexual orientation. According to the fraternal birth-order effect, each additional older brother that a male has increases the odds that the male is homosexual by 33%. The fraternal birth-order effect may be explained by a defensive maternal immune response to foreign substances produced by male fetuses that increases with each consecutive birth (Blanchard, 1997, 2001; Blanchard, Zucker, Siegelman, Dickey, & Klassen, 1998; Ellis & Blanchard, 2001).

BRAIN STRUCTURES AND SEXUAL ORIENTATION

Research into the biological origins of sexual orientation has also looked at structures in the brain. While brain structures can be altered by experience, observed differences in post-mortem studies reveal certain correlations between some brain structures and sexual orientation. For example, a section of the anterior commissure, which connects the two hemispheres of the brain, is larger in homosexual men (Allen & Gorski, 1992), and a set of nodules in the hypothalamus called a hypothalamic cluster is reliably larger in heterosexual men than in homosexual men (LeVay, 1991). Another study has linked the hypothalamus to sexual orientation: In heterosexual women and homosexual men, the scent of the testosterone derivative AND, found in male sweat, activated a hypothalamic response that is commonly related to sexual behaviour. In contrast, heterosexual men showed a similar sexually linked hypothalamic response to EST, an estrogen derivative present in female urine (Savic, Berglund, & Lindström, 2005). Overall, post-mortem studies have found more similarities between homosexual male brains and female brains than between homosexual male brains and heterosexual male brains. While few conclusions can be drawn based on these findings, they may eventually lead to a better understanding of the origins of sexual orientation.

∧∧∧ **Several species have been known to engage in occasional same-sex relations**, including grizzlies, gorillas, monkeys, flamingos, and owls. **About 8% of rams** are **exclusively homosexual** (Cloud, 2007).

Summary

WHAT ARE THE BIOLOGICAL AND SOCIETAL INFLUENCES ON GENDER? p.110

- X and Y chromosomes control a person's sex—the biological categorization of that person as either male or female.
- Sex roles and conditioning affect the behaviours and characteristics that define gender, and a person's gender identity can be fluid. This socialization of gender begins at birth and continues throughout the lifespan. The gender learning theory and the gender schemata theory explain the many ways we learn to be a specific gender.
- Therefore, sex is biologically determined, whereas gender is environmentally determined.

WHAT ARE THE TYPICAL AND ATYPICAL PROCESSES INVOLVED IN AN INDIVIDUAL'S DEVELOPMENT OF A GENDER IDENTITY? pp.110 and 114

- Typically, a child has male or female genitals at birth and develops secondary sexual characteristics during puberty. An individual identifies with either gender based on these biological characteristics and the responses they receive from others.
- Atypically, a person can be born with ambiguous genitalia. A person born with one set of sexual characteristics may identify with the opposite sex and choose gender reassignment surgery.
- Some individuals experience gender identity disorder, a feeling that they are born in the body of the wrong sex.

- Androgynous individuals consider themselves to be equal in male and female traits.
- Sexism can arise when we hold strict and unchanging views of what men and women can do, known as gender stereotypes.

WHAT SIMILARITIES AND DIFFERENCES BETWEEN THE GENDERS HAVE BEEN OBSERVED AND STUDIED? p.114

- Women tend to be shorter than men. They generally have more fat and less muscle than men do, and they tend to live longer.
- The male brain seems to be thicker in areas related to spatial abilities, while the female brain seems to be thicker in areas related to verbal abilities.
- In general, men tend to be aggressive and socially dominant, and women tend to value interdependence and social connectedness.
- In Canada, women make less money than men, are employed less often, and hold fewer high-powered managerial positions.

WHAT DO WE KNOW ABOUT THE BIOLOGICAL AND SOCIETAL INFLUENCES ON SEXUAL ORIENTATION? p.116

- Early psychological research suggested that people's sexuality depended largely on their upbringing.
- Most current research suggests that sexual orientation is largely biological in origin, dependent on such factors as genetics and birth order.

Test Your Understanding

1. Which of the following distinguishes gender from sex?
   a. self-perception
   b. brain structures
   c. physical characteristics
   d. reproductive capacities

2. Primary sex characteristics:
   a. make reproduction possible
   b. develop at puberty
   c. are not directly involved in reproduction
   d. develop earlier in males than females

3. Which of the following is a secondary sex characteristic?
   a. penis
   b. labia
   c. pubic hair
   d. uterus

4. Michael watches his father fixing a car's engine on the driveway. Later, Michael picks up one of his toy cars and pretends to fix it. Michael's behaviour demonstrates:
   a. gender schema theory
   b. benevolent sexism
   c. social learning theory
   d. male answer syndrome

5. A female fetus exposed to excess androgens will most likely grow up to be:
   a. more masculine than most females
   b. more feminine than most females
   c. genetically male
   d. hormonally male

6. Individuals are characterized as intersex if they have:
   a. gender identity disorder

b. non-standard male or female genitalia

c. gender reassignment surgery

d. androgen insensitivity syndrome

7. Dylan is an attorney known both for his competitive, aggressive presence in the courtroom and for his ability to nurture strong, caring relationships with his clients and co-workers. Which of the following terms best describes Dylan?

a. sexist

b. androgynous

c. gender-typed

d. transgendered

8. When Yuan-Chun gives birth to a baby boy, her friends all comment on how strong the child looks. This is an example of:

a. benevolent sexism

b. gender typing

c. gender identity disorder

d. androgyny

9. Ayana and Vinay have four sons. According to the fraternal birth-order effect, which son is most likely to be homosexual?

a. the oldest son

b. the second-born son

c. the third-born son

d. the youngest son

10. The fact that gender roles have changed over time suggests that:

a. gender roles are the result of sexism

b. women and men have the same biological construction

c. gender construction has a social dimension

d. biology plays no role in gender construction

11. Marco and Ana go on a date to a fancy restaurant. Marco helps Ana take her coat off, pulls out her chair for her, and orders her meal for her. Marco is displaying:

a. negative stereotyping

b. benevolent sexism

c. social connectedness

d. feminist behaviour

12. Which of the following statements about gender differences between men and women is true?

a. The average female enters puberty later than the average male and has a slightly lower life expectancy.

b. Men are biologically predisposed to have greater spatial awareness than women.

c. Aggressive tendencies in men are primarily due to nurture and have little biological relevance.

d. Gender bias may influence the diagnosis of particular mental disorders in men and women.

13. According to supporters of the male answer syndrome theory, a man who does not know the answer to a question is most likely to:

a. guess the answer

b. research the answer

c. ask a friend for the answer

d. admit that he does not know the answer

14. At what stage of life is gender segregation most prevalent?

a. ages 13 to 18

b. early adulthood

c. early childhood

d. ages eight to 11

15. An absence of androgens during the third month of pregnancy will result in:

a. the development of the Wolffian system

b. androgen insensitivity syndrome

c. an intersex child

d. the development of the Müllerian system

16. With which of the following statements would the Intersex Society of North America most likely agree?

a. Infants born with non-standard genitalia should immediately be allowed to have surgical sex assignment.

b. Infants born with non-standard genitalia should be raised according to their parents' wishes.

c. Infants born with non-standard genitalia should not have surgical sex assignment forced upon them in infancy.

d. Infants born with non-standard genitalia should never be told about their condition in order to avoid irreversible psychological damage.

17. Bem's theory of homosexuality assumes that:

a. children should identify with their own gender

b. sexual orientation can be changed with therapy

c. there is a relationship between gender identity and sexuality

d. biology plays a direct role in sexual orientation

18. Sibling, twin, and birth-order studies all support the idea that homosexuality is:

a. at least partly due to genetics

b. primarily a result of environment

c. linked to particular structures in the brain

d. functionally different in men and women

19. Post-mortem studies on the brains of men and women reveal that:

a. there are very few differences between the brains of homosexual men and the brains of heterosexual men

b. the brains of homosexual males have more in common with the brains of females than with the brains of heterosexual males

c. parts of the hypothalamus are larger in homosexual men than they are in heterosexual men

d. the scent of testosterone activates the hypothalamus in both homosexual men and homosexual women

20. A person with gender identity disorder is most likely to:

a. live as a member of the opposite sex

b. be homosexual

c. refuse sex reassignment surgery

d. experience erotic plasticity

Remember to check www.thethinkspot.ca for additional information, downloadable flashcards, and other helpful resources.

Answers: 1) a; 2) a; 3) c; 4) c; 5) a; 6) b; 7) b; 8) b; 9) d; 10) c; 11) b; 12) d; 13) a; 14) d; 15) d; 16) c; 17) c; 18) a; 19) b; 20) a

EDITORIAL

Sex and Gender Differences: New Perspectives and New Findings Within a Psychobiosocial Approach

Markus Hausmann[1] and Barbara Schober[2]

[1]Department of Psychology, Durham University, UK, [2]Faculty of Psychology, University of Vienna, Austria

> **In this chapter, you learned the difference between sex and gender. How do you define each of these terms?**

> **What psychological differences do you believe exist between men and women?**

> **Do you think this claim is valid? What factors may influence a young mother's willingness to work 80 hours a week?**

Sex and gender are among the most heavily investigated interindividual factors in all areas of psychology. Although sex and gender have been studied for more than a hundred years, there has been an explosion of theories and research in this area in the past several years. Whether psychological differences between men and women truly exist, and where they originate, is still under debate. Although the majority of experts would deny that sex and gender differences in mind and behavior are either purely biological or purely social in origin, it seems that the proportions attributable to nature and nurture are still being negotiated. New research takes into account biological and social factors, as well as the interaction between them, and addresses "the small difference" within a psychobiosocial approach. This topical issue integrates research on sex and gender differences from various psychological disciplines and emphasizes a psychobiosocial approach as a promising new perspective in this field.

In January 2005, Larry Summers, then president of Harvard University, gave a speech at the "Diversifying the Science and Engineering Workforce" conference held by the National Bureau of Economic Research in Cambridge, MA, that elicited a political and social earthquake. In his attempt to answer the question why women are underrepresented in top academic careers, he offered three potential explanations: (1) He argued that more young mothers than fathers are unwilling to spend 80 hr per week at work. (2) More boys than girls tend to be at the highest or lowest end of mathematical performance in high schools. Although boys and girls do not show significant differences in mean mathematical performance, a higher proportion of boys reveal extremely high mathematical aptitude, which might explain why women are underrepresented in the upper echelons of academic and professional life. (3) Finally, Summers admitted that discrimination at universities exists, including at Harvard University, but this may be less relevant because women are already underrepresented below the top level of academic leadership. His second point especially not only led to many attendees indignantly leaving the hall, but also revived a worldwide debate.

Is there empirical evidence for "innate" sex differences in cognitive abilities? Is there new empirical support for a biological basis for cognitive differences between men and women? What are the social factors that elicit or promote sex and gender differences? Although a lot of research has been done on these issues, many questions remain unanswered and an appraisal of new perspectives and new findings thus appears necessary from time to time (see, e.g., Schober, Reimann, & Wagner, 2004).

In light of this, the present topical issue "Sex and Gender Differences Revisited–New Perspectives and New Findings", on the one hand, contains contemporary studies of sex differences in specific cognitive variables, focusing on some relevant biological and social factors underlying the "small difference," and, on the other hand, presents new findings on mechanisms behind gender differences from more applied research on education, work, and science. Finally, it includes two opinion papers with the explicit aim of discussing new perspectives and possible reconciliations between very different research approaches to sex and gender.

Cognitive tests favoring men mainly include specific mathematical and spatial problems such as mental rotation, an ability that involves the ability to imagine and mentally manipulate 3D objects. Because mental rotation is particularly sexsensitive so that men outperform women with effect sizes up to one standard deviation, sex differences in mental rotation are the focus of various psychological approaches.

> **Where else does discrimination based on sex and gender exist?**

> **In this chapter, you read about gender typing, gender stereotypes, and sexism. How does society influence our beliefs about males and females?**

Neuburger, Jansen, Heil, and Quaiser-Pohl (2012) focus on gender stereotypes and their effects on mental rotation performance in primary school children. Gender stereotype effects on cognitive abilities in general, and mental rotation in particular, have been reported before (e.g., Hausmann, Schoofs, Rosenthal, & Jordan, 2009). It has remained unclear, however, at what age gender stereotypes begin to affect cognitive behavior. Specifically, Neuburger and colleagues (2012) reveal that the male advantage in mental rotation disappears when children, at around 10 years of age, are told prior to experimental testing that girls are usually better at this task or that no differences between boys and girls exist in this task.

Beyond this experimental developmental perspective on gender stereotypes, Hirnstein, Freund, and Hausmann (2012) investigate effects of stereotypes on cognitive sex differences. While the majority of studies in this field have focused on cognitive domains in which men outperform women, far fewer studies have investigated whether gender stereotyping also affects men when men are seen as the vulnerable group. The authors conducted an experimental study in which the gender stereotype of adult women having better verbal abilities (verbal fluency) than men was activated in both male and female participants. Instead of a decline in men's verbal fluency after confronting them with negative stereotypes about their sex's verbal abilities (stereotype threat; Steele, 1997), both men and women performed significantly better on these tests when both sexes were stereotyped. While the detailed mechanisms are up for

discussion, the results show that cognitive performance can change if individuals are aware that gender differences are being investigated. This strongly suggests that researchers in all psychological disciplines should be very careful with the way they frame their experimental tasks.

The extent to which sex differences in visuospatial abilities also account for sex differences in specific mathematical skills is investigated in children by Krinzinger, Wood, and Wilmes (2012). This study is based on the assumption that the use of spatial/conceptual strategies may be more advantageous for mathematical problem solving than verbal/syntactical strategies (Casey, Nuttal, & Benbow, 1995; Van Garderen, 2006). Although no sex differences in general spatial abilities were found, this study reveals that children's attitudes toward mathematics (more positive in boys than in girls) and general spatial abilities predict multi-digit number processing. Visual-spatial working memory capacity is not a significant predictor. These results strongly suggest an interaction between specific (spatial) cognitive abilities and attitudes in children's development of cognitive sex differences, which is in line with the psychobiosocial model. Moreover, Krinzinger and colleagues (2012) support the idea that sex differences in a specific task may be misclassified as a sex difference in mathematics, when in fact the task measures something else in addition or instead (Caplan, MacPherson, & Tobin, 1985), such as visuospatial abilities. This can obviously result in incorrect conclusions and overgeneralization of sex differences in specific cognitive domains.

Although sex differences in specific spatial abilities are widely

accepted, the study by Sänger, Schneider, Beste, and Wascher (2012) reveals that women do not necessarily show a general deficit in the processing of spatial information. However, in this electrophysiological study it was found that women are more distracted by irrelevant (spatial) cues, probably because women show a tendency to integrate (spatial) information more than men. In other words, the neurocognitive mechanisms that promote an augmented integration of information may be less efficient in situations in which relevant information is accompanied by irrelevant but salient information in the surroundings. It is also important to note that the results by Sänger and colleagues (2012) were not only observed behaviorally (error rates and response times) but there were also corresponding effects in an event-related electroencephalogram component (N2pc) that is assumed to reflect spatially selective attentional processing. It is generally assumed that, if sex differences in cognitive behavior are found, the neural correlate of this behavior should also be sexually differentiated. Although this is probably true, it should be borne in mind that male and female brain processes might differ even if no sex differences in (cognitive) behavior are found. In other words, neural correlates of cognitive processes can significantly differ between men and women, although the cognitive performance is almost identical between sexes (Cahill, 2006). For example, Jordan, Wüstenberg, Heinze, Peters, and Jäncke (2002) revealed overlapping but also different areas being activated in men and women during a mental rotation task, however, there were no differences in performance.

Callout boxes:

What are the implications of this statement?

Why might researchers find this result?

What can be done to prevent these sex biases in children?

What parts of the brain differ between men and women (Chapter 8)?

The above studies consider sex differences in cognitive variables at different ages and vary in their link to psychosocial variables. Braun, Peus, and Frey (2012) exclusively focus on the explanatory power of gender stereotypes and connected psychological mechanisms. Their study on possible negative consequences of attractiveness in female leaders confirmed gender-specific effects on followers' trust and loyalty–but only for female followers and only when combined with a specific leadership style. In an extension to prior literature on this "beauty is beastly effect" (e.g., Braun & colleagues, 2012; Heilman & Stopeck, 1985), data indicate the relevance of powerful mediators. A differentiated view of moderating effects of this kind is necessary in order to understand the paucity of women in leadership positions.

Adding new insight into the determinants of this so-called "glass ceiling effect" (Lyness & Thompson, 1997) is a central aim of Jöstl, Bergsmann, Lüftenegger, Schober, and Spiel (2012). Their study is concerned with science as a field of careers, where a "leaky pipeline" for women is often diagnosed (see also Larry Summers' statements above). The authors investigate young male and female scientists with regard to their research self-efficacy and the degree to which they are affected by the "impostor phenomenon" (IP). The IP integrates several motivational and cognitive characteristics and refers to objectively successful persons who fear that their deficits will be unmasked one day (e.g., Clance, 1985). The results show that the IP should be considered a psychological barrier for female university careers. This is the first study of the university context in German-speaking countries with

the theoretical aim of testing the explanatory power of the integrating construct IP.

Beyond a more integrated perspective on individual variables, we also need new and integrated perspectives on the structural barriers faced by women (e.g., Oakley, 2000). Mutz, Bornmann, and Daniel (2012) investigate gender differences in science at a systemic level: They evaluate the peer-reviewing process of one of Austria's biggest science funding sources (Austrian Science Fund – FWF) with regard to its gender fairness. In contrast to some previous studies on a possible gender bias in the review system and studies on individual differences described above, Mutz and colleagues (2012) found that sex and gender do not decisively matter in terms of the evaluation of research project proposals.

All aforementioned contributions of this topical issue are based on empirical studies and are focused on new findings on specific variables. They are thematically rather wide ranging, mostly following one specific research approach. Some researchers have already taken an integrative view and their results suggest why this is necessary. In contrast to these, the goal of Kaiser (2012) and Campbell (2012) is to explicitly elaborate new perspectives in research on gender and sex differences at a conceptual level. These two opinion papers discuss the integration of psychological, social, and biological approaches and traditions. Kaiser (2012) addresses reasons for and consequences of the difficulty of defining a clear-cut distinction between sex and gender–both terminologically and neurologically. The author suggests rethinking what is meant by male and female,

especially in neuropsychological settings, and elaborates why this should be seen as the starting point for further research. Campbell's contribution (2012) summarizes the contradictory positions of feminist and evolutionary psychology. The author reviews the sources of this conflict and identifies areas of convergence between them.

With the approach of identifying convergences, Campbell (2012) directly reflects on the basic aims of this topical issue. On the one hand, the present literature suggests that sex and gender differences still need to be investigated even after decades of research many questions remain open. On the other hand, an immense number of unconnected theories and evidence exist. Bearing this in mind, one clear issue becomes evident: Even if researchers on gender differences agree in principle on a complex interaction of biological, psychological, and social aspects (e.g., Ceci, Williams, & Barnett, 2009; Halpern, 2000), most research is so far conducted from only one of these perspectives. New approaches, realizing a systematic psychobiosocial approach, are therefore necessary as they can contribute substantially to a better understanding of sex and gender differences and their development (e.g., Hausmann, 2011).

So far, only a few studies have tried to realize this. This is perhaps understandable as this approach makes stringent demands on experimental designs and methods, and requires much more communication and coordination between different and very specialized (sub)disciplines than has been realized so far. In this sense, this topical issue can be a starting point by (a) presenting a number of studies that integrate different approaches and

---

In Chapter 14, you will learn more about the attractiveness bias and the "Beauty is Beastly" effect.

Self-efficacy is your belief about your ability to successfully perform a task (Chapter 15). Can you think of a task for which you have high self-efficacy and one for which you have low self-efficacy?

What makes a study "empirical" (see Chapter 2)?

What do you think is meant by male and female?

(b) being one of the rare topical issues in which researchers from psychological, biological, and social research traditions publish together.

But one final question remains: Was Larry Summers right when he said that there are innate sex differences in cognitive abilities that must be considered as one relevant explanation for deficits of gender equity in high positions? According to the present state of knowledge (as it is also presented in this topical issue), there seem to be differences between men and women in some specific cognitive abilities. However, for most of them, the magnitude of sex-related differences is usually quite small and they seem not necessarily relevant for daily life. Finding the reasons for the gender gap in many fields of daily life, such as the male dominance in academic leadership positions, seems to be complicated and we are far from understanding the full range of relevant mechanisms. But it is clear that we have to integrate knowledge from different disciplines and we have to find new perspectives by combining psychological, biological, and social approaches. This requires some changes in our present science culture of increasing specialization and differentiation. We hope this topical issue will encourage researchers of various psychological disciplines to contribute to this ambitious endeavor.

REFERENCES

Braun, S., Peus, C., & Frey, D. (2012). Is beauty beastly? Gender-specific effects of leader attractiveness and leadership style on followers' trust and loyality. *Zeitschrift für Psychologie, 220*, 98–108. doi: 10.1027/2151-2604/a000101

Cahill, L. (2006). Why sex matters for neuroscience. *Nature Review Neuroscience, 7*, 477–484.

Campbell, A. (2012). The study of sex differences: Feminism and biology. *Zeitschrift für Psychologie, 220*, 137–143. doi: 10.1027/2151-2604/a000105

Caplan, P. J., MacPherson, G. M., & Tobin, P. (1985). Do sex-related differences in spatial abilities exist? A multilevel critique with new data. *American Psychologists, 40*, 785–799.

Casey, M. B., Nuttall, R., & Benbow, C. P. (1995). The influence of spatial ability on gender differences in Mathematics College entrance test-scores across diverse samples. *Developmental Psychology, 31*, 697–705.

Ceci, S., Williams, W., & Barnett, S. (2009). Women's underrepresentation in science: Sociocultural and biological considerations. *Psychological Bulletin, 135*, 218–261.

Clance, P. R. (1985). *Imposter phenomenon: When success makes you feel like a fake.* Atlanta, GA: Peachtree.

Halpern, D. F. (2000). *Sex differences in cognitive abilities* (3rd ed.). Mahwah, NJ: Erlbaum.

Hausmann, M. (2011). Sex oder gender? Neurobiologie kognitiver Geschlechtsunterschiede [Sex or gender? The neurobiology of cognitive sex differences]. In M. Gottfried, R. Neck, & C. Spiel (Eds.), *Wissenschaft und Gender* (pp. 55–79). Vienna, Austria: Böhlau.

Hausmann, M., Schoofs, D., Rosenthal, H. E. S., & Jordan, K. (2009). Interactive effects of sex hormones and gender stereotypes on cognitive sex differences–a psychobiosocial approach. *Psychoneuroendocrinology, 34*, 389–401.

Heilman, M. E., & Stopeck, M. H. (1985). Being attractive, advantage or disadvantage? Performance-based evaluations and recommended personnel actions as a function of appearance, sex, and job type. *Organizational Behavior and Human Decision Processes, 35*, 202–215.

Hirnstein, M., Freund, N., & Hausmann, M. (2012). Gender stereotyping enhances verbal fluency performance in men (and women). *Zeitschrift für Psychologie, 220*, 70–77. doi: 10.1027/2151-2604/a000098

Jöstl, G., Bergsmann, E., Lüftenegger, M., Schober, B., & Spiel, C. (2012). "When will they blow my cover?" The imposter phenomenon among Austrian doctoral students. *Zeitschrift für Psychologie, 220*, 109–120. doi: 10.1027/2151-2604/a000102

Jordan, K., Wüstenberg, T., Heinze, H. J., Peters, M., & Jäncke, L. (2002). Women and men exhibit different cortical activation patterns during mental rotation. *Neuropsychologia, 40*, 2397–2408.

Kaiser, A. (2012). Re-conceptualising "sex" and "gender" in the human brain. *Zeitschrift für Psychologie, 220*, 130–136. doi: 10.1027/2151-2604/a000104

Krinzinger, H., Wood, G., & Willmes, K. (2012). What accounts for individual differences in the multi-digit number processing of primary school children? *Zeitschrift für Psychologie, 220*, 78–89. doi: 10.1027/2151-2604/a000099

Lyness, K. S., & Thompson, D. E. (1997). Above the glass ceiling? A comparison of matched samples of female and male executives. *Journal of Applied Psychology, 82*, 359–375.

Mutz, R., Bornmann, L., & Daniel, H.-D. (2012). Does gender matter in peer review? An empirical investigation using the example of the Austrian Science Fund. *Zeitschrift für Psychologie, 220*, 121–129. doi: 10.1027/2151-2604/a000103

Neuburger, S., Jansen, P., Heil, M., & Quaiser-Pohl, C. (2012). A threat in the classroom: Gender stereotype activation and the mental rotation performance of elementary school children. *Zeitschrift für Psychologie, 220*, 61–69. doi: 10.1027/2151- 2604/a000097

Oakley, J. G. (2000). Gender-based barriers to senior management positions: Understanding the scarcity of female CEOs. *Journal of Business Ethics, 27*, 321–334.

Sänger, J., Schneider, D., Beste, C., & Wascher, E. (2012). Sex differences in competition-based attentional selection. *Zeitschrift für Psychologie, 220*, 90–97. doi: 10.1027/2151-2604/a000100

Schober, B., Reimann, R., & Wagner, P. (2004). Is research on gender-specific underachievement in gifted girls an obsolete topic? New findings on an often discussed issue. *High Ability Studies, 15*, 43–62.

Steele, C. M. (1997). A threat in the air: How stereotypes shape intellectual identity and performance. *American Psychologist, 52*, 613–629.

Van Garderen, D. (2006). Spatial visualization, visual imagery, and mathematical problem solving of students with varying abilities. *Journal of Learning Disabilities, 39*, 496–506.

CHARLOTTETOWN

EMOTION AND MOTIVATION

Military members

experience great pressure to be unemotional. The ability to contain, conceal, and hide emotions is fostered within the military, and conforms to stereotypical masculine norms (Burns & Mahalik, 2011). Although most of us are not in the military, we are all acutely aware of what emotions are appropriate to display in each of our social encounters. Most of us have become experts at hiding or masking inappropriate behaviours, while displaying more socially acceptable behaviours. For example, when we receive a gift that we do not like, we smile and feign appreciation; we do not frown or cry. But for some the ability to control their emotions is a difficult, even impossible, goal.

At the funeral of a friend's father, Marina Darco begins to laugh. She looks at the solemn people weeping around her, but she can't control her emotions and fears she is losing her mind. Kathy Owen Coon looks at the man to whom she is happily married and begins crying. Thomas Shea's normally polite demeanour suddenly becomes short-tempered, and a kind gesture from his sister causes

him to leave the room in tears. Are Marina, Kathy, and Thomas, suffering from a serious psychiatric disturbance? No: They all suffer from a condition known as Involuntary Emotional Expression Disorder (IEED).

People with IEED struggle with a disconnect between their emotions and their motor responses. The disorder looks very similar to depression or emotional instability and healthcare professionals may misdiagnose the condition. It is not uncommon for people who suffer from Alzheimer's disease (Mimica, Stipe, & Presecki, 2009), multiple sclerosis (Multiple Sclerosis Society of Canada, 2012), stroke, and other neuro-degenerative diseases (Petracca, Jorge, Ación, Weintraub, & Robinson, 2009) to suffer from IEED.

Biological disorders, such as IEED, and professions, such as the military, are two ends on the continuum of emotional expression. Both raise questions about the nature of our emotions. What makes us burst into laughter or tears, anyway? Can we control our love, happiness, and anger, or is it possible for us to fall victim to our own intense feelings? What motivates us to behave the way we do?

<<< There are approximately 80 000 Canadians currently serving in the Canadian Forces. Canadians may be motivated to join the military for several reasons, including patriotism, the drive for service, or even job security. The Canadian Forces also stands as an example of how our work environment, stereotypes, and social norms influence how and when we express our emotions. While most of us may not wish to join the military, we all have internal drives that push us toward our individual goals, and outside influences, such as cultural and gender expectations, that influence how we show our feelings. What factors influence your emotions and motivations?

CHAPTER **09**

Theories of Emotion

THE NATURE OF EMOTIONS

Laughing and crying are both expressions of emotions, but what do we mean when we talk about emotions themselves? Based on all the words we have for our emotions and all the artistic ways we express them, we know that emotions are complex. When we experience a subjective reaction to an object, event, person, or memory, we are experiencing **emotion**. Emotion includes an **affective component,** or the feelings associated with emotion. It also involves **mood,** a free-floating emotional feeling that does not relate directly to a stimulus.

Emotion includes three distinct but related parts: **physiological arousal, expressive behaviour,** and **cognitive experience.** If your heart pounds in fear when you must present in front of your class, or you feel choked up watching sad movies, you are experiencing physiological arousal. If you turn around and run out of the classroom or cry during the film, you are exhibiting expressive behaviours. Your cognitive experience might include feeling embarrassed and deciding never to watch sad movies in public or to speak to a room full of people. Or you might feel moved and continue to rent sad movies. For people with IEED, these three components can fail to coincide, or do so in ways that are not appropriate for the situation.

> **Emotion** is a subjective reaction to an object, event, person, or memory.
>
> **Affective component** describes feelings associated with emotion.
>
> **Mood** is a free-floating emotional feeling that does not relate directly to a stimulus.
>
> **Physiological arousal** is a heightened bodily reaction to a stimulus.
>
> **Expressive behaviour** is an outward sign that a person is experiencing an emotion.
>
> **Cognitive experience** is the brain's remembered response to experiencing an emotion.
>
> **Universality hypothesis** supposes that facial expressions are understood across all cultures.
>
> **James-Lange theory** proposes that the physiological experience of heart pounding or tears flowing causes a person to feel afraid or sad.
>
> **Cannon-Bard theory** proposes that the mental and physiological components of emotions happen simultaneously.

THE UNIVERSALITY HYPOTHESIS

At some point in your life, you might have experienced emotions so painful that you wished you couldn't feel any emotions at all, but humans have evolved emotions in order to help us survive and reproduce. Fear might make us run away, anger might lead us to defend ourselves, and love might encourage us to bond with others. The facial expressions that indicate our emotions also help us communicate. In *The Expression of the Emotions in Man and Animals*, Charles Darwin (1872/1965) states his **universality hypothesis,** which supposes that facial expressions are understood across all cultures. For instance, a frown means sadness or disapproval in Japan, England, or Botswana, but gestures and other expressions of emotions can vary between cultures. But regardless of cultural norms, the expression of emotion seems so fundamentally tied to the emotion itself that IEED episodes seem especially jarring.

THE JAMES-LANGE THEORY

Many psychologists have attempted to answer the question of whether the physiological experience, the expression, or the awareness of an emotion comes first and produces the other parts. At the end of the 19th century, American psychologist William James and Danish physiologist Carl Lange both simultaneously but independently arrived at the same theory of emotion. They believed that the physiological experience of emotion precedes our cognitive understanding of it. Instead of fear causing your heart to race or sadness causing tears to flow, the **James-Lange theory** proposes that the physiological experience of heart pounding or tears flowing causes you to feel afraid or sad (James, 1890/1950; Lange, 1887).

THE CANNON-BARD THEORY

Walter Cannon and Philip Bard, on the other hand, believed that physiological reactions did not precede emotions because sudden emotions don't allow for the delay in experiencing and then processing. According to the **Cannon-Bard theory,** the mental and physiological components of emotions happen simultaneously (Cannon, 1927). When a 5.4 magnitude earthquake hit Los Angeles on July 30, 2008, Huntington Beach resident Danny Casler woke up from his sleep and ran out of the house in boxer shorts. According to the Cannon-Bard theory, Casler would have simultaneously felt fear and made the decision to run out of the house.

Emotions involve **physiological arousal, expressive behaviour, and cognitive experience.**

SCHACHTER AND SINGER'S TWO-FACTOR THEORY

In the 1960s Stanley Schachter and Jerome Singer (1962) developed the **Schachter and Singer two-factor theory,** which says that the cognitive evaluation happens alongside our physiological arousal to create the emotion we experience. Labels become important since physiological experiences can be very similar. **Schachter's cognition-plus-feedback theory** says that how we perceive an environment feeds back into the physiological arousal and influences what we feel. During a pilgrimage to a temple in India in August 2008, pilgrims were led to believe that they were experiencing a landslide because of a broken railing. As the landslide rumour spread through the crowd, an environment of panic was created, and the pilgrims rushed down the hill, killing 145 people in the stampede.

ZAJONC AND THE MERE EXPOSURE EFFECT

While cognition may be part of emotion, Robert Zajonc (1980, 1984) believed that some emotional reactions could bypass our conscious minds. A flashed image of a smiling or angry face influenced people's emotions, although they had no conscious awareness of having seen the face (Murphy, Monahan, & Zajonc, 1995; Duckworth, Bargh, Garcia, & Chaiken, 2002). Prior experience of a stimulus causes an **exposure effect;** the familiarity of the stimulus primes us to react a certain way (Zajonc, 1968). Some messages can go directly to the **amygdala,** a structure in the brain essential for

> If you are taking an exam while sitting next to someone, you might think that you feel attracted to that person, when in fact you are simply terrified of failing the exam.

unconscious emotional responses such as the fight-or-flight response, leaving our cortex to process the information afterwards. More messages go to the cortex from the amygdala than the other way around.

COGNITIVE-APPRAISAL THEORY

In contrast to Zajonc, Richard Lazarus (1991, 1998) believes that we have to think about our physiological responses in order to develop an emotion. According to the **cognitive-appraisal theory,** if you notice a particular physiological response, you first have to decide what it means before you can feel an emotion. For instance, your heart could be pounding because you're nervous that you didn't prepare for an exam or because you're excited that the person you went on a date with last weekend just walked into the room. Having to decide what emotion a physiological response indicates could lead to **misattribution.** If you are taking an exam while sitting

Schachter and Singer two-factor theory states that cognitive evaluation happens alongside a person's physiological arousal to create the emotion he or she experiences.

Schachter's cognition-plus-feedback theory states that how a person perceives an environment feeds back into physiological arousal and influences what the person feels.

Exposure effect is caused by the prior experience of a stimulus.

Amygdala is part of the limbic system; it is involved in fear detection and conditioning and is essential for unconscious emotional responses such as the fight-or-flight response.

Cognitive-appraisal theory states that if a person notices a particular physiological response, that person has to decide what it means before he or she can feel an emotion.

Misattribution is assigning the incorrect meaning to an emotion because of a particular physiological response.

Thalamus is part of the brain located just above the brainstem that receives sensory information, processes it, and sends it to the cerebral cortex; it helps to regulate the states of arousal, sleep and wakefulness, and consciousness.

next to someone, you might think that you feel attracted to that person, when in fact you are simply terrified of failing the exam.

PLUTCHIK'S MODEL OF PRIMARY EMOTIONS

Robert Plutchik (1980) proposed understanding emotions by organizing them around a wheel. He believed that the eight primary emotions were fear, surprise, sadness, disgust, anger, anticipation, joy, and acceptance. Emotions on the opposite ends of the wheel contrasted with each other just as colours on a colour wheel do. Joy would be the opposite of sadness, and disgust the opposite of acceptance. The pie shape of each emotional sector indicated that emotions could vary in intensity, and emotions such as anger and anticipation could combine to produce aggression.

Emotion and the Body

BRAIN STRUCTURES
The Amygdala

The amygdala, a small structure in the brain that assesses the emotional significance of stimuli, receives information from external stimuli in two different ways: (1) through a short and fast route directly from the **thalamus,** and

Plutchik's Emotion Wheel

Love · Submission · Awe · Disappointment · Remorse · Contempt · Aggressiveness · Optimism

Joy · Acceptance · Fear · Surprise · Sadness · Disgust · Anger · Anticipation

Prefrontal cortex is the very front of the brain and part of the neocortex; it is responsible for the executive functions, such as mediating conflicting thoughts and making choices between right and wrong. It is essential for the cognitive experience of emotion.

Prefrontal lobotomy is a type of surgery in which the prefrontal area of the brain is disabled, causing people to feel less intense emotions but also leaving them unable to plan or manage their lives.

Autonomic nervous system (ANS) is the part of the peripheral nervous system that performs tasks that are not consciously controlled.

Sympathetic division is the part of the autonomic nervous system that tells the hypothalamus to release epinephrine and norepinephrine to prepare the body for action.

Parasympathetic division is the part of the autonomic nervous system that brings the body back to its resting state after actions caused by intense emotions.

Nucleus accumbens is an area of the brain underneath the frontal cortex that is involved in experiencing pleasure.

(2) by a long, slow, and more precise route, from the cortex. The short and fast route keeps us alive by allowing us to prepare even in situations where we do not know the nature of the danger. In such cases, the time it would have taken for the message to reach our cortex and then travel to the amygdala, could very well cost us our life. "Suppose you are walking through a forest when you suddenly see a long, narrow shape coiled up at your feet. This snake-like shape very quickly, via the short route, sets in motion the physiological reactions of fear that are so useful for mobilizing you to face the danger. But this same visual stimulus, after passing through the thalamus, will also be relayed to your cortex. A few fractions of a second later, the cortex, thanks to its discriminatory faculty, will realize that the shape you thought was a snake was really just a discarded piece of garden hose. Your heart will then stop racing, and you will just have had a moment's scare" (Canadian Institutes of Health Research, 2012).

>>> **Communication between the amygdala, thalamus, and cortex** allows us to attach **emotional significance** to what we experience.

Canadian researcher Frederic Gosselin and colleagues have examined the role of the amygdala in humans' ability to recognize emotions. They studied the ability of SM, an adult with bilateral damage to her amygdala, to recognize emotions from facial expressions and music (Adolphs et al., 2005; Gosselin, Peretz, Johnsen, & Adolphs, 2007). They found that SM was not able to detect fear from facial expressions, and she showed a diminished ability to "feel" scary or peaceful music. Researchers from the Hospital for Sick Children in Toronto (Hung, Smith, & Taylor, 2012) found that the amygdala and other parts of the limbic system process emotions differently as we age. Their findings have important implications for our understanding of how and why emotion, perception, and regulation change through the lifespan.

The Prefrontal Cortex

At the anterior of the frontal lobes, the **prefrontal cortex** is essential for the cognitive experience of emotion. As a treatment for severe mental disorders, from 1949 to 1952 about 50 000 people in the United States were given **prefrontal lobotomies,** which left people feeling less intense emotions but also unable to plan or manage their lives. Because the prefrontal cortex receives input from the amygdala and the somatosensory cortex in the parietal lobes, emotion may be essential to the prefrontal cortex's ability to carry out the life functions it controls, such as planning, setting goals, and reasoning.

AUTONOMIC NERVOUS SYSTEM

In fight-or-flight crises, the **autonomic nervous system (ANS)** prepares our bodies for action and controls unconscious processes

such as perspiration and respiration. The two divisions of the autonomic nervous system help us prepare for and recover from emotionally charged actions.

Sympathetic Division

Imagine that you suddenly realize the building you're in is on fire or the bus you need to catch is driving off. Your emotions are high, and you need to act. To prepare for action, the **sympathetic division** of the ANS tells the hypothalamus to release epinephrine (adrenaline) and norepinephrine (noradrenaline). The pituitary gland secretes thyrotrophic hormone (TTH), causing the thyroid gland to make more energy available to the body. Adrenocorticotrophic hormone (ACTH) stimulates the adrenal cortex on the outer part of the adrenal glands, which release epinephrine and norepinephrine. The arousal response causes dilated pupils, decreased salivation, increased perspiration and respiration, accelerated heart rate, and inhibited digestion. These changes allow the body to focus on what it needs to do to get out of the building or catch the bus. Interestingly, this state of arousal aids performance on well-known tasks but hinders new or complex ones. This is referred to as the Yerkes-Dodson law and will be discussed later in the chapter.

The Parasympathetic Division

Once the crisis is over, the **parasympathetic division** takes over and brings the body back to its resting rate. As the adrenal glands stop releasing stress hormones, the heart rate and breathing slow down, perspiration decreases, the pupils contract, and digestion resumes.

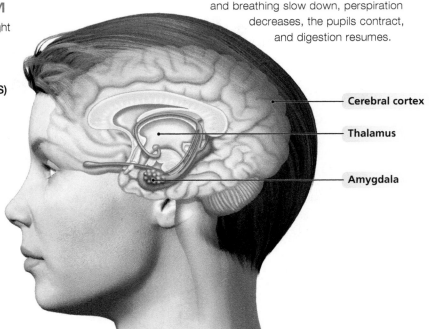

Cerebral cortex

Thalamus

Amygdala

COMPARING SPECIFIC EMOTIONS

Just as your heart might pound as a result of nervousness over an exam or an attractive person, arousal levels for many emotions are similar. Many emotions have physiological similarities. Being ecstatic about winning the lottery produces the same heart rate increase as the fear you might feel while running away from a wild animal. So how can you tell if you're feeling ecstatic or afraid?

You might want to think of emotions as recipes: Each emotion is made up of different physiological ingredients that set it apart. Anger changes finger temperature more than joy or sadness. Anger, fear, or sadness will increase your heart rate far more than happiness, surprise, or disgust. Fear moves different muscles in the face than joy, and the amygdala becomes much more active in someone looking at a fearful rather than an angry face.

Positive and negative emotions also engage different sides of the brain. Negativity, such as resentment or guilt, activates the right side of the prefrontal cortex more than the left. Depressed people often show less activity in the left side of the frontal cortex, which is associated with positive emotions. Research has shown that a major factor in drug addiction involves the way that certain drugs are able to directly tap into the reward system that allows us to feel pleasure functions in a very particular way. Special neurons at the base of the brain send dopamine along a dopaminergic pathway to an area underneath the frontal cortex called the **nucleus accumbens** (Nestler & Malenka, 2004). Electrical stimulation of the nucleus accumbens in depressed people releases dopamine and triggers smiling and laughing.

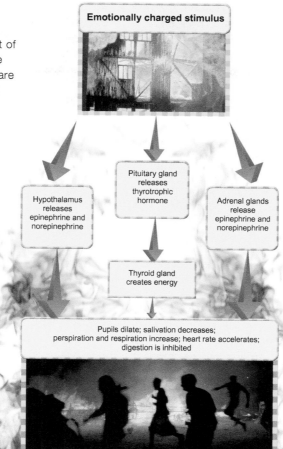

Emotionally charged stimulus

Pituitary gland releases thyrotrophic hormone

Hypothalamus releases epinephrine and norepinephrine

Adrenal glands release epinephrine and norepinephrine

Thyroid gland creates energy

Pupils dilate; salivation decreases; perspiration and respiration increase; heart rate accelerates; digestion is inhibited

Person reacts to stimulus

Non-verbal Emotional Expression

FACIAL EXPRESSION AND EYE CONTACT

It's impressive how much we're able to communicate to each other without words: With just a "look," two people who know each other well can communicate when they want to leave a party or if they've hit on the same idea. Interestingly, not all expressions draw our attention equally. We seem to have radar for threats and

will more easily pick out angry faces from a set of different facial expressions (Fox et al., 2000; Hansen & Hansen, 1988). Experiences also influence which emotions we see more easily. When shown a picture of a face that combined fear, sadness, and anger, physically abused children more frequently classified the expression as angry.

GENDER DIFFERENCES

Gender also informs how we read and express emotions. In general, women can detect and interpret non-verbal cues better than men (Hall, 1984, 1987). When asked to express happiness, sadness, and anger, women expressed happiness better than men, and men expressed anger better than women (Coats & Feldman, 1996). Psychologist Monica Moore found that while flirting, women also communicate better non-verbally and use 52 recorded flirting behaviours, such as hair flipping, head tilting, and smiling coyly, to invite men to approach.

CULTURE

Researchers have shown that people throughout the world use the same facial expressions to show anger, fear, disgust, surprise, happiness, and sadness (Ekman & Friesen, 1975; Ekman et al., 1987; Ekman, 1994). Blind children who have never seen facial expressions will express emotions with the same expressions as sighted people, a fact that argues for the innate biological basis of emotional expression. Although facial expressions seem to be universal, physical gestures and degree of emotional expression vary among cultures. These cultural variations make social interactions challenging in countries like Canada, where there are large populations of multi-ethnic groups.

>>> **A polygraph test** measures vital signs such as blood pressure, heart rate, respiration, and perspiration in order to determine stress levels.

Facial feedback hypothesis states that a person who makes a certain facial expression will feel the corresponding emotion, as long as the person is not feeling some other competing emotion.

Intensification is an exaggeration of emotions.

Deintensification is a muting of emotions.

Masking refers to showing one emotion while feeling another.

Neutralizing refers to showing no emotion, even though the person is actually feeling one.

Morphology is the form or shape of something.

Mood-congruent processing is the selective perception of stimuli congruent with the emotional state of the person experiencing the stimuli.

For example, how do you behave when asked a question in class? Caribbean adults tend to maintain a lot of eye contact when they know the answer to a question, while Canadian adults, followed by Japanese adults, tend to maintain less eye contact. If they have to think about the answer, Canadian and Caribbean adults look up and to the right, while Japanese adults look down (McCarthy et al., 2006, 2008). These differences in gaze behaviour reflect cultural norms. Eye contact is positively perceived in Western society, while looking upward is generally associated with thinking. In Japan, however, looking down is a sign of respect. Understanding cultural differences such as these is necessary for successful cross-cultural communication.

THE FACIAL FEEDBACK HYPOTHESIS AND FACIAL EXPRESSIONS

The **facial feedback hypothesis** says that a person who makes a certain facial expression will feel the corresponding emotion, as long as the person is not feeling some other competing emotion. When people were asked to frown while watching sad films, they felt even sadder than they did while watching the films without

>>> **Canadian Prime Minister Stephen Harper** often gives the "thumbs up" to indicate that **things are going well. How might different cultures** interpret this gesture?

frowning (Larsen, Kasimatis, & Frey, 1992). People who held pencils in their teeth, effectively forcing them to smile, while looking at cartoons reported that the cartoons were more amusing and enjoyable (Strack, Martin, & Stepper, 1988).

DECEPTIVE EXPRESSION
Hiding Emotions

Although forcing yourself to smile might make you feel happy, true expressions actually differ from false ones. If you are pleased to see someone but act overjoyed, you're showing **intensification,** exaggerating your emotions. In public, someone feeling intense grief might find it necessary to use **deintensification** to mute some of their emotions in order to be sociable. Showing one emotion while feeling another is **masking;** the runners-up at award shows smile broadly while feeling miserable about losing the prize. Poker players routinely maintain the "poker face," **neutralizing** whatever they feel, so their opponents have no clues about their hands.

Cognition, or thought, can influence what we feel or believe we feel. **Arousal from one event can spill over into the emotions we experience about other events.**

Detecting Emotions

Regardless of how much people hide their emotions, we can detect them if we know the

signs of true and false emotions. False expressions involve different muscle groups than real ones, and studying their **morphology,** or shape, can tell us if the expressions are real. Sincere emotions have more symmetry than insincere ones, so both sides of the face show the same expression equally. Real expressions last about half a second; false ones can have a longer or shorter duration. Sincere expressions come and go smoothly, but insincere ones start and end abruptly.

Lie Detection

Everyone lies! When someone lies, his or her body shows signs of arousal, which a polygraph test measures. Since many emotions evoke physiological arousal, a person feeling nervous or afraid may appear to be lying. Conversely, spies famously tricked lie detectors because they knew how to control their physiological reactions or confuse results by showing arousal for baseline questions. Thermal imaging can also reveal the different patterns of facial blood flow that accompany a lie. However, many of these techniques may not be reliable. How good are you at hiding your physiological reactions and emotions? Research examining the development of telling lies shows that by the time we are teenagers we can successfully hide, or mask, behaviours, such as eye movements, that would otherwise reveal our deception (McCarthy & Lee, 2009).

Experienced Emotion

COGNITION AND EMOTION

Cognition, or thought, can influence what we feel or believe we feel. Arousal from one event can spill over into the emotions we experience about other events. For example, if someone insults you just after you've completed a long run, you might react more angrily than usual because your body is aroused from physical exercise. Misattribution sometimes leads people to attribute their arousal to the wrong stimulus. When given an injection of epinephrine, a stimulating hormone, subjects attributed their arousal to an attraction to someone in the room (Schachter & Singer, 1962). Sometimes our emotions can influence what we choose to perceive through **mood-congruent processing.** Depressed patients noticed stimuli related to sadness more than to other emotions (Elliott, Rubinsztein, Sahakian, & Dolan, 2002;

Erickson et al., 2005). In general, people will selectively perceive stimuli congruent with their emotional state (Ito, 2000).

Sometimes emotions do not reach our cognitive pathways or even have a cognitive element at all. People tend to prefer an image they have seen before, even if they didn't know they saw it (Elliott & Dolan, 1998). Since the message about the stimulus goes directly from the thalamic nuclei to the amygdala without reaching the cortex, the stimulus can elicit an emotional response without the element of cognition.

When we engage in **emotion regulation,** we use cognitive strategies to control and influence our own emotional responses. For example, if you see your boyfriend or girlfriend animatedly talking to another person, you could stop yourself from feeling jealous or worried by reappraising the situation and deciding that talking does not necessarily indicate romantic involvement. Thoughts can also help us make better decisions. You might have perused college Web sites to decide where to apply and imagined yourself as a student at each school. If so, you engaged in **affective forecasting,** imagining how you would feel about something that might happen in the future.

VALENCE AND AROUSAL

All emotions have a **valence,** a positive or negative value along a continuum, and also vary in degree of arousal. An unpleasant feeling, fear has a negative valence. As a strong emotion, its high arousal makes you act quickly in a frightening situation. Because people don't enjoy feeling bored, boredom would have a negative valence but a low arousal, as a low-energy emotion. By contrast, elation has a positive valence and a high arousal; an elated person feels happy and excited. Sadness has a negative valence and low arousal; sadness feels unpleasant but does not feel particularly stimulating.

FEAR

Fear may not be a comfortable feeling, but it is an adaptive alarm system that prepares us for a fight-or-flight response when faced with danger. Children learn fear by watching others and by experiencing fear-inducing situations. But some fears, such as a fear of snakes and spiders, seem to be biologically hard-wired into us. In a classic experiment of conditioning (that would never be conducted today), researchers Watson and Rayner (1920) taught

an infant named Albert to transfer and generalize his fears. Initially, the child showed fear of loud noises. The researchers synchronized loud noises with the presence of a rat, and the child gradually learned to feel frightened of the rat (as well as of all furry white things—for more on the "Little Albert" study, see Chapter 11). Likewise, children learn to fear heights by repeatedly falling or almost falling (Campos, Bertenthal, & Kermoian, 1992).

ANGER

Facial expressions of anger may be universal, but elements of anger expression can be culturally specific. To preserve group harmony, individuals from cultures that emphasize interdependence tend to express anger less often (Markus & Kitayama, 1991). Tahitians are particularly polite, and Japanese express anger less often than Westerners. In the West, the **catharsis theory,** the idea that expressing emotions to prevent them from building up and exploding, is generally accepted. Many forms of therapy encourage expressions of anger to release pent-up feelings, but studies have shown that "venting" does not decrease rage and actually makes people angrier (Bushman, Baumeister, & Stack, 1999). Venting may give temporary relief, but distracting yourself or redirecting feelings are more effective coping mechanisms.

> Children learn fear by watching others and by experiencing fear-inducing situations. But some fears, such as a fear of snakes and spiders, seem to be biologically hard-wired into us.

HAPPINESS

What's so great about happiness anyway? According to the **feel-good, do-good phenomenon,** when people are already happy, they are more likely to be helpful. Psychologists use **subjective well-being**—a person's self-perceived satisfaction with life—along with objective measures, such as income and health, to evaluate quality of life. Martin Seligman, one of the founders of a field known as positive psychology, believes that psychology should also study highly functioning, not just maladaptive, people. Positive psychology tries to determine the inner strengths, virtues, resources, and character traits that enable people to be happy. Studies have found that negative feelings caused by unpleasant

daily events tend to last for a short period of time and often result in more positive feelings the next day (Affleck, Tennen, Urrows, & Higgins, 1994; Bolger, DeLongis, Kessler, & Schilling, 1989; Stone & Neale, 1984). Similarly, an extremely positive event makes people feel only temporarily happier, and they soon return to their normal state (Brickman, Coates, & Janoff-Bulman, 1978).

We tend to judge our present state by our previous ones, so because of the **adaptation-level phenomenon,** an elevated mood, more money, or greater prestige becomes the new norm (Campbell, 1975), and we start to want even more.

As the saying goes, money can't buy happiness. Those who value and pursue money often feel less happy than those who value love and friendship (Kasser, 2002; Perkins, 1991). People in affluent countries don't seem to be any happier than those in poor countries (Diener & Biswas-Diener, 2002; Eckersley, 2000). However, Canadian psychologist Elizabeth Dunn believes that money CAN buy us happiness—if we spend it right (Dunn, Gilbert, & Wilson, 2011). Dunn and her colleagues outline eight principles for maximizing the happiness we get from money. These principles include: Buy experiences instead of things, help others instead of yourself, and buy many small pleasures instead of a few big ones.

Our happiness also depends on how happy we perceive others to be. While not everyone rejoices in other people's miseries,

Relative deprivation relates to a person's comparison of himself or herself to others; when the person compares himself or herself to someone of higher social standing, he or she feels worse, and when the person compares himself or herself to someone of lower social standing, he or she feels better.

Motivation is a need or desire that energizes and directs behaviour.

Dispositional forces are internal factors involved in motivation.

Situational forces are external factors involved in motivation.

Motivation states are internal conditions that make a person tend toward certain goals.

Drives are internal conditions that make a person tend toward certain goals; this is caused by a departure from optimal states.

Conscious motivation is a motivation that remains in a person's awareness.

Subconscious motivation is a motivation that is not in a person's awareness but can be easily accessed.

Unconscious motivation is a motivation that operates without a person's awareness.

Approach motivation is a motivation involved with striving to achieve a positive result.

Avoidance motivation is a motivation involved with striving to avoid a negative result.

Instincts are unlearned complex behaviours with a fixed pattern throughout a species.

Hedonic principle states that people want to experience pleasure and avoid pain.

Drive-reduction theory states that a person reacts when a physiological need creates an aroused state that drives him or her to reduce the need.

Homeostasis describes a steady and balanced inner state.

Regulatory drives seek to preserve homeostasis.

Non-regulatory drives initiate activities not required to preserve homeostasis.

Social learning theory emphasizes the role of cognition in motivation and the importance of expectations in shaping behaviour.

Central-state theory explains drives by understanding them as corresponding to neural activity.

Central drive system is a set of neurons that create a drive.

most of us do judge our **relative deprivation** by comparing ourselves to others. When we compare ourselves to those of higher social standing, we feel worse; when we compare ourselves to those of lower social standing, we feel better. In a 2012 study on happiness, Canada ranked as the fifth happiest country in the world. Denmark came in first, the United States came in eleventh, and Sierra Leone came in last (Helliwell, Layard, & Sachs, 2012).

So what does make people happy? Although the predictors for happiness vary somewhat by culture, they include optimism, close relationships, faith, meaningful work, good sleeping and eating patterns, and, in individualistic countries, high self-esteem. Age, gender, education levels, parenthood, and physical attractiveness are not reliable predictors of happiness (Diener, Oishi, & Lucas, 2003).

Perspectives on Motivation, Drives, and Incentives

MOTIVATION

In 2009, Bernie Madoff was sentenced to 150 years in prison. He had pleaded guilty to defrauding thousands of investors of billions of dollars in one of the world's largest investment scams. Was it just greed that motivated Madoff or were his reasons more complex?

Motivation is the need or desire that energizes and directs behaviour. It is made up of internal factors— **dispositional forces**—and external factors—**situational forces**—that drive us to do specific things in a particular situation. Motivation answers the question "Why did I do that?" Our **motivation states** and **drives** are internal conditions that make us tend toward certain goals, which may change over time. **Conscious motivations** remain in our awareness, but we can also be motivated by **subconscious motivations,** which are not in our awareness but can be easily accessed, and **unconscious motivations,** which operate without our awareness. Studying to get a good grade on an exam—a positive result—is an example of **approach motivation. Avoidance motivation** would involve pulling an all-nighter so you don't fail. When we act to satisfy a requirement by eating a healthy meal, we fulfill a physical need

∧ ∧ **Why might** ∧ **offering chocolate to a loved one on Valentine's Day make sense physiologically?**

and our drive for food. By eating ice cream after the meal, we satisfy a want, something not considered a requirement.

THEORIES OF MOTIVATION

As Darwin's theories of evolution became popular, so did labelling human instincts. William James (1890) believed that **instincts**— unlearned complex behaviours with a fixed pattern throughout a species—are purposeful in humans and other animals. Sigmund Freud, who believed in the **hedonic principle**—that people want to experience pleasure and avoid pain—described the force of psychic energy initiated by drives as the root of life instincts (including sexuality).

According to Clark Hull's **drive-reduction theory,** we act when a physiological need creates an aroused state that drives us to reduce the need. If we feel tired, we take the action of going to bed to restore **homeostasis**—a steady and balanced inner state. Reducing the tension reinforces the behaviour (Hull, 1943, 1952). Departures from optimal states create drives. **Regulatory drives,** such as hunger and thirst, preserve homeostasis. **Non-regulatory drives,** such as sex or social drives, initiate other activities. A drive to preserve safety motivates feelings of fear, anger, and even the need for sleep. Sexual drives and drives to protect offspring motivate sexual and family relationships. Social drives make people want to co-operate, and educative drives inspire curiosity and play, as well as the pursuit of art and literature.

Julian Rotter (1954) developed the **social learning theory** that emphasizes the role of cognition in motivation and the importance of expectations in shaping behaviour. According to this theory, people do things based on the expectation of obtaining a goal and the importance of that goal to them. If individuals find that behaving in a specific way does not get them what they want, they might change their behaviour. **Central-state theory** explains drives by understanding them as corresponding to neural activity. Different drives have different **central drive systems**—sets of neurons that create the drive. For example, hunger and sex have different but overlapping drive systems. Italian researchers have found a relationship between chocolate consumption and sexual desire, and women with low libido seem to become more interested in sex after eating chocolate.

Located in the base of the brain, the hypothalamus connects to the brainstem and the forebrain and plays a significant role in regulating many central drive systems. The hypothalamus is directly connected to nerves carrying input from internal organs and carrying autonomic motor output back to internal organs. The hypothalamus also connects to and works with the pituitary gland to control hormone release.

INCENTIVES

You may buy a soda because you feel thirsty, but you might also buy it because you watched a commercial touting its refreshing qualities. In addition to drives, **incentives**—positive or negative stimuli in the environment—motivate us to act. A strong drive can increase an incentive's value. If you are thirsty, you feel more influenced by the appearance of a refreshing drink.

Achieving a reward or a goal also reinforces incentives. An **intrinsic reward,** such as a desire to help others or learn new skills, creates its own joy just in performing the action. An **extrinsic reward,** such as studying to get a good grade, means we are motivated to perform an action that produces a separate, tangible reward.

Wanting and Liking

Both winning and enjoying a sport give an athlete a feeling of **liking**—a subjective feeling of pleasure derived from a reward. **Wanting** to win a medal at the Olympics gives athletes the desire to work hard for the reward. **Reinforcement** is the effect of the reward on learning and explains why athletes continue the pursuit of their sports.

Animals with **reward neurons** that are missing or damaged will lose all motivation and die unless artificially fed. The **medial forebrain bundle,** the brain's reward pathway, winds from the midbrain through the hypothalamus into the nucleus accumbens, the synaptic terminal for medial forebrain neurons. Because this pathway controls reward, animals will work long and hard to stimulate it. Rats with electrodes attached to the nucleus accumbens pressed a lever thousands of times to stimulate the brain reward areas (Wise, 1978).

The **liking system** involves pleasure and does not depend on dopamine. For instance,

neuroscientists have found sweet tastes activate the liking system regardless of the level of dopamine. When rats received dopamine-reducing drugs, they still engaged in liking behaviours and only sought out rewards that were directly available. **Endorphins**, morphine-like substances released by the medial forebrain bundle, inhibit pain and may be involved in the immediate pleasure of rewards, such as the runner's high.

By contrast, the **wanting system** depends heavily on dopamine. Rats trained to press a lever for a reward have a short burst of dopamine activity in the nucleus accumbens just before but not after pressing the lever (Phillips et al., 2003). Dopamine also plays a role in learning. When rats are exposed to light just before they receive food, their dopamine activity starts occurring in response to the light. When they expect food, the rats start feeling an anticipation of reward, a feeling well known to those with addictions.

Like a bad romantic relationship, an addiction creates "wanting" without much "liking." Addictions basically hijack the brain's reward system. Cocaine, amphetamines, and narcotics imitate the effects of dopamine and endorphins in the nucleus accumbens. They also stimulate mechanisms that control reward-based learning that activate every time the drug is used, reinforcing the behaviour.

Gambling and games of chance also activate the nucleus accumbens and the reward pathway. In Canada, gambling is a multi-million dollar industry and more and more Canadians are risking their financial security for a shot at the big win. According to Statistics Canada (2010), revenue from gambling brings in over $13 million each year. Over 60% of Canadians have gambled at least once in the last year, with lottery tickets being the most common form of gambling. Young adults, age 18 to 24, have the highest rate of gambling problems (Wiebe, Mun, & Kauffman, 2006). For gamblers, the simple

> **Once** an individual had met biological and safety needs, he or she would seek a feeling of belongingness—the need to feel loved and avoid alienation.

Incentive is a positive or negative stimulus in the environment.

Intrinsic reward is a task that is pleasurable in and of itself.

Extrinsic reward is a reward that is achieved through the completion of a task.

Liking is a subjective feeling of pleasure derived from a reward.

Wanting is a desire to achieve a particular goal in order to receive a reward.

Reinforcement describes an act that causes a response to be more likely to recur.

Reward neurons are neurons involved with experiencing the positive emotions associated with receiving a reward.

Medial forebrain bundle is the brain's reward pathway.

Liking system is a system involved with experiencing pleasure; it does not depend on dopamine.

Endorphins are morphine-like chemicals that inhibit pain signals and are released by the medial forebrain bundle.

Wanting system is a system involved with achieving a goal to receive pleasure; it depends heavily on dopamine.

Optimal arousal is an arousal state in which a person has enough motivation but not so much that he or she feels anxious and unable to perform.

Yerkes-Dodson law states in general that performance peaks with a moderate level of arousal.

anticipation of payoff causes dopaminergic activity and overrides dopamine-conserving mechanisms.

OPTIMAL AROUSAL

Olympic athletes need an **optimal arousal** that gives them enough motivation but not so much that they feel anxious and unable to perform. The **Yerkes-Dodson law** states in

How might gambling addiction resemble drug addiction?

general that performance peaks with a moderate level of arousal (Yerkes & Dodson, 1908). Described graphically, the Yerkes-Dodson law resembles an inverted U: Performance levels increase as arousal increases, but only up to a certain point (the peak of the inverted U). After that, performance levels decrease as arousal increases. Easier tasks have higher optimal levels of arousal, and more difficult tasks have lower optimal levels of arousal. Tasks requiring persistence also generally require more arousal than intellectual ones. Optimal arousal to compete in a sport would be higher than to play chess.

MASLOW'S HIERARCHY OF NEEDS

Abraham Maslow (1970) described motivation through a **hierarchy of needs** in which more basic levels had to be fulfilled before higher levels. **Physiological needs,** such as hunger and thirst, appeared at the bottom of the hierarchy as the most basic level. **Safety,** a feeling of being in a secure and safe environment, came next on the hierarchy. Once an individual had met biological and safety needs, he or she would seek a feeling of **belongingness**—the

need to feel loved and avoid alienation. Then come **esteem needs,** feelings of worthiness and achievement. At the very top of the hierarchy, Maslow (1971) placed **self-actualization,** a complete feeling of self-acceptance and an awareness of fulfilling one's unique potential. (For more information about the hierarchy of needs, see Chapter 15).

Hunger

THE PHYSIOLOGY OF HUNGER

If you've ever skipped breakfast before an early-morning class, you've probably experienced the embarrassment of your stomach growling loud enough to alert everyone in the room of your hunger. A. L. Washburn swallowed a balloon to monitor stomach contractions and discovered that feelings of hunger did indeed correspond to stomach contractions (Cannon & Washburn, 1912). But removing the stomach in rats and humans did not eliminate hunger, leading to new theories about its source.

Hunger, Body Chemistry, and the Brain

The levels of **glucose**—blood sugar—help determine hunger and satiety. When glucose levels drop, we feel hungry. If glucose levels rise, the hormone **insulin** reduces them by telling the body to convert glucose to fat. As the body monitors these chemical levels, it sends messages to the brain about whether or not to eat.

Research has shown the role the hypothalamus plays in regulating hunger along a dual centre model. The lateral hypothalamus secretes the hormone **orexin,** which brings on feelings of hunger, an orexogenic response. When the lateral hypothalamus was electrically stimulated, rats that already felt full started eating. When the area was damaged or removed, even starving rats had no desire to eat (Sakurai et al., 1998). The ventromedial hypothalamus suppresses hunger and sends out **anorexogenic** signals that stop an animal from eating. The hypothalamus's **arcuate nucleus** contains both appetite-stimulating and -suppressing neurons.

Not all hunger originates in internal body states. Many people seem to have room for dessert even when they already feel full after a meal. In this case, the **gustatory sense**— taste—mediates hunger. Satiety, a feeling of satisfaction, also involves sensory stimuli in the

environment. The dessert looks appetizing, so we feel like eating it. Animals that eat a certain food until they feel satisfied will eat again if introduced to a novel food or taste. The sweet taste of dessert presents a new taste compared to the savoury one of the meal.

> "Many people seem to have room for dessert even when they already feel full after a meal. **In this case, the gustatory sense— taste—mediates hunger**."

Sexual Motivation

SYNCHRONY

Most mammals' sexual drives synchronize with their hormonal levels and chemical signals. The female cyclic production of estrogen and progesterone is the menstrual cycle in humans and the estrous cycle in other animals. In female rats, the ventromedial area of the hypothalamus corresponds to the preoptic area in males. For female mammals, estrogen peaks at ovulation, when the female becomes sexually receptive. Testosterone levels in male mammals remain more constant but still influence sexual behaviour.

The human female's sex drive synchronizes less with her hormonal levels than in most other mammals. The female sex drive increases somewhat during ovulation but has more to do with testosterone levels than estrogen levels (Harvey, 1987; Meuwissen & Over, 1992; Meston & Frohlich, 2000; Reichman, 1998). Testosterone therapy, such as the testosterone patch, increases sex drive in women who feel a reduced desire for sex due to removal of the ovaries or adrenal glands. In males, testosterone also controls sex drive. For humans, sexual activity may be about pleasure as much as it is for procreation—that is, biological as well as social factors play a role in our sexuality.

CASTRATION

In 17th- and 18th-century Europe, prepubescent boys who were castrated to preserve their high singing voices did not develop adult male sex characteristics or sexual desire. Castrated adult males also lose their desire for sex as their testosterone levels decline. Male sexual offenders given Depo-Provera to reduce testosterone to prepubescent levels also report less interest in sex. Some studies show a decrease in repeat offences, but others indicate that the treatment does not reduce the rapist's desire to express aggression through sex (Criminal Justice Special Report, 1988).

Belongingness

When high school students try to be part of a clique or adults join professional groups, they are responding to a human need to belong. In *Nicomachean Ethics*, Aristotle called humans the "social animal." Belonging does not simply make life more fulfilling; social bonds may have evolved to boost our ancestors' survival rates. Attachments between parents and children keep children close and protected. The word *wretched* comes from the Middle English word *wrecche*, meaning to be without kin nearby. Early humans probably fought, hunted, and foraged together to give themselves protection against predators and enemies.

Wanting to belong seems to be a cross-cultural need. A Zulu saying goes, "Umuntu ngumntu ngabantu," meaning "a person is a person through other persons." We act to increase our social acceptance because self-esteem tends to waver based on how valued and accepted we feel. Our need to maintain relationships means that we stay in close contact with our friends and relatives. Being excluded hurts, and groups use social ostracism as a means of control. An online study showed that even the mildest forms of ostracism can control behaviour powerfully (Williams et al., 2000). Participants playing a virtual game felt upset as other (computer-generated) participants began excluding them. In a second study, the ostracized participants complied more readily on tasks. Rejection literally hurts; social pain causes increased activity in the anterior cingulate cortex, an area involved in physical pain (Eisenberger & Lieberman, 2004). University students told during an experiment that they would be excluded from a group started showing more self-defeating and destructive behaviours (Twenge et al., 2001; Twenge et al., 2002). Conversely, social safety nets and a sense of belonging can improve and preserve health.

Developing a sense of belonging can be particularly difficult, but even more important, for new immigrants. With changes in customs, the absence of previous social networks, new jobs, and new expectations, moving to a new country can be scary, frustrating, and isolating. But Statistics Canada's Ethnic Diversity Survey (2007) shows that as Canadian immigrants and their children grow older, their attachment to Canada strengthens.

∧ How do changing schools, moving
∧ to a new country, or starting a new
∧ job affect our **sense of belonging?**

Motivation at Work

JOB SATISFACTION

Given the current world economy, it is not surprising that unemployment causes as much unhappiness as bereavement and separation, while job security and good relationships lead to greater job satisfaction than pay or flexible work (Helliwell, Layard, & Sachs, 2012). Mihaly Csikszentmihalyi (1990, 1999) defined the feeling of being fully and comfortably engaged in work as "flow." We experience flow when tasks absorb us completely and demand enough from us, not too much or too little. A musician playing onstage, a chef busily preparing a dish, or a scientist engaged in research may all experience flow.

According to **equity theory,** workers decide how satisfied they feel with their jobs by comparing themselves to others. If they notice that they do a certain amount of work and get a specific reward while others do less work and get the same reward, they may feel unfairly treated. They may ask for a raise, work less, or leave their positions.

∧ What lessons can **employers learn**
∧ about how to increase employee job
satisfaction, so that they experience flow?

Review

Summary

WHAT ARE THE COMPONENTS OF EMOTION AND MOTIVATION? p.122

• Emotions are made up of three distinct but related parts: physiological arousal, expressive behaviour, and cognitive experience.

• We are motivated by both dispositional forces (internal states and drives) and situational forces (external stimuli).

WHAT ARE THE DOMINANT THEORIES OF EMOTION AND MOTIVATION? p.122

• Theories of emotion are the James-Lange theory (physiological response precedes cognition), Cannon-Bard theory (physiology and cognition are simultaneous), Schachter-Singer two-factor theory (perception along with physiological response produces emotion), cognitive-appraisal theory (cognitive evaluation follows physiological response to produce emotion), and Plutchik's emotion wheel (eight primary emotions combine to form more complex emotions).

• Theories of motivation are drive-reduction theory (actions are motivated by a drive to reduce physiological need), social learning theory (actions are motivated by the expectation of achieving goals), and central-state theory (drives are created by neural systems).

WHAT PARTS OF OUR BRAIN ARE INVOLVED IN MOTIVATION AND EMOTION? p.123

• Emotions are processed in many parts of our brain including the prefrontal cortex, amygdala, and somatosensory cortex.

• When we are in danger, the fight-or-flight response is initiated by the sympathetic nervous system. Once the crisis is over, the parasympathetic nervous system brings the body back to its resting state.

HOW DO WE EXPLAIN THE EMOTIONS OF FEAR, ANGER, AND HAPPINESS? p.127

• Fear protects us by initiating a fight-or-flight response.

• Anger is a universal emotion, but its expression is culturally specific.

• Happiness tends to be temporary, makes people helpful, depends on our sense of success relative to others, and can be bought.

WHAT MOTIVATES PHYSIOLOGICAL AND SOCIAL BEHAVIOURS? p.128

• Our physiological and social needs and behaviours are subject to motivational states.

• Hunger depends on stomach contractions, glucose levels, hypothalamic secretions of orexin, and the gustatory sense.

• The levels of testosterone, estrogen, and other hormones in our bodies influence our sex drives. However, other social or recreational motivations may influence sexual behaviour.

• Job security, equity, and good relationships are key for job satisfaction.

• A feeling of belonging maximizes survival, and its absence resembles physical pain.

• People find intrinsically rewarding work to be most satisfying.

Test Your Understanding

1. People with IEED can feel one emotion but express another because emotions have:
   a. learned and innate dimensions
   b. control over cognition and behaviour
   c. their origin in neurological structures
   d. cognitive and expressive components

2. According to Darwin's universality hypothesis, which of the following would signify happiness or approval across all cultures?
   a. a "thumbs up" gesture
   b. a smile
   c. a wink
   d. an outstretched arm

3. If you were to find yourself in some remote area of the world inhabited by people who were unknown to the rest of the world, you would:
   a. be able to recognize all of their facial expressions of emotion
   b. be able to recognize only their facial expressions of anger and happiness
   c. have great difficulty recognizing any of their facial expressions of emotion
   d. be able to recognize many of their facial expressions of emotion

4. The attempt to hide an emotion is called:
   a. modulation
   b. masking
   c. simulation
   d. emotional deception

5. In laughter therapy, people lift their mood by standing in a circle and saying "ha ha" as a way to make themselves laugh. Which theory of emotion does this technique demonstrate?
   a. James-Lange
   b. Cannon-Bard
   c. cognitive-appraisal
   d. Schachter-Singer two-factor

6. Which of the following concepts is present in both the Schachter-Singer two-factor theory and the cognitive-appraisal theory?

   a. Cognitive experience primes us to react in particular ways.
   b. Cognitive experience precedes physiological arousal.
   c. Physiological arousal and evaluation of emotion occur simultaneously.
   d. Different emotions have similar physiological expressions.

7. How might the principle of mere exposure be used to ensure that moviegoers feel scared during a horror film?

   a. Cold air could be pumped into the theatre.
   b. A fearful face could be flashed onto the screen prior to the film.
   c. Moviegoers could be required to watch the film by themselves.
   d. Moviegoers could be asked to record their physiological reactions.

8. Which sequence of events describes emotions according to the cognitive-appraisal theory?

   a. Your heart pounds as you feel fear and then decide to run.
   b. Your heart pounds, you run, and you realize that you feel fear.
   c. Your heart pounds; then you decide you feel fear, and you run.
   d. You feel fear; then you notice that your heart is pounding, and you run.

9. Yoko is feeling angry, and Li is feeling sad. Which of the following is most likely to be true?

   a. Yoko is experiencing flow and Li is not.
   b. Yoko's finger temperature has changed more than Li's has.
   c. Yoko's heart rate has decreased and Li's heart rate has risen.
   d. Both Yoko and Li are exercising the same facial muscles.

10. Damien is in love, and he finds himself paying particular attention to the sunny, beautiful weather outside. Damien's experience is an example of:

    a. affective forecasting
    b. facial-feedback hypothesis
    c. mood-congruent processing
    d. adaptation-level phenomenon

11. Which of the following best describes the valence and arousal of extreme embarrassment?

    a. positive valence and low arousal
    b. negative valence and low arousal
    c. positive valence and high arousal
    d. negative valence and high arousal

12. Which of the following do polygraph tests measure?

    a. arousal
    b. truthfulness
    c. eye movement
    d. amygdala activity

13. Which of the following best exemplifies William James's conception of an instinct?

    a. dogs pulling sleds
    b. people going to work
    c. beavers building dams
    d. horses running in races

14. A teacher ignores students who don't raise their hands before asking a question. Which theory is the teacher employing?

    a. drive-reduction theory
    b. social learning theory

    c. central-state theory
    d. dispositional force theory

15. According to the Yerkes-Dodson law, which of the following states is an optimal level of arousal?

    a. extreme relaxation and calmness
    b. moderate relaxation and calmness
    c. moderate nervousness and excitement
    d. extreme nervousness and excitement

16. Kristen, a 13-year-old girl, is teased by her classmates and excluded from parties and other social activities. As a result, Kristen most likely experiences:

    a. increased levels of dopamine in the brain
    b. increased activity in the anterior cingulate cortex
    c. decreased levels of adrenaline in the brain
    d. decreased activity in the prefrontal cortex

17. Which best summarizes the rationale behind Maslow's hierarchy of needs?

    a. Everyone has different basic needs.
    b. All needs are equally important.
    c. Basic survival needs motivate us before other needs.
    d. Humans are only able to fulfill one need at a time.

18. What do we know about the mechanisms of hunger?

    a. The lateral hypothalamus controls hunger.
    b. Stomach contractions are the only cause of hunger.
    c. When glucose levels in the blood rise, we feel hungry.
    d. Mental, physical, and environmental factors contribute to hunger.

19. A woman with a low sex drive is most likely to have:

    a. high estrogen levels
    b. high adrenaline levels
    c. low testosterone levels
    d. low progesterone levels

20. Which of the following is more likely to lead to job satisfaction?

    a. job security
    b. flexible work hours
    c. pay increase
    d. being the boss

Remember to check www.thethinkspot.ca **for additional information, downloadable flashcards, and other helpful resources.**

Answers: 1) d; 2) b; 3) d; 4) b; 5) a; 6) d; 7) b; 8) c; 9) b; 10) c; 11) d; 12) a; 13) c; 14) b; 15) c; 16) b; 17) c; 18) d; 19) c; 20) a

133 / Emotion and Motivation

CONSCIOUSNESS

Greg Koons

heard strange noises coming from his neighbours' backyard. Peering over the cinder-block wall, he saw a woman writhing on the ground near the swimming pool. Koons's neighbour, Scott Falater, was calmly walking toward the struggling woman, wearing a pair of canvas gloves. With a dawning sense of horror, Koons watched his neighbour drag the woman toward the swimming pool, push her in, and hold her head under the water. Koons immediately called 911, but by the time the emergency services arrived, the woman—Falater's wife, Yarmila—was dead from multiple stab wounds and drowning.

The incident, which took place in Phoenix, Arizona, in 1997, seemed like an open-and-shut case. An eyewitness saw his neighbour brutally murder his wife of 20 years. And Scott Falater, a 43-year-old father of two, certainly didn't deny the killing. But Falater had an unusual defence, which he hoped would spare him from a conviction of murder in the first degree—he claimed he had been sleepwalking at the time.

Claiming to be unconscious while committing a brutal act is not unheard of; in 1981, Steven Steinberg was acquitted of murder under the temporary insanity defence, after stabbing his wife 26 times. Witnesses testified that Steinberg may have been sleepwalking or in a dissociative mental state while committing the crime. Falater was not

so lucky. Jurors did not believe that a sleepwalking man would have the foresight to change his bloody clothes, hide the hunting knife used in the stabbing, and stash incriminating evidence in the trunk of his car—all actions that Falater managed to complete before his arrest. Although sleep experts at his trial testified that Falater's story was possible, skeptics theorized that his actions would have taken much more time to complete than a normal sleep cycle would permit. In 1999, Falater was convicted of murder in the first degree and sentenced to life imprisonment without the possibility of parole. Although, these "murder while sleepwalking" cases happened quite a while ago, there is still great debate over whether actions such as murder are possible while asleep. Just how much awareness do we have while we are asleep, and are we responsible for our actions? Should sleepwalking be a valid defence for a crime? If so, how can a jury distinguish between genuine, tragic cases and instances of cold-blooded killers providing convenient excuses? Would the verdicts have been different if the defendants' consciousness were altered as a result of drugs rather than sleep? An in-depth study of consciousness and the physiological changes the body goes through during altered states of consciousness may enable us to make more informed judgments.

<<< *Unlike most states of consciousness, sleep has its own holiday: World Sleep Day, which occurs every March, raises awareness of sleep disorders and sleep health worldwide. In China, where one man dozed next to a sculpture of a dragon, studies have found that nearly 40% of the population suffers from a sleep disorder such as insomnia or sleep apnea.*

CHAPTER **10**

Consciousness and Information Processing

Today, most psychologists define **consciousness** as our awareness of ourselves and our environment. This definition, however, may be deceptively straightforward. We each look at the world from a slightly different perspective, and our observations and experiences tend to be subjective. Since none of us see the world—or ourselves—in exactly the same way, it is likely that consciousness is a unique experience for each individual.

Phenomenology is the study of individual consciousness that addresses subjective experience. You know what the colour red looks like, and if you pointed at a stop sign or a fire truck and asked your friend what colour it was, she'd probably say, "It's red, of course." But how do you know that your friend's perception of red is identical to your perception of red? The colour that your friend describes as red might actually look green or purple to you. Unfortunately, there's no way to determine whether your experience of the colour red matches your friend's. This fundamental difficulty of trying to understand the consciousness of others is known as the **problem of other minds**: Because the nature of consciousness is internal, we can't possibly determine how similar or different another person's perceptions are to our own.

LEVELS OF CONSCIOUSNESS

Was Falater consciously aware of stabbing his wife 44 times? If he was truly sleepwalking, it is possible that he was not functioning at the same level of awareness as a person in a wakened state. Someone who is not fully alert to his or her mental processes may be experiencing an **altered state of consciousness**—bizarre, disorganized, or dreamlike thought patterns. We enter these altered states naturally when we sleep or daydream, but they can also be purposely induced through drugs, meditation, or hypnosis.

When we sleep, we experience **minimal consciousness**—a relatively fragmented connection between self and environment in which we might respond to a stimulus without being aware of it at a more thoughtful level.

Full consciousness, on the other hand, describes not only an awareness of one's environment but also an awareness of one's mental state and the ability to provide information about it. Metacognition, or thinking about thoughts, is a feature of this level. During Falater's trial, prosecutors argued that because he had the presence of mind to hide crucial evidence immediately following his wife's murder, he was clearly in a state of full consciousness—and thus criminally responsible for his actions.

The most self-aware state of consciousness, **self-consciousness,** allows us to focus on our individual selves. We enter a state of self-consciousness every time we examine ourselves in the mirror: Recognizing one's own reflection is a fairly advanced skill that requires self-consciousness to perform, and most animals can't achieve it. In fact, researchers have used mirror self-recognition tests to prove that humans, orangutans, and chimpanzees are among the relatively few species to possess some level of self-consciousness. In humans, this skill usually develops around the age of 18 months.

When we focus on ourselves, we tend to notice our successes and our shortcomings; self-evaluation and self-criticism are two aspects of self-consciousness.

NONCONSCIOUS, PRECONSCIOUS, AND UNCONSCIOUS INFORMATION

Are we aware of everything we do? Not entirely. In fact, our brains store a significant amount of nonconscious, preconscious, and unconscious information. If you're skeptical of this claim, try to remember the last time you checked to make sure your heart kept beating while you were asleep. We don't consciously monitor and adjust our body's vital processes like blood flow, pulse rate, and oxygen intake, but we each carry out hundreds of these **nonconscious activities** every day.

Other types of information are **preconscious,** which means that we might not always be aware of them, but we can bring them into

∧ If you weren't **self-conscious,**
∧ how might you **interpret** what
you see in the **mirror?**

Consciousness is a person's awareness of himself or herself and his or her environment.

Phenomenology is the study of individual consciousness that addresses subjective experience.

Problem of other minds states that because the nature of consciousness is internal, a person can't possibly determine how similar or different another person's perceptions are to his or her own.

Altered state of consciousness is a state characterized by bizarre, disorganized, or dreamlike thought patterns.

Minimal consciousness describes a relatively fragmented connection between self and environment in which a person might respond to a stimulus without being aware of it at a more thoughtful level.

Full consciousness is a state of consciousness in which a person is aware of his or her own environment and also is aware of his or her mental state and is able to provide information about it.

Self-consciousness is the most self-aware state of consciousness; it allows a person to focus on his or her individual self.

Nonconscious activity is a process that occurs in the body that people do not have to consciously monitor or regulate.

Preconscious information is usually outside a person's awareness, but is able to be brought into consciousness on demand.

consciousness on demand. For example, with a little effort, we can bring preconscious memories into our conscious minds. A familiar scent or a vivid photograph can make old, preconscious memories memorable again; that's why a whiff of pumpkin pie can trigger memories of that long-ago Thanksgiving dinner you thought you'd forgotten. (For more information about memory, see Chapter 12.)

> " Fortunately for us, we're able to focus our consciousness by **paying attention only to the things that are most important at any given time**. "

According to Sigmund Freud, some experiences, ideas, and motives are so threatening or unacceptable that we have permanently removed them from our consciousness. Freud believed that we bury this **unconscious information** through the process of repression (see Chapter 15). Contemporary psychologists have reinterpreted these ideas by developing the concept of a **cognitive unconscious**—a collection of mental processes that affect the way we feel or behave, even though we are not consciously aware of them. For example, if a photo of a smiling person flashes very briefly before your eyes, you may not even be aware that you've seen the picture. However, it's likely that you'll feel happier than you did before, even though you can't quite explain why. This process, which enables unconsciously perceived stimuli to affect our thoughts and feelings, is part of the cognitive unconscious.

SURVIVAL ADVANTAGES OF CONSCIOUSNESS

Our ability to be conscious of information on a number of different levels—and to move some pieces of information in and out of consciousness as necessary—gives us a significant advantage when it comes to survival. If we were completely unaware of ourselves and our environments, we wouldn't last long in a group of predators (or on a four-lane highway, for that matter). At the same time, if we were conscious of every single thing going on around and inside us, we would likely be completely overwhelmed and unable to function effectively.

The Restrictive Function

Thanks to the **restrictive function** of consciousness, we don't waste our attention on information that is not immediately relevant to our situations. The restrictive function allows us to exercise selective attention, or a conscious focus on one stimulus or perception at a given time (see Chapter 4). For example, when you take an exam, the restrictive function of consciousness lets you focus on reading and answering the questions without becoming preoccupied by the feeling of your shirt against your skin or the pressure of the pencil against your finger. This function is also responsible for the cocktail party phenomenon, or our ability to selectively tune in to particular messages while filtering out others in a crowded, noisy, or chaotic environment (see Chapter 4).

Selective Storage Function

Closely linked to the restrictive function, the **selective storage function** of consciousness allows us to selectively analyze, interpret, and act on stimuli. In other words, we are able to choose the sights, sounds, and other sensations that we want to pay particular attention to. For example, if you wore a special set of headphones designed to play two messages simultaneously, one in each ear, you would most likely be able to choose to listen only to the message in your right ear and ignore the message in your left. Then, if you decided to pay attention to the message in your left ear instead,

Unconscious information consists of experiences, ideas, and motives that are so threatening or unacceptable that a person has permanently removed them from his or her consciousness.

Cognitive unconscious is a collection of mental processes that affect the way a person feels or behaves, even though he or she is not consciously aware of them.

Restrictive function is an aspect of consciousness that allows people to exercise selective attention, or a conscious focus on one stimulus or perception at a given time.

Selective storage function is an aspect of consciousness that allows people to selectively analyze, interpret, and act on stimuli.

you would be able to consciously refocus your attention.

The "selectivity" of the selective storage function can vary over time, as things to which we once devoted our attention become less important for us to think about consciously. When we first learn a novel, complex task—such as driving, for example—we must consciously focus on each aspect of the activity. During this learning period, other stimuli or thoughts—the sound of thunder in the distance, plans for the upcoming weekend—tend to be selectively restricted from our conscious awareness. As we gain mastery over the individual aspects of driving, it becomes an automatic process. This change "frees up" our consciousness to focus on other thoughts; we can simultaneously consider the weekend's events while safely navigating through traffic.

Executive Control Function

Imagine that a friend breaks a promise to help you study, leaving you woefully unprepared for a big exam. You're furious, but rather than pummelling your

>>> The **restrictive function of consciousness** allows you to **focus awareness** on the person you're talking to **in a crowded room**.

Executive control function is an aspect of consciousness that helps people inhibit urges they have that are not moral, ethical, or practical; it equips people with the conscious self-awareness necessary to analyze and evaluate their thoughts before they act on those thoughts.

Planning function see *executive control function.*

Sleep is a natural loss of consciousness.

Circadian rhythm is a biological clock that regulates body functions on a 24-hour cycle.

Suprachiasmatic nucleus is the part of the hypothalamus that controls the circadian clock.

Melatonin is a sleep-inducing hormone.

Adenosine is a sleep-inducing hormone.

Rapid eye movement (REM) sleep is a recurring stage of sleep during which vivid dreams usually occur.

Beta wave is a type of brainwave that characterizes active wakefulness.

Alpha wave is a type of brainwave that characterizes a relaxed state of wakefulness.

Theta wave is a type of brainwave that characterizes the first stage of sleep.

Hypnagogia is a period of transition between wakefulness and stage one sleep.

K-complex is a biphasic wave form that occurs spontaneously during sleep.

Sleep spindle is a burst of fast, sharply pointed brainwaves.

Delta wave is a type of brainwave with a high amplitude that characterizes stage three sleep.

---

friend with a physical or verbal assault, you express your frustration through pointed, but tactful, words. What helped you make this wise, conscious choice? The **executive control function** (also called the **planning function**) of consciousness. The executive control function helps us to inhibit urges we have that are not moral, ethical, or practical, and it equips us with the conscious self-awareness necessary to analyze and evaluate our thoughts before we act on them. This high-level conscious processing enables us to avoid saying or doing inappropriate things. While most people would agree that the executive control function is crucial, especially in social situations, it's not particularly speedy: Because it happens serially, or in sequence, rather than all at once, high-level conscious processing takes place relatively slowly compared to other types of information processing. If you want to confront your friend about his broken promise as coolly and rationally as possible, you might need to wait a few minutes to give your executive control function a chance to step in.

> " Our temperatures rise in the morning, peak during the day, and decline both in early afternoon and before we go to sleep. Recent research suggests that thinking and memory peak consistently with circadian arousal. "

Sleep

Sleep—the natural loss of consciousness— often seems like it's beyond our control. This notion formed the basis of Scott Falater's defence against the murder charges filed against him: He claimed that he was not in control of, or responsible for, his actions while sleeping. But, if our conscious minds aren't in control of our sleeping bodies' behaviours, what is in control?

CIRCADIAN RHYTHM

One force that controls our sleep patterns is the body's **circadian rhythm,** a biological clock that regulates body functions on a 24-hour cycle. Circadian rhythms affect whether we are awake or asleep as well as our body temperatures and levels of arousal during periods of sleep and wakefulness. Our temperatures rise in the morning, peak during the day, and decline both in early afternoon and before we go to sleep. Recent research suggests that thinking and memory peak consistently with circadian arousal. While this peak occurs at different times for different people, it seems to occur at increasingly earlier times of day as we age (Roenneberg et al., 2004). This explains why many older adults rise at dawn, eat dinner by 5 p.m., and are asleep by 8 or 9 p.m. For college students, perhaps like you, who feel lively and energetic at night but struggle to make it to 9 a.m. classes, this likely comes as no surprise. New Canadian research indicates that dopamine plays a critical role in our circadian rhythm. In fact, it is the daily fluctuations in the levels of dopamine that determine the rhythm of the "clock protein" that regulates our circadian rhythm (Hood et al., 2010).

Circadian rhythms are not immune to effects from external factors. For example, light can alter or reset our circadian clocks. When light

hits the eye, it activates light-sensitive proteins in the retina. These, in turn, signal the **suprachiasmatic nucleus**—the part of the hypothalamus that controls the circadian clock. The suprachiasmatic nucleus causes the pineal gland to either increase (in the evening) or decrease (in the morning) production of **melatonin,** a sleep-inducing hormone. When we stay up until 1 a.m. in a well-lit place, we're exposed to artificial light, which tricks our bodies into producing less melatonin at a time when it should be producing more, delaying sleep and pushing back our biological clocks (Oren & Terman, 1998). Thus many young people operate on a 25-hour cycle because they stay up late and don't rise until late morning or early afternoon.

Because the suprachiasmatic nucleus plays a key role in regulating sleep, damage to this area of the brain can have devastating effects, such as causing random periods of sleep throughout the day. It is like taking the batteries out of the circadian clock.

Adenosine, another sleep-inducing hormone, increases as the night wears on, inhibiting certain neurons and making us drowsy. However, if we need to hold off adenosine's soporific effects late into the evening, we can block its activity by ingesting a few cups of coffee, a Red Bull, or any other potent source of caffeine. But this disruption to our circadian rhythm could harm our health. Canadian researchers (Martino et al., 2008) have found that hamsters whose circadian rhythms were disrupted experienced cardiovascular and renal disease and died sooner compared to hamsters with undistributed rhythms.

SLEEP STAGES

Before the 1950s, scientists assumed that all sleep was essentially created equal; that is, they believed that there were no distinguishing physiological or psychological factors between the sleep you experience in the first 10 minutes after lying down and the sleep that occurs in the middle of the night. In 1952, however, University of Chicago graduate student Eugene Aserinsky made a serendipitous discovery that paved the way for research into the distinct rhythms and patterns that characterize sleep. In an effort to repair a malfunctioning electroencephalogram (EEG) machine, Aserinsky decided to test the machine on his sleeping eight-year-old son, Armond. EEG machines collect amplified recordings of the brain's electrical activity through electrodes placed on a person's skull. After attaching the electrodes near Armond's eyes, Aserinsky was astounded to find the machine recording a dramatic zigzag pattern (Aserinsky, 1988; Seligman & Yellen, 1987). The pattern, which coincided with Armond's perceptible jerky eye movements, recurred several times throughout the night. Even more interestingly, when Armond was awakened during one of these periods, he told his father he had been in the middle of a dream. Aserinsky realized that the darting eyes, lively brainwaves, and the dream were related and, most importantly, indicative of a distinct stage of sleep—**rapid eye movement (REM) sleep,** a recurring stage of sleep during which vivid dreams usually occur.

Aserinsky went on to collaborate with Nathaniel Kleitman on similar studies, and their research, among that of others, yielded the discovery of other sleep stages characterized by specific brainwave activity (Aserinsky & Kleitman, 1953). We now know, through the use of EEGs on sleeping participants, that sleep comprises five distinct stages that we cycle through every 90 minutes.

> Some people report feeling as though they are floating weightlessly above the bed during the hypnagogic period. Although there's nothing otherworldly about these strange sensations, their existence may explain individuals' accounts of alleged alien abductions or other "supernatural" experiences (Moody & Perry, 1993).

Stage One and Stage Two

If you used an EEG to measure the neural activity of someone who was on the verge of falling asleep, what would you discover? You'd most likely get evidence of a few different types of brainwaves. As we prepare for sleep, our brains transition from producing the low-amplitude, fast, and irregular **beta waves** that characterize active wakefulness to producing the slower **alpha waves** that characterize a relaxed state of wakefulness. As we enter the first stage of sleep, alpha wave activity decreases and larger, slower **theta wave** activity increases. Stage one lasts approximately 10 minutes on average.

Awake	Stage 1	Stage 2	Stages 3 & 4	REM Sleep

Several strange, often disconcerting sensations can occur during **hypnagogia,** or the period of transition between wakefulness and sleep that typifies stage one. One of these is the hypnagogic jerk—a sudden jerk of the body just as one is drifting off to sleep. A less common hypnagogic sensation is referred to as "exploding head syndrome," characterized by what sounds like a loud internal bang just as one falls asleep. Some people report feeling as though they are floating weightlessly above the bed during the hypnagogic period. Although there's nothing otherworldly about these strange sensations, their existence may explain individuals' accounts of alleged alien abductions or other "supernatural" experiences (Moody & Perry, 1993).

As we continue to doze, we become increasingly relaxed, and soon we enter stage two of sleep. This stage lasts about 20 minutes and is marked by the periodic appearance of **K-complexes,** biphasic wave forms that occur spontaneously, and **sleep spindles,** which are bursts of fast, sharply pointed brainwaves. Although the physiological roles of K-complexes and sleep spindles are still unclear, many researchers believe that their function is to inhibit conscious awareness to protect the sleeper from awakening (Hess, 1965). However, during stage two, we can still be woken up fairly easily.

Stage Three and Stage Four

Sleep stages three and four feature the kind of sleep most of us covet: deep, refreshing, and largely immune to disturbances. During the transitional stage three, slow, irregular, high-amplitude **delta waves** begin to appear. These patterns continue into stage four, another slow-wave, deep-sleep stage that lasts about 30 minutes (although it gets shorter and eventually disappears as the night progresses). People in

stages three and four are usually difficult to wake up, and if they are awoken, they tend to be groggy and disoriented. For reasons that scientists don't completely understand, children who wet the bed or sleepwalk tend to do so at the end of stage four. Among three- to 12-year-olds, approximately 20% had at least one instance of sleep-walking that lasts two to 10 minutes and 5% had more than one episode (Giles, Dahl, & Coble, 1994). Because young children experience stage four sleep for longer periods of time than adults do, they are far more likely than adults to experience sleepwalking; sleepwalking after age 40 is quite rare. (This fact didn't prevent Scott Falater from blaming his criminal actions on sleepwalking, but it did raise questions as to the validity of such a defence.)

REM Sleep

About an hour after we fall asleep and complete one cycle of the four non-REM sleep stages, we return through stages three and two and enter REM sleep, which can last anywhere from a few minutes to an hour. We spend about 20% to 25% (about 100 minutes) of an average night in REM sleep.

At the beginning of REM sleep, our brainwaves resemble those that appear during stage one sleep. In contrast to stage one, however, the REM sleep stage is a time of physiological arousal rather than of increasing tranquility: Our heart rate increases, our breathing becomes rapid and irregular, and our eyes dart around behind our eyelids in quick bursts of activity about every 30 seconds. And yet, in the midst of all this excitement, our muscles remain relaxed. For this reason, REM sleep is also referred to as paradoxical sleep; even though the brain's motor cortex remains active, hyperpolarized, or overexcited, neurons in the brainstem and spinal cord are unable to transmit messages to the rest of the body. This causes our muscles to be still to the point of paralysis. Researchers have discovered that glycine—the inhibitory neurotransmitter that causes muscle paralysis during sleep—does not inhibit the motor nuclei of the cranial nerves, explaining the occasional facial twitch during REM sleep. It is generally thought that REM-associated muscle paralysis occurs in order to prevent the body from acting out the dreams that occur during this stage, thus avoiding potential injuries while we ride purple horses or save the universe from robot aliens.

REM sleep is the primary venue for the often disjointed, hallucinatory imaginings we call dreams. Although about 37% of people claim they rarely or never dream, people, on average, spend about 600 hours each year dreaming and have more than 100 000 dreams over a typical lifetime (Moore, 2004). In fact, of those people who reported they never dreamed, a full 80% remembered a dream when woken during REM sleep.

Although some sleep researchers have suspected that the rapid eye movements characteristic of REM sleep are related to the visual aspects of dreaming, most scientists believe that these eye movements are a result of overflow to the active nervous system. Dreams that take place during REM tend to be narrative, emotional, and fantastical in quality (e.g., "My friend and I were taking a walk when all of a sudden we morphed into lions"), as opposed to the vague, impressionistic ones experienced at other stages (e.g., "I had left something somewhere").

As the night wears on, we tend to spend more time in REM sleep and less time in the stages of deep sleep, stages three and four. Our periods of REM sleep generally increase in both duration and frequency the longer we sleep.

> **It's generally believed that a "good night's sleep" should be about eight hours in duration, but the amount of sleep needed for optimal functioning varies across individuals. Some people are well rested from six hours of sleep each night, but others can't function on less than ten.**

STIMULI AWARENESS AND LEARNING

If you've ever seen a cat napping, you may have noticed that even while it's asleep, its ears continue moving around in response to sounds. Since so much of our information processing

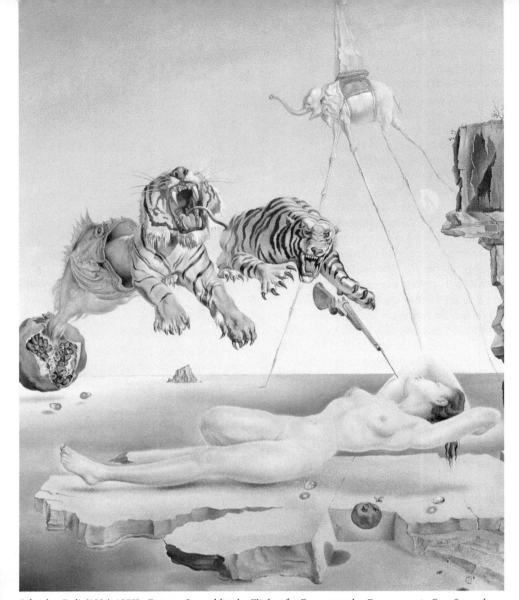

Salvador Dali (1904–1989), *Dream Caused by the Flight of a Bee around a Pomegranate One Second before Waking up*, 1944, (oil on panel), Dali, Salvador (1904-89)/Thyssen-Bornemisza Collection, Madrid, Spain/Giraudon/The Bridgeman Art Library/Salvador Dali, Gala-Salvadro Dali Foundation/SODRAC (2012).

∧
∧ One way to **remember your dreams** is to write
∧ **them down** as soon as you wake up. You could also **paint them,** like Salvador Dali did in his *Dream Caused by the Flight of a Bee around a Pomegranate One Second before Waking up.*

takes place outside of conscious awareness, humans are also capable of processing certain stimuli while we sleep. EEG recordings show that the auditory cortex is responsive to sound stimuli while we sleep, which explains why we're able to awake from a deep sleep when someone calls our name or a baby cries in the next room (Kutas, 1990). We also manage to roll around while sleeping without falling out of bed or kicking the dog napping at our feet.

Some studies even make the case for **hypnopaedia**—learning while asleep. For example, participants in one study were able to link a certain sound to a mild electric shock during sleep (Graves, Heller, Pack, & Abel, 2003), and others were able to stop problematic nail-biting after repeatedly hearing a phonograph recording of the phrase "My fingernails taste terribly bitter" during sleep (LeShan, 1942). While we may be able to engage in behavioural learning tasks like these while we sleep, it's less likely that we can engage in cognitive learning: Although it seems like it would be particularly convenient to listen to podcasts of study materials while we sleep, there is little evidence to support the notion that we can remember information we hear while we're sleeping. We also usually forget anything that happens during the five minutes just before we fall asleep or anything that wakes us briefly from sleep.

PURPOSE OF SLEEP

While psychologists have a fairly solid understanding of what happens in the brain and body as we sleep, exactly why we sleep remains a topic of debate. Several theories attempt to shed light on this intriguing question. The **preservation and protection theory** explains sleep as a mechanism evolved to preserve energy and provide protection during the night, when danger from predators was low and opportunities to get food were few. Sleep patterns do not depend on an animal's physical exertion levels but on how the animal finds food and protects itself. If predators hunt an animal during the day, the animal would be more likely to be nocturnal and out of harm's way during the daylight hours. Similarly, visually reliant species, such as human beings, tend to be diurnal to take advantage of sunlight for daily activities.

The **body restoration theory** explains sleep as a time for necessary rest and recuperation. During sleep, the metabolic rate goes down, muscles relax, and the body secretes growth hormones to promote tissue repair. Rats deprived of sleep experience tissue breakdown and eventually die (Rechtschaffen & Bergman, 1965). Sleep-deprived humans also experience declines in health and functioning.

Sleep seems to be necessary to consolidate memories of the things we learn during the day and to promote learning (Leproult, Copinski, Buxton, & Van Cauter, 1997; Guzman-Marin et al., 2005). Memory storage requires long-term potentiation (LTP), two neurons firing together to extend the communication at the synapse, the junction where neurons meet. Rats that had been kept awake showed less long-term potentiation than those that had been allowed to sleep (Vyazovskiy et al., 2008).

The **activation-synthesis theory** understands sleep as a side effect of the visual and motor area neurons firing during REM sleep, the stage of sleep characterized by rapid eye movements. Dreams occur because neurons in different parts of the brain fire randomly, and the cortex synthesizes them into some kind of coherent story, but activation theory does not attribute any purpose to dreams or argue against any psychoanalytic theories.

SLEEP NEEDS AND PATTERNS

It's generally believed that a "good night's sleep" should be about eight hours in duration, but the amount of sleep needed for optimal functioning varies across individuals. Some people are well rested from six hours of sleep each night, but others can't function on less than ten. Newborns spend about two-thirds of the day asleep, while most adults doze for about half that time. In rare cases, people known as **nonsomniacs** can sleep far less than what most would consider normal without feeling tired during the day. Domestic diva Martha Stewart and late-night talk show host Jay Leno, for example, reportedly get by on about four hours of sleep each night.

Our sleep patterns seem to have some genetic influence. When researchers studied the sleep patterns of identical and fraternal twins, they found that only the sleep patterns of identical twins were similar (Webb & Campbell, 1983). When allowed to sleep unhindered by alarm clocks, energetic children, or hungry pets, most people will sleep at least nine hours in a night; these people generally wake up invigorated and experience an overall boost in mood and performance (Coren, 1996). However, cultural habits can alter these natural patterns. Modern light bulbs, shift work, and social diversions have created industrialized societies in which people sleep much less than they did a century ago.

SLEEP DEPRIVATION

Does sleep deprivation make you feel like a walking zombie most of the time? If it does, you're not alone; in fact, according to psychologist James Maas (1999), a sleep expert at Cornell University, we have become "a nation of walking zombies." Sleep deprivation is all too common and especially problematic not only because of how it affects our ability to function, but also because a sleep debt isn't easily paid off. Have you ever tried to make up for several nights of only five or so hours of sleep with one 10-hour sleep? Unfortunately, this strategy doesn't usually work as well as we might like, and we're left feeling groggy even after a long sleep.

Young people, especially teenagers, are highly prone to skimping on sleep. Teenagers need about eight to nine hours of sleep each night, but on average, they only get about seven hours—two hours less than teens got 80 years ago (Holden, 1993; Maas, 1999). A study

Hypnopaedia is learning while asleep.

Preservation and protection theory states that sleep is an evolutionary adaptation that keeps us out of harm's way when darkness sets in.

Body restoration theory states that sleep is necessary for our bodies to recuperate from the day's activities.

Activation-synthesis theory states that sleep is a side effect of neural firing during REM sleep.

Nonsomniac is a person who requires much less than eight hours of sleep each day.

examining the sleeping patterns of 1600 grade nine Toronto students found that their sleep patterns were disturbed because they stay up late watching television, playing video and computer games, and using social networking sites (McCrindle, 2010). To make matters worse, teens who suffer from sleep deprivation during the day often get a "second wind" around 11 p.m., preventing them from going to bed earlier and getting more sleep. Stanford researcher William Dement (1997) reports that 80% of students are sleep deprived at dangerous levels that cause difficulty studying, irritability, fatigue, a lowered rate of productivity, and a tendency to make mistakes. Moreover, high-achieving secondary students with good grades average 25 more minutes of sleep each night and go to bed 40 minutes earlier than their lower-achieving counterparts.

> Unfortunately, the effects of sleep deprivation are not limited to merely feeling lethargic or moody; sleep deprivation can have tragic consequences.

Dangers of Sleep Deprivation

Unfortunately, the effects of sleep deprivation are not limited to merely feeling lethargic or moody; sleep deprivation can have tragic consequences. Car accidents are far more common during the morning after daylight savings time begins, when people change their clocks and lose an hour of sleep (Coren, 1996). Sleep deprivation leads to slowed reaction times and increased errors on visual tasks, resulting in potentially catastrophic mishaps both for drivers and for those whose jobs rely on these skills: pilots, airport baggage screeners, surgeons, and X-ray technicians, to name a few (Horowitz,

> As a child, you may have sent your parents into a panic by sitting bolt upright in bed, screaming, and uttering a stream of gibberish through ragged, frightened breaths. **People who display these symptoms suffer from night terrors, a relatively benign, albeit disturbing, sleep disorder most common in young children.**

Cade, Wolfe, & Czeisler, 2003). The 1989 *Exxon Valdez* oil spill; the 1984 Union Carbide Bhopal, India, disaster; the 1979 Three Mile Island nuclear accident; and the 1986 Chernobyl nuclear accident all occurred after midnight, when operators were likely to be most tired.

Sleep deprivation can have dire consequences for our general health, too. For children, sleep deprivation can have great consequences. According to Canadian researcher Brian McCrindle (2010), sleep deprivation can lead to higher blood pressure and cholesterol, to poor food choices, and to a lack of physical activity. Sleep deprivation can lead to obesity—which can lead to premature hardening of the arteries, diabetes, joint pain, and depression (Harris, 2010). Older adults who have no difficulty falling or staying asleep and people who sleep seven to eight hours each night tend to live longer than those who are chronically sleep deprived (Dement, 1999; Dew et al., 2003). Sleep deprivation has also been shown to weaken the immune system, which explains why exhaustion and illness seem to go hand in hand, as well as why we sleep more when we feel sick (Beardsley, 1996; Irwin et al., 1994). Not only does sleep deprivation make us more susceptible to infection, but it can also make us feel and appear older. When we don't get enough sleep, our metabolic and endocrine systems actually change in ways that resemble aging, making us more susceptible to obesity, hypertension, and memory loss (Spiegel, Leproul, & Van Cauter, 1999; Taheri, 2004).

SLEEP DISORDERS

Often, sleep deprivation is a by-product of a busy schedule that allows little time for sleep. Sometimes, however, it is caused by **insomnia,** a sleep disorder characterized by recurring difficulty falling or staying asleep. Insomnia is the most common sleep disorder in Canada (Schur, 2010). About 10% of Canadians suffer from chronic insomnia and the need to sleep can be so strong that many people will gladly pop a sleeping pill in the hope of catching some zzz. People who do experience insomnia, however, should avoid relying on "quick fixes" such as alcohol and sleeping pills, which can make the problem worse by reducing REM sleep and creating next-day fatigue. Moreover, people who use these substances on a regular basis can quickly build up a tolerance, leading to unpleasant withdrawal and worsening insomnia if and when the "sleep aids" are discontinued. Most alarmingly, according to Canadian psychologist Genevieve Belleville (2010), the use of sleeping pills could be deadly—Canadians who reported using medication to treat insomnia had a higher mortality rate (15.7%) compared to individuals who did not (10.5%). Relaxing, exercising, abstaining from caffeine, and sticking to a regular sleep schedule are natural, effective treatments for insomnia.

In stark contrast to insomnia is **narcolepsy,** a sleep disorder characterized by periodic, uncontrollable sleep attacks. These unexpected periods of sleep usually last less than five minutes, but because they occur at unexpected times—in the middle of a conversation, for example, or while driving—they can seriously impair one's quality of life, not to mention safety (Dement, 1978, 1999). However, for the approximately one in 2000 people suffering from narcolepsy (Stanford University Center for Narcolepsy, 2002), there is hope: Neuroscientists have found a relative absence of the hypothalamic neural centre that produces hypocretin, an alerting neurotransmitter, in the brains of those afflicted. Armed with this knowledge, scientists are now working to develop a drug that mimics hypocretin and might relieve the symptoms of narcolepsy. Until such a drug is developed, narcoleptics must live their lives cautiously, lest they unexpectedly fall asleep while driving, cooking, or carrying out other potentially hazardous activities.

Sleep apnea, a disorder that literally leaves people breathless, affects about 3 million Canadians (Sleep Well Canada, 2010). Those afflicted with sleep apnea intermittently stop breathing during sleep, which in turn causes the level of oxygen in the blood to plummet. As a result, sufferers may wake up around 400 times a night to gasp in air. These excessive, non-stop interruptions deprive sufferers of slow-wave sleep, leaving them chronically groggy and irritable during the day. Because they often don't remember waking up briefly during the night, many people suffering from sleep apnea don't even realize they have the disorder. Sleep apnea is particularly common among those who are obese, and as obesity rates have gone up in North America, so too have the rates of sleep apnea. Treatment for sleep apnea usually involves wearing a masklike device that forces air into the lungs during sleep.

Some sleep disorders are most commonly observed in children. As a child, you may have sent your parents into a panic by sitting bolt upright in bed, screaming, and uttering a stream of gibberish through ragged, frightened breaths. People who display these symptoms suffer from **night terrors,** a relatively benign, albeit disturbing, sleep disorder most common in young children and characterized by episodes of high arousal and terrified appearance. Unlike nightmares, night terrors usually occur within two to three hours of falling asleep, during stage four sleep (Garland & Smith, 1991). Children rarely wake up during episodes of night terrors, and they tend not to remember these episodes the next morning. Because stage four sleep decreases in length as we age, so too do incidences of night terrors.

Dreams

Dreams—the sequences of images, feelings, ideas, and impressions that pass through our minds as we sleep—are among the most fascinating aspects of human consciousness. They can leave us quaking with fear or with laughter, transport us through time, and make the impossible seem tantalizingly possible. Often, they're completely indecipherable. This fact hasn't stopped humans from attempting

At least once in your life, you've probably woken from a memorable dream and wondered, "What was that about?" In their studies of dreams and dreaming, psychologists ask similar questions: What do we dream, and why?

to decipher dreams, however: At least once in your life, you've probably woken from a memorable dream and wondered, "What was that about?" In their studies of dreams and dreaming, psychologists ask similar questions: What do we dream, and why?

DREAM CONTENT

As you've learned, dreams experienced during REM sleep tend to involve bizarre imagery and vivid, though highly illogical, plots. Nevertheless, when we dream, we uncritically accept these strange elements and, at times, even confuse them with reality. Our dreams often seem to be influenced by the events in our waking lives; for example, people tend to have nightmares

after traumatic events, and in one study, psychologists found that people who played Tetris for seven hours before sleep were highly likely to report dreaming of images of falling blocks (Stickgold, Hobson, Fosse, & Fosse, 2001).

Sigmund Freud, who based much of his theory around the significance of dreams and dream analysis (see Chapters 15 and 17), classified the content of dreams into two sets: the manifest content and the latent content. **Manifest content** refers to what we explicitly remember about a dream—its storyline, characters, and details. Manifest content often includes pieces of experiences and concerns from daily life, such as having a meeting at work, taking an exam, or interacting with family members (De Koninck, 2000). Manifest content also may incorporate sensory stimuli from the sleeper's environment. For instance, people who had cold water lightly sprayed on their faces while sleeping were more likely to dream about water (Dement & Wolpert, 1958). When your alarm clock goes off in the morning, you might find yourself incorporating its drone into your dream.

Studies of manifest content have found that our dreams follow certain trends, and those trends, unfortunately for us, can be a bit disturbing. For both men and women, eight in 10 dreams are characterized by negative emotions, such as failing, experiencing misfortune, or being attacked, pursued, or rejected (Domhoff, 2002). Although many people assume that sex dreams are frequent occurrences, only one in

10 young men and one in 30 young women who were awakened during REM sleep reported dreams containing sexual imagery (Domhoff, 1996; Foulkes, 1982; Van de Castle, 1994). And researchers have noted one interesting gender difference: While women dream of men and women with equal frequency, 65% of the people in men's dreams are male (Domhoff, 1996).

Occasionally, we achieve an awareness of a dream as a dream while dreaming—a phenomenon known as **lucid dreaming** that's been illustrated in both Richard Linklater's 2001 rotoscoped film *Waking Life* and Cameron Crowe's film *Vanilla Sky*. Lucid dreamers can test whether or not they're dreaming by assessing the manifest content of their dream. Obviously dreamlike features (such as clocks that keep irregular time, an ability to fly, talking purple bananas, or light switches that don't work) allow lucid dreamers to determine that they're not actually awake.

THE PURPOSE OF DREAMS

Have you ever felt like a dream you had the previous night was trying to tell you something? Did it seem so cryptic that you decided it must have a deeper meaning and couldn't resist trying to decode it? Many believe that our dreams can help us solve the problems of our waking lives or give us clues about our futures. Just as several different theories attempt to explain why we sleep, there are also many competing theories regarding the purpose of dreams.

Freud and *The Interpretation of Dreams*

In *The Interpretation of Dreams* (1900), Freud argues that dreams allow us to fulfill our wishes and express our unacceptable feelings in a safe environment. Freud believed that in addition

<<< During a **lucid dream**, you can be pretty sure you're dreaming if your attempt to fly is successful.

> For both men and women, eight in 10 dreams are characterized by negative emotions, such as failing, experiencing misfortune, or being attacked, pursued, or rejected (Domhoff, 2002).

to manifest content, dreams also contain **latent content**—the underlying meaning of the dream through which threatening or unacceptable drives and wishes are discharged. Freud theorized that most adults' wishes expressed through dreams are erotic, even when overt sexual imagery is not present. According to Freud, our inner conflicts and unconscious desires can be identified and analyzed through dream interpretation. There are plenty of critics of Freud's dream theory, however. Some of these critics point out that dreams can be interpreted to mean nearly anything, depending on the creativity of the interpreter; others argue that dreams don't hide anything below the surface and don't seem to contain subtle clues to our unconscious desires.

Information Processing

A more recent dream theory suggests that dreams help us sort and place the day's experiences into our memories. Deep, slow-wave REM sleep stabilizes our memories and experiences, converting them into long-term learning. One study of rats' brains illustrated this potential connection between dreams and learning: Researchers measured rats' brain activity as they ran through two different mazes during the day. When researchers measured the rats' brain activity as the rats slept afterwards, they noticed patterns that suggested the rats were not only dreaming of running through each of the mazes they had encountered that day, but also of a hybrid maze that seemed to synthesize characteristics of both mazes (Louie & Wilson, 2001; Maquet, 2001). These results suggest that dreams play a part in memory consolidation (see Chapter 12).

Activation Synthesis

We may be unconscious during sleep, but the neurons in our brain fire away even while we slumber.

The activation-synthesis theory of dreaming states that dreams are the result of the brain's attempt to make sense of this random neural activity. PET scans of the brain during REM sleep show stimulation in the visual processing area of the brain, which is responsible for generating images, and the limbic system, which is linked to emotions (Maquet & Franck, 1996). According to the activation-synthesis theory, our brains produce dreams by weaving these image-based, emotion-laced signals into stories. Moreover, since the frontal-lobe regions of the brain (responsible for our powers of reason and logic) are largely inactive during sleep, dreams tend toward the nonsensical (Maquet et al., 1996). The activation-synthesis theory is further supported by research indicating that damage to either the visual processing areas or the limbic system may lead to impairment in dreaming (Domhoff, 2003).

Development

Some psychologists theorize that dreams are not merely the fanciful inventions of a sleep-activated brain; instead, they may be key components in our cognitive development (Domhoff, 2003; Foulkes, 1999). The brain activity associated with dreaming may help to develop and preserve neural pathways, especially for infants, who spend ample time in REM sleep and who are also in a state of rapid neural development. The way dreams change over time also seems to indicate a developmental role. Up until about age nine, our dreams take the form of a series of individual scenes or images; only in late childhood and early adolescence do our dreams come to resemble interconnected narratives. Eventually, dream content reflects our waking thoughts and intelligence, featuring coherent speech and drawing on our knowledge and learning.

Hypnosis

What comes to mind when you hear the term *hypnosis*? You might think of the carnival

>>> What **aspects of hypnotism** are probably more grounded in **showmanship** than in **psychology?**

performer who dangles a pocket watch in front of his audience and proclaims that they are getting very sleepy, the stage-show magician who convinces her subjects to act like chickens, or the highway billboard that touts hypnosis as a quick fix for obesity or smoking. These popular conceptions of hypnosis—as a parlour game, a form of entertainment, and a miracle cure—can obscure the term's true meaning, and merits, within the field of psychology.

At its most basic level, **hypnosis** is an exercise in suggestion. During hypnosis, one person, the hypnotist, makes suggestions to another person, the subject, regarding the perceptions, feelings, thoughts, or behaviours that the subject can expect to experience. Austrian physician Anton Mesmer is credited with developing the techniques employed in modern hypnosis.

SUSCEPTIBILITY

Since hypnosis revolves around the power of suggestion, it makes sense that its effectiveness—that is, whether or not it works for a given subject—is dependent on the subject's susceptibility to suggestion. That's not to say that highly hypnotizable people are especially gullible. Rather, those with **hypnotic ability,** or a high susceptibility to hypnotism, are able to focus their attention deeply and intensely on given tasks, to the point of absorption. Researchers have discovered that a person's susceptibility to hypnosis may be linked to the efficiency of the frontal system—the area of the brain associated with inattentional action. According to Gruzelier's (1998) three-stage model of

> Given that hypnosis enables people to entertain new and often bizarre possibilities, it's not surprising, then, **that people with hypnotic ability tend to be highly imaginative and inventive in their thoughts.**

hypnosis, a person who is particularly susceptible to hypnosis is easily able to focus his attention. During the initial stages of hypnosis, the person pays close attention to the hypnotist, increasing activity in the frontal brain regions. The person then "lets go" of his controlled attention and gives executive control to the hypnotist, reducing frontal activity. During the third stage, the person engages in passive imagery, increasing posterior cortical activity. By exhausting his frontal abilities during the initial stages of hypnosis, the person becomes frontally impaired in a hypnotic state. Given that hypnosis enables people to entertain new and often bizarre possibilities, it's not surprising, then, that people with hypnotic ability tend to be highly imaginative and inventive in their thoughts, the types that easily become lost in the pages of a novel or transfixed by the images on a movie screen (Barnier & McConkey, 2004; Silva & Kirsch, 1992).

Although hypnotic ability varies with each individual, anyone who can turn his or her attention inward and imagine something—in other words, almost all of us—can experience some degree of hypnotism. Whether or not we realize it, we are all susceptible to suggestion in some ways. For example, it turns out that when people stand with their eyes closed and are told repeatedly that they are swaying, nearly everyone actually begins to sway. This test, called the postural sway test, is just one of the items on the Stanford Hypnotic Susceptibility Scale, which is used to assess individuals' relative degree of hypnotic ability. Other items on the scale—such as the spontaneous sensation of sweet and sour tastes on the tongue—are not as universal. Keep in mind, also, the power of expectation: People who believe that they can be hypnotized and who expect hypnotic responsiveness are far more likely to experience it than are determined doubters.

Proponents of hypnotism put forth myriad claims about its usefulness, and not all hypnotists

have the same goals in mind. From memory recovery to smoking cessation to pain relief, hypnotism has many purported benefits, with varying evidence to support each promised result.

RECALL

Many people believe that hypnosis allows us to access the past, to recover long-buried memories from the annals of our brains (Johnson & Hauck, 1999). This belief has given rise to the use of hypnosis to induce "age regression" within a therapeutic setting, the goal being for clients to relive experiences from childhood in order to uncover and address the roots of psychological problems. However, research demonstrates that claims of successful age regression are, in fact, questionable at best. As it turns out, age-regressed people under hypnosis tend to act as they think children of a certain age would act rather than how they actually act. For example, a client "hypnotized" to return to the age of four or five may start speaking in ungrammatical sentence fragments, not realizing that most four- and five-year-olds are highly adept at grammatical speech.

The use of hypnosis as a tool to aid (or not aid) memory also has implications for the legal system. It sounds great in theory—witnesses can't recall exactly what the perpetrator of a robbery looked like? Take them back to the scene of the crime, if only in their mind's eye, through hypnosis. Unfortunately, this method not only does not work, but also can actually do more harm than good: It can cause people to develop false memories (see Chapter 12). Regardless of the best intentions of both hypnotist and subject, a hypnotist's questions can shape a subject's memory of an event simply through the power of suggestion. If a hypnotist asks, "What colour was the burglar's beard?" the subject may falsely "remember" that the burglar had a beard, even if he was actually clean shaven. Because of the unreliability of hypnosis-induced "memories," court systems around the world, including those in the United States and United Kingdom, have begun banning testimony from witnesses who have been hypnotized (Druckman & Bjork, 1991; Gibson, 1995; McConkey, 1995).

THERAPY

Although the link between hypnosis and memory enhancement is largely unsubstantiated, hypnosis does have some real, valuable uses within a therapeutic environment. Hypnosis can, in fact, help people control undesirable behaviours or symptoms. Much of its success revolves around the implementation of

Latent content describes the unconscious meaning of a dream.

Hypnosis is an exercise in suggestion during which one person makes suggestions to another person regarding the perceptions, feelings, thoughts, or behaviours that the subject can expect to experience.

Hypnotic ability is high susceptibility to hypnotism.

Post-hypnotic suggestion is a suggestion made during hypnosis that is executed by the participant when he or she is no longer hypnotized.

Hypnotic analgesia consists of pain relief through hypnosis.

Dissociation is a split in consciousness that allows simultaneous thoughts and behaviours to occur apart from each other.

post-hypnotic suggestion—a suggestion made during hypnosis that is executed by the participant when he or she is no longer hypnotized. For example, a hypnotherapist might suggest that a client whose anxiety causes her to break out in unsightly hives imagine swimming in a pool of soothing, cleansing water whenever she becomes anxious. Post-hypnotic suggestion has been shown to be effective in alleviating headaches, asthma, and stress-related skin disorders. Unfortunately, drug, alcohol, and smoking addictions do not respond well to hypnosis; however, hypnosis seems very helpful in the treatment of obesity (Nash, 2001).

PAIN RELIEF

Hypnosis also has promising implications in the area of pain relief. Hypnotic pain relief, known as **hypnotic analgesia,** can benefit about half of us, and 10% of people can become so hypnotized that major surgery can be performed on them without traditional anaesthesia (Hilgard & LeBaron, 1984; Reeves, Redd, Storm, & Minogawa, 1983). While the prospect of unmedicated surgery may seem rather ambitious, keep in mind that even light hypnosis can help calm us down and reduce our apprehension of (and subsequent oversensitivity to) pain. Canadian research findings support the use of hypnosis to manage children's pain during medical procedures and after surgery. Hypnosis is also useful in decreasing children's anxiety and chronic headache (Rogovik & Goldman, 2007). Further, Canadian research into sexual health has found that hypnosis is a promising treatment for the pain experienced by some women during intercourse (Pukall, Kandyba, Amsel, Khalifé, & Binik, 2007).

How does hypnotic analgesia work? One theory suggests that it causes **dissociation**—a

Psychoactive substances are drugs that alter our consciousness.

Agonists are drugs that increase neural activity.

Antagonists are drugs that inhibit or decrease neural activity.

Tolerance occurs when an increasing amount of a drug is needed to produce intoxication.

Withdrawal symptoms occur when we stop taking a drug for which we have developed a tolerance.

Physical drug dependence is caused by compulsive drug use and leads to the development of tolerance and withdrawal symptoms.

Psychological drug dependence refers to the cravings for a drug's pleasurable effects. This type of dependence is harder to overcome and can lead to a relapse.

> Many people believe that hypnosis allows us to access the past, to recover long-buried memories from the annals of our brains (Johnson & Hauck, 1999). This belief has given rise to the use of hypnosis to induce "age regression" within a therapeutic setting, the goal being for clients to relive experiences from childhood in order to uncover and address the roots of psychological problems.

split in consciousness that allows simultaneous thoughts and behaviours to occur apart from each other. Through hypnosis, the sensation of pain can be disconnected from the emotional suffering that characterizes the experience of pain. For example, in one study, participants were hypnotized to dissociate a typically painful stimulus—putting their arms in ice water—from the emotional reaction of discomfort that normally accompanies such an experience. The technique worked: Instead of screaming in pain after submerging their arms in the freezing water, the subjects tended to respond calmly and thoughtfully, saying things like, "Hmmm. That's very cold, but not really painful" (Miller & Bowers, 1993).

Hypnotic analgesia may owe its success in part to the power of selective attention. Think of athletes who sustain serious injuries during sporting events but who keep playing, claiming afterwards that they didn't even feel the pain of the injury until the game was over. These athletes are often so focused on the competition that they easily ignore their injuries. Similarly, people treated with hypnotic analgesia may be so relaxed or distracted by the hypnosis process that they don't attend to their pain.

Although these theories attempt to explain how hypnosis relieves pain, they still assume that the participant experiences the pain stimulus at some level. This is supported by laboratory studies showing that participants who report feeling no pain from an electric shock still register increased heart rates. Moreover, PET scans of hypnotized people show reduced activity in the brain areas that process painful stimuli but not in the sensory cortex, which receives the raw sensory input (Rainville, Duncan, Price, Carrier, & Bushnell, 1997). It seems that although hypnosis can alter our perception of a painful stimulus, it's not powerful enough to block the sensory input itself.

Meditation

In the past, meditation—an altered state of consciousness that aims to enhance self-knowledge and well-being through an extreme sense of calm and relaxation— seemed, to many, a fringe practice reserved for "New Age" hippie types. In recent years, however, bolstered by high-profile celebrity endorsements and, more importantly, scientific research findings, meditation has gone mainstream.

Valued by many Eastern cultures and religions as a way of directing consciousness away from worldly preoccupations, meditation may involve focused and regulated breathing, specific body positions, minimization of external distractions, mental imagery, and mental clarity. In a meditative state, sensory input is gradually diminished, creating what Carrington (1998) called a "mental isolation chamber." Although the person is awake, he or she is in a deeply relaxed state. During deep meditation, the brain shows similar brainwave activity to that seen during sleep. In concentrative meditation, participants attempt to achieve complete mental tranquility by focusing on something specific, such as a particular physical pose, mental picture, or word. Mindfulness meditation, on the other hand, involves a focused awareness of everything you experience, from walking to class to doing laundry to talking with friends. You might think of it as "being in the moment." (For more information about mindfulness meditation, see Chapter 17.)

Physiological changes resulting from meditation are well documented. EEGs show that meditation is associated with the alpha waves typical of a relaxed state, as well as with significantly low levels of activity in the posterior superior parietal lobe (Herzog et al., 1990/1991; Newberg et al., 2001). Meditating Buddhist monks have also been studied for their ability to use meditation to raise their body temperature and decrease their metabolism (Wallace & Benson, 1972). Some researchers have even found evidence of meditation's ability to increase intelligence and improve cognitive performance (So & Orme-Johnson, 2001).

The ultimate goal of many programs of meditation is enlightenment—a transcendent state of wisdom. While this might not necessarily seem practical or attainable, keep in mind that meditation, at the very least, can free your perceptions and thoughts, allowing you to see familiar things in new ways. Most scientists agree that it

∧∧∧ Specific body postures, or asanas, may be used during meditative yoga to help the practitioner focus attention inward.

can be a powerful, natural antidote to anxiety and stress (Kabat-Zinn et al., 1992; Bahrke & Morgan, 1978).

Drugs

The last time you were at a bar, club, or party did you witness the way alcohol affects a person's level of consciousness? Perhaps you have experienced this yourself. Drugs that alter our consciousness are called **psychoactive substances.**

Whether these psychoactive substances, or drugs as we commonly call them, are legal or illegal, they produce a "high," or intoxication effect, when taken. The "high" produced by psychoactive drugs results from changes in neural transmission in the brain. There are two types of psychoactive drugs. **Agonists** increase neural activity by causing the release of more neurotransmitter, by mimicking a neurotransmitter and binding to receptor sites itself, or by inhibiting the reuptake process, thereby keeping the neurotransmitter in the synapse longer. Caffeine, amphetamines, cocaine, and heroin are agonists. **Antagonists** inhibit or decrease neural activity by decreasing the production or release of neurotransmitter or by blocking receptor sites and preventing the binding of a neurotransmitter. Alcohol and LSD are antagonistic drugs.

When we take these drugs, we activate the "wanting system" in our brain (see Chapter 9). This wanting system releases dopamine and other neurotransmitters, thereby stimulating reward-based learning so that drug use is reinforced. In other words, when we take drugs, we feel good, and that good feeling acts as encouragement or reinforcement for us to use the drug again. In the beginning, a small amount of drug is enough to produce intoxication, but after repeated use more and more drug is needed to achieve a high. When this happens we have developed a **tolerance** for the drug. Once we develop a tolerance for a drug and we stop taking a drug, we experience **withdrawal symptoms.** Withdrawal symptoms are very unpleasant and can be dangerous—even leading to death. Withdrawal symptoms tend to be "opposite" of the effects that the drugs caused (see table below). A person is **physically drug dependent** when he or she has developed a tolerance for a drug and experiences withdrawal symptoms when drug use is stopped. Once the period of withdrawal is over—the person has "detoxed"—the desire for the drug may still continue. A person is **psychologically drug dependent** when he or she craves the pleasurable effects of a drug. Psychological drug dependence is more difficult to overcome and is a major reason relapse is so common.

Drugs differ in their potential to be addictive. Most of us would agree that heroin is more addictive than caffeine. But why? A drug's addictive potential depends on the following factors:

1 **How quickly the effects of the drug are felt.** The faster we feel the effects the more addictive the drug. How the drug is taken affects how quickly we feel the effects. Drugs that are ingested, such as caffeine and alcohol, take the longest to reach our bloodstream, while drugs that are smoked or injected, such as crack cocaine, enters our bloodstream the quickest, and its effects are felt within seconds.

2 **How long the effects of the drug last.** If a drug's effects last a long time, we do not need to take more of it as often, thereby decreasing the likelihood that we will develop tolerance. However, if the drug's effects last only a short time, we will need to take the drug more often to maintain the high, increasing the probability that we will develop a tolerance. The most addictive drugs produce a high for only a few minutes.

3 **How good the drugs make us feel.** The stronger the pleasurable effects of a drug the more addictive it is.

4 **The severity of withdrawal symptoms.** The more discomfort we feel after stopping a drug the more likely we are to take it again.

Table 10.01: The Effects of Psychoactive Drugs on Consciousness

Classification of Psychoactive Substance	Example	Effect on Consciousness	General Effect on Neural Communication	Some Withdrawal Symptoms
Stimulants	Caffeine, nicotine, cocaine, amphetamine, methamphetamine, MDMA (ecstasy)	Increases arousal, increases alertness, increases sociability, reduces appetite, increases heart rate, respiration, body temperature	Agonist—Increases neural activity	Irritability, anxiety, headache, fatigue, depression
Depressants	Alcohol, barbiturates, Rohypnol, ketamine	Decreases anxiety, lessens inhibitions, causes drowsiness, increases relaxation and calm	Antagonist—Decreases neural activity	Anxiety, tremors, nausea, vomiting, seizures, anxiety, heart attack, death
Opiates	Morphine, heroin, opium, codeine	Provides pain relief, causes drowsiness and sleep	Antagonist—Decreases neural activity; Agonist—Increases neural activity	Anxiety, chills, restlessness, diarrhea, nausea
Hallucinogens	LSD, mescaline, psilocybin (magic mushroom), salvia divinorum	Produces euphoria, delusions, and hallucinations	Antagonist—Decreases neural activity	Anxiety, hyperactivity, increased arousal
Hallucinogen & depressant	Marijuana	Increases relaxation and calm, increases appetite	Antagonist—Decreases neural activity	Anxiety, hyperactivity, increased arousal, decreased appetite

10

Review

Summary

HOW DO DIFFERENT LEVELS OF CONSCIOUSNESS FUNCTION? p.136

• During minimal consciousness, we only dimly perceive the environment and might respond to a stimulus without full awareness of it (for example, during sleep).

• During full consciousness, we are aware of our environment and of our own thoughts and mental state.

• Self-consciousness is the highest level of consciousness; it enables us to reflect on our own identity.

HOW DOES CONSCIOUSNESS CHANGE WHILE WE SLEEP AND DREAM, AND WHY? p.138

• The body's circadian rhythm controls sleep patterns.

• The sleep cycle consists of several stages. Stage one is a very short period characterized by slow breathing and irregular brainwaves, stage two is a brief period characterized by bursts of brain activity, and stages three and four are longer periods of deep sleep.

• After we complete stage four sleep, we cycle back through stages three and two sleep and enter REM sleep, in which heart rate and breathing increase and brainwaves become fast and irregular.

• This cycle occurs every 90 minutes throughout the night. Stages three and four sleep periods decrease in length and eventually disappear, while REM sleep periods lengthen over the course of the night.

HOW CAN HYPNOSIS AND MEDITATION ALTER CONSCIOUSNESS? p.144

• Hypnosis is an altered state of consciousness achieved through social interaction. It may cause dissociation, a split in consciousness that allows some simultaneous thoughts and behaviours to occur separately from others.

• Meditation is a process by which people can achieve a state of deep mental calm through concentration or mindfulness.

HOW DO PSYCHOACTIVE SUBSTANCES ALTER OUR CONCIOUSNESS? p.147

• Drugs that alter our consciousness are called psychoactive substances.

• Psychoactive drugs include stimulants (caffeine, nicotine, cocaine), depressants (alcohol, marijuana), opiates (morphine, heroin), and hallucinogens (LSD, marijuana).

• All psychoactive substances affect our consciousness by either increasing or decreasing neural activity.

• Antagonists, such as alcohol, reduce neural activity while agonists, such as cocaine, increase neural activity.

• Drugs activate the wanting system in our brain and can lead to physical and psychological dependence.

• Withdrawal symptoms occur after we develop a tolerance for a drug, and these are signs that physical drug dependence (addiction) has occurred.

• Psychological dependence is a major cause for relapse because recovering drug users continue to crave the effects of the drug.

• Drugs differ in their addictive potential. The quicker the drug's effects are felt, the shorter the effects last, the more intense the effects are, and severe withdrawal symptoms make a drug highly addictive.

Test Your Understanding

1. Which of the following best states the problem of other minds?
   a. We unconsciously allow other people to influence our own perceptions.
   b. We cannot determine how other people's perceptions compare to our own.
   c. We are more susceptible to the power of suggestion when we are with others.
   d. We cannot access unconscious, preconscious, and nonconscious information in the brain.

2. Antonio has a guitar lesson today and needs to practise. Although he has a lot going on in his life, including relationship problems and pending exams, he manages to focus on learning a new chord. Which function of consciousness is Antonio most likely utilizing?
   a. the executive control function

   b. the unconscious function
   c. the planning function
   d. the restrictive function

3. The suprachiasmatic nucleus in the hypothalamus controls circadian rhythms by causing the pineal gland to:
   a. adjust melatonin production
   b. produce adenosine
   c. inhibit certain neurons
   d. induce rapid eye movement

4. As the brain prepares for sleep, brain activity transitions from:
   a. beta waves to alpha waves
   b. alpha waves to beta waves
   c. theta waves to beta waves
   d. theta waves to alpha waves

5. John sleeps for less than four hours a night but does not feel tired during the day. He functions well at work and leads an active social live. John is probably:

   a. an insomniac
   b. a nonsomniac
   c. narcoleptic
   d. suffering from sleep apnea

6. A child who wets the bed is probably in:

   a. stage two sleep
   b. stage one sleep
   c. REM sleep
   d. stage four sleep

7. REM sleep is characterized in part by:

   a. motor cortex activity and a lack of muscular activity
   b. visual cortex activity and a lack of dreams
   c. sleepwalking and a lack of theta waves
   d. physiological arousal and a lack of rapid eye movement

8. Which of the following statements about sleep deprivation is NOT true?

   a. Sleep deprivation can cause irritability, fatigue, lowered productivity, and a tendency to make mistakes.
   b. Traffic accidents are more common the morning after daylight savings time begins, when people are likely to be sleepy.
   c. Sleep deprivation weakens the immune system and makes us susceptible to obesity.
   d. It is possible to reduce the effects of sleep deprivation during the week by sleeping for longer periods of time at weekends.

9. How does a night terror differ from a nightmare?

   a. A person can usually be easily awakened from a night terror.
   b. A night terror occurs during stage four sleep, not REM sleep.
   c. Children have night terrors; adults have nightmares.
   d. A night terror is more frightening than a nightmare.

10. According to the preservation and protection theory, we sleep in order to:

   a. problem solve
   b. avoid predators
   c. repair body tissue
   d. establish memories

11. After a visit to the dentist, Keerthi dreams that her teeth are falling out. According to Freudian theory, the teeth in Keerthi's dream are the:

   a. manifest content
   b. latent content
   c. hidden content
   d. symbolic content

12. While Navid is sleeping, his malfunctioning MP3 player turns on quietly and plays a few songs. Navid is most likely to:

   a. sing along to the songs in his sleep
   b. stop dreaming for the rest of the night
   c. wake up and be unable to go back to sleep
   d. incorporate the music into his dreams

13. During a dream, Eric jumps from the roof of a tall building. When he doesn't immediately plummet to the ground, Eric realizes he is dreaming. Eric is experiencing:

   a. lucid dreaming
   b. a night terror
   c. sleep apnea
   d. narcolepsy

14. Damage to the visual processing areas or limbic system may lead to:

   a. symbolic dreaming
   b. impairment in dreaming
   c. more frequent dreams
   d. more lucid dreams

15. Abena has hypnotic ability. Which of the following statements is most likely to be true about Abena?

   a. She is able to persuade people easily.
   b. She can control people's thoughts and actions.
   c. She is highly imaginative and inventive.
   d. She is not susceptible to the power of suggestion.

16. Hypnosis has been successfully used to:

   a. regress people back to childhood
   b. assist with pain relief
   c. force people to behave against their will
   d. treat addictions to drugs and alcohol

17. Which of the following indicates that meditation is a state of altered consciousness?

   a. Meditation helps people reduce their anxiety.
   b. Meditation involves focused and regulated breathing.
   c. Meditation causes physiological changes on EEG recordings.
   d. Meditation can be used to decrease metabolism.

18. Any drug that alters our consciousness is called a(n):

   a. agonist
   b. antagonist
   c. illegal substance
   d. psychoactive substance

19. Horace requires progressively more and more of a drug to get the same effect. He has developed:

   a. withdrawal symptoms
   b. a drug addiction
   c. a drug tolerance
   d. the ability to feel more alert and energetic

20. Stimulants do each of the following EXCEPT:

   a. make a person feel more alert and energetic
   b. increase the body's store of energy
   c. increase blood pressure, heart rate, and respiration rate
   d. suppress appetite

Remember to check www.thethinkspot.ca for additional information, downloadable flashcards, and other helpful resources.

Answers: 1) b; 2) d; 3) a; 4) a; 5) b; 6) d; 7) a; 8) d; 9) b; 10) b; 11) a; 12) d; 13) a; 14) b; 15) c; 16) b; 17) c; 18) d; 19) c; 20) b

Effects of Acute Nicotine Administration on Resting EEG in Nonsmokers

Derek J. Fisher, Natalia Jaworska, Richelle Daniels, Amy Knobelsdorf, Verner J. Knott

Institute of Mental Health Research and Royal Ottawa Mental Health Centre, Carlton University

Smoking/nicotine has been shown to increase brain-arousal states, yet previous studies have failed to distinguish between absolute improvements due to nicotine versus relief from withdrawal symptoms in smokers. This study examined the electrocortical response to nicotine in a nonsmoking population, in order to negate potential withdrawal symptoms. Twenty right-handed, nonsmoking participants were administered nicotine (6 mg) or placebo gum within a double-blind, repeated-measures design. In each session, EEG was recorded during a 2-min, resting, eyes-open condition. Nicotine administration (vs. placebo) resulted in significantly greater frontal (specifically left-frontal) $alpha_2$ power. Similar to previous findings in smokers. The absence of slow-wave changes following nicotine in nonsmokers suggest that these previous results in smokers may be related to withdrawal state.

Functional or "psychological-tool" models of smoking motivation have argued that smokers maintain their habit not simply to avoid the negative consequences associated with smoking abstinence but to experience the positive-reinforcing effects of nicotine (Stepney, 1979; Warburton, 1995). Smoking/nicotine not only increases brain-arousal states (Knott, 2001), but it also has been shown to improve both mood and cognitive functioning (Heishman, Kleykamp, & Singleton, 2010; Henningfield, Schuh & Jarvik, 1995; Le Houezac, 1998; Waters & Sutton, 2000).

Increased nicotinic acetylcholine receptor (nAChR)-mediated dopamine neurotransmission has been implicated in the cognition-facilitating actions of smoking nicotine (Mansvelder, van Aerde, Couey, & Brussard, 2006). Although smoking/nicotine-induced electrocortical activation is prominent at posterior brain regions, frontal regions are progressively recruited in a dose-dependent fashion with increasing smoking doses of nicotine (Knott, 1989a). This smoking/nicotine-activation profile is likely mediated by nAChR dopaminergic function, as its appearance is affected by the administration of the dopamine antagonist haloperidol (Walker, Mahoney, Ilivitsky, & Knott, 2001).

Although not possessing the spatial sensitivity of other functional neuroimaging methodologies, the superior temporal resolution (on the order of ms) and the more direct probing of neural activity associated with brain-electric recordings make electroencephalography (EEG) a viable tool for investigating resting brain activity in response to drug administration. EEG recordings are typically quantified to yield specific oscillatory bands (including delta, theta, $alpha_1$, $alpha_2$, and beta) and activities within these frequency bands have been linked to states of behavioral arousal. Acute smoking and nicotine typically induces a pharmaco-EEG profile similar to that seen with psychostimulants, by increasing alpha2 and beta frequency power, while decreasing power in delta, theta, and alpha1 bands (Knott, 1988; Knott, 1999b; Knott & Fisher, 2007; Knott et al., 2005; Knott & Venables, 1977). These observed neuroelectric power shifts, however, have been limited to smokers following smoking abstinence, a state that has been associated with a sedation-like EEG pattern (i.e., power shift from $alpha_2$/beta to delta, theta, and alpha1 bands) and they have been restricted to resting (eyes closed) states with no behavioral or task demands. Early research on the effects of nicotine on cognition showed that abstinence disturbs cognitive functioning and that smoking/nicotine administration restores it (Levin & Simon, 1998; Rezvani & Levin, 2001). Thereby, the effects of nicotine in smoking-deprived smokers cannot provide conclusive evidence regarding nicotine's effects on cognition, because any improvements may simply be related to the reversal of withdrawal-associated cognitive impairments (Levin, McClernon, & Rezvani, 2006; Parrott & Roberts, 1991).

Studies using nonsmokers have reported cognitive-enhancing effects in both healthy controls and patients with cognitive disorders, thus eliminating the possibility that nicotine's procognitive actions are withdrawal dependent (Evans & Drobes, 2009; Foulds, 1993; Mansvelder et al., 2006). There has been one previous pilot study

---

Do you remember what you read about withdrawal symptoms? What withdrawal symptoms might you experience if you stop smoking after becoming physically dependent on nicotine? (see p.147)

Smoking activates the "Wanting System" in our brain and releases dopamine. How does this lead us to smoke again? (see p.147).

In Chapter 3, we discussed brain-imaging techniques. How many of these techniques do you remember?

Nicotine is a stimulant and as such will affect our brains in a similar manner as other stimulants (e.g., caffeine, cocaine).

Why would withdrawal symptoms affect our ability to perform cognitive tasks?

What are the roles of the frontal and parietal lobes? (see Chapter 3)

In Chapter 2, we discussed scientific methods. Why do you think the researchers in this study used the design they did?

examining the effects of nicotine on EEG (theta, beta, global alpha) activity at two leads in four nonsmokers (Foulds et al., 1994); however this study did not find any main effect of nicotine (vs. placebo) on EEG power, only reporting a statistically significant shift in mean dominant alpha with nicotine from 8.75 Hz to 9.63 Hz.

Given that it is difficult to interpret smoking/nicotine-induced EEG changes in smokers as evidence of either normalization (i.e. of withdrawal deficits) or true stimulation (Domino, 2001; Knott & Harr, 1995), the primary objective of this study was to examine the electrocortical response to nicotine in a nonsmoking population, unfettered by potential withdrawal symptoms. We aimed to examine this across five EEG bands (delta, theta, $alpha_1$, $alpha_2$, beta) in both hemispheres at frontal and parietal recording sites.

METHODS

Participants

Twenty (18–40 years of age) right-handed, non-smoking participants were recruited (7 male, 13 female, mean [M] age 23.79, standard error [SE] ± 1.13). All participants had smoked less than 10 cigarettes in their lifetime and none within the past year. Additionally, participants could not have exposed themselves to other sources of nicotine, including pipes, cigars, chewing tobacco, or any form of nicotine replacement (patch or gum).

All volunteers were right-handed, as indicated by the Edinburgh Handedness Inventory (Oldfield, 1971) and were medication-free (with the exception of the oral contraceptive pill). Additionally, volunteers were required to have no neurological, psychiatric, or alcohol/substance abuse history, nor the presence of seizures or a history of serious head injuries (including loss of consciousness).

Prior to their sessions, all volunteers were informed about the nature of the study and possible adverse experiences. Informed consent was obtained from all participants and the study was approved by the Research Ethics Boards of the Royal Ottawa Health Care Group and the Carleton University Ethics Committee for Psychological Research.

Design

The testing was carried out in a randomized, placebo-controlled, double-blind, repeated-measures design. There were two experimental sessions, which were separated by at least 24 hours, with participants receiving nicotine one day and placebo on the other day. The order of nicotine administration was counterbalanced across sessions, so that half (randomly selected) were administered nicotine in the first session and placebo in the second session, and the remaining half were administered nicotine and placebo in the reverse order.

Procedure

Test sessions were conducted between 12 p.m. and 4:30 p.m. All participants were asked to abstain from caffeine, alcohol, recreational drugs, medication, and food for a minimum of 8 hours prior to their scheduled testing, and abstain from liquids (with the exception of water) for 2 hours prior in order to avoid interference with nicotine absorption. If any participants did not comply with abstinence constrictions (verified by self-report at the beginning of each session), sessions were rescheduled. All participants reported compliance in this study. Sessions were completed in a dimly lit, sound-attenuated chamber situated adjacent to the control room housing the monitoring and testing computers. Participants were seated in a large semi-reclining chair facing a computer monitor, and nicotine or placebo was administered concurrently with EEG electrode hook-up. Thirty minutes after nicotine/placebo administration, the time of peak nicotine venous blood levels (Hukkanen et al., 2005), vital signs were assessed and then EEG was recorded during a 2-min, resting, eyes-open condition. As this particular investigation was part of a larger study, we only recorded eyes-open EEG for comparison with (eyes-open) cognitive tasks.

Nicotine

Nicotine was administered as a single dose (6 mg) that consisted of one piece of cinnamon-flavored Nicorette (2 mg) and one piece of cinnamon-flavored Nicorette Plus (4 mg) gum; this dose yields a nicotine venous blood level of ~15–30 ng/mL, which

In addition to affecting nicotine absorption, what other affects might additional drug use have on participants' performance in this study?

How reliable are self-report measures? What other techniques could the experimenters use to determine whether participants had taken other drugs?

Based on what you read about a drug's addictive potential, which of these methods would be the most addictive for nicotine? Which would be the least addictive?

approximates levels seen after smoking a cigarette of mild-to-moderate nicotine content (Hukkanen, Jacob & Benowitz, 2005). The placebo-gum treatment (which contained no nicotine) consisted of two commercial cinnamon-flavored gum pieces, similar in flavor, size, shape, and texture to the nicotine gum. A blindfold was placed over the participants' eyes to conceal gum type. The participants also wore a nose plug for the duration of gum administration in order to control for any perceived sensory differences between the two gums. Each participant was instructed to chew the gum according to manufacturer's guidelines, which required them to bite the gum twice every minute and to "park" the gum between the teeth and cheeks between bites. The gum was removed after approximately 20 min of instructed chewing, and replaced with a "cleansing" gum: a strong commercial mint gum to disguise any taste differences between the placebo and nicotine gums. After this gum was chewed for 2–3 min, both the blindfold and the nose plug were removed. At the end of each test session, participants were asked to guess whether they had received nicotine or placebo gum, to ensure that double-blind conditions were upheld. Overall, participants were able to correctly guess which gum they had received exactly 50% of the time, which is exactly that expected by chance.

EEG

EEGs were digitally sampled at 256 Hz from an electrode cap (Electro-Cap International, Eaton, Ohio) that positioned tin electrodes at 28 scalp sites, including frontal Fp1, Fp2, F7, F8, F3, Fz and F4; frontal-central FC5, FC1, FC2, and FC6; central C3, Cz, and C4; parietal P3, Pz, P4, P7, P8; centro-parietal CP5, CP1, CP2, and CP6; temporal T7 and T8; occipital O1, Oz and O2, with all sites based on the 10–10 system (Chatrian, Lettich & Nelson, 1985). Linked-mastoid sites A1 and A2 were used as references. A midforehead electrode served as the ground and additional electrodes were placed on the orbital ridges and external canthus of one eye to monitor vertical and horizontal electro-oculographic activities. Electrode impedances were kept below 10 kΩ, and all electrical signals were amplified with a bandpass filter of 0.1–30.0 Hz (Embla, Ottawa). For each task condition, a minimum of twenty 2-s, artifact-free epochs

were subjected to a Fast Fourier Transform (FFT) algorithm (with a high-pass, auto-regressive filter, weighted by a 5% cosine taper) for computation of average log-transformed power (μV^2) at each scalp site for: delta (1.5–4.0 Hz), theta (4.0–8.0 Hz), alpha$_1$ (8.0 –10.5), alpha$_2$ (10.5–13.0 Hz), and beta (13.0 –20.0 Hz) frequency bands. For this study, EEG was analyzed from four scalp sites, including left (F3) and right (F4) frontal and left (P3) and right (P4) parietal regions, consistent with previous research (Allen, Iacono, Depue, & Arbisi 1993; Gilbert et al., 1999). In addition to log power, a R–L hemisphere asymmetry index (derived by subtracting left hemisphere power scores from right hemisphere power scores) was calculated for both frontal and parietal regions, and a F–P anterior–posterior index (derived by subtracting combined left and right parietal power scores from left and right frontal power scores) were analyzed.

Self-Reports

A physical-symptoms checklist used by Harkrider and Hedrick (2005), was employed to measure the severity of nicotine-related adverse symptoms perceived by the individual participants. They were instructed to indicate the severity of their symptoms on a 5-point scale: 0 = "no symptoms," 1 = "mild symptoms," 2 = "moderate symptoms," 3 = "strong symptoms," and 4 = "extreme symptoms." Symptoms included such events as heart-pounding, headache, dizziness, and nausea.

Vital Signs

Systolic blood pressure (SBP), diastolic blood pressure (DBP), both in millimetres of mercury [mmHg], and heart-rate (HR) level (beats per min) were measured before and after gum administration while participants were sitting (semireclined) without task involvement.

Statistics

Statistical analysis of the data was carried out with the Statistical Package for Social Sciences (SPSS). Repeated-measures general linear model (GLM) procedures were carried out for EEG log-power measures of individual band indices with treatment (placebo vs. nicotine), region (frontal vs.

> As discussed in this chapter, these are common effects of stimulants.

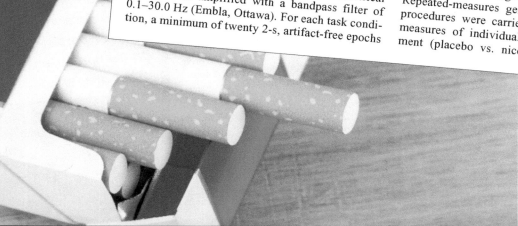

parietal), and hemisphere (left vs. right) serving as within-subjects factors. Gender was included as an exploratory between-subjects factor. When the GLMs indicated significant ($p < .05$) effects, follow-up of main and interaction effects involved pair-wise comparisons. Regardless of analysis of variance significance, planned comparisons testing study hypotheses were carried out, but were mainly limited to placebo–nicotine contrasts.

In order to determine the effect of treatment on physiological measures (SBP, DBP, HR), we calculated treatment change scores (pre–post) for each of the two treatments. We then compared nicotine and placebo change scores using paired-samples t tests.

RESULTS

Resting EEG Measures

Overall, there were no significant main treatment effects or interactions with treatment for any of the resting baseline measures (power, R–L index, F–P index) within delta, theta, alpha$_1$, alpha$_2$, or beta frequency bands. There was, however, a trend, $F(1, 19) = 3.48, p = .078$, for alpha$_2$ to be larger in response to nicotine ($M = 2.37$ μV2, $SE \pm 0.046$) than placebo ($M = 0.17$ μV^2, $SE \pm 0.038$). Regional effects generally found in the EEG literature were observed in the placebo condition ($p < .05$), with alpha band and beta band activities being greater in posterior than anterior sites, and with theta and delta being greater in anterior versus posterior regions. There were no main or interaction effects of gender.

With planned comparisons, nicotine administration ($M = 0.23$ μV^2, $SE \pm 0.052$) was found to yield significantly ($p = .05$) larger alpha$_2$ activity than did placebo ($M = 0.13$ μV^2, $SE \pm 0.028$) at frontal sites. Specifically, alpha$_2$ power was found to be greater ($p = .032$) with nicotine ($M = 0.17$ μV^2, $SE \pm 0.035$) versus placebo treatment ($M = 0.12$ μV^2, $SE \pm 0.025$) in the frontal region of the left hemisphere (i.e., F$_3$; Figure 1).

Adverse Events

No significant effect of treatment was observed for self-reported adverse events.

Vital Signs

Treatment with nicotine significantly ($t = 2.09$, $p \leq .05$) increased DBP ($M = -1.67$ mmHg, $SE = 1.32$) as compared with placebo ($M = 3.17$ mmHg, $SE = 1.94$), but did not alter HR or SBP.

Discussion

This report is the first full study to examine the effects of nicotine on EEG (delta, theta, alpha$_1$, alpha$_2$, beta) power in nonsmokers across the scalp. Assessing nicotine effects on resting EEG in nonsmokers provided an opportunity to determine whether the spectral EEG changes previously reported in smokers with acute smoking/nicotine were withdrawal dependent. During the resting EEG, it was found that nicotine only increased alpha$_2$ power, and this was evident in the left hemisphere of the frontal region. This corroborates a previous pilot report of nicotine affecting alpha (albeit global alpha), and not beta or theta, in nonsmokers (Foulds et al., 1994). Smokers have also exhibited an increase in alpha power, typically within the left frontal region (Gilbert et al., 1999) and, additionally, increasing nicotine dose has been shown to produce greater frontal alpha activity (Knott, 1989). The absence of alpha$_1$ and theta changes in the current study in response to nicotine administration may suggest that previous nicotine administration may suggest that previous alpha$_1$ and theta results found in mostly abstaining smokers may be related to withdrawal effects that are not evident with nonsmokers. It is of note that

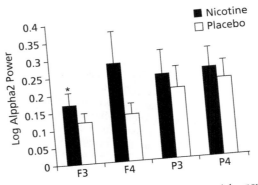

Figure 1. Mean ($\pm SE$) resting, eyes-open log alpha$_2$ power during placebo and nicotine treatment ($p = .032$).

previous studies in smokers administered nicotine doses of 4 mg (via polacrilex; Knott & Fisher, 2007; Knott et al., 2005), whereas the present study administered 6 mg of nicotine gum, suggesting appropriate dosing of nicotine. This suggestion is further supported by nicotine-related alterations of DBP and, although nicotine's peripheral (i.e., vital sign) effects were minimal, they are in line with what might be expected following the smoking of a single cigarette, consistent with the dosing used (Hukkanen et al., 2005).

Although the neurochemical basis of nicotine alterations in alpha$_2$ is uncertain, as neither nAChR or dopamine antagonists block its enhancement with smoking (Knott, Harr, Ilivitsky, & Mahoney, 1998; Walker et al., 2001), increases in left-frontal alpha$_2$ EEG activity may reflect an activation of neural circuitry in this region, which regulates both approach/motivational systems and positive emotions (Davidson, 1998), consistent with nicotine's mood-enhancing effects (Kalman, 2002). Additionally, this activation of motivational/emotional systems may contribute to nicotine's addictive properties.

Several limitations existed within this study, therefore the findings must be treated with caution. First, EEG was obtained during an eyes-open resting condition and, therefore, the reported results may not be seen under eyes closed conditions. Certainly, the effects of nicotine on eyes-closed EEG in nonsmokers should be investigated. Another possible confound in the study relates to nicotine administration, as only a single dose was used and the slow absorption with gum may have favored nAChR desensitization, rather than activation. The results would more accurately reflect the true effects of acute nicotine through smoking if other methods of nicotine administration were explored. Specifically, nicotine inhalation may mimic the effect of smoking more accurately than the administration of nicotine gum. Furthermore, as this study did not assess venous blood nicotine level, there was no way to ensure that each participant had similar nicotine blood levels. Another limitation is the recruitment of unequal numbers from each sex, hindering the investigation as to whether nicotine differentially affects male and female nonsmokers. Future studies should recruit an equal number of men and women in order to elucidate the potential presence and

nature of nicotine-related electrocortical sex differences. Finally, we did not track what phase of the menstrual cycle our female participants were in on their days of participation. Future studies may wish to track this in order to ensure no confounding effects stemming from hormonal fluctuations.

In summary, in this first full report of the effects of nicotine on resting EEG, we document increased left-frontal alpha$_2$ power, consistent with previous reports in smokers. The absence of changes in slow-wave (alpha$_1$, theta) bands following nicotine in nonsmokers may suggest that these previously reported results in smokers are related to alleviation of withdrawal state with nicotine.

REFERENCES

Allen, J. J., Iacono, W. G., Depue, R. A., & Arbisi, P. A. (1993). Regional electroencephalographic asymmetries in bipolar seasonal affective disorder before and after exposure to bright light. *Biological Psychiatry, 33,* 642–646. doi:10.1016/0006-3223(93)90104-L

Chatrian, G. E., Lettich, E., & Nelson, P. L. (1985). Ten percent electrode system for topographic studies of spontaneous and evoked EEG activity. *American Journal of EEG Technology, 25,* 83–92.

Davidson, R. (1998). Anterior electrophysiological asymmetries, emotion, and depression: Conceptual and methodological conundrums. *Psychophysiology, 35,* 607–614. doi:10.1017/S0048577298000134

Domino, E. F. (2001). Nicotine and tobacco dependence: normalization or stimulation? *Alcohol, 24,* 83–86.

Evans, D. E. & Drobes, D. J. (2009). Nicotine self-medication of cognitive-attentional processing. *Addictive Biology, 14,* 32–42. doi:10.1111/j.1369-1600.2008.00130.x

Foulds, J. (1993). Does nicotine replacement therapy work? *Addiction, 88,* 1473–1478. doi:10.1111/j.1360-0443.1993.tb03132.x

Foulds, J., McSorley, K., Sneddon, J., Feyerabend, C., Jarvis, M. J., & Russell, M. A. (1994). Effect of subcutaneous nicotine injections of EEG alpha frequency in non-smokers: A placebo-controlled pilot study. *Psychopharmacology, 115,* 163–166. doi:10.1007/BF02244767

Gilbert, D. G., McClernon, F. J., Rabinovich, N. E., Dibb, W. D., Plath, L. C., Hiyane, S., . . .Gehlbach, B. A. (1999). EEG, physiology, and task-related mood fail to resolve across 31 days of smoking abstinence: Relations to depressive traits, nicotine exposure, and dependence. *Experimental and Clinical Psychopharmacology, 7,* 427–443. doi:10.1037/1064-1297.7.4.427

Harkrider, A. W. & Hedrick, M. S. (2005). Acute effect of nicotine on auditory gating in smokers and non-smokers. *Hearing Research, 202,* 114–128. doi:10.1016/j.heares.2004.11.009

Henningfield, J. E., Schuh, L. M., & Jarvik, M. E. (1995). Pathophysiology of tobacco dependence. In F. E. Bloom & D. J. Kupfer (Eds.), *Psychopharmacology: The fourth generation of progress* (pp. 1715–1729). New York, NY: Raven Press, Ltd.

Hukkanen, J., Jacob, P., & Benowitz, N. L. (2005). Metabolism: Clinical and Experimental and disposition kinetics of nicotine. *Pharmacological Reviews, 57,* 79–115. doi:10.1124/pr.57.1.3

Kalman, D. (2002). The subjective effects of nicotine: Methodological issues, a review of experimental studies, and recommendations for future research. *Nicotine & Tobacco Research, 4,* 25–70. doi:10.1080/14622200110098437

Knott, V. J. (1988). Dynamic EEG changes during cigarette smoking. *Neuropsychobiology, 19,* 54–60. doi:10.1159/000118434

Knott, V. J. (1989a). Brain electrical imaging the dose-response effects of cigarette smoking. *Neuropsychobiology, 22,* 236–242. doi:10.1159/000118623

Knott, V. J. (1989b). Effects of low-yield cigarettes on electroencephalographic dynamics. *Neuropsychobiology, 21,* 216–222. doi:10.1159/000118580

Knott, V. J. (2001). Electroencephalographic characterization of cigarette smoking behavior. *Alcohol, 24,* 95–97. doi:10.1016/S0741-8329(00)00140-3

Knott, V. J. & Fisher, D. J. (2007). Naltrexone alteration of the nicotine-induced EEG and mood activation response in tobacco-deprived cigarette smokers. *Experimental and Clinical Psychopharmacology, 15,* 368–381. doi:10.1037/1064-1297.15.4.368

Knott, V., & Harr, A. (1995). Smoking-induced alterations in brain electrical profiles: normalization or enhancement? In P. B. S. Clarke, M. Quik, F. Adlkofer, & K. Thurau (Eds.), *Effects of Nicotine on Biological Systems II* (pp. 191–187). Basel: Birkhauser Verlag.

Knott, V. J., Harr, A., Ilivitsky, V., & Mahoney, C. (1998). The cholinergic basis of the smoking-induced EEG activation profile. *Pharmacoelectroencephalography, 38,* 97–107. doi:10.1159/000026524

Knott, V. J., Raegele, M., Fisher, D., Robertson, N., Millar, A., McIntosh, J., & Ilivitsky, V. (2005). Clonidine pre-treatment fails to block acute smoking-induced EEG arousal/mood in cigarette smokers. *Pharmacology Biochemistry and Behavior, 80,* 161–171. doi:10.1016/j.pbb.2004.10.025

Knott, V. J. & Venables, P. H. (1977). EEG alpha correlates of non-smokers, smokers, smoking, and smoking deprivation. *Psychophysiology, 14,* 150–154. doi:10.1111/j.1469-8986.1977.tb03367.x

Le Houezac, J. (1998). Nicotine: Abused substance and therapeutic agent. *Journal of Psychiatric Neuroscience, 23,* 95–108.

Levin, E. D., McClernon, F. J., & Rezvani, A. H. (2006). Nicotine effects on cognitive function: Behavioural characterization, pharmacological specification, and anatomic localization. *Psychopharmacology, 184,* 523–539. doi:10.1007/s00213-005-0164-7

Levin, E. D. & Simon, B. B. (1998). Nicotinic acetylcholine involvement in cognitive function in animals. *Psychopharmacology, 138,* 217–230. doi:10.1007/s002130050667

Mansvelder, H. D., van Aerde, K. I., Couey, J. J., & Brussaard, A. G. (2006). Nicotinic modulation of neuronal networks; from receptors to cognition. *Psychopharmacology, 184,* 292–305. doi:10.1007/s00213-005-0070-z

Oldfield, R. C. (1971). The assessment and analysis of handedness: The Edinburgh inventory. *Neuropsychologia, 9,* 97–113. doi:10.1016/0028-3932(71)90067-4

Parrott, A. C. & Roberts, G. (1991). Smoking deprivation and cigarette reinstatement: Effects upon visual attention. *Journal of Psychopharmacology, 5,* 404–409. doi:10.1177/026988119100500435

Rezvani, A. H. & Levin, E. D. (2001). Cognitive effects of nicotine. *Biological Psychiatry, 49,* 258 –267. doi:10.1016/S0006-3223(00)01094-5

Stepney, R. (1979). Smoking as a psychological tool. *Bulletin of the British Psychological Society, 32,* 341–345.

Walker, D., Mahoney, C., Ilivitsky, V., & Knott, V. J. (2001). Effects of haloperidol pretreatment on the smoking-induced EEG/mood activation response profile. *Neuropsychobiology, 43,* 102–112. doi:10.1159/000054875

Warburton, D. M. (1995). The functional conception of nicotine use. In P. Clarke, M. Guik, F. Adlkofer, & K. Thurau (Eds.), *Effects of nicotine on biological systems II* (pp. 257–264). Basel, Switzerland: Birkhauser Vorlag.

Waters, A. J. & Sutton, S. R. (2000). Direct and indirect effects of nicotine/smoking on cognition in humans. *Addictive Behaviors, 25,* 29–43. doi:10.1016/S0306-4603(99)00023-4

LEARNING

WHAT ARE THE PRINCIPLES OF LEARNING?
HOW DO REFLEXES CONDITION OUR RESPONSES TO STIMULI?
HOW DOES ASSOCIATION SHAPE OUR BEHAVIOUR?
WHAT CAN WE LEARN FROM WATCHING OTHERS?
WHAT BRAIN PROCESSES TAKE PLACE WE LEARN?

Imagine

being stuck in the world's worst traffic jam and instantly being able to calculate an alternative route. Or being given an unfamiliar address and immediately visualizing the quickest way to get there. For many of us, a near-perfect sense of direction would be a dream come true. But a study of London cab drivers has revealed that practice may in fact make perfect—extensive navigation experience increases the size of the human brain.

Researchers at University College, London, took structural MRI scans of 16 licensed London cab drivers and compared those scans with the scans of 50 people who did not drive cabs for a living. The researchers discovered that the posterior hippocampus—the area of the brain associated with spatial navigation—was larger in the brains of the cab drivers. Furthermore, the longer the cab drivers had been doing their job, the higher the hippocampal volume. In other words, the hippocampus is able to expand with spatial knowledge, enabling experienced London cab drivers to retain a complete mental map of the city.

Given that it takes about two years of extensive training to learn the complex network of streets in central London, it is perhaps unsurprising that cab drivers' hippocampi must expand to retain all the information needed to circumnavigate Buckingham Palace. Researchers have similarly observed increased hippocampal volume relative to brain and body size in mammals and birds that require spatial memory. Ever wondered how a squirrel remembers where it stored all its nuts? If you could run fast enough to catch a squirrel and put it in an MRI scanner, you might find that the squirrel's hippocampus is relatively large for its size.

Our ability to learn enables us to adapt to our environment—without this faculty, we would be unable to survive as a species. But how much of our behaviour is a result of reflex action? How much do we learn from watching others? What motivates us to learn, and what is happening in our brains as we do?

<<< This scene would have been unthinkable just a few decades ago, but with an increasing number of cars on the road, highways are expanding to accommodate them. Learning to adapt to our environment is a vital part of modern life, with researchers continually developing new ways to tackle air pollution and increased traffic volume. Every time we remember to avoid a busy route or take a newly discovered shortcut, the change in our behaviour indicates that learning has taken place.

CHAPTER 11

Principles of Learning

For psychologists, **learning** is the process through which experience results in a relatively permanent change in future behaviour. Imagine never having learned that it is a bad idea to touch a pot of boiling water, step on a nail, or leave the front door unlocked. Learning is involved in nearly everything we do.

BEHAVIOURISM

How should we study learning? Some early psychologists believed that we should focus on directly observable responses and discard any references to inner thoughts, feelings, and motives. This approach is known as **behaviourism.** Psychologists such as B. F. Skinner and John B. Watson believed that most behaviour can be explained as the product of simple forms of learning. They maintained that introspection is too subjective to be scientifically viable, whereas observing behaviour directly enables psychologists to analyze how organisms respond to stimuli in their environments. While few researchers today would agree that studying mental processes is of little significance, nearly all would agree that observing behaviour is a very important means by which to study learning.

SOME GENERAL TERMS

Learning-Performance Distinction

Imagine that you wanted to drive from British Columbia to New Brunswick and studied a road map for several days. You learned the route by heart, but on the day of the trip, you found yourself horribly lost. The difference between what you learned and its application on that particular day is known as a **learning-performance distinction.** Although learning gives us the capability to perform, we may not always be able to exercise this capability.

Associative Learning

Humans are not the only species with the capacity to learn. Have you ever watched a dolphin and its trainer at an aquarium? The dolphin will jump through hoops and balance a ball on its nose, knowing it will receive fish as a reward. By linking two events that occur together, the dolphin exhibits **associative learning.** We learn to associate certain stimuli all the time—a clap of thunder with a bolt of lightning, the smell of cooking with the possibility of food, an upturned nail on the floor with a sharp twinge of pain. This process of learning associations is known as **conditioning.**

Extinction and Spontaneous Recovery

What would happen if a dolphin trainer suddenly stopped rewarding Flipper for jumping through hoops? The dolphin would probably continue to perform for a while, but as the prospect of food becomes less likely, he will be less inclined to show off his trick. The gradual elimination of a learned response that occurs when an unconditioned stimulus such as a treat or reward is taken away is known as **extinction.**

Extinction does not completely erase what has been learned. A learned behaviour may reoccur after a rest period—a phenomenon known as **spontaneous recovery.** Having refused to perform his trick for several weeks, Flipper may decide to give it one more go in the hope of getting a treat.

If his trainer decided to reintroduce the treat, even after a long period without practice, Flipper would be able to perform the trick almost as well as he could originally. The ability to reacquire a learned behaviour in a shorter period of time than it took to learn originally is known as **savings.**

Generalization and Discrimination

If a particular object or situation closely resembles another, a learner may react to both in the same way—a process known as **generalization.** A dog trained to fetch a ball when it hears a whistle may also fetch a ball if it hears a loud buzzer or bell. A child learning to speak may associate every woman she sees with the word *Mama*.

Psychologist Gregory Razran (1949) proved that we generalize not only objects that are physically similar, but also stimuli that have similar subjective meanings. When shown a list of words, adults will generalize the semantically related words *style* and *fashion*, rather than the phonetically similar words *stile* and *style*, even though the latter pair look and sound more alike. Razran's research suggests that we've learned to generalize words based on their meanings rather than on their sounds or appearances.

Through a process of **stimulus discrimination,** learners can be trained to distinguish between similar but distinct stimuli. The child

Dolphins are conditioned to associate performing tricks with receiving tasty rewards.

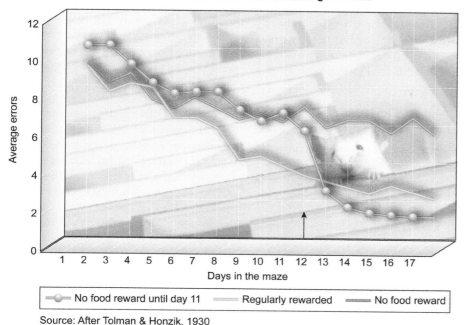

Evidence for Rats' Latent Learning in a Maze

Average errors

Days in the maze

No food reward until day 11 — Regularly rewarded — No food reward

Source: After Tolman & Honzik, 1930

∧
∧ The **group of rats** that is awarded food on **Day 10**
∧ immediately begins to make fewer navigational
errors, suggesting **prior learning** of the maze.

who calls every woman *Mama* will learn to distinguish her actual mother by a process of positive reinforcement. She will be praised when she correctly identifies her mother and unrewarded when she incorrectly labels other female figures. The child's mother becomes a **discriminative stimulus**—a cue signalling that a particular response will be positively reinforced.

Cognition and Learning

Just as behavioural conditioning is exhibited across different species, so too is cognitive learning. Researchers have found evidence of cognitive processes in animals by studying rats in mazes. Psychologist Edward Tolman performed an experiment in which he taught three groups of rats the same maze (Tolman & Honzik, 1930). Rats in the first group were individually placed in the maze and rewarded with food for making their way out the other side. The process was repeated over a period of several weeks. Rats in the second group were treated the same way but were not rewarded for making their way out of the maze until the tenth day of the experiment. The third group, the control group, was not rewarded at all during the experiment.

Tolman discovered that the second group of rats, which appeared to be wandering aimlessly around the maze for the first nine days, immediately solved the puzzle once food was presented as a reward for escaping from the maze. He concluded that the rats had learned how to solve the maze but had no incentive to do so before they were rewarded for demonstrating their behaviour. Learning that is exhibited only in the presence of an incentive is known as **latent learning.**

Just as London taxi drivers seem to create mental representations of the city in their brains, the rats appeared to develop **cognitive maps,** or mental representations of the maze. Tolman's experiment showed that learning can occur without reinforcement or punishment.

Motivation

Why do we behave as we do? Those of us who perform activities for their own sake are **intrinsically motivated**—we do things because they are interesting, satisfying, challenging, or enjoyable. **Extrinsic motivation** is the desire to complete a behaviour because it will lead to a reward or avoid punishment. Sometimes excessive rewards can undermine intrinsic motivation, a concept known as **overjustification.** Children promised a payoff for

playing with a particular toy will play with that toy less than children who are not paid to play (Deci, Koestner, & Ryan, 1999).

BIOLOGICAL PREDISPOSITIONS IN LEARNING

An animal's natural predispositions create a propensity for learning some kinds of associations rather than others. It is easy to teach a chicken to "dance" for treats because as the chicken waits for food, it naturally scratches at the ground in a manner that resembles (fairly bad) dancing. However, if you try to teach a chicken to stand still in order to obtain food, you will find the process much harder: Chickens are not biologically predisposed to wait patiently for dinner. The tendency for an animal to revert back to its instinctual behaviour over time is known as **instinctual drift.**

Food Preferences

If you've ever gotten food poisoning from a bad hamburger and discovered afterwards that you no longer have any interest in eating hamburgers, you've experienced **taste-aversion learning,** a form of conditioned learning in which exposure to a flavour paired with sickness will produce a consistent aversion to that flavour. Psychologist John Garcia discovered that rats given a sweetened liquid and then injected with a drug or exposed to radiation that caused nausea would not touch the liquid again (Garcia & Koelling, 1966). Even if we

Fear-Related Learning Biases

Most of us have never been attacked by a shark, but plenty of people still hear the *Jaws* theme music in their heads every time they set foot in the ocean. Humans are biologically predisposed to acquire fears of situations and objects that posed a threat to our ancestors or that threaten our survival as a species. We quickly learn to fear storms, snakes, spiders, and cliffs, while our instincts leave us unprepared for modern dangers such as electricity and global warming, even though they now pose a bigger threat (Lumsden & Wilson, 1983).

Place-Learning Abilities

Some animals appear to have specialized learning abilities to help them locate important places. A squirrel is able to recall numerous locations of buried food stores, while salmon are biologically predisposed to return to their own hatching grounds when it is time to spawn. Remember how both taxi drivers and squirrels have unusually large hippocampi? One study suggests that in the case of the squirrels, this might be seasonal. In spring and fall, when squirrels are actively gathering and retrieving nuts, they show a 15% increase in hippocampus size compared to the rest of the year (Lavenex, Steele, & Jacobs, 2000).

ingest food several hours before we feel nauseated, we can still develop strong taste aversions.

If we are deprived of essential nutrients, do we automatically turn to foods that can provide us with the supplements we need? Studies of sodium-deprived and calcium-deprived rats show that the animals preferentially seek out foods rich in these minerals (Richter, 1936; Richter & Eckert, 1937). This is true even of rats that have never been exposed to sodium or calcium before, suggesting that the preference is an unlearned response.

However, food preference is not just a biological response; animals (including humans) also learn what's good to eat through social observation. Studies on Norway rats showed that the rodents expressed a preference for food that had already been successfully ingested by their fellow rats (Galef & Wigmore, 1983).

∧ **How does a squirrel**
∧ **remember where it**
∧ **stored all its nuts?**

Classical Conditioning

Although the idea of learned associations was not new at the time, Russian physiologist Ivan Pavlov's classic studies in the early 20th century proved that it was possible to learn to associate two stimuli and thus create a reflex response. This phenomenon became known as **classical conditioning.** While Pavlov was studying canine digestion, he noticed that his dogs were salivating at the mere sight of food. Even the sound of a dog bowl clattering in the kitchen made them drool. Pavlov studied the dogs' reflexes by sounding a bell every time he was about to give them food. After many occasions of hearing the bell and immediately receiving food, the dogs learned to associate the two. They began to salivate at the sound of the bell, even in the absence of food, indicating that they had learned there was a connection between the bell's ring and the arrival of food (Pavlov, 1927).

The **unconditioned stimulus (US)** is the original, unlearned stimulus that elicits a certain reflex action, known as an **unconditioned response (UR).** In this case, the unconditioned stimulus is the food that the dogs expect to eat, while salivation is the unconditioned response. When a **conditioned stimulus (CS)**—an event that is repeatedly paired with the unconditioned stimulus—is introduced, it will eventually trigger a learned reaction even without the unconditioned stimulus. This is known as a **conditioned response (CR).** Through a period of acquisition, Pavlov taught the dogs to associate the sound of a ringing bell with the expectation of food, causing the dogs to salivate whenever they heard a bell.

TYPES OF CLASSICAL CONDITIONING

Pavlov experimented with several types of classical conditioning. In **delayed conditioning,** the conditioned stimulus is presented before the unconditioned stimulus, and the termination of the conditioned stimulus is delayed until the unconditioned stimulus is made available.

>>> 1. A neutral stimulus (NS) produces no salivation response. 2. An unconditioned stimulus (US) produces an unconditioned response (UR). 3. The unconditioned stimulus is repeatedly presented just after the neutral stimulus and continues to produce an unconditioned response. 4. The neutral stimulus produces a conditioned response without the unconditioned stimulus. The neutral stimulus becomes a conditioned stimulus (CS).

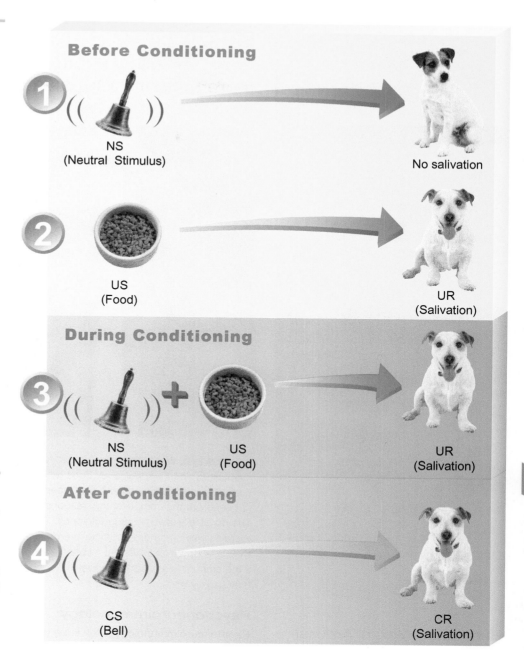

Before Conditioning

1. NS (Neutral Stimulus) → No salivation

2. US (Food) → UR (Salivation)

During Conditioning

3. NS (Neutral Stimulus) + US (Food) → UR (Salivation)

After Conditioning

4. CS (Bell) → CR (Salivation)

For example, Pavlov would continue ringing his bell until the dogs were able to see the food in front of them.

In **trace conditioning,** the conditioned stimulus is discontinued before the unconditioned stimulus is presented. For example, Pavlov would sound the bell once and then bring the food in after an interval with no stimuli. Pavlov found that the conditioned stimulus and unconditioned stimulus should occur within a few seconds of each other in order to work effectively.

In **simultaneous conditioning,** the conditioned stimulus and unconditioned stimulus are presented at the same time. Pavlov found this method to be ineffective: When the bell rang and the food appeared simultaneously, the dogs did not have time to anticipate the food and did not associate it with the ringing bell.

In the procedure called **backward conditioning,** the conditioned stimulus is presented after the unconditioned stimulus, signalling the end of the food. This rarely results in learning, supporting the idea that classical conditioning is biologically adaptive—it helps organisms prepare for an event. It would be of little use to hear a footstep behind us in a dark alley (a conditioned stimulus that signals danger) if we have already been clonked over the head by

an attacker (an unconditioned stimulus that causes a fight-or-flight reflex action).

Second-order conditioning occurs when a conditioned stimulus is paired with a neutral stimulus. It is possible for the neutral stimulus to become a second conditioned stimulus, even though it has never been directly related to the unconditioned stimulus. For example, Pavlov later paired the learned bell with a black square. Eventually, the dogs would salivate at the mere sight of the square, even though it had never been directly linked to food.

CLASSICAL CONDITIONING AND OUR EVERYDAY LIVES

You may not realize it, but classical conditioning is present in our everyday lives.

Fear

Psychologists John Watson and Rosalie Rayner proved that it is possible to condition human emotions such as fear. They took an 11-month-old infant named Albert who, like most children, was afraid of loud noises but not of white rats. Watson and Rayner presented Albert with a white rat and, just as he was about to touch it, struck a hammer against a steel bar directly behind the infant's head. After this procedure had been repeated several times, Albert burst into tears at the mere sight of the rat (Watson & Rayner, 1920). Thanks to the principle of generalization, Albert also developed an unhealthy fear of all things furry: Rabbits, cotton wool, and even Santa Claus's beard caused the child to dissolve into tears.

What other things may become **associated with drug use? How might these associations make it more difficult to break a drug dependence?**

Fear conditioning is highly resistant to extinction. In severe cases, just one pairing of a neutral stimulus with an unconditioned stimulus can create a serious phobia. After the 9/11 attacks, tens of thousands of children in New York City experienced nightmares and fear of public places (Goodnough, 2002).

> "Advertisers pair their products with beautiful women, successful and handsome men, catchy jingles, and promises of wealthier and happier lives. We as consumers begin to associate these positive attributes to their products. Want a better life? Then just buy this car, or beer, or pair of shoes."

Hunger and Sexual Arousal

Both hunger and sexual arousal can be associated with different locations, smells, signals, objects, and sights. For example, the smell of cookies may make your stomach growl, while the smell of a specific cologne or perfume may remind you of a sexual partner.

Drug Tolerance

Canadian researcher Shepard Siegel and his colleagues (1982) found that drug taking could become associated with a specific location. When we are in the "drug associated" location, our body produces a compensatory or protective response to the drug that decreases its effect—leading us to take more of the drug to produce the same high. This phenomenon, known as drug tolerance, refers to the lessening of physiological and behavioural effects caused by a drug because of repeated use.

However, when we are not in our "drug associated" location, our body does not expect drugs to be taken and so it does not send out the compensatory response. The result is a lowered drug tolerance. This explains why some drug addicts overdose if they take drugs in a different location—even if the amount is smaller or equivalent to what they usually take.

Psychoneuroimmunology

Psychoneuroimmunology is the study of how psychology relates to events involving the nervous system and the immune system. Have you ever heard someone talk about head lice and immediately felt your scalp itch all over?

Classical conditioning affects not only the body's physiological responses, but also its immune system. Researchers paired rats' drinking of saccharine-sweetened water with injections of a drug that suppressed immune functioning. After repeated pairings, the saccharine water alone triggered immune suppression, as if the drug had been given (Ader & Cohen, 1985).

Advertising

Advertisers pair their products with beautiful women, successful and handsome men, catchy jingles, and promises of wealthier and happier lives. We as consumers begin to associate these positive attributes to their products. Want a better life? Then just buy this car, or beer, or pair of shoes.

Self-esteem and Other Emotions

Canadian researchers report that self-esteem can be increased by pairing self-relevant information with smiling faces (Baccus, Baldwin, & Packer, 2004). In addition, those around us can influence how we feel. How do you feel when you are around people you love? How do you feel when you are around people you hate?

Operant Conditioning

Whereas classical conditioning occurs with reflexive, involuntary behaviour, **operant conditioning** is a type of learning in which organisms associate their actions with consequences. This type of conditioning is active, meaning it requires action from the organism. In classical conditioning, the organism is passive and simply learns to associate a stimulus with an outcome; it need not respond in any specific way. It is therefore more likely to repeat rewarded behaviours and less likely to continue performing actions that are punished.

OPERANT BEHAVIOUR

Operant conditioning involves **operant behaviour**—responses that an organism makes to produce an effect on the environment. According to Skinner, most of our behaviour is a result of **reinforcement**—an act that causes the response to be more likely to recur.

Take Edward Thorndike's "puzzle box," for example. Thorndike (1898) placed a hungry cat in a wooden cage that required a simple act (such as pushing a lever) to open it. To heighten feline frustration and further motivate an escape attempt, he then placed a bowl of food just outside the door of the cage so that the cat could see it. To reach the food, the cat had to figure out how to press the lever to open the door, a process that Thorndike timed. After pushing and rubbing up against the walls of the cage, the cat accidentally stood on the lever, opening the door. The cat did not learn the connection between the lever and the road to freedom immediately. However, after numerous trials, the cat was able to open the door very quickly, demonstrating that it had learned an association between the lever and the path to food and freedom.

Based on his research, Thorndike developed the **law of effect:** If a response produces a satisfying effect, it is likely to occur again.

PRINCIPLES OF REINFORCEMENT

Building on Thorndike's law of effect, Skinner developed some of the principles of behaviour control. He developed his own version of a puzzle box, called a "Skinner box," or "operant-conditioning chamber." By pressing a bar in the chamber, a rat could release food pellets or water, while a device recorded the animal's responses.

Skinner believed that to analyze human and animal behaviour, each act could be broken into three parts, known as a **three-term contingency.** This includes the discriminative stimulus (the bar to be pushed), the **operant response** (the act of pushing the bar), and the **reinforcer/punisher** (receiving food or water). Through this process, organisms learn that in the presence of certain stimuli, their behaviour is likely to have a particular effect on the environment.

If you spend a few hours a week working out at the gym, what motivates you to go? Achieving a good level of personal fitness? Receiving compliments on your lean

appearance? There are many health-related reasons to jump on a treadmill, but there are also fringe benefits such as spending time with your gym buddies or avoiding an unpleasant household chore. For every

> Give a young child a 100 dollar bill and she probably won't have much of a reaction. But once she learns how many toys that 100 dollar bill could purchase, she will learn to appreciate money as a strong motivating factor.

repeated action we take, there are different types of reinforcers.

Types of Reinforcers

Positive reinforcers strengthen a response by presenting a pleasurable consequence. We receive compliments for a job well done. We feel good about taking our recycling to the local recycling centre or donating blood to the blood bank.

In contrast, **negative reinforcers** strengthen a response by removing an unpleasant consequence. We block our ears to shut out the piercing sound of a fire alarm. We rock a baby to sleep to stop it from crying.

A **primary reinforcer** satisfies a basic biological need, such as hunger or thirst. A **secondary reinforcer** becomes satisfying or pleasurable through experience. Give a young child a 100 dollar bill and she probably won't have much of a reaction. But once she learns how many toys that 100 dollar bill could purchase, she will learn to appreciate money as a strong motivating factor.

Unlike other animals, humans have the ability to respond to **delayed reinforcement,** or a reward that does not immediately follow an action. We can wait a week or a month before we receive our paycheques, and we do not immediately demand to know an exam result at the end of a test. Even though we can respond to delayed reinforcement, however, we still often reject long-term, delayed consequences in favour of short-term, immediate pleasures. It's hard to convince ourselves to change our lifestyles drastically in order to

reduce our carbon footprint when we may not see any tangible environmental results of this decision for several years.

Reinforcement Schedules

Continuous reinforcement ensures that a desired response is reinforced every time it occurs. This schedule results in rapid learning, but if the reinforcement stops, extinction also occurs rapidly. If a rat suddenly stops receiving food pellets every time it presses a bar, it will soon stop pressing it.

Often, we do not experience continuous reinforcement in our daily lives. A telemarketer may be lucky if one person in a hundred gives him or her the time of day, and the people who create "junk" mail see the bulk of their labour immediately consigned to the nearest trash can. Yet if these people were completely unsuccessful, their companies would go out of business.

Partial (intermittent) reinforcement occurs when responses are sometimes reinforced and sometimes not. This produces slower initial learning, but the learning is more resistant to extinction. It seems that we are more persistent when we achieve rare but satisfying results. There are several types of partial reinforcement:

Fixed-ratio schedules. Behaviour is reinforced after a set number of responses. For example, you might get one free latte after every 10 purchases at the local coffee place. Fixed-rate schedules bring forth high rates of responding with only a brief pause following reinforcement.

Variable-ratio schedules. Behaviour is reinforced after varying and unpredictable numbers of responses. A gambler at a slot machine may put in thousands of coins and receive no payout, or insert a single quarter into the slot and win thousands of dollars. Variable-ratio schedules have high response rates and produce behaviour that's difficult to extinguish.

Fixed-interval schedules. Behaviour is reinforced for the first response after a fixed time period. If we know that our dinner is almost ready, we will check the oven more frequently, producing rapid responses at the expected time of reward and slower responses until then.

Variable-interval schedules. Behaviour is reinforced after variable periods of time. We may obsessively check our e-mail for new messages and be rewarded for our efforts at varying time intervals. This generally produces slow and steady behavioural responses.

Accidental Reinforcement

Is behaviour reinforced when it is accidentally linked to a fortunate outcome? You can probably answer this question by assessing your closet. If you have a "lucky" shirt that achieved its moniker because your team once made it to the championships while you were wearing it, you have experienced accidental reinforcement.

Skinner (1948) demonstrated similar "superstitious" behaviour with pigeons. He placed the hungry birds in individual cages containing food hoppers and dropped grains of food into each hopper at random intervals. The pigeons repeated whatever they had been doing just before the food was dropped into the cage—hopping from side to side, turning around, or making a pendulum-like motion with their heads. Although there was no actual link between the pigeons' actions and the outcome (just as your team is equally likely to win or lose regardless of whether you wear your lucky shirt), they continued to demonstrate the same behaviour.

Attractive Rewards and Reward Expectations

Some theorists argue that the stimulus-response relationship is an oversimplification of the learning process and suggest that there is a cognitive component involved with regard to the expectation of reward. For example, if a rat knows that it will receive a larger amount of food than usual when it completes a maze, will it be motivated to run faster? A sudden shift in the attractiveness of a reward is called a **reward contrast effect** (Crespi, 1942, 1944). Response rates decrease when a strong reinforcer is exchanged for a weaker one, creating a negative contrast effect. Conversely, if a reward becomes more enticing, response rates will increase, creating a positive contrast effect. Institutions such as rehabilitation centres and psychiatric facilities use **token economies** to capitalize on this theory. Desired behaviours such as grooming and taking medication are rewarded with token payoffs such as free time or extra dessert.

Enticing rewards tend to be good motivators. The **Premack principle** states that a preferred activity can be used to reinforce a non-preferred task. For example, you might promise yourself a trip to the movies as a reward for finishing the paper that's been hanging over your head for weeks.

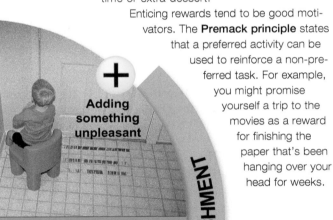

REINFORCEMENT

Adding something valuable or desirable

Avoiding something unpleasant

PUNISHMENT

Adding something unpleasant

Removing something valued or desired

+ POSITIVE — NEGATIVE

> Reinforcement is generally acknowledged to be more effective than punishment when disciplining children.

PUNISHMENT AND SHAPING

Most of us probably remember being sent to our rooms to "think about what we've done." Some of us may have even thought twice about locking our younger brother in the closet again. Whereas reinforcement increases a behaviour, **punishment** decreases it. If a high school student cuts class, he or she might receive punishment in the form of after-school detention or extra assignments. Since most of us would prefer not to spend our time in either of these ways, we're likely to respond to this threat of punishment by making sure to show up for class.

Is it possible to gradually teach good table manners to a badly behaved child? The process of **shaping** behaviour uses reinforcers to guide an organism's actions toward a desired behaviour. This is achieved using **successive approximations,** or behaviours that are incrementally closer to the overall desired action. For example, on the first day, you might encourage the child to simply sit at the table for a short period of time before allowing him to watch TV. The next day, you might extend the time period, gradually moving to more complex behaviours such as using a napkin and not talking with a mouth full of food.

> Skinner's theories that external influences shape behaviour, as opposed to thoughts and feelings, were highly controversial. His critics argued that he dehumanized people by neglecting their personal freedom.

One method of shaping complex behaviour is **chaining,** a process in which the final step in a sequence is reinforced first, becoming a conditioned reinforcer for the preceding response. This method is often used in animal training. For example, you might place a rat on a top platform in a cage where it is able to eat food. You might then place the rat on a lower platform so that it has to climb a ladder in order to reach the top platform and eat the food. These steps can be expanded to shape a complex chain of events. Skinner managed to train a rat to wait to hear "The Star-Spangled Banner" before sitting up on its hind legs, pulling a string to hoist the U.S. flag, and finally saluting the banner in a remarkable but atypical display of rodent patriotism.

Punishment is a penalty given in an attempt to decrease the occurrence of a certain behaviour.

Shaping is a process in which reinforcers are used to guide an organism's actions toward a desired behaviour.

Successive approximations are behaviours that are incrementally closer to the overall desired action.

Chaining is a process in which the final step in a sequence is reinforced first, becoming a conditioned reinforcer for the preceding response.

APPLICATIONS OF OPERANT CONDITIONING

Skinner's theories that external influences shape behaviour, as opposed to thoughts and feelings, were highly controversial. His critics argued that he dehumanized people by neglecting their personal freedom. Whatever the objections to Skinner's ideas, applications of operant conditioning are evident in schools, homes, and businesses.

Skinner believed that it was possible to achieve an ideal education. He stated: "Good instruction demands two things. Students must be told immediately whether what they do is right or wrong and, when right, they must be directed to the step to be taken next." We can see Skinner's vision to some extent in modern classrooms that use online learning programs and interactive student software.

Reinforcement principles have been shown to enhance athletic abilities. Thomas Simek and Richard O'Brien (1981, 1988) used these techniques to improve the performances of students learning to play golf and baseball. For example, golf students would start with very short putts and gradually increase their distance from the tee. This behavioural method of training showed faster skill improvement than students who had been taught using conventional methods.

Both punishment and reinforcement are most effective when they immediately follow the performed behaviour. IBM bigwig Thomas Watson would immediately write an employee a cheque whenever he spotted an achievement worthy of praise (Peters & Waterman, 1982). While it would be great to have such a generous boss, a simple "thank you" for a job well done is equally effective.

<<< **Do high gas prices** affect your driving decisions?

If you suddenly became responsible for the entire electricity bill in a shared house, would you be more careful about turning the lights off? You would probably find yourself painfully aware of how many lights your housemates were leaving on, too. Economists and psychologists believe that people's spending behaviour is controlled by the consequences of that behaviour. Al Gore (1992) pointed out that when the government decides to tax a commodity, people use less of that commodity (because they don't want to pay taxes), whereas when the government subsidizes a commodity, that commodity is more heavily used (because people want to take advantage of the relatively cheap price). He suggested that a good policy move would be to increase taxes on the burning of fossil fuels to encourage people to use less gas. Recent surges in fuel prices and the subsequent outcry suggests that there is a limit to how much Canadians are willing to spend on their love of the open road.

Observational Learning

We didn't directly experience many of the behaviours we learned about as children. Instead, we learned by watching others. Take Michigan youngster Adrian Cole, who in 2005, at the age of four, was picked up by police officers in the middle of the night after driving his mother's car to the local video store. When the officers asked him how he learned to drive, Adrian told them that he just watched what his mom did. **Observational learning,** in which we observe and imitate others, plays a large part in our overall learning process.

ELEMENTS OF OBSERVATIONAL LEARNING

Stimulus enhancement is the tendency to pay attention to a particular place or object that someone else has shown interest in. Learning how to play a particular instrument will become more desirable if we see a friend or sibling playing that same instrument.

Our drive to receive the rewards we've obtained in the past is called **goal enhancement.** We are more motivated to act out behaviours that have previously resulted in being rewarded. An undesired piano lesson may become more appealing if previous

> In nature, animals are active learners, acquiring new behaviours by observing others or simply by going about their day-to-day business. **Both animals and humans learn via play and exploration.**

lessons have ended with a trip to the movies, or if we have watched a sibling receive a treat for correctly playing the scales.

To learn by observation, an organism must be able to reproduce the action that is being observed—a concept known as **modelling.** A toddler may be able to imitate a sibling drinking out of a cup, but more complex actions such as performing a backflip or playing Beethoven's Fifth Symphony are generally not possible through mere observation.

Latent learning, which we discussed earlier, is another type of observational learning. Learning that an observer does not immediately demonstrate may still be added to his or her knowledge base. Observational learning helps us understand how the children of abusive parents may grow up to be more aggressive (Stith et al., 2000). These children may not necessarily display aggressive behaviour at the time, but they are learning it through observation.

BANDURA'S EXPERIMENTS

How do children react when they see adults behaving aggressively? Canadian psychologist Albert Bandura conducted a famous experiment in which he attempted to answer this question (Bandura, Ross, & Ross, 1961). Using a group of preschool children, a researcher invited one child at a time to sit in a room and complete some artwork. Having shown the child how to design pictures with potato prints, the experimenter moved to the opposite side of the room and began playing with a Tinkertoy set and a five-foot inflatable Bobo doll. The experimenter then began acting aggressively toward the doll, using easily imitable actions such as placing the doll on its side and repeatedly punching it on the nose while chanting aggressive remarks.

After the child observed the aggressive outburst, the experimenter took the child to another room full of appealing toys. The experimenter allowed the child to play for a few minutes before interrupting, explaining that these particular toys were reserved for other children. The frustrated child was then taken to another room that contained a few toys, including a Bobo doll. Making herself as inconspicuous as possible, the experimenter watched the child's reactions toward the doll.

Children that had been exposed to violent outbursts were much more likely to lash out at the doll. The experimenters noted that the children imitated the exact same acts that they had witnessed and used the same aggressive verbal remarks. Bandura concluded that children imitate violent behaviour they see in adults, and he began to research links between children's exposure to violence on television and aggressive behaviour toward others.

APPLICATIONS OF OBSERVATIONAL LEARNING

Based on Bandura's study, we might be tempted to conclude that observational learning is not a good thing. Negative role models can create anti-social effects, encouraging crime and gang violence. Some studies conclude that violence seen on television and in the movies can have a negative impact on children's behaviour (Comstock & Lindsey, 1975; Eron, 1987).

However, observational learning is not all bad news. **Prosocial** models—those that

^
^
^ What **skills** might these children be **learning** as they play?

are positive and helpful—can have beneficial effects on people's behaviour. Humanitarian figures such as Martin Luther King Jr. and Mahatma Gandhi used their influence to direct people's behaviour through non-violent action. Parents and teachers can also be strong role models, encouraging children through their own actions to be kind and helpful to others and to have a positive impact on the world.

LEARNING-BASED ACTIVITIES

In nature, animals are active learners, acquiring new behaviours by observing others or simply by going about their day-to-day business. Both animals and humans learn via play and exploration.

Play

It is easy to dismiss play as a form of entertainment that serves no real purpose, but have you ever watched a kitten wiggle its rump and pounce on a piece of string or a dog's tail? This behaviour is helping the kitten learn to hunt. Play activity in animals serves as natural training for behaviours that will

> When we learn we create new connections between neurons in our brain. Just like the muscles in our bodies, **the more we use the information we have learned the stronger the neural connections will become.**

prove useful in serious situations. Similarly, two young children role-playing nurturing games with dolls are actually learning important behavioural lessons that will improve their social development (see Chapter 7).

Exploration

If you place a rat in an unfamiliar cage and watch its reactions, you will probably see it scurry from corner to corner, as it assesses its

new surroundings. Exploring an environment is generally considered to be more primitive and widespread than play behaviour. New surroundings inspire both curiosity and fear in an organism.

Once the rat is satisfied that it has familiarized itself with its new environment, you may see it **patrolling**—periodically scanning the cage by rearing up on its hind legs to make sure that nothing has changed.

Learning in the Brain

EARLY STUDIES

What processes take place in the brain when we learn?

When we learn we create new connections between neurons in our brain. Just like the muscles in our bodies, the more we use the information we have learned the stronger the neural connections will become. This strengthening of neural connections is called **long-term potentiation (LTP),** the process that is needed to learn or remember information for a long time.

Canadian psychologist Donald Hebb (1949) was the first to recognize that learning was tied to neural activity and that we need to strengthen neural connections in order to learn.

Studies have shown that if we prevent the strengthening of neural connections, that is we prevent LTP, then learning is impaired or does not occur at all (Lynch & Staubli, 1991). Conversely, we can increase learning potential by increasing LTP. Mice can be genetically engineered to have heightened learning capacities, by increasing the number of neurons involved in forming connections when we learn something new (Tsien, 2000).

HOW CAN WE BECOME SMARTER?

The question of how we can become smarter is really a question about how we can learn more effectively and consequently how we can maximize our brain's ability. Studies have demonstrated that rats living in enriched environments show enhanced learning abilities—a phenomenon that disappears when the rodents are placed in impoverished cages deprived of stimuli (Rosenzweig, Bennett, & Diamond, 1972). Like the brains of London taxi drivers, which increase with spatial knowledge, the structures of rats' brains alter with experience.

Missing an early morning lecture for a bit of extra sleep might ironically improve your chances of graduating. Learning, or the strengthening of neural connections (also known as LTP), is more difficult following prolonged periods of wakefulness (Vyazovskiy et al., 2008).

Sleep plays an important role in the stabilization of long-term memory—after learning, we need sleep in order to consolidate the new information. That is we need sleep to strengthen the new neural connections we have created. Research has found that sleep deprivation can lead to the depletion of proteins that help neurons grow and survive (Sei, Saitoh, Yamamoto, Morita, & Morita, 2000) and can hinder the creation of cells in the hippocampus (Guzman-Marin et al., 2003). Sleep deprivation has also been found to impair subsequent learning (Yoo, Hu, Gujar, Jolesz, & Walker, 2007), making it a good idea to leave the Thursday night party relatively early if you want to retain any information from Friday's lecture.

Neurobiologists identify two types of memory consolidation. The first, known as **synaptic consolidation,** takes place within a few hours after learning. It involves the morphological changes necessary for the successful transference of information into our long-term memory.

The second type of memory consolidation takes place at a system level. **System consolidation** is a more gradual process (taking weeks or months), involving the reorganization of the brain regions that support memory. According to **Ribot's law,** memory loss following brain damage affects recent memories to a greater extent than remote memories. Think of your brain as a computer saving a file—if the computer crashes, it will retain all the information on that file except for the most recent data that has not automatically been saved. Similarly, if the consolidation process is disrupted before your brain has had a chance to organize the information properly, the new memories that were being created may be lost.

WHAT PARTS OF THE BRAIN ARE INVOLVED IN LEARNING?

Many studies have shown the changes that occur in our brain when we learn. Several parts of our brain are involved in the learning process, including the somatosensory cortex, the basal ganglia, the cerebellum, and the hippocampus.

The somatosensory cortex is involved in sensory learning. For example, neurobiologist Gregg Recanzone and his colleagues (1992) trained adult owl monkeys to detect the difference in frequency between two stimuli that are placed on one of their fingers. They found that larger areas of the somatosensory cortex were activated after training compared to before training occurred.

The basal ganglia are associated with learning that occurs from operant conditioning (i.e., the use of reinforcement). Remember how the reward areas of a mother's brain light up on brain-scan images when she sees a photo of her smiling infant? Behaviour that results in a reward causes dopamine neurons to fire in bursts. Conversely, if an expected reward is not received, the dopamine cells stop firing altogether. In the basal ganglia, actions that are rewarded (i.e., causes a release of dopamine) result in stronger neural connections than actions that not rewarded with a release of dopamine.

The amygdala is involved in emotional learning. Remember Little Albert, the toddler who was conditioned to fear white rats? He developed an unhealthy fear of all things furry because he associated them with loud noises. The amygdala was responsible for the conditioning of this fear. Imagine a rat when it is frightened: It gets into a crouching position and sits motionless, a defensive reaction called **freezing.** Physiological reactions also take place, such as an increase in heart rate and blood pressure. If the rat is conditioned to fear a particular stimulus, both the behavioural and physiological reactions will occur. This is ultimately how classical conditioning leads to learned fear of a stimulus. Once connections from the amygdala are severed, these reactions no longer take place (Kim, Rison, & Fanselow, 1993) and fear conditioning does not occur.

The hippocampus and the cerebellum are also involved in learning that occurs through classical conditioning. The hippocampus is involved in learning that occurs when there is a delay between the presentation of the unconditioned and conditioned stimuli (called trace conditioning); the cerebellum is involved in learning that occurs when the conditioned stimuli is presented before the unconditioned stimuli (called delayed conditioning).

The hippocampus is also involved in spatial learning. Psychologists John O'Keefe and Lynn Nadel (1978) proposed the **cognitive map theory,** in which the hippocampus provides a spatial framework, enabling us to create a mental map of our surroundings. In contrast, supporters of the **relational memory theory** suggest that the hippocampus processes events by linking them into frameworks based on the relationships between events, people, places, and so on (Cohen & Eichenbaum, 1993). For example, you might hear your favourite childhood TV show's theme song and suddenly be reminded of a multitude of associations—the characters on that show, what you liked to eat while you were watching it, the childhood friends who also used to watch the show and act out scenes with you at school the following day.

We know that specific parts of our brain are involved in learning that occurs through operant and classical conditioning, but what happens when we learn just by watching other people? Are the same processes involved even if we do not complete the task ourselves? It appears the answer is *yes*. Regardless of whether completion of a task is witnessed or is done first-hand, the same neurons are activated. For example, neuroscientists have discovered that the same neurons, called **mirror neurons,** are activated in the macaque monkey both when a task is completed and when they watch another monkey perform the task. Humans have these neurons in the frontal lobe, and they appear to also be involved in learning through observation (Fabbri-Destro & Rizzolatti, 2008; Ramachandran, 2000).

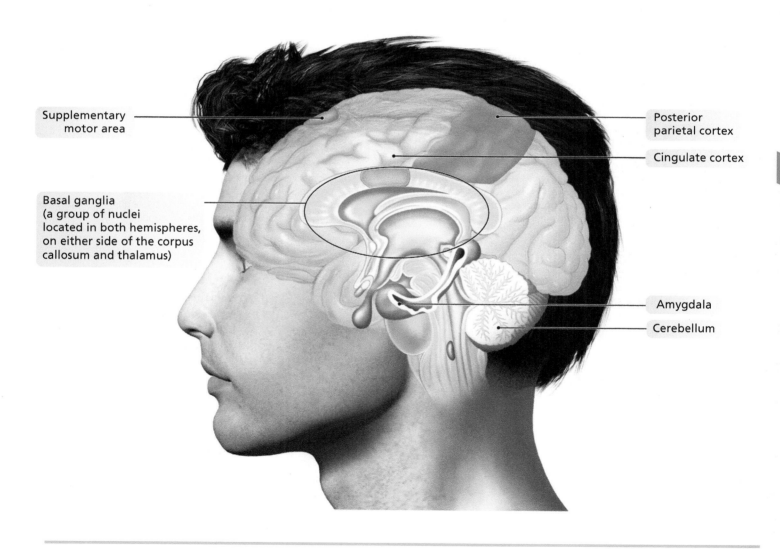

Supplementary motor area

Posterior parietal cortex

Cingulate cortex

Basal ganglia (a group of nuclei located in both hemispheres, on either side of the corpus callosum and thalamus)

Amygdala

Cerebellum

∧ ∧ ∧ The amygdala is critical for **emotional conditioning** and damage to this area may cause a lack of fear. What **disadvantages** might you encounter if you became fearless?

Summary

WHAT ARE THE PRINCIPLES OF LEARNING? p.152

• Learning is the process through which experience results in a relatively permanent change in future behaviour.

• Behaviourists B. F. Skinner and John B. Watson believed that most behaviour can be explained as the product of simple forms of learning.

• Organisms have biological predispositions to learn certain types of associations such as natural fear of situations that threaten survival.

HOW DO REFLEXES CONDITION OUR RESPONSES TO STIMULI? p.154

• We naturally respond in certain ways to certain stimuli. Classical conditioning takes advantage of these reflexive responses by teaching us to respond reflexively to formerly neutral stimuli.

HOW DOES ASSOCIATION SHAPE OUR BEHAVIOUR? p.156

• When we associate our actions with either positive or negative consequences, we undergo operant conditioning. We are likely to repeat behaviours that have positive consequences and abandon behaviours that have negative consequences.

WHAT CAN WE LEARN FROM WATCHING OTHERS? p.160

• We can learn to perform certain actions by watching others performing those actions and imitating their actions ourselves. This technique is known as observational learning.

• Through observational learning, we can learn both aggressive and prosocial behaviours.

WHAT BRAIN PROCESSES TAKE PLACE WHEN WE LEARN? p.161

• When we learn, we create new connections between neurons. The more we use the information we have just learned the stronger we make these connections, a process known as long-term potentiation.

• There are two types of memory consolidation: synaptic consolidation, which takes place hours after learning, and system consolidation, which takes place days or weeks after learning. Sleep helps us retain new information.

• Different parts of our brain seem to be involved in specific types of learning. For example, the amygdala is involved in learning fear through classical conditioning methods. The cerebellum and the hippocampus are involved in learning that depends on the pairing of the unconditioned and conditioned stimulus. The hippocampus is also involved in spatial learning. The basal ganglia are involved in learning that occurs through operant conditioning.

Test Your Understanding

1. While attempting to condition his cat to associate a red flag with the arrival of food, Tariq presents the flag and the food at the same time. Tariq is using:
   a. trace conditioning
   b. simultaneous conditioning
   c. delayed conditioning
   d. second-order conditioning

2. Erica rewards her dog with a treat every time it stands on its hind legs. When she stops rewarding her dog for performing the trick, the dog stops standing on its hind legs. This phenomenon is known as:
   a. extinction
   b. spontaneous recovery
   c. savings
   d. generalization

3. Which type of learning is NOT immediately reflected in a behaviour change?
   a. cognitive learning
   b. operant conditioning
   c. classical conditioning
   d. latent learning

4. Chloe is participating in an experiment. She is seated in front of a table on which a set of four coloured wooden blocks is placed. The experimenter instructs Chloe to pick up a block. When she picks up the blue block, the experimenter gives her a candy bar. When she picks up any of the other blocks, nothing happens. What is the discriminative stimulus in this experiment?
   a. the experimenter's instruction
   b. the set of four blocks
   c. the blue block
   d. the candy bar

5. When Jamal completes his chores, his mother typically allows him to watch his favourite show. Today, Jamal's mother asks him to clean his room. Jamal is motivated by:
   a. stimulus enhancement
   b. goal enhancement
   c. intrinsic motivation
   d. modelling

6. According to Ribot's law, which of the following statements is true?
   a. Memory loss following brain damage affects recent memories more than remote memories.

b. Memory loss following brain damage affects remote memories more than recent memories.

c. Memory loss following brain damage affects remote memories and recent memories equally.

d. Memory loss following brain damage is permanent in remote memories, but temporary in recent memories.

7. Which part of the brain is critical for emotional conditioning?

   a. the basal ganglia
   b. the cerebellum
   c. the hippocampus
   d. the amygdala

8. As a young child, Tara is knocked over by a horse. She later develops a fear of all large four-legged creatures with long tails, including donkeys and zebras. Which of the following explains Tara's fear?

   a. stimulus discrimination
   b. generalization
   c. the law of effect
   d. the Premack principle

9. Which statement best explains why people who use illegal street drugs need to consistently increase their dosage in order to experience the drug's effect?

   a. People who repeatedly use a drug develop a tolerance of that drug.
   b. People's bodies begin to reject drugs after a long period of drug use.
   c. People are classically conditioned to increase their dosage regularly.
   d. People stop associating commonly used drugs with pleasurable feelings.

10. Which of the following is an example of positive reinforcement?

    a. A child is sent to his bedroom for refusing to tidy his toys.
    b. A mother rocks her baby to sleep to stop it from crying.
    c. An employee receives a bonus for managing a successful project.
    d. A dog retrieves a stick in hopes of receiving a treat from its owner.

11. Which of the following statements about the relationship between sleep and learning is NOT true?

    a. Sleep deprivation can deplete the proteins that help neurons survive.
    b. Sleep prevents us from consolidating recently learned information.
    c. Sleep deprivation impairs our ability to learn new information.
    d. Sleep helps to preserve an overall balance of synaptic strength.

12. Mia completes her homework because her teacher has threatened to give a detention to anyone who fails to hand in his or her work. Mia is motivated by:

    a. intrinsic motivation
    b. extrinsic motivation
    c. goal enhancement
    d. stimulus enhancement

13. Every time a rat presses a bar, it is rewarded with a food pellet. The rat is receiving:

    a. partial reinforcement

b. continuous reinforcement
c. delayed reinforcement
d. negative reinforcement

14. Which of the following learning methods would be most useful if you were trying to train a dog to complete an obstacle course?

    a. chaining
    b. taste-aversion learning
    c. cognitive learning
    d. classical conditioning

15. Which of the following demonstrates the Premack principle?

    a. A student revises an essay in order to avoid failing the class.
    b. A mother buys her children ice cream even though they have behaved badly.
    c. A girl sees her brother playing the flute and asks her parents for lessons.
    d. A boy completes his least favourite homework assignment and rewards himself with a snack.

16. Damage to the hippocampus is most likely to impair:

    a. delay conditioning
    b. trace conditioning
    c. motor skill learning
    d. all types of learning

17. Chantel learned to play the piano at the age of seven. She did not practise for many years, but when she took lessons again as an adult she discovered that she could pick up the skill again very quickly. Which learning concept explains Chantel's experiences?

    a. spontaneous recovery
    b. savings
    c. overjustification
    d. extinction

18. Every year, Keiko's parents promise her an expensive present as an incentive to do well on her exams. This year, they are unable to afford an expensive present, so they offer her a smaller gift instead. As a result, Keiko does not try as hard on her exams. This is due to a:

    a. negative contrast effect
    b. positive contrast effect
    c. primary reinforcer
    d. secondary reinforcer

19. Which part of the brain plays a crucial role in spatial learning?

    a. cerebellum
    b. hippocampus
    c. amygdala
    d. occipital lobe

20. As a young child, Mike calls every four-legged creature "dog." As he grows older, he begins to distinguish between different animals. This learning process is known as:

    a. learning-performance distinction
    b. overjustification
    c. successive approximation
    d. stimulus discrimination

Remember to check www.thethinkspot.ca **for additional information, downloadable flashcards, and other helpful resources.**

Answers: 1) b; 2) a; 3) d; 4) c; 5) b; 6) a; 7) d; 8) b; 9) a; 10) c; 11) b; 12) b; 13) b; 14) a; 15) d; 16) b; 17) b; 18) a; 19) b; 20) d

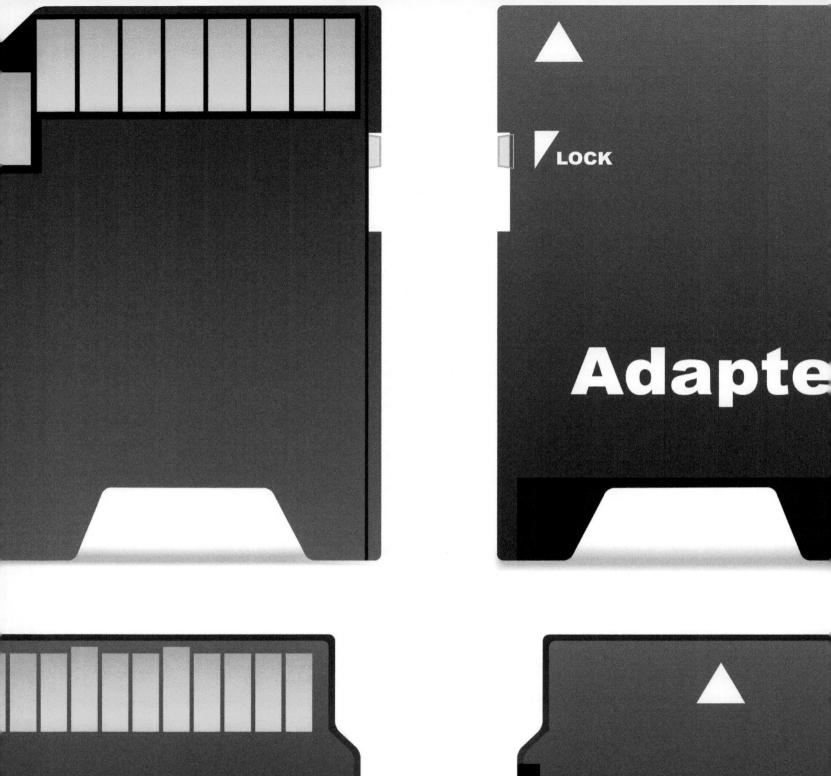

What is

your earliest memory? Your happiest memory? Your saddest memory? Each of us is able to reflect back on our lives, the good and the bad, thanks to our memory. But, our memories are not like movies that replay unchanging sequences of events. Instead our memory is dynamic and ever changing. Our current experiences affect how we interpret our past memories, and as such the human memory is quite different from that of a computer or memory key.

We need our memory to be successful in our everyday tasks, from the mundane and automatic, like brushing our teeth, to the complex and effortful, like recalling course material for your Introductory Psychology exam. And in using our memory we will fall victim to its limitations.

Psychologist and memory expert Daniel Schacter put forth a description of the errors that often plague our memory, including errors that lead to forgetting and distortions of our memories.

Forgetting

1. **Absent-mindedness.** Misplacing your sunglasses isn't so terrible. But it's caused by absent-mindedness, which occurs when we don't pay attention to what we're doing. This lack of attention results in a failure to encode information into working memory.
2. **Transience.** Most of our memories are not permanent; they fade over time.
3. **Blocking.** Retrieval failure keeps us from accessing stored memories. If you've ever felt as though the answer to a question was right on the tip of your tongue, but you couldn't quite remember it, you've experienced blocking.

Memory Distortions

1. **Misattribution.** When we misattribute a memory, we may remember some parts of an event accurately but misremember their context. If you remember a joke your sister told you on the phone but think your roommate told you the joke at dinner, your memory has committed the sin of misattribution. This phenomenon is more specifically known as **source amnesia**. We remember information, but we forget or misremember its source.
2. **Suggestibility.** The brain has no filter for determining which memories are truly autobiographical and which are not; furthermore, it can be extremely prone to suggestion. Our memories can be tweaked, and false memories can be implanted, with only a few simple words and the power of suggestion.
3. **Bias.** Our memories reflect and support our personal biases, sometimes at the expense of accuracy. Say, for example, that you are an outspoken advocate of environmentalism. Although you've only recently realized the importance of being eco-friendly, you believe strongly in doing what you can to help the planet. Because your beliefs colour your memories, you might remember recycling on a constant basis for the past five years, even if, in reality, you started recycling regularly only a year ago.

Can you identify which errors in memory you have experienced? The more we know about our memory, such as how it works and how we can improve it, the less likely we are to experience these errors.

167

<<< *Memory is critical to life as we know it. But, our memories are not perfect. How is our memory similar and different from that of the memory of a computer?*

CHAPTER **12**

The Function of Memory

The things that we remember—and forget—can have a significant impact on our lives. **Memory,** our brain's system for filing away new information and retrieving previously learned data, is important to us both when it succeeds and when it fails. The ability to create and access memories is an evolutionary advantage; in fact, it's often necessary for survival. (Imagine trying to survive in a world in which none of us could remember our names, our families, or where we'd left our groceries.) Memory is an essential human attribute, but it can also be a flawed one. In terms of accuracy, memory is not a videotape: It doesn't always present us with a clear, factually accurate account of events. Like a videotape, though, our memories can be edited, tampered with, or lost forever.

How Is Memory Organized?

TYPES OF MEMORY

Not all memories are created equal. There are three basic types of memory: **sensory memory, working memory,** and **long-term** memory. Sensory memories last no more than a few seconds. However, we can retain information we store in our working, or short-term, memory for longer periods of time. Our long-term memories can last our entire lives. These three types of memory can be further divided into subtypes as shown in the graphic above:

Our brains can store many different types of information in memory. (You might remember where you live, your friend's phone number, and the muscle movements required for rollerblading, to name only a few possibilities.) Some memories are lost quickly, while others are more permanent; some memories are formed and stored consciously, while others are created without your conscious knowledge. Each of your day-to-day experiences, remarkable or mundane, has the potential to be preserved in your mind as a memory. Whenever you find yourself remembering the sight of exploding fireworks or the moves to a dance you choreographed, take a minute to appreciate your brain's remarkable capacity to process myriad types of memorable information.

INFORMATION PROCESSING: THE BACKBONE OF HUMAN MEMORY

How do we put our observations and experiences into memory, and how do we get them out later? Think of your memory as your own personal administrative assistant: Just as an assistant organizes hundreds of files, puts them away in specific filing cabinets, and finds your stored files for you when you need them, your memory encodes information, stores it away, and retrieves it for later use. This process of **encoding, storage,** and **retrieval** is known as the information-processing model of memory.

Although our memory's information-processing techniques consist of three basic steps, the work of memory isn't quite as easy as one, two, three. Sometimes, memory

Types and Subtypes of Memory

∧∧∧ The process of **memory encoding, storage, and retrieval** is similar to a filing system. What kinds of memories might be stored in each "drawer"?

Source amnesia is a phenomenon in which a person remembers information but forgets or misremembers where that information came from.

Memory is the brain's system for filing away new information and retrieving previously learned data.

Sensory memory is a type of memory lasting no more than a few seconds in which the impression of a sensory stimulus is stored.

Working memory is a type of memory in which information for short-term use is stored.

Long-term memory is a type of memory in which information that can last a lifetime is stored.

Encoding is the process by which sensory information is converted into a form that can be stored.

Storage is the process by which encoded information is placed into memory.

Retrieval is the process by which previously stored information is moved from long-term memory to working memory.

Forgetting is the inability to retrieve information that has been previously stored.

Sensory registers are the parts of the brain that make up sensory memory.

Visual cortex is the part of the brain that mediates the human sense of sight by encoding visual information.

Auditory cortex is the part of the brain that mediates the human sense of hearing by encoding auditory information.

Sensory cortex is the part of the brain that mediates the human sense of touch by encoding tactile information.

Frontal lobe is a part of the brain involved in the encoding and storage of working and long-term memory and, to a lesser extent, in sensory memory processing.

Iconic memory is a type of sensory memory involving visual stimuli.

Eidetic memory is the ability to recall detailed images vividly after looking at them for a short period of time.

Echoic memory is a type of sensory memory involving auditory stimuli.

Attention is the act of applying the mind to a sense or thought.

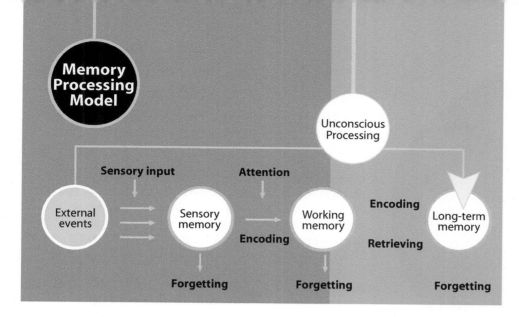

<<< This modified three-stage model of memory, based on Atkinson and Shiffrin's 1968 model, illustrates the process through which external events are transformed into long-term memories.

follows a basic three-stage processing model (first proposed by Atkinson and Shiffrin, 1968):

1) When you experience an event, your senses collect information about the event and hold those details in sensory memory.

2) Some of the sensory information you've collected is then encoded and stored in working memory.

3) If you need to remember the information for more than a few seconds or minutes, it can go through a second encoding process and become stored in your long-term memory. (You can later retrieve stored information from long-term memory and bring it back into working memory.)

The Atkinson-Shiffrin model isn't quite complete, however. For example, you may not be able to retrieve information you've previously stored. You probably know this phenomenon better as **forgetting.** Additionally, recent research has suggested that not all memories pass through working memory before arriving at long-term storage. Sometimes, without our conscious knowledge, our brains skip over the first two stages of the model and deposit information directly into long-term memory. As a basic framework, though, the three-stage model can help us understand the functions of—and connections between—our three types of memory.

Sensory Memory

No matter what its specific content, a memory is the product of a sensory experience—a series of images, sounds, tastes, smells, and feelings. We constantly use our five senses to collect information about the world around us. This information is the raw material from which memories are formed. It is transmitted from

the senses into the brain's **sensory registers,** which together make up sensory memory. Each sense has its own register for holding information. These registers are capable of containing a large amount of data, but if we don't pay attention to the information in our sensory registers, it disappears in less than a second.

Certain areas of the brain are active during the creation of sensory memory. These areas—the **visual cortex,** the **auditory cortex,** and the **sensory cortex**—receive input from the senses. When you listen to the radio, your auditory cortex is actively encoding the music you hear; when you look at a photograph, your visual cortex is hard at work processing the image. In short, when your senses encounter a stimulus, the corresponding sensory area of the brain processes that stimulus. While the **frontal lobe** plays a more prominent role in the encoding and storage of working and long-term memory, it is also involved to some extent in sensory memory processing.

> Like iconic memory, echoic memory comes and goes quickly.

ICONIC AND ECHOIC MEMORY

You've probably heard of "photographic memory," or the ability to accurately remember every detail in an image after looking at it for a short time. While research suggests that true photographic memory does not exist, most people have the capacity to recall exact images for very brief periods of time (a few tenths of a second). This ability is facilitated by a form of sensory memory called **iconic memory.** Research by

George Sperling (1960) demonstrated that our visual registers are able to store accurate representations of images. Almost immediately, however, these images are replaced by new images, so our "photographic memories" have severely limited lifespans.

If photographic memory is a myth, then what's **eidetic memory?** A handful of people, known as "eidetikers," have the ability to recall detailed images vividly after looking at them for a short time (about 30 seconds in some experiments). As they describe the image they have just seen, eidetikers' eyes move as though they are looking at the image itself, suggesting that they are "seeing" their memories. According to psychologist Alan Searleman, however, eidetic memory isn't truly photographic: Eidetikers sometimes make errors, and unlike photographs, their vivid memories last only for a few minutes.

The other sensory register about which scientists have the most information is the auditory register. Our ability to briefly and accurately remember sounds is called **echoic memory.** Like iconic memory, echoic memory comes and goes quickly: If we are not paying attention to a sound, we are able to recall it from our echoic memory only for the next three or four seconds before it disappears.

Working Memory

ENCODING INTO WORKING MEMORY
Attention

While most memories in the sensory registers are quickly overwritten, some of these memories are retained, encoded, and stored in working memory. But how do we determine which memories to store and which to discard?

The answer is **attention.** At any given moment, we are processing dozens of images, sounds, and other sensory information from our environment, but we're

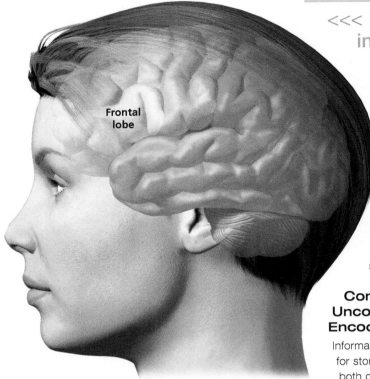

Frontal lobe

<<< The brain's **frontal lobe** plays a key role in the **encoding** and **storage** of **working memory.** Damage to the frontal lobe hinders the memory process.

not paying attention to all of these sensory memories. When a sensation grabs our attention, however, we're likely to pay attention to it and transfer it to our working memory. This is particularly true for highly interesting or unusual events. For example, if you're asked to imagine and remember a bright pink chicken, this bizarre image is likely to capture your attention. Attention also takes centre stage in the cocktail party effect mentioned in 2011. When you're in a room full of laughing, chatting people, you're able to tune out the background chatter and pay attention only to the people who are talking to you. You'll also probably notice if

someone across the room says your name—it grabs your attention. Attention allows us to extract meaningful information from a background of sensory "noise."

Conscious and Unconscious Encoding

Information can be encoded for storage in working memory both consciously and unconsciously. **Conscious encoding,** also called effortful processing, requires paying explicit attention to the information to be remembered. This strategy is particularly useful when we need to remember novel information. When you meet a new acquaintance, for example, you have to pay attention to her name (and maybe repeat it silently to yourself once or twice) in order to remember that she's "Lara," not "Laura."

Unconscious encoding, also called automatic processing, refers to the fact that we often pay attention to certain things without being consciously aware that we are doing so. If someone asks you where you were at 6 p.m., you can say, "I was at dinner," even though it's unlikely that you

took a few seconds at 6 p.m. to note and explicitly memorize your location. You're using automatic processing even as you read this paragraph: You can store the last few words you read in your working memory without even thinking about it.

What Do We Encode? Images, Sounds, and Meanings

The way in which our brains encode information depends on the type of information being processed. **Visual encoding** is the encoding of images, **auditory encoding** is the encoding of sounds, and **semantic encoding** is the encoding of meaning. Some pieces of information can be encoded in multiple ways: If you look at a graph that shows the results of a political poll, you can encode it both visually (by remembering what it looks like) and semantically (by thinking about what the poll results mean for each candidate).

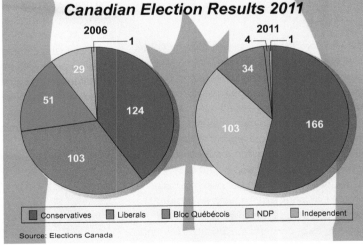

Canadian Election Results 2011

2006
1
29
51
124
103

2011
4   1
34
103
166

■ Conservatives ■ Liberals ■ Bloc Québécois ■ NDP ■ Independent

Source: Elections Canada

∧
∧
∧ The **pie chart** illustrates the distribution of seats for the different political parties after the 2011 general election. How would you **encode this graph visually?** How would you **encode it semantically?**

Conscious encoding is a process of encoding that involves paying specific attention to the information to be remembered.

Unconscious encoding is a process of encoding that does not involve any deliberate thought or action.

Visual encoding is the process of encoding images.

Auditory encoding is the process of encoding sounds.

Semantic encoding is the process of encoding meaning.

● ● ●

Although we are capable of encoding images, sounds, and meanings, not all types of encoding are equally effective. In general, we find it easier to remember information that means something to us. A 20-letter sentence in a textbook, for example, is much easier for us to remember than a random, meaningless string of 20 letters.

STORAGE IN WORKING MEMORY

Although information remains in working memory longer than it can be held in the sensory registers, working memory does not have a particularly large capacity for storage. Research has found that people can hold approximately seven different pieces of information in working memory at any one time (Miller, 1956). If someone gives you a number that's seven digits long, you will most likely be able to remember all seven numbers for a short time, though it might be difficult to do so. If you need to remember a longer number, however, you may need to use a strategy for storing that number in your working memory.

Organization and Rehearsal

If we can hold only seven pieces of information in our working memory at one time, how are we able to remember 10-digit phone numbers? Why is 807-555-8342 easier to remember than 8075558342? Chalk it up to **chunking.** By organizing pieces of information into chunks, we can store more of that information in working memory. The phone number above consists of 10 digits, but the digits are divided into three chunks, giving working memory only three pieces of information to store instead of 10. This strategy works only up to a point, however: The larger each chunk gets, the fewer chunks working memory can store.

We can use organizational strategies to remember things other than numbers, of course. Words that are organized into categories, for example, are easier to remember than words listed in a random order (Bower, Clark, Lesgold, & Winzenz, 1969).

Left untended, information is stored in working memory for only a few seconds. Through rote rehearsal, however, we can increase the length of

time that information lingers in working memory. **Rote rehearsal,** also known as **maintenance rehearsal,** is the process of repeating information, either out loud or silently, with the intent of learning that information. When you "cram" for an exam, for example, you might use rote rehearsal to keep a long list of dates, facts, and historical figures in your memory. The intent to learn plays a large role here: If you repeat something over and over but are not paying attention to the information you are repeating, that information won't get stored in working memory (Nickerson & Adams, 1979). Rote rehearsal alone can't cause memories to last for years—when your exam is over, you probably won't be able to remember the material you memorized by "cramming"—but it is an effective strategy for

> While our long-term memories can sometimes seem almost impossible to retrieve, this isn't the case when it comes to working memory. For the short time during which memories are stored in working memory, they are "at the ready": We don't have to rack our brains or dig through metaphorical layers of sludge in order to retrieve them.

Chunking is the process of organizing large pieces of information into smaller pieces, or chunks.

Rote (or maintenance) rehearsal is the process of repeating information, either out loud or silently, with the intent of learning that information.

Recency effect is the ability to recall information most recently stored when given a list of things to remember.

Primacy effect is the ability to recall information given first when given a list of things to remember.

Serial position effect is the ability to recall (or not recall) information in a list depending on that information's position in the list.

keeping information in working memory for longer than a few seconds.

RETRIEVAL FROM WORKING MEMORY

It's easy enough to store information in working memory, but what happens when you need to get that information back out? In general, items stored in working memory are fairly easy for us to retrieve. This is illustrated by the **recency effect:** When given a list of items to remember, we will be able to remember the last few items on the list without much difficulty. Since they were presented most recently, they are still in our working memory. We also won't have much trouble remembering the first few items on the list, thanks to the **primacy effect:** Since we had a lot of time to rehearse those first items, they have benefited the most from rote rehearsal and may have already moved into long-term memory. The items in the middle of the list are hardest to recall because they are no longer stored in working memory, but we didn't have the opportunity to rehearse them or move them to long-term memory. The middle items probably also suffered from a lack of attention: Since we were busy rehearsing the first few items on the list, we probably didn't pay as much attention to the items that came after them. Our ability to recall (or not recall) items depending on their position in a list is known as the **serial position effect.**

<<< **What information might a blackjack player store in his or her working memory?**

<<< The skills and movements necessary for riding a bicycle are stored in our brains as procedural memories.

While our long-term memories can sometimes seem almost impossible to retrieve, this isn't the case when it comes to working memory. For the short time during which memories are stored in working memory, they are "at the ready": We don't have to rack our brains or dig through metaphorical layers of sludge in order to retrieve them.

FORGETTING

Although our memories are easily accessible when they're in working memory, they're also easily lost. Working memory is limited not only in capacity but also in duration: Without rehearsal, information can be stored in working memory for about 15 or 20 seconds. Over a very short time, information in working memory decays until it's been forgotten altogether.

Interference with Encoding

When the encoding process does its job well, information from the sensory registers is stored in working memory. But what happens when something interferes with the encoding process? One cause of forgetting is ineffective or interrupted encoding of information (Brown & Craik, 2000). Say, for instance, that your friend is trying to tell you

about his weekend plans while you're trying to read a novel. In psychological terms, your friend's story is interfering with your attention to your book. Since you're not really paying attention to your book, you'll probably find it hard to remember what you just read. Assuming you manage to encode any information from the book at all, you may be engaging in visual or auditory encoding rather than semantic encoding—you're processing the words themselves but not their meanings. Since these types of encoding aren't as effective as semantic encoding, you're more likely to forget the information you encoded.

It's possible, too, that while you think you're encoding information as you attempt to read, your attention has been interfered with to the point that you're not actually storing any information in working memory at all. When you go to retrieve your memories and find them missing, it may be because they were never encoded into working memory in the first place. Technically, this isn't an example of forgetting information—it's impossible to forget something you never really knew. Rather, this type of encoding interference is called **pseudoforgetting.**

If, however, you're paying reasonably close attention to your book, you'll probably remember most of what you read. Do you remember which brightly coloured animal was described a few pages ago?

Cued or Intentional Forgetting

Some types of forgetting are intentional. If we don't intend to remember information, we usually have no trouble removing that information from working memory. **Cued forgetting** is one example of this process. Participants in cued forgetting studies

are given information to study and told to remember some of that information and forget the rest. This instruction to forget is, generally speaking, quite effective: Participants do not remember the information that they are told to forget. Children, however, have more difficulty forgetting the "forget-cued" information than adults do, suggesting that as we grow older, we become more able to control (and inhibit) our own encoding processes (Cruz, Hall, Lehman, Renkey, & Srokowski, 2003). A real-world example of this phenomenon is the experience of calling information for a phone number. Once the number is dialled and you hear the phone ringing, you might be cued to forget the number that the operator gave you.

While many of our memories are forgotten only seconds after they're formed, not all memories meet a tragic fate at the hands of forgetting. Some information is stored so effectively in working memory that it is transferred to a more secure place: long-term memory.

Long-Term Memory

ORGANIZATION OF LONG-TERM MEMORY

We store information in our long-term memory as either explicit memories or implicit memories. **Explicit memories** are memories of which we are consciously aware: We remember certain facts or experiences, and we are able to state that we remember these things. Some explicit memories are **semantic**—that is, they contain factual and conceptual information that is not directly linked to life events. If you bought a dozen pizzas for a party, how many pizzas did you buy? When you answered "12," you accessed a semantic memory: The word *dozen* means "12." This information is an example of one of the vast number of semantic facts stored in your long-term memory.

Often, though, we don't just remember bare-bones facts; we remember entire sequences of events, or episodes, as

<<< Friend or foe? Your emotional reaction to this clown may be influenced by conditioning.

Pseudoforgetting is a type of encoding interference in which information is never actually stored because of some kind of attention interference.

Cued forgetting is a type of forgetting in which a person is specifically told to forget certain information.

Explicit memories are memories of which a person is consciously aware.

Semantic means containing factual and conceptual information that is not directly linked to life events.

Episodic memories are memories in which a person remembers an entire sequence of events.

Implicit memories are memories of which a person is not consciously aware.

Priming is the process of activating associations in memory just before starting a certain task.

Procedural memory is a type of implicit memory consisting of habits and skills people perform.

Conditioning is a process in which an implicit memory forms because of repeated exposure to a certain stimulus that causes a reaction in a person.

instance, you and your friends got unabashedly lost on the way to pick up your dozen pizzas, arriving at the pizza place so late that the party was already over and you had to eat most of the slices yourself, you would probably have a vivid personal memory of this experience. Since many autobiographical memories are particularly emotionally salient, they are often easier for us to recall than episodic or semantic memories to which no particular emotion is attached. (We'll talk about the link between emotion and memory later in the chapter.)

By contrast, we are not consciously aware, however, of our **implicit memories.** When we remember information implicitly, that information is retained in our minds, but we are not necessarily aware that we have remembered it.

But if we're not conscious of our own implicit memories, how do we know that implicit memories exist at all? Some evidence for the existence of implicit memory comes from the phenomenon of **priming.** In psychological studies, researchers prime subjects by presenting them with a stimulus (usually very quickly) before asking the subjects to complete a task. The stimulus is designed to activate certain unconscious associations in the subjects' minds. In their seminal research on priming and implicit memory, Graf and Schacter (1985) primed subjects with a list of words. Later, they gave the subjects several unfinished words and asked the subjects to complete the words. The results of the study suggested that people who see the word *trees* on a list, for example, are likely to complete the word tre__ as *trees*, even if they don't remember seeing *trees* on the original list. In other words, the priming process can form implicit memories.

One type of implicit memory, **procedural memory,** consists of habits and skills that we perform. Riding a bike and playing a musical instrument are both examples of procedural memory. Both of these skills take time and practice to learn, but once they're learned, they are stored in long-term

episodic memories. When you think about the process of solving a long division problem, you're accessing an episodic memory, or a specific sequence of events. Many episodic memories are autobiographical. If, for

"While many of our memories are forgotten only seconds after they're formed, not all memories meet a tragic fate at the hands of forgetting. Some information is stored so effectively in working memory that it is transferred to a more secure place: long-term memory."

memory, and we don't need to consciously access them. Additionally, in this case, the appearance of the behaviour serves as evidence of the memory.

Other implicit memories are formed through **conditioning.** For example, let's say that you're scared of clowns: After watching a few horror movies featuring creepy supervillains decked out in red noses and floppy shoes (not to mention that harrowing trip to the circus when you were a kid), you've started to associate the sight of clowns with feelings of fear. The next time you see a real clown, you'll feel fearful, although you might not be aware of the source of your fear. There may be nothing inherently scary about a clown, but your implicit memories inform you that when a clown comes along, a scary situation won't be far behind.

ENCODING INTO LONG-TERM MEMORY

Just as information can be encoded into working memory both consciously and unconsciously, there are both conscious and unconscious processes for encoding long-term memories. Not all information passes through working memory before being stored in long-term memory. For example, particularly emotional events can become immediately

173

Memory

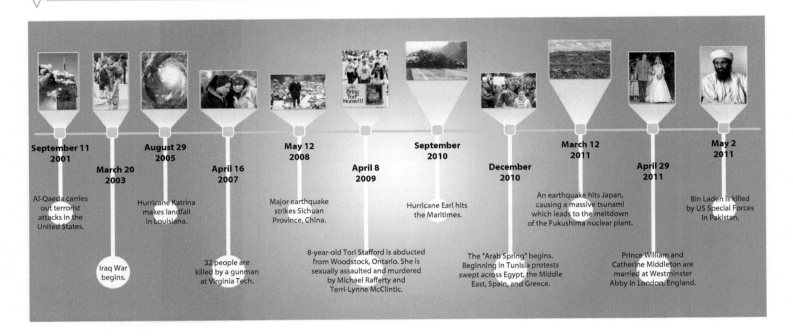

September 11
2001

Al-Qaeda carries
out terrorist
attacks in the
United States.

March 20
2003

Iraq War
begins.

August 29
2005

Hurricane Katrina
makes landfall
in Louisiana.

April 16
2007

32 people are
killed by a gunman
at Virginia Tech.

May 12
2008

Major earthquake
strikes Sichuan
Province, China.

April 8
2009

8-year-old Tori Stafford is abducted
from Woodstock, Ontario. She is
sexually assaulted and murdered
by Michael Rafferty and
Terri-Lynne McClintic.

September
2010

Hurricane Earl hits
the Maritimes.

December
2010

The "Arab Spring" begins.
Beginning in Tunisia protests
swept across Egypt, the Middle
East, Spain, and Greece.

March 12
2011

An earthquake hits Japan,
causing a massive tsunami
which leads to the meltdown
of the Fukushima nuclear plant.

April 29
2011

Prince William and
Catherine Middleton are
married at Westminster
Abby in London, England.

May 2
2011

Bin Laden is killed
by US Special Forces
in Pakistan.

seared into long-term memory as **flashbulb memories.** Flashbulb memories can be shared by many people, or they can be highly personal. Many people point to the terrorist attacks of September 11, 2001, as an example of a powerful, emotional event that most North Americans remember vividly. You may also have a vivid memory of your first kiss, which was a highly unique and personally relevant event. Other (less dramatic) events and skills can also be encoded unconsciously into long-term memory.

If we could unconsciously store all the information we needed to remember in long-term memory, our lives might be a lot simpler. Some memories, however, need our conscious help in order to stick. Rote rehearsal can be useful for transferring information from working memory to long-term memory, but a much more effective strategy is **elaborative rehearsal.** When we elaborate, we give meaning to the information we want to memorize (even if the information itself is fairly meaningless). We also make connections between the new information and information that we already remember. This form of semantic encoding is particularly useful for getting information into long-term memory. If you wanted to memorize the first several digits of pi, rather than using rote rehearsal to repeat 3.14159265 over and over again, you could

use elaborative rehearsal to attach meaning to the digits (your area code is 314; the year 1592 marked the hundredth anniversary of Christopher Columbus's voyage; your favourite aunt is 65 years old).

If your very educated mother has ever served you nine pizzas, you are probably familiar with **mnemonics.** Mnemonic devices are memory aids that give rhyme and reason to lists or other pieces of information. For example, before Pluto lost its planetary status, the phrase *My Very Educated Mother Just Served Us Nine Pizzas* was used to help students remember the order of the planets in the solar system. The first letter of each word in the phrase corresponds to the first letter of each planet's name (Mercury, Venus, Earth, etc.). Other mnemonics are short rhyming poems or memorable phrases. By arranging information in a meaningful order or a memorable context, we can help ourselves remember that information for years instead of seconds.

STORAGE IN LONG-TERM MEMORY

If you took a journey through the brain in search of a central long-term memory processing and storage centre, you'd be searching for a long time. No single area of the brain is in charge of processing and storing long-term memories. A few areas, however, have been

recognized as particularly crucial to memory formation.

Explicit and implicit long-term memories don't just seem different to us; they're actually processed in different areas of the brain. The **hippocampus** is largely responsible for processing our explicit memories, and it is assisted in memory formation by some areas of the frontal lobe. After semantic, episodic, and autobiographical memories are formed in the hippocampus, they are sent to other regions of the brain for storage. The hippocampus is also pivotal to the recognition and recall of long-term memories: People and animals with hippocampus damage struggle to remember explicit memories (Luu et al., 2012; Milne, McQueen, & Hall, 2012; Sherry & Vaccarino, 1989; Schacter, 1996).

Do you want to improve your memory? Then you might be wise to get some sleep. Researchers at MIT report that rats displayed the same hippocampus activity while sleeping as they had while running a maze earlier during their waking hours. This suggests that rats (and humans) replay daily activities during sleep, strengthening these memories. In addition, researchers at Harvard found that people who sleep after studying images of Easter eggs remember the eggs' positions better than those who remain awake do. While we don't know everything about the link between sleep and memory, it seems likely that our brains remain focused on the task of processing and storing memories even when we're fast asleep.

You may also consider taking a multivitamin as recent research suggests that the use of multivitamins may also improve memory (Macpherson, Ellis, Sali, & Pipingas, 2012).

How about going right to the source and using electrical stimulation? Toronto surgeons discovered that electrical stimulation to the limbic system created vivid memories, making deep brain stimulation a possible treatment for Alzheimer's disease (Laxton et al., 2010). Where are implicit memories processed and stored? Three regions of the brain—the hippocampus, the **cerebellum,** and the **basal ganglia**—play large roles in the formation and storage of implicit long-term memories. The hippocampus and cerebellum are essential for successful conditioning, one process through which implicit memories are formed. Because both the cerebellum and the basal ganglia are linked to the development of motor skills, they are necessary for the formation of procedural memories and habits related to movement. The basal ganglia and the cerebellum may be linked to different types of motor skills, but patients with damage to either area have difficulty creating new procedural memories (Gabrieli, 1998).

Many parts of the brain are involved in long-term memory storage, but a significant amount of recent research has focused particularly on the **synapses** (the areas between neurons across which nerve impulses travel from one neuron to the next, as described in Chapter 2). When we learn, neurotransmitters travel across the synapses associated with the information we're learning. Each time we review that information, those specific neural connections are strengthened, and it becomes easier for neurotransmitters to travel across those certain synapses. In 1949, Canadian psychologist Donald Hebb theorized that a relationship existed between these strong neural connections and the creation and maintenance of memories. When Hebb's theory was confirmed in the 1970s, scientists dubbed this strengthening of neural connections **long-term potentiation (LTP).** As Hebb suggested, LTP is a biological basis for memory: When memories form strong neural connections, we remember those memories more easily.

RETRIEVAL FROM LONG-TERM MEMORY
Recognition or Recall?

When you retrieve information from memory, you either recall it or recognize it. What's the difference between **recognition** and **recall?** Say you're given a list of breakfast foods and asked to circle the foods you ate for breakfast that day. This exercise is an example of recognition: You are matching an external stimulus (a word on the list) to a stored memory (the contents of your breakfast). If, however, you're given a blank sheet of paper and asked to write down what you ate for breakfast, you are engaging in recall. You have no external cues or stimuli on which you can rely as you retrieve your breakfast memories.

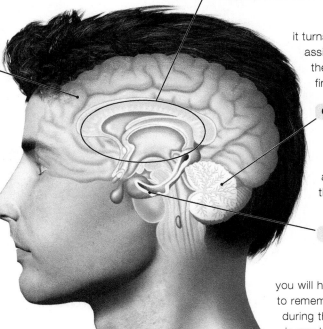

Basal ganglia
(a group of nuclei located in both hemispheres, on either side of the corpus callosum and thalamus)

Frontal lobe

Cerebellum

Hippocampus

The **hippocampus** and **frontal lobe** process **explicit memories,** while the **cerebellum and basal ganglia** contribute to the creation of **implicit memories.** >>>

Retrieval Cues

Assigned classroom seating: terrific or torturous? As it turns out, the monotony of having an assigned seat may be outweighed by the stellar grades you receive on the final exam—as long as you take that exam in that same assigned seat. When you encode information in a specific context, you are likely to find it easier to retrieve that information in the same context. So if you sit in one seat for every lecture and return to that seat for the exam, you will have an advantage when it comes to remembering the information you learned during those lectures. This **context effect** is one kind of **retrieval cue**—a stimulus

State-dependent memory is a stored memory that is more easily retrieved when a person is in the same state as they were when the information was first encoded.

Proactive interference is a phenomenon in which previously learned information interferes with a person's ability to recall new information.

Retroactive interference is a phenomenon in which new information interferes with a person's ability to recall previously learned information.

Forgetting curve is a graphical representation of how quickly a person tends to forget information.

Storage decay is a phenomenon in which many of a person's memories fade over time.

RETRIEVAL FAILURE: FORGETTING

Despite our best efforts, not all information that we store in long-term memory can be retrieved. Do the memories that we forget disappear from our brains entirely? Or is the problem just that we can't figure out how to find the memories we've stashed away? In many cases, retrieval failure, or forgetting, occurs in long-term memory not because our memories have been "thrown away" or overwritten but because we are unable to access them.

Interference

Most of us have forgotten more than a handful of e-mail passwords, computer log-ons, and PINs in our lives. Maybe you just changed your e-mail password, and although you can't remember what your new password is, you have no trouble remembering the old one. This phenomenon is known as **proactive interference,** and it occurs when previously learned information interferes with your ability to recall new information. Conversely, maybe it's been a while since you've changed your password, and now that you've gotten used to the new code, you no longer remember what your old code was. This is an example

of **retroactive interference,** which occurs when new information causes you to forget older memories.

Storage Decay

Interference isn't the only thing that causes us to forget the things we've learned. In 1885, German psychologist Hermann Ebbinghaus memorized a list of nonsense syllables and measured how many of those syllables he could recall over the next 30 days. His results, described graphically as the **forgetting curve,** suggest that we are quick to forget most things that we learn. After a few days, however, our rate of forgetting levels off: If we haven't forgotten something after three or four days, we're likely to remember it after 30 days as well. Ebbinghaus's findings have contributed to the theory of forgetting known as **storage decay.** Simply put, many of our memories, like paintings or photographs, fade over time.

Memory Mishaps

When memory functions well, it's an invaluable resource. When things go wrong, however, the consequences can range from irritating (forgetting where you left your cellphone) to devastating (incorrectly identifying someone as the person you saw commit a crime). How do these memory mishaps occur?

> *If you learn something in one state (when you're deeply in love, scared to death, or just plain happy), you'll probably be able to recall that information more easily when you're in a similar state.*

that helps us retrieve information from memory. Like labels on the "file folders" in which your memories are stored, the pieces of information that you associate with a memory can help you access that memory later. Take the phenomenon of **state-dependent memory,** for example: If you learn something in one state (when you're deeply in love, scared to death, or just plain happy), you'll probably be able to recall that information more easily when you're in a similar state.

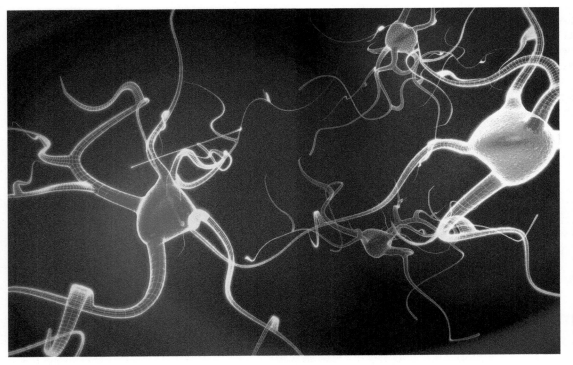

∧ Connections between neurons serve as a biological basis
∧ for memory.

EMOTION, STRESS, AND MEMORY

As the phenomenon of flash-bulb memories illustrates,

it's often very easy for us to remember emotional or stressful events. Arousal from heightened emotion or stress can facilitate the storage of information in long-term memory, while weaker emotions tend to create weaker memories. But stress isn't always so beneficial. Canadian researcher Sonia Lupien and her colleagues (Lupien et al., 2005) gave participants medication that either increased or decreased their normal levels of stress hormone. They found that participants in both conditions had impaired memory abilities. When participants were given medication that brought their stress hormone levels back to normal, their memory performance returned to normal levels. So, stress hormones are essential for normal memory function. But too little or too much stress hormone can impair memory performance—an example of the **Yerkes-Dodson law,** which states that, in general, performance peaks with moderate levels of arousal (Lupien, 2009; Yerkes & Dodson, 1908).

> "Stress hormones are essential for normal memory function. But too little or too much stress hormone can impair memory performance—an example of the Yerkes-Dodson law, which states that, in general, performance peaks with moderate levels of arousal.

AMNESIA

"According to Hollywood," writes neuropsychologist Sallie Baxendale, "[amnesia] is something of an occupational hazard for professional assassins." Baxendale is referring to *The Bourne Identity* and other popular movies that, although they feature characters who struggle from various forms of memory loss, hardly ever present an accurate picture of amnesia. Outside the borders of the silver screen, there are two distinct types of amnesia: retrograde amnesia and anterograde amnesia. **Retrograde amnesia** is characterized by the loss of past memories (usually memories formed before the time of the injury). **Anterograde amnesia,** in contrast, affects the future: Although people with anterograde amnesia can remember events from their past, they struggle to create new long-term memories. (Baxendale points to the 2000 movie *Memento* as a fairly accurate representation of anterograde amnesia.)

Yerkes-Dodson law states that, in general, performance peaks with a moderate level of arousal.

Retrograde amnesia is memory loss characterized by the loss of past memories.

Anterograde amnesia is memory loss characterized by an inability to form new long-term memories.

Both types of amnesia are linked to brain damage, which is often caused by accident, surgery, or illness. The type of amnesia a patient develops depends on the affected area of the brain: A patient with a disease like dementia that affects the whole brain (particularly the hippocampus) may show signs of retrograde amnesia, while someone who sustains frontal lobe injuries in a car accident will have difficulty encoding memories and may suffer from anterograde amnesia. The famous patient H. M. developed anterograde amnesia in 1953 when doctors removed his temporal lobes in an attempt to cure his severe epilepsy. H. M. could no longer create new long-term memories, but his working memory remained functional, as did many of his procedural memories. Although H. M. never knew it, his case was instrumental in leading scientists to research the biological connections between memory, memory loss, and the brain.

CHAPTER

12

Review

Summary

HOW IS MEMORY ORGANIZED? p.168

- Memory is the brain's system for filing away new information and retrieving previously learned data.
- There are three different types of memory: sensory memory, working memory, and long-term memory.
- Sensory memory is a type of memory lasting no more than a few seconds in which the impression of a sensory stimulus is stored.
- Working memory is a type of memory in which information for short-term use is stored.
- Long-term memory is a type of memory in which information that can last a lifetime is stored.
- According to the information-processing model, our brains encode information, store it as a memory, and retrieve it when we need to remember it.

WHAT ARE THE CHARACTERISTICS OF SENSORY, WORKING, AND LONG-TERM MEMORY? p.169

- Sensory memory consists of sights, sounds, smells, and other information that the senses transmit to the corresponding sensory cortices in the brain. Sensory memories last for no more than a few seconds.
- Iconic memory is the type of sensory memory that comes from visual stimuli.
- Eidetic memory is not truly photographic.
- Echoic memory is the type of sensory memory that comes from auditory stimuli.
- Working memory contains memories that we can access immediately. Images, sounds, and meanings can all be encoded

in working memory. We can store approximately seven pieces of information in our working memory.

- Long-term memory includes both implicit and explicit memories. Meaningful or emotional information is often encoded into long-term memory. Long-term memories can last a lifetime but can be difficult to retrieve.

HOW ARE MEMORIES ENCODED, STORED, AND RETRIEVED? p.169

- Attention enables us to consciously or unconsciously encode memories.
- We use rehearsal, mnemonics, chunking, and other organizational strategies to store memories.
- The frontal lobe, hippocampus, basal ganglia, and cerebellum are active in memory encoding and storage.
- Retrieval cues such as the context effect help us move long-term memories into working memory, where stored information is "at the ready."
- Forgetting can be due to interference, cued forgetting, pseudo-forgetting, storage decay, or memory mishaps, such as amnesia or too much stress.

WHAT ARE THE WEAKNESSES AND LIMITATIONS OF MEMORY? p.176

- Memory is not perfect. Our memories, and our abilities to store and retrieve memories, change.
- Stress can inhibit memory storage and recall.
- Brain damage can lead to retrograde and anterograde amnesia.
- Memories are easily forgotten and prone to distortion, and they can persist even when we try to forget them.

Test Your Understanding

1. Which of the following statements about the "sins of memory" is true?
   a. The brain rarely allows us to misattribute the source of information.
   b. Absent-mindedness results in a failure to encode information into sensory memory.
   c. The brain has a precise filter for determining autobiographical memories.
   d. False memories can be implanted with suggestive language.

2. Which piece of information would most likely be retained longest in memory?
   a. the scent of the ocean
   b. a photograph of the ocean
   c. the sound of ocean waves
   d. a definition of the word *ocean*

3. Which area of the brain would likely be most active as you encode the lyrics to a song you hear on the radio?
   a. the frontal lobe
   b. the visual cortex
   c. the auditory cortex
   d. the sensory cortex

4. Which of the following images are you most likely to transfer from your sensory memory to your working memory?
   a. a green flamingo
   b. a green tree
   c. a green frog
   d. a green car

5. Arjun repeats the names of people he meets at a party to himself so that he will better remember them. Arjun is using:
   a. iconic memory

    b. automatic processing

    c. effortful processing

    d. eidetic memory

6. Semantic encoding allows you to remember that stop signs:

    a. are red octagons with white letters

    b. appear at intersections

    c. measure about 3.7 metres in height

    d. mean you must bring your vehicle to a halt

7. Carla's friend asks her to pick up 12 items at the grocery store and lists the names of the items. Carla tries to remember all of the items without writing them down. According to the serial position effect, which items will Carla most likely remember?

    a. Carla will remember the first few items and the last few items on the list.

    b. Carla will only remember the first few items on the list.

    c. Carla will only remember items in the middle of the list.

    d. Carla will not remember any items on the list.

8. Which conclusion does the phenomenon of cued forgetting best support?

    a. We cannot forget very emotional information or events.

    b. We become better at memorizing information as we grow older.

    c. We have significant control over the information we choose to remember.

    d. We are not able to create new memories unless we consciously try to do so.

9. Which of the following is an example of an episodic memory?

    a. the smell of cake

    b. the taste of cake

    c. the process of baking a cake

    d. the weight of 250 millilitres of cake flour

10. Faima, a college student, has been playing basketball since she was five. The skill of dribbling the basketball is stored in her:

    a. explicit memory

    b. echoic memory

    c. procedural memory

    d. priming memory

11. Although most Canadians have seen hundreds of nickels, many of them find it difficult to remember which way the beaver faces on the coin. Which explanation best accounts for this paradox?

    a. Most people do not pay attention to the beaver's image when they handle nickels.

    b. Most people have difficulty remembering an object's direction or orientation.

    c. Most people experience source amnesia when they try to recall what a nickel looks like.

    d. Most people's memories of dimes and quarters proactively interfere with their memories of nickels.

12. In which of the following ways are flashbulb memories and post-traumatic stress disorder similar?

    a. Both are types of state-dependent memory.

    b. Both tend to be formed during states of low arousal or relaxation.

    c. Both can be caused by extremely emotional events.

    d. Both are examples of Schacter's "sins of commission."

13. Which of the following statements about mnemonic devices is true?

    a. They are popular, but unproven as memory aid devices.

    b. They aid memory by giving meaning to information.

    c. They must take the form of a short rhyming poem to be effective.

    d. They are less effective than rote rehearsal in transferring information to long-term memory.

14. Damage to the hippocampus would likely interfere most with which type of memories?

    a. autobiographical

    b. procedural

    c. elaborative

    d. eidetic

15. If you were to write an autobiography, most of the content would be retrieved from your:

    a. episodic memory

    b. nondeclarative memory

    c. semantic memory

    d. sensory memory

16. Which of the following would indicate the presence of vivid, easily recalled memories?

    a. constant activity in the visual cortex

    b. a lack of damage to the frontal lobes

    c. an increase in the size of the hippocampus

    d. strong neural connections between synapses

17. When Jason visits his old elementary school as an adult, he is flooded with memories of what he did and learned in fifth grade. Which of the following likely accounts for this phenomenon?

    a. the context effect

    b. basal ganglia arousal

    c. cued forgetting

    d. flashbulb memories

18. You often dial a friend's old phone number rather than her new phone number. Which of the following most likely caused you to dial the old number?

    a. proactive interference

    b. retroactive interference

    c. storage decay

    d. retrieval cues

19. Which of the following scenarios does the Yerkes-Dodson law explain best?

    a. An assault victim recalls her assault in vivid detail.

    b. An assault victim becomes conditioned to fear specific situations.

    c. An assault victim has difficulty recalling her assault in detail.

    d. An assault victim experiences a high level of alertness when recalling her assault.

20. A person who suffers severe frontal lobe injuries is most likely to:

    a. suffer retrograde amnesia

    b. suffer source amnesia

    c. suffer transient amnesia

    d. suffer anterograde amnesia

Remember to check www.thethinkspot.ca **for additional information, downloadable flashcards, and other helpful resources.**

Answers: 1) d; 2) d; 3) c; 4) a; 5) c; 6) d; 7) a; 8) c; 9) c; 10) c; 11) a; 12) c; 13) b; 14) a; 15) a; 16) d; 17) a; 18) a; 19) c; 20) d

COGNITION

WHAT IS COGNITIVE PSYCHOLOGY?

WHAT IS INTELLIGENCE, AND HOW C
MEASURE IT?

HOW DO WE REASON, SOLVE PROBL
AND MAKE DECISIONS?

HOW DOES ATTENTION HELP US PRC
INFORMATION?

HOW ARE VERBAL AND VISUAL COGN
RELATED?

Imagine being

able to immediately recall every phone number you needed to know or being able to list every element in the periodic table from memory. These days, slight differences in cognitive performance can determine the difference between success and failure in the professional and academic world. To get ahead, you might find yourself training your brain as vigorously as professional athletes train their bodies.

Step one on the road to peak mental fitness might include a look at the variety of software on the market that claims to improve cognitive function by exercising certain functions of the brain, such as memory and puzzle solving. The surging popularity of cognitive-enhancement programs such as Nintendo's *Brain Age* resulted in earnings of $225 million in 2007. Some studies have even shown that the software benefits those whose cognition is impaired, including subjects with attention deficit hyperactivity disorder (ADHD) and dyslexia. But while the effectiveness of most programs is unconfirmed, research suggests that the programs help build our working memories, ultimately leading to better problem-solving capabilities.

<<< *The question of whether artificial intelligence could ever match the highly complex cognitive abilities that humans have remains a real possibility. Robots now have the ability to develop language through interactions with humans. In June 2012, Dr. Caroline Lyon and colleagues introduced the world to Dr. DeeChee, a childlike humanoid robot that learns to speak. At first, DeeChee is only able to babble until it engages in conversation with humans. After the conversation, DeeChee is able to produce some word forms—giving researchers insight into how human children may acquire language skills. Although, at present, DeeChee does not know the meanings of the words it speaks, researchers are working on achieving that cognitive advancement for artificial intelligence.*

But what if you're not so computer savvy, or if you don't like crossword puzzles? A new trend of chemical cognitive enhancers is emerging, giving the trusty double-shot cappuccino a run for its $4.50. Two of the leading drugs are Modafinil and Ritalin, which were developed to treat narcolepsy and ADHD, respectively. Studies have shown that Modafinil can improve certain aspects of memory, such as working memory and ability to stay on task. However, Modafinil does not improve the user's attention or enhance spatial memory span—bad news if you were hoping that the drug would help you remember where you put your car keys every morning.

Some adults especially worried about declining cognitive performance are turning to Ritalin or Adderall, drugs that are typically prescribed for children with ADHD. The drugs help to focus attention by increasing dopamine levels in the brain. In young adults, Ritalin can improve spatial working memory and cognitive flexibility. However, its effects are varied, and can result in anxiety, tiredness, and low moods.

Which method do you prefer? A good brain-building exercise regimen, or a cognitive-enhancement drug? Of course, you can always find the answer at your local bookstore. Just ask the barista.

CHAPTER 1

Cognitive Psychology

The science of studying what makes our minds work isn't new. Study of **cognition,** the mental activities associated with thinking, knowing, remembering, and communicating, has been going strong since the 1950s and 1960s (Miller, 2003). Before this, however, many psychologists were behaviourists who tended to dismiss the study of cognition. Instead they preferred the study of mental processes that are readily observable.

In opposition to the behaviourists before them, cognitive psychologists such as Chomsky and Piaget showed that we must understand cognition in order to understand behaviour.

MENTAL PROCESSES

Think of all the stimuli around you when you are in class: the size of the room, familiar faces, the questions of the professor, the smell of the classroom, the sounds coming from outside. What if you had to give equal attention to all these stimuli at once? You couldn't possibly concentrate. Luckily, our minds use a variety of processes to take in and work with large doses of stimuli. Cognitive scientists have categorized processes in two general categories: (1) how much attention they involve and (2) whether they must be done in sequence rather than simultaneously.

The mental processes associated with seemingly simple tasks are surprisingly intricate. For example, a job requiring multi-tasking, such as a serving job at a restaurant, involves an average of six different forms of mental processing.

As you can probably tell by this point, our mental processes don't get much of a break in our day-to-day lives. Whether we're learning, creating, solving problems, reasoning, making judgments and decisions, or communicating, we rely on cognition to live our daily lives, go to school, do our jobs, and make sense of our world.

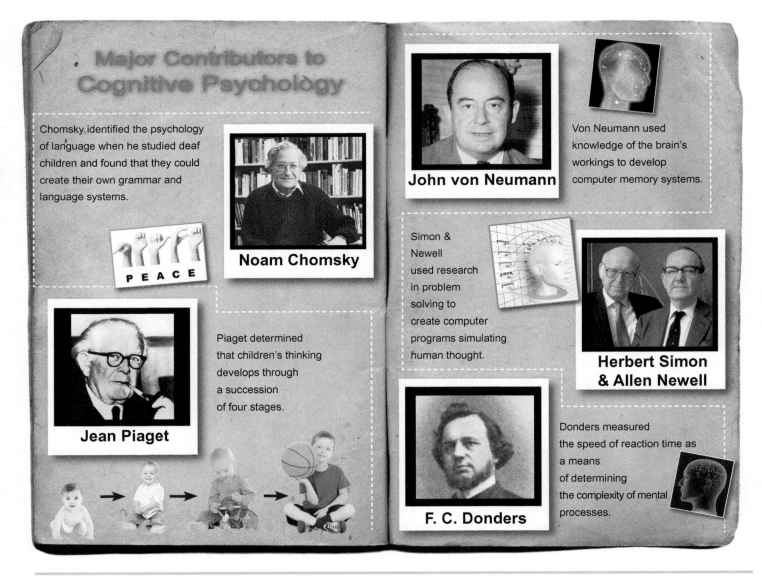

Major Contributors to Cognitive Psychology

Chomsky identified the psychology of language when he studied deaf children and found that they could create their own grammar and language systems.

Noam Chomsky

PEACE

Piaget determined that children's thinking develops through a succession of four stages.

Jean Piaget

John von Neumann

Von Neumann used knowledge of the brain's workings to develop computer memory systems.

Simon & Newell used research in problem solving to create computer programs simulating human thought.

Herbert Simon & Allen Newell

F. C. Donders

Donders measured the speed of reaction time as a means of determining the complexity of mental processes.

∧∧∧ How might these contributions help us understand **human behaviour** and **cognition?**

Theories of Intelligence

Not everyone processes information the same way. Some of us are adept at solving complex math problems, while others are able to memorize mind-boggling amounts of text. Which skill is a better indication of mental prowess? For more than a century, psychologists have argued various theories of **intelligence**—the capacity to reason, solve problems, and acquire new knowledge. But is intelligence really that easy to define? How can we measure a person's intelligence level when different people have different areas of expertise? Is intelligence genetic, or does our environment play a role in determining our ability to organize, understand, and communicate information?

INTELLIGENCE TESTING

In 1904, French scientist Alfred Binet was asked to develop a test that could help teachers identify students with special needs. Binet developed a test that determined a child's **mental age,** or ability typical of a child of the same chronological age. The test was a great success and was administered throughout Europe and the United States. In 1916, Lewis Terman published an adaptation of Binet's test, called the Stanford-Binet Intelligence Scale. A mathematical formula

used the test score and the child's age to determine an intelligence quotient (IQ) score:

$$IQ = \frac{Mental\ age}{Chronological\ age} \times 100$$

Using this scale, if a child's mental age and chronological age are the same, the score is 100. Terman's formula is particularly helpful in comparing children of various ages.

In response to the Stanford-Binet Intelligence Scale, David Wechsler developed a derivative of the test to assist him in his work with adults at Bellevue Hospital in New York City. He first published the Wechsler Adult Intelligence Scale (WAIS) in 1939. The scale contained fewer verbal items than Stanford-Binet, and it used normal distribution rather than IQ. According to **normal distribution,** scores are tracked on a bell-shaped curve with a concentration of data in the centre. Today's intelligence tests are often still referred to as IQ tests, yet for the most part they use deviation IQ scores. These scores place subjects at a certain point within the normal distribution of intelligence regardless of age. The standard deviation curve enables a comparison of scores, by showing how close a particular IQ score is to the average (the score of 100 is deemed to indicate average intelligence).

Intelligence tests like these are designed to measure **aptitude,** which is a person's potential ability, rather than **achievement,** which is a person's knowledge and progress.

Cognition consists of mental activities associated with sensation, perception, thinking, knowing, remembering, and communicating.

Intelligence is the capacity to reason, solve problems, and acquire new knowledge.

Mental age refers to the level of ability typical of a child of the same chronological age.

Normal distribution is an instance of frequency distribution in which scores are tracked on a bell-shaped curve with a concentration of data in the centre.

Aptitude is a person's potential ability.

Achievement is a person's knowledge and progress.

However, critics question if aptitude is really measurable. Test questions are inherently bound to tap into the subject's factual knowledge, despite efforts to mostly test common knowledge (Ackerman & Beier, 2005; Cianciolo & Sternberg, 2004). If a test taker shares the same knowledge as the test makers, then he or she will obviously perform exceedingly well. Despite criticism, psychologists perceive IQ results to be consistently reliable. Studies show that IQ test scores correlate relatively well with performance in academics and employment. However, these correlations are directly related to the type of work subjects do in these environments.

Routine Mental Processes of a Restaurant Server

Mental Processes	Examples
Attentional: distribute resources to the most immediate or important needs	Greeting new customers is a server's most important task.
Serial: thoughts/actions that must be done consecutively	A server must take a customer's order before delivering food.
Parallel: able to be done simultaneously	A server can walk and carry beverages at the same time.
Controlled: require attention	Answering a customer's questions requires attention.
Automatic: do not generally require attention	Taking a customer's menu doesn't require attention.
Bottleneck: occurs when two processes cannot be done simultaneously and must be done serially	When serving a large party, a server may need to make two separate deliveries of food to the table.

What other types of jobs require multiple mental processes?

GENERAL INTELLIGENCE

Are some of us more intelligent than others overall? Psychologist Charles Spearman would likely say yes. He identified **general intelligence (g)** as a common factor that underlies certain mental abilities. In contrast, psychologist Raymond Cattell argued that intelligence was not a single entity, but that different types of intelligence were, in fact, distinct from one another. He defined **fluid intelligence** as the ability to process information and act accordingly and described **crystallized intelligence** as the mental ability derived directly from previous experience. Cattell's research found that as people age, they accumulate more crystallized knowledge, but their fluid intelligence levels decrease (Aizpurua & Koutstaal, 2010; Cattell, 1963; Horn, 1982).

In other attempts to identify what makes up general intelligence, psychologists have found that quick speeds in processing information often contribute to high IQ scores (Deary, 2001). The high capacity of a person's working memory has also been identified as an important factor in general intelligence (Kyllonen & Christal, 1990). Besides these factors, mental self-monitoring also plays a role. Researchers find that strong **central executive functioning,** the set of mental processes that governs goals, strategies, and coordination of the mind's activities, is related to higher intelligence (Duncan, 2000). They've been able to chart brain activity to support these ideas. Prefrontal cortex areas show an increased activity during taxing tasks. In addition, prefrontal cortex size is linked to IQ more closely than the size of any other area in the brain (Reiss et al., 1996).

NATURE OR NURTURE?

Parents might try to improve their children's intellect by reading to them and buying media such as Baby Mozart and Baby Einstein. But to what degree is a child's intelligence predetermined by his or her genetics? In a study of twins, siblings, and unrelated siblings raised in the same household

> It is important to remember that IQ tests are likely to be subject to cultural bias. People raised in a different culture or economic status from the person who designed the IQ test are likely to perform poorly on that particular test, meaning that group differences in scores are not necessarily reflective of group differences in intelligence.

(McGue, Bouchard, Iacono, & Lykken, 1993), results indicated that genetics are ultimately more influential than environment. Identical twins raised in different households

showed some difference in IQ score, indicating that environment plays a slight role. However, in cases of unrelated siblings raised in the same home, IQ correlations existed in childhood, but the correlation waned over time.

Do culture and socio-economic status influence IQ scores? While some studies indicate that they do, it is important to remember that IQ tests are likely to be subject to cultural bias. People raised in a different culture or economic status from the person who designed the IQ test are likely to perform poorly on that particular test, meaning that group differences in scores are not necessarily reflective of group differences in intelligence. Many test designers have come to the conclusion that it may be impossible to create a test completely free of cultural bias (Carpenter, Just, & Shell,1990). Instead, designers aim to create tests that are culturally fair, for example, by minimizing or eliminating the use of language and downplaying skills and values that vary from culture to culture, such as speed.

Why are IQ scores currently on the rise? Environment may be playing a crucial role. Every 30 years, IQ test scores have risen about 9–15 points. Scores measuring fluid intelligence have increased the most while scores reflecting school learning have seen the least change. With greater travel and communication opportunities in today's world, our enriched learning environment seems to be boosting our intelligence.

DIFFERENT TYPES OF INTELLIGENCE

Why are some of us math scholars while others excel at poetry or sports? Some scholars would argue that the skills we have in specific domains reflect different kinds of intelligences.

Sternberg's Triarchic Theory of Intelligence

So how many different types of intelligence exist? On this point, psychologists and other experts disagree. One psychologist, Robert Sternberg (1985), identified three aspects of successful intelligence. The aspect that most

Gardner's Multiple Intelligences

> *Every 30 years, IQ test scores have risen about 9–15 points. Scores measuring fluid intelligence have increased the most while scores reflecting school learning have seen the least change.* **With greater travel and communication opportunities in today's world, our enriched learning environment seems to be boosting our intelligence.**

Each of Gardner's eight intelligences is distinct from the others, which means that we may be very talented in some of these areas and completely untalented in others. Someone who's a great dancer may have bodily-kinesthetic intelligence, musical intelligence, and spatial intelligence, but she might have difficulty making friends or interacting with people, meaning that interpersonal intelligence is probably not her strong suit. Gardner's theory is of particular interest to educators, who can tailor their lesson plans according to individual students' strengths and weaknesses. For example, a musical learner may find it easier to memorize facts if the teacher encourages that learner to create a song or rhyme incorporating the information.

Social Intelligence

The ability to negotiate new social environments is called **social intelligence**

General intelligence (g) is a common factor that underlies certain mental abilities.

Fluid intelligence is the ability to process information and act accordingly.

Crystallized intelligence is mental ability derived from previous experience.

Central executive functioning is a set of mental processes that governs goals, strategies, and coordination of the mind's activities.

Analytic intelligence is a type of intelligence generally assessed by intelligence tests that present well-defined problems with only one correct answer.

Creative intelligence is a type of intelligence characterized by the ability to adapt to new situations, come up with unique and unusual ideas, and think of novel solutions to problems.

Practical intelligence is the ability to find many solutions to complicated or poorly defined problems and use those solutions in practical, everyday situations.

Social intelligence is the ability to negotiate new social environments.

Emotional intelligence is a person's ability to perceive, understand, manage, and utilize his or her emotions.

people probably think of when they hear the word *intelligence* is **analytic intelligence,** or academic problem-solving intelligence. This is the type of intelligence generally assessed by intelligence tests that present well-defined problems with only one correct answer. The second aspect, **creative intelligence,** isn't a skill that only people in the creative arts can tap into. If you're a creative thinker—if you can adapt to new situations, come up with unique, unusual ideas, and think of novel solutions to problems—you have creative intelligence.

Practical intelligence, the third aspect in Sternberg's schema, is the ability to find many solutions to complicated or poorly defined problems and use those solutions in practical, everyday situations. For example, when you've discovered that the birthday bash you're hosting for a friend is the same day as your brother's college graduation, you might use practical intelligence to hash out a solution to your scheduling woes.

Gardner's Multiple Intelligences

Along with his Harvard colleagues, Howard Gardner (1983, 2004) developed a theory of multiple intelligences that's fairly well known today. According to Gardner, there are eight different types of intelligence.

Some researchers believe that the prefrontal cortex is an area of the brain crucial to intelligence.

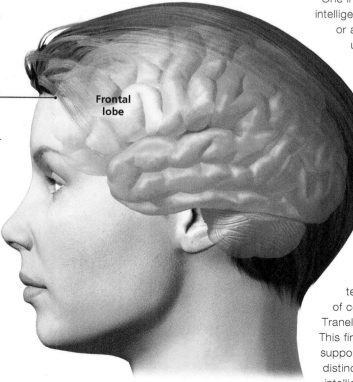

Prefrontal cortex

Frontal lobe

(Cantor & Kihlstrom, 1987). If you are socially intelligent, you can easily understand social situations and the part you should play in order to be a successful group member.

One important facet of social intelligence is **emotional intelligence,** or a person's ability to perceive, understand, manage, and utilize his or her emotions. Further, researchers from the University of Western Ontario (Vernon et al., 2009) report a relationship between people's emotional intelligence and sense of humour. People who exhibit a high degree of emotional intelligence are usually very self-aware. Interestingly, research has found that people who suffer brain damage that impairs their emotional intelligence tend to have unimpaired levels of cognitive intelligence (Bar-On, Tranel, Denburg, & Bechara, 2003). This finding provides biologically based support for the idea that we have many distinct and independent types of intelligence.

NEUROLOGICAL MEASUREMENTS OF INTELLIGENCE

Since larger muscles often indicate greater strength, you might think that a larger brain indicates greater intelligence. In fact, several studies have indicated that there is a slight correlation between brain size and intelligence. However, uncontrolled variables such as nutrition and environmental stimulation could cause both above-average intelligence and large brains, so it's not clear that brain size has much to do with intelligence.

Instead, the neural component of intelligence might be more closely related to the brain's **plasticity,** or its flexible ability to grow and change (first discussed in Chapter 3). A study by neuroscientist Philip Shaw and his colleagues (2006) on a group of children who were "highly intelligent" according to intelligence tests revealed a link between the thickening and thinning rate of the brain's cortex and intelligence: Very intelligent children tended to have a thinner cortex than their peers during childhood, but the cortex thickened more rapidly during the pre-teen years. These results suggest that there's a relationship, at least in childhood, between the rate at which the brain matures and IQ.

Does intelligence reside in a particular part of the brain? Some believe that there is a "global workspace for organizing and coordinating information" in the brain's frontal lobe (Duncan, 2000), but this assertion is the subject of hot debate among intelligence researchers. However, there are a few correlations that may help us pin down the connections between intelligence and the brain. First, there are correlations between a person's intelligence test score and his or her **perceptual speed,** or the time it takes a person to perceive and compare stimuli. People with higher scores tended to take in perceptual information more quickly than their lower-scoring counterparts. There also seems to be a relationship between high intelligence test scores and the speed and complexity of activity in the brain. People with high intelligence scores tended to exhibit complex, fast-moving brainwave

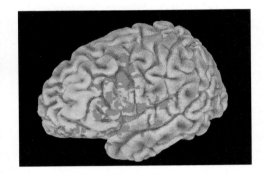

activity in response to simple stimuli. While this finding is certainly interesting, its significance is uncertain: We still don't know why fast reactions to simple tasks should be a good predictor of intelligence.

∧
∧ A new study found
∧ that **specific structures, primarily on the left side of the brain, are vital to general intelligence and executive function (the ability to regulate and control behaviour). Brain regions that are associated with general intelligence and executive function are shown in colour, with red indicating common areas, orange indicating regions specific to general intelligence, and yellow indicating areas specific to executive function.**

(Credit: Photo courtesy Aron Barbey)

Problem Solving and Reasoning

CONCEPTS

Think about everything you've learned and all the information you've collected in your life so far. Directions to the town recycling centre, the poem you memorized when you were eight, the blog post about your cat that you're composing in your head, a litany of dates and facts and events. . . . How can we possibly keep track of everything that's stored in our brains?

For starters, we use concepts. **Concepts** are mental groupings of similar objects, events, and people. We are able to comprehend vast amounts of information with concepts by creating a mental representation that categorizes shared features of related objects, events, or other stimuli. For example, the concept *car* contains everything from a shiny BMW to a jalopy with a bad paint job to smart cars. Once we form a concept category, we can classify it even more by organizing it into category **hierarchies.** The category *car* might contain the hierarchies *fuel-efficient*, *sedan*, and *race car*.

Sometimes we form concepts by definition. We might define an athlete as one who excels in one or more sports. However, we usually form our concepts by creating a mental image or a typical example that exhibits all of the features associated with a certain category. This mental image or example is called a **prototype.** We more readily identify a thing as an example of the concept if the thing closely resembles the prototype (Rosch, 1978).

Theories of Concepts and Categories

We use categories to organize the world around us, but how exactly does this cognitive process work? Wittgenstein's (1953) **family resemblance theory** suggests that we put items in categories together if they share certain characteristics, even if not every member of the category has similar features. Wittgenstein used the example of games: Table tennis, poker, and hopscotch have very little in common, but they are united by a common thread—a family resemblance—that allows us to group them together in a single category.

Exemplar theory claims that we make category judgments by comparing new things that we encounter with examples of other things that we remember that fit into that category (Ashby, 1992). For example, your concept of a dog is informed not by a single prototype but rather by all the dogs you've ever interacted with.

PROBLEM SOLVING

Think about the last time you got lost. What did you do to find your way? You might have checked a map to get back on track. Maybe you used trial and error, trying different routes until you arrived at your destination. You may have just asked for directions. Whatever strategy you chose, you were probably ultimately able to reach your destination thanks to problem solving. **Problem solving** is the act of combining current information with information stored in your memory to find a solution to a task.

Newell and Simon (1972) examine a problem in terms of the **initial state,** the **goal state,** and the **set of operations.** In the initial state, you have incomplete or unsatisfactory information. (You got lost on the way to Thanksgiving dinner at your aunt's house, and you don't know any of the roads in this part of town.) You're trying to reach the goal state, or the state in which you have all the information that you need. (You get a set of clear directions from your current location to your aunt's house.) The set of operations consists of the steps that you need to take to reach the goal state from the initial state. (You pull out your cellphone, call your aunt, ask her for directions, and write down her response.)

Problem-Solving Strategies

It's all well and good to identify a problem—to figure out your initial state and your goal state—but eventually, you're going to want to come up with a solution. We use a variety of different methods for solving different sorts of problems.

Algorithms are step-by-step procedures that we can follow in order to arrive at a solution to a particular problem. To do long division or decipher an encoded message, you might follow the steps of an algorithm. As long as you follow the correct process, you're sure to come up with the correct solution.

We all approach problems with a **mental set,** or a pre-existing state of mind that we use to solve problems because it's helped us solve similar problems in the past. A mental set is especially helpful for simple, everyday tasks. However, our mental sets can sometimes interfere with problem solving. Try solving the problem at the bottom of this page.

How'd you do? If you couldn't find the solution, you probably were a victim of **functional fixedness,** a bias that limits your ability to think in unconventional ways. You might not have considered an unconventional use of the pliers, which were the key to solving the problem. By attaching the pliers to the end of one string, you could swing them like a pendulum to reach the other string and tie a knot (Maier, 1931).

As the "two strings" problem demonstrates, it can help to take a novel perspective or pay attention to unusual or seemingly unimportant elements when you're trying to solve a difficult problem. It also doesn't hurt to keep your chin up: Your mood can affect your success with a problem (Fredrickson, 2000). When you're in a bad mood, your perceptions and thoughts become restricted, and you'll probably find it harder to "think outside the box."

Sometimes, of course, we don't need to use algorithms or analyses or complicated methods to solve problems. On those rare and wonderful occasions, we experience **insight:** Without warning, the solution we've been looking for suddenly pops into our heads. If you've ever had a flash of inspiration while taking a test or struggling with a seemingly impossible project, you're probably familiar with the joys that insight can bring. It turns out that scientists can spot insight in the brain: Recently, psychologists used fMRI and EEG imaging technology to map the brains of participants who were solving word problems. The researchers noticed

Problem solving is the act of combining current information with information stored in memory to find a solution to a task.

Initial state is a problem-solving state in which a person has incomplete or unsatisfactory information.

Goal state is a problem-solving state in which a person has all the information he or she needs.

Set of operations consists of the steps that a person needs to take to get from the initial state to the goal state.

Algorithm is a step-by-step procedure that a person can follow to arrive at a solution to a particular problem.

Mental set is a pre-existing state of mind that a person uses to solve problems because that state has helped the person solve similar problems in the past.

Functional fixedness is a bias that limits a person's ability to think in unconventional ways.

Insight refers to the sudden realization of the solution to a problem.

Reasoning is a cognitive process of organizing information or beliefs into a series of steps to reach conclusions.

that when participants had an insight that helped them solve a problem, there was increased activity in the participants' right temporal lobes (Jung-Beeman et al., 2004). Insight has also been connected to heightened brain activity in the cingulate, lateral, prefrontal, and posterior parietal cortices (Vogeley et al., 2001).

REASONING

Reasoning is the cognitive process of organizing information or beliefs into a series

>>> **Can you find a way** to tie the two **strings together?** You can use any of the **objects** in the room.

Practical reasoning is a type of reasoning in which a person considers what to do or how to act.

Theoretical reasoning is a type of reasoning directed toward arriving at a belief or conclusion rather than at a practical decision.

Discursive reasoning see *theoretical reasoning*.

Syllogistic reasoning is a type of reasoning in which a person decides whether a conclusion logically follows from two or more statements that the person assumes to be true.

Syllogism is a deductive pattern of logic in which a conclusion is made based on two or more premises.

Deductive reasoning is a top-down method of arriving at a specific conclusion based on broader premises.

Inductive reasoning is a method of using specific examples to arrive at a general conclusion.

Overconfidence is a person's tendency to think that he or she is more knowledgeable or accurate than he or she really is.

Hindsight bias describes a person's erroneous belief that he or she knew something all along after an event has occurred.

Belief bias describes the effect that occurs when a person's beliefs distort his or her logical thinking.

Belief perseverance is a person's tendency to continue believing something even when presented with evidence refuting that belief.

Heuristics are informal rules that make the decision-making process quick and simple.

" Reasoning is the cognitive process of organizing information or beliefs into a series of steps to reach conclusions. When we reason, we generally think about facts we already know and use those facts to come up with new assumptions. "

---

of steps to reach conclusions. When we reason, we generally think about facts we already know and use those facts to come up with new assumptions. There are a few different flavours of reasoning: We engage in **practical reasoning** when we consider what

to do or how to act. **Theoretical reasoning,** or **discursive reasoning,** is directed toward arriving at a belief or conclusion rather than at a practical decision. Your religious beliefs might be shaped by theoretical reasoning. We use **syllogistic reasoning** when we decide whether a conclusion logically follows from two or more statements that we assume to be true. For example, assume that all professional baseball players have excellent hand-eye coordination. James is a professional baseball player. You should logically conclude that James has excellent hand-eye coordination. This pattern of logic is called a **syllogism.**

Syllogisms are a good example of **deductive reasoning,** a top-down method of arriving at a specific conclusion based on broader premises. In the case of the example above, you can use two general pieces of information (baseball players have good hand-eye coordination and James is a baseball player) to arrive at a specific conclusion (James has good hand-eye coordination). Using deductive reasoning can be a bit like solving a math problem: When you follow certain rules in the proper order, you arrive at a correct and logical conclusion.

In contrast to deductive reasoning, which starts with generalizations and moves to specifics, **inductive reasoning** is a method of using specific examples to arrive at a general conclusion. For example, you may have noticed that all the ice you've ever seen in your life has been cold. Using inductive reasoning, you can logically conclude that all ice is cold. Inductive reasoning does leave some room for error, however: If you've observed only female field hockey players, you might reason that all field hockey players are female, but many male field hockey players around the world would beg to differ with you. When we use analogies to solve problems about unknown situations by comparing them to situations we've experienced in the past and drawing conclusions from those past situations, we're using inductive reasoning.

ERRORS IN REASONING

Have you ever been 100% sure that you were right about something, only to find out that you were completely mistaken? It happens to the best of us: Sometimes, despite our best efforts, our reasoning can be quite faulty.

Overconfidence

One common error in reasoning is **overconfidence,** or our tendency to think we are more knowledgeable or accurate than

we really are. The subprime mortgage crisis that reared its head in 2008 was due in part to overconfidence on the part of both lenders and home buyers, many of whom were wrongly convinced that they'd be able to make payments on time or make huge amounts of money from home sales. Of course, many people who didn't get caught up in this housing debacle believed after the fact that they'd never have gotten involved in such a risky action, but this response may simply be an example of a form of overconfidence called **hindsight bias,** our tendency to overestimate our previous knowledge of situations (see Chapter 2).

Belief Bias

Logic is sometimes at odds with our reasoning. Consider the following statements:

- Premise 1: Women enjoy watching romantic comedies.
- Premise 2: Men are not women.
- Conclusion: Men do not enjoy watching romantic comedies.

Does this conclusion sound logical to you? If it does, you've fallen victim to **belief bias,** the effect that occurs when our beliefs distort our logical thinking. The two premises allow for the possibility that some men might like watching romantic comedies, but your own beliefs about men's preferred movies might have led you to conclude the opposite. Our beliefs have incredible power over our judgments and reasoning skills: Even when we are presented with evidence that refutes our beliefs, we find it difficult to abandon those beliefs. This tendency is known as **belief perseverance.**

Heuristics

Which is a more probable cause of death, a plane crash or a car crash? If you can, answer that question as quickly as possible, and try not to think too much about it. When you need to make a quick decision like this one, you often follow your intuition in lieu of extended logical analysis. To reach a quick solution, you use mental shortcuts called **heuristics.** Like rules of thumb, heuristics are informal rules that make the decision-making process quick and simple. We use them all the time; in fact, psychologists Daniel Kahneman and Amos Tversky (1979) argue that human judgment rests more heavily on heuristics than on purely rational analytic processes. However, heuristics can easily lead us astray: While deaths from car accidents are actually far more common than

> *Have you ever been 100% sure that you were right about something, only to find out that you were completely mistaken? It happens to the best of us: Sometimes, despite our best efforts, our reasoning can be quite faulty.*

deaths from airplane crashes, plane crashes are much more heavily reported in newspapers and on the 6 o'clock news, and we tend to remember them when we hear about them. If you said that dying in a plane crash was more likely than dying in a car crash, you were probably misled by the **availability heuristic,** which tells us that if we can bring examples of an event (like a plane crash) to mind easily, that event must be common. This rule of thumb, while true in many cases, is not always accurate.

Confirmation Bias

If you're a member of a political party, you probably laugh when you hear claims that the media are unbiased.
It seems clear to
you, if you're
liberal, that news
stories tend to
have a con-
servative bent.
On the other
hand, if you're

conservative, it's equally clear that reporters across the country have a distinct liberal bias.

When we already believe that something is true, we tend to look for evidence that proves our beliefs, and we tend not to notice evidence that disproves those beliefs. This phenomenon is known as **confirmation bias**—although we may think we're being objective, we're actually trying to confirm our previously held opinions. If you already think that the media are biased against your particular political beliefs, you're more likely to notice those news stories that are biased against your beliefs, but you may not notice those stories that are unbiased or those that are biased toward your beliefs.

The Conjunction Fallacy

Gabe was a psychology major in college. He recently watched and enjoyed the documentary *An Inconvenient Truth*, about the dangers of global warming. Gabe takes cloth bags to the supermarket with him instead of using plastic bags to carry his groceries.

Which of the following statements is more likely?

- Gabe is a newspaper reporter.
- Gabe is a newspaper reporter who's active in an environmental group.

From what we know
about Gabe, it's clear
that he cares about
the environment,

Availability heuristic is a type of heuristic that tells a person that if he or she can bring examples of an event to mind easily, that event must be common.

Confirmation bias is a person's tendency to look for evidence that proves his or her beliefs and to ignore evidence that disproves those beliefs.

Conjunction fallacy is a phenomenon that causes people to believe that additional information increases the probability that a statement is true, even though that probability actually decreases.

so you might think that the second statement is more likely than the first. However, it's far more probable that Gabe is a reporter than it is that he is a reporter and an environmentalist. Since the first statement is contained in the second, and the second statement includes additional pieces of information that may or may not be true, the first statement is more likely. If you thought otherwise, you experienced the **conjunction fallacy,** a phenomenon that causes people to believe that additional information increases the probability that a statement is true, even though that probability actually decreases.

> If you wanted to **prove media bias,** what **evidence** would you look for? What evidence might you **unconsciously ignore?**

Judgment is a skill that allows people to form opinions, reach conclusions, and evaluate situations objectively and critically.

Decision making is the process of selecting and rejecting available options.

Framing describes the perspective from which people interpret information before making a decision.

Decision aversion is the state of attempting to avoid making any decision at all.

Rational choice theory states that people make decisions by determining how likely each outcome of that decision is, as well as the positive or negative value of each outcome.

Prospect theory states that people will more likely avoid risk in situations where they stand to gain but will seek risk when they stand to lose something.

Dopamine is a neurotransmitter that helps people make decisions that lead to good outcomes and avoid bad outcomes.

Decision Making, Judgment, and Executive Control

Would you consider trying any of the cogn enhancement methods mentioned at the beginning of this chapter, or are you skep cal? You have probably formed an opinioi about these methods using your judgmer **Judgment** is a skill that allows us to form opinions, reach conclusions, and evaluate situations objectively and critically.

DECISION MAKING

Judgment informs our **decision making**— process of selecting and rejecting available options. The presentation, or **framing,** of ε issue can greatly influence the decisions th we make. For example, people are more li to purchase ground beef that is "75% lean rather than ground beef that's "25% fat" (L & Gaeth, 1988; Sanford, Fray, Stewart, & Moxley, 2002). Sometimes, if we're preser with a decision that can be viewed through too many conflicting frames, or if we have too many alternatives to choose from, we develop **decision aversion,** the state of attempting to avoid making any decision at all.

Theories of Decision Making

Once we've been given a decision to make, how do we arrive at a conclusion? **Rational**

choice theory states that we make decisions by determining how likely each outcome of that decision is, as well as the positive or negative value of each outcome. If you were asked to decide whether to purchase a new iPhone, what would you do? According to rational choice theory, you'd determine the pros and cons of buying the phone versus not buying it, as well as the likelihood of each of these pros and cons. Then, if the value of buying the phone outweighed the value of not buying it, you'd head over to the Apple store and make the purchase.

Kahneman and Tversky proposed an alternative decision-making theory called **prospect theory,** which describes how people make decisions in situations that involve elements of risk. In general, we avoid risk in situations where we stand to gain, but our behaviour becomes more risk-seeking when we face a loss. Let's say you're a contestant on a game show. The host gives you a cheque for $1000. You can either keep the cheque, netting a certain $1000, or you can

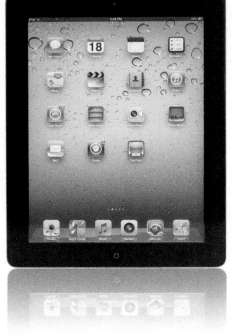

^ ^ **What outcomes would you consider before spending your money on the latest technology?**

> In general, we avoid risk in situations where we stand to gain, **but our behaviour becomes more risk-seeking when we face a loss.**

exchange the cheque for the envelope in the host's hand. There's a 50% chance that the envelope contains $2500, but there's a 50% chance that the envelope contains nothing at all. In this situation, most people choose to avoid risk and stick with the $1000 they're sure to win. However, try to imagine a slightly more sadistic game show: The host says that if you do nothing, he's going to take $1000 from you. However, he offers you another envelope. There's a 50% chance that the envelope contains a card that will let you keep all your money, and there's a 50% chance that it contains a card that will allow the host to take $2500 from you. Do you take the envelope? Faced with this decision, most people would rather run the risk of losing $2500 in order to have a chance to keep all their money. Prospect theory suggests that we have different attitudes toward risk depending on the situation we're facing.

Neural Contributions to Decision Making

When your friend makes a decision that you don't agree with, you may wonder what could possibly have been going through her brain when she made that choice. What was going through her brain? One answer might be the neurotransmitter **dopamine.** Research has found that the presence of dopamine in the brain helps us make decisions that lead to good outcomes and avoid bad outcomes (St. Onge & Floresco, 2008). A large amount of dopamine is present in the basal ganglia, an area of the brain that seems to be crucial to decision making. When we're faced with a decision, activity in the basal ganglia picks up, and bursts of dopamine help us choose the most rewarding or favourable potential outcome.

What happens, though, if a choice that makes us feel good isn't necessarily the best choice for us? For instance, if you want to eat more healthily, you probably don't want to decide to eat a delicious frosted cupcake, but the dopamine in your brain will cause you to identify that cupcake as a tasty

> Conscious attention is selective, meaning that although we are aware of alternative interpretations, we can experience only one perception at any given time.

reward. Luckily, your brain has **executive control systems** that inhibit the pleasurable response to the cupcake so you can stick to your original plan and snack on a salad instead. These systems are generally thought to be centred in the brain's frontal regions (with significant additional input from the thalamus). Specifically, the **ventromedial prefrontal cortex** helps us adhere to social and behavioural rules and plays a role in allowing us to link our behaviours to their potential consequences. The **dorsolateral prefrontal cortex** initiates our behaviour, but it can also shift or inhibit that behaviour based on the decisions we make. The **anterior cingulate cortex** is also involved in controlling our behaviour, and the **parietal cortex** plays a critical role in directing our attention during the decision-making process.

Attention

How do you maintain focus when that all-important exam is approaching? Do you use one of the cognitive-enhancement programs mentioned earlier in the chapter or listen to classical music while you study? Whatever method you choose, **attention**—the way the brain selectively processes important information—plays a vital role.

FOCUS OF ATTENTION

Conscious attention is selective, meaning that although we are aware of alternative interpretations, we can experience only one perception at any given time (see Chapter 4). According to one study, we consciously process about 40 of the 11 000 000 bits of information we receive per second (Wilson, 2002).

Cognitive scientists Corbetta and Schulman (2002) proposed that there are two types of attention. In **goal-directed selection,** or **endogenous attention,** we make an explicit choice to pay attention to something—we look for a particular face in the crowd, or try to memorize a particular section of text.

Stimulus-driven capture, or **exogenous attention,** occurs when our attention is driven by external stimuli. When something novel or unexpected happens (a deer jumps through the living room window, for example), our attention is automatically drawn to the scene.

How do we decide how much attention to devote to a particular task? We might be able to keep up with a slow-moving romantic comedy while calling a friend for the latest gossip, but multi-tasking would not be recommended if our to-do list included cutting down a tree and writing a nuclear physics essay. **Perceptual load** is the level of processing difficulty or complexity of

Executive control systems are parts of the brain that inhibit pleasurable responses so that people can avoid making decisions that feel good but are bad for them.

Ventromedial prefrontal cortex is an area of the brain that serves as an executive control system that helps a person adhere to social and behavioural rules; it also plays a role in allowing a person to link his or her behaviour to its potential consequences.

Dorsolateral prefrontal cortex is an area of the brain that serves as an executive control system that initiates a person's behaviour; it can also shift or inhibit that behaviour based on the decisions the person makes.

Anterior cingulate cortex is an area of the brain that serves as an executive control system that helps control a person's behaviour; it is involved in the perception of physical pain.

Parietal cortex is an area of the brain that serves as an executive control system that plays a critical role in directing a person's attention during the decision-making process.

Attention is the act of applying the mind selectively to a sense or thought.

Goal-directed selection is a type of attention in which a person makes an explicit choice to pay attention to something.

Endogenous attention see *goal-directed selection*.

Stimulus-driven capture is a type of attention that is motivated by external factors.

Exogenous attention see *stimulus-driven capture*.

Perceptual load refers to the processing difficulty or complexity of a task.

a task. Because human brains have limited resources, the perceptual load of a task often determines the amount of attention allocated to it.

When we stop paying attention to a task there is less activity in the areas of our brain that receive external stimuli. Canadian researcher Daniel Smilek and his colleagues (2010) found that we blink more when our minds wander away from a task. These frequent blinks create a type of physical barrier, limiting the input of sensory information and allowing our brain to "tune out."

<<< We are able to multi-task if the perceptual load of each chore is fairly low.

UNATTENDED STIMULI

Filter Theory

Our attention is limited to just a few stimuli at any one given time. So how do we choose what to concentrate on? Broadbent's (1958) **filter theory** proposed that we select stimuli early in the perception process, even before we assess the meaning of the input. When participants in a dichotic listening task use headphones to listen to two simultaneous messages, one in each ear, they are told to pay attention only to the message they hear in one ear. Then, they're able to repeat, or shadow, the words that they hear in that ear. The attended message is generally the only portion of the stimuli that can

be reported. Broadbent suggested that two messages presented at the same time reach a **sensory buffer,** which holds information for a short time before it is accepted or rejected by the filter. One of the messages would then be allowed through the filter on the basis of its physical characteristics. For example, if participants have been told to listen to a male voice and the other voice on the tape is female, they can filter out the female voice fairly easily. When two messages are presented in the same tone with few physical differences, they become harder to separate (Cherry, 1953).

Inattentional Blindness

For a variety of reasons, we often fail to process certain stimuli, a concept known as inattentional blindness (see Chapter 4). One type of processing failure is called **attentional blink.** Imagine that you are shown a series of words and told to remember every word that could be used to describe a tree. Pretty easy, right? But if you are shown the words *tall* and *leafy* within a very short period of time, you will be unable to recall seeing the second word. This is due to the **psychological refractory period**—the interval during which your brain is too busy processing the first stimulus to comprehend the second.

FEATURE INTEGRATION

Since Broadbent developed his filter theory, many other models of attention have been proposed.

> "Imagine that you are shown a series of words and told to remember every word that could be used to describe a tree. Pretty easy, right? But if you are shown the words *tall* and *leafy* within a very short period of time, you will be unable to recall seeing the second word."

Psychologist Anne Treisman developed the influential **feature integration theory,** suggesting that we organize stimuli based on knowledge about how their features should be combined (Treisman, 1987). Treisman argues that most stimuli are both similar and yet sufficiently different so that there are a limited number of sensible ways to combine their features (see Chapter 4). For example, while you may not have seen an Irish wolfhound before, you know that an animal with particular physical features is likely to be a dog. Previous sensory experience allows you to categorize the animal, while still being able to distinguish it from other four-legged creatures with a tail.

Broadbent's Filter Theory

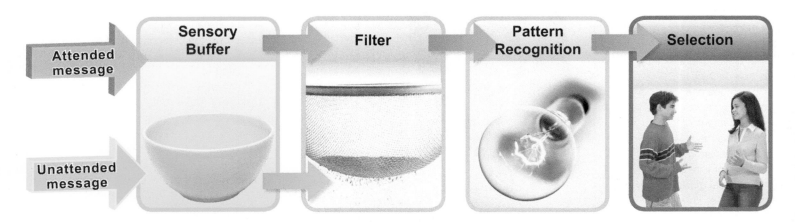

∧
∧ **Both messages reach a sensory buffer and are temporarily stored, like ingre-**
∧ **dients being held in a mixing bowl. The messages are filtered according to their physical characteristics, as though they are sifted through a sieve. The desired physical characteristic is recognized. Attention is devoted to a single message, enabling focused conversation.**

Language and Verbal Cognition

Language—the system of symbols that enables us to communicate our ideas, thoughts, and feelings—plays a vital part in how we think. So does this mean that the language we use can shape our attitudes toward others? Do people who speak different languages also see the world a different way? What processes take place when we use language, and how are people able to comprehend more than one language?

MULTIPLE LANGUAGES

People who speak multiple languages often learn their second language at a young age. Children who acquire a new language before the age of seven can develop near-perfect fluency, and you would find it difficult to distinguish them from native speakers. Asian immigrants to the United States were given a grammar test, which showed that those who had arrived in the country as young children understood American English grammar as proficiently as native speakers (Johnson & Newport, 1991). However, fluency tends to decrease with age, even when learning sign language. Why is this? Research shows that some areas of the brain are more active in children than in adults during language-based tasks. This may account for some disparity in learning capacity between children and adults.

Adults can learn second languages after this critical period has passed. They use different cognitive strategies than babies and young children. Indeed, the brains of people who learn a second language late in life look different from the brains of people who are bilingual from infancy (Marian et al., 2007). Early bilingualism does not interfere with normal cognitive development. In fact, learning a second language early in life increases the density of grey matter in the lower left parietal area. This area of the brain is associated with performance of verbal fluency tasks.

LANGUAGE PRODUCTION

You might have heard the expression, "Put your brain in gear before you put your mouth

> Children who acquire a new language before the age of seven can develop near-perfect fluency, **and you would find it difficult to distinguish them from native speakers.**

in action," meaning that we should think before we speak. But what actually does go through our minds the moment before we say something? Sociolinguist Allan Bell (1984) theorized that everything we say is directed to a particular audience, a concept known as **audience design.** Bell claimed that we adapt our style of speaking in accordance with the person we are talking to, either to express solidarity or to keep our distance. He called this habit **style shifting.** You may have noticed the painfully awkward process of a parent trying to utilize modern slang in order to better relate to his or her teenage child.

Cognitive scientist H. P. Grice (1975) described the **co-operative principle,** which instructs speakers that utterances should be truthful, informative, relevant, and clear. Both the speaker and the addressee have to follow certain semantic and syntactic rules in order to communicate effectively. Another critical consideration is whether a speaker has an accurate understanding of the listener's knowledge, enabling them to find "common ground" (Clark & Marshall, 1981). For example, it would be pointless to use the baseball metaphor "cover all your bases" in a conversation with someone who had never heard of the ball game.

Audience design is a concept that states that everything people say is directed to a particular audience.

Style shifting describes the habit of a person to adapt his or her style of speaking in accordance with the person he or she is talking to, either to express solidarity or to maintain distance.

Co-operative principle instructs speakers that utterances should be truthful, informative, relevant, and clear.

>>> **Motherese is effective in communicating with infants, but it would not be appropriate in conversations with adults. In what ways can style shifting come across as false, inappropriate, or even insulting?**

Errors in speech are evidence that multiple levels of processing are at work during language production. A **spoonerism** is a common execution error in which a person exchanges the initial sounds of two or more words in a phrase, such as *cast far* instead of *fast car*. Studies suggest that spoonerisms are more likely to result when the exchanges result in actual words. Other errors, such as word switching, are more likely when two idioms from which the words are taken carry the same meaning. For example, a person might confuse *meet your maker* and *kick the bucket*, resulting in the befuddling expression *kick your maker*. **Opportunism**—the necessity of rapid speech production—is also the cause of many execution errors. Few of us can come up with a perfectly phrased witty retort on the spur of the moment, usually resulting in a poorly worded reply that has us kicking ourselves for the rest of the day as we think of increasingly eloquent responses.

LANGUAGE COMPREHENSION

The above headline, attributed to the *Toronto Star*, shows how even the experts struggle with **lexical ambiguity**—the multiple meanings of a word or phrase (in this case *joint*). We differentiate homonyms, such as *carrot* and *karat*, based on context and the relative frequency of the word's use. When resolving **structural ambiguity**—the multiple meaning of a sentence depending on syntax, we differentiate between different possible sentence structures that produce different meanings. Take the following headline as an example: "Stolen painting found by tree." Did the tree find the painting? Probably not! Most of the time we are able to make logical inferences about the intended meaning of a word or sentence based on previous experience.

LANGUAGE AND THOUGHT

Do people from different cultures perceive the world differently? Many studies suggest that they do (Nisbett & Norenzayan, 2002; Peng & Nisbett, 1999). A group of Japanese and American students were shown an animated underwater scene in which one larger, "focal" fish swum among smaller fish and other aquatic life. When asked to describe

Marijuana Issue Sent to Joint Committee

what they saw, the Japanese students were much more likely to begin by describing the background and how the parts of the scene related to one another—the rocky pool, the colour of the water, the fish swimming past seaweed. In contrast, American students were far more likely to begin by describing prominent individual aspects of the scene—the largest, fastest, brightest fish. Nisbett and his colleagues found that the

> "Few of us can come up with a perfectly phrased witty retort on the spur of the moment, **usually resulting in a poorly worded reply that has us kicking ourselves for the rest of the day as we think of increasingly eloquent responses.**"

Japanese were similarly sensitive to context in the social world and could pick up how situational pressures were affecting people's behaviour far quicker than Americans. The results suggest that there are fundamental differences in the way Easterners and Westerners perceive the world.

Does language also affect the way we think? Linguists Edward Sapir and Benjamin Whorf proposed that the language we speak influences our conception of reality. Their ideas became known as the **linguistic relativity hypothesis** (Whorf, 1956). For example, English and other European languages have an egocentric frame of reference. In other words, space is represented with

ourselves at the centre. You might describe a local grocery store as being two kilometres from your house, whereas someone with an absolute frame of reference might give the specific geographic location. Similarly, the Japanese have many words for interpersonal emotions such as *sympathy*, while the English language contains many self-focused emotions, such as *anger* (Markus & Kitayama, 1991). Might this influence the differences in culture? Many bilingual speakers report feeling a different sense of self depending on which language they are using (Matsumoto, 1994).

Consider this riddle: A famous surgeon was a passenger in a car driven by his teenage son. "I'll drop you at the hospital, Dad," said the young man. "Fine, son," said his father. Those were his last words; a wildly careening convertible crossed the centre strip and ran headlong into the car. At the emergency room the father was pronounced dead on arrival; the son was taken for emergency surgery. The surgeon called to the scene reached for a scalpel but paused: "I can't operate," the surgeon said, "this is my son." Is this possible?

Did you figure it out? If it took you more than a few seconds to work out that the surgeon was the boy's mother, some psychologists would argue that the generic use of *he* and *man* has influenced the way you perceive certain professions. Twenty studies have consistently found that the supposedly generic *he* is not interpreted as including women (Henley, 1989).

Linguistic determinism is the theory that different languages impose different conceptions of reality. However, some research undermines this theory. Whorf discovered that the Hopi Indian tribe had no words for *past*, *present*, or *future*, yet they still had a sense for the continuum of time. It's clear, though, that language and thought influence each other to a large degree: Our cognition shapes our language, and our language, in turn, may help to shape our cognition.

> **Think of a house you used to live in, or a favourite family vacation. You probably just conjured up a whole host of mental images. Visual representations are a useful way of helping us remember our experiences.**

Visual Cognition

Think of a house you used to live in, or a favourite family vacation. You probably just conjured up a whole host of mental images. Visual representations are a useful way of helping us remember our experiences. Now try using visual images to think of a process or a concept. Not so easy, is it? According to Paivio's (1986) **dual-coding theory,** concrete words are mentally represented both visually and verbally, whereas abstract terms, such as *choice*, are coded only verbally, requiring more complex coding and making them more difficult to retrieve. Event-related potential (ERP) studies, which measure electrical activity in the brain, indicate distinct patterns of brain activity when people are processing words that are easily visualized compared to words that are not (Kounios & Holcomb, 1994).

Studies of visual cognition have found that when imagining an activity, the same brain areas are activated as when physically performing the activity. We also think in images while we sleep. After learning something, such as the way through a maze, the

Spoonerism is a common execution error in which a person exchanges the initial sounds of two or more words in a phrase.

Opportunism refers to the necessity of rapid speech production.

Lexical ambiguity occurs when a word or phrase has multiple meanings.

Structural ambiguity occurs when syntax causes a sentence to have multiple meanings.

Linguistic relativity hypothesis states that the language a person speaks influences his or her conception of reality.

Linguistic determinism states that different languages impose different conceptions of reality.

Dual-coding theory states that concrete words are represented both visually and verbally, whereas abstract terms are coded only verbally, requiring more complex coding and making them more difficult to retrieve.

mind retraces its steps during sleep (O'Neill, Senior, & Csicsvari, 2006). This behaviour is a purported mechanism for learning (see Chapter 11), providing a convenient excuse for taking that afternoon nap.

∧
∧ The **Japanese** have a **proverb** that says "The nail that sticks up gets hammered down." Whereas North Americans treasure individualism, collectivist cultures emphasize the good of the group over the individual. How might this affect language use and cultural understanding?

Summary

WHAT IS COGNITIVE PSYCHOLOGY? p.182

- Cognition comprises the mental activities associated with thinking, knowing, remembering, and communicating.

- Cognitive scientists assess the attention and steps associated with mental processes.

WHAT IS INTELLIGENCE, AND HOW CAN WE MEASURE IT? p.183

- Intelligence is the capacity to reason, solve problems, and acquire new knowledge.

- Intelligence tests, such as the Wechsler Adult Intelligence Scale, measure aptitude rather than achievement. They give you an intelligence quotient (IQ) score that is based on your mental age and chronological age.

- Genetics are believed to influence intelligence levels more than environmental factors do.

- Intelligence seems to be located in many parts of our brain.

- Many psychologists believe there are multiple types of intelligence.

HOW DO WE REASON, SOLVE PROBLEMS, AND MAKE DECISIONS? p.186

- We group similar objects, events, and people into concepts. We develop typical examples that represent key features of a concept, called prototypes.

- We use current and remembered information to find a solution to a task. We can use specific strategies (such as algorithms) to solve problems, and we occasionally experience insight. If we are unable to find a solution to a problem, it may be due to functional fixedness, an inability to think in unconventional ways.

- Reasoning is the process of organizing information into a series of steps to reach conclusions. Overconfidence, belief bias, confirmation bias, and the conjunction fallacy may all lead to errors in reasoning.

- Decision making is the process of selecting and rejecting available options. Rational choice theory and prospect theory both explain aspects of human decision making.

HOW DOES ATTENTION HELP US PROCESS INFORMATION? p.191

- Attention—the way the brain selectively processes important information—is either endogenous (goal-directed) or exogenous (stimulus-driven).

- Our attention is limited to a few stimuli at any one given time.

HOW ARE VERBAL AND VISUAL COGNITION RELATED? p.193

- Language is the system of symbols that enables us to communicate. We modify our style of speaking depending on our audience, called style shifting.

- According to the linguistic relativity hypothesis, the language we speak influences the way in which we perceive the world.

- According to dual-coding theory, we process words for concrete concepts both visually and verbally, but we code words for abstract concepts only verbally.

Test Your Understanding

1. Sharmi is very good at meeting new people and making them feel comfortable. Some cognitive psychologists would argue that Sharmi has:
   a. analytical intelligence
   b. practical intelligence
   c. social intelligence
   d. creative intelligence

2. Which of the following determines the level of attention we need to pay to a particular task?
   a. stimulus-driven capture
   b. attentional blink
   c. sensory buffer
   d. perceptual load

3. David is deciding whether to change jobs. He writes down a list of things he likes and dislikes about his current job, followed by a list of things he likes and dislikes about the new job. David's decision-making process is an example of:
   a. exemplar theory
   b. family resemblance theory
   c. prospect theory
   d. rational choice theory

4. Which of the following statements about intelligence tests is true?
   a. Intelligence tests are unreliable because they do not correlate with academic performance.
   b. Many designers believe it is impossible to create a test completely free of cultural bias.
   c. Intelligence test scores that measure school learning have risen dramatically since 1960.
   d. A score of 150 on an intelligence test indicates average intelligence.

5. When Nora talks to her young niece, she adopts a childish tone of voice and only uses words that her niece will understand. Nora is:

a. using lexical ambiguity
b. style shifting
c. talking in spoonerisms
d. practising opportunism

6. The correlation of intelligence is most likely to be highest for:

a. fraternal twins
b. identical twins
c. a brother and a sister
d. a husband and a wife

7. Phil reads a newspaper report about hurricane victims who refused to evacuate their homes and, as a result, were severely injured in the storm. Phil thinks, "If I had been in the hurricane's path, I definitely would have evacuated." Phil is guilty of:

a. confirmation bias
b. belief bias
c. hindsight bias
d. belief perseverance

8. Which of the following statements is true about people who speak multiple languages?

a. Fluency peaks in the early 20s and decreases thereafter.
b. Early bilingualism negatively affects normal cognitive development.
c. Most adults are unable to learn a second language once they have passed the critical period of language development.
d. Children who learn a second language before the age of seven are nearly indistinguishable from native speakers.

9. Which of the following is an example of a spoonerism?

a. writing the word *hair* instead of *hare*
b. saying the word *run* instead of *sprint*
c. saying the words *lack of pies* instead of *pack of lies*
d. writing the words *enormous vehicle* instead of *big car*

10. Every blade of grass that Qing has ever seen is green. As a result, she concludes that all grass is green. Qing is using:

a. practical reasoning
b. theoretical reasoning
c. inductive reasoning
d. discursive reasoning

11. Miguel is trying to design a culturally fair intelligence test. Which of the following pieces of advice should he follow?

a. focus on speed
b. incorporate general knowledge questions
c. eliminate puzzle-based questions
d. avoid using language-based questions

12. Andy is convinced that the government has had contact with alien life forms. He decides to research his theory on the Internet. Ignoring all of the sites that are skeptical of his beliefs, Andy only converses with people online who share his views. This is an example of:

a. functional fixedness
b. heuristics
c. confirmation bias
d. belief bias

13. When Marla thinks of her house, she is able to conjure up a mental picture in her head. Yet when she tries to create mental pictures of words associated with her house, such as *peaceful* or

safe, her mind goes blank. Which of the following explains Marla's experience?

a. linguistic determinism
b. dual-coding theory
c. feature integration theory
d. filter theory

14. According to Gardner, scientists, researchers, and engineers would most likely have which of the following types of intelligence?

a. musical
b. spatial
c. bodily-kinesthetic
d. logical-mathematical

15. In which of the following scenarios would we use exogenous attention?

a. studying a textbook for an important exam
b. hearing a car's brakes squealing loudly
c. memorizing a speech for a recital
d. seeking out an empty seat at a theatre

16. Lions, dogs, seals, and horses do not appear to have much in common. Which of the following theories suggests that we categorize them together?

a. family resemblance theory
b. exemplar theory
c. dual-coding theory
d. feature integration theory

17. Tyrus has locked himself out of his house and does not have a key. He has several items with him that might help him open the door, including a credit card and a wire hanger, but he does not think to use them. This is an example of:

a. syllogistic reasoning
b. functional fixedness
c. the conjunction fallacy
d. belief perseverance

18. Which of the following statements about prospect theory is true?

a. Behaviour becomes more risk-seeking when faced with a loss.
b. Behaviour becomes less risk-seeking when faced with a loss.
c. Most people would rather face a definite loss than risk losing everything.
d. Most people would risk a definite win in the hope of gaining more.

19. According to Broadbent's filter theory, we choose what to pay attention to:

a. once we have analyzed the input
b. before stimuli reach the sensory buffer
c. before we assess the meaning of the input
d. at the end of the perception process

20. According to the linguistic relativity hypothesis:

a. language and thought influence each other
b. language and thought develop independently
c. the way we think influences language
d. language influences the way we think

Remember to check www.thethinkspot.ca **for additional information, downloadable flashcards, and other helpful resources.**

Answers: 1) c; 2) d; 3) d; 4) b; 5) b; 6) b; 7) c; 8) d; 9) c; 10) c; 11) d; 12) c; 13) b; 14) d; 15) b; 16) a; 17) b; 18) a; 19) c; 20) d

THINK READINGS

Positive Mood Effects on Delay Discounting

Jacob B. Hirsh, Alex Guindon, Dominique Morisano, and Jordan B. Peterson
University of Toronto

The reward centre, also known as the wanting system, is also activated by food and psychoactive substances (Chapters 10 and 11).

Do you remember the roles of the frontal and parietal lobes (see Chapter 3)?

Can you think of a situation in your life in which you chose to work towards a long-term goal instead of focusing on immediate rewards?

In Chapter 11, you learned about operant conditioning, which uses reinforcement and punishment to shape behaviour. What effect does reward have on behaviour?

In Chapter 9 you read about other factors that motivate our behaviour.

In Chapters 6 and 7, you read about developmental milestones. Do you think children and adolescents are able to delay immediate gratification?

How do we know when someone is addicted to a drug (see Chapter 10)?

Delay discounting is the process by which the value of an expected reward decreases as the delay to obtaining that reward increases. Individuals with higher discounting rates tend to prefer smaller immediate rewards over larger delayed rewards. Previous research has indicated that personality can influence an individual's discounting rates, with higher levels of Extraversion predicting a preference for immediate gratification. The current study examined how this relationship would be influenced by situational mood inductions. While main effects were observed for both Extraversion and cognitive ability in the prediction of discounting rates, a significant interaction was also observed between Extraversion and positive affect. Extraverted individuals were more likely to prefer an immediate reward when first put in a positive mood. Extraverts thus appear particularly sensitive to impulsive, incentive-reward-driven behavior by temperament and by situational factors heightening positive affect.

Delay discounting describes the psychological tendency for the subjective value of a given reward to decrease as the delay to obtaining that reward increases.

Higher discounting rates indicate a preference for smaller immediate rewards over larger delayed rewards. It is important that this preference has been associated with negative outcomes in a variety of life domains, including worse academic performance and poor self-regulation (Kirby, Winston, & Santiesteban, 2005; Mischel, Shoda, & Rodriguez, 1989). Additionally, higher discounting rates have been associated with a variety of addictive and impulsive behaviors such as alcoholism, pathological gambling, heroin use, and cigarette smoking (Bickel & Marsch, 2001; Kirby, Petry, & Bickel, 1999). The ability to work toward long-term goals instead of focusing on immediate gratification appears to be an important psychological process with real-world consequences.

Behavioral models of delay discounting have identified the competing influence of the "hot" and "cool" psychological processes that are involved when choices are made between current and future rewards (Metcalfe & Mischel, 1999). According to such models, "hot" processes are driven by the motivational appeal of the immediately available rewards, while "cool" processes reflect the strength of top-down cognitive-control networks that emphasize the importance of long-term goals. The relative strength of these "hot" and "cool"

systems is thought to determine whether an individual ultimately chooses to pursue immediate gratification or a delayed reward. Neuropsychologically, this decision process appears to be instantiated as a conflict between the reward centers of the mesolimbic dopamine system and the cognitive control networks in frontal and parietal cortex (McClure, Laibson, Loewenstein, & Cohen, 2004). When greater activity is observed in frontal-parietal regions, it is the preference for the larger, delayed reward that holds greater sway. When greater activity is observed in the mesolimbic reward circuits of the ventral striatum, by contrast, the desire for the immediate reward dominates an individual's behavior. This process can be seen most clearly in the extreme case of addictive behavior, in which the midbrain dopaminergic circuitry gains disproportionate control over an individual's actions (Hyman & Malenka, 2001).

The strength of these "hot" and "cool" systems appears to vary substantially across individuals, with some people experiencing a stronger incentive pull toward rewards of a given size, and others demonstrating a greater capacity to control and regulate their motivational impulses. In the former case, a stronger incentive pull is associated with the strength of the mesolimbic dopamine system. The perception of reward cues is associated with phasic releases of dopamine (Schultz, 2002), as well as the experience of positive affect (Burgdorf & Panksepp, 2006), both of which appear to facilitate incentive motivation during goal pursuit. In terms of individual differences, the dopaminergic response to a potential reward has been linked to the personality trait of Extraversion (Depue & Collins, 1999; Wacker, Chavanon, & Stemmler, 2006). Extraverted individuals appear to have more responsive dopaminergic circuits and, as a result, tend to be more sensitive to rewards in general, while also experiencing greater positive affect (Cohen, Young, Baek, Kessler, & Ranganath, 2005; Lucas, Diener, Grob, Suh, & Shao, 2000). Thus, when compared to introverts, extraverts experience a stronger subjective reward for any given objective reward. It therefore appears easier to trigger the "hot" motivational systems of extraverts. As predicted by behavioral and neuropsychological models of delay discounting, extraverts also tend to prefer immediate gratification over delayed rewards (Hirsh, Morisano, & Peterson, 2008; Ostaszewski, 1996).

The strength of the "cool" cognitive process, meanwhile, appears to be reflected in measures of general cognitive ability, with higher IQ scores predicting reduced discounting rates (partly mediated through the improved anterior prefrontal cortical function of intelligent individuals; Shamosh et al., 2008; Shamosh & Gray, 2007). With more cognitive resources available, intelligent individuals are better able to deliberatively regulate their motivational impulses, calculate the optimal choice strategy, and integrate their decisions within more long-term goals.

Discounting behavior also appears to be influenced by the situational manipulation of these "hot" and "cool" systems, as well as their dispositional status. The "cool" system can, for example, be disrupted by manipulations that reduce the availability of cognitive resources. Increasing an individual's working memory load ties up cognitive resources, leading to higher discounting rates (Hinson, Jameson, & Whitney, 2003). In the case of the dopaminergic "hot" system, discounting rates tend to increase following the presentation of cues for incentive reward (Wilson & Daly, 2004). Indeed, during states of "hot" emotional arousal, people tend to increase the value that is given to immediate gratification (Ariely & Loewenstein, 2006). Based on neuropsychological models of discounting behavior, this appears to be due to the increased dopaminergic activity that follows exposure to reward cues (Schultz, 2002).

There is reason to suspect, however, that the consequences of emotional arousal for decision-making processes might not be the same for all individuals. In particular, the net activation of the "hot" circuitry should reflect a combination of its dispositional strength and the current situational influence. Because extraverted individuals appear to have higher dispositional levels of "hot" reward-related dopaminergic activity, they should exhibit even stronger motivational impulses during situations of emotional arousal. As a result, the previously observed relationship between Extraversion and higher discount-ing rates should be strengthened following the induction of positive mood. The current study tested this possibility by examining the personality predictors of delay discounting following a positive mood manipulation. It was hypothesized that higher levels of induced positive affect would result in greater discounting of future rewards among extraverted individuals (hypothetically due to increased dopaminergic responsivity). Conversely, induced negative affect was not expected to influence the discounting behavior of extraverts, as it should not be related to the heightened incentive motivation associated with dopaminergic activity.

METHOD

Participants

Participants included 137 undergraduate students (99 female) from the University of Toronto, with an age range of 18 to 25 years ($M = 20.1$, $SD = 1.5$). Participants were recruited from an introductory psychology class for a study on decision making, and were given course credit for completion of the experiment. The sample consisted of mostly European-Canadian (46%) and East-Asian (35%) participants.

Materials

Delay discounting measure. Participants were asked to choose repeatedly between receiving various amounts of money now or in the future on a computerized task that took approximately 15 minutes to complete. This type of hypothetical monetary choice task has been validated as an effective measure of actual monetary

---

Extraversion, and other personality traits, will be discussed in Chapter 15.

What do you remember about the way our memory works? What is the role of our working memory (see Chapter 12)?

Do you think that culture affects the way we think and make decisions? In what ways?

In this chapter you read about cognitive abilities and IQ tests. Whose theory of intelligence most closely supports the idea of a "general cognitive ability"?

Can you think of some examples to show how our emotions may have a positive effect on our decision-making ability? How about when our emotions have a negative effect on our decisions?

You will read more about the Big Five personality traits in Chapter 15.

Why did the researchers choose to present the tasks randomly to participants instead of in increasing order of monetary amount (see Chapter 2)?

In this chapter you read about intelligence tests. What are some of the limitations of these tests?

In Chapter 2, you read about the ethical procedures that must be involved when conducting research with humans. Is informed consent ALWAYS necessary?

Can you identify the independent and dependent variables in this study (Chapter 2)?

decisions, with no differences being observed between real and hypothetical choices (Johnson & Bickel, 2002; Lagorio & Madden, 2005; Madden, Begotka, Raiff, & Kastern, 2003; Madden et al., 2004). While the size of the immediate reward option varied on each trial, the delayed reward option was always $1,000 (large) or $20 (small) after a short (1 week), medium (6 months), or long (1 year) delay. Altogether, the task presented 114 separate monetary choices, one at a time, in random order, from a predetermined list of delays and immediate amounts (ranging from $2 to $20 for small rewards and $100 to $1,000 for large rewards). For each delay and reward size, the indifference point was obtained at which the participant was equally likely to choose the immediate and delayed rewards. Most decisions were consistent with the observed indifference points ($M = 92\%$, $SD = 5\%$), such that immediate rewards were chosen primarily on trials that were below the indifference point and delayed rewards were chosen primarily on trials that were above the indifference point.

A hyperbolic discounting rate was estimated using the formula $V = A/(1 + kD)$, where k is the rate at which delayed rewards are discounted, A is the size of the delayed reward, V is the present value of the delayed reward (i.e., the indifference point), and D is the delay in days toward obtaining the delayed reward (cf. Kirby et al., 1999). Discounting rates for each reward magnitude (small, large, overall) were estimated by fitting the equation above to the obtained data with the Solver subroutine in Microsoft Excel, 2007. Statistical analyses employed the log-transformed discounting rates, to ensure normality. Higher discounting rates indicate a preference for immediate rewards.

Big Five Inventory (BFI; John & Srivastava, 1999). The Big Five personality traits were measured with the BFI, a reliable and widely used measure of the five factors. The BFI contains 44 items spread across the five dimensions. Participants rate the extent to which they can be described by the items on a 5-point scale (1 = *strongly disagree*; 5 = *strongly agree*). Sample items include "Is helpful and unselfish with others," and "Is a reliable worker."

Positive and Negative Affective Schedule (PANAS; Watson, Clark, & Tellegen, 1988). The PANAS was used to assess the participants' levels of positive affect (PA) and negative affect (NA) following the mood manipulation. The questionnaire features two 10-item Likert scales assessing an individual's current levels of positive and negative affect.

Wonderlic Personnel Test (WPT; Wonderlic, 1983). The WPT was used as a brief (12-min) measure of cognitive ability. The 50 items on the WPT are based on those from the original *Otis Test of Mental Ability*, and scores correlate highly with full-scale IQ as measured by the *Wechsler Adult Intelligence Scale*, Third Edition ($r = .92$; McKelvie, 1989).

Procedure

After signing an informed consent form, each participant completed the WPT, and computerized versions of the BFI and PANAS. As a cover story, each participant was told that the next section of the study required manual administration, and would be completed simultaneously with another participant (a confederate). As part of this task, the participant and the confederate were brought together at a table with the experimenter to complete three commercially available puzzles: "Tangled Nails," "Tangoes," and "Crazy Blocks." For each of these puzzles, it typically requires between 2 and 5 minutes to discover the correct solution. The confederate was already familiar with the puzzle solutions, and could modify his or her behavior to contrast with the true participant's performance.

In the "participant success" condition, the confederate did not complete the puzzles until after the participant had already done so. In the "participant failure" condition, the confederate completed the puzzles quickly, and always prior to the participant. In the neutral condition, there was no confederate. The use of puzzles instead of a written or computerized task allowed the progress of both the participant and the confederate to be readily apparent to both parties. At no time was any type of competition or social comparison explicitly indicated, and no explicit performance feedback was given. Upon completion of the puzzle session, the participant returned to the original computer workstation, and was again asked to complete the PANAS, followed by the delay-discounting task. Participants were fully debriefed at the end of the experiment.

RESULTS

The PANAS was characterized by high alpha reliability before

(PA = .88, NA = .84) and after (PA = .93, NA = .89) the mood manipulation. Similar alpha reliabilities were obtained when independently examining the postmanipulation affect scores in the positive (PA = .94, NA = .83), negative (PA = .92, NA = .85), and neutral (PA = .88, NA = .95) conditions. No baseline differences were observed between the three groups for either positive, $F(2, 134) = 1.46, p = .24$, or negative affect, $F(2, 134) = 0.09$, $p = .91$. Postmanipulation differences, however, were observed across groups for positive affect, $F(2, 134) = 3.02, p < .05$, and negative affect, $F(2, 134) = 3.78$, $p < .05$. As a manipulation check, paired sample t tests were used to confirm the emotional consequences of the success and failure conditions. After the puzzle task, participants in the success condition were characterized by increased positive affect ($M_1 = 2.23, M_2 = 2.59$), $t(45) = 2.96$, $p < .01, d = 0.40$, with no significant change in negative affect, whereas participants in the failure condition were characterized by increased negative affect ($M_1 = 1.44, M_2 = 1.79$), $t(49) = 4.11$, $p < .01, d = 0.55$, and decreased positive affect ($M_1 = 2.47, M_2 = 2.23$), $t(49) = -2.59, p < .05, d = 0.28$. No significant changes in positive or negative affect were observed in the neutral condition. As situationally induced affect (rather than dispositional levels of affect) was the variable of interest, PANAS difference scores (Time 2 minus Time 1) were utilized in subsequent analyses.

Multiple regression analyses were employed to examine whether Extraversion interacted with positive affect to predict

discounting behavior across the entire sample. As in previous research, discounting rates were smaller when using the large reward (mean $k = 0.0091, SD = 0.0501$) compared to the small reward (mean $k = 0.0415, SD = 0.1534$). Separate regressions were therefore employed to predict the discounting of small and large rewards, as well as overall discounting rates. Variables entered in the model were Extraversion, WPT performance, difference scores for positive and negative affect (postmanipulation minus premanipulation values), and the Extraversion by affect interaction terms. Table 1 displays the beta weights and significance values for all three regression analyses.

As found in previous studies, delay discounting was significantly predicted by Extraversion and cognitive ability. While no main effects were observed for situationally induced changes in positive or negative affect, Extraversion and induced positive affect interacted significantly in predicting discounting behavior. Both the main effects and the interaction term were stronger predictors in the large compared to the small reward condition. Probing the interaction for the overall discounting rate confirmed

that Extraversion became a stronger predictor of discounting rates as levels of induced positive mood increased: For $Z = -1, \beta = -.20$, $p = .26$; for $Z = 0, \beta = .18, p < .05$; for $Z = 1, \beta = .56, p < .001$ (see Figure 1). In contrast, negative affect did not interact with Extraversion in predicting discounting behavior. Controlling for gender made no significant difference to the observed results, although the sample was biased somewhat toward female participants.

DISCUSSION

As in previous studies, preferences for immediate gratification were positively associated with Extraversion and negatively associated with cognitive ability. Individual differences in Extraversion are thought to reflect the dispositional strength of "hot" incentive motivation systems, and differences in cognitive ability appear to reflect the strength of the "cool" cognitive-control networks involved in the pursuit of long-term goals. While measures of personality and cognitive ability reflect the dispositional strength of these networks, the present findings suggest that situational inductions

Table 1

Standardized Regression Weights for Predicting Delay-Discounting Rates

	Small reward ($20)	Large reward ($1000)	Overall
Positive affect	.04	.04	−.02
Negative affect	−.03	.07	.06
Cognitive ability	−.17*	−.26*	−.24*
Extraversion	.17*	.19*	.18*
E × PA	.18*	.38*	.36*
E × NA	.05	.12	.12

* Significant at $p < .05$. E = extraversion; PA = positive affect; NA = negative affect

What does p < .05 indicate (Chapter 2)?

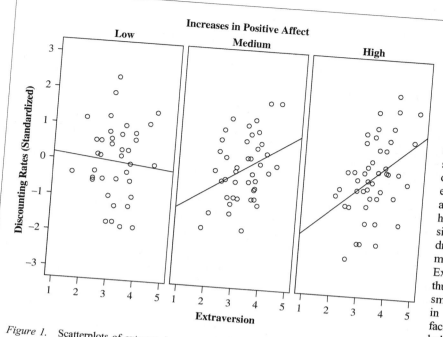

Increases in Positive Affect

Figure 1. Scatterplots of extraversion and standardized delay discounting rates. The three panels reflect a tertiary split of the sample based on increases in positive affect as a result of the mood manipulation.

of positive affect can also influence discounting behavior. In particular, induced positive affect interacted with Extraversion to predict a preference for immediate rewards. Previous research has suggested that discounting rates increase when "hot" motivational systems are situationally activated (Metcalfe & Mischel, 1999; Wilson & Daly, 2003), and the current results suggest that this affective influence is most pronounced for individuals with high levels of Extraversion.

Neuropsychologically, this interaction appears to be due to the increased sensitivity of extraverted individuals to the release of dopamine in response to reward cues (Cohen et al., 2005; Depue & Collins, 1999; Wacker et al., 2006). Positive affect is associated with an increased release of dopamine in the ventral striatum (Burgdorf & Panksepp, 2006). When extraverted individuals experience high levels of positive affect, the

increased dopaminergic response to potential rewards appears to tilt decision-making processes even further toward a preference for immediate gratification. This finding is in keeping with neuropsychological models of inter-temporal choice (McClure et al., 2004). In contrast, levels of negative affect did not influence the discounting rates of extraverts. It is worth noting that while the current study examined only general positive affect, it is possible that greater differentiation could be observed when looking at specific positive emotions. However, models of discounting behavior would predict that any approach-related emotional activity would have a similar effect.

It is worth noting that while positive mood inductions interacted with Extraversion in predicting discounting rates, there was no main effect for positive mood. In light of previous research linking states of "hot" emotional arousal to increased impulsivity (e.g.,

Metcalfe & Mischel, 1999), the lack of main effect for positive emotion in the current study might be due to the use of a relatively mild mood manipulation. This manipulation appears to have been sufficient to alter the decision making of extraverted individuals, who already have higher levels of dispositional positive affect driving their "hot" motivational systems. Extraverted individuals thus appeared to require smaller increases in positive mood to facilitate the observed behavioral consequences. It is possible that less extraverted individuals would require a stronger mood manipulation to produce the same behavioral effects (cf. Larsen & Ketelaar, 1989).

Positive affect is generally considered to be highly desirable. Indeed, high levels of positive affect have been associated with increased creativity (Isen, Daubman, & Nowicki, 1987), successful life outcomes (Lyubomirsky, King, & Diener, 2005), and personal growth and flourishing (Fredrickson, 2004). However, the current findings suggest that among extraverted individuals, who already have higher dispositional levels of positive affect, situational inductions of positive mood can bias decision making toward immediate rewards and away from long-term investments. From an evolutionary perspective, an increased focus on immediate rewards during periods of positive affect is a strategy for taking advantage of spontaneous opportunities as they arise (Wilson & Daly, 2004). Indeed, high levels

In Chapter 14, you will learn more about dispositional and situational attribution.

of Extraversion have been linked with strategies that promote the immediate pursuit of available rewards over more cautious and deliberative approaches (Nettle, 2005). Although such impulsivity is designed to maximize immediate rewards, it can also have a number of negative long-term consequences, as reviewed earlier. The current results indicate that high levels of positive affect can serve to increase this reward-focused impulsivity among extraverted individuals.

REFERENCES

Ariely, D., & Loewenstein, G. (2006). The heat of the moment: The effect of sexual arousal on sexual decision making. *Journal of Behavioral Decision Making, 19*, 87–98.

Bickel, W., & Marsch, L. (2001). Toward a behavioral economic understanding of drug dependence: Delay discounting processes. *Addiction, 96*, 73–86.

Burgdorf, J., & Panksepp, J. (2006). The neurobiology of positive emotions. *Neuroscience and Biobehavioral Reviews, 30*, 173–187.

Cohen, M., Young, J., Baek, J., Kessler, C., & Ranganath, C. (2005). Individual differences in extraversion and dopamine genetics predict neural reward responses. *Cognitive Brain Research, 25*, 851–861.

Depue, R. A., & Collins, P. F. (1999). Neurobiology of the structure of personality: Dopamine, facilitation of incentive motivation, and extraversion. *Behavioral and Brain Sciences, 22*, 491–517.

Fredrickson, B. (2004). The broaden-and-build theory of positive emotions. *Philosophical Transactions of the Royal Society B: Biological Sciences, 359*, 1367–1378.

Hinson, J., Jameson, T., & Whitney, P. (2003). Impulsive decision making and working memory. *Journal of Experimental Psychology Learning, Memory, and Cognition, 29*, 298–306.

Hirsh, J. B., Morisano, D., & Peterson, J. B. (2008). Delay discounting: Interactions between personality and cognitive ability. *Journal of Research in Personality, 42*, 1646–1650.

Hyman, S., & Malenka, R. (2001). Addiction and the brain: The neurobiology of compulsion and its persistence. *Nature Reviews Neuroscience, 2*, 695–703.

Isen, A., Daubman, K., & Nowicki, G. (1987). Positive affect facilitates creative problem solving. *Journal of Personality and Social Psychology, 52*, 1122–1131.

John, O. P., & Srivastava, S. (1999). The Big Five Trait Taxonomy: History, measurement, and theoretical perspectives. In L. A. Pervin & O. P. John (Eds.), *Handbook of personality: Theory and research* (pp. 102–138). New York: Guilford Press.

Johnson, M., & Bickel, W. (2002). Within-subject comparison of real and hypothetical money rewards in delay discounting. *Journal of the Experimental Analysis of Behavior, 77*, 129–146.

Kirby, K., Petry, N., & Bickel, W. (1999). Heroin addicts have higher discount rates for delayed rewards than non-drug-using controls. *Journal of Experimental Psychology: General, 128*, 78–87.

Kirby, K., Winston, G., & Santiesteban, M. (2005). Impatience and grades: Delay-discount rates correlate negatively with college GPA. *Learning and Individual Differences, 15*, 213–222.

Lagorio, C., & Madden, G. (2005). Delay discounting of real and hypothetical rewards III: Steady-state assessments, forced-choice trials, and all real rewards. *Behavioural Processes, 69*, 173–187.

Larsen, R., & Ketelaar, T. (1989). Extraversion, neuroticism and susceptibility to positive and negative mood induction procedures. *Personality and Individual Differences, 10*, 1221–1228.

Lucas, R., Diener, E., Grob, A., Suh, E., & Shao, L. (2000). Cross-cultural evidence for the fundamental features of extraversion. *Journal of Personality and Social Psychology, 79*, 452–463.

Lyubomirsky, S., King, L., & Diener, E. (2005). The benefits of frequent positive affect: Does happiness lead to success? *Psychological Bulletin, 131*, 803–855.

Madden, G., Begotka, A., Raiff, B., & Kastern, L. (2003). Delay discounting of real and hypothetical rewards. *Experimental and Clinical Psychopharmacology, 11*, 139–145.

Madden, G., Raiff, B., Lagorio, C., Begotka, A., Mueller, A., Hehli, D., & Wegener, A. (2004). Delay discounting of potentially real and hypothetical rewards: II. Between-and within-subject comparisons. *Experimental and Clinical Psychopharmacology, 12*, 251–261.

McClure, S., Laibson, D., Loewenstein, G., & Cohen, J. (2004). Separate neural systems value immediate and delayed monetary rewards. *Science, 306*, 503–507.

McKelvie, S. J. (1989). The Wonderlic Personnel Test: Reliability and validity in an academic setting. *Psychological Reports, 65*, 161–162.

Metcalfe, J., & Mischel, W. (1999). A hot/cool-system analysis of delay of gratification: Dynamics of willpower. *Psychological Review, 106*, 3–19.

Mischel, W., Shoda, Y., & Rodriguez, M. (1989). Delay of gratification in children. *Science, 244*, 933–938.

Nettle, D. (2005). An evolutionary approach to the extraversion continuum. *Evolution and Human Behavior, 26*, 363–373.

Ostaszewski, P. (1996). The relation between temperament and rate of temporal discounting. *European Journal of Personality, 10*, 161–172.

Schultz, W. (2002). Getting formal with dopamine and reward. *Neuron, 36*, 241–263.

Shamosh, N., DeYoung, C., Green, A., Reis, D., Johnson, M., Conway, A., et al. (2008). Individual differences in delay discounting: Relation to intelligence, working memory, and anterior prefrontal cortex. *Psychological Science, 19*, 904–911.

Shamosh, N., & Gray, J. (2007). Delay discounting and intelligence: A meta-analysis. *Intelligence, 36*, 289–305.

Wacker, J., Chavanon, M., & Stemmler, G. (2006). Investigating the dopaminergic basis of extraversion in humans: A multilevel approach. *Journal of Personality and Social Psychology, 91*, 171.

Watson, D., Clark, L., & Tellegen, A. (1988). Development and validation of brief measures of positive and negative affect: The PANAS scales. *Journal of Personality and Social Psychology, 54*, 1063–1070.

Wilson, M., & Daly, M. (2004). Do pretty women inspire men to discount the future? *Proceedings of the Royal Society of London, Series B: Biological Sciences, 271*, 177–179.

Wonderlic, E. F. (1983). *Wonderlic Personnel Test manual*. Northfield, IL: E. F. Wonderlic & Associates.

Username | Password | **Sign in**

■ Remember me | Forgot it?

Follow your interests

Instant updates from your friends, industry experts, favorite
celebrities, and what's happening around the world.

New to Twitter? Join today!

Full name

Email

Password

Sign up

Search Twitter 🔍

SOCIAL
PSYCHOLOGY

Facebook

goes public! And with that announcement Facebook's crown as the king of social media has been secured—it is the most popular social networking site in the world. It connects people around the world and the neighbours who live next to each other. With the average user spending over 400 minutes on Facebook each month, we are led to ask, "What is the appeal"? Why are so many of us driven to log on to Facebook each morning to read the statuses of our friends and families and to post events, from the grand to the mundane, for everyone to read? What does online social networking give us that keeps us coming back for more? Perhaps online social networking provides the best of both worlds for us—we can be connected to others yet still be alone. Whether it's Facebook, Twitter, or LinkedIn, we provide glimpses into our hopes, dreams, fears, and behaviours to others, who do the same in return. Humans are social beings, and we actively seek

out interactions with others and in so doing we learn about them and ourselves.

Researchers have found that social networking sites are extremely popular for peer socialization (e.g., Luo, 2010), the establishment of support networks (e.g., Horvath, 2012), and increased business success (e.g., Indrupati & Henari, 2012). In fact, online social networking played a pivotal role in the Egyptian revolution, also known as the "Arab Spring," that took place in 2011 (Mansour, 2012). Without a doubt, social networking has changed human interaction and is an extremely powerful force shaping world, societal, and individual events.

But, there are dangers associated with social networking sites. These include ever-changing privacy policies, cyberbullying and harassment, and the unrecognized consequences of our daily updates and posted pictures. Like the schoolyard and the business office, online social networks are also prone to elitism, cliques, and popularity scores. How many Facebook friends do you have? How many blog readers? How many Twitter followers? Will your Klout score get you hired? The domain may have changed, but many of the same issues with social interactions still remain.

<<< Online social networking has forever changed human interaction. What benefits does this bring to social engagement and a feeling of belonging? What concerns should we have about the prevalence of this type of social interaction?

CHAPTER **14**

Foundations of Social Psychology

Human beings may be individuals, but we are all individuals within a group. **Social psychologists** study how the thoughts, emotions, and behaviour of individuals influence and are influenced by interactions between people. Our interactions with others (and sometimes with ourselves) depend to a great extent on our **social perception,** the process through which we understand and categorize the behaviour of others.

ATTRIBUTION THEORY

Psychologist Fritz Heider would not be surprised by our desire to connect with others through social networking. He believed that we are all "naive scientists," naturally interested in analyzing other people's personalities and attitudes. According to Heider's (1958) **attribution theory**, we understand the behaviour of others by attributing their behaviour either to their internal dispositions or their external situations.

When you attribute a person's behaviour to his or her personality or characteristics, you are making a **dispositional attribution.** Alternatively, when you attribute behaviour to external factors such as the person's situation or environment, you're making a **situational attribution.**

Often, we don't have enough information about people to determine why they act the way they do. Since we can't read other people's minds, we try to compensate by observing their behaviour in a variety of situations and environments. Our observations are based on three characteristics: the behaviour's distinctiveness (Is the behaviour specific to a situation?), its consistency (Does the person usually behave this way?), and consensus (Do other people behave similarly in similar situations?). We can then use our observations to draw conclusions about why people act the way they do. This process of attribution is known as the **covariation principle** (Kelley, 1967).

The Fundamental Attribution Error

Both personal characteristics and external factors play an important role in determining our actions, but it turns out that most people tend to attribute behaviour to character rather than the situation. Social psychologist Lee Ross (1977) has dubbed this phenomenon the **fundamental attribution error (FAE).** Amazingly, studies have shown that even when people know that a situation has actually caused a certain behaviour, they still make a dispositional attribution. For example, participants who were told that an experiment collaborator had been instructed to behave coldly or warmly toward them still persisted in believing that the behaviour reflected the collaborator's real personality (Napolitan & Goethals, 1979). Factors such as culture and religion play a role in how we explain the behaviours of others. For example, a 2012 study examined whether Catholics and Protestants differed in their attribution styles. Yexin Li and colleagues (2012) found that Protestants made more dispositional attributes compared to Catholics. The authors discussed that this difference may be the result of the increased focus on the soul emphasized in Protestantism.

Despite the prevalence of the fundamental attribution theory, we can change the way we think of others. Canadian researcher Kerry Kawakami and her colleagues (Stewart, Latu, Kawakami, & Myers, 2010) found that participants could be trained to focus on situational attributes instead of dispositional attributes when thinking about negative racial stereotypes. In the study, white participants received **Situational Attribution Training** that taught them to choose situational over dispositional explanations for negative stereotyped behaviours commonly associated with black men. Kawakami and colleagues found that these participants showed reduced racial stereotyping compared to the control group who did not receive the Situational Attribution Training. It is important to realize that the attributions we make about other people can have significant consequences for our own behaviour: If your friend stands you up at the movie theatre, you might attribute her behaviour to thoughtlessness or cruelty and call her to leave a nasty message, not realizing that she's been delayed because of a parent's illness.

Bias in Attribution

Since we don't have a lot of information to go on when we make conclusions about other people, we take shortcuts by using our prior knowledge, personal beliefs, and biases to make assumptions about strangers. We all

Social psychologist is a psychologist who studies how the thoughts, emotions, and behaviour of individuals influence and are influenced by interactions between people.

Social perception is the process through which a person understands and categorizes the behaviour of others.

Attribution theory states that a person understands other people by attributing their behaviour either to their internal dispositions or their external situations.

Dispositional attribution is an attribution based on a person's personality or characteristics.

Situational attribution is an attribution based on a person's situation or environment.

Covariation principle is a process of attribution in which behaviour is observed based on three characteristics: the behaviour's distinctiveness, its consistency, and consensus.

Fundamental attribution error (FAE) is a phenomenon in which people make an attribution based on character, even when they know that the behaviour is situational.

Situational Attribution Training is a new technique designed to reduce our attribution biases by teaching us to focus on situational rather than dispositional explanations for the behaviours of others.

∧ Who is most likely to be a **banker?** An **engineer?**
∧ An **athlete?** Racial stereotyping can be **decreased**
∧ through Situational Attribution Training. Is this type of training a **good idea?**

have **pre-existing schemata**, sets of ideas or beliefs about others that lead us to perceive people in a way that conforms to our expectations. For example, someone who believes that athletes are not as intelligent as non-athletes won't perceive the school's best hockey player as an academic superstar, even though that player may graduate with honours and later receive a doctorate in astrophysics.

Although we know intellectually that appearances can be deceiving, we often subconsciously base our opinions about people on their physical appearance. An **attractiveness bias** leads us to rate physically attractive people as more intelligent, competent, sociable, and sensitive than their less-attractive counterparts (Eagly, Ashmore, Makhijani, & Kennedy, 1991; Feingold, 1992; Hatfield & Sprecher, 1986; Rohner & Rasmussen, 2012; Sanderson, 2012). In the literature this is referred to as the "what is beautiful is good" heuristic. This positive view of attractive individuals is evident in social gatherings, job interviews, and even the court system. Toronto researchers (Esses & Webster, 2006) report that attractive and average-looking sexual offenders are seen as less likely to reoffend compared to unattractive sexual offenders. Further, Halifax researcher Marc Patry (2008) found that mock jurors were less likely to find an attractive-looking defendant guilty compared to a plain-looking defendant, if there was no jury deliberation. The attractiveness bias also has implications for financial success with the more attractive individuals having higher incomes and less financial strain (Judge, Hurst, & Simon, 2009).

We even see the attractiveness bias in our romantic relationships. Perhaps it's no surprise that we prefer our romantic partners to be attractive (e.g., Eastwick, Eagly, Finkel, & Johnson, 2011), even in adolescence (Ha, Overbeek, & Engels, 2010). But, it may surprise you to find out that we actually judge our romantic partners as being more attractive than objective ratings (Barelds, Dijkstra, Koudenberg, & Swami, 2011). Also, our perception of our own attractiveness is affected by the attractiveness of those who are romantically interested in us. This effect is especially seen in men, who rated their attractiveness lower when an unattractive, compared to attractive, individual expressed interest in them.

The attractiveness bias does not always favour the more attractive individuals. For example, researchers who study the "beauty is beastly" effect (e.g., Braun, Peus, & Frey, 2012; Heilman & Stopeck, 1985; Shahani-Denning, Dudhat, Tevet, & Andreoli, 2010) have found that attractiveness can have a negative effect on the perception of women's abilities, whereas attractive men are judged quite positively. This effect is especially prominent in stereotypical male professions and political leadership.

CONSTRUCTING SOCIAL REALITY

We may make dispositional attributions when we judge other people's behaviour, but when it comes to judging our own behaviour, we tend to be a little kinder: We often show a **self-serving bias** that causes us to attribute our failures to external events and our successes to our personal characteristics and skills (Gilovich, 1991). When we get into a car accident or get rejected from a team, we keep our self-esteem intact by placing the blame on the other drivers on the road or the obviously inept coach. This self-serving bias can be seen in assessments about job performance (e.g., Libby & Rennenkamp, 2012), ethical decision making (Dalton & Ortegren, 2011), and overall skill and ability level (Ludwig & Nafzinger, 2011).

Pre-existing schema is a set of ideas or beliefs about others that leads a person to perceive others in a way that conforms to that person's expectations.

Attractiveness bias is the tendency for a person to rate physically attractive people as more intelligent, competent, sociable, and sensitive than their less-attractive counterparts.

Self-serving bias is the tendency for a person to attribute his or her failures to external events and his or her successes to personal characteristics and skills.

Pygmalion effect is the tendency for people to behave in accordance with others' expectations.

Self-fulfilling prophecy is a belief that causes itself to become true.

Culture is one factor that affects our self-serving bias. Canadian researchers (Higgins & Bhatt, 2001) compared the self-serving biases found among undergraduate students in Canada (an individualistic culture) and India (a collectivist culture). They report that the Indian participants gave more situational explanations for life events and had a stronger self-serving bias compared to Canadian participants.

The self-serving bias can also distort our perceptions of responsibility—"it's not my fault." Recent research suggests that individuals attribute their racial biases to cultural socialization rather than to themselves (Uhlmann & Nosek, 2012).

In George Bernard Shaw's play *Pygmalion* (and the musical version, *My Fair Lady*), arrogant linguist Professor Henry Higgins demonstrates that he can pass a London flower girl off as an aristocrat simply by changing the way she speaks. The **Pygmalion effect**, named after Shaw's play, describes people's tendency to behave in accordance with others' expectations: If you expect someone to be an aristocrat, she will behave in an aristocratic manner. The Pygmalion effect is one type of **self-fulfilling prophecy**, or a belief that causes itself to become true.

Social psychologists have noticed that these beliefs can be particularly powerful in the classroom and in business (e.g., Inamori, Farhad, & Kakabadse, 2012;

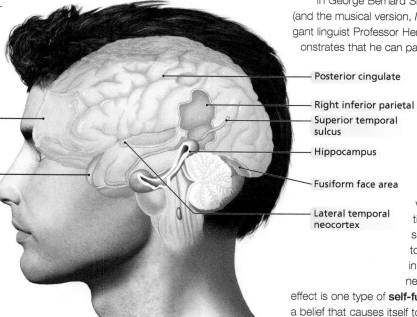

∧ ∧ ∧ **Several parts of the brain are active during the face-recognition process.**

Frontopolar cortex

Temporal pole

Posterior cingulate

Right inferior parietal

Superior temporal sulcus

Hippocampus

Fusiform face area

Lateral temporal neocortex

Rosenthal, 1974). Using a data set of 11 000 secondary school students who were monitored for five years, Hester de Boer and colleagues (2010) examined the effect of teacher expectation on student performance and found that teacher expectation had long-lasting effects on student academic performance. This result is one example of **behavioural expectation confirmation** (Snyder, 1984), a phenomenon that enables us to influence other people to behave in accordance with our expectations.

Social Cognition

Research in **social cognition** focuses on the underlying processes, such as attention and memory, that make social behaviour possible. As we expand our knowledge about the biology of the brain, social cognitive neuroscience has become increasingly important as a way to understand these processes. Biological structures and processes in the brain help us navigate our social environment, whether we're

Social pressure has negative connotations, but can you think of any ways in which social pressure might be a positive influence?

recognizing a friend's face in a crowd, making determinations about a person's age or race, or feeling empathy for others.

PERCEPTION OF SOCIAL CUES: FACIAL RECOGNITION

When you meet a person on the street, you can easily recognize that person as a friend or stranger. Just by looking at that person's face, you can probably tell what type of mood she's in and how she might feel about you. Face recognition forms an integral part of our social interactions. While debate in neuroscience rages about localized and generalized brain function, recent studies have shown that the **fusiform face area,** an area on the underside of the brain where the occipital lobe meets the temporal lobe, plays an essential role in face recognition (e.g., Axelrod & Yovel, 2011; Kanwisher, McDermott, & Chun, 1997; Silverstein et al., 2010). When we recognize a face, the fusiform face area becomes active and sends messages to the lateral temporal neocortex, where neurons specifically linked to face recognition fire (Gross & Sergent, 1992; Susac, Ilmoniemi, Ranken, & Supek, 2011). The temporal pole at the back of the temporal lobe connects the visual information to emotional association (Olson, Plotzker, & Ezzyat, 2007; Pujol et al., 2009). Finally, the hippocampus retrieves memories necessary for recognition (Rissman, Gazzaley, & D'Esposito, 2008). These reciprocal exchanges of information between different areas of the brain happen so quickly that we can instantly distinguish a familiar face from an unfamiliar one. People with damage to the ventral region of the temporal lobe have difficulty processing information about facial features. This condition, known as **prosopagnosia,** prevents people from recognizing faces; however, these people can usually recognize facial expressions of emotion. Often, people with prosopagnosia are able to identify their loved ones using information from their voices or the way that they walk and move.

Have you ever picked up a friend's belly laugh or favourite figure of speech without realizing what you were doing? You weren't just being a copycat: When we mimic others, we are better able to understand what those others are feeling and thinking.

SOCIAL CATEGORIZATION

We often refer to social categories such as age, race, and gender, to make inferences about the people we meet. In fact, our brains are amazingly speedy when it comes to processing information about social categories: Researchers have measured electrophysiological responses in the brain and found that when we view faces of people of different ages and genders, our brains respond to these changing social categories in as little as 145 milliseconds (Mouchetant-Rostaing & Giard, 2003). While it might take us a while to determine someone's personal qualities (such as compassion, intelligence, or aggression) from his or her facial features, it usually doesn't take us long at all to categorize that person by age, race, and gender. In fact, we process faces that are similar to ours, in terms of race, age, and gender, differently than we process faces that are different from ours.

Can we learn about people's racial biases by observing the way they process faces that are different from their own? Yes. For over a decade researchers have been able to assess unconscious racial biases using face-recognition experiments. For example, researchers have shown that white participants displayed unconscious racial bases when asked to look at unfamiliar African American faces (Phelps et al., 2000; Richeson et al., 2003). When they looked at unfamiliar male African American faces, those participants who associated African American faces with negative traits also showed a stronger startle eye-blink response and greater amygdala activity than other participants did (Phelps et al., 2000). Since both amygdala activity and startle eye-blink response indicate fear, unfamiliar male African American faces probably evoked fear in these experiment participants. However, these results diverged completely from the participants' conscious or professed positive beliefs about African Americans, suggesting that it's possible for our biological responses to people to be at odds with our conscious, socially controlled responses (Richeson et al., 2003). This other-race face processing seems to begin in infancy (Hayden, Bhatt, Zieber, & Kangas, 2009).

MENTALIZING

To empathize with others, neurologically speaking, we must walk a mile in their shoes. Experiencing empathy means feeling for others, understanding their position, and wanting to help them. It involves **mentalizing,** or understanding that our behaviour and that of others reflects our mental states: our thoughts, beliefs, and feelings.

The brain assists us in this type of social cognition in several different ways. For example, mirror neurons in the brain fire both when we perform an action and when we watch others performing that same action, helping us relate our actions and intentions to those of others (Ferrari, Rozzi, & Fogassi, 2005). We also have

>>> **Edmonton company Empire Avenue measures a person's social worth by tracking activity on sites like Facebook and Twitter. Is this an accurate way to measure someone's social worth?**

the mental flexibility to put ourselves in someone else's position and attempt to see things from his or her perspective. In fact, mirror neurons may provide a built-in mechanism for the benefit of support groups, social support, and group psychotherapy (Schermer, 2010).

Social Influence

A presidential candidate asks for your vote; an animated gecko on television wants you to buy his company's car insurance; you want a friend to come out with you after work although she feels exhausted—every day we encounter and exert forms of **social influence,** or behavioural control. For example, a study examined the role of social influence in impaired driving among adults in Alberta. The data from 1211 participants indicated that social influence was a significant factor in whether someone drove while intoxicated (Nurullah, 2009). Closely related

> " It appears that other people have a certain amount of influence on our own emotional states, to the extent that catching a glimpse of a sad-looking person could put a slight frown on your face. "

to the concept of social influence is **social pressure,** the real or imagined psychological forces that others exert over us through their example, judgments, and demands. Social pressure comes in too many forms to count, but when you face it, it can be hard to resist.

HEDONIC, APPROVAL, AND ACCURACY MOTIVES

"Call now!" the TV commercial begs you. "We'll even throw in an extra set of steak knives!" This tantalizing bargain is an example of one type of social influence called a **hedonic motive,** a pleasurable incentive or reward for acting in a certain way. Not all hedonic motives are as exciting as free steak knives, however: We can also be hedonically motivated by the threat of pain if we fail to act a certain way. (The traffic fine that doubles if you fail to pay it by a specific date is one such example.)

The **approval motive,** or the desire to be accepted by our peers, can also convince us to take action. Being well liked by others helps us survive. Research has found that social acceptance actually boosts our health, while isolation and loneliness can make us more vulnerable to illness (Devine & Dawson, 2010; Oberle, Schonert-Reichl, & Thomson, 2010; Pressman et al., 2005).

Since most of us don't enjoy being wrong, the **accuracy motive,** or our desire to be correct or accurate, can have a strong pull on our behaviour. If you're in a group of people who are discussing their shared belief that the government should support the development of sustainable, renewable energy, you might listen to their opinions and decide to jump on the renewable-energy bandwagon because you've been persuaded that their position is the correct one.

CONTAGIOUS BEHAVIOUR

As Elvis and Cher impersonators in Las Vegas know, human beings cannot help imitating each other. Even in North America, where individuality and independence are strong cultural values, there's a streak of imitation: When Kate Middleton married Prince William, her wedding dress and the dress her sister, Pippa, wore became the hottest new styles for brides-to-be and their bridesmaids. But

imitation isn't always a conscious choice. Take, for example, the **chameleon effect,** our unconscious mimicry of other people's expressions, behaviours, and voice tones (Chartrand & Bargh, 1999; Dalton, Chartrand, & Finkel, 2010). Have you ever picked up a friend's belly laugh or favourite figure of speech without realizing what you were doing? You weren't just being a copycat: When we mimic others, we are better able to understand what those others are feeling and thinking.

If you've ever met someone with "infectious enthusiasm," you know that emotions, like behaviours, can be contagious. Emotional contagion happens quickly and unconsciously. In fact, when researchers ran a study in which they flashed stimuli of emotional faces in front of participants, they discovered that although the participants were not consciously aware that they had seen facial expressions, the participants' faces took on the same expressions that they had unconsciously processed from the images (Dimberg, Thunberg, & Elmehed,

2000). It appears that other people have a certain amount of influence on our own emotional states, to the extent that catching a glimpse of a sad-looking person could put a slight frown on your face.

CONFORMITY

While imitation may be the sincerest form of flattery, **conformity** requires adjusting our behaviour or thinking to conform to a group standard. We can feel the pressure to conform

> When Asch asked experiment participants to match the length of a stimulus line with the length of one of three other lines, they had no problem performing this matching task correctly. When they were asked to perform the same task in a group with experiment confederates who kept offering the wrong answer, however, participants changed their answers to conform with those of the group one-third of the time.

in a wide variety of situations, but certain conditions facilitate conformity.

Whenever people conform by buying the latest style of jeans, joining a religious community, or ostracizing an outsider, social influence is at work. **Normative social influence,** influence that draws on our desire for others' approval and our longing to be part of a group, can cause us to conform to the norms, or social expectations about attitudes and behaviours, that a group values. **Informational social influence,** influence exerted by information that

Conditions that

feelings of **incompetence** or **insecurity**

a **group** of **at least three people**

a **unanimous** group **without dissenters**

being among **admired** people

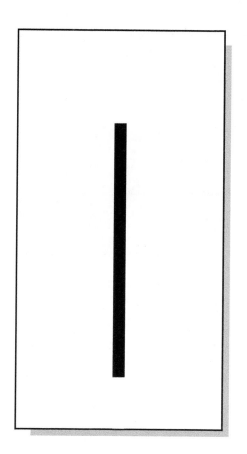

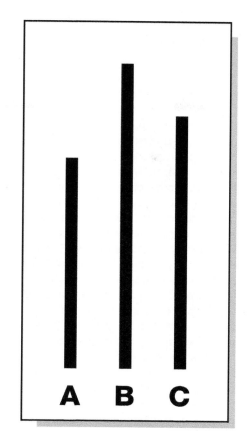

A B C

of the group one-third of the time. Both normative and informational social influence may have played a role in these results: Normative social influence may have caused participants to change their answers to match the group's answers, and informational social influence may have made the participants think that their original perceptions were factually incorrect. After all, if 10 other people say two lines are the same and you are the only one who thinks the lines are different, it seems very likely that you've missed something that everyone else has seen. (For more information about Asch's experiment, see Chapter 2).

The Bystander Effect

In April 2010, a 79-year-old man was mugged on the Toronto subway and no one helped. In September 2010, a 12-year-old Alberta girl was sexually assaulted outside her school while a dozen of her schoolmates looked on—but no one called for help. In October 2011, Canadian teenager Jamie Hubley committed suicide after years of being bullied because he was openly gay. How could someone just watch while others are victimized and not help in some way? The answer lies in the bystander effect. According to the **bystander effect,**

others give us, can shed new light on the objective nature of an event or situation. Normative social influence appeals to the approval motive and our desire to be liked, while informational social influence appeals to the accuracy motive and our desire to obtain correct information.

Asch's Conformity Studies

Renowned social psychologist Solomon Asch (1940, 1956) showed how **suggestibility,** or

susceptibility to the opinions of others, can cause people to conform. When Asch asked experiment participants to match the length of a stimulus line with the length of one of three other lines, they had no problem performing this matching task correctly. When they were asked to perform the same task in a group with experiment confederates who kept offering the wrong answer, however, participants changed their answers to conform with those

Influence Conformity

lack of a prior commitment to a particular response

a public setting

a culture that encourages adherence to social standards

the need to make difficult decisions of high personal relevance

Reference group consists of those people to whom a person feels affiliated.

Total situation is a situation in which people are isolated from alternative viewpoints and given strict rewards and punishments from leaders.

Compliance is a change in a person's behaviour that occurs in response to a direct request.

Cognitive dissonance is a disconnect between a person's internal attitudes and his or her external behaviour.

Lowball technique encourages compliance by offering an attractive deal, only to change the terms of the deal later.

Bait-and-switch technique encourages people to comply with an attractive offer but substitutes that offer with a less-attractive option once the person has agreed.

Foot-in-the-door technique involves asking people to comply with a small request and then making a much larger request, to raise funds.

Shared identity is a person's feeling that he or she is similar to other people in thought, feeling, and behaviour.

Norm of reciprocity is a socialized norm that involves a person's tendency to desire to return favours.

Door-in-the-face technique is a procedure for gaining compliance that involves making a large request and then, when that request is refused, making a smaller request that seems reasonable in comparison.

OBEDIENCE
Stanley Milgram and Obedience to Authority

The genocides in Cambodia, Bosnia, Rwanda, and Darfur have joined the Holocaust in Nazi Germany as testaments to the fact that ordinary human beings can perform extraordinarily inhuman acts. To understand how and why people obey immoral and unethical commands, Stanley Milgram (1963, 1974) conducted experiments that became some of the most famous and infamous in social psychology. In 20 experiments, Milgram cast 1000 people as "teachers" and instructed them to deliver an electric shock to learners for every wrong answer. The "learners," actually experiment confederates, voiced discomfort, pain, and even agony, but most of the "teachers" continued delivering progressively stronger shocks, despite having said explicitly that they would stop as soon as the learner experienced any discomfort. Even after the "learner's" voice became silent, suggesting that he had been severely injured by the shocks, the experimenter ordered participants to continue administering shocks, and although many of the participants seemed very uncomfortable about it, a surprisingly large number of them dutifully followed orders. In fact, 65% of the participants showed total obedience by administering "lethal" shocks at the maximum level of 450 volts.

What allowed typical college students to behave like sadistic torturers? Milgram

> We don't always behave the way others would like us to, but we make both small and large gestures of compliance all the time. Why are we so willing to change our behaviours because of other people's requests?

determined that certain conditions encouraged participants to follow commands. For example, we generally follow the norm of obeying legitimate authority figures such as the university psychologists who directed the experiment. The experimenter seemed self-assured and accepted responsibility for the outcome of the experiment, making participants feel less responsible for their actions. The experimenter also asked the participants to increase the shocks incrementally; once participants had agreed to give the "learner" a shock of 60 volts, it became more difficult for them to refuse to administer a 70-volt shock. Participants were placed in a separate room from the "learner," increasing their psychological distance from the repercussions of their actions, and participants had no alternative models of behaviour to follow—in other words, all they'd seen anyone do was comply with the experimenter's requests, so they didn't have a model for refusing to comply. Finally, demand characteristics, or the cues in the experimental setting that influenced participants' beliefs about their expected behaviour, most likely played a role in participants' decisions to obey authority.

Milgram noticed that certain conditions created the highest levels of obedience.

Strengths and Weaknesses of Conformity and Obedience Studies

Conformity and obedience studies like Asch's and Milgram's have given us valuable insight into humans' susceptibility to social influence and provided information about why we

in situations where someone requires help, the greater the number of bystanders present, the less likely any individual bystander is to help the person in need. Darley and Latané (1968) showed that people are more likely to intervene to help another person having an epileptic seizure when they believe they are the only person who can hear—and help—the seizing individual. People also look to their **reference group,** those with whom they feel affiliated, to gauge how to behave. If they see people behaving indifferently, they tend to do the same, but if even one person chooses to help, the others will also tend to follow. As in Nazi Germany, **total situations**— situations in which people are isolated from alternative viewpoints and given strict rewards and punishments from leaders—also prompt people to follow social norms closely.

Conditions that Influence Obedience

4 Participant does not have access to models of defiance.

3 Victim is depersonalized or kept at a distance.

5 An intermediary bystander is present.

2 Person giving orders is a legitimate authority figure supported by a prestigious institution.

6 Participant is affected by normative and informational influence.

1 Person giving orders is in physical proximity to the participant.

7 Participant's behaviour is an ingrained habit.

AC VOLTS

sometimes accept false beliefs or capitulate to cruelty. However, Milgram's experiments also raised a number of criticisms. Today, ethical concerns about lasting damage suffered by participants coerced to harm others would have prevented these studies from being conducted. (It's worth noting, however, that 84% of participants in Milgram's experiments felt glad to have taken part in the study, and only 2% regretted it (Milgram, 1964; Errera, 1972). Critics also question the degree to which experimental results explain real-world crimes. Perhaps participants' belief (warranted or not) that the experimenters would never allow them to severely harm others allowed the participants to follow instructions more easily (Orne & Holland, 1968), but people who genuinely and purposefully harm others hold no such belief. Although Milgram's results may be limited to the lab, his experiments offer us clues about how ordinary people can obey orders to commit genocide and mass murder.

COMPLIANCE

If you wanted your friend to turn down his obnoxiously loud stereo or cheer up about his favourite football team's poor performance, you would need to figure out how to get your friend to comply with your wishes. **Compliance** is a change in a person's behaviour that occurs in response to a direct request. We don't always behave the way others would like us to, but we make both small and large gestures of compliance all the time. Why are we so willing to change our behaviours because of other people's requests?

Cognitive Dissonance

Let's say you agreed to see a movie with friends even though you would rather stay home. This disconnect between your internal attitudes and your external behaviour is called **cognitive dissonance.** Social psychologist Leon Festinger (1957) coined the term, and he and others have shown that our desire to counteract cognitive dissonance can play a major role in the phenomenon of compliance: We often comply with requests in order to make our actions match our attitudes (or vice versa).

Festinger and his colleagues asked participants to undertake incredibly boring tasks such as putting spools into a tray and turning square pegs a quarter-turn at a time. The experimenter then asked each participant to

tell the next participant that the tasks were enjoyable, intriguing, and exciting. Half of the participants were promised $20 in exchange for telling this lie; the other participants were offered $1. Festinger and his fellow researchers discovered that, after the participants had lied to their peers and received their money, the participants who had received $1 rated the tasks they'd performed as significantly more interesting than did the participants who had received $20. Festinger used his theory of cognitive dissonance to explain these results: If you say something you don't believe, but you don't have sufficient justification (such as a $20 bill) for saying it, you're likely to change your beliefs in order to reduce the effect of cognitive dissonance (Festinger & Carlsmith, 1959).

A study examining academic dishonesty by Canadian post-secondary students showed that most students who cheated displaced

cognitive dissonance—that is, they knew it was wrong to cheat but did so anyway (Rozzet, Hage, & Chow, 2011). Interestingly, Canadian college students have been shown to have lower cognitive dissonance than their American counterparts, and older students tend to show less cognitive dissonance than younger students (Chow & Wood, 2001).

Motivations for Compliance

It's often all too easy to influence human behaviour, and people with a vested interest in our compliance have come up with several time-honoured methods for convincing people to act in certain ways. Credit card companies, for instance, often use the **lowball technique,** which encourages compliance by offering an attractive deal, only to change the terms of the deal later. You might agree to sign up for a credit card that offers no monthly fees through July, only to find out on August 1 that your monthly fees have skyrocketed. Since you've made a commitment to the credit card by that point, however, you're more likely to continue to use the card.

> It's often all too easy to influence human behaviour, and people with a vested interest in our compliance have come up with several time-honoured methods for convincing people to act in certain ways. Credit card companies, for instance, often use the lowball technique, which encourages compliance by offering an attractive deal, only to change the terms of the deal later.

Advertisers and politicians use the discomfort created by cognitive dissonance to get people to try a new product or vote for a ballot initiative. For example, the **bait-and-switch technique** encourages people to comply with an attractive offer but substitutes that offer with a less-attractive option once the person has agreed. During campaign season, a politician might promise not to raise taxes, but when she's in office, she may choose to keep taxes low only for people making a certain amount of money. To reduce cognitive dissonance, the people who complied with the politician's request for votes may convince themselves that the politician isn't breaking her promise.

Charities and public television stations that ask for small initial contributions and then follow up with larger and larger requests rely on the **foot-in-the-door technique,** a procedure that involves asking people to comply with a small request and then making a much larger request, to raise funds. Once we've given $10 to our favourite local radio station because we strongly believe in community-supported radio, it can feel inconsistent not to give the station the $100 they ask for in their next e-mail, so we adjust our actions to match our attitudes.

We often comply in order to reduce cognitive dissonance, but there are other factors that also encourage compliance. For example, early in our lives we realize that if we help someone they will likely help us in the future; in fact, we learn to expect this reciprocity. Because we feel a connection to someone who has helped us, we want to return favours and we are more likely to comply with requests from others who have granted our requests in the past. Whether we are helping a buddy move, sponsoring someone's "walkathon," or accepting a "friend request" on Facebook, the act of reciprocity helps to maintain relationships.

If a Girl Scout knocked on your door and asked you to buy 100 boxes of cookies, you'd probably refuse. But if she then said, "Okay, would you consider buying just three boxes?" you might comply with her request. This particular Girl Scout used the **door-in-the-face technique**, a procedure for gaining compliance that involves making a large request and then,

Attitude is an evaluative belief or opinion about a person, object, or idea.

Explicit attitude is a belief or opinion that a person holds consciously and can report to others.

Implicit attitude is a belief or opinion that a person can't report and that will automatically influence his or her actions.

Persuasion is a deliberate effort to change an attitude or behaviour.

Central route is a path to persuasion that involves paying careful attention to strong, well-presented arguments that are personally relevant and that appeal to reason.

Peripheral route is a path to persuasion that involves evaluating an argument based on tangential cues rather than on the argument's merits.

Elaboration-likelihood model states that people tend to be persuaded through the central route when their motivation and ability to understand and consider the persuasive message is high, while they are more likely to be persuaded by the peripheral route when their motivation is low or when they need to make a quick decision.

Perseverance effect is a phenomenon in which it is difficult for people to shake their initial impressions.

when that request is refused, making a smaller request that seems reasonable in comparison.

ATTITUDES AND ACTIONS

Attitudes, our evaluative beliefs or opinions about people, objects, and ideas, fundamentally affect our behaviours. We have both **explicit attitudes,** beliefs or opinions that we hold consciously and can report to others, and **implicit attitudes,** beliefs and opinions that we can't (or won't) report and that automatically influence our actions. All attitudes have three component

> *Your implicit attitudes during the 2011 election season probably matched your explicit attitudes, but maybe you decided to consciously fight a lifelong devotion to one political party and vote based on policy issues rather than on your gut instincts.*

parts: affect (our emotions or feelings), cognition (our thoughts), and behaviour. Our feelings, thoughts, and behaviours work together to shape our attitudes. Attitudes can be formed in many ways, including through classical conditioning (see Chapter 11) and through the acceptance of social norms.

Political elections can provide a wealth of examples of both explicit and implicit attitudes. If you have an explicit attitude about a candidate, you have consciously held opinions about him or her: Maybe, during the 2011 Canadian federal election you liked Stephen Harper because of his positions on the economy and the environment, or maybe you disliked him because his social values differed from yours. Your implicit attitudes during the 2011 election season probably matched your explicit attitudes, but maybe you decided to consciously fight a lifelong devotion to one political party and vote based on policy issues rather than on your gut instincts.

In a 2008 study of Italian politics, researchers at the University of Padua discovered that

implicit political attitudes can determine voters' behaviour on election day. Voters who declared themselves "undecided" had no explicit attitude about the candidates, but they often had implicit attitudes about the candidates or their political parties, and these voters tended to ultimately cast their ballots for the party they implicitly favoured, even if they didn't consciously prefer either party (Arcuri et al., 2008).

PERSUASION

Some attitudes that we hold are stronger than others, but nearly all attitudes are susceptible to change. **Persuasion**, a deliberate effort to change an attitude or behaviour, is indigenous to many areas of our lives, but it might help to consider it in one of its natural habitats: the courtroom. Attorneys commonly use persuasive techniques to get jury members on their side. The jury might be swayed through the **central route** to persuasion, which involves paying careful attention to strong, well-presented arguments that are personally relevant and that appeal to reason. Or they might be convinced through the **peripheral route** to persuasion, which involves evaluating an argument based on tangential cues rather than on the argument's merits. For example, a juror might be persuaded by a defence attorney's argument based on the attorney's good looks or sunny disposition rather than on the facts of the case. Emotional appeals can be just as persuasive as appeals to reason, but the former follow the peripheral route, while the latter follow the central route. According to the **elaboration-likelihood model** (Petty & Cacioppo, 1986), we tend to be persuaded through the central route when our motivation and ability to understand and consider the persuasive message is high. When our motivation is low, however, or when we need to reach a quick decision and we don't have time to think critically, we're more likely to be persuaded through the peripheral route.

When and where we learn information can also affect our ability to be persuaded by it. Our initial impressions are hard to shake, a phenomenon known as the **perseverance effect.** If a

<<< What **explicit and implicit attitudes** might Canadians have held about the **Conservative, Liberal, NDP, Bloc Québécois, and Green Party** candidates during the last Canadian election?

Source: http://thetyee.ca/News/2011/05/02/HarperWins/

teacher receives a stellar first paper from his student, he can probably be easily persuaded that the student's subsequent work is of the highest calibre even though unbiased teachers may not hold the same opinion of the student's performance. The **sleeper effect,** which occurs when we forget the unreliable source of a piece of information but remember the information itself and believe that it's trustworthy, can also affect our judgment and our ability to be persuaded by false statements.

GROUP INFLUENCE

Groups of people can influence individual behaviour in powerful ways. In fact, the mere presence of others can affect how well we perform a task. When we're being observed by others, we perform better on easy tasks or ones we know well but worse on difficult or less familiar tasks (Guerin, 1986; Zajonc, 1965). When people believe that their individual efforts don't matter or that they are not personally responsible because they are only one member of a group, they tend to put less effort into a task, a phenomenon called **social loafing** (Ferrari & Pychyl, 2012; Latané, 1981; Jackson & Williams, 1988; Harkins & Szymanski, 1989; Kerr & Bruun, 1983; Woodman, Roberts, Hardy, Callow, & Rogers, 2011).

You would probably not stand up by yourself and cheer loudly at a sporting event or concert, but you might do so very easily as part of a large cheering crowd. Being part of a group can make us feel less restrained and more aroused, a process of **deindividuation** that allows us to relinquish personal responsibility and give ourselves over to the group experience.

Group Interactions and Minority Influence

The strength of group influence means that the more members of the group discuss similar opinions, the more extreme their positions become. This phenomenon, known as **group polarization,** strengthens resolve but can also create more radical behaviour. Group interactions can also lead to **groupthink** when group members' opinions become so uniform that all dissent becomes impossible. Such uniformity of opinion may have been responsible for the behaviour of the U.S. military at Abu Ghraib, where extreme interrogation and torture of prisoners took place (Post & Pannis, 2011).

While social control can be very powerful, committed individuals confident about their viewpoints have the power to influence the majority. **Minority influence,** the power

> **Emotions affect how we behave with others, and social situations affect our emotions.** As social animals, our emotions link inextricably with the social situations in which we find ourselves.

of a few people, allowed Gandhi to lead the movement for the independence of India and civil rights leaders like Martin Luther King Jr. to press for desegregation in the American South. More recently, we are seeing the effects of minority influence in the pro-democratic movements around the world.

Social Relations

EMOTIONAL FOUNDATIONS OF SOCIAL NATURE

Emotions affect how we behave with others, and social situations affect our emotions. As social animals, our emotions link inextricably with the social situations in which we find ourselves.

Ending a romantic relationship may hurt, and having a migraine headache can be very painful, but if you end a relationship while you have a migraine headache, your headache will be even more intense. At least, that's what researchers have found. If we lose a close personal relationship or membership in a group, we feel **social pain.** The pain of rejection or loss feels as real as physical pain because it activates the same areas in the brain, the anterior cingulate cortex and the anterior insula (Eisenberger, Lieberman, & Williams, 2003). If we happen to be experiencing physical pain, social pain will actually magnify our distress (Eisenberger & Lieberman, 2004; Nordgren, Banas, & MacDonald, 2011).

In addition, our ability to empathize with others may make us more sensitive to pain. Researchers from McGill University found that this type of "emotional contagion" can be found even in rats and highlights the critical role of social interactions in pain management (Mogil, 2006). Emotion contagion can also help us perform better. For example, researchers (Moll, Jordet, & Pepping, 2010) found that the celebratory actions of one soccer teammate after a

Sleeper effect is a phenomenon that occurs when a person forgets the unreliable source of a piece of information but remembers the information itself and believes that it's trustworthy.

Social loafing is a phenomenon that occurs when people believe that their individual efforts don't matter or that they are not personally responsible because they are only one member of a group, so they tend to put less effort into a task.

Deindividuation is a process that allows people in a group to relinquish personal responsibility and give themselves over to the group experience.

Group polarization is a phenomenon in which the more members of a group discuss similar opinions, the more extreme their positions become.

Groupthink is a phenomenon in which group members' opinions become so uniform that all dissent becomes impossible.

Minority influence refers to the power of a few people.

Social pain is the pain of rejection or loss brought on by losing a close personal relationship or membership in a group.

Self-conscious emotion is an emotion that relates to a person's thoughts about himself or herself and about his or her own actions.

successful penalty kick positively affected the entire team's performance.

Self-conscious emotions, such as guilt or shame, that relate to thoughts about ourselves and our own actions have important functions in social relations (Tangney, 1999). As a motivator for relationship repair, guilt can be an evolutionarily adaptive mechanism for preserving social cohesion, although it can be maladaptive if taken to extremes. Embarrassment motivates people to rectify awkward situations, and those who show embarrassment seem to appear more likable (Keltner & Anderson, 2000; Semin & Manstead, 1982). Shame leads to social withdrawal, especially when someone's failings have been publicly exposed.

PREJUDICE

Prejudice is a negative learned attitude toward particular people or things. Although the detrimental effects of prejudice have been well documented, prejudice against individuals because of race, ethnicity, gender, or other factors still persists. Although most of us overtly deny having feelings of prejudice, many people still display prejudiced implicit attitudes. What causes this disconnection between our outward beliefs and our actions? Can well-intentioned, fair, considerate people still be unconsciously affected by powerful stereotypes?

> Stereotype is a general belief about a group of people.
>
> Stereotype threat refers to a stereotyped group's knowledge that they must work against a negative stereotype.
>
> Explicit stereotype is a stereotype that is consciously held.
>
> Implicit stereotype is an unconscious set of mental representations that guide attitudes and behaviours.
>
> Discrimination consists of negative behaviour toward a group of people and its members.

> " Tests have shown that while most people consciously believe that they are not racially prejudiced, many white students more quickly associate positive adjectives with white faces and negative adjectives with black faces. "

Stereotypes

In and of themselves, **stereotypes,** or general beliefs about a group of people, can be useful schemas for interpreting the world around us. They can help us make rapid determinations about an individual, saving us cognitive time and energy. For example, if you see a man wearing a wedding ring and holding a baby, you might quickly intuit that the man is committed, mature, and caring—all positive stereotypes associated with married fathers. While stereotypes might provide us with some useful basic information, however, very often they can lead us to draw false conclusions and ultimately contribute to acts of prejudice and discrimination. Stereotypes can be hard to disprove: When we hold stereotypes about a certain group, we're likely to discredit information that does not support those stereotypes. Thanks to the confirmation bias (see Chapter 13), we tend to selectively accept only information that supports our

preconceived views (Mercier & Sperber, 2011; Munro & Ditto, 1997).

The mere existence of negative stereotypes can be harmful. Those subject to stereotyping may not be able to perform as well on tasks as they normally would because of **stereotype threat,** the knowledge that they must work against a negative stereotype (Inzlicht & Kang, 2010; Neuburger, Jansen, Heil, & Quaiser-Pohl, 2012; Steele & Aronson, 1995). For example, women who are aware of the stereotype that women are not supposed to be good at math and science may feel particularly pressured to perform well on a math test and disprove the stereotype, but the extra pressure they put on themselves may actually hurt their performance, leading them to inadvertently support the stereotype. Of course, a variety of other factors often contribute to the performance gap between men and women in math and

science; stereotype threat alone is only part of the complex picture.

When people hold an **explicit stereotype,** they consciously adhere to a set of beliefs about a group of people. But many beliefs actually operate as **implicit stereotypes,** an unconscious set of mental representations that guide attitudes and behaviours. Because of the way our implicit memories function, priming the mind with one concept facilitates the access of associated concepts. Tests have shown that while most people consciously believe that they are not racially prejudiced, many white students more quickly associate positive adjectives with white faces and negative adjectives with black faces, suggesting that these students hold implicit negative stereotypes about black people. Black students tend to show the inverse preference (Fazio, Jackson, Dunton, & Williams, 1995). The Implicit Association Test, developed by Mahzarin Banaji and Tony Greenwald to access implicit attitudes by measuring the time required to pair certain concepts (such as "white" and "good"), has also revealed people's implicit beliefs about race and gender (Banaji & Greenwald, 1995; Carlsson & Bjorkland, 2010; Greenwald, McGhee, & Schwartz, 1998, Greenwald, Oakes, & Hoffman, 2003).

Discrimination

The racial segregation practised in parts of the United States until the 1950s showed how prejudiced attitudes lead to **discrimination,** negative behaviour toward a group of people and its members. In the landmark Supreme Court case *Brown v. Board of Education,* Thurgood Marshall and other attorneys referred to studies by social psychologists Kenneth and Mamie Clark as evidence for the tremendously damaging effects of discrimination. During the "doll test," black children showed an overt preference for white dolls, and when asked to colour pictures of children, they chose white or yellow crayons (Clark & Clark, 1947). By showing how the "separate but equal" education system fosters a sense of inferiority in children, the "doll test" helped end segregation in the United States.

<<< How might stereotype threat affect your life? How can it be combatted?

People taking an Implicit Association Test might be asked to match **African American** faces with the word *good*.

∨ ∨
∨

BAD   GOOD

Racism is hardly the only prominent form of discrimination. Unfortunately, in many countries, discrimination is often conducted on the basis of gender, religion, or sexual preference, to name only a few categories.

Foundations of Prejudice

As social animals, human beings tend to form groups and derive some portion of their identity from these groups. They treat their own group as the **ingroup** and favour their group positions and members; those outside their group might be considered part of an **outgroup** (Shamdasani & Jung, 2011; Tajfel, 1982; Wilder, 1981). When taken to extremes, the ingroup and outgroup dichotomy can erupt into violence, as happens during a time of war or even at sporting events when conflict erupts between supporters of rival teams.

Prejudice also often has an emotional basis, and our feelings of fear and anger are particularly likely to lead us toward discrimination. When we're frustrated by our own failings, we often look for scapegoats whom we can blame for our problems. Often, those scapegoats are outgroup members: After the attacks of September 11, 2001, for example, some people's fears and feelings of anger led them to stereotype and act out against members of the worldwide Muslim community.

A number of cognitive processes help people justify both their position at the "top of the food chain" and their poor treatment of those who are worse off. For instance, the **just-world phenomenon** leads us to believe that the world is a fair place in which good people are rewarded and bad people are punished. If this is really the case, we convince ourselves, then we must be doing well because we are good people, while those who are suffering are simply getting what they deserve.

Reversing Prejudice

Although we might intuitively believe that contact between hostile groups should reduce prejudice, **mere exposure,** or simple contact between two groups, does not usually reverse prejudice unless groups co-operate with each other to achieve a common goal (Allport, 1954; Dovidio, Gaertner, & Kawakami, 2003; Pettigrew

& Tropp, 2006). This principle of co-operation also works to soothe relationships in the classroom: In "jigsaw" classrooms, each student must manage one part of a project in order for the group to complete the entire assignment (Aronson & Gonzalez, 1988). Learning more about an outgroup through friendship or collaborative efforts can make people more tolerant of the norms and customs of other groups, a process called **deprovincialization.** Recently, researchers have found that non-invasive brain stimulation to the anterior temporal lobe significantly reduced prejudice scores on the Implicit Associations Test (Gallate, Wong, Ellwood, Chi, & Snyder, 2011). This research suggests that we may be able to reduce negative stereotypes using brain stimulation.

AGGRESSION
What Causes Aggressive Behaviour?

Whether it occurs between warring nations, feuding first graders, or romantic partners, any physical or verbal behaviour intended to harm others qualifies as **aggression.** Given the pervasiveness of aggression in animals, it's no surprise that biology influences aggression. From an evolutionary perspective, we can explain aggression as a quality that has developed from a struggle for survival and resources. Aggression may also be influenced by genetics: If a child has a violent temper, his or her siblings are likely to be aggressive, too (Miles & Carey, 1997; Rowe, Almeida, & Jacobson, 1999; Simons et al., 2011; Takahashi, Quadros, de Almeida, & Miczek, 2011). In the brain, the amygdala and other limbic structures help to initiate aggression, and it's likely that the frontal lobes play a role in controlling aggression as well (Lewis, Pincus, Feldman, Jackson, & Bard, 1986; Taylor, Stanek, Ressler, Huhman, 2011). For example, researchers have found that when participants were exposed to stress their left frontal lobe became more activated compared to the right frontal lobe, and these participants subsequently displayed more aggression compared to participants in the no-stress condition (Verona, Sadeh, & Curtin, 2009).

Alcohol and violence are commonly linked in the media, and it's true that the biological effects of alcohol can increase aggressive behaviour (Davis et al., 2012; Levinson, Giancola, & Parrott, 2011; Reyes, Foshee, Bauer, & Ennett, 2011). In addition, as the amount of alcohol consumed increases so does the intensity of aggression (Duke, Giancola, Morris, Holt, & Gunn, 2011). This is likely because alcohol is known to reduce inhibition by compromising frontal lobe function.

While some factors that influence aggression are biological, others are linked to our environments and our external situations. Canadian researchers (Huijbregts, Séguin, Zoccolillo, Boivin, & Tremblay, 2008) have found a link between a mother's cigarette smoking during pregnancy and later aggressive behaviours of her child. Many violent criminals have experienced abuse as children. When humans and other animals experience aversive events such as abuse, they tend to pay it forward (Berkowitz, 1983, 1989; Davis et al., 2012). Hot weather also seems to contribute to hot tempers, and a number of studies point to the influence of uncomfortable heat in aggressive acts (Anderson & Anderson, 1984). Aggressive behaviour also seems to be influenced by the seasons—with researchers reporting more dating aggression by adolescence in the Spring rather than Fall semesters (Reyes, Foshee, Bauer, & Ennett, 2011). Anyone who has experienced road rage while stuck in traffic can agree with the **frustration-aggression hypothesis** that frustration occurs when people feel blocked in obtaining their goals (Dollard, Doob, Miller, Mowrer, & Sears, 1939; Reio, 2011). Unemployment also creates economic frustration so that violence rates increase as unemployment rates rise (e.g., Hall & Pizarro, 2010), up to a given point. After that, the general anxiety over job loss supersedes aggressive feelings (Catalano, Novaco, & McConnell, 1997, 2002).

Cultural Constraints

Cultural constraints about acceptable levels of aggression may control how much aggression we feel free to show. In one experiment, American children displayed more verbal aggression in hypothetical situations of conflict than did Japanese children (Zahn-Waxler et al., 1996). More recently, researchers examined the cultural differences in physical dating aggression among Canadian and Italian adolescents (Nocentini et al., 2011). Based on a sample of 1628 adolescents (704 Italians and 924 Canadians; 800 males and 828 females) aged 14 to 16 years, they found that although participants from both cultures expressed similar perceptions about dating violence, the specific forms of violence differed across cultures. Norms of aggression can also be set by models of aggression in everyday life. While there is no data to suggest that children's exposure to violent TV programs and video games leads to violent behaviour later in life, the media and entertainment industries do provide numerous models of violence for children (Bushman & Anderson, 2002; Anderson & Bushman, 2001). Real-life models of violence seem to have more of an impact on behaviour than do violent games or movies: Children who have either experienced or watched physical abuse often become violent themselves (Berkowitz, 2003; Salzinger et al., 2006).

CONFLICT

In 2010, Toronto hosted the G20 Summit. Although most of the protests surrounding the event were peaceful, a small group of radical protestors did clash with police. They smashed windows, looted, and vandalized banks and businesses in downtown Toronto. They even set several police cruisers on fire. This is just one recent example of **conflict,** or a disparity between people's or groups' actions, goals, or ideas. We tend to engage in conflict in pursuit of our own self-interests, but the "winners" of

∧
∧ What types of conflict are more likely to turn
∧ violent? What factors play a role in the peaceful resolution of a conflict?

a conflict don't always emerge from the fight in a better position than the one they started in. Sometimes, conflicting parties engage in mutually destructive behaviours, causing them to end up in a **social trap:** As everyone tries to win, no one actually does.

The Psychology of Genocide

On July 21, 2008, Radovan Karadzic, the Bosnian Serb president who presided over the genocide in Bosnia, was arrested after 10 years in hiding. **Genocide,** the systematic destruction of one group by another, begins when living conditions become very strained, as they did after the breakup of Communist regimes in Eastern Europe. Faced with economic, social, and political uncertainty, old ethnic conflicts resurfaced as Bosnian Serbs identified themselves as the ingroup and Bosnian Muslims as a scapegoated outgroup. Feeling legitimized by the just-world phenomenon and under attack by Croatians and other outgroups, many Bosnian Serbs massacred their former neighbours, Bosnian Muslims. The lethargy of the world community in reacting to the genocide in Bosnia also reinforced feelings of righteousness among Serbians. Currently, the genocide in Darfur and the violence in Syria have also evoked little intervention by the United Nations and the international community.

Co-operation

Although we can easily think of recent examples of genocide, the picture isn't entirely bleak—some seemingly intractable conflicts have also been recently resolved. For example, positive political developments in Northern Ireland have proven that **co-operation,** or working together for the good of the group, can lead to more benefit than **defection,** promoting one's own interest at the expense of others. Co-operation is beneficial, but it isn't easy: We face a social dilemma when a certain course of action that benefits an individual hurts the group as a whole and will do more harm than good as a whole if everyone takes the same course. This dilemma often plays out on a global scale. Industrialized countries have about 20% of the world's population but produce about 40% of the global carbon emissions (Sierra Club, 2008). As China and India have also become increasingly industrialized and contribute more to carbon emissions, the planet as a whole suffers the consequences of each individual country promoting its own economic interests with little regard for the environmental consequences.

There are plenty of factors that can convince us to co-operate with others, however. When people feel a high level of personal accountability, for example, they feel more inclined to co-operate. People may also co-operate in order to protect their reputation or follow the norms of reciprocity that dictate that we should help others if they have helped us. Norms of fairness (such as punishing cheaters and rewarding helpful individuals) can encourage co-operation, as can a shared social identity with a group. In the aftermath of Hurricane Igor's devastating blow to Newfoundland in 2010, volunteers worked together to help their neighbours.

It's hard to co-operate with someone else if you can't (or won't) communicate, so communication is a particularly crucial element of co-operation. When conflicting groups can't reach a mutually agreeable solution, mediators can help the groups communicate with each other and develop a plan that's beneficial to both sides.

ALTRUISM AND PROSOCIAL BEHAVIOUR

What makes us put the interests of others first, even risking our own well-being in the process? **Prosocial behaviour,** behaviour carried out with the goal of helping others, becomes **altruism** when it is carried out without concern for one's own safety or self-interest. We don't gain any sort of advantage from performing an altruistic act; in fact, we might even put ourselves at a disadvantage. (Some psychologists and philosophers argue that if we feel good after performing an altruistic act, the act wasn't purely altruistic after all.) While displays of altruism don't commonly grip reality TV show audiences, it's important to remember that humans are capable of selfless social acts as well as selfish ones.

What might cause us to act altruistically? The theory of **reciprocal altruism** suggests that people may carry out altruistic acts with the expectation of being the recipient of altruism at some point in the future or because they have been helped by altruism sometime in the past (Trivers, 1971). In general, people

> We face a social dilemma when a certain course of action that benefits an individual hurts the group as a whole and will do more harm than good as a whole if everyone takes the same course. This dilemma often plays out on a global scale.

Frustration-aggression hypothesis states that frustration occurs when people feel blocked in obtaining their goals.

Conflict is the disparity between people's or groups' actions, goals, or ideas.

Social trap is a situation in which conflicting parties all try to win a conflict by engaging in mutually destructive behaviours, resulting in no one winning.

Genocide is the systematic destruction of one group by another.

Co-operation is the act of working together for the good of the group.

Defection is the act of promoting one's own interest at the expense of others.

Prosocial behaviour is behaviour carried out with the goal of helping others.

Altruism is prosocial behaviour that is carried out without concern for one's own safety or self-interest.

Reciprocal altruism is a theory that suggests that people may carry out altruistic acts with the expectation of being the recipient of altruism at some point in the future or because they have been helped by altruism sometime in the past.

Egoism describes the act of doing something beneficial for others in the hopes of receiving something in return.

Collectivism describes the act of contributing something beneficial to the whole group to which a person belongs.

Principlism is a desire to engage in prosocial behaviour out of principle.

show altruism toward their relatives (nepotism), but perhaps we look after our families because we know that they will do the same for us (Burnstein, Crandall, & Kitayama, 1994). Altruism can even enhance our attractiveness: In one study, college women who perceived altruism in certain men evaluated those men as more physically and sexually attractive (Jensen-Campbell, Graziano, & West, 1995).

According to C. Daniel Batson (1994), altruism constitutes only one motive for prosocial behaviour. Corporate sponsors who receive promotional benefits from charitable contributions practise **egoism,** doing something beneficial for others in the hopes of receiving something in return. Social security could be considered a form of **collectivism:** Everyone contributes to the community chest to help the group as a whole. Religious values that encourage helping others would count as examples of **principlism,** the desire to engage in prosocial behaviour out of principle. No matter what drives us, however, our prosocial behaviour helps us improve society and nurture and sustain our relationships.

Summary

WHAT IS SOCIAL PSYCHOLOGY? p.200

- Social psychology examines how the thoughts, actions, and behaviour of individuals influence and are influenced by groups.
- Humans are social beings, meaning that we actively seek out others to interact with, and in so doing we learn about them and ourselves.
- Our interactions depend on social perception. But this perception can be flawed: The fundamental attribution theory, pre-existing schemas, the attractiveness bias, and the self-fulfilling bias can all affect our ability to interact with others.

WHAT COGNITIVE PROCESSES UNDERLIE SOCIAL BEHAVIOUR? p.202

- Social cognition focuses on the underlying processes, such as attention and memory, that make social behaviour possible. Biological structures and processes in the brain help us navigate our social environment.
- The fusiform face area of the brain allows us to recognize faces.
- The amygdala is involved in social category processing.
- The superior temporal sulcus processes biological motions.
- Mirror neurons in the inferior frontal gyrus help us feel empathy.

HOW DOES SOCIAL INFLUENCE AFFECT OUR THOUGHTS AND ACTIONS? p.203

- Through social pressure, social influence can lead people to conform, obey, and mimic others.
- Social influence affects performance and plays a role in persuasion.
- Social influence can have a positive or negative effect on us.
- The chameleon effect, conformity, obedience, compliance, and the bystander effect are all examples of the power that others have on our thoughts and behaviours.

HOW ARE SOCIAL RELATIONS INFLUENCED BY PSYCHOLOGICAL PHENOMENA? p.209

- Fear and anger can affect social relations through prejudice, stereotyping, and conflict. Prejudice can be conscious or unconscious.
- Aggression and conflict represent negative aspects of social interaction, with complex biological, societal, and cultural influences.
- Self-conscious emotions such as guilt can lead to social repair.
- Group relations can be improved through co-operation and altruism.

Test Your Understanding

1. Jane is waiting in line at the grocery store when another woman bumps into her, does not apologize, and then steps in line in front of her. According to the theory of the fundamental attribution error, which of the following is most likely to be Jane's reaction?

   a. That woman must be in a hurry for some reason.
   b. That woman must not have been able to see me well.
   c. That woman must be incredibly rude and thoughtless.
   d. That woman must not be used to shopping in large stores.

2. Elijah believes that he failed to land a job because the hiring manager was in a bad mood on the day of his interview. Which of the following is most likely affecting Elijah's reasoning?

   a. a baby-face bias
   b. a self-serving bias
   c. an attractiveness bias
   d. a pre-existing schema

3. Which of the following statements about social cognition is NOT true?

   a. Theories of social cognition attempt to explain the relationship between attention, memory, and social behaviour.
   b. Theories of social cognition generally acknowledge the importance of biological processes in social behaviour.

   c. According to social cognitive theory, our ability to recognize faces can be traced to specific structures in the brain.
   d. According to social cognitive theory, our social interactions are guided almost entirely by external, environmental factors.

4. What do neurological findings about racial biases suggest about the nature of prejudice?

   a. Our prejudices are impossible to change.
   b. Everyone grows up without racial biases.
   c. It is difficult for us to unlearn old prejudices.
   d. Prejudice is determined entirely by genetics.

5. A person who buys a lottery ticket is acting in response to the:

   a. hedonic motive
   b. approval motive
   c. accuracy motive
   d. chameleon effect

6. In a discussion about who to vote for in the federal election, which of the following conditions would most likely facilitate conformity?

   a. a discussion among several people in a crowded restaurant
   b. a discussion between a Liberal and a Conservative
   c. a discussion between a woman and a man
   d. a discussion that takes place in a private home

7. Which of the following is a primary explanation for the existence of the bystander effect?
   a. People are too busy to help others in need.
   b. People in a group relinquish personal responsibility.
   c. People tend to pay attention only to their own problems.
   d. People in a group are easily distracted by other group members.

8. Which of the following conclusions is best supported by the findings of Milgram's experiments?
   a. People are inherently immoral.
   b. People enjoy inflicting pain on others.
   c. People prefer not to think for themselves.
   d. People tend to obey others under certain conditions.

9. Why are Milgram's findings limited in their ability to explain real-world phenomena?
   a. Milgram performed his experiments on naturally violent people.
   b. Milgram's experiments were not considered ethical by today's standards.
   c. The experimental conditions did not simulate a plausible real-world experience.
   d. Real-world phenomena can never be explained by experimental results.

10. Which of the following best accounts for how false information from tabloids sometimes becomes accepted as fact?
    a. persuasion
    b. implicit attitudes
    c. the sleeper effect
    d. cognitive dissonance

11. Karimah, who is usually shy and reserved, dances and sings loudly at a crowded rock concert. Karimah's actions serve as an example of:
    a. groupthink
    b. deindividuation
    c. group polarization
    d. minority influence

12. How might self-conscious emotions serve a social function?
    a. They can reduce groupthink.
    b. They can increase social loafing.
    c. They can lead to relationship repair.
    d. They can hinder minority influence.

13. Which of the following statements about stereotypes is true?
    a. Stereotypes serve no useful purpose.
    b. Stereotypes are hard to disprove due to minority influence.
    c. Stereotypes are often supported by the confirmation bias.
    d. Stereotypes have become significantly less powerful over the years.

14. Results from Implicit Association Tests about race reveal that:
    a. people think racism is socially acceptable
    b. people are often unaware of their biases
    c. racial prejudice has decreased over the years
    d. racist attitudes can only be accessed implicitly

15. Given that Mika's opinion about homelessness is affected by the just-world phenomenon, which statement most likely reflects Mika's opinion?
    a. "If I ignore homelessness, I'll be happier."
    b. "Helping the homeless is not very important to me."
    c. "It's not fair that so many people should be homeless."
    d. "Only bad people who don't work hard end up homeless."

16. Which of the following scenarios would be most likely to effectively reduce prejudice between two groups of people?
    a. Members of both groups live near each other.
    b. Members of both groups work together to solve a puzzle.
    c. The two groups participate in Implicit Association Tests.
    d. The two groups compete against each other in an athletic contest.

17. Which of the following statements about aggression is supported by research findings?
    a. Genetics likely play no significant role in aggression.
    b. Aggression is a quality that likely developed from our need to belong.
    c. Large limbic structures in the brain are associated with lack of aggression in humans.
    d. Frontal lobe damage may compromise an individual's ability to control aggression.

18. Which of the following behaviours best illustrates the frustration-aggression hypothesis?
    a. arguing after drinking too much
    b. competing for a promotion at work
    c. conducting an armed robbery at a bank
    d. yelling after being put on hold on the phone

19. Faizah volunteers to help his professor with administrative tasks because he wants to get on his professor's good side and receive a better grade in class. Faizah's behaviour is an example of:
    a. altruism
    b. egoism
    c. collectivism
    d. principlism

20. Phoebe is an advertiser who has created several ads in order to convince people to buy a new brand of toothpaste. Which of the following ad concepts best illustrates Phoebe's use of the peripheral route to persuasion?
    a. a picture of a popular celebrity holding a tube of toothpaste
    b. a diagram that illustrates how the toothpaste removes plaque
    c. a local dentist's explanation of the toothpaste's proven health benefits
    d. a price comparison chart that shows people how affordable the toothpaste is

Remember to check www.thethinkspot.ca for additional information, downloadable flashcards, and other helpful resources.

Answers: 1) c; 2) b; 3) d; 4) c; 5) a; 6) a; 7) b; 8) d; 9) c; 10) c; 11) b; 12) c; 13) c; 14) b; 15) d; 16) b; 17) d; 18) d; 19) b; 20) a

THINK READINGS

Decades Later, Still Asking: Would I Pull That Switch?

By Benedict Carey

Some of psychology's most famous experiments are those that expose the skull beneath the skin, the apparent cowardice or depravity pooling in almost every heart.

The findings force a question. Would I really do that? Could I betray my own eyes, my judgment, even my humanity, just to complete some experiment?

The answer, if it's an honest one, often gives rise to observations about the cruelties of the day, whether suicide bombing, torture or gang atrocities. And so a psych experiment—a mock exercise, testing individual behavior—can become something else, a changing prism through which people view the larger culture, for better and for worse.

Consider the psychologist Stanley Milgram's obedience studies of the early 1960s that together form

one of the darkest mirrors the field has held up to the human face. In a series of about 20 experiments, hundreds of decent, well-intentioned people agreed to deliver what appeared to be increasingly painful electric shocks to another person, as part of what they thought was a learning experiment. The "learner" was in fact an actor, usually seated out of sight in an adjacent room, pretending to be zapped.

Researchers, social commentators and armchair psychologists have pored through Milgram's data ever since, claiming psychological and cultural insights. Now, decades after the original work (Milgram died in 1984, at 51), two new papers illustrate the continuing power of the shock experiments—and the diverse interpretations they still inspire.

In one, a statistical analysis to appear in the July issue of the journal *Perspectives on Psychological Science*, a postdoctoral student at Ohio State University verifies a crucial turning point in Milgram's experiments, the voltage level at which participants were most likely to disobey the experimenter and quit delivering shocks.

The participants usually began with what they thought were 15-volt shocks, and worked upward in 15-volt increments, as the experimenter instructed. At 75 volts, the "learner" in the next room began grunting in apparent pain. At 150 volts he cried out: "Stop, let me out! I don't want to do this anymore."

At that point about a third of the participants refused to continue, found Dominic Packer, author of the new paper. "The previous expressions of pain were insufficient," Dr. Packer said. But at 150 volts, he continued, those who disobeyed decided that the learner's right to stop trumped the experimenter's right to continue. Before the end of the experiments, at 450 volts, an additional 10 to 15 percent had dropped out.

Many of the most infamous studies to which Carey is referring, such as the Milgram experiments discussed in this article, were performed decades ago and would not be sanctioned by today's institutional review boards, which impose rigorous ethical standards.

Milgram's studies are discussed in detail in Chapter 14 (p.206).

Why do you think Milgram's experiments are still so famous over 40 years after they took place?

This appreciation of another's right is crucial in interrogation, Dr. Packer suggests. When prisoners' rights are ambiguous, inhumane treatment can follow. Milgram's work, in short, makes a statement about the importance of human rights, as well as obedience.

In the other paper, due out in the journal *American Psychologist*, a professor at Santa Clara University replicates part of the Milgram studies—stopping at 150 volts, the critical juncture at which the subject cries out to stop—to see whether people today would still obey. Ethics committees bar researchers from pushing subjects through to an imaginary 450 volts, as Milgram did.

The answer was yes. Once again, more than half the participants agreed to proceed with the experiment past the 150-volt mark. Jerry M. Burger, the author, interviewed the participants afterward and found that those who stopped generally believed themselves to be responsible for the shocks, whereas those who kept going tended to hold the

experimenter accountable. That is, the Milgram work also demonstrated individual differences in perceptions of accountability—of who's on the hook for what.

Thomas Blass, a psychologist at the University of Maryland, Baltimore County, and the author of a biography of Milgram, "The Man Who Shocked the World" (Basic Books, 2004), said establishing the demand by the subject to stop as the turning point was itself a significant achievement. "It's a simple but important discovery," Dr. Blass said. "I had been mining this data for years and somehow missed it."

He added that extrapolating Milgram's findings to larger events like the Holocaust, as Milgram himself did, or Abu Ghraib was a big leap. "The power of the Milgram work was it showed how people can act destructively without coercion," he said. "In things like interrogations, we don't know the complexities involved. People are under enormous pressure to produce results."

The Milgram data have unappreciated complexities of their own. In his new report, Dr. Burger argues that at least two other factors were at work when participants walked into the psychologist's lab at Yale decades ago. Uncertainty, as it was an unfamiliar situation. And time pressure, as they had to make decisions quickly. Rushed and disoriented, they were likely more compliant than they would otherwise have been, Dr. Burger said.

In short, the Milgram experiments may have shown physical, biological differences in moral decision making and obedience, as well as psychological ones. Some people can be as quick on the draw as Doc Holliday when they feel something's not right. Others need a little time to do the right thing, thank you, and would rather not be considered sadistic prison guards just yet.

"The most remarkable thing," Dr. Burger said, "is that we're still talking about the work, almost 50 years after it was done. You can't say that about many experiments."

The bystander effect, discussed in Chapter 14 (p.205), is also related to issues of accountability and personal responsibility. How does our perception of our own accountability seem to influence our actions?

This could be a reference both to the events at Abu Ghraib and to Zimbardo's famous Stanford Prison Experiment, which is described in Chapter 2 (p.29).

Do you think this new study is more ethical than Milgram's original study was? Can we really draw an ethical line based on voltage?

Remember that all of these experiments were conducted in laboratory settings, so it's hard to generalize their findings to real-world situations.

At 150 volts he cried out: "Stop, let me out! I don't want to do this anymore."

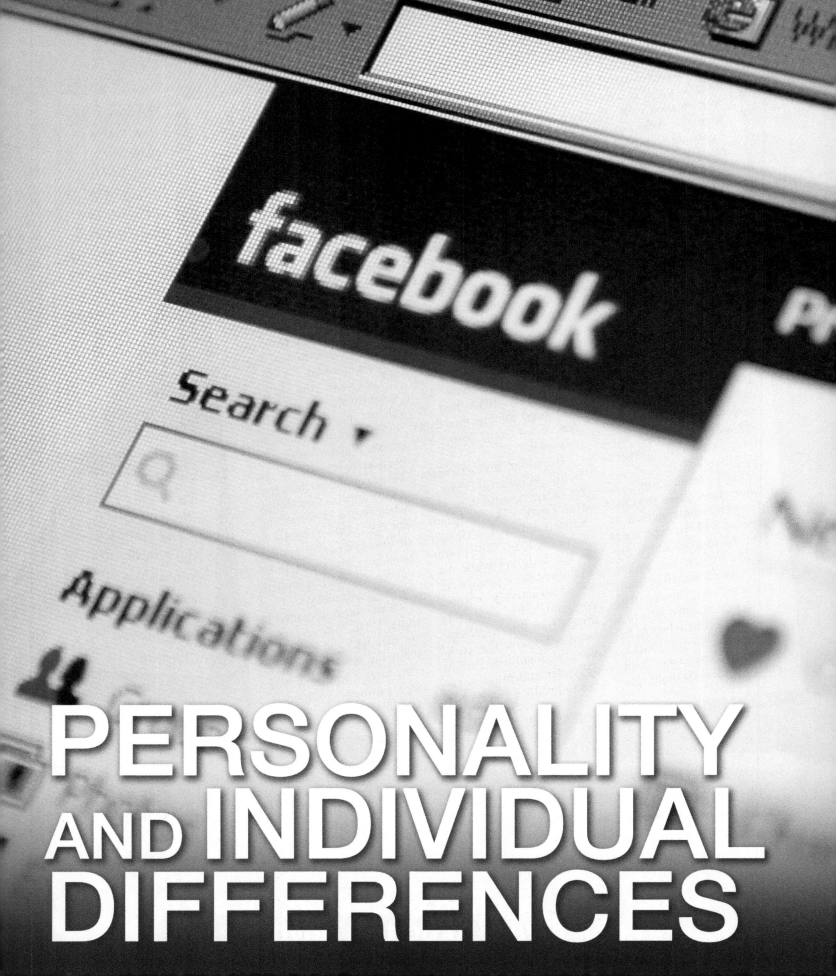

PERSONALITY
AND INDIVIDUAL
DIFFERENCES

WHAT IS PERSONALITY, AND HOW IS IT STUDIED?

WHAT ARE THE MAJOR TRAIT THEORIES, HOW ARE TRAITS ASSESSED, AND HOW DO GENES AFFECT INDIVIDUALS' TRAITS?

HOW DID FREUD CONCEPTUALIZE HUMAN PERSONALITY, AND HOW HAS PSYCHODYNAMIC THEORY EVOLVED OVER THE YEARS?

WHAT ARE THE MAJOR TENETS OF THE HUMANISTIC APPROACH TO PERSONALITY?

HOW DO SOCIAL COGNITIVE THEORIES OF LEARNING AND BEHAVIOUR APPLY TO THE STUDY OF PERSONALITY, AND HOW DO CONCEPTIONS OF PERSONALITY VARY ACROSS CULTURES?

It is

a jarring, eerie case that has fascinated psychologists for decades: Identical twins, separated at birth, raised in starkly contrasting households by different adoptive parents, turn out to share some remarkable similarities. They both struggled with thumb sucking, nail biting, and bedwetting throughout their childhoods. They are both intensely afraid of the dark and of being alone. They both have raging cases of hypochondria, and they both display an unusual tendency to cling to an artificial world characterized by role-playing and pretence. It's no wonder that this, the story of Amy and Beth, has made such a lasting impression on the world of psychology (Wright, 1997).

In the late 1960s, two blonde-haired, button-nosed little girls—referred to in psychological literature as Amy and Beth—were adopted by separate families in New York. Before their placement, Dr. Peter Neubauer, a psychiatrist at New York University's Psychoanalytic Institute, enlisted them in a twin study. As part of the study, Neubauer tracked the twins from infancy to the age of 10, recording details about their respective environments—family dynamics, parenting styles, etc.—as well as their personalities and behaviours.

Amy's adoptive mother was socially awkward, insecure, and stingy with her love and affection. Amy's brother, an academic standout, assumed the role of the "star" of the family, while Amy was viewed by both her mother and father as the "problem child."

As a result, Amy spent much of her childhood feeling alienated and rejected. Many of her disturbing behaviours and qualities—the thumb sucking, the bedwetting, the rampant fears and fantasies that largely defined her—seemed fitting, logical reactions to a difficult environment. Shy, indifferent, and pathologically immature, Amy appeared to be the product of a dismissive and alienating family.

But what about Beth? Neubauer found her troubles to be equally pronounced. Could they also be traced to an unsupportive family and problematic upbringing? The answer was no. Beth's mother was doting and attentive, going to great lengths to make Beth feel included in the family. Beth's parents regarded her as the centre of the family, heaping her with attention and praise. And yet, despite all of the advantages that her long-lost twin sister lacked, Beth turned out very much the same—shy, disconnected, and terrified of being left alone.

Amy and Beth's case continues to fascinate us because of what it suggests about the relative effects (or lack thereof) of genetics and environment on human personality. When it comes to personality, are we merely pre-programmed puppets of destiny? What forces shape us into the people we are today?

CHAPTER **15**

Introduction to Personality

In today's world, personality is an all-encompassing concept. Fashion magazines instruct us on how to "express our personalities" through clothing, while online dating Web sites promise to analyze the many dimensions of our personalities to successfully find our best romantic match. What, exactly, is personality?

In psychology, **personality** refers to the style in which we interact with the world, particularly with other people. Spending time with friends and family members, you've probably noticed that individual people's behaviour tends to stay relatively consistent. You might have a friend who volunteers to take charge of every situation from working on a major class project to ordering pizza. You might know someone who is painfully shy and someone else who converses easily with anyone on any occasion. We are innately interested in and attuned to the ways in which people are different from ourselves and from one another. In addition, we tend to focus on the characteristics that make us different rather than those characteristics that we all share. This focus helps us to decide who we should choose as partners and friends, and it provides us with cues for interacting with specific individuals.

STRATEGIES FOR STUDYING PERSONALITY

In general, psychologists who study personality rely on five different sources of data, to varying degrees and in varying combinations: self-report data (information you provide about your own thoughts, feelings, behaviours, or qualities), observer-report data (information about you provided by friends or family), specific behavioural data (information about specific things

> **Personality** is the style in which a person interacts with the world, particularly with other people.
>
> **Idiographic approach** is a method of interpreting personality data that is person-centred and focuses on how the unique parts of a person's personality form a consistent whole.
>
> **Nomothetic approach** is a method of interpreting personality data that is variable-centred and focuses on finding consistent patterns of relationships among individuals' traits.
>
> **Trait** is a person's relatively stable disposition to behave in a certain way.
>
> **State** is a person's transient disposition to behave in a certain way.

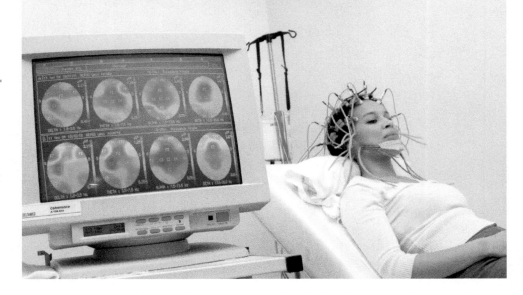

∧ **One way psychologists study personality is through**
∧ **the use of physiological data.** By measuring changes in **brain waves** or **blood pressure** in response to certain **stimuli**, psychologists aim to uncover patterns that point to specific **personality tendencies** or **traits**.

you have done), life-events data (information about things that have happened to you), and physiological data (information about the goings-on in your body, such as heart rate, blood pressure, and brain activity). In addition, psychologists interpret the data they collect through the use of two contrasting approaches. The **idiographic approach** is person-centred, focusing on how the unique parts of our personalities form a consistent whole. Studies that use this approach are primarily concerned with describing and analyzing individuals' personalities. In contrast, the **nomothetic approach** is variable-centred, focusing instead on finding consistent patterns of relationships among individuals' traits. Studies that use the nomothetic approach often involve many participants and are most concerned with determining general principles and theories of behaviour. Both approaches have played, and continue to play, an important role in personality research.

Personality Traits

Quick—list a few words that describe your personality. What did you choose? Chances are good that the words you selected, whether they were honest and kind or aggressive and ambitious, are linked to certain personality traits. A **trait** is a relatively stable disposition to behave

in a certain way. Traits are part of the person rather than part of the environment, although the environment, by triggering people to behave in certain ways, may play a key role in how traits are revealed. Although traits effectively describe how people are different, they do not offer explanations for what causes these differences.

An important distinction exists between traits and **states.** While both traits and states

> While both traits and states can be examined through someone's observable behaviour, traits are lasting, while states are transient. Moreover, a trait can determine the likelihood that someone enters into a temporary state. For example, a person who possesses the trait of insecurity is more likely to enter a state of depression than is someone who is very secure.

can be examined through someone's observable behaviour, traits are lasting, while states are transient. Moreover, a trait can determine the likelihood that someone enters into a temporary state. For example, a person who possesses the trait of insecurity is more likely to enter a state of depression than is someone who is very secure.

In addition, traits are continuous characteristics, meaning that people can differ in the degree to which they express a trait. An extremely sociable person may, for instance, have hundreds of friends, whereas a moderately sociable person could have a dozen.

TRAIT THEORIES

Since there are myriad traits and words to describe them, it can be challenging for psychologists to describe people's personalities briefly and consistently. That's why several researchers have come up with **trait theories,** sets of meaningful and distinct personality dimensions that can be used to describe how people differ from one another. In the 1930s, psychologist Gordon Allport became a pioneer in trait theory when he and his colleague H. S. Odbert attempted to identify all of the possible words in the dictionary that could be used to describe people's personality traits. It was a noble goal, but the results were a little overwhelming: They came up with a list of nearly 18 000 trait descriptors (Allport & Odbert, 1936).

Cattell's 16 Personality Factors

Psychologist Raymond Cattell (1965) developed the earliest well-known trait theory by first condensing Allport's extensive list of traits into about 170 distinct adjectives. Next, he had large samples of people rate themselves on each of these adjectives. Cattell then used a statistical technique called **factor analysis** to identify patterns of correlations in these responses. He used these patterns to determine factors, areas in which certain responses tended to cluster. For example, Cattell found that individuals who rated themselves as given to perfectionism were also likely to describe themselves as organized and self-disciplined, but unlikely to be described as impulsive or lax. Based on this research, Cattell identified 16 distinct personality dimensions, measured in the 16 PF Questionnaire ("PF" stands for "Personality Factors"). In this questionnaire, there are almost 200 statements about specific aspects of behaviour, such as "I plan my work carefully" and "I stay calm even when I'm angry," to which participants can respond yes, occasionally, or no. Psychologists still use the questionnaire today.

Eysenck and Gray's Two Central Dimensions

Psychologist Hans Eysenck (1967) believed that personality could be described in terms of two central dimensions: emotional stability vs. instability and introversion vs. extraversion. Emotional stability refers to our ability to cope with life's stressors in healthy ways and avoid extremes in mood or behaviour, while introversion and extraversion refer to our tendency to be shy, serious, and reserved (introverted) or social, high-spirited, and affectionate (extroverted). Eysenck thought differences in introversion and extraversion stemmed from individual differences in alertness. He hypothesized that the **reticular formation,** a part of the brain that controls arousal, is more sensitive in outgoing people than in shy people.

Jeffrey Gray (1972), another personality researcher, refined Eysenck's ideas, proposing that two basic brain systems are reflected

> ❝ Psychologist Hans Eysenck (1967) believed that personality could be described in terms of two central dimensions: emotional stability vs. instability and introversion vs. extraversion. ❞

in Eysenck's two personality dimensions. According to Gray, the **behavioural activation system (BAS)** activates approach behaviour in response to the anticipation of a reward. For example, if a student expects to achieve a high grade by studying hard, activity in the BAS will cause the student to review thoroughly in order to move toward the goal. Gray believed that the BAS is also responsible for experiencing positive feelings such as hope, elation, and happiness. In contrast, the **behavioural inhibition system (BIS)** inhibits approach behaviour in response to the anticipation of punishment. Gray believed that the BIS is also responsible for experiencing negative feelings, such as fear, anxiety, frustration, and sadness. Gray's theory may help to explain certain personality traits. For example, a person with particularly high BIS sensitivity may be extremely anxious when faced with impending punishment (a parking ticket, for example), compared to someone with lower BIS sensitivity.

Trait theory states that a set of meaningful and distinct personality dimensions can be used to describe how people differ from one another.

Factor analysis is a statistical technique that is used to identify patterns of correlations in responses to questionnaires.

Reticular formation is a part of the brain that controls arousal.

Behavioural activation system (BAS) is a part of the brain that activates approach behaviour in response to the anticipation of a reward.

Behavioural inhibition system (BIS) is a part of the brain that inhibits approach behaviour in response to the anticipation of a punishment.

Five-factor model ("Big Five" theory) is a model that is used to describe personality by assessing a person's score on each of five dimensions: extraversion/introversion, agreeableness/antagonism, conscientiousness/undirectedness, emotional stability/instability, and openness to experience/non-openness.

The Five-factor Model

The "Big Five" may sound like a global trade organization or a band of evildoers, but in fact, it's a popular trait theory. Robert McCrae and Paul Costa, who believe that Cattell's 16-factor theory is overly complex and redundant, reanalyzed Cattell's data and identified five factors of personality. According to this **five-factor model ("Big Five" theory)**, we can describe personality by assessing a person's score on each of five dimensions:

 extraversion/introversion

 agreeableness/antagonism

 conscientiousness/undirectedness

 emotional stability/instability

 openness to experience/non-openness

In addition, each trait dimension consists of six facets, which correlate with one another. For example, agreeableness correlates with facets such as trust, straightforwardness, and modesty (McCrae & Costa, 1994). Within the field of psychology, the Big Five theory has become a useful and generally accepted construct for describing personality.

In fact, researchers have studied how individuals in 56 nations scored on the Big Five personality traits. The results showed that, despite claims to the contrary, Canadians are actually very similar to their American counterparts on all five dimensions. Quebec participants, however, more closely resembled

Personality inventory is a long, scientifically rigorous questionnaire that asks questions about many different behaviours and assesses several traits at once.

Minnesota Multiphasic Personality Inventory (MMPI) is the most widely used personality inventory, initially developed to identify emotional disorders but now used for a variety of other purposes.

Consistency paradox is the observation that personality ratings are consistent across time and among different observers, but that behaviour ratings are not.

France than the United States and English-speaking Canada (Schmitt et al., 2007).

ASSESSING TRAITS

In psychology, **personality inventories** refer to a long, more scientifically rigorous questionnaire that asks questions about many different behaviours and assesses several traits at once. The most widely used and researched of all personality inventories is the **Minnesota Multiphasic Personality Inventory (MMPI).** Originally developed to identify emotional disorders, the MMPI is now used for a variety of other purposes.

One major problem with virtually all personality questionnaires is that the questions tend to be transparent, meaning that it's possible for you to present yourself not as you are but as you'd like to be. The usefulness of a personality test's results depends on how honest and insightful the respondents are about their own behaviours and attitudes. One way to address this potential bias is to have others rate you on a personality inventory—a relatively underused but highly valuable method to assess personality (Connelly & Ones, 2010).

The Predictive Value of Personality Inventories

The validity of a personality measure is determined by the degree to which the scores for each trait correlate with the corresponding aspects of the person's actual behaviour. For example, if world leaders like Vladimir Putin, David Cameron, Barack Obama, and Angela Merkel scored low on ambition and leadership qualities on a personality assessment, it would be clear that the inventory had failed to accurately describe them. Interestingly, one study compared Canadian Prime Minister Stephen

Harper to 87 heads of state/government and 122 other political leaders across seven key leadership traits. The results showed that, compared to other political leaders, Harper ranked in the low-to-moderate range in his belief in his own ability to control events. He also ranked low in the need for power and distrust of others. Harper did, however, rank in the moderate range for self-confidence and in the moderate-to-high range for task focus (Carter, 2008).

Researchers (e.g., Furguson, 2010) have found that personality remains relatively stable across the lifespan—a trend that is seen cross-culturally. Researchers have also uncovered something called the **consistency paradox**—the observation that personality ratings are consistent across time and among different observers, but that behaviour ratings are not (Mischel, 1968, 1984, 2004). This accounts for how our actions vary, depending on the situation. A disciplined athlete who always shows up for practice on time might be late to a friend's party or a job interview. Although we have persistent underlying traits, people, like the situations we encounter, are dynamic.

G8 SUMMIT 2012

∧ How might these **prominent individuals** describe themselves on **personality**
∧ **inventories?** Do you think this **assessment** would be accurate?

THE EFFECTS OF GENETICS ON PERSONALITY

As Beth and Amy's story illustrates, **heritability**—the degree to which a trait is able to be passed on genetically—plays a significant role in personality. Beth had many of the advantages that Amy lacked, including an affectionate and attentive mother and a supportive, inclusive family. But both twins battled anxiety and developed detached personalities. Was there something in the twins' genetic makeup that made this outcome inevitable?

Researchers have discovered that traits identified by trait theories are relatively heritable. Because they share the same genes, identical twins like Amy and Beth are more likely than fraternal twins to have many similar personality traits. Psychologist David Lykken administered personality tests to twins raised in the same home and to twins, like Beth and Amy, who were separated at birth and raised in different homes (Lykken et al., 1988). He still found that identical twins were more similar than fraternal twins, regardless of whether the twins had been raised in the same home. The Big Five traits of extraversion and openness to new experiences have a very high genetic component (Shane, Nicolaou, Cherkas, Spector, 2010). Moreover, cross-cultural studies indicate that the Big Five personality traits exist in all human groups (McCrae et al., 2005). These traits even seem to persist across species; researchers have detected such traits in monkeys, dogs, cats, and pigs (Gosling & John, 1999).

How, then, do genes influence personality traits? Genes may impact the physiological characteristics of the nervous system, particularly neurotransmission in the brain. One theory is that genes influence our temperament—the characteristics and personality traits we are born with—which in turn influence the ways in which we behave. These behavioural patterns and styles soon come to define our personalities.

EVALUATING THE TRAIT PERSPECTIVE

Looking at personality through the lens of the trait perspective can give us plenty of insight into the actions of our friends, our families, and ourselves—but traits have their limitations, too. While the trait perspective effectively describes how people are, it fails to offer much insight into why people are that way. And the question about whether people's behaviours are more influenced by situational factors than by personality traits, known as the **person-situation controversy,** persists (e.g., Bleidorn et al., 2010; Schermer, Johnson, Vernon, & Jang, 2011). Although people's traits may endure over time, their specific behaviour may vary in different situations, so traits alone may not always help us predict behaviour.

The Psychodynamic Perspective

SIGMUND FREUD

As discussed in Chapter 1 and Chapter 10, Sigmund Freud pioneered the clinical approach to understanding personality. The image that many of us associate with psychological counselling—a bearded doctor asking his patient (who is, naturally, lying on a leather couch) to "Tell me about your mother"—originates here. A controversial figure who shocked Victorian Britain with his theories of sexual repression, Freud was initially ridiculed for his ideas. Today,

> Looking at personality through the lens of the trait perspective can give us plenty of insight into the actions of our friends, our families, and ourselves—but traits have their limitations, too. While the trait perspective effectively describes how people are, it fails to offer much insight into why people are that way.

his theories about the unconscious frequently undergo similar tongue-lashings from psychology students, and most professionals view his ideas with great skepticism. However, the influence Freud has had on the modern world is undeniable—ask any member of the public to explain a basic Freudian concept and he or she will most likely be able to do so. Despite the professional skepticism, many Freudian concepts still form a basis for modern personality theories.

Freud believed that our problems in adulthood are caused by our memories, especially disturbing ones from childhood. These memories, according to Freud, are impossible for us to access consciously—they're buried deep in the unconscious mind. Freud thought that to understand his patients' actions, problems, and

Heritability describes the degree to which a trait is able to be passed on genetically.

Person-situation controversy focuses on the question of whether people's behaviours are more influenced by situational factors than by personality traits.

Psychic determinism is the concept that unconscious processes underlie all conscious thoughts and actions.

Psychoanalysis is a type of psychotherapy that relates closely to Freudian concepts like the influence of the unconscious. It requires patients to talk to a psychiatrist about their lives while the psychiatrist listens, analyzes, and interprets each word.

Psychodynamic theory is a personality theory that focuses on the interaction of mental forces.

Id is the part of the psyche that tries to satisfy a person's basic drives and survival instincts.

Pleasure principle states that a person should seek immediate gratification and pay no attention to societal expectations or constraints.

personalities, he had to access the contents of their unconscious minds. This concept—that unconscious processes underlie all conscious thoughts and actions—is known as **psychic determinism.** The method of treatment that Freud invented, called **psychoanalysis,** requires patients to talk to a psychiatrist about their lives while the psychiatrist listens, analyzes, and interprets each word.

Freud's psychoanalytic theory was the first **psychodynamic theory,** a personality theory that focuses on the interaction of mental forces. Psychodynamic theories are based on two beliefs: We don't usually know what our true motives are, and we have defence mechanisms that keep our unpleasant thoughts and motivations in our unconscious mind. How do these "mental forces" interact, why are we unaware of our motives, and what, exactly, are these defence mechanisms (see Chapter 1)? Psychodynamic theory provides some interesting answers.

The Id, Ego, and Superego

Freud conceptualized the mind as three interacting systems: the id, the *ego*, and the *superego*. The *id* tries to satisfy our basic drives and survival instincts. It operates on the hedonistic **pleasure principle**: Seek immediate gratification and pay no attention to societal expectations or constraints. You might associate the *id* with the behaviour of an infant, who cries

Ego is the part of the psyche that tries to identify the basic drive that the *id* wants to fulfill and to come up with a realistic plan for satisfying that drive.

Reality principle states that basic drives and survival instincts should be achieved through actions that will be pleasurable rather than painful.

Superego is the part of the psyche that forces the *ego* to consider societal constraints and acceptable forms of behaviour.

Collective unconscious is a shared pool of memories and images common to all humans.

Archetype is a particular image, such as mother as caretaker and nurturer, persistent across time and cultures.

Inferiority complex is a drive for perfection and superiority throughout adulthood in an effort to compensate for feelings of both physical and mental inferiority rooted in childhood.

Thematic Apperception Test (TAT) presents a participant with a series of random, unfamiliar images and asks him or her to tell stories about them; these stories supposedly reflect the person's inner hopes, fears, and desires.

Rorschach inkblot test presents a participant with a series of nebulous inkblots and asks him or her to say whatever comes to mind upon viewing the inkblots; interpretations of the inkblots supposedly are related to the viewer's unconscious thoughts.

Humanistic theory is a type of personality theory that emphasizes people's conscious understanding of themselves and their abilities to attain self-fulfillment.

Self-concept is a person's understanding of who he or she is.

Self theory is a personality theory that states that all people want to become their "real" selves; to do so, people need to live according to their own wishes rather than those of other people.

when it needs something (even at a fancy dinner party or in a worship service) and stops when that need is fulfilled.

The *ego*'s role is to identify the basic drive that the *id* wants to fulfill and come up with a realistic plan for satisfying that drive. In contrast to the id, the *ego* operates on the **reality principle,** meaning that it attempts to achieve the *id*'s goals through actions that will be pleasurable rather than painful. The *ego* contains our partly conscious perceptions, thoughts, judgments, and memories.

If the *id* represents some of your more devilish impulses, then the *superego* would be the opposite, the proverbial angel on your shoulder. The *superego* forces the *ego* to consider societal constraints and "acceptable" forms of behaviour. Let's say that you're dying to have a shiny new car. If your *superego* didn't

exist, you might steal the car from the lot, paying no attention to laws, social conventions, or a moral sense of right or wrong. Fortunately for you, your *superego* would probably step in, remind you that stealing is illegal and wrong, and then direct your *ego* to obtain the car in a realistic way: Get a job, earn enough money for a down payment, secure a loan, purchase the car, and continue to make monthly payments.

Freud's idea of the mind is often compared to an iceberg that's partly visible above the surface, which represents consciousness, but mostly hidden in the underwater depths of the unconscious mind. The *id* is a completely unconscious force, while the *ego* and *superego* have both conscious and unconscious components.

POST-FREUDIAN PSYCHODYNAMIC THEORISTS

Freud had a number of followers and disciples who helped propagate his ideas into future generations. At the same time, however, few of these disciples agreed with Freud on all points.

Freud's Theory of the Mind

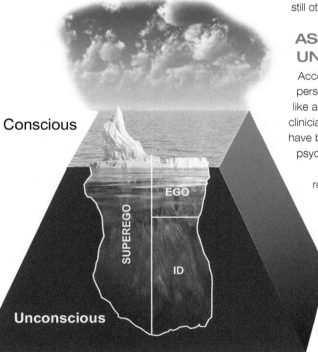

^ ^ ^ How is Freud's conception of the mind similar to an iceberg that is mostly— but not entirely—underwater? What are some limitations of this analogy?

Many prominent post-Freudian psychologists, including Carl Jung, Alfred Adler, Karen Horney, and Erik Erikson, modified or amended Freud's original theories to reflect their own beliefs and concepts regarding personality.

Carl Jung, for example, believed, like Freud, that human personality is strongly influenced by the unconscious. However, Jung placed less emphasis on sexual feelings and pioneered the concept of the **collective unconscious,** a shared pool of memories and images common to all humans. For example, the image of a mother as a caretaker and nurturer exemplifies a common idea persistent across time and cultures. Jung called such images **archetypes.**

Alfred Adler developed the idea of the **inferiority complex** as being an important factor in human personality. Adler believed people often strive for perfection and superiority throughout adulthood in an effort to compensate for feelings of both physical and mental inferiority rooted in childhood.

Psychologist Karen Horney was deeply influenced by Freud's teachings, but she emphasized the importance of social factors, particularly anxiety, as a strong shaper of our personalities. According to Horney, some of us cope with anxiety by becoming submissive, others by becoming aggressive, and still others through detachment.

ASSESSING THE UNCONSCIOUS

Accessing, exploring, and assessing a person's unconscious processes sounds like a tall order, even for the most skilled clinician. Fortunately, a number of tests have been developed over the years to aid psychologists in this endeavour.

Many psychodynamic psychologists rely on projective tests when helping people understand their unconscious thoughts and feelings. These tests present an ambiguous stimulus and then ask the participant to describe it or tell a story about it. For example, the **Thematic Apperception Test (TAT),** developed by Henry Murray, presents people with a series of random, unfamiliar images and asks them to tell stories about them. These stories supposedly reflect their inner hopes, fears, and desires.

Similarly, the **Rorschach inkblot test** presents a series of nebulous inkblots to participants, who are instructed

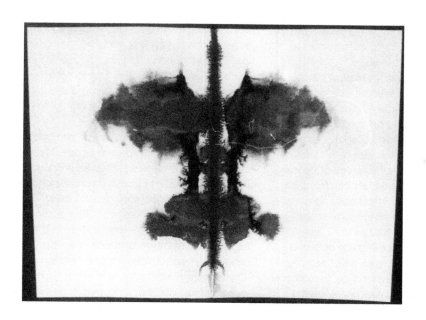

<<< The Rorschach inkblot test represents psychodynamic approaches to personality assessment. From this psychoanalytic perspective, the scenarios that participants evoke from the images on the test reflect the inner workings of their minds.

to say whatever comes to mind upon viewing them. The test assumes that our interpretations of the inkblots are related to our unconscious thoughts. For example, if you see threatening storm clouds in the blurry inkblots, a psychologist might infer that you have feelings of fear or anxiety about something; if you see a dog, you might be longing for a best friend or trusty companion. While this may seem like an unreliable and subjective way to assess the unconscious mind, psychologists use a scoring system to measure participants' responses. For example, frequency tables indicate how often a particular response is given by the general population. Test administrators also look for qualities such as the vagueness of a response, rather than merely focusing on what participants see in the inkblot.

EVALUATING PSYCHODYNAMIC THEORY

Several of Freud's terms and theories have become familiar cultural mainstays, but how popular is the Freudian approach to personality today? Given its emphasis on the unconscious, childhood, and sexuality and aggression, it's probably not too surprising that psychodynamic theory has remained controversial ever since Freud first introduced it to the world. While Freud's theory explains individuals' personality traits after they have developed, it offers no insight or methods to predict these qualities, making its usefulness more or less limited to after-the-fact analysis (Hall & Lindzey, 1978). Strangely, although Freudian theory is developmental, it's not supported by observations or studies of children. Many critics, including Karen Horney, point out that much of the theory seems to have a male-centred bias.

Despite these criticisms, however, Freudian-based, psychodynamic theories endure because both psychologists and people in general continue to see merit in many of their foundational concepts (Huprich & Keaschuk, 2006; Westen, 1998; Shedler, 2010; Town, Abbass, & Hardy, 2011). The idea that we sometimes act in ways that we don't completely understand because of partially unconscious processes makes sense to most of us, as does the concept that our personalities are influenced, at least in part, by our early experiences as children. Although we might hesitate to look to Freud for all of the answers to our questions about why we are the way we are, we shouldn't write him off completely, either.

> The Rorschach inkblot test assumes that our interpretations of the inkblots are related to our unconscious thoughts. For example, if you see threatening storm clouds in the blurry inkblots, a psychologist might infer that you have feelings of fear or anxiety about something; if you see a dog, you might be longing for a best friend or trusty companion.

The Humanistic Approach

The humanistic approach represents yet another way psychologists attempt to understand and analyze human personality. **Humanistic theories** of personality emphasize people's conscious understanding of themselves and their abilities to attain self-fulfillment. Many humanistic theories were developed in the middle of the 20th century as a reaction to the dominance of psychodynamic theories like Freud's. With their emphasis on human capacity for generosity, self-improvement, high achievement, and happiness, humanistic theories tend to appeal to the optimists in all of us.

ROGERS AND SELF-CONCEPT

The humanistic approach to personality centres on the principle of **self-concept**, or a person's understanding of who he or she is. Humanistic theories contend that our self-concept makes up a key part of our reality. Take a moment to consider the question, Who am I? A college student, a son or daughter, a sister or brother, a friend? A kind person, a funny person, an ambitious person, a laid-back person? Answering this question can be a daunting task, and your responses will probably change depending on your mood and outlook. The way you think about yourself, however, represents your self-concept.

Psychologist Carl Rogers (1980) expanded on this idea to develop a theory of personality called **self theory.** Rogers believed that all people want to become their "real" selves. To achieve this goal, we need to live according to our own wishes rather than those of other people. At the same time, however, other people can help us become our real selves by accepting us, acting genuinely, and showing empathy. When people value us despite our problems and weaknesses, they show us **unconditional positive regard,** an ingredient that Rogers considered crucial to self-development.

For Rogers, our self-concept and access to unconditional positive regard is inextricably linked to our personalities and our interactions with the world at large. A positive self-concept, according to Rogers, manifests itself in positive interactions with the world, productive relationships, and personal satisfaction and happiness. Those people who lack unconditional positive regard and have a negative self-concept tend to struggle with feelings of anxiety or doubt.

MASLOW AND SELF-ACTUALIZATION

Humanistic theorists also believe in the importance of **self-actualization,** the experience of becoming your real self and realizing your full potential. Since everyone is individual and unique, everyone reaches self-actualization differently. However, whatever route you take toward self-actualization, it must be a route you've chosen for yourself. It makes sense: The only person who can tell you how to become your real self is you!

That's not to say that external circumstances play no role in self-actualization. In fact, many humanists would argue that we need a nurturing environment in order to achieve full self-actualization. However, we

alone are responsible for taking advantage of that environment and using its resources to help ourselves reach our goals.

Like Rogers, Abraham Maslow devoted a large portion of his career to developing the major tenets of humanistic psychology. Maslow (Maslow, 1954) believed that in order to self-actualize, we must satisfy five sets of needs. He envisioned this idea as a pyramidal structure, known as the **hierarchy of needs**.

According to Maslow, we can focus on higher needs only if our most basic needs have been satisfied. For example, you're unlikely to pay much attention to your need for love or self-expression if you are starving or desperate for a glass of water. Maslow's hierarchy makes sense from an evolutionary perspective: Our physiological and safety needs are the

Maslow's Hierarchy of Needs

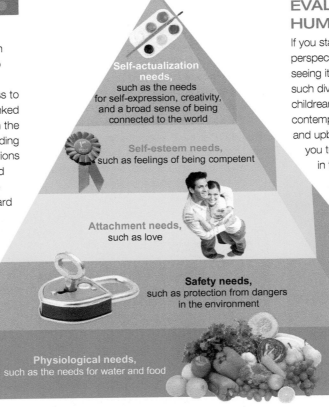

Self-actualization needs, such as the needs for self-expression, creativity, and a broad sense of being connected to the world

Self-esteem needs, such as feelings of being competent

Attachment needs, such as love

Safety needs, such as protection from dangers in the environment

Physiological needs, such as the needs for water and food

most basic because they are most immediately linked to survival.

In Maslow's view, some needs are more essential than others, but they are all nonetheless interconnected. Although you can technically live without friends, as opposed to food or water, maintaining strong social bonds actually helps you meet your physiological, safety, and reproductive needs. Additionally, you might think of self-actualization as the result of years of learning experiences. You acquire skills and

knowledge through both formal education and activities such as playing, exploring, and creating. These acquired skills not only help you self-actualize but also make it easier for you to get food, escape threats, and find a mate. Even your "less essential" needs turn out to be pretty essential after all.

By focusing on the capacity for psychologically healthy people to grow and achieve happiness, Maslow represented a marked shift from the psychodynamic emphasis on uncovering the roots of individual's psychological troubles. "Tell me about your mother" became "Tell me about yourself—your hopes, dreams, and vision of the future." From Maslow's perspective, our personalities are self-directed and self-determined. Those who strive for higher-level needs such as self-actualization, he found, tend to be more generous, accepting, and patient than those focused on satisfying only their basic needs.

EVALUATING THE HUMANISTIC APPROACH

If you start looking around for the humanistic perspective in your everyday life, you might start seeing it everywhere. Its ideas have influenced such diverse areas as counselling, education, childrearing, and management, not to mention contemporary pop psychology. Self-help books and upbeat magazines have probably urged you to read about "finding yourself," "getting in touch with the real you," or "living the life you were meant to live." This type of language has become a ubiquitous part of self-help literature, talk show chatter, and general conversation. If you listen closely, you can hear the voices of humanistic psychology echoing in the background.

The appeal of the humanistic approach is obvious. It is person-centred, accessible to the masses, and refreshingly optimistic. Cultivating a positive self-concept is the key to being happy and successful, and most people think they're capable of seeing themselves in this positive light. In addition, humanists' focus on the individual self reinforces Western cultural values, so people in the Western world find it easy to relate to the humanist perspective.

Despite, or perhaps because of, its popularity, critics of the humanistic perspective have said that its concepts are vague and subjective. A self-actualized person sounds great in theory, but what, exactly, does this person look like?

What evidence exists to differentiate that person from his or her non-self-actualized peers? Some psychologists also criticize the humanistic approach on the grounds that the individualism and focus on self that this perspective demands may lead to selfishness and narcissism. If realizing yourself, thinking well of yourself, and making yourself happy are all that you are concerned about, critics argue, will you bother to think of the rest of the world? (Campbell & Specht, 1985; Wallach & Wallach, 1983).

Like any approach, the humanistic perspective has its limitations and non-believers. Nevertheless, humanists such as Rogers and Maslow, in their interpretation of humans as malleable, dynamic, and capable of great things, offer a hopeful view of personality.

The Social Cognitive Perspective

"You are the company you keep": Whoever first uttered this old saying would probably have been a proponent of the social cognitive perspective on personality. Social cognitive theories of personality place emphasis on the beliefs and habits of thought, both conscious and automatic, that we form through our interactions with society. Social cognitive theories overlap to some extent with humanistic ideas, but unlike most humanistic theories of personality, social cognitive theories rely heavily on laboratory research and are concerned with predicting people's behaviour in specific situations rather than with predicting people's more general life choices.

Social cognitive theorists believe our behaviours can be traced to our attempts to model

what we have observed others doing or to practise what we have learned through conditioning. We are fun-loving and affectionate because our parents were fun-loving and affectionate, and we naturally model their behaviour. Or, we continue to be responsible because every time we have acted responsibly in the past, we were praised and rewarded.

Psychologists who support social cognitive theories generally believe that our unique perceptions and thinking—about ourselves and our situations—play a major role in determining our behaviour. In their view, personality is less determined by underlying traits or childhood traumas than it is by the current situation, our acquired knowledge from past situations, and the way we think about both. For social cognitive psychologists, personality tends to be highly dynamic and reflective of a combination of social cues and norms as well as individual thought patterns.

ROTTER AND PERSONAL CONTROL

If you've ever felt like you have no control over a situation, you know that feeling this way can be depressing and difficult. One idea central to many social cognitive theories of personality is that of **personal control**, or our sense of controlling our environment rather than feeling helpless. Julian Rotter, one of the principal founders of the social cognitive perspective on personality, devoted much of his research to exploring the relationship between individuals' sense of personal control and their behaviours, personalities, and states of mind.

Do you act differently when you play a game of poker as opposed to a game of bingo? In one laboratory study, Rotter (Rotter, 1954) found that people behave differently at different tasks and games, depending on whether they believe that the game requires skill or luck. When we think a game requires skill, we work hard and improve our performance. When we think a game requires only luck, however, we believe that

we can't control the game's outcome, so we don't work hard and we tend not to improve at all. Based on these findings, Rotter argued that our behaviour depends on our perception of the amount of control that we have over a certain situation. He called this disposition the **locus of control**. According to Rotter, people with an **internal locus of control** believe that they control their own rewards and, therefore, their own fate. People who have an **external locus of control** believe that rewards and fate are controlled by outside forces. Rotter (1966) developed a locus-of-control questionnaire that can be used to identify which locus of control an individual most displays.

Since Rotter's initial experiments, many studies have demonstrated links between scores on this questionnaire and actual behaviour. People who demonstrate an internal locus of control are more likely to excel in school, take preventive healthcare measures, resist group pressure, effectively deal with stress, and handle illness better (Injeyan et al., 2011; Lachman & Weaver, 1998; Lefcourt, 1982; Presson & Benassi, 1996; Waldron et al., 2010). In addition, people who demonstrate an internal locus of control tend to be less anxious and more content with life than people who demonstrate an external locus of control.

Recent research has explored the idea that we each have many different loci of control, each of which corresponds to a certain area of our lives. In other words, you may feel that your performance in school is entirely in your own hands, but your performance on the

<<< Our perception of how much control we have on the outcome of a game affects our behaviour. Many people devote ample time to improving their skills at poker. Would you do the same for a game like bingo? Why or why not?

soccer team is more or less determined by fate. According to this theory, our **outcome expectancies,** or our assumptions about the consequences of our behaviour, greatly influence the degree to which we may exhibit an internal or external locus of control.

Consistently being unable to control important situations may eventually cause us to develop **learned helplessness,** a feeling of hopelessness and passivity caused by being unable to avoid or control traumatic events. Psychologist Martin Seligman (Seligman, 1968) found that dogs, after being exposed to electric shocks with no chance to escape, did not even bother trying to escape later when put in the same situation, even when they had the opportunity to get away. Repeated exposure to painful or traumatic events can cause us to feel depressed and resigned to our fate.

BANDURA, RECIPROCAL DETERMINISM, AND SELF-EFFICACY

Canadian psychologist Albert Bandura was another pioneer of the social cognitive perspective. His cognitive social-learning theory emphasizes the cognitive processes that are involved in acquiring and maintaining patterns of behaviour and, as a result, personality. At the centre of this theory is the idea of **reciprocal determinism,** which provides a basis for understanding how environmental factors coexist with and influence personality, just as personality factors coexist with and influence the environment. Our personalities are a

> Bandura believed that high self-efficacy not only predicts high performance but also causes it. From Bandura's standpoint, the "I think I can" attitude results in actual achievement.

potent mix of our unique thought patterns, our environments, and our behaviours, all of which are engaged in a constant series of cyclical causes and effects. For example, you might love being in the limelight; you feel great when you're the centre of attention. As a result, you sign up for a drama class and start hanging out with a group of gregarious friends. This

> From a **social cognitive perspective, your feelings, your behaviour, and your environment interact to determine your personality.**

new environment reinforces your thoughts and feelings, and soon enough, your behaviours reflect increased extroversion: You audition for *Canadian Idol*; you perform at a local open mike night; you start conversations with strangers while standing in line. Your thoughts and personality helped you choose an environment, which in turn further shaped your thoughts, behaviours, and personality.

Much of Bandura's (Bandura, 2003) research also focused on self-efficacy. **Self-efficacy,** a concept similar to self-confidence, describes people's expectations about their own abilities to perform certain tasks: The higher your level of self-efficacy, the greater your belief that you can perform a given task. Like locus of control, self-efficacy can refer to a specific task or to a large category of tasks.

Self-efficacy consistently predicts high performance in areas such as math, physical exertion, and pain tolerance. In fact, Bandura believed that high self-efficacy not only predicts high performance but also causes it. From Bandura's standpoint, the "I think I can" attitude results in actual achievement (a comforting idea to keep in mind the next time you find yourself scaling a mountain, literally or figuratively). For example, researchers have found that Canadians with higher self-efficacy are more likely to be physically active (Cutumisu & Spence, 2012), have higher levels of confidence (Guerrero & Rothstein, 2012), and remain sober after alcohol recovery (Solomon & Annis, 2006).

THE POWER OF THINKING POSITIVELY

For some, the seemingly inexhaustible perkiness and cheer of daytime talk show hosts like Rachael Ray and Kelly Ripa is comforting and inspiring; for others, it can be grating and annoying. Nonetheless, psychological research shows that regardless of our feelings about these high-spirited, bubbly television personalities, we could all benefit from a healthy dose of optimism.

The roles that optimism and pessimism play in shaping personality are an important part of **social cognitive theory.** Psychologists have designed a number of different questionnaires that assess

Reciprocal Determinism

BEHAVIOUR

PERSONAL FACTORS (Thoughts and feelings)

ENVIRONMENT

people's general ability to think either positively or negatively. For example, Rick Snyder and colleagues (1996) designed a questionnaire that assesses hope, and Martin Seligman designed a questionnaire that assesses how optimistically or pessimistically people explain negative events in their lives.

Questionnaires like these have been used in several correlational studies, which have found that optimistic people tend to cope more effectively with negative events than do people who are pessimistic. For example, students who adopt a positive attitude about school are more likely to start earning higher grades than are students who hold on to negative thought patterns like "This is too hard" or "I'm going to fail no matter what" (Noel, Forsyth, & Kelley, 1987; Peterson & Barrett, 1987). In fact, students achieved greater academic success when they attended schools in which the faculty was optimistic that their students would be successful (Kirby & DiPaola, 2011) Optimism has other benefits, too: An optimistic state of mind benefits our health by giving the body's immune system its best chance at remaining strong. Research has even shown that optimists outlive pessimists and are generally healthier overall (e.g., Piko, Kovacs, & Fitzpatrick, 2009; Taylor et al., 2010).

CROSS-CULTURAL DIFFERENCES IN PERSONALITY

If you grew up in Tokyo, Japan, would your personality be different than it would be if you grew up in Timmins, Ontario? It's certainly possible. People around the world are exposed to a wide, rich variety of cultural values, philosophies, economic conditions, and expectations for how to behave. One major way in which cultures differ is the degree to which they are formed around collectivist or individualist ideals. **Collectivist cultures** emphasize people's interdependence: Our relationship to others is a defining aspect of our identities, and we all have responsibilities to our families and communities. The dominant cultures of East Asia, Africa, and South America tend to be collectivist. As a result, people raised in these cultures are likely to possess an **interdependent construal of self**, to see themselves as parts of a larger network of family and community members.

In contrast, **individualist cultures** place emphasis on each person's individual rights and freedoms and de-emphasize the social roles that we play in relation to others. The dominant cultures of North America, Australia, and Western Europe tend to be individualist, and people who grow up in cultures like these tend to have an **independent construal of self**, viewing themselves as self-directed, self-contained entities.

What does all of this have to do with personality? If you exhibit a personality trait called **allocentrism**, you tend to think and act in a collectivist manner. If you exhibit **ideocentrism**, on the other hand, you tend to have a more individualistic focus. Allocentric people care deeply about their personal relationships and the interests of their friends, families, and other groups. They generally focus on the similarities between themselves and other group members, and they believe that their thoughts and actions are responses to their social environment. Ideocentric people, on the other hand, tend to focus not on their roles in society but on their roles as individuals. These people see themselves as unique, and they believe that their personal hopes, dreams, and desires are the driving forces in their lives.

The culture in which we're raised affects not only our personality but also our views of the concept of personality. If you were raised

> "People around the world are exposed to a wide, rich variety of cultural values, philosophies, economic conditions, and expectations for how to behave. One major way in which cultures differ is the degree to which they are formed around collectivist or individualist ideals."

in a collectivist culture, individualists' fascination with personality tests and "finding your true self" might seem bewildering to you, since people in collectivist cultures tend to believe that individual differences stem not from our deep-seated personality traits but from situational or environmental variations. And the cultural differences don't end there. For example, East Asians emphasize different personality trait dimensions than the dimensions that individualist cultures usually come up with. The Chinese believe in the importance of traits such as harmony (inner peace of mind and harmonious interactions with others), face (concern with maintaining reputation or dignity), and *ren qing* (emphasis on the mutual exchange of favours in relationships). You might notice that these traits don't correspond at all to

Collectivist culture is a culture that emphasizes people's interdependence.

Interdependent construal of self refers to a person's view of himself or herself as part of a larger network of family and community members.

Individualist culture is a culture that emphasizes each person's individual rights and freedoms and de-emphasizes the social roles that people play in relation to others.

Independent construal of self refers to a person's view of himself or herself as a self-directed, self-contained entity.

Allocentrism is a personality trait exhibiting the tendency to think and act in a collectivist manner.

Ideocentrism is a personality trait exhibiting the tendency to think and act in an individualistic manner.

the dimensions described in the Big Five. This means that personality tests are not necessarily cross-culturally applicable: Fundamental differences in how Western and non-Western cultures understand personality prevent us from creating a truly global measure of personality.

EVALUATING THE SOCIAL COGNITIVE PERSPECTIVE

Critics charge that the social cognitive approach to personality places too much importance on external situations and does not fully appreciate the importance of the roles that biology and genetics play in establishing our inner traits. Some critics also point out that the social cognitive perspective often fails to account for the dramatically different ways in which people react to the same situations. For example, some people become panicked and uncontrollably anxious during emergency situations, while others are the picture of tranquility. Or think back to Amy and Beth. You could argue that Amy's detachment and anxiety was reflective of the environment in which she was raised. But what about Beth? Her mother was kind and loving, but Beth was equally detached.

Although the social cognitive approach to personality has its limitations, it's been embraced to some extent in popular culture. It gives us valuable insight into potential connections between our thoughts, our environments, and our actions. Even better, it offers us strategies for improving our lives: For example, the social cognitive perspective suggests that if we change the way we think, we can often change the way we act, effectively creating positive situations for ourselves. If you maintain a positive attitude about your upcoming exam, for example, you may be more likely to pass it with flying colours.

Summary

WHAT IS PERSONALITY, AND HOW IS IT STUDIED? p.218

• Personality is the style in which one interacts with the world, particularly with other people.

• Researchers study personality by using either the ideographic or the nomothetic approach to examine self-report data, observer-report data, specific behavioural data, life-events data, and physiological data.

WHAT ARE THE MAJOR TRAIT THEORIES, HOW ARE TRAITS ASSESSED, AND HOW DO GENES AFFECT INDIVIDUALS' TRAITS? p.219

• Trait theories are sets of meaningful and distinct personality dimensions that can be used to describe how people differ from one another.

• Research has shown that personality remains relatively stable across the lifespan, and that genetics plays a significant role in the individual differences for most traits. Genes may impact the chemical makeup of the brain, which in turn influences behavioural patterns and personality.

HOW DID FREUD CONCEPTUALIZE HUMAN PERSONALITY, AND HOW HAS PSYCHODYNAMIC THEORY EVOLVED OVER THE YEARS? p.221

• Freud believed that the mind comprises three interacting systems: the *id*, the *ego*, and the *superego*.

• Post-Freudian theorists include Carl Jung (collective unconscious), Alfred Adler (inferiority complex), and Karen Horney (social factors).

WHAT ARE THE MAJOR TENETS OF THE HUMANISTIC APPROACH TO PERSONALITY? p.223

• Humanistic theories of personality emphasize people's conscious understanding of themselves and their abilities to attain self-fulfillment.

• Humanistic theorists include Carl Rogers (self theory) and Abraham Maslow (hierarchy of needs).

HOW DO SOCIAL COGNITIVE THEORIES OF LEARNING AND BEHAVIOUR APPLY TO THE STUDY OF PERSONALITY, AND HOW DO CONCEPTIONS OF PERSONALITY VARY ACROSS CULTURES? p.225

• Social cognitive theories hold that personality is a function of beliefs and habits of thought acquired through unique social experiences.

• People in collectivist cultures tend to have interdependent construals of self, while people in individualist cultures tend to have independent construals of self.

Test Your Understanding

1. Which of the following is likely to be true of a personality study that employs the idiographic approach?
   a. It involves hundreds of participants.
   b. It provides detailed descriptive analyses of each participant's personality.
   c. It uses factor analysis to find patterns among the traits of participants.
   d. It aims to develop a general theory regarding human personality.

2. Andre feels anxious before big exams but is otherwise an easy-going guy. Laura tends to be anxious about most things, most of the time. Which of the following is probably true?
   a. Both Andre and Laura possess the trait of anxiety.
   b. Andre possesses the trait of anxiety, but Laura experiences a state of anxiety.
   c. Andre experiences a state of anxiety, but Laura possesses the trait of anxiety.
   d. Andre has an anxiety disorder, but Laura does not.

3. According to the Big Five theory, a daredevil who enjoys skydiving and bungee jumping would likely score high in the personality dimension of:
   a. extraversion
   b. agreeableness
   c. conscientiousness
   d. emotional stability

4. Anya is known for being honest and straightforward. However, when Anya's friend asks her what she thinks of her new haircut, Anya lies and tells her she likes it. Anya's behaviour exemplifies:
   a. reciprocal determinism
   b. factor analysis
   c. the consistency paradox
   d. psychic determinism

5. Which of the following would a trait theorist most likely provide?
   a. an explanation of why you are conscientious

b. an evaluation of how past experiences caused you to be conscientious

c. an analysis of how being conscientious leads to self-actualization

d. a description of how you exhibit conscientiousness

6. Fritz considers himself to be a highly insecure person. A psychologist employing the Freudian approach to personality would most likely:

a. identify the thought patterns that compound Fritz's insecurity

b. determine how to satisfy Fritz's safety needs so that he feels less insecure

c. identify other facets of Fritz's personality related to his insecurity

d. trace Fritz's insecurity to unconscious conflicts and childhood experiences

7. According to Freud, a person controlled by his or her *id* would be likely to:

a. always act in a morally upright way

b. have a difficult time making decisions

c. frequently display socially inappropriate behaviour

d. have a highly developed sense of self

8. Mayu, who has an intense fear of medical procedures, forgets to go to her doctor's appointment. From a Freudian standpoint, Mayu's behaviour is an example of:

a. repression

b. sublimation

c. reaction formation

d. displacement

9. The universal image of the hero as a protector of good and defeater of evil exemplifies:

a. Adler's conception of the inferiority complex

b. Jung's conception of the collective unconscious

c. Horney's criticism of Freudian theory as male-centred

d. Rogers's conception of self-concept

10. Which of the following would most likely strengthen psychodynamic theory in the eyes of many critics?

a. a strict focus on psychosexual stages of development

b. a complete dismissal of the theory's foundational concepts

c. a detailed theoretical construct of the mind

d. a series of studies involving observations of child development

11. Which of the following statements exemplifies the idea of unconditional positive regard?

a. "I want to improve my self-concept."

b. "I am working to reach self-actualization."

c. "I love you even though you are flawed."

d. "I have an interesting life story."

12. According to Maslow and his hierarchy of needs, which of the following is true?

a. Physiological needs are identical to safety needs.

b. Physiological needs must be met before other needs can be considered.

c. Physiological needs are the least important.

d. Physiological needs have no bearing on self-actualization.

13. Which of the following does NOT accurately describe the humanistic perspective on personality?

a. It appeals mainly to scientists and the academic elite.

b. It has become a ubiquitous part of pop culture.

c. It is often criticized as promoting narcissism.

d. It focuses on the potential of healthy people.

14. A psychologist looks for correlations between the personality characteristics of children and their best friends in order to determine if they tend to model each other's behaviour. This psychologist likely subscribes to the:

a. trait theory approach

b. psychodynamic approach

c. humanistic approach

d. social cognitive approach

15. Cate possesses an internal locus of control. She is most likely to:

a. earn straight As in school

b. succumb to peer pressure

c. have a strong belief in luck

d. neglect her health

16. The theory of reciprocal determinism accounts for how:

a. people don't try to improve at games requiring skill

b. people tend to feel helpless after repeated traumatic experiences

c. people choose friends whose interests are similar to their own

d. people work harder when there is a promise of a reward

17. Tamika possesses a high level of self-efficacy in her mathematical abilities. Tamika will most likely:

a. perform poorly on math tests

b. earn high scores on math tests

c. have a high level of self-efficacy in athletics

d. have a high level of self-efficacy in all academic areas

18. According to psychological studies, a highly optimistic person is most likely to:

a. give up on games depending on luck

b. cope effectively with stress

c. become chronically ill

d. earn high grades in all subjects

19. An allocentric person is most likely to:

a. express his or her personality through a unique clothing style

b. move far away from friends and family

c. invest a great deal of time and effort in cultivating friendships

d. disagree vehemently with friends' opinions on most topics

20. Which of the following individuals would be most likely to DISAGREE with the principles of the social cognitive theory of personality?

a. a preschool teacher

b. a humanistic psychologist

c. a fan of the self-help book *The Secret*

d. a genetic scientist

Remember to check www.thethinkspot.ca for additional information, downloadable flashcards, and other helpful resources.

Answers: 1) b; 2) c; 3) a; 4) c; 5) d; 6) d; 7) c; 8) a; 9) b; 10) d; 11) c; 12) b; 13) a; 14) d; 15) a; 16) c; 17) b; 18) b; 19) c; 20) d

THINK READINGS

PSYCHOLOGICAL SCIENCE

Short Report

Facebook Profiles Reflect Actual Personality, Not Self-Idealization

Mitja D. Back, Juliane M. Stopfer, Simine Vazire, Sam Gaddis, Stefan C. Schmukle, Boris Egloff and Samuel D. Gosling

More than 700 million people worldwide now have profiles on on-line social networking sites (OSNs), such as MySpace and Facebook (ComScore, 2008); OSNs have become integrated into the milieu of modern-day social interactions and are widely used as a primary medium for communication and networking (Boyd & Ellison, 2007; Valkenburg & Peter, 2009). Despite the increasing integration of OSN activity into everyday life, however, there has been no research on the most fundamental question about OSN profiles: Do they convey accurate impressions of profile owners?

A widely held assumption, supported by content analyses, suggests that OSN profiles are used to create and communicate idealized selves (Manago, Graham, Greenfield, & Salimkhan, 2008). According to this *idealized virtual-identity hypothesis*, profile owners display idealized characteristics that do not reflect their actual personalities. Thus, personality impressions based on OSN profiles should reflect profile owners' ideal-self views rather than what the owners are actually like.

A contrasting view holds that OSNs may constitute an extended social context in which to express one's actual personality characteristics, thus fostering accurate interpersonal perceptions. OSNs integrate various sources of personal information that mirror those found in personal environments, private thoughts, facial images, and social behavior, all of which are known to contain valid information about personality (Ambady & Skowronski, 2008; Funder, 1999; Hall & Bernieri, 2001; Kenny, 1994; Vazire & Gosling, 2004). Moreover, creating idealized identities should be hard to accomplish because (a) OSN profiles include information about one's reputation that is difficult to control (e.g., wall posts) and (b) friends provide accountability and subtle feedback on one's profile. Accordingly, the *extended real-life hypothesis* predicts that people use OSNs to communicate their real personality. If this supposition is true, lay observers should be able to accurately infer the personality characteristics of OSN profile owners. In the present study, we tested the two competing hypotheses.

METHOD

Participants

Participants were 236 OSN users (ages 17–22 years) from the most popular OSNs in the United States (Facebook; N = 133, 52 male, 81 female) and Germany (StudiVZ, SchuelerVZ; N = 103, 17 male, 86 female). In the United States, participants were recruited from the University of Texas campus, where flyers and candy were used to find volunteers for a laboratory-based study of personality judgment. Participants

In Chapter 15 (p.224), you read about Maslow's hierarchy of needs. What needs do social networking sites such as Facebook fulfill?

Think about what you learned about research methods in Chapter 2. How does this step demonstrate good research practice? What might have happened had the researchers not thought to do this?

were compensated with a combination of money and course credit. In Germany, participants were recruited through advertisements for an on-line study on personality measurement. As compensation, they received individual feedback on their personality scores.

To ensure that participants did not alter their OSN profiles, we saved their profiles before the subject of OSNs was raised. Scores on all measures were normally distributed.

MEASURES

Accuracy criteria. Accuracy criteria (i.e., indices of what profile owners were actually like) were created by aggregating across multiple personality reports, each of which measured the Big Five personality dimensions (John, Naumann, & Soto, 2008). In the U.S. sample, profile owners' self-reports and reports from four well-acquainted friends were obtained using the Ten Item Personality Inventory (TIPI; Gosling, Rentfrow, & Swann, 2003). In the German sample, self-reports on the short form of the Big Five Inventory (BFI-10; Rammstedt & John, 2007) and the NEO Five-Factor Inventory (Costa & McCrae, 1992) were combined.

Ideal-self ratings. We measured ideal-self perceptions by rephrasing the TIPI and the BFI-10 rating instructions: Participants were asked to "describe yourself as you ideally would like to be."

Observer ratings. Observer ratings (how profile owners were perceived) were obtained from 9 (U.S. sample) and 10 (German sample) undergraduate research assistants, who perused each OSN profile without time restrictions and then rated their impressions of the profile owners using an observer-report form of the TIPI (U.S. sample) or BFI-10 (German sample). Each observer rated only profiles of participants from his or her own country. Observer agreement (consensus) was calculated within each sample using intraclass correlations (ICCs) for both single, ICC(2,1), and aggregate, ICC(2, k), ratings. Consensus was then averaged across samples using Fisher's r-to-z transformation (see Table 1, column 1).

ANALYSES

In each sample, we determined accuracy by correlating the aggregated observer ratings with the accuracy criterion. To gauge the effect of self-idealization, we computed partial correlations between profile owners' ideal-self ratings and aggregated observer ratings, controlling for the accuracy criterion; this procedure removed the reality component from ideal-self ratings to leave a pure measure of self idealization.[1] To determine whether results were consistent across samples, we computed a dummy-coded variable, "U.S. versus German sample," and ran general linear models, including all interactive effects. No significant interactions emerged. Thus, to obtain the most robust estimates of the effect sizes, we first z-standardized all data within each sample, then combined the samples, and then ran the analyses again. To provide an estimate of accuracy and self-idealization effects for a single observer (not inflated by aggregation), we also calculated the effects separately for each observer and then averaged across observers using Fisher's r-to-z transformation (Hall & Bernieri, 2001). Significance testing was done by means of one-sample t tests, using observer as the unit of analysis.

RESULTS AND DISCUSSION

Our results were consistent with the extended real-life hypothesis and contrary to the idealized virtual-identity hypothesis. Observer

Review the "Big Five" in Chapter 15 (p.219).

Experimenters compared average observer ratings with participants' ideal-self ratings to come to their conclusions.

Table 1

Consensus, Accuracy, and Self-Idealization: Agreement Among Observer Ratings Elicited by Facebook Profiles and Correlations With Actual Personality and the Ideal Self

Observer rating	Actual personality			Ideal self	
	ICC (consensus)	r (accuracy)	$r_{partial}$	r	$r_{partial}$ (self-idealization)
Extraversion					
Average observer	.81***	.39***	.32***	.13	.01
Single observer	.31***	.25***	.21***	.08*	.00
Agreeableness					
Average observer	.59***	.22**	.20*	.16	.08
Single observer	.13***	.11**	.11**	.08*	.04
Conscientiousness					
Average observer	.77***	.27**	.26**	.05	-.02
Single observer	.27***	.17***	.16***	.03	-.01
Neuroticism					
Average observer	.48***	.13	.13	.12	.11
Single observer	.09***	.06	.06*	.04	.04
Openness					
Average observer	.72***	.41***	.37***	.24**	.11
Single observer	.23***	.24***	.21***	.14***	.06

Note: Consensus among observers was calculated using the intraclass correlation (ICC). Accuracy was determined by correlating observer ratings with the criterion measure of actual personality. The effect of self-idealization was determined by the partial correlation between the ideal-self ratings of the profile owners and observer ratings, controlling for the criterion measure of actual personality. In addition, the table shows simple correlations between the ideal-self ratings of the profile owners and observer ratings, as well as partial correlations between the criterion measure of actual personality and observer ratings, controlling for ideal-self ratings. In the case of single-observer scores, means of the correlations for single observers are presented.

*$p_{rep} > .95$. **$p_{rep} > .99$. ***$p_{rep} > .999$.

accuracy was found, but there was no evidence of self-idealization (see Table 1), and ideal-self ratings did not predict observer impressions above and beyond actual personality. In contrast, even when controlling for ideal-self ratings, the effect of actual personality on OSN impressions remained significant for nearly all analyses. Accuracy was strongest for extraversion (paralleling results from face-to-face encounters) and openness (similar to research on personal environments). Accuracy was lowest for neuroticism, which is consistent with previous research showing that neuroticism is difficult to detect in all zero-acquaintance contexts (Funder, 1999; Kenny, 1994). These results suggest that people are not using their OSN profiles to promote an idealized virtual identity.

Neuroticism is a mental disorder accompanied by disturbances such as anxieties or phobias.

Robert McCrae and Paul Costa were fundamental in developing the Big Five theory. You can read more about their work in Chapter 15 (p.219).

Instead, OSNs might be an efficient medium for expressing and communicating real personality, which may help explain their popularity.

Our findings represent a first look at the accuracy of people's self-portrayals on OSNs. To clarify the processes and moderating factors involved, future research should investigate (a) older users and other OSNs, (b) other personality traits, (c) other forms of impression management, (d) the role of specific profile components (e.g., photos, preferences), and (e) individual differences among targets (e.g., self-monitoring) and observers (e.g., OSN experience).

DECLARATION OF CONFLICTING INTERESTS

The authors declared that they had no conflicts of interests with respect to their authorship and/or the publication of this article.

NOTE

1. As expected, accuracy criteria and ideal-self ratings were moderately correlated, mean $r = .28$ (neuroticism: $r = .08$; extraversion: $r = .36$; openness: $r = .33$; agreeableness: $r = .22$; conscientiousness: $r = .26$).

REFERENCES

Ambady, N., & Skowronski, J. (Eds.). (2008). *First impressions*. New York: Guilford.

Boyd, D.M., & Ellison, N.B. (2007). Social network sites: Definition, history, and scholarship. *Journal of Computer-Mediated Communication, 13*, 210–230.

ComScore. (2008). *Social networking explodes worldwide as sites increase their focus on cultural relevance*. Retrieved August 12, 2008, from http://www.comscore.com/press/release.asp?press=2396

Costa, P.T., Jr., & McCrae, R.R. (1992). *Revised NEO Personality Inventory (NEO-PI-R) and NEO Five-Factor Inventory (NEOFFI) professional manual*. Odessa, FL: Psychological Assessment Resources.

Funder, D.C. (1999). *Personality judgment: A realistic approach to person perception*. San Diego, CA: Academic Press.

Gosling, S.D., Rentfrow, P.J., & Swann, W.B., Jr. (2003). A very brief measure of the Big Five personality domains. *Journal of Research in Personality, 37*, 504–528.

Hall, J.A., & Bernieri, F.J. (Eds.). (2001). *Interpersonal sensitivity: Theory and measurement*. New York: Erlbaum.

John, O.P., Naumann, L.P., & Soto, C.J. (2008). Paradigm shift to the integrative Big Five trait taxonomy: History, measurement, and conceptual issues. In O.P. John, R.W. Robins, & L.A. Pervin (Eds.), *Handbook of personality: Theory and research* (pp. 114–154). New York: Guilford.

Kenny, D.A. (1994). *Interpersonal perception: A social relations analysis*. New York: Guilford.

Manago, A.M., Graham, M.B., Greenfield, P.M., & Salimkhan, G. (2008). Self-presentation and gender on MySpace. *Journal of Applied Developmental Psychology, 29*, 446–458.

Rammstedt, B., & John, O.P. (2007). Measuring personality in one minute or less: A 10-item short version of the Big Five Inventory in English and German. *Journal of Research in Personality, 41*, 203–212.

Valkenburg, P.M., & Peter, J. (2009). Social consequences of the Internet for adolescents: A decade of research. *Current Directions in Psychological Science, 18*, 1–5.

Vazire, S., & Gosling, S.D. (2004). E-perceptions: Personality impressions based on personal websites. *Journal of Personality and Social Psychology, 87*, 123–132.

> **Online** social networking **sites** might be an efficient medium **for** expressing and communicating real personality, **which may help** explain their popularity.

POLICE LINE DO NOT CROSS

PSYCHO-PATHOLOGY

Am I

normal? This is a question that many of us will ask at some time in our lives. We are reassured that we are in fact "normal" based on the behaviours of others, social norms, and by comparisons to those who clearly function outside the realm of normality. In psychology, "normal" refers to average behaviour, with behaviours existing on a continuum. If you deviate from the norm, you are said to be abnormal. Individuals such as Paul Bernardo, Karla Homolka, Robert Pickton, and Russell Williams clearly illustrate the dangerous and negative extremes of abnormality. What causes these abnormalities? Can mental illness account for such extremes in behaviour? And are all abnormal behaviours necessarily bad? Let's examine the other extreme of abnormality, the one that is coveted and admired by us, that of the genius.

Picture a creative genius and you will probably come up with a mental image of someone who is slightly eccentric, odd, and abnormal. The stereotype of the mad professor is often perpetuated in novels and science fiction movies. But is genius really linked to madness and abnormality? Can having a mental disorder actually heighten creativity?

The answer to the first question appears to be yes. The rates of psychological disorders are about twice as high among people who work in creative fields than in the general population. Looking back at some historical legends, we find that Isaac Newton, Ludwig van Beethoven, Virginia Woolf, and Winston Churchill all suffered from mental illness. Today, the list of creative thinkers that suffer from mental illness is long and ever growing. As an artist's prominence increases, so too do the chances of developing psychopathological symptoms, in particular, depression, alcoholism, and attempts at suicide. Artistic creators are more likely to develop these symptoms than scientific creators. How many creative artists can you name who have suffered from mental disorders?

But does madness actually result in creative genius? Psychologist Robert Weisberg (1994) believes the answer is no. Studying the works of composer Robert Schumann, who suffered from bipolar disorder, Weisberg noted that the quality of Schumann's work remained consistent. Although the quantity of Schumann's compositions increased during his manic years, he was no better able to produce great music than he had been without the mania. Weisberg concluded that although mania increases energy levels, it does not give a person access to ideas that he or she wouldn't have had otherwise. Further, researchers (e.g., Silvia & Kimbrel, 2010) have reported that mental illnesses such as depression and anxiety have only a very small relationship with creativity.

Could environment be the missing link between creativity and depression? Weisberg notes that the creative lifestyle is often far from emotionally stable; many artists struggle with poverty and public indifference throughout their lives. Those who do achieve recognition within their lifetimes suffer from the stress of having to live up to previous successes, a heavy burden to carry. Artists are also more likely to live self-reflective lives, constantly mulling over issues. This style of thinking is symptomatic of depression, and can even lead to it. Rather than the disorder causing the creativity, creative people and people suffering from mental disorders appear to share some common personality and cognitive traits (Fink, Slamar-Halbedl, Unterrainer, & Weiss, 2012). Whether we are trying to understand the behaviour of murderers or that of geniuses, the role of mental illness remains prominent because such individuals deviate so much from the average, normal person. But, mental illness is not reserved for the outliers of the population; far from it. In Canada, one in five individuals suffers from a mental illness, 33% of all hospitalizations are the result of mental illness, and 90% of people who commit suicide have a diagnosable mental illness (Mood Disorders Society of Canada [MDSC], 2009). So how are psychological disorders categorized? What causes them, and how can they be identified?

<<< **What do the names Paul Bernardo, Karla Homolka, Clifford Olson, Robert Pickton, Russell Williams, and Luka Magnotta bring to mind? Fear, anger, disgust, the resounding and never-ending question of "Why"? Why would these individuals commit such heinous, violent crimes? Clearly, we can see that something is wrong—they do not think, feel, or behave as we do. But, can mental illness, even severe and untreated, account for the behaviours of these murderers?**

CHAPTER 10

Psychological Disorders

Most people agree that a mother who throws herself in front of a train while holding her young child is not behaving normally. But how do we distinguish between someone who is temporarily unable to get out of bed after going through a traumatic divorce and someone who is suffering from severe depression? How do we know which person is likely to recover after a period of grieving and which person needs immediate counselling? **Abnormal psychology,** or **psychopathology,** is the study of disorders of mind, mood, and behaviour.

A precise definition for a psychological disorder is difficult to put into words—behaviour that one person might see as a symptom of mental illness, another person may view as creative eccentricity. The American Psychiatric Association's (APA) *Diagnostic and Statistical Manual of Mental Disorders* (DSM-IV-TR) is the current authoritative scheme for classifying psychological disorders. It defines a mental disorder as a disturbance in a person's emotions, drives, thought processes, or behaviour that:

- involves serious, prolonged distress
- impairs the person's ability to maintain social and occupational relationships
- is not a normal response to an event
- cannot be explained by poverty, prejudice, or other social forces
- is viewed by mental health professionals as persistently harmful, deviant, distressful, and dysfunctional.

Just as physical illnesses can produce particular physical effects, people suffering from psychological disorders may exhibit **symptoms**—characteristics of thought or behaviour that indicate a potential mental disorder. A combination of interrelated symptoms observed in an individual is known as a **syndrome.** For example, a child with Asperger syndrome might display symptoms such as performing repetitive rituals, interacting inappropriately with peers, and making clumsy, uncoordinated movements. A syndrome is considered to be a mental disorder if it involves impairment of functioning, is internally driven, and is not under voluntary control.

Sometimes a person may suffer from two or more mental disorders, a condition known as **comorbidity.** For example, a patient may simultaneously experience both depression and anxiety. Often, substance abuse problems such as alcoholism are linked to mental illness. Attempts to self-medicate symptoms of mental illness by abusing alcohol or prescription drugs are widely assumed to be a contributing factor to the high rate of psychiatric illness and substance abuse comorbidity. The comorbid existence of a mental disorder and substance abuse is referred to as **dual diagnosis.**

When a person is diagnosed with a physical or mental illness, he or she is given a **prognosis**—a prediction of the typical course of the disease and the likelihood of recovery. Just as some people respond to chemotherapy while others succumb to cancer, treatment of mental illness and subsequent recovery depends on a number of factors, including the individual patient and the severity of the disease.

DIAGNOSING PSYCHOLOGICAL DISORDERS

The DSM-IV-TR (the fourth edition of the manual, updated as a 2000 "text revision") is the American Psychiatric Association's current official guide for diagnosing mental disorders. It provides a complete list of approximately 250 disorders, each defined in terms of significant behaviour patterns. Mental health professionals use this guide to give a **psychological diagnosis,** or assign a label to a person's mental disorder by identifying and classifying patterns of behaviour. For example, a person who is hallucinating, talking incoherently, suffering from delusions, and acting

Axes of Diagnosis

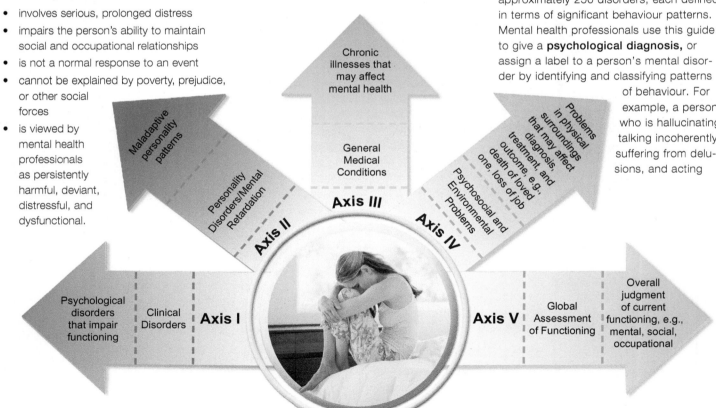

The **DSM-IV-TR** divides mental health disorders into five categories, or axes. The newest version of the DSM, DSM-5 will be published in the next year.

socially withdrawn may be classified as schizophrenic. Classifying mental illnesses is helpful for clinicians who, thanks to the DSM-IV-TR, have a common shorthand language, common understandings of the causes of particular mental disorders, and comprehensive treatment plans for each disorder. However, while they provide clinicians with a common language, labels do very little to describe a specific individual. Proper diagnosis and treatment must be centred on the careful understanding of every individual's situation.

LABELLING PSYCHOLOGICAL DISORDERS

While it can be helpful for psychologists and psychiatrists to categorize psychological illnesses, labels can lead to damaging preconceptions. Psychologist David Rosenhan (1973) recruited eight mentally healthy volunteers and had them attempt to gain admission to various psychiatric facilities. The volunteers complained of hearing voices in their heads that were saying the words *empty, hollow*, and *thud*. The volunteers gave false names and occupations, but they answered all other questions truthfully, describing real

> **A precise definition for a psychological disorder is difficult to put into words**—behaviour that **one person might see as a symptom of mental illness, another person may view as creative eccentricity.**

relationships with friends, colleagues, and family members. All eight were admitted into the psychiatric facilities, and seven were diagnosed with schizophrenia. The clinicians later interpreted normal behaviour, such as the volunteers' taking notes or pacing the corridors out of boredom, as symptoms of mental illness.

Abnormal psychology is the study of disorders of mind, mood, and behaviour.

Psychopathology see *abnormal psychology*.

Symptom is a characteristic of thought or behaviour that indicates a potential mental disorder.

Syndrome is a combination of interrelated symptoms observed in an individual.

Comorbidity is a condition in which a person suffers from two or more mental disorders.

Dual diagnosis is the comorbid existence of a mental disorder and substance abuse.

Prognosis is a prediction of the typical course of a disease and the likelihood of recovery.

Psychological diagnosis is a label for a person's mental disorder assigned by identifying and classifying patterns of behaviour.

Clinical disorders in Axis I and personality disorders in Axis II are further divided into diagnostic categories.

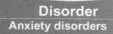

Disorder	Examples
Anxiety disorders	Phobias, panic disorder, post-traumatic stress disorder, obsessive-compulsive disorder
Mood disorders	Depression, mania, bipolar disorders
Somatoform disorders	Hypochondria, conversion disorders
Schizophrenia and psychotic disorders	Schizophrenia, delusional disorders
Dissociative disorders	Multiple personality, dissociative amnesia
Disorders usually diagnosed in infancy, childhood, or adolescence	ADHD, learning disabilities, autism, hyperactivity disorder
Delirium, dementia, amnesia, and other cognitive disorders	Alzheimer's, Parkinson's
Eating disorders	Anorexia nervosa, bulimia nervosa
Substance-related disorders	Alcohol dependence, nicotine dependence
Sexual and gender-identity disorders	Hypoactive sexual desire disorder, male erectile disorder, vaginismus
Impulse-control disorders not classified elsewhere	Kleptomania, pyromania, pathological gambling
Sleep disorders	Insomnia, sleepwalking, narcolepsy
Adjustment disorders	Mixed anxiety, conduct disturbance
Personality disorders	Borderline personality disorder, antisocial personality disorder, narcissistic personality disorder

Cultural relativity refers to the need to consider the individual characteristics of a culture in which a person with a disorder was raised in order to diagnose and treat the disorder.

Culture-bound syndrome is any disorder that is limited to a particular cultural group.

Medical model refers to the concept that psychological abnormalities are diseases that, like biological diseases, have symptoms, causes, and cures.

"Crazy" or just slightly eccentric? Controversial artists such as Lady Gaga aren't afraid to differ from the norm.

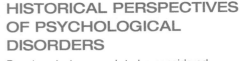

Psychiatrist Thomas Szasz (1960) argued that the notion of mental illness is a myth. He believed that disease can affect only the body, whereas there is no evidence for the biological causes of mental illness. According to Szasz, a person who is locked away because he is labelled as mentally ill is being locked away because he behaves differently from other people. Szasz argued that as long as people don't pose a threat to others, they should have the same rights and freedoms as everybody else. Some psychologists believe that labelling people as mad can suppress creativity and individuality: People who don't want to risk being thought of as "crazy" or "disturbed" aren't likely to put forward controversial or alternative ideas. Vincent van Gogh walked a fine line between genius and madness, but if he had been locked away without his art materials, the world would be deprived of several cultural masterpieces.

It's not uncommon for mental illness to walk hand in hand with cultural stigmas. When an associate of psychologist Stewart Page (1977) called 180 people in Toronto who were advertising rooms for rent, the rooms were nearly all still available. When the associate mentioned that she was about to be released from a mental health facility, 75% of the rooms were suddenly no longer vacant. Mysteriously, when a second person called back later, the rooms had become available again. Recently, however, the stigma associated with mental illness seems to be disappearing. Psychological disorders are now more widely recognized as diseases of the brain rather than character impediments (Solomon, 1996), and there has been a dramatic increase in the number of public figures willing to talk about their mental health disorders. Movie stars Brooke Shields (2005) and Gwyneth Paltrow have both publicly discussed their struggles with postpartum depression, a talk show topic that would have been unthinkable just a few years ago. In addition, more recently, researchers (e.g., Perry, 2011) have

reported that individuals who suffer from mental illness have increasingly strong and broad social networks that provide necessary support and further diminish the stigma attached to mental illness diagnoses.

CULTURAL VARIATIONS

What passes for normal behaviour in one culture may look remarkably abnormal in another. **Cultural relativity** refers to the need to consider the individual characteristics of a culture in which a person with a disorder was raised in order to diagnose and treat it (Castillo, 1997). For example, in most Asian cultures, mental illness is considered shameful. As a result, many Asian people

> Some psychologists believe that labelling people as mad can suppress creativity and individuality: People who don't want to risk being thought of as "crazy" or "disturbed" aren't likely to put forward controversial or alternative ideas.

suffering from disorders such as depression or schizophrenia report bodily symptoms rather than mental ones because physical illness is more acceptable than mental illness (Federoff & MacFarlane, 1998). In addition, according to Ahtoy Wonpat-Borja and colleagues (2012) Asian communities view genetic mental illnesses more favourably than mental illnesses with non-genetic causes.

Some disorders, known as **culture-bound syndromes,** are limited to specific cultural groups. For example, koro is a psychological disorder primarily found in South Asian and East Asian countries in which the sufferer believes that his or her external genitals or breasts are retracting into the body, and that this will cause death. Taijin kyofusho (TKS) is a social anxiety disorder found primarily in Japan that causes people to fear they will do something inappropriate in public and cause embarrassment to others. Western cultures have unique disorders too—anorexia and bulimia nervosa are rarely found outside of North America and Western Europe.

Cultural values influence not only manifestations of particular disorders, but also their labels. It might seem difficult to believe now, but homosexuality was classified as a mental disorder by the American Psychiatric Association until 1973. In the 1940s, smoking was considered a harmless social pastime; less than 40 years later, nicotine dependence was added to the APA's list of psychological disorders.

HISTORICAL PERSPECTIVES OF PSYCHOLOGICAL DISORDERS

People unlucky enough to be considered "mad" in the Middle Ages were caged, beaten, burned, exorcised, or castrated in vain attempts to cure them of their aberrant behaviours. Fortunately, the **medical model**—the concept that psychological abnormalities are diseases that, like biological diseases, have symptoms, causes, and cures—emerged in the 1800s. Reformers such as French physician Philippe Pinel (1745–1826) and German psychiatrist Emil Kraepelin (1856–1926) worked on developing a classification system of psychological disorders.

Contemporary Views of Psychopathology

There is a wide range of contemporary views of psychological disorders. A clinician taking the **biological approach** looks for physical problems as a root cause—structural abnormalities in the brain, biochemical processes, or hereditary factors. For example, depression is commonly thought to be caused by a chemical imbalance in the brain.

A clinician using the **psychoanalytic approach** investigates unconscious conflicts and other possible underlying psychological factors. These factors can usually be traced back to childhood. A woman who was abandoned by her father when she was a young child may be clingy with romantic partners because she has an unconscious fear of being left alone again.

The **behavioural approach** focuses on people's current behaviour and the learned responses that sustain this behaviour. For example, a man who convinces himself that he is a poor communicator is less inclined to practise his public speaking skills. He flubs an important job interview because he hasn't rehearsed any practice questions, reinforcing his belief that he is a poor communicator. Behavioural therapists aim to modify people's dysfunctional behaviours by analyzing the self-fulfilling prophecies or reinforcements that cause them. Similarly, the **cognitive approach** focuses on thought processes that contribute to psychological distress, such as pessimism and poor self-esteem.

Today, most mental health workers have an interdisciplinary approach to psychological disorders, taking into account all of the aforementioned approaches, as well as the social context in which the disorder takes place. The **biopsychosocial approach** recognizes that it is not possible to separate body and mind—negative emotions can contribute to physical illness, while physical abnormalities may increase the likelihood of psychological disorders.

Possible Causes of Psychological Disorders

BRAIN DAMAGE

Irreversible brain damage can result in irreversible psychological damage and in some cases, the loss of ability to function in a normal social setting. Neuroscientist Antonio Damasio (1994) discovered that the removal of a brain tumour had left one patient, a corporate lawyer named Elliot, without any emotion. When shown disturbing images of injured people, destroyed communities, and natural disasters, Elliot reported feeling nothing. His emotional detachment cost him his job and his marriage.

Alzheimer's disease, which primarily affects the elderly, is a degenerative memory disease resulting from a deterioration of neurons that produce the neurotransmitter acetylcholine. As the disease runs its course, the patient becomes emotionally flat, then disoriented, then incontinent, and finally mentally incapable of comprehending anything at all.

MULTIPLICITY OF CAUSES

Most mental disorders are episodic—they recur and subside throughout a person's life. Why does this happen? Genetic, biological, and social circumstances all play a role.

Predisposing causes are existing underlying factors that make an individual particularly susceptible to a certain disorder. Birth defects, environmentally damaging effects on the brain, toxins such as alcohol, and viruses or bacteria can all be predisposing causes.

Let's say that you are predisposed to alcohol dependency and have a family history of alcoholism. You have been deliberately staying away from the liquor cabinet, but when your new job becomes overwhelming, you suddenly find it harder to resist the urge to drink. **Precipitating causes** are the events in our day-to-day lives that bring on a particular disorder.

Imagine that your alcohol consumption distracts you from pressures at work. You also gain attention of friends and family members, who notice that your drinking has increased and make a concerted effort to help you quit. **Perpetuating causes** are the consequences of a disorder that help keep it going once it has manifested. These can be positive (your behaviour gains attention, so you continue to pursue it) or negative (excess drinking affects your performance at work, so you drink even more to numb the emotional pain of receiving a poor review).

Biological approach is a method of analyzing a psychological disorder in which physical problems are looked for as the root cause.

Psychoanalytic approach is a method of analyzing a psychological disorder in which unconscious conflicts and other possible underlying psychological factors are examined.

Behavioural approach is an approach to psychology that concentrates on observable behaviour that can be directly measured and recorded.

Cognitive approach is a method of analyzing a psychological disorder that focuses on thought processes that contribute to psychological distress.

Biopsychosocial approach is a method of analyzing a psychological disorder that recognizes that it is not possible to separate body and mind; negative emotions can contribute to physical illness, while physical abnormalities may increase the likelihood of psychological disorders.

Predisposing cause is an existing underlying factor that makes an individual particularly susceptible to a certain disorder.

Precipitating cause is an event in a person's day-to-day life that brings on a particular disorder.

Perpetuating cause is a consequence of a disorder that helps keep it going once it has manifested.

GENDER DIFFERENCES

Statistically, women are more often diagnosed with depression and anxiety than men. However, this discrepancy does not indicate that women are more prone to mental disorders. In Western society, it's more culturally acceptable for women to discuss their emotional problems than it is for men, so women may be more likely to seek treatment. Conversely, men have higher rates of substance abuse and antisocial personality disorder (characterized by reckless and irresponsible behaviour) than women do. When men behave abnormally, they are more likely to drink too much and display aggressive behaviour, externalizing their stress, whereas women are more

> Neuroscientist Antonio Damasio discovered that the removal of a brain tumour had left one patient, a corporate lawyer named Elliot, without any emotion. When shown disturbing images of injured people, destroyed communities, and natural disasters, Elliot reported feeling nothing. His emotional detachment cost him his job and his marriage.

Anxiety disorder is a mental disorder in which a person feels anxious all the time without any identifiable reason.

Generalized anxiety disorder (GAD) is a type of anxiety disorder in which a person feels inexplicably and continually tense and uneasy.

Phobia is a persistent, irrational fear of a specific object, activity, or situation.

Social phobia is an irrational fear of being publicly humiliated or embarrassed.

Panic disorder is a condition in which sufferers come to fear the possibility of another panic attack following an initial attack.

Agoraphobia is intense fear of being in a situation from which there is no escape.

Obsessive-compulsive disorder (OCD) is an anxiety disorder in which a person feels driven to think disturbing thoughts or to perform senseless rituals.

Rates of Psychological Disorders in Men and Women

Men	Disorder	Women
4%	Alcohol abuse or dependence	2%
9%	Anxiety disorder	16%
5%	Major depression	11%
1%	Bipolar disorder	1%
1%	Schizophrenia	1%

Source: Mood Disorders Society of Canada, 2009; Statistics Canada, 2011

^ Why are women more likely to suffer from
^ depression and anxiety, while men suffer more
from alcohol dependence?

likely to become depressed and hopeless, internalizing their emotional pain. This distinction suggests that gender-based socialization often plays a significant role in the development and diagnosis of psychiatric disorders.

Diagnoses may also be influenced by clinicians' expectations of each gender (Schwartz, Lent, & Geihsler, 2011). For example, researchers (Ford & Widiger, 1989) sent fictitious case studies to clinical psychologists for diagnosis. One case described a patient with antisocial personality disorder (usually diagnosed in males); the other described a patient with histrionic personality disorder (usually diagnosed in females). The subject of each case study was identified as male in some cases and female in others. When the antisocial personality disorder case was identified as male, most clinicians diagnosed it correctly. However, when the subject was identified as female, most clinicians identified it as histrionic personality disorder. Similar results occurred in reverse with the histrionic personality disorder case indicating

that, like the rest of us, clinicians are subject to expectation bias when it comes to gender.

Anxiety Disorders

Whether we're facing a tough exam or a skydiving expedition, we all feel anxious or fearful from time to time. But what if we persistently feel anxious even though we cannot identify the source of our worries? This type of vague, unidentifiable, prolonged anxiety may be a symptom of an anxiety disorder.

Anxiety disorders are the most common type of mental illness in Canada. On average, 12% of Canadians will suffer from an anxiety disorder in a given year (MDSC, 2009).

GENERALIZED ANXIETY DISORDER

People who are inexplicably and continually tense and uneasy may have generalized anxiety disorder (GAD). Sufferers worry about multiple issues and tend to experience muscle tension, irritability, difficulty sleeping, and occasional gastrointestinal upset as a result of an overactive autonomic nervous system. For diagnosis, a person must exhibit at least three of the symptoms listed above in addition to general feelings of anxiety.

Rates of GAD have dramatically increased in Western cultures since the middle of the 20th century. GAD affects 1.1% of the Canadian population (MDSC, 2009). Most sufferers of GAD will also suffer from depression. GAD typically precedes the onset of major

> "Most mental disorders are episodic—they recur and subside throughout a person's life. Why does this happen? Genetic, biological, and social circumstances all play a role."

depressive disorder. Two-thirds of people diagnosed with GAD are women.

PHOBIAS

Does the photo of the spider cause beads of sweat to appear on your forehead while your heart pounds furiously? If so, you may be arachnophobic. **Phobias** are persistent, irrational fears of specific objects, activities, or situations. While some species of spiders may be venomous, unless you live in the Amazon Rainforest you are unlikely to encounter one, making your debilitating fear of every eight-legged arachnid unreasonable (though fairly common). Specific phobias of objects or situations affect 6% to 8% of Canadians and are more commonly diagnosed in women than men (MDSC, 2009). To be classified as a phobia, the fear must be significant enough to disrupt everyday life in some way. Someone with a fear of thunderstorms would not spend a week inside after seeing an ominous weather report, but someone with a phobia of thunderstorms might. Other common specific phobias include fear of heights (acrophobia), confined spaces (claustrophobia), and snakes (ophidiophobia). Psychologist Martin Seligman (1971) suggests that people are genetically predisposed to be wary of objects and situations that posed realistic threats to humans throughout evolutionary history.

<<< Arachnophobia is an intense, irrational fear of spiders.

Some people suffer from **social phobias,** irrational fears of being publicly humiliated or embarrassed. Common social phobias include speaking in public, using public restrooms, or meeting new people. Roughly 7% of Canadians suffer from social phobias, which affect both men and women equally (MDSC, 2009).

PANIC DISORDER

Many people who have a panic attack mistakenly believe they are having a heart attack: They suddenly experience chest pain, shortness of breath, heart palpitations, sweating, and an intense feeling of terror and panic. This attack usually lasts around 10 to 15 minutes. Recurring episodes lead to a diagnosis of **panic disorder,** a condition in which sufferers come to fear the possibility of another attack. Feelings of dread often last for days or even weeks after the original attack. Less than 1% of Canadians suffer from panic disorder (MDSC, 2009).

For some people, panic disorder can lead to **agoraphobia,** an intense fear of being in a situation from which they cannot escape. The fear of having a panic attack in public may cause sufferers to avoid being in crowds, travelling on trains or buses, or visiting unfamiliar places.

OBSESSIVE-COMPULSIVE DISORDER

Most of us have probably had a sudden fear that we left our car unlocked or forgot to turn off the gas. A quick check is usually enough to put our minds at ease. For many people with **obsessive-compulsive disorder (OCD),** though, a quick check wouldn't be sufficient. Obsessions are disturbing and intrusive thoughts that repeatedly interrupt a person's consciousness even if the person knows these thoughts are irrational. Compulsions are repetitive, ritualistic behaviours usually performed in response to an obsession. Someone with OCD may need to repeatedly wash her hands, persistently check to make sure a task has been completed, or step in and out of a doorway a certain number of times whenever she enters a room.

How would having OCD or another anxiety disorder affect someone's life?

There is a fine line between normal behaviour and OCD, and we cross it when our obsessions become so persistent that they disrupt our normal lives. Almost 2% of Canadians have OCD (MDSC, 2009)

How does OCD develop? Trauma, poison, or disease can all initiate the onset of OCD, which seems to be closely linked to brain abnormalities in the portions of the frontal lobes and parts of the limbic system and basal ganglia involved in the circuit controlling voluntary action. PET scans of people with OCD reveal unusually high activity in these areas (Del Casale et al., 2011; Maia, Cooney, & Peterson, 2008; Rauch & Jenike, 1993). Sufferers report that they do not experience the normal sense of task completion when they carry out an action, prompting them to repeat it over and over again.

POST-TRAUMATIC STRESS DISORDER

Traumatic stress, caused by experiencing or witnessing out-of-control events with feelings of helplessness or fear, can cause **post-traumatic stress disorder (PTSD).** Victims of abuse, accident and disaster survivors, people who live in war zones, and combat veterans are all likely to develop PTSD. According to Stéphane Grenier, the Canadian military's special adviser on operational stress injuries (which includes PTSD, anxiety, and depression), as many as 60 soldiers a year will need in-patient care for severe PTSD (CBC News, May 2010). PTSD is the only anxiety disorder brought on by a particular traumatic experience; therefore, its symptoms will be directly linked to that trauma.

Sleeplessness, emotional numbing, high arousal, irritability, survivor's guilt, and depression are all common symptoms experienced by people suffering from PTSD. Around 7% of the population suffers from the disorder at some point in their lives, with women twice as likely as men to develop PTSD. In addition, PTSD appears be a spectrum disorder ranging from an acute stress reaction that resolves on its own without treatment to "classic" or "simple" PTSD in the middle to "complex" PTSD at the other end (Hegadoren, Lasiuk, & Coupland, 2006). This may make diagnosing PTSD a more complex process given the variations in symptoms and intensity of illness.

EXPLAINING ANXIETY DISORDERS

We inherit Mom's green eyes and Dad's brown hair. Is it also possible to inherit

tendencies toward psychological disorders? Yes—researchers have located specific genetic sites that may predispose people toward anxiety disorders (Shienle, Hettema, Cáceda, & Nemeroff, 2011; Goddard et al., 2004; Hamilton et al., 2004; Zavos, Gregory, & Eley, 2012). Twin studies also support this theory, although other research suggests that phobias are primarily caused by environmental factors rather than genetics (Skre et al., 1993).

The psychodynamic approach views anxiety as a signal that repressed urges are attempting to surface (Freud & Gay, 1977). According to this perspective, we transfer this anxiety to an outside object or situation, which then becomes the source of fear. Rather than viewing anxiety disorders as the result of unconscious fears, however, behaviourists believe that anxious behaviour is learned. Remember Little Albert in Chapter 11 who was taught to fear white rats? The child's fear

The **dark winter months** can initiate **seasonal affective disorder,** making us feel **gloomy** and **lethargic.**

> Usually, people can snap out of a bad mood in a relatively short period of time, but when it lasts much longer and prevents everyday functioning, it is classified as a disorder.

became a conditioned response once it was reinforced through repetition. Similarly, people with OCD find that their obsessive-compulsive habits reduce anxiety levels, reinforcing the behaviour.

Cognitive psychologists view anxiety disorders as the result of distorted negative thoughts. People with anxiety disorders tend to overestimate the dangers they are facing and underestimate their ability to cope with them, leading to complete avoidance of the perceived threat.

The precise cause of anxiety disorders continues to elude scientists and is likely a complex interaction of genetics and environment that varies with each individual.

Mood Disorders

Although we can experience emotions ranging from deep despair to intense elation, we're usually somewhere in between these two extremes. People with **mood disorders,** however, experience these emotional extremes as a matter of course. Mood disorders come in two main forms: **depressive disorders,** characterized by prolonged or extreme periods of depression, and **bipolar disorders,** characterized by alternating episodes of depression and mania (a state of hyperactivity).

DEPRESSIVE DISORDERS

Clinical depression is different from the doldrums we all get into from time to time when nothing seems to be going right. Usually, people can snap out of a bad mood in a relatively short period of time, but when it lasts much longer and prevents everyday functioning, it is classified as a disorder. Because predispositions toward depression and anxiety are linked to the same genes, they are often comorbid.

There are several types of clinical depression. **Major depressive disorder (MDD) is** characterized by signs of severe depression that last for more than two weeks with no apparent cause. Symptoms include changes in appetite, sleep disturbances, feelings of guilt, poor concentration, or thoughts of suicide. MDD is the most commonly diagnosed mood disorder. By the year 2020, MDD will be the second leading cause of disability in the world, following heart disease (MDSC, 2009).

Dysthymia, from the Greek words for "bad spirit," is a chronic, but less severe form of depression that lasts for two years or more. The lifetime risk for developing dysthymia is approximately 2% to 3%, with women again being twice as likely to suffer from the condition as men. When bouts of major depression and dysthymia occur together, a person has **double depression.**

Some people find that they get depressed only at certain times of the year, particularly in the winter. This condition, known as **seasonal affective disorder (SAD),** is characterized by increased appetite and general lethargy. It is caused by the body's reaction to low levels of light present during the winter months (Boyce & Barriball, 2010; Partonen & Lonnqvist, 1998), which may cause decreased levels of serotonin—the hormone that helps to regulate a person's sleep-wake cycles, energy, and mood.

> *People in a manic state may initially become more productive and creative but tend to suffer from poor judgment that can lead to reckless financial decisions, spending sprees, and unsafe sex.*

In Canada, 15% of individuals will experience the "winter blues." But only 2% to 3% of Canadians will have symptoms severe enough to be diagnosed with SAD. SAD is more common in women and decreases with age (MDSC, 2009).

BIPOLAR DISORDERS

Virginia Woolf, Ernest Hemingway, and Edgar Allan Poe all wrote their masterpieces while suffering from bipolar disorder. People with bipolar disorders suffer from alternating episodes of major depression and **mania**—periods of euphoria characterized by elevated self-esteem, increased talkativeness, enhanced energy, and a decreased need for sleep. People in a manic state may initially become more productive and creative but tend to suffer from poor judgment that can lead to reckless financial decisions, spending sprees, and unsafe sex. Cycles of at least one manic episode followed by at least one depressive episode are classified as bipolar I disorder. Canadians suffering from bipolar disorder have a two to three times higher mortality rate, including suicide, compared to the general population (MDSC, 2009).

A milder form of mania, called hypomania, causes less severe mood elevations and does not interfere with normal daily functioning to the same extent as mania. People with milder forms of mania may find that increased energy levels fuel creativity, perpetuating the stereotype of the mad genius. Cycles of at least one episode of **hypomania** followed by at least one depressive episode are classified as bipolar II disorder.

People who suffer from more than four episodes of either mania or depression a year are said to go through **rapid cycling,** which occurs in approximately 10% of cases and is more common in women.

Post-traumatic stress disorder (PSTD) is an anxiety disorder caused by experiencing or witnessing out-of-control events with feelings of helplessness and fear.

Mood disorder is a mental disorder in which a person regularly experiences emotional extremes.

Depressive disorder is a mood disorder characterized by prolonged or extreme periods of depression.

Bipolar disorder is a mood disorder characterized by alternating episodes of depression and mania.

Major depressive disorder (MDD) is a mood disorder characterized by signs of severe depression that last for more than two weeks with no apparent cause.

Dysthymia is a chronic, but less severe form of depression that lasts for two years or more.

Double depression is a condition in which bouts of major depression are superimposed over a state of dysthymia.

Seasonal affective disorder (SAD) is a mood disorder in which a person gets depressed only at certain times of the year.

Mania is a period of euphoria characterized by elevated self-esteem, increased talkativeness, enhanced energy, and a decreased need for sleep.

Hypomania is a milder form of mania that causes less severe mood elevations and does not interfere with normal daily functioning to the same extent as mania.

Rapid cycling occurs when a person with bipolar disorder experiences more than four episodes of either mania or depression a year.

Negative cognitive style describes a pattern of pessimistic or negative thoughts.

EXPLAINING MOOD DISORDERS
Cognitive Theories of Depression

The rate of diagnosed depression is increasing with each successive generation. From 1936 to 1945, the prevalence of major depression in the population was about 3%, with the onset of symptoms occurring around the ages of 18 to 20. Between 1966 and 1975, rates skyrocketed to about 23%, with the age of onset dropping to the early teens. What could be causing this trend? Many experts agree that depression is exacerbated, if not brought on, by **negative cognitive styles,** or patterns of thought.

Psychologist Aaron Beck (1967) noticed that depressed clients tended to negatively distort their perceptions of experiences. They

Attributional-style questionnaire is a type of questionnaire that seeks to assess how people view the events that happen in their lives based on three criteria: stability, globality, and locus.

Learned helplessness describes a feeling of hopelessness and passivity caused by being unable to avoid or control traumatic events.

Schizophrenia is a mental disorder that causes a person to experience distorted perceptions, inappropriate emotions or reactions, and confusion.

Delusion is a persistent false belief.

Hallucination is a false sensory perception that a person believes to be real.

Positive symptom is a symptom that reflects an excess or distortion of normal functions, such as delusions and hallucinations.

Negative symptom is a symptom that indicates a decrease in normal functions such as attention or emotion.

made "mountains out of molehills" by viewing simple, everyday problems as major setbacks. Patients also believed that future events would turn out badly and overgeneralized, by interpreting one single negative event as a never-ending pattern of defeat. If you have a habit of using the phrase "Nothing ever goes right" whenever you lose your house keys or break a glass, you may be an occasional overgeneralizer.

Studies using **attributional-style questionnaires** support Beck's findings. Researchers gave people questionnaires containing 12 hypothetical events, half describing positive occurrences (a friend compliments you on your new haircut) and half describing negative incidents (you go on a disastrous blind date). By asking people to assess the events in terms of stability (how likely they are to reoccur), globality (how important they are), and locus (who or what caused the events), the researchers were able to analyze people's attitudes. They discovered that negative thinking is not merely a symptom of depression—a depressive cognitive style can trigger the disorder (Peterson et al., 1982). Lyn Abramson, Gerald Metalsky, and Lauren Alloy (1989) proposed that negative thinking results in a sense of hopelessness. If you have a problem that you believe is permanent, will affect every other aspect of your life, and is entirely your own fault, you are more likely to become depressed.

So why can't people just "snap out of it" by thinking more positively? Martin Seligman theorized that depression can be explained by the idea of **learned helplessness**—the tendency to fail to attempt to escape a situation because of a history of repeated failures in the past. This sense of powerlessness may explain why people living in abusive households eventually stop trying to leave their abusers, even when given the opportunity.

The Depressed Brain

Depression seems to be at least partially related to the chemicals in our brains—it's often attributed to low levels of the neurotransmitters norepinephrine and serotonin. Antidepressant medications called serotonin and norepinephrine reuptake inhibitors (SNRIs) increase the levels of these neurotransmitters by inhibiting their reabsorption into cells in the brain (see Chapters 3 and 17). However, while an SNRI will elevate a patient's norepinephrine and serotonin levels in only a few days, it won't cause noticeable behavioural changes for at least two weeks. Neuroimaging studies have shown that localized areas in the brain are affected by depression (e.g., Kroes, Rugg, Whalley, & Brewin, 2011). People with depression exhibit reduced activity in the left dorsolateral prefrontal cortex, while the right dorsolateral prefrontal cortex shows increased activation.

Can ordering lox on our bagels improve our mental health? Recently, studies have linked depression to a low level of omega-3 fatty acids, typically found in cold-water fish such as salmon and trout. Clinically depressed people often have a lower level of omega-3 in their blood, and several studies have shown that supplementing diets with omega-3 helps alleviate depression (Sarris, Mischoulon, & Schweitzer, 2012; Kiecolt-Glaser et al., 2007).

Evolutionary Bases of Depression

Are our ancestors to blame for modern mood disorders? Some psychologists believe that

> Have you ever seen a puppy roll onto its back with its legs in the air, in deference to its mother? Signals of helplessness by depressed people may similarly express submission and a need for care.

depression may have evolved from simple self-protective instincts into an extreme form of self-preservation. Depressive behaviour can signal a lack of threat to others, invite care, and minimize unrealistic optimism.

Take the symptoms of seasonal affective disorder. Just as bears hibernate during the winter to conserve energy, humans could benefit evolutionarily from the increased appetite and extra sleep that characterize SAD during the winter months. The fact that SAD does not typically cause the levels of sadness, self-reproach, and crying characterized by other forms of depression supports the idea of an evolutionary basis (Keller & Nesse, 2005).

Have you ever seen a puppy roll onto its back with its legs in the air, in deference to its mother? Signals of helplessness by depressed people may similarly express submission and a need for care. People who are bereaved typically suffer from depressed moods characterized by sadness and crying—signs that they are looking for love and support from other people.

Biological Causes of Depression and Bipolar Disorders

Although stressful experiences can bring on periods of depression, studies have also shown that some people are genetically predisposed to mood disorders. The risks of major depression and bipolar disorder increase if you have a depressed parent or sibling (Sullivan, Neale, & Kendler, 2000). Twin studies have shown that if one identical twin has major depression or bipolar disorder, the chances that the other twin will also develop a mood disorder are between 40% and 70% (Muller-Oerlinghausen, Berghofer, & Bauer, 2002). Women are twice as vulnerable to major depression as men, a discrepancy not yet fully understood but explained by psychologists as a combination of psychological, social, economic, and biological factors.

Schizophrenia

Literally meaning "split mind," **schizophrenia** is often mistaken for dissociative identity disorder, a controversial condition in which people claim to have multiple personalities. However, schizophrenia actually refers to a person's split from reality, characterized by distorted perceptions, inappropriate emotions or reactions, and confusion. Schizophrenia affects only 1% of the Canadian population, but the direct and indirect costs of schizophrenia are an alarming $4.35 billion a year (MDSC, 2009).

To be diagnosed with schizophrenia, a person must display two or more symptoms for at least a month. People with schizophrenia often think or speak in ways that are disorganized, illogical, or incoherent. Schizophrenics may also suffer from **delusions**, persistent false beliefs. For example, patients may believe that they are being spied on, that someone is controlling their thoughts and actions, or that people are being unfaithful to them. These delusions may be supported by illogical thinking.

A third symptom of schizophrenia is the existence of **hallucinations**—false sensory perceptions that a person believes to be real. Hearing voices is the most common type of hallucination; many schizophrenics report that they hear insulting comments or receive orders from voices inside their heads. Research using fMRI scans shows that verbal hallucinations in schizophrenics are accompanied by activity in the brain regions normally associated with thought processing (Sharma, 2003; Shergill et al., 2000). While auditory hallucinations are most common, people may also see, feel, smell, or taste things that aren't really there.

Schizophrenics often have difficulty acting appropriately in social situations. They may become catatonic and remain motionless for several hours, or they may become wildly agitated and talk or shout constantly.

Clusters of symptoms can help to categorize schizophrenia. People who show **positive symptoms** reflect an excess or distortion of normal functions, such as delusions and hallucinations. These symptoms tend to appear and disappear as the disorder recurs and goes into remission. Disorganized symptoms, such as confused speech and flat emotion, follow the same pattern. However, schizophrenics who display **negative symptoms,** or decreases in normal functions such as attention or emotion, tend to exhibit more constant symptoms that are less responsive to antipsychotic medications.

EXPLAINING SCHIZOPHRENIA
Cognitive and Neural Abnormalities

Cognitive deficits are a core feature of schizophrenia. People with schizophrenia tend to perform poorly on many information-processing tasks, particularly activities that require sustained attention. Working memory is permanently and consistently impaired, while long-term memory involving the acquisition and recall of new information may be relatively severely impaired (Saykin et al., 1991). Since it is difficult for people with schizophrenia to remember the source of a piece of information, it is likely that they will be unable to distinguish between factual information and fiction or imagination, resulting in the delusions characteristic of the disorder.

Poor cognitive function may serve as an early warning system for diagnosing children with schizophrenia. Deficits in attention and memory in childhood correlate positively to the subsequent development of the disorder. One study found that children with early-onset schizophrenia display poorer verbal memory function than older adults with the disorder (Tuulio-Henriksson et al., 2004).

Can chemical imbalances in the brain explain schizophrenia? When researchers examined the brains of schizophrenic patients after death, they discovered up to six times

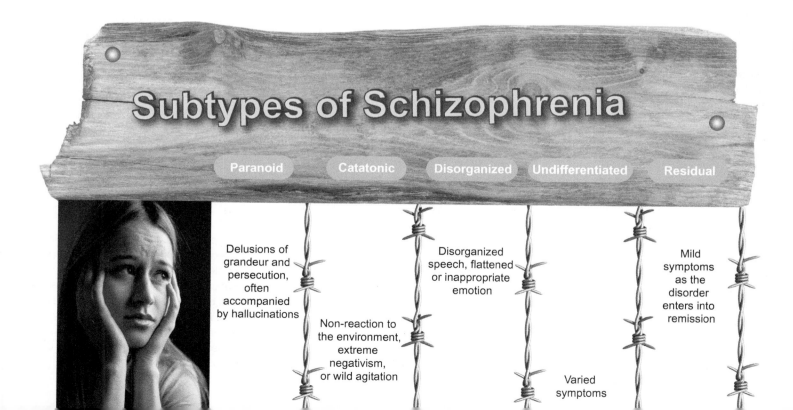

Subtypes of Schizophrenia

Paranoid · Catatonic · Disorganized · Undifferentiated · Residual

Delusions of grandeur and persecution, often accompanied by hallucinations

Non-reaction to the environment, extreme negativism, or wild agitation

Disorganized speech, flattened or inappropriate emotion

Varied symptoms

Mild symptoms as the disorder enters into remission

Diathesis-stress hypothesis suggests that people are genetically predisposed to a particular mental disorder but will develop the disorder only if exposed to environmental or emotional stress during critical developmental periods.

Personality disorder is a rigid, maladaptive pattern of behaviour that makes it difficult for individuals to have normal social relationships.

Schizotypal personality disorder is characterized by peculiar or eccentric mannerisms and difficulty forming social relationships.

Paranoid personality disorder is characterized by extreme suspicion and distrust of others.

Schizoid personality disorder causes people to show very little interest in others and have few personal relationships.

Borderline personality disorder is characterized by unstable moods, intense and stormy relationships, and manipulation and distrust of others.

Antisocial personality disorder is characterized by a complete lack of conscience.

Histrionic personality disorder is characterized by a tendency to overreact to situations, excessive emotionality, and the use of manipulation to gain attention from others.

Narcissistic personality disorder is characterized by an inflated sense of self-importance and a deep need for admiration.

> "Hearing voices is the most common type of hallucination; many schizophrenics report that they hear insulting comments or receive orders from voices inside their heads."

the normal number of dopamine receptors (Seeman, Guan, & Van Tol, 1993). The researchers believe that this elevated level of dopamine may intensify brain signals in schizophrenic patients, causing positive symptoms such as hallucinations and paranoia. Drugs that block dopamine transmission have proved effective at reducing many of the symptoms of schizophrenia, whereas drugs that increase dopamine action, such as cocaine or amphetamines, can exacerbate symptoms (Swerdlow & Koob, 1987).

Recent research suggests that defects in the major receptor molecules for glutamate, another neurotransmitter, may cause symptoms of schizophrenia. This would account for general cognitive defects, as well as explaining the effects of street drugs such as PCP (commonly known as "angel dust"), which interfere with glutamate transmission and temporarily induce schizophrenia-like symptoms in otherwise normal people.

Brain scans reveal that people with schizophrenia tend to have abnormal brain structures. Enlarged brain ventricles in some patients indicate a deficit in the volume of surrounding brain tissue. There is also evidence of abnormally low activity in the frontal lobes

(Pettegrew, Keshavan, & Minshew, 1993). What is clear from studies of the schizophrenic brain is that there are clearly a number of brain regions whose compromise may contribute to schizophrenia.

Remember how the brain selectively prunes unused neurons and connections during adolescence? (See Chapter 6.) Some neuroscientists believe that abnormal pruning may lead to the loss of too many cell bodies, potentially causing symptoms of schizophrenia. Australian researcher Christos Pantelis and his colleagues took MRI scans of three groups of young people—one group of people who had recently been admitted to hospital with schizophrenia, one group of people without schizophrenia, and one group of people who had suffered from the disorder for around 10 years (Fornito, Zalesky, Pantelis, & Bullmore, 2012). Pantelis discovered that the brains of the first group were shrinking at twice the rate of those without schizophrenia, suggesting that the normal developmental pruning process is accelerated in the brains of people with schizophrenia (Ho, Andreasen, Ziebell, Pierson, & Magnotta, 2011; Boksa, 2012; Salleh, 2003).

Genetics and Environment

Numerous studies indicate that schizophrenia has a strong genetic component. Irving Gottesman (1991) compiled data showing that the risk of developing schizophrenia increases with the degree of biological closeness to someone suffering from the disorder. While the general population has a 1% risk of developing schizophrenia, the chance of being diagnosed with the disorder increases to 9% if a sibling is afflicted. If an identical twin is diagnosed with schizophrenia, the likelihood of the other twin developing the disorder jumps to 50%.

The fact that dizygotic twins show a higher rate of concordance than non-twin

siblings (17% compared to 9%) indicates that the prenatal environment may play a role in developing schizophrenia. Mothers who contract rubella or influenza during the second trimester of pregnancy are twice as likely to give birth to children who develop the disorder (Brown et al., 2000). However, whether this risk factor is due to the virus itself, the mother's immune response, medications taken to combat the virus, or another, unknown factor is still unclear.

If schizophrenia were entirely controlled by genes, the risk of two identical twins both developing the disorder should be close to 100%. That the concordance rate is half this suggests that both genetics and environment play significant roles in the development of schizophrenia. Some psychologists propose the **diathesis-stress hypothesis,** which suggests that people are genetically predisposed to a particular mental disorder but will develop the disorder only if they are exposed to environmental or emotional stress during critical developmental periods.

Personality Disorders

Personality disorders are rigid, maladaptive patterns of behaviour that make it difficult for individuals to have normal social relationships. There are 10 recognized types of personality disorders, divided into three clusters: odd or eccentric behaviours, dramatic or impulsive behaviours, and anxious or inhibited behaviours.

ODD/ECCENTRIC PERSONALITY DISORDERS

People with eccentric personality disorders are classified as schizotypal, paranoid, or schizoid. Those with **schizotypal personality disorder** display peculiar or eccentric mannerisms, and find it difficult to form social relationships. They often hold peculiar or magical beliefs. Schizotypal personality disorder is often considered to be a mild form of schizophrenia and can occasionally develop into the full disorder.

Paranoid personality disorder is characterized by extreme suspicion and distrust of others. People with paranoid personality disorder are often jealous, critical of others, yet unable to accept criticism themselves. By quickly counterattacking perceived threats, people with this disorder may frequently become involved in legal disputes.

People with **schizoid personality disorder** are loners. Showing very little interest in others, they have few friendships and often do not marry. People with schizoid personality disorder often show emotional coldness or flattened affect.

DRAMATIC/ERRATIC PERSONALITY DISORDERS

People with dramatic or erratic personality disorders exhibit impulsive behaviours. A person with **borderline personality disorder** may have unstable moods, experience intense and stormy personal relationships, and be manipulative and untrusting of others. Periods of depression, excessive spending, drug abuse, or suicidal behaviour are also characteristic of the disorder. Lacking a sense of identity, the person may cling to others, often using suicidal behaviour as a form of manipulation.

One of the most dangerous and well-researched personality disorders is **antisocial**

personality disorder. Formerly called a sociopath or psychopath, a person with this disorder typically displays a complete lack of conscience by the age of 15. This usually leads to behaviours such as lying, stealing, cheating, or even murder, without remorse. Nearly three to six times as many males as females are diagnosed with antisocial personality disorder (APA, 2000). Several brain-imaging studies have demonstrated that those who commit murder show reduced activity in their frontal lobes—the area that helps us control impulses. These studies also show deficits in the ability to regulate emotions and memory (e.g., Hughes, 2010; Kiehl, 2004). For example, researchers (Raine, 1999; Raine et al., 2000) compared PET scans of 41 murderers' brains and noted that this was especially true for those who murdered impulsively. They also found that criminals who repeatedly committed violent crimes had 11% less frontal lobe tissue than non-violent control subjects, suggesting that they may have greater difficulty controlling their behaviour than non-violent criminals.

While antisocial personality disorder is primarily diagnosed in men, the frequency of **histrionic personality disorder** is two to three times greater in women (APA, 2000). Characterized by a tendency to overreact to situations, excessive emotionality, and the use of manipulation to gain attention from others, people with histrionic personality disorder often use sexually provocative behaviour in order to be the centre of attention.

Plenty of people believe they're more important than everyone else, but when this characteristic is taken to the extreme, it may be symptomatic of **narcissistic personality disorder.** People with this disorder have an inflated sense of self-importance and a deep need for admiration. They may have little regard for the feelings of others and be preoccupied with fantasies of their own success.

ANXIOUS/INHIBITED PERSONALITY DISORDERS

A person who consistently expresses feelings of anxiety may be suffering from an anxious or

inhibited personality disorder, categorized as avoidant, dependent, or obsessive-compulsive. **Avoidant personality disorder** is characterized by high levels of social anxiety and feelings of inadequacy. People with this disorder yearn for social interaction, but their extreme shyness and fear of rejection make it very difficult for them to socialize.

A person with a **dependent personality disorder** may display similar insecurities in the form of clingy, needy behaviour. The person may require excessive approval and reassurance, ask others to make decisions for them, and have difficulty expressing disagreement with others in case of a loss of support or approval.

Anxiety that manifests in excessive orderliness may be a symptom of **obsessive-compulsive personality disorder.** A person with this type of personality disorder may be obsessively neat, find it difficult to delegate tasks because of a fear the tasks will be completed in a substandard manner, and become preoccupied with rules, schedules, and order. However, people with this disorder do not feel the need to repeatedly complete ritualistic actions, distinguishing it from OCD.

> "One of the most dangerous and well-researched personality disorders is antisocial personality disorder. Formerly called a sociopath or psychopath, a person with this disorder typically displays a complete lack of conscience by the age of 15."

Dissociative Disorders

If you have ever driven the familiar route home and then realized you can't remember anything of the journey, you are already familiar with dissociation. Our conscious minds are able to focus on the term paper due next week, while another part of our brains somehow navigates us through traffic lights and stop signs. **Dissociative disorders** are conditions in which the normal cognitive processes are fragmented, causing a sudden loss of memory or change in personality. These take several forms and can vary in length from a matter of minutes to many years.

Dissociative amnesia is a disorder that causes sudden, selective memory loss. It is usually preceded by a traumatic event, such as rape or childhood abuse (Chu, Frey, Ganzel, & Matthews, 1999). Dissociative amnesia differs from retrograde amnesia (see Chapter 12), in which memory loss is typically caused by a blow to the head rather than psychological trauma.

Imagine waking up in a strange place with no idea who you are or how you got there. While it sounds like the plot to a bad Hollywood movie, **dissociative fugue** is a real condition, characterized by a sudden loss of memory accompanied by an abrupt departure from home. A person suffering from dissociative fugue may forget all personal history and take on a whole new identity.

Is it possible to have more than one personality? Psychologists are now debating the existence of **dissociative identity disorder,** formerly known as multiple personality disorder, in which a person seems to experience two or more personalities in one body. Each personality has its own voice and mannerisms, and may or may not be aware of the others. Skeptics find it suspicious that this disorder became so prevalent in the late 20th century, with the number of diagnosed cases in North America jumping from two per decade between 1930 and 1960 to more than 20 000 cases in the 1980s (McHugh, 1995). However, there are some neurological findings that support the existence of dissociative identity disorder. Whether a person is right- or left-handed sometimes switches with personality (Henninger, 1992). In one study, ophthalmologists detected shifting visual acuity and eye-muscle balance as patients shifted between one patient and another—a change that control subjects simulating multiple personality were unable to achieve (Miller et al., 1991).

Somatoform Disorders

Somatoform disorders are characterized by physical symptoms that do not have an identifiable cause. For example, a person with **somatization disorder** may frequently and dramatically complain of vague, unverifiable symptoms such as dizziness and nausea. Although the person is not making up these symptoms, the ailments have no physical cause and treatment is often related to underlying psychological problems such as stress and depression.

> "Is it possible to have more than one personality? Psychologists are now debating the existence of dissociative identity disorder, formerly known as multiple personality disorder, in which a person seems to experience two or more personalities in one body."

Conversion disorder is a somatoform disorder rarely seen in North America and Western Europe (although it was fairly common 100 years ago). Characterized by the sudden, temporary loss of a sensory function, a person may experience blindness, paralysis, deafness, or numbness of particular body parts. The disorder usually occurs when the person has been exposed to a traumatic event. For example, there was a high rate of psychological blindness among Cambodian women after the Khmer Rouge reign of terror in the 1970s. These symptoms have no physical cause, but people with conversion disorder are not being intentionally deceitful. Although they may appear to be "acting out" symptoms, people suffering from blindness as a result of conversion disorder actually believe that they are blind.

People suffering from **hypochondriasis** become so preoccupied with minor symptoms that they develop an exaggerated belief that the symptoms are indicative of a life-threatening illness.

Unlike someone with hypochondriasis, a person with somatization disorder may not exaggerate the seriousness of the symptoms.

Childhood Disorders

Some disorders are characteristic of children or may first be evident in childhood. The diagnostic criteria used to assess psychological disorders in children are less standardized and more contextualized than criteria used for adults, and diagnosis can be difficult because symptoms may differ in children and adults. In Canada, 15% of children and youth are affected by mental illness. Anxiety is the most common disorder, affecting 6.5% of Canadian children and youth (MDSC, 2009). The following disorders are just a few of the prevalent mental illnesses experienced or diagnosed in childhood.

ATTENTION-DEFICIT HYPERACTIVITY DISORDER

Children diagnosed with **attention-deficit hyperactivity disorder (ADHD)** typically find it difficult to focus their attention and are easily distracted. They may fidget, find it difficult to take turns, impulsively blurt out an answer before hearing the entire question, and consistently fail to remain seated. Affecting 3% to 5% of school-age children, ADHD is two to three times more prevalent in boys than girls. It is treated with stimulant drugs such as Ritalin or methylphenidate, which increase levels of dopamine in the brain, stimulating attentional and motivational circuits.

AUTISM

Children who fail to form normal attachments to their parents and who withdraw into their own separate worlds may be suffering from **autism,** a developmental disorder that impedes social development and communication skills. Autistic children avoid eye contact and may display repetitive movements such as rocking back and forth or self-abusive behaviour such as headbanging.

Researchers believe that autism is a polygenic disorder, meaning that when a number

of particular genes combine, the risk of developing the disorder increases. In families with one autistic child, the risk of having a second child with the disorder is 3% to 8% higher than the risk for the general population. Autism has also been linked to underlying medical conditions, including metabolic disorders (untreated PKU), genetic disorders (fragile X syndrome), and developmental brain abnormalities (microcephaly). However, these disorders alone do not cause autism—most children with these conditions are not autistic.

ASPERGER SYNDROME

Autism has recently come to be viewed as part of a spectrum of disorders known as autism spectrum disorder (ASD). **Asperger syndrome,** named after Viennese physician Hans Asperger, is part of this spectrum. In 1944, Asperger wrote a paper about children who had normal levels of intelligence and cognitive abilities, but displayed autistic-like social behaviours. Often viewed as eccentric or odd, people with Asperger syndrome show marked deficiencies in social skills, have obsessive routines, and may be preoccupied with a particular subject they find interesting. The disorder was added to the DSM-IV in 1994.

Summary

WHAT ARE MENTAL DISORDERS? p.232

• A mental disorder is a disturbance that impairs a person's ability to form social and occupational relationships, involves serious, prolonged distress, and is viewed by mental health professionals as harmful, deviant, and dysfunctional.

• Mental disorders may vary across cultures. Culture-bound syndromes and cultural expectations affect the diagnosis and treatment of mental illnesses across cultures.

WHAT ARE THE POSSIBLE CAUSES OF MENTAL DISORDERS? p.235

• Irreversible brain damage can cause psychological damage. Degenerative memory diseases such as Alzheimer's occur because of neuron deterioration in the brain.

• Predisposing factors such as genetics, birth defects, and toxins such as alcohol make individuals susceptible to particular psychological disorders.

• Environmental influences can trigger mental disorders in individuals who are biologically predisposed to develop those disorders.

WHAT ARE THE MAJOR TYPES OF MENTAL DISORDERS, AND WHAT ARE THEIR CHARACTERISTICS? p.236

• Anxiety disorders are characterized by persistent, often unidentifiable feelings of anxiety. Generalized anxiety disorder, phobias, panic disorder, obsessive-compulsive disorder, and post-traumatic stress disorder are all types of anxiety disorders.

• Mood disorders come in two main forms: depressive disorders, characterized by long, extreme periods of depression, and bipolar disorders, characterized by alternating episodes of depression and mania. Major depressive disorder, dysthymia, and seasonal affective disorder are all types of clinical depression.

• Schizophrenia is often characterized by delusions, hallucinations, and disorganized or catatonic behaviour.

• Personality disorders are characterized by rigid, abnormal patterns of behaviour that affect normal social functioning. There are three types of personality disorders: odd/eccentric, dramatic/erratic, and anxious/inhibited.

• Dissociative disorders cause a sudden loss in memory or change of personality. Dissociative amnesia, dissociative fugue, and dissociative identity disorder are types of dissociative disorders.

• Somatoform disorders, including somatization disorder, hypochondriasis, and conversion disorder, are characterized by physical symptoms without an identifiable cause.

• Childhood disorders are characteristic of children or first evident in childhood. Prevalent childhood disorders include ADHD, autism, and Asperger syndrome.

Test Your Understanding

1. When Binda visits a mental health expert, the clinician asks her a lot of questions about her family medical history. Binda is then given an MRI scan. Which approach to psychopathology is the clinician most likely using?

   a. a cognitive approach
   b. a biological approach
   c. a psychoanalytic approach
   d. a behavioural approach

2. Tomas has a family history of substance abuse, although Tomas himself has never used drugs. When Tomas's father dies suddenly, Tomas tries cocaine for the first time and quickly becomes addicted. The death of Tomas's father is a:

   a. perpetuating cause
   b. predisposing cause
   c. precipitating cause
   d. psychoanalytic cause

3. A person with an irrational fear of heights is suffering from:

   a. a social phobia
   b. agoraphobia
   c. panic disorder
   d. a specific phobia

4. Which type of schizophrenic is most likely to suffer from delusions of persecution?

   a. disorganized
   b. catatonic
   c. paranoid
   d. residual

5. Priyanka constantly worries that she has left her car unlocked. She wakes up several times in the night and checks that her car is secure. Priyanka's constant checking of the car is:

   a. a compulsion
   b. an obsession
   c. a phobia
   d. a panic disorder

6. Dave has little regard for the feelings of others and considers himself to be extremely important. He craves the admiration and respect of the people he works with. Dave is most likely suffering from:

   a. histrionic personality disorder
   b. avoidant personality disorder

c. narcissistic personality disorder

d. antisocial personality disorder

7. Which of the following causes some people with panic disorder to develop agoraphobia?

   a. a need to be able to sit down quickly

   b. a fear of having a panic attack in a public place

   c. a desire to seek medical treatment

   d. an inability to walk long distances

8. Hannah is married and has a good job. Recently, she has lost her appetite and is having difficulty sleeping. She is unable to concentrate at work and constantly feels guilty for no apparent reason. Despite taking part in regular activities, Hannah no longer enjoys anything she does and spends long periods of time lying in bed. Hannah is most likely suffering from:

   a. generalized anxiety disorder

   b. bipolar disorder

   c. histrionic personality disorder

   d. clinical depression

9. Which of the following statements about schizophrenia is true?

   a. People with schizophrenia are typically able to memorize lots of facts and figures.

   b. People with schizophrenia usually have decreased levels of dopamine in their brains.

   c. People with schizophrenia often show symptoms of having more than one personality.

   d. People with schizophrenia often have abnormal brain structures, including low activity in the frontal lobes.

10. According to the diathesis-stress hypothesis, people who are genetically disposed to a particular mental disorder will:

    a. inevitably develop the disorder

    b. develop the disorder if a sibling has it

    c. develop the disorder if they are exposed to environmental or emotional strain

    d. develop the disorder if their mother contracted rubella or influenza during pregnancy

11. Daku is a seven-year-old boy who is having problems at school. He constantly fidgets, moves around the classroom, and interrupts the teacher. Daku would most likely be treated with:

    a. stimulant drugs

    b. antipsychotic drugs

    c. antidepressant drugs

    d. mood-stabilizing drugs

12. Which psychological approach posits that abnormal behaviour is caused by negative thought processes?

    a. the biological approach

    b. the behavioural approach

    c. the cognitive approach

    d. the psychoanalytic approach

13. Which of the following statements about antisocial personality disorder is true?

    a. A person with antisocial personality disorder typically displays a lack of conscience.

    b. Males and females are diagnosed with antisocial personality disorder at equal rates.

    c. Violent criminals with antisocial personality disorder have more frontal lobe tissue in their brains than normal.

    d. Symptoms of antisocial personality disorder include excessive emotionality, the use of manipulation, and sexually provocative behaviour.

14. People who suffer from generalized anxiety disorder are also likely to develop which of the following disorders?

    a. bipolar disorder

    b. schizophrenia

    c. histrionic personality disorder

    d. major depressive disorder

15. A decrease in the hormone serotonin is believed to create the biological conditions for which of the following disorders?

    a. conversion disorder

    b. seasonal affective disorder

    c. schizophrenia

    d. autism

16. Tania is painfully shy and believes that she is not worthy of having friends. She feels awkward in social situations and fears that if she tries to talk to people they will laugh at her or tell her to go away. Tania is most likely suffering from:

    a. dependent personality disorder

    b. antisocial personality disorder

    c. borderline personality disorder

    d. avoidant personality disorder

17. Etsuko suffers from both generalized anxiety disorder and depression. Etsuko's doctor would likely describe her conditions as:

    a. dual diagnosis

    b. comorbid

    c. double depression

    d. dissociative

18. Which of the following symptoms is most likely to indicate that a person is suffering from schizotypal personality disorder?

    a. a belief in clairvoyance

    b. excessive spending

    c. an inflated sense of self-importance

    d. obsessive neatness

19. Fadna, a woman from Darfur, witnesses a brutal massacre. After she escapes, Fadna realizes that she has gone blind. Doctors, however, are unable to find anything physically wrong with her eyes. Fadna is most likely suffering from:

    a. somatization disorder

    b. conversion disorder

    c. dissociative fugue

    d. dissociative amnesia

20. A child with Asperger syndrome is most likely to display:

    a. above-average physical abilities

    b. below-average intelligence

    c. impaired cognitive abilities

    d. impaired social development

Remember to check www.thethinkspot.ca **for additional information, downloadable flashcards, and other helpful resources.**

Answers: 1) b; 2) c; 3) d; 4) c; 5) a; 6) c; 7) b; 8) d; 9) d; 10) c; 11) a; 12) c; 13) a; 14) d; 15) b; 16) d; 17) b; 18) a; 19) b; 20) d

TREATMENT OF PSYCHO-PATHOLOGY

HOW HAS THE MENTAL HEALTH SYSTEM EVOLVED OVER THE YEARS, AND HOW IS IT STRUCTURED TODAY?

HOW DO BIOMEDICAL THERAPIES TREAT PSYCHOLOGICAL DISORDERS?

HOW DO PSYCHODYNAMIC AND HUMANISTIC THERAPIES TREAT PSYCHOLOGICAL DISORDERS?

HOW DO COGNITIVE AND BEHAVIOURAL THERAPIES TREAT PSYCHOLOGICAL DISORDERS?

WHAT FACTORS MAKE PSYCHOTHERAPY AN EFFECTIVE TREATMENT, AND HOW DOES IT COMPARE IN USE TO BIOMEDICAL TREATMENTS?

On the

surface, clinical psychologist Kay Redfield Jamison seemed to have it all: good looks, plenty of friends, a supportive family, and a promising future as a psychologist. She was bright, energetic, vibrant, and gifted—on the surface.

Sometimes, though, Jamison was too bright, too energetic, too vibrant. And then, sometimes, she was not; she was the opposite, in fact: depressed, lethargic, wilting in an abyss of pain and nothingness. Jamison knew the details of her academic specialty, mental illness, far too intimately: She was bipolar.

In her 1995 memoir *An Unquiet Mind*, Jamison, a psychologist and professor of psychiatry at Johns Hopkins University, recalls her struggle with a debilitating mental illness that threatened both her livelihood and her life. As a graduate student at UCLA in the mid-1970s, Jamison experienced dramatic mood swings that made her fun-loving and buzzing with creativity one minute and deeply despondent the next. Like many sufferers of bipolar disorder, Jamison was at first afraid to admit she was sick and afraid to get help. Despite her qualms, however, Jamison did seek treatment. Under the guidance and supervision of a psychiatrist, she began taking lithium, an elemental salt that controls bipolar mood swings for many sufferers. Lithium wasn't magic; there were unpleasant side effects, and in truth, Jamison missed the mania sometimes, the surge of raw energy that made her feel unstoppable, invincible, electric. Several times, Jamison even stopped taking the medication, only to find that without it, her life would quickly spin out of control. As difficult as it was, Jamison eventually realized that in order to continue working and living, she needed to continue treating her illness.

Treatment allowed Jamison to continue her pursuits as a researcher, author, and professor in the field of psychology. Her book *Manic-Depressive Illness* is the classic textbook on bipolar disorder, she was chosen by *Time* magazine as a "Hero of Medicine," and she was a 2001 MacArthur Fellowship recipient. In 2007, she was awarded the Robert S. Liebert Award in Applied Psychoanalysis from Columbia University. In 2009, she was named an Honorary Fellow by the American College of Psychiatrists. In 2010, she received the David Mahoney Prize, from Harvard University, and she served as Honorary President and Board Member of the Canadian Psychological Association from 2009 to 2010. In all, Jamieson has received seven honorary degrees, ranging from literature to medical science. Jamison has dedicated her life and career to unlocking the mysteries surrounding mental illness, helping countless other sufferers in the process. Jamison's recovery from and maintenance of her illness, in addition to her long list of professional and personal accomplishments, is a testament to the belief that with the proper treatment, people who suffer from psychological disorders can take their lives back.

<<< *Beloved Canadian children's author Robert Munsch recently revealed his struggle with obsessive-compulsive disorder and bipolar disorder. Munsch revealed that he used cocaine and alcohol to help him cope with his mental illness and had become dependent on these drugs. Munsch is just one of many public figures to seek treatment for mental illness.*

CHAPTER **17**

Clinical Psychology and the Mental Health System

Kay Redfield Jamison occupies a unique position in that she is both a patient and practitioner of **clinical psychology,** a field of practice and research that aims to help people suffering from psychological problems and disorders. When people find themselves struggling with the kinds of problems detailed in Chapter 16, psychological problems, they can turn to clinical psychology for help.

These days, seeking psychological help from a therapist is anything but uncommon. It's not unusual to hear people flippantly reference "getting their heads shrunk," or to even cite advice or directives from psychological professionals in casual conversations with friends. As you've likely noticed, therapists and therapy sessions also dot the cinematic and television landscape, from Meredith Grey discussing her commitment issues with Dr. McDreamy on *Grey's Anatomy* to Dr. Phil McGraw demanding that the troubled guests on his eponymous talk show "get real." Whether serious, as in Jamison's *An Unquiet Mind*, or tinged with humour, as in many contemporary movies and sitcoms, cultural references to psychological treatments have helped demystify and destigmatize such measures for many people. This represents a significant change, and significant progress, within the realm of mental health.

<<< Actor **Patrick Dempsey** stars on the hit show *Grey's Anatomy*, which occasionally dramatizes the **mental health system.** Do you think that depictions of **clinical psychology** in pop culture help to **destigmatize mental illness?**

Clinical psychology is a field of psychology that deals with the diagnosis and treatment of people with specific mental or behavioural problems.

Patient is a person with a psychological disorder who is being treated using a biomedical approach.

Client is a person with a psychological disorder who is being treated with the view that his or her psychological distress is caused by behavioural issues and faulty thought processes.

● ○ ○

THE HISTORY OF MENTAL HEALTH PRACTICES

From the Middle Ages through the 17th century, most people considered mental disorders to be a form of bedevilment or possession by evil spirits. As a result, treatment was ineffective—or worse. Many "treatment" methods, such as torture, hanging, and burning at the stake, were particularly cruel and inhumane. Some sufferers were even sent off in "ships of fools," relegated to a fate of either drowning or being miraculously saved by divine providence.

In 1792, Philippe Pinel, director of a large mental hospital in Paris, initiated the reform movement in the treatment of the mentally ill. He advocated treating those in mental institutions like patients rather than prisoners. Under his direction, patients, rather than being locked in their rooms or even chained

---

to their beds, were allowed to move around freely and exercise outdoors. By the mid-19th century, Canada had established asylums for the mentally ill in New Brunswick, Nova Scotia, Prince Edward Island, Newfoundland, Ontario, and Quebec. By the 20th century, asylums were also established in Western Canada. By 1950, the asylum population in Canada had grown to an estimated 66 000 patients (Davis & Marshall, 2009).

In the middle of the 20th century, a growing trend of disenchantment with large institutions to house the mentally ill took hold. As a result, treatment of psychological disorders began to be deinstitutionalized, thanks in part to advances in psychopharmacology. For the first time, people with severe mental illness were able to live and function independently with the help of carefully monitored medications and treatments. In Canada, it costs over $34 000 per year to support someone with a serious mental illness living in the community. It would cost over $170 000 per year to keep this same individual in the hospital for treatment of their mental illness (Mood Disorders Society of Canada [MDSC], 2009).

Nevertheless, the deinstitutionalization movement has hardly been an unqualified success. Lacking adequate transitional support, many patients stop taking necessary medication and end up unemployed, homeless, and unable to care for themselves. In Canada, the unemployment rate for individuals with serious mental illness is 70% to 90%. Roughly one-third of homeless Canadians suffer from a mental illness, with mood disorders being the most common illness (MDSC, 2009).

THE STRUCTURE OF THE MENTAL HEALTH SYSTEM

When it comes to choosing a mental health professional, there is no shortage of choices. Mental health professionals take on a variety of titles and roles, depending on their education, training, expertise, and area of focus.

There is one additional distinction worth noting—that is, the one between **patient** and **client**. In general, professionals who take a biomedical approach to treating psychological disorders refer to those whom they treat as patients. In contrast, professionals who conceptualize psychological distress as "problems in living" (rather than as illness) call those who seek their help clients.

PSYCHIATRIST

Medical doctors who specialize in the treatment of psychological disorders. Because they have medical degrees, they can prescribe drugs. Some psychiatrists conduct psychotherapy sessions with patients.

PSYCHIATRIC NURSE

Have degrees in nursing with specific training for care of mental patients; generally work in hospitals or medical settings.

CLINICAL PSYCHOLOGIST

Specialists who hold doctoral degrees in psychology and have undergone extensive training in research and clinical practice.

COUNSELLING PSYCHOLOGIST

Similar in training and degree to a clinical psychologist, with an emphasis on counselling.

COUNSELLOR

Generally have master's degrees in counselling with less training in research and diagnostics than a clinical or counselling psychologist has; work primarily in school or institutional settings.

PSYCHIATRIC SOCIAL WORKER

Hold master's degrees in social work and have training and experience working with those with psychological problems. They usually are employed by public social-work agencies.

PREVENTIVE CARE AND MENTAL HEALTH

In the past few decades, much of the focus in the field of psychiatric treatment has shifted toward preventive care—taking measures to prevent people from developing mental health problems in the first place by addressing the conditions thought to cause or contribute to them. For example, poverty, racism, and abusive households can have an enduring and significant effect on people's abilities to effectively cope with the stresses of life (Albee, 1986; Danshiff, DiMicco, Myers, & Sheppard, 2009; Yoshikawa, Aber, & Beardslee, 2012). Advocates for preventive care believe that reducing the incidence of these traumas in people's lives through social justice programs, community assistance, and educational opportunities will also decrease the number of people afflicted with psychological problems (Nikulina, Widom, & Czaja, 2011; Wadsworth et al., 2011). Obviously, there are no easy solutions for complex social problems such as poverty; however, the investment of time, money, and resources into alleviating some of these issues is a worthy cause from both a social and a mental health perspective.

CLINICAL SOCIAL WORKER

Similar to psychiatric social workers, but have taken part in specialized training that has prepared them for working with psychiatrists, psychologists, and other mental health professionals.

The availability of care and treatment in the current mental health system remains a challenge for many people because of a shortage of qualified mental health professionals coupled with a difficult-to-navigate system that often neglects the under- or uninsured. Even people with health insurance often find that their insurance has strict limits on mental health care and doesn't cover treatments for certain psychological disorders. As a result, many people with psychological problems seek care and don't receive it to an adequate degree or, even worse, simply give up and continue suffering. As a result, these people's psychological problems often continue to deteriorate, with potentially tragic results. It's clear that there is still considerable room for improvement in the mental health system.

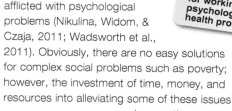

<<< Extreme poverty is just one of the social problems thought to contribute to mental illness. Do you think a difficult social environment contributes to a person's likelihood of developing psychological problems?

Biological Treatments: Biomedical Therapies

For Kay Redfield Jamison and legions of others afflicted with bipolar disorder, biomedical therapies are a major part of an effective treatment plan. Over the past 50 years or so, **psychopharmacology,** the study of how drugs affect the mind and behaviour, has led to the development of a wide array of **psychoactive medications.** These medications, such as the lithium Jamison takes, alleviate symptoms of mental disorders by acting on the bodily processes that may cause those symptoms.

Canada has the most users of psychoactive medications in the world. In 2007, 58 million prescriptions were filled for psychoactive medications (MDSC, 2009).

ANTIPSYCHOTIC DRUGS

Antipsychotic drugs are a class of psychoactive medications used to treat disorders in which psychotic symptoms, such as hallucinations, paranoia, and delusions, predominate. There are two types: typical and atypical.

Although many typical antipsychotics have been around since the 1950s, they continue to be as effective as newer medications at treating psychotic illnesses such as schizophrenia. Examples of typical antipsychotics include chlorpromazine and haloperidol. These drugs effectively reduce or eliminate the positive symptoms of disorders like schizophrenia, such as delusions and hallucinations (see Chapter 16), by decreasing dopamine activity at certain synapses in the brain (Lehman et al., 1998; Lenzenweger, Dworkin, & Wethington, 1989). The relative effectiveness of these drugs indicates that too much dopamine is at least partially responsible for schizophrenia (Howes & Kapur, 2009; Kendler & Schaffner, 2011; Pickar et al., 1984; Taubes, 1994). A notable limitation of typical antipsychotics, however, is that they do not treat negative symptoms. In addition, side effects of typical antipsychotics can include sluggishness, tremors, and even tardive dyskinesia, a serious and often irreversible motor disturbance in which the tongue, face, and other muscles involuntarily jerk or contract (Ling, Klainin, & Ignacio, 2011; Kaplan & Saddock, 1989). As a result of these potentially severe side effects, people with psychotic illnesses often find it difficult to continue taking antipsychotics for extended periods of time.

For those afflicted with negative symptoms of schizophrenia, such as apathy or prolonged lack of movement (see Chapter 16), atypical antipsychotics can provide relief. These drugs alter the activity of other neurotransmitters, such as serotonin, in addition to dopamine, and are also less likely to produce major side effects. Examples of atypical antipsychotics include clozapine, risperidone, and olanzapine. Although atypical antipsychotics generally produce fewer side effects than do typical antipsychotics, both types of drugs can cause symptoms such as dizziness, weight gain, constipation, sexual impotence in men, and nausea.

> **ABC News political analyst George Stephanopoulos, actress Brooke Shields, and comedian Rosie O'Donnell have all publicly credited SSRIs with helping them reclaim their lives after bouts with depression.**

ANTIDEPRESSANTS

Given the prevalence of major depressive disorder in Canada, it's no wonder that antidepressant medications have become well known to the general public in recent years (Kessler et al., 2005; Thase, 2011). **Antidepressants** work to alleviate symptoms of depression by altering how certain neurotransmitters—usually serotonin and norepinephrine—are circulated throughout the brain. Serotonin and norepinephrine are associated with arousal and feelings of well-being, and people suffering from depression often have serotonin or norepinephrine deficiencies.

The earliest forms of antidepressants, most popular from the 1960s to the 1980s, are called tricyclics. Examples include imipramine (Tofranil) and amitriptyline (Elavil). Typically, serotonin and norepinephrine are reabsorbed by the synapses in the brain (see Chapter 3). By blocking the reuptake of these neurotransmitters, tricyclics can elevate patients' moods. However, tricyclics have a number of unpleasant side effects, including dry mouth, fatigue, and blurred vision, and are more likely to cause death in the case of an overdose than are other types of antidepressants (Anderson, 2000; Mulrow, 1999; Smith & Curry, 2011).

Selective serotonin reuptake inhibitors, or SSRIs, are a newer alternative to tricyclics. These antidepressants, which began appearing in the mid-1980s, only block the reuptake of serotonin in the brain and have relatively few side effects. Fluoxetine (Prozac), paroxetine (Paxil), and sertraline (Zoloft) are all SSRIs. Tricyclics and SSRIs tend to have similar effectiveness in treating depression, but because SSRIs have fewer unpleasant side effects, they are more popular. Testimonial evidence indicates that these drugs can be powerfully effective; ABC News political analyst George Stephanopoulos, actress Brooke Shields, and comedian Rosie O'Donnell have all publicly credited SSRIs with helping them reclaim their lives after bouts with depression. "The gray has gone away. I am living in bright Technicolor," O'Donnell wrote of her experience with the medication.

Monoamine oxidase (MAO) inhibitors are another type of antidepressant. MAO is an enzyme that metabolizes monoamines such as norepinephrine, so by inhibiting this enzyme, these drugs allow for increased amounts of norepinephrine in the brain.

Because they can have severe side effects, including lethal food and drug combinations, MAO inhibitors are usually used as a last resort, for people who don't respond to other drug therapies.

The newest types of antidepressants, atypical antidepressants, affect neurotransmitters (including serotonin, norepinephrine, and dopamine) in specific combinations. Bupropion (Wellbutrin) and duloxetine hydrochloride (Cymbalta) are examples of these drugs. Interestingly, Wellbutrin, which works as an antidepressant by inhibiting the reuptake of norepinephrine and dopamine, has also been shown to be moderately effective in helping people quit smoking.

Millions of people have benefited from antidepressants—more than 38 million alone from Prozac (Goode, 2000; Isacsson, Rich, Jureidini, & Raven, 2010). The title of journalist Elizabeth Wurtzel's 1994 memoir—*Prozac Nation*—serves as a facetious commentary on the pervasiveness of antidepressants in North America. Indeed, our use of these drugs has become quite common over the last two decades, in part because of highly visible marketing campaigns. You're probably familiar with the cartoonish butterfly-chasing egg featured in Zoloft commercials or the emotionally wrought voice-overs that reverberate throughout Cymbalta ads. Some people even blithely refer to antidepressant medications as "happy pills." Yet the fact remains that antidepressants are serious, psychoactive medications. They are most effective and safe when they are used in conjunction with psychotherapy, and they should be taken only under close supervision of a physician who is hyperaware of the circumstances of treatment. Recent findings of a correlation between antidepressant use and increased suicide rates among children and young adolescents only strengthen the case for careful physician supervision (Wilkinson, Kelvin, Roberts, Dubicka, & Goodyer, 2011; Jureidini, 2009; Katz et al., 2008; Olfson, Marcus, & Shaffer, 2006).

ANTI-ANXIETY MEDICATION

For those suffering from anxiety disorders, anti-anxiety medications can provide relief. These drugs reduce the symptoms, such as tension and nervousness, associated with many anxiety disorders by slowing down the central nervous system's activity. The first anti-anxiety drugs were barbiturates, commonly known as tranquilizers, and were highly addictive. **Benzodiazepines,** a safer class of drugs, largely replaced barbiturates during the 1960s. These medications, including Valium and Xanax, are mostly effective for treating generalized anxiety disorder and panic disorder. Side effects can include drowsiness and a decline in motor coordination. Although benzodiazepines are less addictive than barbiturates, they have several unpleasant withdrawal symptoms. Furthermore, many practitioners believe that anti-anxiety drugs

relieve the symptoms of the disorder without addressing the underlying causes; these practitioners often recommend treatment plans that consist of both medication and therapy. Other anxiety disorders, including OCD and PTSD, are more likely to be treated with antidepressants, specifically SSRIs.

> Widespread advertising for **antidepressant medications** has helped make them **acceptable** to the mainstream. What do you think of such ads? Are they **helpful** or **harmful**?

MOOD-STABILIZING DRUGS

When people like Kay Redfield Jamison experience the rapid mood changes that are the hallmark of bipolar disorder, doctors often prescribe mood-stabilizing drugs—namely, lithium—in response. Lithium is a simple salt element that has been shown to benefit about seven in 10 bipolar patients when used on a long-term basis (Solomon et al., 1995). Exactly how and why the drug works remains a mystery to medical professionals. The important thing is, however, that it does work for so many afflicted with the disorder; journalist and

Benzodiazepines are anti-anxiety medications used mainly to treat generalized anxiety disorder and panic disorder.

Electroconvulsive therapy (ECT) is a type of therapy in which electric shocks are sent to patients' brains to treat certain psychological disorders in patients who don't respond to other treatment methods.

television host Jane Pauley, diagnosed as bipolar in 2001, says of lithium: "It just is stabilizing. It allows me to be who I am."

ELECTROCONVULSIVE THERAPY

If you have ever read Ken Kesey's *One Flew Over the Cuckoo's Nest,* or seen the film adaptation, you likely have a very negative impression of **electroconvulsive therapy (ECT).** Early uses of ECT—which involves sending electric shocks to patients' brains—were largely ineffective and, even worse, barbaric. However, with modern technology and careful medical supervision, ECT is now used to successfully treat people suffering from severe depression who do not respond to either psychotherapy or antidepressant medications.

ECT today is administered much differently than it used to be. Practitioners use muscle relaxants and other drugs to block nerve and muscle activity so the patient feels little pain and is not in danger of physical harm. Studies have shown that up to 80% of patients experience significant improvement in their depressive symptoms after six to 12 ECT sessions over the course of two to four weeks (Bergshlom, Larsen, Rosendahl, & Holsten, 1989; Coffey, 1993; Dawkins, 2012). Memory loss is typically the most troubling side effect; however, a new method called unilateral administration has helped to reduce its occurrence. During unilateral administration, physicians administer shocks only to the right hemisphere of patients' brains, lessening the treatment's impact on conscious, verbal memories.

As with lithium, the mechanism that makes ECT an effective treatment remains unknown. While ECT continues to be controversial, it is increasingly gaining a reputation as a promising, effective treatment option

Psychosurgery is a treatment method in which parts of the brain are surgically altered to treat mental disorders.

Psychotherapy is the interaction between a therapist and someone suffering from a psychological problem, the goal of which is to provide support or relief from the problem.

Eclectic psychotherapy is a type of psychotherapy involving the use of multi-faceted treatments that vary depending on each person's unique problem and take into account biological, psychological, and social influences.

Psychodynamic therapy is a type of therapy based on Freudian psychodynamics, the theory of which states that unconscious conflicts underlie mental disorders, and these conflicts make their way to the surface through a person's speech and behaviour.

Psychoanalysis is a type of psychotherapy that relates closely to Freudian concepts like the influence of the unconscious. It requires patients to talk to a psychiatrist about their lives while the psychiatrist listens, analyzes, and interprets each word.

Free association is a psychoanalytic technique in which the therapist encourages the client to relax his or her mind and, starting from a recent experience, a memory, or a dream, report every image or idea that enters awareness, refraining from logic or self-editing.

for those who have been unable to find relief from their depression elsewhere (Consensus Conference, 1985; Parker, Roy, Hadzi, & Pedic, 1992; Glass, 2001). ECT is also an effective treatment for people suffering from schizophrenia (Phutane, Thirthalli, Kesavan, Kumar, & Gangadhar, 2011), post-traumatic stress disorder (Margoob, Ali, & Andrade, 2010), and other mental illnesses (e.g., Zisselman & Jaffe, 2010).

PSYCHOSURGERY

Like ECT, **psychosurgery,** for many, conjures grotesque images of cruel, practically slapdash medical procedures from the past. Fortunately, modern medicine has ended the age of ill-advised lobotomies (a procedure that disconnects the frontal lobe from the rest of the brain and results in a near vegetative state) and transformed psychosurgery—in which parts of the brain are surgically altered to treat mental disorders—into a humane treatment option. These refined versions of psychosurgery are highly localized and targeted to specific areas of the brain. However, because psychosurgery is irreversible and carries all of the risks of surgery, it is used only in rare or extreme cases.

For example, OCD that's untreatable by other means can sometimes be treated with

psychosurgery. Doctors implant electrodes in areas of the brain shown to be overactive in OCD patients—the cingulum and basal ganglia—and then stimulate these electrodes with radio-frequency currents. Destroying these small segments of brain tissue can reduce OCD symptoms (Sachdev & Sachdev, 1997). In addition, a newer treatment called deep brain stimulation can be used for rare cases of otherwise untreatable OCD. Surgeons implant a thin wire electrode in the patient's brain; when activated, this electrode can stimulate (not destroy) neurons lying near it. Scientists believe this treatment effectively combats OCD by disrupting the ongoing neural loop that may underlie obsessions and compulsions. Deep brain stimulation may also be promising for treatment-resistant depression (Hirschfeld, 2011; Mohr, Rodriguez, Slavícková, & Hanka, 2011).

Psychodynamic and Humanistic Psychotherapy

As a clinical psychologist and a sufferer of bipolar disorder, Kay Redfield Jamison knows the ins and outs of psychotherapy better than most. **Psychotherapy** refers to an interaction between a therapist and someone suffering from a psychological problem, the goal of which is to provide support or relief from the problem. Although some people view psychotherapy as an alternative to biomedical treatments, it is often used along with psychotropic drugs. This blended approach—the use of multi-faceted treatments that vary depending on each person's unique problem and take into account biological, psychological, and social influences—is called **eclectic psychotherapy,** and it has become increasingly

> Not all psychotherapies are the same. In fact, each approach to psychotherapy represents a different perspective on how the mind works and how to best address 'problems of the mind.'

popular among therapists over the past two decades (Beitman, Goldfried, & Norcross, 1989; Lydecker et al., 2010; Castonguay & Goldfried, 1994; Livesley, 2012; Schnyder, Muller, Maercker, & Wittmann, 2011).

Not all psychotherapies are the same. In fact, each approach to psychotherapy represents a different perspective on how the mind works and how to best address "problems of the mind."

PSYCHODYNAMIC THERAPIES

Psychodynamic therapies are based on Freudian psychodynamics (see Chapter 15). According to psychodynamic theory, unconscious conflicts underlie mental disorders, and these conflicts make their way to the surface through our speech and behaviour. This perspective leads psychodynamic therapists to tend to view the symptoms of a disorder as side effects of a deep, underlying problem that needs to be resolved. Psychodynamic therapists apply Freud's ideas not only to their view of psychological disorders but also to their treatments. They tend to trace their clients' problems to childhood or past experiences and focus strongly on understanding symptoms in the context of the client's important personal relationships.

Psychoanalysis

Although its popularity has waned considerably over the years due to its tendency to be expensive and time intensive (requiring several sessions a week for several years), some psychodynamic therapists still employ psychoanalysis when treating patients (Goode, 2003). **Psychoanalysis** is a type of psychotherapy that relates closely to Freudian concepts like the influence of the unconscious. It involves a number of specific techniques and concepts, all with the aim of helping clients "work through" their issues and resolve their psychological problems.

"I went to the zoo yesterday . . . elephants . . . grey . . . charcoal . . . campfire . . . oak tree." This seemingly random string of thoughts is an example of what might be produced during an exercise in free association. **Free association** is a psychoanalytic technique in which the therapist encourages the client to relax his or her mind and, starting from a recent experience, a memory, or a dream, report every image or idea that enters awareness, refraining from logic or self-editing. The therapist then tries to discern whether these seemingly random associations point to particular underlying conflicts or anxiety in the client's unconscious mind.

Manifest content is what a person explicitly remembers about a dream—its storyline, characters, and details.

Latent content describes the unconscious meaning of a dream.

Resistance refers to a client's attempt to avoid doing therapeutic work.

Transference is an instance in which a client's unconscious feelings about a significant person in his or her life are instead directed toward the therapist.

Catharsis is healing emotional release.

Interpersonal psychotherapy is a type of psychotherapy that focuses on helping clients improve their relationships, particularly their current relationships, as a means to resolving their psychological problems.

∧
∧ Psychodynamic therapists may use **psychoanalytic**
∧ **techniques,** including free association and **dream analysis.** Do you think these methods can produce great insights and **relieve psychological problems?**

Freud believed that dreams are the purest forms of free association, and dream analysis is another notable psychoanalytic technique. When analyzing clients' dreams, therapists wade through the **manifest content**—the way the dream is experienced and remembered by the dreamer—in order to uncover the **latent content,** or the unconscious meaning of the dream.

Throughout sessions in psychoanalysis, therapists remain on the lookout for instances of resistance and transference in their clients. **Resistance** refers to a client's attempts to avoid doing therapeutic work. For example, a client might "forget" to go to sessions or refuse to talk about certain topics. During **transference,** a client's unconscious feelings about a significant person in his or her life are instead

directed toward the therapist. From a psychoanalytic perspective, a client who begins to resent her therapist might in fact be transferring her unconscious, unresolved resentment of her mother. By identifying these instances and analyzing their roots, therapists attempt to provide insights that will lead clients toward **catharsis,** or a healing emotional release.

Neo-Freudian Therapies

Several psychologists subscribe to Freud's fundamental ideas but have tweaked or amended his techniques to develop what are known as neo-Freudian therapies. Harry Sullivan, for example, believed that interpersonal relationships have a significant impact on psychological problems. His philosophy

contributed to the rise of **interpersonal psychotherapy,** which focuses on helping clients improve their relationships, particularly their current relationships, as a means to resolving their psychological problems. Like traditional psychoanalysis, interpersonal psychotherapy is based on the concept that patients need to uncover the roots of their problems, but it tends to be briefer, less intense, and more practical and immediate than psychoanalysis. This type of therapy seems to be particularly helpful for people suffering from depression (Poleshuck et al., 2010; Swartz, Levenson, & Frank, 2012; Weissman, 1999).

HUMANISTIC THERAPIES

If you believe that all people have the potential to grow, improve, and become their best selves, you might look at life from a humanistic perspective. The humanistic approach to psychology emphasizes humans' promise and our capacities for health, happiness, and

> "Humanistic psychologist Carl Rogers believed that in order to feel motivated to move forward in life, we have to feel good about ourselves and feel accepted and approved of by others, regardless of our flaws."

Person-centred therapy is a type of humanistic therapy in which the therapeutic process focuses squarely on the client's abilities and insights rather than the therapist's thoughts and skills.

Client-centred therapy see *person-centred therapy.*

Gestalt therapy is a type of humanistic therapy in which the therapist attempts to make the client feel whole by helping the client feel aware of and responsible for his or her thoughts, behaviours, experiences, and feelings.

Group therapy is a type of therapy that is led by a therapist and involves a group of clients experiencing psychological disorders.

Family therapy is a type of therapy in which the therapist views the family as a single unit and attempts to resolve conflicts and stresses that arise among the family members.

generosity toward others (see Chapter 15). It makes sense, then, that humanistic therapies address psychological problems through a lens of positivity and optimism. Psychological problems are not necessarily problems at all, a humanistic therapist might say, but opportunities for us to pause, reflect on our lives, and make changes that enhance our potential. Humanistic therapies tend to focus not on treating illness but on achieving wellness, even greatness, and they're particularly concerned with recognizing and igniting individuals' inner potential for positive growth.

Humanistic therapies centre on the notion that when it comes to happiness, the power lies with the people; that is, the choices we make regarding our own behaviour can effectively promote our survival and well-being. Humanistic therapists aim to help their clients develop the self-awareness and self-confidence necessary to achieve happiness. They don't "fix" clients so much as show clients how to "fix" themselves. You might think of them as the unrelentingly upbeat cheerleaders of the psyche.

Person-Centred Therapy

Humanistic psychologist Carl Rogers believed that in order to feel motivated to move forward in life, we have to feel good about ourselves and feel accepted and approved of by others, regardless of our flaws. This principle underlies a popular humanistic therapy developed by Rogers (1961, 1980) called **person-centred, or client-centred, therapy.** In this model, the therapeutic process focuses squarely on the client's abilities and insights rather than the therapist's thoughts and skills. Person-centred therapists assume the roles of motivators, collaborators, and facilitators of their clients' mental

health. They believe their clients are worthy and capable, even when the clients in question don't agree. The therapists' expressions of genuine acceptance are intended to help clients begin to feel more positive and self-confident, paving the way for clients to advance on their quest for personal fulfillment (Hill & Nakayama, 2000).

You might have heard a character on TV complain, "You're not really hearing me!" or you might have said something similar yourself once or twice. The idea of being "heard," or fully understood and listened to, comes from a key component of Rogers's person-centred therapy called active listening. When a therapist actively listens to a client, he or she tries to understand what the client is saying from the client's point of view, without judgment. Active listening involves echoing, restating, and seeking clarification of clients' statements. At the same time, therapists are careful to allow the client to maintain control of the discussion and direct its topics. An active listening session might sound something like this:

Client: Sometimes I feel like such a failure. Like I can't do anything right.

Therapist: So you feel like you're failing in some ways, that you can't do things right? Is that correct?

Client: Yeah, it's like every time I try to do something, I just mess it up.

Therapist: That sounds painful and frustrating. Is there an example you'd like to discuss?

According to Rogers, "hearing" clients in this fashion can be a powerful, uplifting force in the lives and minds of clients seeking help.

Gestalt Therapy

Gestalt means "whole," so it makes sense that in **gestalt therapy**, another humanistic method, therapists aim to "fill in the holes . . . to make the person whole" (Perls, 1969). Developed by psychologist Fritz Perls, gestalt therapy helps clients become aware of, and take responsibility for, their thoughts, behaviours, experiences, and feelings. Gestalt therapists move their clients toward this goal by encouraging them to speak in the active voice ("I called my parents" rather than "my parents were called") and to confront their fears, conflicts, or other troubles head-on.

Group and Family Therapies

For some people, the prospect of sitting down one-on-one with a therapist is too intimidating to bear, no matter how open, accepting, and empathic the therapist may be. **Group therapy** can be an effective alternative for these people since it tends to be less threatening than a one-on-one session. Additionally, group therapy gives

> *Additionally, group therapy gives clients the opportunity to observe others, practise their interpersonal skills, and change their thinking and behaviours based on other people's influence and input. People often find that hearing about others' experiences dealing with similar problems can be enormously comforting and helpful.*

clients the opportunity to observe others, practise their interpersonal skills, and change their thinking and behaviours based on other people's influence and input. People often find that hearing about others' experiences dealing with similar problems can be enormously comforting and helpful. Community support groups and self-help groups, such as Alcoholics Anonymous, are examples of highly effective group therapies (Galanter, Hayden, Castaneda, & Franco, 2005; Kurtz, 2004; McKellar, Stewart, & Humphreys, 2003; Cabello et al., 2012; Ouimette et al., 2001; Van Ingen & Novicki, 2009).

When families experience significant conflict or stress, they might look to a family therapist for help. **Family therapy** treats the family as a system or unit and can be an effective tool in helping families cope with and resolve conflict. The therapist focuses on how conflict or stress manifests itself in the relationships among the family members rather than on each individual's unique set of problems. Individual therapy often accompanies family therapy as part of the overall treatment plan.

Cognitive and Behavioural Psychotherapy

"I think, therefore I am": Even if you aren't an expert in philosophy, you're probably familiar with this statement from René Descartes, 17th-century scholar and thinker. Although

Descartes wasn't a psychologist, his belief about the interaction between thought, action, and existence is a convenient starting place for a discussion of cognitive and behavioural therapy as treatments for psychological disorders.

Cognitive and behavioural therapies are based on the idea that psychological problems are caused by faulty or irrational thinking, which in turn produces faulty or irrational behaviours. Essentially, you are what you think you are. As a result, cognitive and behaviour therapies, which are often combined in the form of **cognitive-behaviour therapy (CBT),** try to get people to change the way they think (cognition) and the way they act (behaviour). This approach is significantly different from both the psychodynamic and humanistic approaches: The client's goal isn't to gain insights into the unconscious mind or to realize personal potential. Rather, CBT asks clients to identify the thought and behaviour patterns that create their problems,

and then make immediate, quantitative changes to break these patterns. Interestingly, the use of CBT to treat phobias has been shown to have similar brain effects to SSRI treatments: Both reduce amygdala and hippocampus reactivity or activation (Coull & Morris, 2011; Furmark et al., 2002; Wannemueller et al., 2011). This finding indicates that there is a biophysiological aspect to CBT, and that changing the way you think and act can literally change your brain circuitry.

COGNITIVE THERAPY

Cognitive therapy, which can be either part of CBT or a stand-alone treatment option, first gained notice in the 1960s and is based on the theory that people's psychological problems can be traced to their own illogical or disturbed beliefs and thoughts. For example, people are depressed because they have depressive, self-defeating, negative thoughts; people

are anxious because they have apprehensive, fearful, panic-laced beliefs. Because these maladaptive thoughts and beliefs can make reality seem worse than it is, cognitive therapies attempt to replace them with healthier cognitive patterns.

Cognitive restructuring is an important part of most cognitive therapies. With this technique, therapists teach clients to question the automatic beliefs, assumptions, and predictions that often lead to negative emotional states and to replace negative thinking with realistic and positive thinking. Psychologist Aaron Beck and colleagues (1979) developed a widely used method based on this concept.

For instance, a client suffering from depression might be consumed by self-defeating thoughts like, "I failed that math exam, which means I'm going to fail the class, and I'll probably never get my degree or a decent job. I'm such a loser." A cognitive therapist applying Beck's technique would encourage the client to understand the illogical reasoning behind this "awfulizing" of an isolated situation: Failing one math exam doesn't make anyone a loser. "What does failing a math test have to do with your status as a human being? You made some mistakes in solving some math problems. Does that mean that everyone who struggles with math is a loser?" the therapist might say. The therapist would continue to work with the client to replace these thoughts with productive, effective ones grounded in reality: "I failed an exam, but it counts for only 10% of the final

∧
∧ Cognitive therapists work with clients to replace
∧ negative thought patterns with more adaptive
ones that can help them avoid depression.

Stress inoculation training (SIT) is a therapeutic technique in which clients are taught how to evaluate and cope with various stressors and are then exposed to increasingly stressful situations in a controlled environment to strengthen these coping mechanisms.

Behavioural therapy is a type of therapy that attempts to change behaviours associated with psychological distress.

Counterconditioning is a process that involves replacing unwanted responses to particular situations with new responses.

Exposure treatment is a type of counterconditioning in which people who have a fear or phobia are repeatedly exposed to what they fear over several sessions until they become so accustomed to it that they no longer fear it.

∧
∧ **Mindfulness meditation,** most often associated
∧ with **Buddhist practices,** has also found a place in cognitive therapy. Clients may work on **gaining self-awareness** through attending structured meditation sessions and **paying close attention** to their everyday **thoughts** and **actions.**

grade. If I work hard and ask the professor for extra help, I can still pass the class. Even if I don't, I can retake it in summer school. I'll still graduate on time. Failing one test is not going to destroy my future job prospects."

Once the client understands how harmful certain thought patterns can be, the therapist and client work together to create clear-cut, attainable goals as part of the treatment plan. These goals might include completing homework assignments like keeping a diary or filling out a form that describes troubling situations, thoughts, and emotions. The client and therapist discuss and analyze the results of the assignments in future sessions.

Sometimes, cognitive therapists encourage their clients to practise mindfulness meditation, a technique based on Buddhist teachings that emphasizes being fully present in each moment. When clients are acutely aware of their thoughts, feelings, and sensations, they can better detect symptoms before those symptoms become problems. According to psychologist Donald Meichenbaum (1977, 1985), this awareness can help people effectively self-edit their own harmful thoughts in negative situations. Meichenbaum called this **stress inoculation training (SIT).** For example, a client struggling with social anxiety may, at a party, begin to have doubts and fears: "Everyone is looking at me and judging me. They're wondering why I'm even here." Mindfulness meditation and stress inoculation training might allow the client to recognize these anxious thoughts and change them before they spiral out of control: "I feel anxious, but there's no reason to. I feel like people are judging me, but I realize that's probably not really true. People are more concerned with themselves than they are with me. I'm going to let go of my anxiety and enjoy the party."

SIT is effective in reducing psychological stress (Flaxman & Bond, 2010), depression, and post-traumatic stress disorder (e.g., Owens, Walter, Chard, & Davis, 2012).

Ultimately, cognitive therapists hope to move from a teaching to a consulting role in their clients' lives. Therapists hope that with the techniques learned during the therapeutic process, clients can achieve self-directed control of their problems and rely on the therapist for guidance rather than treatment.

> For Indiana Jones, receiving exposure treatment **might mean spending some serious quality time with snakes.**

BEHAVIOURAL THERAPY

The other half of CBT, as well as a treatment method in its own right, **behavioural therapy** attempts to change behaviours associated with psychological distress. This type of therapy has two foundational assumptions:

- The behaviours associated with psychological problems are not signs of a disorder or

indications of an underlying issue; they are the problems themselves.
- Because these behaviours are learned, through conditioning or modelling, they can be "unlearned" through similar methods.

As a result of these assumptions, many of the treatment plans that behavioural therapists prescribe involve training the mind and body to react differently to various stimuli.

Counterconditioning is a process that involves replacing unwanted responses to particular situations with new responses. For example, if a child is afraid of the dark, a behavioural therapist might ask her to listen to her favourite song while sitting in the dark. The song makes the child feel happy and relaxed, and she begins to associate darkness with happiness and relaxation rather than with fear. Ideally, the child will eventually become completely habituated, or familiarized, to darkness. (For more information about conditioning and habituation, see Chapters 6 and 11.)

Exposure Treatments

Exposure treatment, a specific type of counterconditioning, takes the mantra "Face your fear" to a clinical level: Over several sessions, people who have a fear or phobia are repeatedly exposed to what they fear until they become so accustomed to it that they no longer fear it

(Wolpe, 1958; Wolpe & Plaud, 1997). Exposure treatment is effective for PTSD (e.g., Yoder et al., 2012) and anxiety disorders, such as phobias (e.g., Pan, Huey, & Hernandez, 2011).

Systematic desensitization is a variation of exposure treatment in which people, within a therapeutic environment, learn to pair states of deep relaxation with thoughts of anxiety-provoking situations. For example, a therapist might begin a systematic desensitization treatment for a client who's terrified of enclosed spaces by helping the client achieve a deeply relaxed, almost drowsy state. Then, the therapist might ask the person to engage in imaginative exposure by imagining a series of increasingly anxiety-inducing settings, from a large enclosed room, to a smaller enclosed room, to a car, to an elevator. The therapist would work with the client to replace any anxiety evoked by each image with relaxation, effectively "desensitizing" the client to the stimulus. Eventually, clients practise the desensitization by participating in real-life situations—such as riding in an elevator—that they previously feared and avoided.

For clients who have difficulty conjuring vivid imagery in their heads, virtual reality exposure provides a helpful alternative. Using computer simulations, clients can learn to be increasingly desensitized to anxiety-inducing situations, from speaking in public to taking an airplane ride. Systematic desensitization, whether through imaginative exposure or virtual reality exposure, has been shown to be an effective tool in the treatment of phobias (Hazel, 2005; McNeil & Zvolensky, 2000; Triscari, Faraci, D'Angelo, Urso, & Catalisano, 2011; Wang & Chen, 2000).

You might think of **implosion therapy** as the "tough love" approach to exposure treatment. While systematic desensitization eases clients gently into facing their phobias,

implosion therapy does virtually the opposite: It habituates clients by exposing them to very intense stimuli. For example, a person afraid of spiders might be asked to imagine having hundreds of spiders crawling all over his body; all of a sudden, that lone arachnid in the bathroom sink doesn't seem so scary. A technique called **flooding** takes implosion therapy a step further, exposing the client (with his or her permission) to the fear-inducing stimulus in a direct, intense way. Someone with an intense fear of dark underground spaces, for instance, might experience flooding in the form of spending several hours in a subway station.

What if you could overcome your deepest anxieties simply by moving your eyes? It sounds too good to be true, but it's the premise of a relatively new form of exposure therapy for phobias and PTSD called **eye movement desensitization and reprocessing (EMDR).** EMDR therapists instruct clients to focus on a disturbing image or traumatic memory as they move their eyes back and forth. Research supports the effectiveness of EMDR for anxiety disorders and PTSD (Triscari et al., 2011; Marich, 2010; Shapiro, 1989, Shapiro, 2002; Van den Berg & Van der Gaag, 2012).

Aversive Conditioning

Therapists often use behavioural therapies to treat clients who have phobias, but what if phobias aren't at the root of your problem? People who struggle with alcoholism, for example, aren't confronting a phobic behaviour; they're facing an addiction. In cases like these, therapists sometimes implement a treatment called **aversive conditioning.** The goal of aversive conditioning is to replace a positive response to a harmful stimulus, such as alcohol, with a negative response. For example, a therapist might pair a drink or a cigarette with a nausea-inducing

---

Systematic desensitization is a variation of exposure treatment in which people, within a therapeutic environment, learn to pair states of deep relaxation with thoughts of anxiety-provoking situations, with the goal of replacing the anxiety felt during these situations with relaxation.

Implosion therapy is a type of exposure treatment in which clients are exposed to very intense stimuli by being asked to imagine an extreme version of their fears or phobias.

Flooding is a type of exposure treatment in which clients are exposed to fear-inducing stimuli in an intense way by directly exposing them to the stimuli.

Eye movement desensitization and reprocessing (EMDR) is a form of exposure therapy in which therapists instruct clients to focus on a disturbing image or traumatic memory as they move their eyes back and forth, with the goal of helping them deal with the psychological issues brought on by the disturbing or traumatic event.

Aversive conditioning is a type of therapy in which a harmful stimulus is paired with a negative response, with the goal of replacing the usual positive response (such as the pleasure a client may feel when drinking alcohol or smoking) with the negative one.

Contingency management is an operant conditioning strategy that involves altering the relationship between a person's actions and those actions' consequences to replace unwanted behaviours with desirable ones.

---

chemical. When the client drinks or smokes, he or she becomes violently ill and begins to associate drinking or smoking with feelings of sickness. Although aversive conditioning has been shown to treat alcoholism effectively in the short run, its long-term usefulness seems fairly limited (Wiens & Menustik, 1983).

Operant Conditioning

Operant conditioning, or behaviour shaping, forms the basis of another category of behaviour therapies. These therapies are centred on the idea that rewards (or a lack thereof) strongly influence our behaviour. One strategy, **contingency management,** involves altering the relationship between a person's actions and those actions' consequences to replace unwanted behaviours with desirable ones.

<<< **Therapists** can use **virtual reality** exposure to treat people for their **phobias** and **anxieties** through a process of **desensitization.**

Token economy is a term for an operant conditioning procedure in which individuals earn tokens when they exhibit desirable behaviour; later, people who've earned tokens can redeem them for privileges or treats.

Behavioural contract is an explicit agreement that thoroughly explains the consequences of several behaviours as well as expectations of the client and the therapist.

Social learning therapy is a type of therapy designed to modify clients' problematic behaviour patterns through observation and behaviour reinforcement.

This type of technique can, among other outcomes, successfully change the behaviour of withdrawn autistic children. For example, parents saw great improvements in the children's behaviour and intellectual achievements after they reinforced their children's good behaviour with attention and rewards and punished or ignored negative behaviours, such as hitting or screaming (Lovaas, 1987). In institutional settings, contingency management is sometimes enacted in token economies, an operant conditioning procedure in which individuals earn tokens when they exhibit desirable behaviour. Later, people who've earned tokens can redeem them for privileges or treats.

In behavioural therapy based on operant conditioning, it's important for both the client and the therapist to reach a clear understanding about positive and negative behaviours and their consequences, so a therapist might draw up a behavioural contract, an explicit agreement that thoroughly explains the consequences of several behaviours as well as expectations of the client and the therapist.

> If you're wondering which type of therapy is 'best,' however, there's only one safe answer: Each client, each therapist, and each disorder is different. As a result, the usefulness of any therapy depends on the client, the therapist, and the nature of their relationship.

Social Learning Therapy

Social learning therapy draws on the idea that we learn to act the way that we do through observing and modelling others' behaviour. Based on Canadian psychologist Albert Bandura's research (see Chapter 11), social learning therapy is designed to modify clients' problematic behaviour patterns through observation and behaviour reinforcement. In a famous study, Bandura and his colleagues helped people overcome their phobia of snakes by watching films in which others interacted comfortably with snakes (Bandura, Blanchard, & Ritter, 1969). Clients learn to perform desirable behaviours by visualizing those behaviours and their consequences, and they receive positive reinforcement when they actually perform the behaviours themselves.

Evaluating Psychotherapies

Does talking with a therapist really work? Does it relieve psychological problems and help people achieve happier, healthier lives? And which therapy is best—psychodynamic, humanistic, cognitive, or behavioural? Are certain therapies more useful for certain types of disorders, or for certain types of people? And what about medications—where do they fit in?

There's plenty of controversy and debate in the world of psychology, and the field of treatment is no exception. Psychologists don't all agree as to whether any type of psychotherapy is effective, and each type of psychotherapy has its champions and skeptics. If you're wondering which type of therapy is "best," however, there's only one safe answer: Each client, each therapist, and each disorder is different. As a result, the usefulness of any therapy depends on the client, the therapist, and the nature of their relationship.

THE EFFICACY OF PSYCHOTHERAPY

Every year Canadians pay $278 million in fees to psychologists and social workers (MDSC, 2009). But, is this expense justified? Research indicates that it is. In one classic study, psychologist R. B. Sloane and colleagues (1975) took a group of participants with generalized anxiety and assigned them to one of three groups: a control group that received no psychotherapy, a group that received psychodynamic psychotherapy, and a group that received behavioural psychotherapy. After the participants were double-blindly assessed both before and after treatment (or no treatment in the control group),

Sloane found that although all groups improved, the two treatment groups improved significantly more than the control group did. Furthermore, although the behavioural group improved slightly more than the psychodynamic group, the difference was insignificant.

Other studies have confirmed these findings: In a meta-analysis of 475 investigations into the efficacy of psychotherapy, Mary Lee Smith and colleagues (1980) concluded that people who receive psychotherapy improve more than about 80% of people who do not receive this treatment. Additional research has yielded similar results, showing that in general, most people who receive psychotherapy report improvement, and that some therapy appears to be better than no therapy at all (Cuijpers, van Straten, Hollon, & Andersson, 2010; Nathan & Gorman, 2002; Shadish, Matt, Navarro, & Phillips, 2000; Kopta, Lueger, Saunders, & Howard, 1999), and you don't have to stay in therapy very long to see the benefits (Bhar et al., 2010). It's important to keep a few points in mind in the context of these findings. In general, these experiments are carried out in research institutions with highly experienced, highly trained clinicians who are aware that they are also being assessed. This, in many instances, leads to optimal therapy conditions, which may or may not be available to the average person who seeks psychotherapy. In addition, the clients recruited to participate in these experiments may be a slightly biased group; their willingness to seek help may indicate an already existing belief that it can, and will, work.

It has been repeatedly shown that psychotherapy is effective for treating the conditions for which people most commonly seek help—generalized anxiety and major depression. Interestingly, however, research on the effectiveness of different therapeutic techniques has not discovered a single therapeutic strategy that is uniquely effective in treating all people with any disorder. However, some therapies do tend to treat certain disorders more effectively than others. For example, cognitive, interpersonal, and behaviour therapy have been shown to be most effective in treating depression, while cognitive and exposure therapy have proven useful in anxiety treatment. Behavioural therapy tends to be effective for impulse-control disorders. For those struggling with bulimia, CBT is perhaps the best option (Chambless et al., 1997; Norcross, 2002).

FACTORS OF EFFECTIVE PSYCHOTHERAPY

What makes psychotherapy an effective treatment? Its success can be attributed to a number of identifiable factors (Frank, 1982;

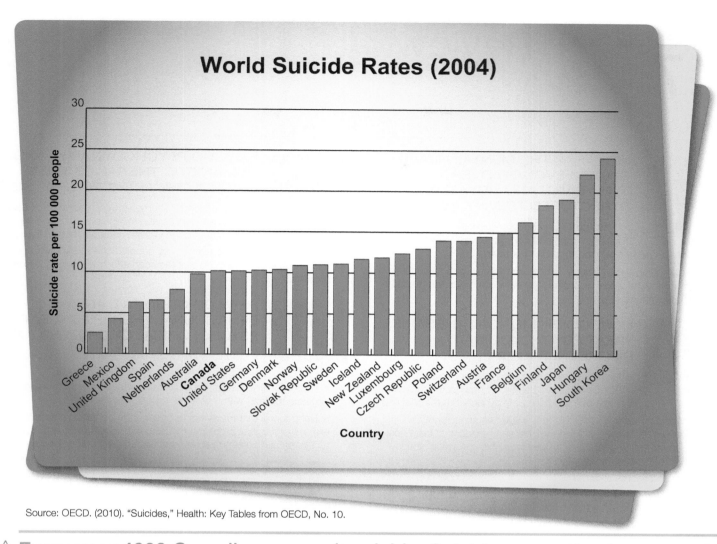

World Suicide Rates (2004)

Suicide rate per 100 000 people

Country

Source: OECD. (2010). "Suicides," Health: Key Tables from OECD, No. 10.

> ∧∧ Every year 4000 Canadians commit suicide. Suicide prevention is one goal of treatment for mental illness. What other goals would an effective treatment have for patients?

Goldfried & Padawer, 1982; Strupp, 1986; Wampold, 2001).

Support. For people struggling with depression and self-doubt, psychotherapy can provide a welcome dose of acceptance, empathy, and encouragement. Studies have shown these qualities to be highly valuable in treatment success, and many therapists consider providing support to be the first and foremost task when treating clients (Blatt, Sanislow, Zuroff, & Pilkonis, 1996; Torrey, 1986).

Hope. Catching sight of a light at the end of the tunnel—the expectation that things can and will get better—can be enormously helpful and comforting to individuals in psychological distress. Therapy often provides clients with this sense of hope.

New perspective. Therapists can give their clients the ability to see alternative views of the situation at hand. A therapist's expertise and experience often allows clients to see themselves, and their problems, in ways they had never before considered. "I have a problem that no one else has and will never be fixed" can become, "I have a problem that many others have struggled with and overcome, and by implementing these strategies, I can overcome it, too."

Motivation. Therapists sometimes explain a client's lack of response to treatment by saying that the client was not "ready to do the work." Therapy is not a passive process, and the patient or client must be motivated to get better and be willing to put in the time and effort that such measures require.

PSYCHOTHERAPY VS. PHARMACOLOGY

The question of which is the most effective treatment for psychological problems—psychotherapy or medications—can stir impassioned debate from both sides. Clearly, some conditions, such as schizophrenia and bipolar disorder, call for one above the other. For Kay Redfield Jamison, for example, CBT alone was not going to be enough to control her bipolar mood swings; she needed lithium.

For other conditions, such as depression and anxiety, psychotherapy, medications, or both may prove to be the most effective treatment for a given patient. Some patients with depression respond immediately and enduringly to SSRIs; some don't. Some benefit greatly from a combination of SSRIs and humanistic therapy; some don't. Some can use what they learn in CBT to overcome their problems; some can't. Each person, each situation, and each treatment is different. As inexact as it may sound, it's the truth: When it comes to treatment of psychopathology, it just depends.

17

· Review

Summary

HOW HAS THE MENTAL HEALTH SYSTEM EVOLVED OVER THE YEARS, AND HOW IS IT STRUCTURED TODAY? p.250

• Until the 17th century, the mentally ill were often treated in cruel and inhumane ways. Reformers such as Pinel campaigned for moral treatment.

• Today, clinical psychology, which aims to help people suffering from psychological disorders, lies at the centre of the mental health system structure.

HOW DO BIOMEDICAL THERAPIES TREAT PSYCHOLOGICAL DISORDERS? p.252

• Psychopharmacology, the study of how drugs affect the mind and behaviour, has led to the development of a wide array of psychoactive medications.

• Antipsychotic drugs treat disorders such as schizophrenia. Typical antipsychotics (chlorpromazine and haloperidol) treat positive symptoms by decreasing dopamine activity. Atypical antipsychotics treat negative symptoms.

• Antidepressants alleviate depression by altering how neurotransmitters, usually serotonin and norepinephrine, are circulated throughout the brain.

• Benzodiazepines treat anxiety disorders by slowing down the central nervous system, while lithium controls bipolar mood swings for many sufferers.

HOW DO PSYCHODYNAMIC AND HUMANISTIC THERAPIES TREAT PSYCHOLOGICAL DISORDERS? p.254

• Psychodynamic therapies trace clients' problems to past experiences and focus on understanding symptoms through clients' personal relationships.

• Humanistic therapies aim to help people achieve self-awareness and positive self-regard so that they can effectively solve their own problems.

HOW DO COGNITIVE AND BEHAVIOURAL THERAPIES TREAT PSYCHOLOGICAL DISORDERS? p.256

• Cognitive-behaviour therapy aims to help people change the way they think and act.

• With cognitive restructuring, therapists teach clients to replace negative thinking with realistic and positive thinking.

• Behavioural therapy seeks to change the behaviours associated with psychological problems by using exposure treatments, such as systematic desensitization, implosion therapy, and flooding.

WHAT FACTORS MAKE PSYCHOTHERAPY AN EFFECTIVE TREATMENT, AND HOW DOES IT COMPARE IN USE TO BIOMEDICAL TREATMENTS? p.260

• In general, most people who receive psychotherapy report improvement; some therapy appears to be better than no therapy.

• Psychotherapy often works because it provides clients support, hope, and a new perspective on their problems. Clients must be motivated to get better in order to improve.

Test Your Understanding

1. Which of the following describes a similarity between a psychiatrist and a clinical psychologist?

   a. Both can write prescriptions for psychoactive medications.
   b. Both always work in private practice.
   c. Both specialize in counselling patients.
   d. Both have the title of "Dr."

2. An advocate for preventive care most likely believes which of the following statements?

   a. Investing in social programs will have no effect on the incidence of mental illness.
   b. Psychotropic drugs are preferable over psychotherapy for the treatment of most mental illnesses.
   c. Exposure to extreme poverty, abuse, or racism can make one more vulnerable to mental illness.

   d. Group therapy is not as effective as one-on-one humanistic therapy for most people suffering from mental illness.

3. A person afflicted with delusions and hallucinations would most likely be prescribed:

   a. typical antipsychotics
   b. SSRIs
   c. benzodiazepines
   d. atypical antipsychotics

4. Which of the following conclusions is supported by the efficacy of SSRIs in treating depression?

   a. Excessive amounts of serotonin and norepinephrine contribute to depression.
   b. High levels of serotonin promote feelings of well-being.

   c. MAO inhibitors are safer but less effective than SSRIs in treating depression.

   d. Serotonin levels play no role in the incidence of depression.

5. Who would most likely be a candidate for ECT?

   a. a patient who experiences dramatic mood swings

   b. a patient who suffers from severe depression

   c. a patient who experiences obsessions and compulsions

   d. a patient who hears voices and constantly feels paranoid

6. From a psychoanalytic perspective, a patient may demonstrate resistance by:

   a. reporting every idea and image that comes to mind

   b. expressing feelings of love and affection toward the therapist

   c. refusing to talk about a past trauma

   d. describing dreams in detail

7. Which of the following is NOT true of active listening?

   a. It involves echoing, restating, and seeking clarifications from clients.

   b. It is a key component of Perls's gestalt therapy.

   c. Its goal is to make clients feel "heard."

   d. It is intended to help clients feel positive and self-confident.

8. Which of the following would a humanistic therapist be most likely to say during a session with a client?

   a. "Let's talk about your childhood."

   b. "It sounds like you've been feeling anxious lately. Is that right?"

   c. "Imagine yourself in a situation that makes you feel very anxious."

   d. "Try replacing your anxious thoughts with soothing thoughts."

9. A client receiving gestalt therapy might be guided to make which of the following statements?

   a. "I feel wounded when he makes insensitive comments."

   b. "His insensitive comments make me feel wounded."

   c. "Insensitive comments are wounding."

   d. "He will never understand how wounding his insensitive comments are."

10. One of the primary advantages of group therapy is that:

   a. it acts on the physiological mechanisms that cause psychological disorders

   b. it forces clients to speak at length about their problems

   c. it allows therapists to observe clients' interpersonal interactions

   d. it helps clients understand the purpose of aversive conditioning

11. Which of the following is NOT true of family therapy?

   a. It treats the family as a cohesive unit.

   b. It is often performed in conjunction with individual therapy.

   c. It focuses on how problems manifest themselves in family relationships.

   d. It involves the analysis of each family member's problems by the entire group.

12. Which of the following is an underlying premise of cognitive restructuring?

   a. We must achieve self-love before loving others.

   b. We control our mental states through our thoughts.

   c. We must learn to do things without the promise of rewards.

   d. We should put the needs of others before ourselves.

13. A therapist who specializes in CBT would most likely combine the techniques developed by which two psychologists?

   a. Beck and Bandura

   b. Rogers and Bandura

   c. Beck and Freud

   d. Rogers and Freud

14. Which of the following is true of both SSRIs and CBT in the treatment of phobias?

   a. They are advocated by most psychodynamic therapists.

   b. They have a powerful placebo effect.

   c. They have been shown to reduce amygdala activation.

   d. They always require a secondary form of treatment.

15. To deal with her intense fear of taking exams, Leslie participates in systematic desensitization. At the end of her treatment, Leslie practises desensitization in which of the following real-life situations:

   a. visualizes herself passing her physics exam

   b. avoids taking her physics exam

   c. takes her physics exam

   d. describes taking her physics exam

16. For people afraid of heights, flooding might involve:

   a. repeatedly visualizing a skydiving experience

   b. moving the eyes back and forth while visualizing climbing a mountain

   c. repeating the mantra "I am not afraid of heights" while meditating

   d. standing on the rooftop observation deck of a very tall building

17. Which of the following describes what might occur in a token economy?

   a. A schizophrenic patient receives a redeemable ticket for making his or her bed.

   b. An autistic child sits in a time-out chair for hitting a classmate.

   c. A woman phobic of dogs receives praise for petting a golden retriever.

   d. A teenager is reprimanded for displaying anti-social behaviour.

18. Which of the following sayings relates most closely to the concept on which social-learning therapy is based?

   a. Work hard, play hard.

   b. You can choose your friends, not your family.

   c. Monkey see, monkey do.

   d. Sometimes a cigar is just a cigar.

19. Which of the following is NOT true of psychotherapy?

   a. Its efficacy has been shown to increase over time.

   b. It is often used in conjunction with biomedical therapies.

   c. It has been shown to work regardless of clients' motivation to get better.

   d. It offers clients a new perspective on their problems.

20. Experiments that attempt to study the efficacy of psychotherapy:

   a. are completely unreliable

   b. tend to be conducted under optimal therapy conditions

   c. show that psychotherapy is no more effective than a placebo

   d. reveal that CBT is the most effective of all therapies

Remember to check www.thethinkspot.ca for additional information, downloadable flashcards, and other helpful resources.

Answers: 1) d; 2) c; 3) a; 4) b; 5) b; 6) c; 7) b; 8) b; 9) a; 10) c; 11) d; 12) b; 13) a; 14) c; 15) c; 16) d; 17) a; 18) c; 19) c; 20) b

THINK READINGS

BRIEF REPORT

Motivation and Maltreatment History Among Youth Entering Substance Abuse Treatment

Susan E. Rosenkranz
York University and Centre for Addiction and Mental Health, Toronto, Ontario

Joanna L. Henderson
University of Toronto and Centre for Addiction and Mental Health, Toronto, Ontario

Robert T. Muller
York University

Ilana R. Goodman
University of Toronto and Centre for Addiction and Mental Health, Toronto, Ontario

> **In Chapter 9 you read about the theories of motivation.**

> **What do you remember about incentives? Why do you think internal motivations are more powerful in changing behaviour than external motivations (Chapter 9)?**

Research has established that maltreatment experiences are common in the life histories of youth with substance abuse problems, and efforts are now moving in the direction of enhancing our understanding of the unique clinical presentations and treatment needs of this population. The current study endeavored to contribute to this body of research by examining associations between experiences of maltreatment and levels of motivation among youth entering outpatient substance abuse treatment. Upon admission, 188 youth (131 males, 57 females) completed a package of self-report questionnaires including measures of motivation to change, motivation for treatment, and history of maltreatment experiences. Results indicated that youth with histories of all forms of maltreatment examined tended to be more aware of the problematic aspects of their substance use, more ready to engage in treatment, more motivated by feelings of shame, and more motivated by external influences. Emotional abuse was the form of maltreatment that predicted level of motivation most strongly. Emotional abuse was particularly strongly associated with the form of motivation reflecting shame regarding substance use, predicting this form of motivation over and above other factors previously reported to be associated with motivation, such as severity of substance abuse and age. While clinicians are increasingly attending to exposure to traumatic events among youth entering substance abuse treatment, these findings suggest that attending to experiences of emotional abuse is also important. Such experiences appear to be related to treatment motivation and may be important to treatment processes and outcomes for these vulnerable youth.

A body of research has established that maltreatment experiences are significant risk factors for the development of substance abuse problems among youth (Clark, Lesnick, & Hegedus, 1997; Kilpatrick et al., 2000). Research is now beginning to turn to the complex clinical presentations and greater treatment needs of substance-using youth with maltreatment histories (Grella, Hser, Joshi, & Rounds-Bryant, 2001; Grella & Joshi, 2003). An area in which knowledge is currently lacking is the association between maltreatment and motivation among youth entering substance abuse treatment, an important issue as lack of treatment engagement presents a significant barrier to service provision. Gaining greater understanding of the factors that bring these particularly vulnerable youth to treatment will be important for enhancing their retention in treatment and ultimately assisting them in moving toward a more adaptive developmental trajectory.

Research has indicated that the broader construct of motivation comprises two separate, but related, forms of motivation: *motivation to change* and *motivation for treatment*. Motivation to change refers to a willingness to recognize behavior as problematic and take steps toward change. Motivation for treatment refers to a willingness to seek help and act in accordance with a treatment program (DiClemente, Schlundt, & Gemmell, 2004). Examining motivation for treatment more closely, Ryan, Plant, and O'Malley (1995) reported that adults seeking outpatient substance abuse treatment with high levels of internal motivation (i.e., seeking treatment for personal benefit, such as improved functioning) had greater involvement in treatment, higher retention rates, and more positive treatment response than those reporting that they were primarily accessing treatment in response to external social pressures. These findings have been replicated in a variety of populations by other authors (e.g., Fickenscher, Novins, & Beals, 2006; Joe, Simpson, & Broome, 1998). Wild, Cunningham, and Ryan (2006) extended these findings by proposing that internal treatment motivation is itself comprised of two separate constructs: *introjected motivation*, which refers to a desire to enter treatment because of feelings of shame related to substance use, and *identified motivation*, which refers to personal identification with the goals of treatment and commitment to those goals. Examining differential associations with treatment engagement, the authors reported that identified motivation was significantly associated with engagement, whereas introjected and external motivation were not.

Similar to findings in the adult substance abuse literature, research has indicated that pretreatment internal motivation is a significant predictor of youth treatment engagement and retention (Broome, Joe, & Simpson, 2001; Melnick, DeLeon, Hawke, Jainchill, & Kressel, 1997). Moreover, higher levels of pretreatment problem recognition and internal treatment motivation are significant predictors of positive outcomes among youth (Cady, Winters, Jordan, Solberg, & Stinchfield, 1996). Unfortunately, research has indicated that youth tend to be less internally motivated than adults to change their substance use and enter treatment (Battjes, Gordon, O'Grady, Kinlock, & Carswell, 2003; Melnick et al., 1997), and non-completion rates in youth outpatient substance abuse treatment may be as high as 70% (Hser et al., 2001).

Despite the importance of internal motivation in treatment outcomes, and findings that youth may present in a manner different from adults with respect to motivation, few studies have examined predictors of motivation among youth. Existing findings indicate that those with more severe substance abuse problems, more negative consequences of their use, or higher levels of internalizing symptoms reported greater motivation (Battjes et al., 2003; Breda & Heflinger, 2007; Slesnick et al., 2009). As one interpretation of these findings is that greater distress may enhance motivation for positive change, one may expect to see a similar effect of maltreatment history on motivation. Two studies were identified that examined such potential associations. Grella and Joshi (2003) reported that youth with histories of physical or sexual abuse were more likely to recognize their substance use as problematic. Battjes and colleagues (2003) reported no association between emotional abuse and youths' motivation for change and perceived need for treatment. Further research in this area is critical in order to clarify potential associations and enhance our understanding of the factors that bring these vulnerable youth to treatment.

Accordingly, the purpose of the current study was to examine the relationship between maltreatment and motivation among treatment-seeking youth. We examined the extent to which various forms of maltreatment were associated with treatment motivation and motivation for change. We also examined whether maltreatment had predictive value over and above the contribution of factors identified by previous research as important to motivation.

METHOD

Participants and Procedure

The sample consisted of 188 youth (131 males and 57 females) entering treatment in an outpatient program for individuals aged 16 to 24 years with substance abuse concerns. Youth completed questionnaires as part of a clinical assessment during their initial session. A research assistant approached each youth to request informed consent to use the clinical information for research; 89% agreed. See Tables 1–3 for descriptive information regarding the sample. This study received university and hospital ethics approval.

Measures

Motivation. The Stages of Change Readiness and Treatment Eagerness Scale, Version 8 (SOCRATES; Miller & Tonigan, 1996) is a 19-item self-report inventory that was used to measure level of motivation to change substance use. The measure yields three subscale scores, of which *Recognition* (level of awareness of substance use as problematic) and *Taking Steps* (evidence that change has already begun) were used in the current study ($\alpha = .84$ to .95). The Treatment Entry Questionnaire (TEQ; Wild et al., 2006) is a 30-item questionnaire that was used to assess the three forms of treatment motivation described previously: external, introjected, and identified motivation ($\alpha = .87$ to .91).

Maltreatment history. The Traumatic Antecedents Questionnaire (TAQ; van der Kolk, 1997) consists of 42 items that gather information about 8 domains of adverse experiences and 2 domains of adaptive experiences across four developmental periods. The scales and suggested scoring (see van der Kolk, 1997) were revised for this study to produce scores reflecting the extent to which the respondent experienced physical abuse (1 item), sexual abuse (4 items), emotional abuse (3 items), emotional or physical neglect (5 items), and exposure to domestic violence (2 items) up to 18 years of age. Item responses across the early childhood, middle childhood, and

Table 1
Participant Demographic Information

Demographic Variables	Males (n = 131)	Females (n = 57)	Full sample (N = 188)
Mean age (SD)	20.49 (2.36)	20.40 (2.46)	20.46 (2.38)
Median education level	Completed high school	Completed high school	Completed high school
Ethnicity			
European-Canadian	69.7%	66.7%	68.8%
Asian-Canadian	11.8%	5.7%	9.9%
African/Caribbean-Canadian	4.2%	7.4%	5.2%
Aboriginal	4.2%	1.9%	3.5%
Latin American/Hispanic-Canadian	3.4%	7.4%	4.6%
Other ethnicities	6.7%	10.9%	8.0%
Employment/School status			
Not a student or employed	36.2%	17.5%	30.5%
Student	20.5%	36.8%	25.5%
Employed part time	25.2%	24.6%	25.0%
Employed full time	18.1%	21.1%	19.0%
Income Source			
Employment	35.0%	43.9%	37.8%
Family support	19.5%	33.3%	23.9%
Disability or unemployment insurance	19.6%	19.3%	19.4%
No income	19.5%	16.1%	18.4%
Legal system involvement			
At present	40.7%	19.2%	34.3%
Previously	22.8%	21.2%	22.3%
Mandated to treatment			
Yes	25.9%	9.3%	20.5%
"Do not know"	9.8%	7.4%	9.0%

Table 2
Descriptive Information Regarding Participant Substance Use

Substance Use Variables	Males (n = 131)	Females (n = 57)	Full sample (N = 188)
Primary Substance			
Cannabis	43.8%	21.8%	36.9%
Alcohol	28.1%	36.4%	30.7%
Cocaine	9.1%	14.5%	10.8%
Opiates	9.1%	10.9%	9.7%
Ketamine	1.7%	10.9%	4.5%
Amphetamines	1.7%	1.8%	1.7%
Others	5.0%	3.6%	5.5%
Polysubstance use	47.2%	52.6%	48.9%
Use substance daily	64.1%	57.9%	62.2%
Mean DAST[a] score out of 20 (SD)	9.61 (4.46)	9.19 (5.10)	9.48 (4.66)
Mean AUDIT[b] score out of 40 (SD)	13.77 (10.10)	15.29 (10.46)	14.23 (10.21)

Note. On the DAST, scores in the range of 6–10 indicate a moderate substance abuse problem (Cocco & Carey, 1998). On the AUDIT, scores in the range of 8–15 indicate a moderate alcohol problem (Babor, Higgins-Biddle, Saunders, & Monteiro, 2001).
[a] Drug Abuse Screening Test (DAST; Skinner, 1982).
[b] Alcohol Use Disorders Identification Test (AUDIT; Saunders et al., 1993).

Do you think a person is more or less likely to stay in treatment if it is mandated?

What does this table tell us about drug use among Canadian youth? Which drugs are used most often? Why?

---

adolescence periods were summed to create the scale scores (α = .70 to .89). All items referred to experiences that occurred within the respondent's family, with the exception of items comprising the sexual abuse scale, which did not refer to a specific perpetrator.

Other predictors. The Alcohol Use Disorders Identification Test (AUDIT; Saunders, Aasland, Babor, de la Fuente, & Grant, 1993) is a 10-item self-report measure that was used to assess severity of alcohol problems (α =.91). The Drug Abuse Screening Test (DAST; Skinner, 1982) is a 20-item self-report measure that assessed the severity of drug problems (α = .72). The Youth Self-Report (YSR/11–18; Achenbach & Rescorla, 2001) and Adult Self-Report (ASR/18–59; Achenbach & Rescorla, 2003) assessed severity of mental health symptoms. T scores on the Internalizing and Externalizing Problems scales were used in the current study. The 14-item Perceived Social Support scale (Procidano & Heller, 1983) assessed the level of social support respondents

Table 3

Descriptive Information Regarding Participant Abuse History

Abuse Variables	Maximum scale score	Males (n = 131)		Females (n = 57)		Full Sample (N = 188)	
		%	Mean (SD)	%	Mean (SD)	%	Mean (SD)
Physical abuse	9	38.2	1.27 (2.03)	48.2	1.54 (2.16)	41.2	1.35 (2.07)
Sexual abuse	36	18.3	0.67 (1.71)	55.4	3.21 (4.22)	29.4	1.43 (2.95)
Emotional abuse	27	—a	5.82 (6.26)	—a	9.00 (6.57)	—a	6.77 (6.50)
Neglect	45	—a	7.99 (6.84)	—a	10.18 (6.19)	—a	8.65 (6.71)
Domestic violence	18	41.2	2.39 (4.31)	50.0	2.45 (3.74)	43.9	2.41 (4.13)

aA cutoff score that could reliably discriminate between those with and without significant emotional abuse and neglect histories was unavailable.

perceived to be available from family and friends (α = .81).

Analyses

We conducted a canonical correlation to examine patterns of association between all maltreatment and motivation variables. We then conducted separate regression analyses in which each of the significant motivation variables from the canonical correlation served as dependent variables. Predictor variables were entered in three steps: (a) abuse variables that emerged as significantly associated with motivation in the canonical correlation, (b) gender and gender by abuse interaction terms, and (c) other factors with prior research support.

Results

Bivariate correlations were run among the motivation and maltreatment variables (see Table 4). Significant correlations among the motivation variables and among the maltreatment variables signaled the importance of examining multivariate relationships using canonical correlation. In the canonical correlation analysis, the first correlation

was .36. A significant result was obtained with all four correlations included, $\chi^2(25)$ = 39.39, p < .05, and subsequent χ^2 tests were not statistically significant, indicating that the first pair of canonical variates accounted for the significant relationships between the two sets of variables. This canonical variate extracted 39.4% of the variance in the motivation variables and 42.0% of the variance in the maltreatment variables. With a cut-off correlation of .3, the variables in the motivation set that were significantly positively correlated with the first canonical variate were introjected, identified, external, and problem recognition. All of the maltreatment variables were significantly positively correlated with the first canonical variate (see Table 5).

Examining the prediction of *introjected treatment motivation*, the abuse variables together accounted for 10% of the variance, and the model was significant at this step, $F(5, 176)$ = 3.76, p < .05 (see Table 6 for regression results). Emotional abuse emerged as the only abuse variable significantly associated with introjected motivation. Model fit did not improve with the addition of the interaction terms, $F(6, 170)$ = 0.83, *ns*. Adding the remaining predictors in the final step produced a significant

Table 4

Bivariate Correlations Among Motivation and Maltreatment Variables

Variables	1	2	3	4	5	6	7	8	9
1. Identified	—								
2. Introjected	.66**	—							
3. External	.26**	-.19**	—						
4. Recognition	.59**	.63**	-.01	—					
5. Taking steps	.25**	.31**	.00	.22*	—				
6. Physical	.11	.09	-.01	.19*	.06	—			
7. Sexual	.08	.11	-.01	.24**	.07	.20*	—		
8. Emotional	.28**	.18*	.18*	.21**	.03	.39**	.22*	—	
9. Neglect	.20*	.17*	.08	.27**	.00	.29**	.28**	.56**	—
10. Domestic violence	.14	.07	.05	.13	.05	.44**	.16*	.28**	.29**

*p < .05.   **p < .001.

In Chapter 2 you read about correlations. What does a correlation tell us?

Table 5
Canonical Correlation Results For Motivation and Maltreatment Variables

Variables	Correlation[a]	Standardized coefficient
Canonical correlation	.36	
Motivation variable set		
Identified	**−.68**	−.34
Introjected	**−.79**	−.15
External	**−.40**	−.44
Recognition	**−.85**	−.58
Taking steps	−.09	.10
Percent of variance	.39	
Redundancy	.05	
Abuse variable set		
Physical abuse	**−.43**	.04
Sexual abuse	**−.55**	−.31
Emotional abuse	**−.88**	−.60
Neglect	**−.79**	−.31
Domestic violence	**−.47**	−.16
Percent of variance	.42	
Redundancy	.05	

[a]Structure correlation coefficients greater than |.30| are bolded.

improvement in model fit, $F(6, 164) = 7.38$, $p < .001$. The final model indicated that more extensive histories of emotional abuse, older age, and more severe drug problems and internalizing symptoms were associated with greater introjected motivation.

The maltreatment variables together accounted for only 5% of the variance in *identified treatment motivation*, and the model was not significant at this first step, $F(5, 175) = 1.85$, *ns*. Model fit did not improve with the addition of the interaction terms, $F(6, 169) = 0.70$, *ns*, but did improve with the addition of the final set of variables, $F(6, 163) = 7.37$, $p < .001$. In the final model, results indicated that maltreatment was not significantly associated with level of identified treatment motivation. This form of motivation was significantly predicted by older age, more severe drug problems, and higher levels of social support.

Examining the prediction of *problem recognition*, the maltreatment variables together accounted for 12% of the variance, and the model was significant at this first stage, $F(5, 174) = 4.61$, $p < .001$. During this step, neglect and sexual abuse emerged as significant predictors. Model fit did not significantly improve with the addition of the

Table 6
Hierarchical Regression Analyses Predicting Level of Motivation: Beta Values and Change In R^2

Predictors	Introjected models 1	2	3	Identified models 1	2	3	Problem recognition models 1	2	3	External models 1	2	3
Emotional abuse	.24*	.33*	.34**	.12	.17	.19	.03	.08	−.02	.23*	.27*	.27*
Neglect	.08	.07	−.03	.11	.10	.09	.19*	.19	.08	−.05	−.05	−.14
Sexual abuse	−.01	.04	.01	.06	.04	.02	.16*	.15	.11	−.03	.02	−.01
Physical abuse	−.01	−.04	−.07	−.02	−.05	−.08	.10	.07	.03	−.12	−.13	−.13
Domestic violence	.06	.07	.04	.02	.06	.04	−.01	.02	−.00	.06	.04	.06
Gender		−.15	−.14		.04	.04		.01	.01		−.14	−.14
Emotional × Gender		.14	.11		.13	.09		.07	.02		.04	.08
Neglect × Gender		−.03	.03		−.02	−.01		.01	.06		−.00	−.02
Sexual Abuse × Gender		−.01	.04		−.05	−.01		−.05	.01		.07	.06
Physical Abuse × Gender		−.00	.05		−.08	−.02		−.09	−.02		.03	.04
Domestic Violence × Gender		.03	−.01		.10	.08		.09	.01		−.11	−.10
Age			.23*			.34**			.20*			−.08
DAST			.27*			.20*			.34**			.05
AUDIT			.04			.07			.22**			−.16
Internalizing			.30*			.16			.29**			.09
Externalizing			−.16			−.11			−.06			.09
Social support			.03			.17*			.14*			−.05
R^2	.10	.12	.31	.05	.07	.17*	.12	.13	.40	.04	.07	.12
F for change in R^2	3.76*	0.83	7.38**	1.85	0.70	7.37**	4.61**	0.38	11.92**	1.41	0.77	1.58

*$p < .05$. **$p < .001$.

How can we use this finding to improve treatment for youth with substance abuse problems?

Why do you think shame is not an effective motivator?

How can psychologists use research findings such as this to better treat abused children and youth?

In Chapter 16 you read about internalizing disorders such as depression and anxiety. In addition to substance abuse, what other mental disorders would abused youth be at risk for developing?

interaction terms, $F(6, 168) = 0.38$, ns. The fit was significantly improved with the addition of the remaining variables, $F(6, 162) = 11.92$, $p < .001$. In the final model, no maltreatment variables significantly predicted problem recognition. This form of motivation was significantly predicted by older age, more severe drug and alcohol problems, more severe internalizing symptoms, and higher levels of social support.

Examining the prediction of *external treatment motivation*, the maltreatment variables together predicted only 4% of the variance in this form of motivation, and the model was nonsignificant at this stage, $F(5, 164) = 1.41$, ns, and at subsequent stages, $F(6, 152) = 1.58$, ns.

DISCUSSION

The findings of the current study replicated and extended the findings of previous research. Consistent with previous research, older age (Melnick et al., 1997), more severe substance abuse problems and internalizing symptoms (Battjes et al., 2003; Breda & Heflinger, 2007; Slesnick et al., 2009), and greater social support (Broome et al., 2001) were associated with higher levels of treatment motivation and problem recognition. Extending previous findings, the results also indicated that all forms of maltreatment examined were associated with higher levels of identified, introjected, and external treatment motivation, as well as problem recognition. Youth with maltreatment histories tended to be more aware of the problematic aspects of their use and more ready to engage in treatment. To the extent that these forms of motivation translate to treatment engagement and positive outcomes, the findings may be seen as consistent with the body of research examining treatment attendance and outcomes among this population. Although research with adults has suggested that maltreatment history is a risk factor for early dropout (Claus & Kindleberger, 2002; Kang, Deren, & Goldstein, 2002) and poorer outcomes (e.g., Ouimette, Ahrens, Moos, & Finney, 1997), the smaller body of research with youth has produced different results. Youth with maltreatment histories have been reported to have similar or better outcomes in substance abuse treatment (Williams et al., 2008) and better treatment attendance (Slesnick, Kang, & Aukward, 2008) compared to those without such histories. Some research has suggested that positive outcomes for these youth may be mediated by such factors as higher treatment intensity (Funk,

McDermeit, Godley, & Adams, 2003), PTSD diagnosis (Jaycox, Ebener, Damesek, & Becker, 2004), and positive therapeutic relationships (Grella & Joshi, 2003). Motivation may be another important mediating variable in the association between maltreatment and outcomes for youth in substance abuse treatment.

Introjected treatment motivation was the only form of motivation for which maltreatment history predicted motivation after considering the effect of other important factors, such that greater severity of emotional abuse predicted higher levels of introjected treatment motivation. Moreover, emotional abuse displayed a stronger association with level of introjected motivation than any of the other factors examined in the full model. As introjected motivation reflects a desire to enter treatment due to the shame associated with substance use, these results are consistent with research indicating elevated levels of shame-proneness among survivors of emotional abuse (Webb, Heisler, Call, Chickering, & Colburn, 2007). Unfortunately, prior research indicated that introjected motivation was not related to treatment engagement among a sample of adults entering substance abuse treatment (Wild et al., 2006), suggesting that the higher levels of shame youth with emotional abuse histories are likely to experience may bring them to the door of treatment but may not be sufficient to keep them there. However, the current study did not include an examination of treatment engagement, and previous research has not examined introjected treatment motivation in relation to engagement among youth or individuals with maltreatment histories. It will be important for future research to examine whether the previous findings hold among these populations.

It is notable that a form of maltreatment that did not consist of direct experiences of interpersonal violence was the most predictive of motivation. One possible explanation for this finding, which requires examination in future research, may lie in the relative impact of different forms of maltreatment. Previous research has reported that emotional abuse has a more detrimental effect on child development and adaptive functioning than forms of abuse that consist of interpersonal violence (see Hart, Binggeli, & Brassard, 1998). Thus, the finding that emotional abuse was more strongly associated with motivation than other forms of maltreatment may indicate that youth with emotional abuse histories experience greater distress and therefore perceive greater need for treatment and change.

Greater severity of internalizing symptoms was also significantly associated with introjected treatment motivation in the current study. Research has indicated an association exists between shame and depression (Webb et al., 2007), and emotional abuse is a consistently reported risk factor for depression (e.g., Bifulco, Moran, Baines, Bunn, & Stanford, 2002). As such, a relationship may exist among emotional abuse, internalizing symptoms, and introjected treatment motivation that should be elucidated in future research.

On a related note, it will be important for future research to expand the scope of investigation to examine predictors of motivation for addressing other aspects of functioning. For youth with maltreatment histories, treatment of the psychological sequelae of their maltreatment histories in conjunction with treatment for their substance use concerns is important (Cohen, Mannarino, Zhitova, & Capone, 2003). Future research should examine the extent to which enhanced motivation for addressing substance use among youth with maltreatment histories may extend to enhanced motivation for addressing other domains of functioning.

There are a number of potential clinical implications of this research. In response to the growing body of literature demonstrating a connection between maltreatment experiences and substance abuse problems, clinicians are increasingly assessing for exposure to sexual and physical abuse among youth entering substance abuse treatment. The current findings suggest that assessing for histories of emotional abuse may also be important. Enhanced feelings of shame may impact the ways in which youth respond to common aspects of the recovery process, such as relapses and missed appointments, and knowledge of a youth's emotional abuse history and resulting self-perceptions may assist clinicians in attending to these issues.

There are some important limitations of the current study to note. Notably, information was not collected that allowed for a contextualization of the abuse experiences, particularly with respect to the sexual abuse data. Research has indicated a number of factors that predict differential outcomes following childhood maltreatment, including the child's relationship to the perpetrator and the availability of a supportive caregiver (Elliott & Carnes, 2001). As such, future research should endeavor to include examinations of the relational context of the abuse. Regarding further limitations in the assessment methods, all variables were assessed through paper-and-pencil self-report measures, which may be subject to biases. Additionally, youth were asked to report on their maltreatment histories in their initial appointment. Some youth may have been uncomfortable disclosing experiences of maltreatment at this early stage. Finally, the sample consisted of more males than females. While this may accurately represent the gender differential in substance abuse treatment, this may have underestimated the impact of forms of maltreatment more frequently reported by females, particularly sexual abuse (Simpson & Miller, 2002). The relatively small number of females also renders the gender by abuse interactions preliminary, and the results should be interpreted with caution.

Despite these limitations, the current study contributes to the body of research examining the clinical presentations of youth with substance abuse problems who have experienced maltreatment. The findings indicate the importance of emotional abuse to level of motivation among youth entering treatment. Clinicians are encouraged to attend to experiences of emotional abuse, as such experiences may be important to treatment processes and outcomes.

REFERENCES

Achenbach, T. M., & Rescorla, L. A. (2001). *Manual for ASEBA schoolage forms & profiles*. Burlington, VT: University of Vermont, Research Center for Children, Youth, & Families.

Achenbach, T. M., & Rescorla, L. A. (2003). *Manual for ASEBA adult forms & profiles*. Burlington, VT: University of Vermont, Research Center for Children, Youth, & Families.

Babor, T. F., Higgins-Biddle, J., Saunders, J. B., & Monteiro, M. G. (2001). The Alcohol Use Disorder Identification Test. *Guidelines for use in primary health care*. Geneva, Switzerland: World Health Organization.

Battjes, R. J., Gordon, M. S., O'Grady, K. E., Kinlock, T. W., & Carswell, M. A. (2003). Factors that predict adolescent motivation for substance abuse treatment. *Journal of Substance Abuse Treatment, 24*, 221–232. doi:10.1016/S0740-5472(03)00022-9

Bifulco, A., Moran, P. M., Baines, R., Bunn, A., & Stanford, K. (2002). Exploring psychological abuse in childhood: II: Association with other abuse and adult clinical depression. *Bulletin of Menninger Institute, 66*, 241–258. doi:10.1521/bumc.66.3.241.23366

Breda, C. S., & Heflinger, C. A. (2007). The impact of motivation to change on substance use among adolescents in treatment. *Journal of Child & Adolescent Substance Abuse, 16*, 109 –124. doi:10.1300/ J029v16n03_06

Broome, K. M., Joe, G. W., & Simpson, D. D. (2001). Engagement models for adolescents in DATOS-A. *Journal of Adolescent Research, 16*, 608–623. doi:10.1177/0743558401166005

Cady, M. E., Winters, K. C., Jordan, D. A., Solberg, K. B., & Stinchfield, R. D. (1996). Motivation to change as a predictor of treatment outcome for adolescent substance abusers. *Journal of Child & Adolescent Substance Abuse, 5*, 73–91. doi:10.1300/J029v05n01_04

Clark, D. B., Lesnick, L., & Hegedus, A. M. (1997). Trauma and other adverse life events in adolescents with alcohol abuse and dependence. *Journal of the American Academy of Child and Adolescent Psychiatry, 36*, 1744–1751. doi:10.1097/00004583-199712000-00023

Claus, R. E., & Kindleberger, L. R. (2002). Engaging substance abusers after centralized assessment: Predictors of treatment entry and dropout. *Journal of Psychoactive Drugs, 34*, 25–31.

Do you think that all youths will be forthcoming with their history of abuse? How can we create an environment in which such disclosure is easier?

Why would researchers continue to use self-report measures despite this limitation (Chapter 2)?

Would you expect gender to play a role in seeking treatment and long-term recovery?

Cocco, K. M., and Carey, K. B. (1998). Psychometric properties of the Drug Abuse Screening Test in psychiatric outpatients. *Psychological Assessment, 10,* 408–414.

Cohen, J. A., Mannarino, A. P., Zhitova, A. C., & Capone, M. E. (2003). Treating child abuse-related posttraumatic stress and comorbid substance abuse in adolescents. *Child Abuse & Neglect, 27,* 1345–1365.

DiClemente, C. C., Schlundt, D., & Gemmell, L. (2004), Readiness and the stages of change in addictions. *The American Journal on Addictions, 13,* 103–119. doi:10.1080/10550490490435777

Elliott, A. N., & Carnes, C. N. (2001). Reactions of non-offending parents to the sexual abuse of their child: A review of the literature. *Child Maltreatment, 6,* 314–331.

Fickenscher, A., Novins, D., & Beals, J. (2006). A pilot study of motivation and treatment completion among American Indian adolescents in substance abuse treatment. *Addictive Behaviors, 31,* 1402–1414. doi: 10.1016/j.addbeh.2005.11.001

Funk, R. R., McDermeit, I. M., Godley, S. H., & Adams, L. (2003). Maltreatment issues by level of adolescent substance abuse treatment: The extent of the problem at intake and relationship to early outcomes. *Journal of Child Maltreatment, 8,* 36–45. doi:10.1177/1077559502239607

Grella, C. E., Hser, Y., Joshi, V., & Rounds-Bryant, J. (2001). Drug treatment outcomes for adolescents with comorbid mental and substance use disorders. *Journal of Nervous and Mental Disease, 189,* 384–392. doi:10.1097/00005053-200106000-00006

Grella, C. E., & Joshi, V. (2003). Treatment processes and outcomes among adolescents with a history of abuse who are in drug treatment. *Child Maltreatment: Journal of the American Professional Society on the Abuse of Children, 8,* 7–18. doi:10.1177/1077559502239610

Hart, S. N., Binggeli, N. J., & Brassard, M. R. (1998). Evidence for the effects of psychological maltreatment. *Journal of Emotional Abuse, 1,* 27–58. doi:10.1300/J135v01n01_03

Hser, Y. I., Grella, C. E., Hubbard, R. L., Hsieh, S. C., Fletcher, B. W., Brown, B. S., & Anglin, M. D. (2001). An evaluation of drug treatments for adolescents in 4 U.S. cities. *Archives of General Psychiatry, 58,* 689–695. doi:10.1001/archpsyc.58.7.689

Jaycox, L. H., Ebener, P., Damesek, L., & Becker, K. (2004). Trauma exposure and retention in adolescent substance abuse treatment. *Journal of Traumatic Stress, 17,* 113–121. doi:10.1023/B:JOTS.0000022617.41299.39

Joe, G. W., Simpson, D. D., & Broome, K. M. (1998). Effects of readiness for drug abuse treatment on client retention and assessment of process. *Addiction, 93,* 1177–1190. doi:10.1080/09652149835008

Kang, S.-Y., Deren, S., & Goldstein, M. F. (2002). Relationships between childhood abuse and neglect experience and HIV risk behaviors among methadone treatment drop-outs. *Child Abuse and Neglect, 26,* 1275–1289. doi:10.1016/S0145-2134(02)00412-X

Kilpatrick, D. G., Acierno, R., Saunders, B., Resnick, H. S., Best, C., & Schnurr, P. (2000). Risk factors for adolescent substance abuse and dependence: Data from a national sample. *Journal of Consulting and Clinical Psychology, 68,* 19–30. doi:10.1037/0022-006X.68.1.19

Melnick, G., DeLeon, G., Hawke, J., Jainchill, N., & Kressel, D. (1997). Motivation and readiness for therapeutic community treatment among adolescent and adult substance abusers. *American Journal of Drug and Alcohol Abuse, 23,* 485–507. doi:10.3109/00952999709016891

Miller, W. R., & Tonigan, J. S. (1996). Assessing drinkers' motivation for change: The Stages of Change Readiness and Treatment Eagerness Scale (SOCRATES). *Psychology of Addictive Behaviors, 10,* 81–89. doi: 10.1037/0893-164X.10.2.81

Ouimette, P. C., Ahrens, C., Moos, R. H., & Finney, J. W. (1997). Posttraumatic stress disorder in substance abuse patients: Relationship to 1-year posttreatment outcomes. *Psychology of Addictive Behaviors, 11,* 34–47. doi:10.1037/0893-164X.11.1.34

Procidano, M., & Heller, K. (1983). Measures of perceived social support from friends and from family: Three validation studies. *American Journal of Community Psychology, 11,* 1–24. doi:10.1007/BF00898416

Ryan, R. M., Plant, R. W., & O'Malley, S. (1995). Initial motivations for alcohol treatment: Relations with patient characteristics, treatment involvement, and dropout. *Addictive Behaviors, 20,* 279–297. doi: 10.1016/0306-4603(94)00072-7

Saunders, J. B., Aasland, O. G., Babor, T. F., de la Fuente, J. R., & Grant, M. (1993). Development of the Alcohol Use Disorders Identification Test (AUDIT): WHO collaborative project on early detection of persons with harmful alcohol consumption II. *Addiction, 88,* 791–804. doi: 10.1111/j.1360-0443.1993.tb02093.x

Simpson, T. L., & Miller, W. R. (2002). Concomitance between childhood sexual and physical abuse and substance use problems: A review. *Clinical Psychology Review, 22,* 27–77. doi:10.1016/S0272-7358(00)00088-X

Skinner, H. A. (1982). *Drug Use Questionnaire (DAST-20).* Toronto, Canada: Centre for Addiction and Mental Health.

Slesnick, N., Bartle-Haring, S., Erdem, G., Budde, H., Letcher, A., Bantchevska, D., & Patton, R. (2009). Troubled parents, motivated adolescents: Predicting motivation to change substance use among runaways. *Addictive Behaviours, 34,* 675–684. doi:10.1016/j.addbeh.2009.04.002

Slesnick, N., Kang, M. J., & Aukward, E. (2008). Treatment attendance among homeless youth: The impact of childhood abuse and prior suicide attempts. *Substance Abuse, 29,* 43–52. doi:10.1300/J465v29n02_05

van der Kolk, B. A. (1997). *The Trauma Center Assessment Package.* Brookline, MA: Trauma Center.

Webb, M., Heisler, D., Call, S., Chickering, S. A., & Colburn, T. A. (2007). Shame, guilt, symptoms of depression, and reported history of psychological maltreatment. *Child Abuse & Neglect, 31,* 1143–1153. doi: 10.1016/j.chiabu.2007.09.003

Wild, T. C., Cunningham, J. A., & Ryan, R. M. (2006). Social pressure, coercion, and client engagement at treatment entry: A self-determination theory perspective. *Addictive Behaviors, 31,* 1858–1872. doi:10.1016/j.addbeh.2006.01.002

Williams, J. K., Smith, D. C., Gotman, N., Sabri, B., An, H., & Hall, J. A. (2008). Traumatized youth and substance abuse treatment outcomes: A longitudinal study. *Journal of Traumatic Stress, 21,* 100–108. doi: 10.1002/jts.20302

HEALTH

You've probably

heard the old cliché, "Laughter is the best medicine." What you might not know, however, is that the saying contains a nugget of scientific truth: Many researchers agree that laughing is one of the easiest and most enjoyable things you can do to benefit your health. In fact, studies have found that humour can actually cause physiological changes that positively affect the health of patients with serious diseases like cancer.

While successful cancer treatment requires much more than a hearty chuckle, humour can be a beneficial addition to a cancer patient's treatment plan. Researchers found that humour and laughter can increase the activity of patients' natural killer cells—lymphocytes that play a crucial role in fighting off infection by attacking tumour cells and other harmful microbes. Humour also seems to help patients tolerate pain, respond to stress, and (perhaps unsurprisingly) feel better during the course of their treatment. Laughter and humour have important psychological benefits as well: Patients who are given "humorous interventions" tend to find it easier to relax, cope with the stressful implications of having a life-threatening disease, and discuss their fears and concerns about cancer with their healthcare providers and family members (Christie & Moore, 2005; Bennet, Zeller, Rosenberg, & McCann, 2003; Lopes Da Silva, 2012; Mora-Ripoll, 2010).

Laughter may be the best medicine for relatively healthy individuals, too. Humour and laughter can improve our health and happiness by reducing stress hormones, enhancing creativity, reducing pain, strengthening the immune system, and reducing blood pressure (Hassed, 2001). Humour may also help in the aging process (Damianakis & Marziali, 2011). And while the life of a cubicle worker isn't always filled with hilarity, humour can help us function effectively in the working world: Studies have shown that when employees laugh purposefully while on the job, they tend to feel more optimistic and confident (Beckman, Regier, & Young, 2007; Mesmer-Magnus, Glew, & Chockalingam, 2012).

Whether you're struggling with a serious condition or simply wishing you could reduce the amount of stress in your life, laughter can improve your health, your well-being, and your outlook on life. The prescription is simple: Laugh long, loud, and often.

<<< Are you stressed? Do you have an exam, assignment, or project due that you have yet to start? Believe it or not, this is a laughing matter. Laughing can help alleviate stress—and ultimately help you complete those stressed-filled tasks. Whether at work, home, or school, laughing and maintaining a positive, optimistic outlook can improve your health in a variety of ways.

CHAPTER **18**

The Mind-Body Connection

As humour's power to create positive physical changes in the body demonstrates, there's a strong connection between our minds and our bodies. Many psychologists study this mind-body connection by examining the ways in which psychological states lead to physical reactions. Take, for example, the case of stress. While stress is a psychological state rather than a physiological ailment, it can significantly increase one's risk of developing any of the four leading causes of serious illness and death: heart disease, cancer, stroke, and chronic lung disease. The prognosis is even worse when people's feelings of stress are combined with unhealthy behaviours, such as smoking, excessive alcohol consumption, or lack of sleep. Unfortunately, as we feel more and more stress in our lives, we may be more likely to use smoking or alcohol as stress relievers, or we may attempt to reduce stress by staying up late and waking up early to get things done. In situations like these, our behaviours and our mental states work together to drag us into a vicious, unhealthy cycle.

How can we keep ourselves mentally and physically healthy in stressful situations or other cases in which our thoughts and behaviours can harm our health? The answer might lie in the field of **behavioural medicine,** an interdisciplinary approach to medical treatment that integrates behavioural, medical, and social knowledge to increase life expectancy and enhance quality of life. The psychologically based aspect of behavioural medicine, known as **health psychology,** is focused on the development of general strategies and specific tactics that people and their doctors can use to eliminate or reduce the risk of illness. For example, health psychologists might develop stress-management techniques, weight-loss plans, or community support groups in an effort to encourage individuals to take a holistic approach to health. As the name

> Unfortunately, as we feel more and more stress in our lives, we may be more likely to use smoking or alcohol as stress relievers, or we may attempt to reduce stress by staying up late and waking up early to get things done. **In situations like these, our behaviours and our mental states work together to drag us into a vicious, unhealthy cycle.**

of the field suggests, health psychology places emphasis on the idea that physical health and mental health are closely related: The mind-body connection is real and powerful, and our psychological states often contribute to our overall level of health.

Stress and Its Impact on Health

STRESS AND STRESSORS

You've got an exam coming up, you're trying to repair your less-than-cordial relationship with your old friend, and you're not sure how you're going to pay off your credit card this month. Even if you've never faced any of these particular circumstances, chances are good that you know what it feels like to be in a stressful situation. **Stress** describes the process by which we perceive and respond to **stressors,** events that we see as threatening or challenging.

Not all stress is created equal. **Acute stress,** for example, is a temporary state of stress that varies in intensity, while **chronic stress** describes a long-lasting state of arousal during which we feel that we don't have the resources available to meet all of the demands placed upon us. If you've experienced either type of stress, you're far from alone: According to the Canadian Mental Health Association, in 2009, there was a 30% increase in stressed-out Canadians from the previous year.

As we begin to understand exactly how predominant stress can be in our daily lives, researchers are paying more attention to studying stress so that they can determine its negative effects on health and, ideally, find ways to reduce it. This increased focus on stress has opened doors to several new areas of study. For example, scientists fairly recently came to the realization that chronic stressors are often linked to specific environments, such as offices, cities, or schools. This discovery led to the development of **environmental psychology,** a field that investigates the physical environment's effects on behaviour and health. For example, air pollution, excess noise, and metal toxins in the water are environmental stressors frequently associated with city living that can negatively affect people's well-being. Another stress-related field, psychoneuroimmunology, explores the ways in which external stressors alter the immune system's responses to internal stressors such as viruses and bacteria.

No matter where we encounter stress or how that stress manifests itself in our bodies, we tend to think of stress in negative terms. For most of us, stress is something to be avoided or overcome. However, while stress can potentially increase your risk for serious illnesses and other health-related problems, it can also help save your life. When stress is short-lived or perceived as a challenge that you feel capable of overcoming, it can have positive effects: It can help activate your immune system so that you can fight off an illness or heal a wound, it can motivate you to find solutions to problems, and it can teach you to become emotionally resilient. For example, feeling a little stressed out before a track meet isn't necessarily a bad thing—that stress might actually help you run faster. This positive type of stress is sometimes known as **eustress.** When stress

---

Behavioural medicine is an interdisciplinary approach to medical treatment that integrates behavioural, medical, and social knowledge to increase life expectancy and enhance quality of life.

Health psychology is the psychologically based aspect of behavioural medicine.

Stress is a physical and mental response to threatening or challenging events.

Stressor is an event that a person perceives as threatening or challenging.

Acute stress is a temporary state of stress that varies in intensity.

Chronic stress is a long-lasting state of arousal during which a person feels that he or she doesn't have the resources available to meet all of the demands placed upon him or her.

Environmental psychology is a field that investigates the physical environment's effects on behaviour and health.

Eustress is a low-level, positive type of stress that helps a person perform a task or achieve a goal.

is prolonged or perceived as a daunting obstacle, however, it is likely to have negative effects and is referred to as **distress.** Children who suffer distress in the form of severe abuse may experience physiological reactions that lead to chronic disease later in life (Kendall-Tackett, 2000; Seifert, Polusny, & Murdoch, 2011). Individuals who have post-traumatic stress responses are also at risk for serious diseases. For example, many veterans of the Vietnam War experienced post-traumatic stress as a result of their participation in heavy combat. Later, these same veterans were found to be more at risk for circulatory, digestive, respiratory, and infectious diseases than were their peers who had not experienced post-traumatic stress (Boscarino, 1997).

THE STRESS RESPONSE SYSTEM

We each perceive stressors differently, and each of us has our own strategies for coping with stress. However, we all have very similar immediate physiological responses to stress. Over the years, in an attempt to simplify and describe these responses, psychologists have developed several models of our stress response system.

Fight or Flight

In 1915, American physiologist Walter Cannon observed that extreme cold, lack of oxygen, and emotion-arousing incidents can trigger an increase in the release of the stress hormones epinephrine and

norepinephrine from the adrenal glands. This observation demonstrated to Cannon that the stress response is a part of the mind-body system: Although stress is a mental state, it produces physical symptoms. Cannon dubbed the body's response to emotional arousal the **fight-or-flight response,** a term that describes our evolutionary options when faced with a stressor—fighting back or fleeing to safety.

> No matter where we encounter stress or how that stress manifests itself in our bodies, we tend to think of stress in negative terms. For most of us, stress is something to be avoided or overcome.

Cannon's description of the fight-or-flight response has become one of the most famous models used to explain animals' responses to stress, but chemically speaking, it doesn't tell the entire story. Following up on Cannon's research, physiologists have identified another stress response system that causes the outer part of the adrenal glands to secrete stress hormones such as cortisol. The stress hormones increase the concentration

of glucose in the blood to make fuel available to the muscles. This finding bolsters Cannon's beliefs about humans' innate responses to stress: Whether we're preparing to fight or running to safer ground, our muscles need fuel to react appropriately, so the secretion of cortisol makes perfect sense in a fight-or-flight framework.

General Adaptation Syndrome

As popular as Cannon's theory is, it's not the only model of stress response. In the 1930s, endocrinologist Hans Selye developed the model of the **general adaptation syndrome (GAS),** which describes how the body adaptively responds to stress in three stages: alarm, resistance, and exhaustion. During the alarm stage, the body's initial reaction to a threat causes the heart rate to increase and blood to be diverted to the skeletal muscles. During the resistance stage, temperature, blood pressure, and respiration remain at high levels, hormones are suddenly released, and the body is ready to fight the challenge being encountered. The exhaustion stage occurs when persistent stress depletes the body of its reserves. During this final stage, the body is more vulnerable to illness and may even collapse or die.

Recent research confirms the implications of the final stage of the GAS: Prolonged stress can lead to physical deterioration and rapid aging (e.g., Kourtis & Tavernarakis, 2011). For example, young women who experience stressful events such as child

<<< Afghanistan War veterans are likely to be at an increased risk for stress-related problems. What might soldiers, their doctors, or their governments do to attempt to minimize this risk?

Catastrophe is an unpredictable, large-scale event.

Burnout is a state of physical, emotional, and mental exhaustion created by long-term involvement in an emotionally demanding situation and accompanied by lowered performance and motivation.

Hassle is a minor nuisance that, when combined with other small problems, can create a stressful environment.

Coronary heart disease is a condition characterized by the clogging of the vessels that nourish the heart muscle.

abuse, violence at the hands of a partner, and increased responsibilities at an early age are more likely to begin menstruating earlier and to experience *physical weathering*, a term that describes accelerated aging and its associated symptoms (Foster, Hagan, & Brooks-Gunn, 2008).

Alternative Stress Responses

Sometimes, stress does not cause us to fight or flee; it causes us to withdraw. If someone close to you passes away, for example, you might respond to this stressful event by spending time alone and avoiding the outside world.

Withdrawal may take the form of leaving a job or relationship or using drugs as a means of escape from reality. While withdrawal can be appealing because it allows us to avoid stressors, it isn't necessarily an effective way to resolve stressful issues or improve emotional well-being.

Social psychologist Shelley Taylor's tend-and-befriend theory, named in homage to Cannon's original model, describes a more effective response to stress. The tend-and-befriend model, which is frequently used to explain women's behaviour, describes our tendency to seek and give support in response to stress. Research has shown that people with support networks of friends and family are often better capable of handling stress than are people who do not have social support networks available.

STRESSFUL LIFE EVENTS

In our daily lives, we encounter stress in varying forms and degrees of severity. Which do you think would cause you more stress: surviving a plane crash, or surviving the traffic jams of your daily commute? Being displaced from your home when a hurricane causes your entire city to flood, or having your

basement flood every time it rains? You may be surprised to discover that the cumulative impact of what we perceive to be minor stressors may be just as significant as the impact of one large-scale event.

Catastrophes

Major stressful life events are characterized as **catastrophes**—unpredictable, large-scale events. The war in Afghanistan and Hurricane Igor are examples of catastrophes, as are the terrorist attacks of September 11, 2001. Catastrophic events like these can have extensive, far-reaching implications for people's stress levels and, subsequently, people's health. For example, after the 9/11 attacks, researchers found that many Americans' blood pressure had increased

> You may be surprised to discover that the cumulative impact of what we perceive to be minor stressors **may be just as significant as the impact of one large-scale event.**

substantially as a result of the attacks and had remained at these increased levels for at least two months (Gerin et al., 2005). The New York area also saw a 28% increase in sleeping pill prescriptions after the attack (HMHL, 2002). Even years after the 9/11 attacks, researchers have documented increased levels of psychosocial stress, including the worry about future attacks and the avoidance of activities because of these fears (Eisenman et al., 2009). People who have experienced catastrophes on this scale may develop post-traumatic stress disorder (PTSD), a stress reaction caused by persistent re-experiencing of

traumatic events (see Chapter 16). Symptoms of PTSD include sleep and concentration problems, anxiety, nightmares, and flashbacks. People may also react with residual stress patterns, which are more persistent and chronic but milder emotional responses of PTSD. When the stressor itself is chronic, stress reactions may be described as **burnout**—a state of physical, emotional, and mental exhaustion created by long-term involvement in an emotionally demanding situation and accompanied by lowered performance and motivation. Burnout is particularly common among those in emotionally stressful helping professions, such as social workers who frequently encounter child abuse cases or healthcare providers who treat casualties of war.

Significant Life Changes

Thankfully, many people never experience catastrophic events first-hand. However, more mundane and common life events, such as moving out of a childhood home, getting married or divorced, losing a loved one, or changing career paths, can cause large amounts of stress in our lives. Many of these significant life changes tend to occur during young adulthood: In your late teens, 20s, and 30s, you may face the challenges and stressors that accompany leaving home for the first time, beginning a career, entering a long-term

>>> Minor hassles can add up to equal major stress.

10 Leading Causes of Death in Canada (2008)

Suicide 1.5%
Kidney Disease 1.6%
Influenza and Pneumonia 2.3%
Alzheimer's Disease 2.5%
Diabetes 3.1%
Accidents 4.2%
Respiratory Disease 4.5%
Cerebrovascular/Stroke 5.9%
Heart Disease 21.5%
Cancer 29.6%

Source: Adapted from Statistics Canada, "Leading causes of death, by sex, numbers, 2008"; http://www40.statcan.gc.ca/l01/cst01/hlth36a-eng.htm

∧
∧ In what ways does stress contribute to the lead-
∧ ing causes of death in Canada?

relationship, starting a family, and coping with the deaths of older relatives. In fact, young adults tend to experience so much change that the term *quarter-life crisis* was recently coined to describe the stressful, overwhelming feelings that people in their 20s commonly grapple with.

Like other stressful events, significant life changes can negatively affect your health. It's been found that people who have recently been widowed, fired, or divorced are more likely to become ill than are those people whose lives have been relatively stable and stress-free.

Daily Hassles

The most frequent and common stressors are daily **hassles,** which include such nuisances as sitting in traffic jams, waiting in long lines, having an overly busy schedule, receiving too much e-mail spam, finding the office coffee pot always empty, tripping over your roommate's shoes every time you walk in the door, and so on. While these hassles may seem relatively minor, their effects on us can add up to create a significant amount of stress. This type of stress can be even more harmful when it is exacerbated by socio-economic or safety-related factors such as

> Thankfully, many people never experience catastrophic events first-hand. However, more mundane and common life events, such as moving out of a childhood home, getting married or divorced, losing a loved one, or changing career paths, can cause large amounts of stress in our lives.

struggling to pay rent or buy groceries, living in an impoverished or high-crime neighbourhood, and experiencing the effects of racism and other types of prejudice. In lower socio-economic areas, where the hassles of everyday life can be particularly stressful and dangerous, residents tend to show signs of high blood pressure, or hypertension—a physical symptom of a stressful environment, and a serious concern for those who are unable to afford or access appropriate medical care.

According to the 2009 Canadian Community Health Survey, over 23% of Canadians (15 years and older) reported that most days were "extremely or quite a bit stressful," with more women reporting higher levels of stress than men.

STRESS AND THE HEART

Just as laughter can improve our health, stress can cause our health to deteriorate. Unfortunately, it often seems as though we spend more time worrying about stressful situations than we do laughing. The amount of stress in our lives may help to explain why coronary heart disease has been a leading cause of death in North America since the 1950s. **Coronary heart disease** is a condition characterized by the clogging of the vessels that nourish the heart muscle. While several factors contribute to the development of coronary heart disease, scientists have found that heart disease and stress are often closely related.

Heart Disease and Personality

Every April 15, taxes are due in the United States ... and every April 15, tax accountants' blood cholesterol climbs to dangerous levels. Is this relationship just a fluke, or could it be indicative of something more? That's the question that Meyer Friedman, Ray Rosenman, and their colleagues asked in the 1950s when they set out to discover whether stress was related to heart disease. They measured tax accountants' cholesterol levels and blood clotting speeds both during peak tax time (mid-April) and during less stressful times of year. The researchers discovered that while the accountants were relatively healthy before and after tax season, their cholesterol and clotting measures spiked around April 15 as they rushed to finish their clients' tax returns. In other words, the accountants' stress levels seemed to be directly correlated with their health (Friedman, Rosenman, Carroll, & Tat, 1958).

This research provided the basis for a classic investigation that studied more than 3000 healthy men age 35 to 59 for nine years. At the onset of the study, researchers interviewed the men to determine which of two personality types they displayed. The study included an approximately equal number of **Type A** men—competitive, impatient, verbally aggressive, easily angered men—and **Type B** men—easygoing, relaxed men. By the end of the study, 257 men in the sample had suffered heart attacks, and 69% of them were Type A. Possibly more impressive was the fact that the men who were the most laid-back and relaxed (the most "Type B-ish" of the Type B men) had all remained heart-attack-free (Rosenman et al., 1975).

What, then, makes the Type A personality so toxic? While Type A people and Type B people have similar levels of arousal in relaxed situations, Type As are more physiologically reactive when they are harassed, challenged, or threatened: Their hormonal secretions, pulse rate, and blood pressure increase drastically. The hormones cause plaque to accumulate more rapidly on artery walls, hardening the arteries, raising blood pressure, and increasing the risk of strokes and heart attacks. The active sympathetic nervous system redistributes blood flow to the muscles and away from internal organs such as the liver, which plays a key role in removing cholesterol and fat from the blood. As a result, the excess cholesterol and fat that the blood is carrying are deposited in the heart.

Negative emotions, especially aggressive anger, may also contribute to Type A toxicity. There are medical reasons why we shouldn't, in the words of one best-selling book, "sweat the small stuff": Adults who react angrily to minor problems or inconveniences are at a higher risk for cardiovascular disease than are their calmer counterparts. Researchers have found that anger, mental illness, and negative personality traits are all risk factors for heart attacks (e.g., Allan & Fisher, 2011; Denollet, 2011; Kubzansky, Sparrow, Vokonas, & Kawachi, 2001; Williams et al., 2000). In short, metaphorically and literally, stress, pessimism, and anger clearly don't do our hearts any favours.

STRESS AND THE IMMUNE SYSTEM

Your immune system is like your own built-in bodyguard—it protects you against damage from the diseases and injuries that try to attack it every day. Although the immune system is strong, it isn't invincible. Factors such as your age, your genetic background, your nutritional intake, and the amount of stress in your life can all influence your immune system's effectiveness. Based on what you already know about the effects of stress on your overall health, it probably comes as no surprise that when you're under stress, your immune system becomes less able to heal your body quickly and effectively.

Two types of white blood cells, or **lymphocytes,** play roles in the immune system. B lymphocytes form in your bone marrow and release antibodies that fight bacterial infections, while T lymphocytes form in your thymus and other lymphatic tissue and attack cancer cells, viruses, and foreign substances (including those substances that may not actually be enemies of the body, such as transplanted organs). When these lymphocytes do their job properly, they keep you healthy and heal your injuries. However, when your immune system isn't functioning properly, it can respond by either overreacting or underreacting. When it underreacts, it may, for example, fail to fight off those bacteria that entered your body after you touched a dirty doorknob and then rubbed your eyes, or it may allow cancer cells to multiply. When it overreacts, your immune system may begin attacking your body's own tissues and could cause problems like arthritis, allergies, lupus, or multiple sclerosis. Since women tend to have stronger immune systems than men, women are generally less vulnerable to infections but more vulnerable to these self-attacking diseases.

How is stress related to the immune system's functions? During periods of stress, the brain causes increased secretion of stress hormones, which then suppress the disease-fighting activities of the B and T lymphocytes. Stress also causes the body to go into "panic mode" and divert much of its energy away from the immune system to the muscles and brain. This reaction to stress may cause surgical wounds to heal more slowly.

One study examined the effect of stress on people's susceptibility to colds. When a cold virus was dropped into the noses of higher-stressed and lower-stressed participants, 47% of the stressed participants and only 27% of the lower-stressed participants developed colds. Follow-up research demonstrated that the happiest and most relaxed people were significantly less vulnerable to an experimentally delivered cold virus (Cohen, Doyle, Turner, Alper, & Skoner, 2003). More recently, researchers have found that chronic psychological stress in childhood is a risk factor for the development of chronic diseases later in life (Miller, Chen, & Parker, 2011).

> "Concentration camp survivors and prisoners of war have experienced some of the most extreme stress possible, **but they do not exhibit a higher incidence of cancer than the regular population.**"

Stress and HIV/AIDS

When a person who is already immunosuppressed experiences stress, the effects of stress on the immune system are even greater. The mere diagnosis of an immunosuppressive disease, such as human immunodeficiency virus (HIV), can be a stressor. HIV, which is spread by the exchange of bodily fluids, such as semen and blood, can lead to acquired immune deficiency syndrome (AIDS). According to the World Health Organization (2011), there are 34 million people worldwide living with HIV. Without regular testing for the disease, many remain unaware that they are infected and can therefore unknowingly transmit the disease to others. By definition, an immunosuppressive disease makes fighting off other diseases difficult, and people with HIV/AIDS commonly die as a result of these other diseases.

Researchers have found that stress and negative emotions correlate with the progression of HIV to AIDS and can speed the decline of those who already have AIDS. Stress-reduction techniques do seem to offer some hope in staving off this decline. For example, many people with HIV have benefited from educational initiatives, bereavement support groups, cognitive therapy, and exercise programs designed to relieve stress.

Stress and Cancer

While laughter and positive emotions can improve cancer patients' health and well-being, stress and negative emotions correlate with the progression of cancer. Researchers have conducted studies with rodents in which the rodents were either given carcinogens—cancer-causing substances—or transplanted with tumours and then exposed to uncontrollable stress, such as unavoidable electric shocks. They found that the rodents who were exposed to these stressors were more prone to tumours that grew larger and more quickly than those rodents who were given carcinogens or transplanted with tumours but were not exposed to uncontrollable stress (Sklar & Anisman, 1981). However, stress does not seem capable of causing cancer on its own. Concentration camp survivors and prisoners of war have experienced some of the most extreme stress possible, but they do not exhibit a higher incidence of cancer than the regular population. There is still controversy surrounding what types of stress may negatively affect cancer recovery and the exact mechanism by which stress affects

>>> Even the most extreme stress can only worsen pre-existing cancer cells, not create them on its own.

cancer (e.g., Surtees, Wainwright, Luben, Khaw, & Bingham, 2010). One possibility is that stress may affect the growth of cancer cells by weakening the body's immune system against a few malignant cells that are already present in the body. Support for this view comes from studies looking at the benefits of massage for cancer patients (e.g., Krohn et al., 2011).

STRESS AND SOMATOFORM DISORDERS

Some people react to stress by experiencing physical symptoms that are not fully explained by a general medical condition. As a group, the psychological disorders characterized by these symptoms are known as somatoform disorders (see Chapter 16). Although the physical symptoms related to these disorders have no physiological cause, people suffering from these symptoms experience them in a very real way.

Migraines, chronic fatigue, and hypertension are just a few of the real physical symptoms that can be caused or worsened by psychological reactions to stress. Once called psychosomatic symptoms, these stress-related symptoms are now referred to as **psychophysiological ("mind-body") illnesses.** It is important to note that, although these physical symptoms have psychological origins, they are not imaginary.

SEEKING TREATMENT

Whether you have a stress-related illness or a common cold, visiting a doctor's office can be a stressful activity in and of itself. However, stress does have potential benefits when it comes to seeking treatment for illness. Some people are far more likely than others to notice physical symptoms of illness: While one person may not pay much attention to a headache or an upset

stomach, another person might decide to see a doctor as soon as she notices these symptoms. What makes these two people react differently to the same symptoms? Stress may be part of the answer. People who notice physical symptoms and report those symptoms to doctors tend to be negative; they often describe themselves as anxious, depressed, and stressed. While no doctor would recommend that his or her patients strive to become anxious, depressed, and stressed, patients who do notice symptoms early on are more likely to receive early, effective treatment. On the other hand, people who are insensitive to symptoms or who wait a while before seeking treatment are in danger of having their conditions worsen. Stress may cause a host of health problems, but it can also motivate you to see a doctor and improve your health.

Improving Health

COPING WITH STRESS

Take a moment to think about it: How do you cope with stress? Your answer is probably different from your friend's answer or your

Coping strategy is a strategy that helps a person reduce or minimize the effects of stressors.

Cognitive appraisal is a thoughtful interpretation and evaluation.

Primary appraisal is a person's initial evaluation of the seriousness of a stressor and the extent of the demands it will put on that person.

Secondary appraisal is a person's reassessment of a stressor that focuses on the actions he or she needs to take and the resources that will help him or her overcome the stressor.

Rational coping is a coping strategy that involves facing a stressor directly and working to overcome it.

Repressive coping is a coping strategy that involves maintaining an artificially positive viewpoint and trying not to think about a stressor.

Reframing is a coping strategy that involves finding a new or creative way to think about a stressor that reduces its threat.

Anticipatory coping is a coping strategy that involves a person foreseeing a potential stressor and considering it in terms of how he or she has previously handled similar stressors, what he or she might do similarly in this situation, and what he or she has learned from past mistakes.

Problem-focused coping is a coping strategy that involves a person's attempt to alleviate stress directly, either by eliminating the source of a stressor or by changing the way he or she behaves in stressful situations.

Emotion-focused coping is a coping strategy that involves attempting to alleviate stress by avoiding the stressor and soothing stress-related emotions.

Stress inoculation is a therapeutic technique in which clients are taught how to evaluate and cope with various stressors and are then exposed to increasingly stressful situations in a controlled environment to strengthen these coping mechanisms.

mother's answer. In fact, there are many different stress-management techniques, each with various advantages and disadvantages. **Coping strategies** help us to reduce or minimize the effect of stressors. People's methods of dealing with stress vary greatly, but common alleviating strategies include cognitive, emotional, and behavioural approaches.

Cognitive Appraisal

Often, we react negatively to stressors before we are able to think about them rationally. You might feel incredibly overwhelmed when you look at your schedule for next week and realize that you have three exams in one day, none of which you've begun to study for yet. However, stressors are often much more manageable

than we originally assume they are. Just giving them some thought can help to minimize their harmful effects.

When we make a **cognitive appraisal** of a stressor, we thoughtfully interpret and evaluate it. Making a cognitive appraisal is usually a two-step process. First, we make a **primary appraisal,** or an initial evaluation of the seriousness of the stressor and the extent of the demands it will put on us. In your primary appraisal of the realization that you have three exams in one day, you may perceive the stressor either as an obstacle that will be impossible to overcome or as a challenge that will require effort to overcome. Later, however, you might make a **secondary appraisal,** or a reassessment that focuses on the actions you need to take and the resources that will help you overcome the stressor. A secondary appraisal can help you re-evaluate the stressor in a more informed and reasonable way. You might realize that you have a three-day weekend before your exams, which will give you extra time to study, or you might decide to seek out study partners to make your exam preparation more effective and fun. By thinking rationally about a stressor and objectively evaluating the resources that are available to you, you may be able to quell your initial emotional reaction and replace it with a plan.

Rational Coping, Repressive Coping, and Reframing

When we make rational, thoughtful cognitive appraisals of stressors, we are engaging

> "However, stressors are often much more manageable than we originally assume they are. Just giving them some thought can help to minimize their harmful effects."

in **rational coping**—we're facing a stressor and working to overcome it. This hands-on approach to stress management tends to be effective, but it can also seem difficult and scary. When we choose not to cope rationally with a stressor, we may decide to use **repressive coping** or **reframing** techniques instead.

Repressive coping is like ignoring the elephant in the room: It involves maintaining an artificially positive viewpoint and trying not to think about the stressor. While some people believe that this method can be effective, especially under short-term circumstances, others worry that failing to adequately face, address, and deal with stressors can lead to long-term negative health consequences. In general, research indicates the repressors are at increased risk of diseases such as high blood pressure and cancer (see Mund & Mittee, 2012 for a meta-analysis of repressive coping and somatic diseases). A more advantageous approach to stress is reframing—finding a new or creative way to think about a stressor that reduces its threat. When you use the reframing technique, you might see your three exams in one day as an opportunity to impress your professors, which will enable them to write you glowing letters of recommendation for graduate school. Or you might decide that it's much easier to get three exams over and done with in one day than to have them spread out over an entire week.

All stress-management techniques have their pros and cons, and you may find that different stressors require different approaches. A person who has recently suffered a heart attack may reframe his vulnerable health situation by speculating that a future attack would enable him to take some time off from work to spend with his family. However, it is probably best not to worry about future heart attacks at all. Researchers discovered that heart attack victims who constantly worried about a future attack were more likely to suffer from symptoms of post-traumatic stress, such as nightmares and insomnia (factors that actually increase the risk of heart attack), than were people who did not dwell on the possibility of future health problems (Ginzburg et al., 2003).

Anticipatory Coping

Worriers react to stressors before they are even a reality. They may anticipate hypothetical situations that might cause them stress in the future, and they tend to ponder the best way to handle potentially non-existent problems. While this can be a tiresome way to live if taken to extremes, it can also be turned into a useful, proactive coping mechanism. **Anticipatory coping** involves foreseeing a potential stressor and considering it in terms of how you have previously handled similar stressors, what you might do similarly in this situation, and what you have learned from past mistakes. For example, if you were unable to cope with your workload last semester and can predict that your classes will be equally demanding this semester, you might minimize potential stress levels by cutting back on extracurricular activities. Like good Boy Scouts, people who use anticipatory coping mechanisms are always prepared.

Problem-Focused Coping

When a stressor is already a reality, attempts to alleviate it may be either problem-focused or emotion-focused. People who engage in **problem-focused coping** attempt to alleviate stress directly, either by eliminating the source of a stressor or by changing the way they behave in stressful situations. We tend to opt for this strategy when we feel a sense of control over a situation. If we feel capable of changing our circumstances or our behaviours in response to a problem, we are more likely to be able to tackle the problem itself. For example, if you are dealing with a particularly challenging project at work, you might talk with your supervisor to see if you can delegate some of your workload (changing the circumstances), or you might decide to work extra hours in order to get the job done (changing your behaviour).

Emotion-Focused Coping

If we feel incapable of changing stressful circumstances, we may resort to **emotion-focused coping**—attempting to alleviate stress by avoiding the stressor and soothing our stress-related emotions. For example, if your relationship with your neighbour has become particularly stressful, you might try to avoid the neighbour and make yourself feel better by spending more time with your good friends instead. While this coping strategy can alleviate stress, it tends to be less effective than problem-focused coping in promoting a healthy, satisfying lifestyle. If you had addressed the problems with your neighbour directly, you might have learned useful strategies for getting along with others that could have helped you avoid the continuing stress of dealing with your neighbour.

Although emotion-focused coping isn't always the most effective way to deal with a stressor, it has certain benefits. For example, when cancer patients laugh, listen to jokes, or watch old comedies on television, they're using emotion-focused coping to alleviate stress. They don't have much control over cancer, but they can make themselves feel better by tending to their emotional well-being.

Stress Inoculation

Those who find dealing with stress especially difficult may seek the help of a therapist, who can assist in the development of effective strategies. One such strategy is **stress inoculation.** Developed by Canadian researcher Donald Meichenbaum in the 1970s, stress inoculation is a three-step process during which one can evaluate, acquire, and apply effective responses to stress.

1 Conceptualization identification of stressors and patient's response to stressors; evaluation of effectiveness of responses

2 Skills Acquisition & Rehearsal rehearsal of stress-reduction techniques, including positive coping statements, relaxation, and realistic appraisals of stressful situations

3 Application & Follow-through application of stress-reduction techniques in increasingly stressful real-world situations

STRESS INOCULATION PROCESS

∧∧∧ Meichenbaum's stress inoculation strategy uses a three-step process to combat stress.

FACTORS THAT REDUCE STRESS

Perceived Control

In humans and non-human animals alike, threats and stressors over which we have no control produce stronger stress responses than do controllable threats. When we believe that we have no control over a situation, our stress hormone levels and blood pressure increase, and our immune responses decrease. These physiological responses help to explain how perceiving a loss of control over stressors in one's life can lead to increased vulnerability and poor health. Having perceived control seems to be similarly important for people in their work environments: One study found that people who have the freedom to adjust their office furnishings and lighting, and who are able to control interruptions and distractions, experience less stress than do those who do not have control over their working environment (Wyon, 2000). In addition, training provided to employees increased their perceived control and decreased their work-related stress (Hafner & Stock, 2010). If we believe that we have the power to control our lives and affect change, we are less likely to experience stress. In short, greater perceived control leads to lower stress levels and improved health.

The relationship between perceived control and stress helps to explain the link between economic status and longevity. High economic status is linked to lower risks for heart and respiratory diseases, infant mortality, low birth weight, smoking, and violence. While money doesn't necessarily lead to health, having enough money to live comfortably can significantly reduce your stress levels and increase your perceived control. If you are fortunate enough to be relatively well off, you can afford to control several aspects of your life: For example, you can choose to live in a healthy neighbourhood, go to a nice gym, and attend thriving schools.

Even if financial resources don't actually give people much control over their lives, it's perceived control that counts when it comes to stress reduction. Studies have found that the positive effects of perceived control over one's situation are very similar to the positive effects of actual control. You may face situations that are truly beyond your control, but if you believe that you can make a difference in those situations, you may reduce your stress levels and improve your overall health.

People with pets tend to be happier and healthier. Many people would consider their pets important members of the family.

Explanatory Style

Do you have a fundamentally positive outlook on life? If so, you may find it relatively easy to cope with stress. One way in which we can try to reduce and combat stress in our lives is to make our **explanatory style,** or the way in which we explain events to ourselves, more optimistic. Psychologists Michael Scheier and Charles Carver (1992) found that optimists have more perceived control, cope better with stressful events, and have better overall health than pessimists do. The researchers also found that during the last month of a semester, optimistic students report less fatigue and fewer coughs, aches, and pains than do their more pessimistic peers, indicating that optimists may be experiencing less stress and, therefore, less illness and less sleeplessness.

Social Support

As beneficial as laughing is on its own, it's even better when you have a group of friends and family members to laugh with. Social support, in the form of an intimate network of supportive friends and family members, plays an important role in reducing stress and promoting happiness and health (Al-Kandari, 2011; Brennan & Spencer, 2012; Thoits, 2011). In fact, people with good social support systems are less likely to die from illnesses or injuries than are those without a strong social network (Kulik & Mahler, 1993). While this correlation may be due in part to the stress relief that friends can provide, people with social support also tend to take better care of themselves in other ways. People with supportive friends and marriage partners tend to eat better, exercise more, sleep better, and smoke less—all of which are activities that are conducive to coping with stress more effectively. One study also found that women who have social support networks are more likely to get breast cancer screenings (Messina et al., 2004).

How Canadians Spend Their Free Time

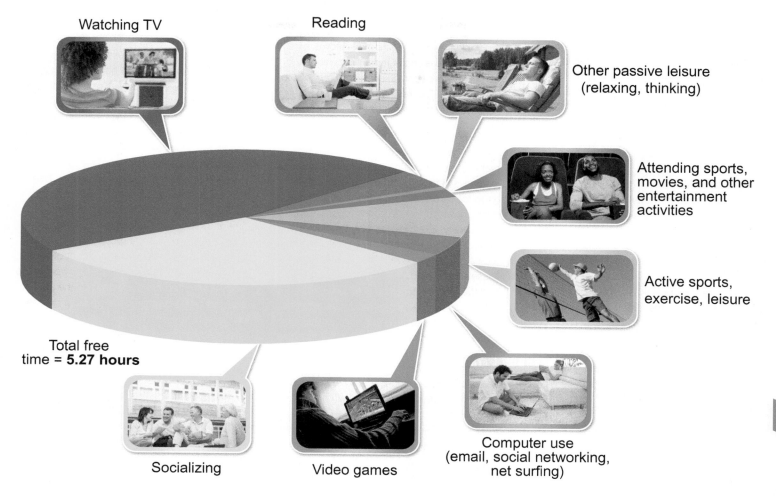

Watching TV

Reading

Other passive leisure (relaxing, thinking)

Attending sports, movies, and other entertainment activities

Active sports, exercise, leisure

Total free time = **5.27 hours**

Computer use (email, social networking, net surfing)

Socializing

Video games

Note: Data include all persons age 15 and over. Data include all days of the week and are annual averages for 2010.

Source: Statistics Canada (2011). General Social Survey - 2010. Overview of the time use of Canadians.

∧
∧ The **average Canadian** has over five hours of free time each day. How do you
∧ spend your free time? How might you use your free time to decrease your
stress and improve your health?

You may be thinking about your turbulent romantic relationships, your nosy parents, and your argumentative siblings and wondering how relationships that sometimes cause so much stress could actually be helping you cope with stress. It is true that relationships can be stressful at times, especially when people live together in crowded conditions without much privacy. However, while family relationships are not always supportive or healthy,

our close family members can provide us with comfort and love when we need it most.

Although marital relationships can be fraught with difficulties, they also happen to be positive predictors of health. Married people live longer, healthier lives than unmarried people.

In successful relationships, a spouse often describes his or her partner as "my best friend." Researchers have found that

having someone to confide in plays an important part in our overall well-being. James Pennebaker and Robin O'Heeron (1984) conducted research with the surviving spouses of people who had committed suicide or died in car accidents—events whose suddenness and unpredictability made them especially stressful. The researchers found that those surviving spouses who were unable to talk about their grief with others had more health problems than did those who had someone to confide in. Although talking about a stressful event may initially be awkward or difficult, the long-term effects can be beneficial. One study of Holocaust survivors found that when they shared their experiences with family and friends in more detail than they ever had before, the survivors exhibited improved health after 14 months (Pennebaker, Barger, & Tiebout, 1989). The sharing of difficult and traumatic experiences also helps those working in war-ravaged countries (e.g., Monson, Fredman, & Dekel, 2010).

People who don't feel able to share their close feelings with others sometimes benefit by writing about their experiences. For other people, man's best friend can provide stress relief, improved health, and slobbery smooches. Even children benefit from having pets (Wagner, 2011): University of Windsor researchers Reza Nakhaie and Robert Arnold (2010) examined the effects of social relationships on the health of Canadians. They found that feeling and expressing love to others had an incredible positive effect on health—producing positive benefits that were three times greater than the negative effects of smoking cigarettes on a daily basis.

STRESS MANAGEMENT

In today's fast-paced society, sometimes it's just not possible to alleviate stress. We still have to face daily commutes, juggle work and family life, compete for scholarships and jobs, and tackle overflowing inboxes. However, a variety of stress-management techniques, including exercise, relaxation, and meditation, can make our bodies more resistant to the negative effects of stress.

Exercise

Regular **aerobic exercise**—sustained exercise that increases heart and lung fitness, such as jogging, swimming, and biking—not only is good for cardiovascular health but also has been shown to reduce stress, depression, and anxiety. Exercise has long been known to have a positive effect on health. It strengthens the heart, increases blood flow, keeps blood vessels open, and lowers blood pressure and the reaction to blood pressure stress. One study estimates that moderate exercise adds two years to a person's life expectancy (Paffenbarger et al., 1993). A regular exercise regime is beneficial for health aging (Geithner & McKenney, 2010).

Researchers frequently examine the relationship between exercise and stress. One

study found that three in 10 Canadians and Americans who participate in some form of aerobic activity three or more times each week manage stressful events better, display more self-confidence, feel more vigour, and experience depression and fatigue less frequently than those who exercise less (McMurray, 2004). Additional research has shown that exercise minimizes the stress on the brain and memory (Head, Singh, & Bugg, 2012). Other studies have considered the direction of cause and effect in the relationship between exercise and stress. Does exercise reduce stress, or are people with less stress more likely to exercise? In an effort to find a causal relationship, Lisa McCann and David Holmes (1984) assigned mildly depressed female college students to one of three groups: a group required to perform aerobic exercise, a group required to perform relaxation exercises, and a control group that received no treatment. After 10 weeks, the women who had been assigned to the aerobic exercise group displayed the greatest decrease in depression. Hundreds of research studies have demonstrated that exercise reduces levels of depression and anxiety and is therefore a useful tool to employ in combination with therapy and/or antidepressant drugs (see Chapter 17 for more information about treatment).

In addition to keeping our hearts healthy and reducing our chances of getting sick, exercise may improve our emotional state by releasing mood-enhancing hormones such as norepinephrine, serotonin, and endorphins.

Group motivation often encourages people to continue along the path to **physical fitness.**

V V V

Exercise also helps us feel good by increasing our warmth and body arousal, helping us relax our muscles and sleep more soundly, improving our physical appearance, and giving us a sense of accomplishment. We can further enhance the benefits of exercise by taking advantage of diverse, interesting outdoor activities and exercising with members of our social support groups.

Biofeedback

While it may sound like a futuristic technique from a sci-fi movie, **biofeedback,** a system for measuring and reporting physiological states, is actually a mind-over-matter form of stress-management therapy. Biofeedback specialists use special electronic equipment to measure people's physiological states, such as blood pressure, heart rate, or muscle tension. The equipment then gives feedback designed to help people control their involuntary body functions and reduce stress. For example, a person may not be aware that he has particularly tense muscles, but when he sees a flashing light informing him that he is experiencing muscle tension, he may make a conscious effort to relax.

When biofeedback was first introduced in the 1960s, people were excited at the prospects of being able to control physiological responses and eliminate the use of certain types of drugs. However, about a decade later, researchers realized that the technique might have been overrated. While biofeedback may cure some people's tension headaches, for example, alternative medicine techniques such as acupuncture and meditation provide similar effects and often do not require expensive equipment.

Relaxation and Meditation

Although biofeedback did not live up to expectations, using relaxation techniques to control physiological responses continues to be a popular therapeutic approach to stress reduction. **Relaxation therapy** involves alternately tensing and relaxing muscles in the body and practising breathing exercises in order to relieve tension. The aim of relaxation therapy is to achieve a **relaxation response**—a condition of reduced muscle tension, cortical activity, heart rate, breathing rate, and blood pressure. Brain scans of people achieving the relaxation response reveal that while the parietal lobe—the area involved in knowing where one is in space—is less active than normal, the frontal lobe—the area involved in focusing attention—is more active than normal (Lazar et al., 2000). When Richard Davidson studied brain scans of Buddhist monks taken during meditation, he

Biofeedback is a system for measuring and reporting physiological states.

Relaxation therapy is a therapeutic technique that involves alternately tensing and relaxing muscles in the body and practising breathing exercises in order to relieve tension.

Relaxation response consists of reduced muscle tension, cortical activity, heart rate, breathing rate, and blood pressure.

discovered that the monks showed increased levels of activity in the left frontal lobe— the area associated with positive emotion (Davidson et al., 2003).

If you ever feel guilty about taking a break, remember that relaxation has plenty of health benefits. Studies have shown that relaxation techniques can help alleviate headaches, hypertension, anxiety, and insomnia (Stetter & Kupper, 2002; Varvogli & Darviri, 2011), and assist in the recovery of illness (Mandel, Hanser, & Ryan, 2010). If you want to reduce the negative health effects of stress, try to stay calm, exercise, emphasize the "Type B" aspects of your personality, and remind yourself that relaxation isn't an unnecessary luxury: On the contrary, it can promote both physical and mental health.

Summary

HOW ARE PSYCHOLOGICAL STATES CONNECTED TO PHYSICAL REACTIONS? p.266

- The field of health psychology places emphasis on the idea that physical health and mental health are closely related.

- Stress significantly increases a person's risk factor for the four leading causes of illness and death: cancer, heart disease, cerebrovascular/stroke, respiratory disease.

- When the body is emotionally aroused, it produces a fight-or-flight response by releasing stress hormones from the adrenal glands.

HOW DOES STRESS AFFECT OUR IMMUNE SYSTEMS AND OUR OVERALL HEALTH? p.268

- Common stressors—events that we see as challenging or threatening—include catastrophes, significant life changes, and daily hassles.

- Stress is related to heart disease. Type A people are more likely than Type B people to suffer from heart attacks because of their different physiological reactions to stress.

- Stress causes the brain to secrete stress hormones that suppress the immune system, making the body more vulnerable to illnesses, including the progression of cancer. Stress also correlates with the progression of HIV to AIDS.

WHAT ARE SOME OF THE DIFFERENT WAYS THAT PEOPLE COPE WITH STRESS? p.271

- Coping strategies, including rational coping, repressive coping, and reframing, help to minimize the effects of stressors.

- Foreseeing a source of stress and considering how to deal with it in advance is known as anticipatory coping.

- Attempts to alleviate stress may be problem-focused (dealing directly with the source of the stress) or emotion-focused (avoiding the stressor).

WHAT TECHNIQUES CAN WE USE TO ALLEVIATE OR MANAGE STRESS? p.274

- People who perceive that they have control over a stressor, who have a positive outlook, and who have social support are better able to deal with stress.

- Aerobic exercise, biofeedback, and relaxation and meditation techniques can help to relieve stress.

Test Your Understanding

1. Jenny has been keeping on top of her studies throughout the semester, but during exam time, she suddenly finds herself feeling overwhelmed and stressed. Jenny is most likely suffering from:
   a. eustress
   b. post-traumatic stress
   c. chronic stress
   d. acute stress

2. Which of the following statements about the effects of stress on health is true?
   a. Adults who are competitive and impatient are more likely to suffer from heart attacks than are adults who are relaxed.
   b. Stress causes the body to divert more energy toward the immune system, causing the immune system to overreact.
   c. A person with high levels of stress is more likely to develop cancerous cells than is a person with low levels of stress.
   d. When a person who is already immunosuppressed experiences stress, the effects of stress have no additional impact on the immune system.

3. Bao has been put in charge of an important project at work that will require a lot of overtime. At first, Bao doesn't think he can handle the project. After a while, though, he begins to think about ways in which he can reduce his workload. Bao is:

   a. making a cognitive appraisal
   b. using repressive coping
   c. using emotion-focused coping
   d. undergoing stress inoculation

4. Which of the following people would be most likely to suffer from burnout?
   a. a part-time lawyer
   b. a professional athlete
   c. a special needs teacher
   d. an elementary school student

5. Which of the following situations does NOT exacerbate stress?
   a. getting married
   b. living in a high-crime neighbourhood
   c. sitting in daily traffic jams
   d. receiving increased levels of personal autonomy at work

6. Stress can actually be good for us because it helps us perform tasks and achieve goals. This type of stress is called:
   a. eustress
   b. adaptive stress
   c. distress
   d. positive stress

7. According to Meichenbaum's stress inoculation strategy, the third stage in treating patients with stress is to:

   a. identify the patients' stressors
   b. have patients apply stress-reduction techniques to real-life situations
   c. practise stress-reduction techniques with patients
   d. evaluate patients' responses to stress

8. Which of the following statements about the relationship between exercise and stress is NOT true?

   a. Exercise may improve our emotional state by releasing mood-enhancing hormones such as norepinephrine, serotonin, and endorphins.
   b. Researchers are unable to prove a causal relationship between exercise and stress because people with lower stress levels usually exercise more.
   c. Regular aerobic exercise increases heart and lung fitness and reduces levels of anxiety and depression.
   d. Moderate exercise on a regular basis can add up to two years to a person's life expectancy.

9. When Tariq's father dies, Tariq begins to separate himself from the rest of the family. He rarely answers his phone and starts using illegal drugs, including heroin and cocaine. Which stress response system is Tariq demonstrating?

   a. fight or flight
   b. tend and befriend
   c. withdrawal
   d. general adaptation syndrome

10. Gwen is undergoing a painful divorce. When people ask how she is doing, she smiles broadly and tells them she has never been better. Which coping mechanism is Gwen using?

   a. reframing
   b. repressive coping
   c. rational coping
   d. anticipatory coping

11. Dewu falls down and breaks his leg, rendering him unable to work for several months. Dewu reminds himself that the time off will enable him to spend more time with his friends and family. Dewu:

   a. has a positive explanatory style
   b. is demonstrating the fight-or-flight response
   c. likely has a Type A personality
   d. is using the stress inoculation strategy

12. Which of the following statements is true about marriage and health?

   a. Being married is a positive predictor of good health even if the marriage is unstable.
   b. The emotional turmoil caused by relationships means that single people are generally healthier than married people.
   c. Married people tend to live longer than unmarried people, regardless of race, age, sex, and income.
   d. There seems to be no relationship between marital status and health.

13. Which of the following topics would an environmental psychologist be most likely to study?

   a. the relationship between excess noise levels and stress
   b. how the immune system responds to the flu virus while under stress
   c. the effects of post-traumatic stress on an Afghanistan War veteran
   d. the relationship between stress levels and life expectancy

14. Which of the following occurs during the alarm stage of Selye's general adaptation syndrome?

   a. Hormones are suddenly released.
   b. Persistent stress depletes the body of its reserves.
   c. Temperature, blood pressure, and respiration remain at high levels.
   d. Heart rate increases and blood is diverted to the skeletal muscles.

15. Which of the following statements about stressful life events is true?

   a. Daily hassles such as traffic jams are minor inconveniences that do not dramatically increase stress levels.
   b. Catastrophes such as hurricanes or war almost always have a greater impact on people's overall health than more common daily stressors do.
   c. Minor stressors can accumulate over time to create health problems that are just as damaging as those caused by major stressful events.
   d. Significant life changes in middle and late adulthood are the most common sources of stress for most individuals.

16. Annie and Lia are identical twins. Annie is currently experiencing several stressful life events, while Lia is relatively relaxed. All other things being equal, which of the following statements about Annie and Lia is true?

   a. Lia is more likely to develop multiple sclerosis than Annie is.
   b. Annie is more likely to have a Type A personality than Lia is.
   c. Lia has a more responsive immune system than Annie does.
   d. Annie is more likely to catch a cold than Lia is.

17. Fang-hua is experiencing problems at work that are causing sleeplessness and irritability. Which of the following is LEAST likely to reduce Fang-hua's stress levels?

   a. getting a pet
   b. drinking two glasses of wine every night
   c. confiding in a friend
   d. writing her feelings in a diary

18. Which of the following is a disadvantage of biofeedback?

   a. It is effective only for women.
   b. It requires the use of expensive equipment.
   c. It has dangerous side effects.
   d. Its effects are not immediately apparent.

19. A person who responds to stress by adhering to Taylor's tend-and-befriend model is most likely to:

   a. avoid communicating with his or her friends
   b. look to friends for comfort and compassion
   c. make new friends only during periods of stress
   d. depend on friends to make important decisions

20. Darnell is a successful businessman who thrives in a competitive environment. He becomes angry easily, and he frequently argues with his colleagues. Darnell is at a high risk of developing:

   a. Alzheimer's disease
   b. conversion disorder
   c. hyperchondriasis
   d. cardiovascular disease

Remember to check www.thethinkspot.ca **for additional information, downloadable flashcards, and other helpful resources.**

Answers: 1) d; 2) a; 3) a; 4) c; 5) d; 6) a; 7) b; 8) b; 9) c; 10) b; 11) a; 12) c; 13) a; 14) d; 15) c; 16) d; 17) b; 18) d; 19) b; 20) d

GLOSSARY

abnormal psychology the study of disorders of mind, mood, and behaviour (233)

absolute threshold the smallest amount of energy needed for a person to detect a stimulus 50% of the time (50)

academic psychologist a type of psychologist who divides his or her time between supervising and teaching students, completing administrative tasks, and carrying out psychological research (11)

accommodation a process in which a person adjusts and refines his or her schemas based on new information (89)

accuracy motive a person's desire to be correct or accurate (204)

achievement a person's knowledge and progress (183)

acquired characteristics useful traits acquired by an organism (73)

action potential an electrochemical ripple that works its way from the cell body to the terminal buttons and terminates in the release of neurotransmitters that will stimulate the next neuron (37)

activation-synthesis theory a theory that explains sleep as a side effect of the visual and motor area neurons firing during REM sleep; it states that dreams are the result of the brain's attempt to make sense of the random neural activity that occurs while a person sleeps (141)

activity theory of aging theory that states that elderly people are happiest when they stay active and involved in the community (102)

acuity sharpness of vision (52)

acute stress a temporary state of stress that varies in intensity (266)

adaptation-level phenomenon a phenomenon in which the things a person is currently experiencing become the norm for that person, causing the person to continually want more (127)

adaptive able to adjust and function according to one's environment (73)

adenosine a sleep-inducing hormone (138)

adolescence the period of transition from childhood to adulthood (84)

adrenal androgen a hormone that increases in production during puberty (101)

aerobic exercise sustained exercise that increases heart and lung fitness, such as jogging, swimming, and biking (274)

affective component feelings associated with emotion (122)

affective forecasting a person's imagining how he or she would feel about something that might happen in the future (127)

age changes developmental changes that track how individuals change as they age (83)

age differences developmental changes that consider how people of varying ages differ from one another (83)

ageism prejudice against the elderly (102)

aggression behaviour intended to harm others (211)

agonist a type of drug that increases neural activity (146)

agoraphobia intense fear of being in a situation from which there is no escape (236)

algorithm a step-by-step procedure that a person can follow to arrive at a solution to a particular problem (187)

alleles pairs of genes located in the same position on the pair of chromosomes in a unit of heredity (69)

allocentrism a personality trait exhibiting the tendency to think and act in a collectivist manner (227)

all-or-none principle a principle that states that once the threshold for a particular neuron is reached, it will transmit all of its information, no matter how many more positive inputs it receives over that threshold (37)

alpha wave a type of brainwave that characterizes a relaxed state of wakefulness (138)

altered state of consciousness a state characterized by bizarre, disorganized, or dreamlike thought patterns (136)

altruism prosocial behaviour that is carried out without concern for one's own safety or self-interest (213)

amplitude the height of a wave (54)

amygdala a part of the limbic system; it is involved in fear detection and conditioning and is essential for unconscious emotional responses such as the fight-or-flight response (40, 123)

analytic intelligence a type of intelligence generally assessed by intelligence tests that present well-defined problems with only one correct answer (185)

androgen insensitivity syndrome a condition in which a genetically male fetus's receptors for androgens fail to function, resulting in the development of external female genitalia (110)

androgens male hormones (110)

androgynous neither specifically masculine nor feminine (112)

andropause gradual sexual changes in men as they age that include declines in sperm count, testosterone level, and speed of erection and ejaculation (84)

anorexogenic signals that stop an animal from eating (130)

antagonist a type of drug that inhibits or decreases neural activity (146)

anterior cingulate cortex an area of the brain that serves as an executive control system that helps control a person's behaviour; it is involved in the perception of physical pain (41, 191)

anterograde amnesia memory loss characterized by an inability to form new long-term memories (177)

anticipatory coping a coping strategy that involves a person's foreseeing a potential stressor and considering it in terms of how he or she has previously handled similar stressors, what he or she might do similarly in this situation, and what he or she has learned from past mistakes (272)

antidepressant a type of medication that works to alleviate symptoms of depression by altering how certain neurotransmitters—usually serotonin and norepinephrine—are circulated throughout the brain (252)

antipsychotic drugs psychoactive medications used to treat disorders in which psychotic symptoms, such as hallucinations, paranoia, and delusions, predominate (252)

antisocial personality disorder a mental disorder characterized by a complete lack of conscience (242)

anxiety disorder   a mental disorder in which a person feels anxious all the time without any identifiable reason (236)

anxious relationship   an intimate relationship characterized by worry about love or lack of love from a partner (101)

applied psychology   the use of psychological theory and practice to tackle real-world problems (11)

approach motivation   a motivation involved with striving to achieve a positive result (128)

approval motive   a person's desire to be accepted by his or her peers (203)

aptitude   a person's potential ability (183)

archetype   a particular image, such as mother as caretaker and nurturer, persistent across time and cultures (222)

arcuate nucleus   a part of the hypothalamus that contains both appetite-stimulating and appetite-suppressing neurons (130)

artificial selection   a concept that contrasts with natural selection in that humans are involved in selecting the desired characteristics to pass on to an organism's offspring (73)

Asperger syndrome   a syndrome in which a person has normal levels of intelligence and cognitive abilities but displays autistic-like social behaviours (245)

assimilation   a process in which a person interprets new experiences in terms of existing schemas (86)

association cortex   a part of the cerebral cortex that helps basic sensory and motor information from a specific lobe integrate with information from the rest of the brain; one exists in each lobe of the cerebral cortex (42)

associative learning   learning characterized by linking two events that occur together (152)

associator   a person who associates colours with letters; he or she does not actually see the colour (63)

attachment   an emotional bond that newborns share with their caregivers (96)

attention   the act of applying the mind selectively to a sense or thought (168, 191)

attentional blink   a type of processing failure characterized by an inability to remember the second element in a pair of rapidly successive stimuli (192)

attention-deficit hyperactivity disorder (ADHD)   a disorder in which a person finds it difficult to focus his or her attention and is easily distracted (245)

attitude   an evaluative belief or opinion about a person, object, or idea (208)

attractiveness bias   the tendency for a person to rate physically attractive people as more intelligent, competent, sociable, and sensitive than their less-attractive counterparts (201)

attribution theory   a theory that states that a person understands other people by attributing their behaviour either to their internal dispositions or their external situations (200)

attributional-style questionnaire   a type of questionnaire that seeks to assess how people view the events that happen in their lives based on three criteria: stability, globality, and locus (240)

audience design   a concept that states that everything people say is directed to a particular audience (193)

auditory cortex   the part of the brain that mediates the human sense of hearing by encoding auditory information (168)

auditory encoding   the process of encoding sounds (170)

autism   a developmental disorder that impedes social development and communication skills (245)

autonomic nervous system   the part of the peripheral nervous system that performs tasks that are not consciously controlled (34, 124)

availability heuristic   a type of heuristic that tells a person that if he or she can bring examples of an event to mind easily, that event must be common (189)

aversive conditioning   a type of therapy in which a harmful stimulus is paired with a negative response, with the goal of replacing the usual positive response (such as the pleasure a client may feel when drinking alcohol or smoking) with the negative one (259)

avoidance motivation   a motivation involved with striving to avoid a negative result (128)

avoidant personality disorder   a mental disorder characterized by high levels of social anxiety and feelings of inadequacy (244)

avoidant relationship   an intimate relationship in which there is ambivalence about commitment and little expression of intimacy (101)

axon   a cable-like extension that transmits a signal away from a neuron's soma toward the target of communication (34)

backward conditioning   a type of classical conditioning in which the conditioned stimulus is presented after the unconditioned stimulus (154)

bait-and-switch technique   a technique that encourages people to comply with an attractive offer but substitutes that offer with a less-attractive option once the person has agreed (206)

bar graph   a representation of a frequency distribution in which vertical or horizontal bars are proportional in length to the value they represent (27)

basal ganglia   a set of interconnected structures in the brain that help with motor control, cognition, different forms of learning, and emotional processing; they are involved in forming procedural memories and habits related to movement (40, 175)

behaviour genetics   a field of study emphasizing the analysis of the effects of genes and environment on behaviour and mental processes (72)

behavioural activation system (BAS)   a part of the brain that activates approach behaviour in response to the anticipation of a reward (219)

behavioural approach   an approach to psychology that concentrates on observable behaviour that can be directly measured and recorded (6, 235)

behavioural contract   an explicit agreement that thoroughly explains the consequences of several behaviours as well as expectations of the client and the therapist (260)

behavioural expectation confirmation   a phenomenon that enables a person to influence other people to behave in accordance with his or her expectations (203)

behavioural inhibition system (BIS)   a part of the brain that inhibits approach behaviour in response to the anticipation of a punishment (219)

behavioural medicine   an interdisciplinary approach to medical treatment that integrates behavioural, medical, and social knowledge to increase life expectancy and enhance quality of life (266)

behavioural therapy   a type of therapy that attempts to change behaviours associated with psychological distress (258)

behaviourism a method of studying learning in which the researcher focuses solely on directly observable responses and discards any references to inner thoughts, feelings, and motives (152)

belief bias the effect that occurs when a person's beliefs distort his or her logical thinking (188)

belief perseverance a person's tendency to continue believing something even when presented with evidence refuting that belief (188)

belongingness a need to feel loved and avoid alienation (130)

benevolent sexism acceptance of positive stereotypes or favourable biased behaviour that propagates unfairness and inequalities based on gender (114)

benzodiazepines anti-anxiety medications used mainly to treat generalized anxiety disorder and panic disorder (253)

beta wave a type of brainwave that characterizes active wakefulness (138)

between-group experiment a study in which different groups of participants are exposed to different independent variables (21)

bias a personal and sometimes unreasonable judgment that a researcher may make that could affect the results of an experiment (27)

biofeedback a system for measuring and reporting physiological states (276)

biological approach a method of analyzing a psychological disorder in which physical problems are looked for as the root cause (235)

biological preparedness the extent to which biological features evolved to promote certain traits (76)

biopsychosocial approach a method of analyzing a psychological disorder that recognizes that it is not possible to separate body and mind; negative emotions can contribute to physical illness, while physical abnormalities may increase the likelihood of psychological disorders (235)

bipedalism the ability to walk on two legs (75)

bipolar disorder a mood disorder characterized by alternating episodes of depression and mania (239)

blind observer an observer who does not know what the research is about and is thus not subject to observer bias (23)

blindsight a condition in which a person experiences blindness in part of his or her field of vision (53)

blood-brain barrier a fatty envelope that filters substances trying to leave the bloodstream and reach the brain (34)

body restoration theory a theory that explains sleep as a time for necessary rest and recuperation (141)

borderline personality disorder a mental disorder characterized by unstable moods, intense and stormy relationships, and manipulation and distrust of others (242)

brainstem the base of the brain; responsible for survival-oriented functions such as breathing, cardiac function, and basic arousal (39)

brightness the intensity of light waves (54)

Broca's area a part of the frontal lobe that initiates the movements needed to produce speech (43)

burnout a state of physical, emotional, and mental exhaustion created by long-term involvement in an emotionally demanding situation and accompanied by lowered performance and motivation (268)

bystander effect a phenomenon in which the likelihood that a person requiring help receives it from an individual bystander is inversely proportional to the number of bystanders present (204)

Canadian Psychological Association (CPA) a scientific and professional organization that represents psychologists in Canada (29)

Cannon-Bard theory a theory that proposes that the mental and physiological components of emotions happen simultaneously (122)

case study an in-depth study of one individual or a few individuals (23)

catastrophe an unpredictable, large-scale event (268)

catharsis healing emotional release (255)

catharsis theory a theory that states that a person should express emotions to prevent those emotions from building up and exploding (127)

caudate part of the basal ganglia; it is involved in the control of voluntary movement and is part of the brain's learning and memory system (40)

central drive system a set of neurons that create a drive (128)

central executive functioning a set of mental processes that governs goals, strategies, and coordination of the mind's activities (185)

central nervous system (CNS) the largest part of the nervous system; it includes the spinal cord and the brain (34)

central route a path to persuasion that involves paying careful attention to strong, well-presented arguments that are personally relevant and that appeal to reason (208)

central-state theory a theory that explains drives by understanding them as corresponding to neural activity (128)

centromere the place where two chromatids meet (68)

cephalocaudal rule the tendency for motor skills to emerge in sequence from top to bottom (83)

cerebellum a part of the brain that coordinates muscle movements and maintains equilibrium; involved in conditioning and forming procedural memories and habits related to movement (40, 175)

cerebral cortex an outer part of the brain that is mainly involved in the coordination of sensory and motor information (40)

chaining a process in which the final step in a sequence is reinforced first, becoming a conditioned reinforcer for the preceding response (159)

chameleon effect a person's unconscious mimicry of other people's expressions, behaviours, and voice tones (204)

change blindness the failure to detect drastic visual changes in a scene (59)

change deafness the failure to detect drastic auditory changes (59)

chemical environment events and conditions inside an organism (69)

choice blindness the failure to detect alterations to choices a person has made (59)

chromatids pairs of duplicated chromosomes (68)

chromosomes long strands of genetic material found in the nuclei of all cells (68)

chronic stress a long-lasting state of arousal during which a person feels that he or she doesn't have the resources available to meet all of the demands placed upon him or her (266)

chronological age the amount of time that has passed since a person was born (83, 101)

chunking the process of organizing large pieces of information into smaller pieces, or chunks (171)

cingulate cortex a part of the brain that is divided into four sections and is involved in various functions such as emotion, response selection, personal orientation, and memory formation and retrieval (40)

circadian rhythm   a biological clock that regulates body functions on a 24-hour cycle (138)

classical conditioning   a phenomenon in which two stimuli are associated, thus creating a reflex response (154)

client   a person with a psychological disorder who is being treated with the view that his or her psychological distress is caused by behavioural issues and faulty thought processes (250)

client-centred therapy   *see* **person-centred therapy**   (256)

clinical psychology   a field of psychology that deals with the diagnosis and treatment of people with specific mental or behavioural problems (11, 250)

clique   a small, same-sex group of three to nine members who share intimate secrets and see themselves as best friends (99)

closure   the tendency to perceive images as complete objects and overlook incompleteness (61)

cocktail party effect   a phenomenon in which selective attention allows a person to concentrate on one voice and ignore many others (59)

cognition   mental activities associated with sensation, perception, thinking, knowing, remembering, and communicating (86, 183)

cognitive appraisal   a thoughtful interpretation and evaluation (272)

cognitive approach   a method of analyzing a psychological disorder that focuses on thought processes that contribute to psychological distress (235)

cognitive dissonance   a disconnect between a person's internal attitudes and his or her external behaviour (206)

cognitive experience   the brain's remembered response to experiencing an emotion (122)

cognitive map   a mental representation of an environment (153)

cognitive map theory   a theory that states that the hippocampus provides a spatial framework that enables a person to create a mental map of his or her surroundings (162)

cognitive psychology   a field of psychology focused on the workings of the human brain and seeking to understand how people process the information that they collect from their environments (6)

cognitive restructuring   a therapeutic technique in which therapists teach clients to question the automatic beliefs, assumptions, and predictions that often lead to negative emotional states and to replace negative thinking with realistic and positive thinking (257)

cognitive therapy   a type of therapy based on the theory that people's psychological problems can be traced to their own illogical or disturbed beliefs and thoughts; therefore, this type of therapy attempts to replace those cognitive patterns with healthier ones (257)

cognitive unconscious   a collection of mental processes that affect the way a person feels or behaves, even though he or she is not consciously aware of them (137)

cognitive-appraisal theory   a theory that states that if a person notices a particular physiological response, that person has to decide what it means before he or she can feel an emotion (123)

cognitive-behaviour therapy (CBT)   a type of therapy centred on the idea that psychological problems are caused by faulty or irrational thinking, which in turn produces faulty or irrational behaviours; therefore, this type of therapy focuses on getting the client to change the way he or she thinks and behaves (257)

cohorts   groups of people raised during the same time period (90)

collective unconscious   a shared pool of memories and images common to all humans (222)

collectivism   the act of contributing something beneficial to the whole group to which a person belongs (213)

collectivist culture   a culture that emphasizes people's interdependence (227)

colour constancy   the inclination to perceive familiar objects as retaining their colour despite changes in sensory information (54)

comorbidity   a condition in which a person suffers from two or more mental disorders (233)

complex cell   a feature detector that only responds to two features of a stimulus (53)

compliance   a change in a person's behaviour that occurs in response to a direct request (206)

concept   a mental grouping of similar objects, events, and people (186)

conditioned response (CR)   a learned reaction triggered by a conditioned stimulus, even in the absence of an associated unconditioned stimulus (154)

conditioned stimulus (CS)   an event that is repeatedly paired with a particular unconditioned stimulus (154)

conditioning   a process of learning associations in which an implicit memory forms because of repeated exposure to a certain stimulus (152, 173)

cone   a photoreceptor cell in the retina that enables a person to see colour (52)

confederate   a person who takes part in an experiment who is seemingly a subject but is really working with the researcher (21)

confirmation bias   a person's tendency to look for evidence that proves his or her beliefs and to ignore evidence that disproves those beliefs (189)

conflict   the disparity between people's or groups' actions, goals, or ideas (213)

conformity   a principle that requires people to adjust their behaviour or thinking to match a group standard (204)

conjunction fallacy   a phenomenon that causes people to believe that additional information increases the probability that a statement is true, even though that probability actually decreases (189)

conscious encoding   a process of encoding that involves paying specific attention to the information to be remembered (170)

conscious motivation   a motivation that remains in a person's awareness (128)

consciousness   a person's awareness of himself or herself and his or her environment (136)

consistency paradox   the observation that personality ratings are consistent across time and among different observers, but that behaviour ratings are not (220)

construct validity   a type of validity that uses a specific procedure that measures or correlates with a theoretical or intangible concept (28)

content words   words that have meaning (90)

context effect   a person's ability to better retrieve information when in the same context in which the information was first encoded (175)

contingency management   an operant conditioning strategy that involves altering the relationship between a person's actions and those actions' consequences to replace unwanted behaviours with desirable ones (259)

continuity the tendency to view intersecting lines as part of a continuous pattern (61)

continuous reinforcement a method of reinforcement that ensures that a desired response is reinforced every time it occurs (157)

continuous traits characteristics such as height, weight, and skin colour that have a range of possible values (71)

contralateral describes a situation in which one side of something controls the opposite side of something else (43)

control group a group of participants in an experiment who are either given no treatment or given treatment that should have no effect (22)

conversion disorder a somatoform disorder characterized by the sudden, temporary loss of a sensory function (245)

co-operation the act of working together for the good of the group (213)

co-operative principle a principle that instructs speakers that utterances should be truthful, informative, relevant, and clear (193)

coping strategy a strategy that helps a person reduce or minimize the effects of stressors (272)

coronary heart disease a condition characterized by the clogging of the vessels that nourish the heart muscle (268)

corpus callosum a large band of axons connecting the two hemispheres of the brain (41)

counterconditioning a process that involves replacing unwanted responses to particular situations with new responses (158)

covariation principle a process of attribution in which behaviour is observed based on three characteristics: the behaviour's distinctiveness, its consistency, and consensus (200)

creative intelligence a type of intelligence characterized by the ability to adapt to new situations, come up with unique and unusual ideas, and think of novel solutions to problems (185)

criterion validity an indication of how closely a measurement correlates with another criterion of the characteristic being studied (28)

critical period the optimal time period shortly after birth during which normal sensory and perceptual development takes place (62, 96)

critical thinking a way of processing information in which a person examines assumptions, evaluates evidence, looks for hidden agendas, and assesses conclusions (18)

cross-sectional studies studies that collect data from different individuals at different ages in order to track age differences (83)

crowd a large, mixed-sex group whose members get together socially (101)

crystallized intelligence mental ability derived from previous experience (185)

cued forgetting a type of forgetting in which a person is specifically told to forget certain information (173)

cultural relativity the need to consider the individual characteristics of a culture in which a person with a disorder was raised in order to diagnose and treat the disorder (234)

culture-bound syndrome any disorder that is limited to a particular cultural group (234)

debrief give a verbal description of the true nature and purpose of a study after the study occurs (29)

decision aversion the state of attempting to avoid making any decision at all (190)

decision making the process of selecting and rejecting available options (190)

deductive reasoning a top-down method of arriving at a specific conclusion based on broader premises (188)

defection the act of promoting one's own interest at the expense of others (213)

deindividuation a process that allows people in a group to relinquish personal responsibility and give themselves over to the group experience (209)

deintensification a muting of emotions (126)

delayed conditioning a type of classical conditioning in which the conditioned stimulus is presented before the unconditioned stimulus, and the termination of the conditioned stimulus is delayed until the unconditioned stimulus is made available (154)

delayed reinforcement a reward that does not immediately follow an action (157)

delta wave a type of brainwave with a high amplitude that characterizes stage three sleep (138)

delusion a persistent false belief (240)

demand characteristic an aspect of a setting that can cause participants in a study to behave as they believe a researcher wants them to (27)

dendrites relatively short, bushy, branch-like structures that emerge from a neuron's cell body and receive signals from adjoining neurons (34)

dependent personality disorder a mental disorder characterized by clingy, needy behaviour (244)

dependent variable a variable that is affected by the independent variable in an experiment (21)

depressive disorder a mood disorder characterized by prolonged or extreme periods of depression (239)

deprovincialization a process in which learning more about an outgroup through friendship or collaborative efforts can make people more tolerant of the norms and customs of other groups (211)

descriptive statistics statistics researchers use to summarize data sets (25)

deterministic fallacy the claim that traits and behaviours can be explained entirely through genetics (77)

developmental age the point at which someone falls among developmental stages; not necessarily related to chronological age (83)

developmental psychologists psychologists who study the physical, cognitive, and social changes that people experience throughout their lives (83)

deviation score the difference between an individual data point's actual value and the mean value of the whole data set (27)

diathesis-stress hypothesis a hypothesis that states that people are genetically predisposed to a particular mental disorder but will develop the disorder only if exposed to environmental or emotional stress during critical developmental periods (242)

difference threshold the minimum difference between two stimuli needed to detect the difference 50% of the time (50)

discrimination negative behaviour toward a group of people and its members (210)

discriminative stimulus a cue signalling that a particular response will be positively reinforced (153)

discursive reasoning *see* **theoretical reasoning** (188)

disengagement theory of aging a theory that states that elderly people gradually and willingly withdraw themselves from the world around them (102)

dispositional attribution an attribution based on a person's personality or characteristics (200)

dispositional force an internal factor involved in motivation (128)

dissociation a split in consciousness that allows simultaneous thoughts and behaviours to occur apart from each other (145)

dissociative amnesia a disorder that causes sudden, selective memory loss (244)

dissociative disorder a condition in which the normal cognitive processes are fragmented, causing a sudden loss of memory or change in personality (244)

dissociative fugue a disorder characterized by a sudden loss of memory accompanied by an abrupt departure from home (244)

dissociative identity disorder a disorder in which a person seems to experience two or more personalities in one body (244)

distal stimulus a stimulus from an object that exists in the surrounding environment (62)

distress a prolonged, negative type of stress characterized by a challenge being perceived as a daunting obstacle (267)

dizygotic twins twins that come from two separate zygotes (70)

DNA a complex molecule that is the main ingredient of chromosomes; it forms the code for all genetic information (68)

dominant genes that suppress the expression of the other gene in a pair of alleles (70)

door-in-the-face technique a procedure for gaining compliance that involves making a large request and then, when that request is refused, making a smaller request that seems reasonable in comparison (206)

dopamine a neurotransmitter that helps people make decisions that lead to good outcomes and avoid bad outcomes (190)

dorsolateral prefrontal cortex an area of the brain that serves as an executive control system that initiates a person's behaviour; it can also shift or inhibit that behaviour based on the decisions the person makes (191)

double depression a condition in which bouts of major depression are superimposed over a state of dysthymia (239)

double-blind experiment an experiment in which both the subject and the observer are kept blind, thus negating the observer-expectancy effect and the subject-expectancy effect (29)

dream a sequence of images, feelings, ideas, and impressions that pass through people's minds as they sleep (142)

drive one of many internal conditions that make a person tend toward certain goals; this is caused by a departure from optimal states (128)

drive-reduction theory a theory that states that a person reacts when a physiological need creates an aroused state that drives him or her to reduce the need (128)

dual diagnosis the comorbid existence of a mental disorder and substance abuse (233)

dual-coding theory a theory that states that concrete words are represented both visually and verbally, whereas abstract terms are coded only verbally, requiring more complex coding and making them more difficult to retrieve (195)

dualism the belief that the mind does not cease to exist when the body dies, and that thoughts and ideas can exist separately from the body (4)

dysthymia a chronic but less severe form of depression that lasts for two years or more (239)

echoic memory a type of sensory memory involving auditory stimuli (168)

echolocation a process in which sound waves are emitted and the environment is analyzed by listening to the frequency of the waves that are reflected back (55)

eclectic psychotherapy a type of psychotherapy involving the use of multi-faceted treatments that vary depending on each person's unique problem and take into account biological, psychological, and social influences (254)

ego the part of the psyche that tries to identify the basic drive that the *id* wants to fulfill and to come up with a realistic plan for satisfying that drive (222)

egoism the act of doing something beneficial for others in the hopes of receiving something in return (213)

eidetic memory the ability to recall detailed images vividly after looking at them for a short period of time (168)

elaboration-likelihood model a model that states that people tend to be persuaded through the central route when their motivation and ability to understand and consider the persuasive message is high, while they are more likely to be persuaded by the peripheral route when their motivation is low or when they need to make a quick decision (208)

elaborative rehearsal a process in which a person gives meaning to information for the purpose of storing that information in long-term memory (175)

electroconvulsive therapy (ECT) a type of therapy in which electric shocks are sent to patients' brains to treat certain psychological disorders in patients who don't respond to other treatment methods (253)

emerging adulthood the period during a person's early 20s in which that person often still greatly depends on his or her parents for financial and emotional support (101)

emotion a subjective reaction to an object, event, person, or memory (122)

emotion regulation the use of cognitive strategies to control and influence a person's own emotional responses (127)

emotional intelligence a person's ability to perceive, understand, manage, and utilize his or her emotions (185)

emotion-focused coping a coping strategy that involves attempting to alleviate stress by avoiding the stressor and soothing stress-related emotions (272)

encephalization an increase in brain size (75)

encoding the process by which sensory information is converted into a form that can be stored (168)

endocrine system the system involved in the release of hormones that regulate metabolism, growth, development, tissue function, and mood (41)

endogenous directed by a person's internal decisions (58)

endogenous attention *see* **goal-directed selection** (191)

endorphin a morphine-like chemical that inhibits pain signals and is released by the medial forebrain bundle (58, 129)

environmental psychology a field that investigates the physical environment's effects on behaviour and health (266)

episodic memories memories in which a person remembers an entire sequence of events (173)

equity theory a theory that states that workers decide how satisfied they feel with their jobs by comparing themselves to others (130)

erotic plasticity   the degree to which the sex drive is shaped by cultural, social, and situational factors (117)

error   random variability that is accidentally introduced into an experiment (27)

esteem need   a need to feel achievement and self-worth (130)

eustress   a low-level, positive type of stress that helps a person perform a task or achieve a goal (266)

evolutionary approach   an approach to psychology that explores ways in which patterns of human behaviour may be beneficial to people's survival (6)

evolutionary psychology   a branch of psychology involved with explaining the development of the human mind and behaviour by studying how adaptive behaviours helped human ancestors survive and reproduce (73)

executive control function   an aspect of consciousness that helps people inhibit urges they have that are not moral, ethical, or practical; it equips people with the conscious self-awareness necessary to analyze and evaluate their thoughts before they act on those thoughts (138)

executive control systems   parts of the brain that inhibit pleasurable responses so that people can avoid making decisions that feel good but are bad for them (191)

exemplar theory   a theory that claims that people make category judgments by comparing new things they encounter with examples of other things they remember that fit into that category (186)

exogenous   directed by external stimuli (58)

exogenous attention   *see* **stimulus-driven capture**   (191)

experimental group   a group of participants in an experiment who are subject to an independent variable (22)

explanatory style   the way in which a person explains events to himself or herself (274)

explicit attitude   a belief or opinion that a person holds consciously and can report to others (208)

explicit memories   memories of which a person is consciously aware (173)

explicit stereotype   a stereotype that is consciously held (210)

exposure effect   an effect caused by the prior experience of a stimulus (123)

exposure treatment   a type of counterconditioning in which people who have a fear or phobia are repeatedly exposed to what they fear over several sessions until they become so accustomed to it that they no longer fear it (258)

expressive behaviour   an outward sign that a person is experiencing an emotion (122)

external environment   events and conditions in the outside world (69)

external genitalia   the penis and scrotum in males and the labia, clitoris, and external vagina in females (110)

external locus of control   a person's tendency to believe that his or her rewards and fate are controlled by outside forces (224)

external validity   a type of validity indicating that a test can be generalized to the rest of the population (28)

extinction   the gradual elimination of a learned response that occurs when an unconditioned stimulus is taken away (152)

extrinsic motivation   the desire to complete a behaviour because it will lead to a reward or avoid punishment (153)

extrinsic reward   a reward that is achieved through the completion of a task (129)

eye movement desensitization and reprocessing (EMDR)   a form of exposure therapy in which therapists instruct clients to focus on a disturbing image or traumatic memory as they move their eyes back and forth, with the goal of helping them deal with the psychological issues brought on by the disturbing or traumatic event (259)

face validity   the extent to which a study superficially measures what it is intended to measure (28)

facial feedback hypothesis   a hypothesis that states that a person who makes a certain facial expression will feel the corresponding emotion, as long as the person is not feeling some other competing emotion (126)

fact   an objective statement made using direct observations (21)

factor analysis   a statistical technique that is used to identify patterns of correlations in responses to questionnaires (219)

false consensus effect   a person's tendency to overestimate the extent to which others share his or her beliefs and behaviours (18)

family resemblance theory   a theory that suggests that people put items in categories together if they share certain characteristics, even if not every member of the category has similar features (186)

family therapy   a type of therapy in which the therapist views the family as a single unit and attempts to resolve conflicts and stresses that arise among the family members (256)

feature detector   a specialized brain cell that only responds to particular elements in the visual field (52)

feature integration theory   a theory that states that people organize stimuli based on knowledge of how their features should be combined (62, 192)

feel-good, do-good phenomenon   the idea that if a person is already happy, he or she is more likely to be helpful (127)

Fetal Alcohol Effects (FAE)   milder mental and cognitive impairments caused by a mother's drinking of alcohol during pregnancy (83)

Fetal Alcohol Spectrum Disorder (FASD)   a continuum of physical and cognitive abnormalities that occur in utero when a mother drinks alcohol during pregnancy; FASD includes fetal alcohol syndrome and fetal alcohol effects (83)

Fetal Alcohol Syndrome (FAS)   the more serious pattern of mental and physical birth defects that results from a mother's heavy drinking of alcohol during pregnancy (83)

field study   a study that is conducted in a setting other than a laboratory (24)

fight-or-flight response   a physiological response to stressors, triggered by the amygdala, in which the body becomes prepared for action (41, 267)

figure   the object on which a person is focusing (61)

filter theory   a theory that states that a person selects stimuli early in the perception process, even before he or she assesses the meaning of the input (192)

five-factor model ("Big Five" theory)   a model used to describe personality by assessing a person's score on each of five dimensions: extraversion/introversion, agreeableness/ antagonism, conscientiousness/undirectedness, emotional stability/instability, and openness to experience/ non-openness (219)

flashbulb memories   memories that are immediately stored in long-term memory and that are caused by emotional events (175)

flooding   a type of exposure treatment in which clients are exposed to fear-inducing stimuli in an intense way by directly exposing them to the stimuli (259)

fluid intelligence the ability to process information and act accordingly (185)

foot-in-the-door technique a technique that involves asking people to comply with a small request and then making a much larger request, to raise funds (206)

foramen magnum the largest opening in the skull; allows the spinal cord to connect to the brain (39)

forgetting the inability to retrieve information that has been previously stored (168)

forgetting curve a graphical representation of how quickly a person tends to forget information (176)

fovea a depressed spot in the retina that occupies the centre of a person's visual field (52)

framing the perspective from which people interpret information before making a decision (190)

free association a psychoanalytic technique in which the therapist encourages the client to relax his or her mind and, starting from a recent experience, a memory, or a dream, report every image or idea that enters awareness, refraining from logic or self-editing (254)

freezing a defensive reaction in which an organism remains motionless (162)

frequency the number of cycles per second in a wave (54)

frequency distribution a summary of how frequently each of the scores in a set of data occurs (27)

frontal lobe a part of the brain that performs a variety of integration and management functions; it is involved in the encoding and storage of working and long-term memory and, to a lesser extent, in sensory memory processing (43, 168)

frustration-aggression hypothesis a hypothesis that states that frustration occurs when people feel blocked in obtaining their goals (213)

full consciousness a state of consciousness in which a person is aware of his or her own environment and also is aware of his or her mental state and is able to provide information about it (136)

functional fixedness a bias that limits a person's ability to think in unconventional ways (187)

functionalism a school of psychology focused on how organisms use their learning and perceptual abilities to function in their environment (4)

fundamental attribution error (FAE) a phenomenon in which people make an attribution based on character, even when they know that the behaviour is situational (200)

fusiform face area an area of the visual cortex that specifically responds to and recognizes faces (53, 203)

gametes reproductive cells in an organism (70)

ganglion cell one of several neurons that connect the bipolar neurons in the eyes to the brain (52)

gate-control theory a theory that states that a "neurological gate" in the spinal cord controls the transmission of pain messages to the brain (58)

gender a set of behaviours and characteristics that define individuals as boys and men or girls and women in society (110)

gender identity a person's sense of being a boy or girl, man or woman (111)

gender identity disorder a condition in which a person feels he or she was born with the body of the wrong sex (112)

gender roles expectations about the way men and women behave (113)

gender schema theory a theory that states that the process of gender differentiation begins at a very young age; as children develop schemas for other things around them, they also develop a schema for their gender and adjust their behaviour to align with it (113)

gender stereotype a widely held concept about a person or group of people that is based only on gender (113)

gender typed referring to boys and men who show traditionally masculine traits and behaviours, and girls and women who show traditionally feminine traits and behaviours (112)

gene complex a group of genes acting together (71)

general adaptation syndrome (GAS) a response to stress that consists of three stages: alarm, resistance, and exhaustion (267)

general intelligence (g) a common factor that underlies certain mental abilities (185)

generalization a process in which a learner reacts to a particular object or situation in the same way that he or she reacts to one that resembles that object or situation (152)

generalized anxiety disorder a type of anxiety disorder in which a person feels inexplicably and continually tense and uneasy (236)

genes sections of DNA that contain specific recipes to make proteins in the body (68)

genocide the systematic destruction of one group by another (213)

genome the complete set of instructions for making an organism (68)

genotype the entire set of genes inherited by an organism (69)

geon a simple three-dimensional shape that, with other geons, makes up all other objects (62)

Gestalt psychology a school of psychology centred on the belief that people naturally seek out patterns, or wholes, in the sensory information available to them (4)

gestalt therapy a type of humanistic therapy in which the therapist attempts to make the client feel whole by helping the client feel aware of and responsible for his or her thoughts, behaviours, experiences, and feelings (256)

glial cells (glia) cells that support neurons by, among other things, keeping neurons in place, creating myelin, and providing nutrition and insulation (34)

globus pallidus a part of the basal ganglia; it relays information from the caudate and putamen to the thalamus (40)

glucose blood sugar (130)

goal enhancement the drive to receive the awards that have been obtained in the past (160)

goal state a problem-solving state in which a person has all the information he or she needs (187)

goal-directed selection a type of attention in which a person makes an explicit choice to pay attention to something (191)

gonads the first sex organs to develop; these are identical in male and female fetuses for the first four weeks of prenatal development (110)

grammatical words words that provide structure (90)

grey matter a substance that makes up the cerebral cortex; it covers the cerebrum and cerebellum (42)

ground the environment surrounding the object of focus, or the figure (61)

group polarization a phenomenon in which the more members of a group discuss similar opinions, the more extreme their positions become (209)

group therapy a type of therapy that is led by a therapist and involves a group of clients experiencing psychological disorders (256)

groupthink a phenomenon in which group members' opinions become so uniform that all dissent becomes impossible (209)

gustatory sense the sense of taste (130)

gyri bulges in the cerebral cortex (42)

habituation decreased responsiveness to a stimulus after repeated exposure to that stimulus (86)

hallucination a false sensory perception that a person believes to be real (240)

hassle a minor nuisance that, when combined with other small problems, can create a stressful environment (268)

health psychology the psychologically based aspect of behavioural medicine (266)

hedonic motive a pleasurable incentive or reward for acting in a certain way (203)

hedonic principle a principle that states that people want to experience pleasure and avoid pain (128)

heritability the degree to which a trait is able to be passed on genetically (72, 221)

heterozygous having non-identical pairs of alleles (70)

heuristics informal rules that make the decision-making process quick and simple (188)

hierarchy a levelled or ranked organization of concept categories based on particular features (186)

hierarchy of needs a pyramidal structure that shows the five needs that must be satisfied for a person to achieve self-actualization (130, 224)

hindsight bias a person's erroneous belief that he or she knew something all along after an event has occurred (18, 188)

hippocampus a part of the brain involved in processing explicit memories, recognizing and recalling long-term memories, and conditioning (40, 175)

histogram a representation of a frequency distribution using rectangles in which the width of a rectangle represents an interval and the area of a rectangle is proportional to the corresponding frequency (27)

histrionic personality disorder a mental disorder characterized by a tendency to overreact to situations, excessive emotionality, and the use of manipulation to gain attention from others (242)

homeostasis a steady and balanced inner state (128)

homozygous having identical pairs of alleles (70)

hue a particular colour (54)

humanistic approach an approach to psychology based on the belief that people have free will and are able to control their own destinies (6)

humanistic theory a type of personality theory that emphasizes people's conscious understanding of themselves and their abilities to attain self-fulfillment (222)

hypercomplex cell a feature detector that responds to multiple features of a stimulus (53)

hypnagogia a period of transition between wakefulness and stage one sleep (138)

hypnopaedia learning while asleep (141)

hypnosis an exercise in suggestion during which one person makes suggestions to another person regarding the perceptions, feelings, thoughts, or behaviours that the subject can expect to experience (145)

hypnotic ability high susceptibility to hypnotism (145)

hypnotic analgesia pain relief through hypnosis (145)

hypochondriasis a disorder in which a person becomes so preoccupied with minor symptoms that he or she develops an exaggerated belief that the symptoms are indicative of a life-threatening illness (245)

hypocretin an alerting neurotransmitter that stimulates wakefulness (142)

hypomania a milder form of mania that causes less severe mood elevations and does not interfere with normal daily functioning to the same extent as mania (239)

hypothalamus a small structure in the brain that links the nervous system to the endocrine system (40)

hypothesis a prediction, based on an existing theory, about a new fact (21)

iconic memory a type of sensory memory involving visual stimuli (168)

id the part of the psyche that tries to satisfy a person's basic drives and survival instincts (221)

identity a person's sense of self (99)

ideocentrism a personality trait exhibiting the tendency to think and act in an individualistic manner (227)

idiographic approach a method of interpreting personality data that is person-centred and focuses on how the unique parts of a person's personality form a consistent whole (218)

illusory conjunction mistakenly combining features of two different stimuli (60, 62)

illusory contour a visual illusion in which lines are perceived without actually being present (60)

implicit attitude a belief or opinion that a person can't report and that will automatically influence his or her actions (208)

implicit memories memories of which a person is not consciously aware (173)

implicit stereotype an unconscious set of mental representations that guide attitudes and behaviours (210)

implosion therapy a type of exposure treatment in which clients are exposed to very intense stimuli by being asked to imagine an extreme version of their fears or phobias (259)

imprinting a process of early attachment in which the first thing a newborn sees is considered its mother (96)

inattentional blindness the failure to perceive a given stimulus (59)

incentive a positive or negative stimulus in the environment (129)

independent construal of self a person's view of himself or herself as a self-directed, self-contained entity (227)

independent variable a variable that a researcher can manipulate in an experiment (21)

individualist culture a culture that emphasizes each person's individual rights and freedoms and de-emphasizes the social roles that people play in relation to others (227)

inductive reasoning a method of using specific examples to arrive at a general conclusion (188)

infant reflexes a set of innate traits in humans (73)

inferential statistics statistics that use probability laws to help researchers decide how likely it is that their results are due to chance and, as a result, how likely it is that the observed results apply to a broader population (25)

inferiority complex a drive for perfection and superiority throughout adulthood in an effort to compensate for feelings of both physical and mental inferiority rooted in childhood (222)

informational social influence influence exerted by information that others give a person (204)

ingroup a group that a person is part of (211)

inhibition a process in which a neuron is instructed not to transmit information to other neurons (37)

initial state a problem-solving state in which a person has incomplete or unsatisfactory information (187)

insight the sudden realization of the solution to a problem (187)

insomnia a sleep disorder characterized by recurring difficulty falling or staying asleep (142)

instinct an unlearned complex behaviour with a fixed pattern throughout a species (128)

instinctual drift the tendency for an organism to revert to instinctive behaviours after being trained to have new behaviours (76, 153)

Institutional Review Board (IRB) an ethics review panel established by a publicly funded research institution to evaluate all proposed research by that institution (29)

insulin a hormone that reduces the level of glucose in the blood (130)

intelligence the capacity to reason, solve problems, and acquire new knowledge (183)

intensification an exaggeration of emotions (126)

interdependent construal of self a person's view of himself or herself as part of a larger network of family and community members (227)

internal locus of control a person's tendency to believe that he or she controls his or her own rewards and fate (224)

internal validity a type of validity indicating that a researcher is able to control all extraneous values in a test so that the only variable influencing the results of the study is the independent variable (28)

interneurons neurons that carry information between sensory neurons and motor neurons (34)

interpersonal psychotherapy a type of psychotherapy that focuses on helping clients improve their relationships, particularly their current relationships, as a means to resolving their psychological problems (255)

intersex referring to people who are born with non-standard male or female genitalia (111)

interview a form of data collection in which people provide oral descriptions of themselves; this can be strictly structured, with a set list of questions, or loosely structured and more conversational (24)

intrinsic reward a task that is pleasurable in and of itself (129)

intrinsically motivated characterized by the desire to do things because they are interesting, challenging, satisfying, or enjoyable (153)

ipsilateral describes a situation in which one side of something controls the same side of something else (43)

James-Lange theory a theory that proposes that the physiological experience of heart pounding or tears flowing causes a person to feel afraid or sad (122)

joint visual attention a behaviour in which a baby looks at an adult's eyes, follows the adult's gaze, and then directs his or her own gaze toward whatever the adult is looking at (89)

judgment a skill that allows people to form opinions, reach conclusions, and evaluate situations objectively and critically (190)

just noticeable difference (jnd) *see* **difference threshold** (50)

just-world phenomenon a phenomenon in which people convince themselves that they are doing well because they are good people, while those who are suffering are just getting what they deserve (211)

K-complex a biphasic wave form that occurs spontaneously during sleep (138)

kinesthetic sense the sense relating to how a person's body parts interact with one another (57)

laboratory observation the study of people or animals in a controlled setting (23)

laboratory study a study in which participants are taken to a location that has been specifically set up to facilitate collection of data and allow control over environmental conditions (24)

language acquisition device (LAD) a theoretical mechanism that provides children with an inherent foundation for the principles of universal grammar (90)

language-acquisition support system (LASS) the social environment into which a baby is born (90)

latent content the unconscious meaning of a dream (145, 255)

latent learning learning that is exhibited only in the presence of an incentive (153)

law of common fate a law that states that if the parts of a stimulus are all moving in the same direction, they are perceived as parts of a whole (61)

law of effect a law that states that if a response produces a satisfying effect, it is likely to occur again (157)

law of pragnanz a law that states that a person organizes a stimulus into the simplest possible form (61)

learned helplessness a feeling of hopelessness and passivity caused by being unable to avoid or control traumatic events (240, 226)

learning the process by which experience results in a relatively permanent change in future behaviour (152)

learning-performance distinction the difference between what a person learns and its application on that particular day (152)

letter/digit colour synaesthesia a condition in which seeing, hearing, or even thinking about a letter or digit creates a visual experience of a specific colour (63)

levels of analysis various ways that psychologists can look at a psychological issue, such as from the level of the brain, the level of the person, and the level of the world (6)

lexical ambiguity confusion caused by multiple meanings of a word or phrase (195)

liking a subjective feeling of pleasure derived from a reward (129)

liking system a system involved with experiencing pleasure; it does not depend on dopamine (129)

limbic system a system in the brain made up of a number of structures that control social and emotional behaviour; it influences cognitive processes, most notably forms of memory (39, 00)

linguistic determinism the belief that different languages impose different conceptions of reality (195)

linguistic relativity hypothesis a hypothesis that states that the language a person speaks influences his or her conception of reality (195)

locus of control a person's perception of whether he or she has control over a given situation (224)

longitudinal studies studies that collect data from the same individuals over a period of time to track age changes (83)

long-term memory a type of memory in which information that can last a lifetime is stored (168)

long-term potentiation (LTP) the process in which neural connections are strengthened through the repetition of neurotransmitters travelling across the same synapses (160, 175)

lowball technique a technique that encourages compliance by offering an attractive deal, only to change the terms of the deal later (206)

lucid dreaming a phenomenon in which a person achieves an awareness of a dream as a dream while dreaming (143)

lymphocyte a type of white blood cell (270)

major depressive disorder (MDD) a mood disorder characterized by signs of severe depression that last for more than two weeks with no apparent cause (239)

male answer syndrome a phenomenon in which males are more likely than females to guess at answers to difficult questions rather than reveal their uncertainty (117)

mania a period of euphoria characterized by elevated self-esteem, increased talkativeness, enhanced energy, and a decreased need for sleep (239)

manifest content what a person explicitly remembers about a dream—its storyline, characters, and details (143, 255)

masking showing one emotion while feeling another (126)

matched pair a set of participants in an experiment, one from one group and the other from another group, who are identical in terms of a particular variable or set of variables (22)

matched sample a group of participants in an experiment that is identical to at least one other group in terms of a particular variable or set of variables (22)

mean the arithmetic average of the scores in a data set, or the sum of all the scores divided by the number of scores (25)

measures of central tendency the three most typical scores in a set of data: mean, median, and mode (25)

medial forebrain bundle the brain's reward pathway (129)

median the middle score in a data set (25)

medical model the concept that psychological abnormalities are diseases that, like biological diseases, have symptoms, causes, and cures (234)

medulla a part of the brain that regulates cardiac and respiratory function (39)

meiosis the process of cell division that results in gamete cells; the process is similar to mitosis but the resulting cells have half the number of chromosomes of the original cell (70)

melatonin a sleep-inducing hormone (138)

memory the brain's system for filing away new information and retrieving previously known data (168)

menarche a girl's first menstruation (84)

Mendelian heredity the idea that units of heredity come in pairs and one pair can dominate another (69)

menopause the end of a woman's menstrual cycle and ability to bear children (84)

mental age the level of ability typical of a child of the same chronological age (183)

mental set a pre-existing state of mind that a person uses to solve problems because that state has helped the person solve similar problems in the past (187)

mentalizing a person's understanding that his or her behaviour and that of others reflects a person's mental states (203)

mere exposure simple contact between two individuals or groups (211)

method a rule or technique that provides a framework for observations (18)

microvillus a tiny hair at the tip of a taste receptor cell (57)

midcingulate cortex part of the cingulate cortex; it is primarily involved in response selection (41)

minimal consciousness a relatively fragmented connection between self and environment in which a person might respond to a stimulus without being aware of it at a more thoughtful level (136)

Minnesota Multiphasic Personality Inventory (MMPI) the most widely used personality inventory, initially developed to identify emotional disorders but now used for a variety of other purposes (220)

minority influence the power of a few people (209)

mirror neuron a neuron that responds both when an organism performs a task and when it watches another organism perform the same task (162)

misattribution assigning the incorrect meaning to an emotion because of a particular physiological response (123)

mitosis the process of cell division in which chromosomes duplicate themselves before the cell divides, creating two cells genetically identical to the original (71)

mnemonics memory aids that give rhyme and reason to lists or other pieces of information (175)

mode the most frequently occurring score in a data set (25)

modelling the ability to reproduce an action that is being observed (160)

molecular genetics a field of study emphasizing the analysis of the molecular structure and function of genes to try to identify the specific genes responsible for a certain disease, trait, or behaviour (72)

monozygotic twins twins that come from a single zygote that divides and separates (70)

mood a free-floating emotional feeling that does not relate directly to a stimulus (122)

mood disorder a mental disorder in which a person regularly experiences emotional extremes (239)

mood-congruent processing the selective perception of stimuli congruent with the emotional state of the person experiencing the stimuli (126)

morphemes the smallest meaningful units of language that represent the objects, events, ideas, characteristics, and relationships in that language's vocabulary (90)

morphology how morphemes may be arranged to form words; the form or shape of something (90, 126)

motivation a need or desire that energizes and directs behaviour (128)

motivation state one of many internal conditions that make a person tend toward certain goals (128)

motor development the emergent ability to execute physical actions (83)

motor neurons neurons that carry information away from the central nervous system to operate muscles and glands (34)

Müllerian system   the precursor of female sex organs (110)

multi-tasking   the act of juggling independent sensory inputs (59)

myelin   a fatty substance that coats and insulates axons (34)

narcissistic personality disorder   a mental disorder characterized by an inflated sense of self-importance and a deep need for admiration (242)

narcolepsy   a sleep disorder characterized by periodic, uncontrollable sleep attacks (142)

natural selection   a theory that states that organisms best adapted to their environment tend to survive and transmit their genetic characteristics to succeeding generations (8, 68)

naturalistic fallacy   the claim that whatever is natural is good or right (77)

naturalistic observation   the study of people or animals in their own environment (23)

nature   inherited characteristics that influence personality, physical growth, intellectual growth, and social interactions (8)

negative cognitive style   a pattern of pessimistic or negative thoughts (239)

negative reinforcer   something that strengthens a response by removing an unpleasant consequence (157)

negative symptom   a symptom that indicates a decrease in normal functions such as attention or emotion (240)

neocortex   the evolutionarily newest part of the brain; it enables symbolic representation (39)

nerve   a tight grouping of neurons (34)

network   a large community of neurons (34)

neurons   excitable cells that receive different types of stimulation; they are the building blocks of the nervous system (34)

neuropathic pain   a negative feeling caused by a malfunction in the central nervous system (57)

neurotransmitter   a chemical message created by a synapse from an electric message transmitted by terminal buttons (37)

neutralizing   showing no emotion, even though the person is actually feeling one (126)

night terrors   a relatively benign, albeit disturbing, sleep disorder most common in young children and characterized by episodes of high arousal and terrified appearance (142)

nociceptive pain   a negative feeling caused by an external stimulus (57)

nodes of Ranvier   parts of an axon that are not insulated by myelin (37)

nomothetic approach   a method of interpreting personality data that is variable-centred and focuses on finding consistent patterns of relationships among individuals' traits (218)

nonconscious activity   a process that occurs in the body that people do not have to consciously monitor or regulate (136)

non-regulatory drives   drives that initiate activities not required to preserve homeostasis (128)

nonsomniac   a person who requires much less than eight hours of sleep each day (141, 000)

Norm of reciprocity   a socialized norm that involves a person's tendency to desire to return favours (206)

normal curve   a graphical representation of an evenly distributed data set in which the curve is symmetrical and bell-shaped due to the even distribution of results and the tendency of data to accumulate around the centre of a set in an even distribution (27)

normal distribution   an instance of frequency distribution in which scores are tracked on a bell-shaped curve with a concentration of data in the centre (183)

normative investigations   research conducted in order to establish norms (83)

normative social influence   influence that draws on a person's desire for others' approval and his or her longing to be part of a group (204)

nucleus accumbens   an area of the brain underneath the frontal cortex that is involved in experiencing pleasure (124)

number-form synaesthesia   a condition in which a person experiences numbers in complex spatial arrangements (63)

nurture   environmental factors such as parental styles, physical surroundings, and economic issues (8)

observational learning   a learning process in which a person observes and imitates others (160)

observational method   the process of observing and recording a subject's behaviour (25)

observer bias   the effect that occurs when an observer expects to see a particular behaviour and notices only actions that support that expectation (23)

observer-expectancy effect   see **observer bias**   (29)

obsessive-compulsive disorder   an anxiety disorder in which a person feels driven to think disturbing thoughts or to perform senseless rituals (236)

obsessive-compulsive personality disorder   a mental disorder characterized by obsessive neatness, difficulty delegating tasks because of a fear the tasks will be completed in a substandard manner, and a preoccupation with rules, schedules, and order (244)

occipital lobes   parts of the brain involved in visual processing; it is the smallest of the four lobes in the human brain (42)

occupational self-direction   a set of desirable characteristics for an occupation comprising work that is complex rather than simple, varied rather than routine, and not closely supervised by another (102)

operant behaviour   responses that an organism makes to produce an effect on the environment (157)

operant conditioning   a type of learning in which organisms associate their actions with consequences (156)

operant response   an act that causes a particular effect on the environment (157)

opportunism   the necessity of rapid speech production (195)

optic chasm   the point near the base of the brain where some fibres in the optic nerve from each eye cross to the opposite side of the brain (52)

optic nerve   a bundle of axons of ganglion cells that carries neural messages from each eye to the brain (52)

optimal arousal   an arousal state in which a person has enough motivation but not so much that he or she feels anxious and unable to perform (129)

orexin   a hormone that brings on feelings of hunger (130)

outcome expectancy   a person's assumption about the consequences of his or her own behaviour (226)

outgroup   a group containing those people outside one's own group (211)

ova   immature eggs (83)

overconfidence   a person's tendency to think that he or she is more knowledgeable or accurate than he or she really is (188)

overextended referring to the relatively broad use of common nouns (90)

overjustification the undermining of intrinsic motivation through excessive rewards (153)

panic disorder a condition in which sufferers come to fear the possibility of another panic attack following an initial attack (236)

papilla a bump on the tongue in which taste buds are embedded (57)

parallel processing the process of doing several things at the same time (53)

paranoid personality disorder a mental disorder characterized by extreme suspicion and distrust of others (242)

parasympathetic division *see* **parasympathetic nervous system** (124)

parasympathetic nervous system the part of the autonomic nervous system that is responsible for functions that do not require immediate action and acts as a brake for organs (34)

parental investment the time, energy, and risk involved in producing and raising offspring (76)

parietal cortex an area of the brain that serves as an executive control system that plays a critical role in directing a person's attention during the decision-making process (191)

parietal lobes parts of the brain primarily concerned with bodily sensations, including those of touch, taste, and temperature (42)

partial (intermittent) reinforcement a method of reinforcement in which responses are sometimes reinforced and sometimes not (157)

participant a person who takes part in an experiment as a subject (21)

patient a person with a psychological disorder who is being treated using a biomedical approach (250)

patrolling periodically scanning an environment to make sure that nothing in the environment has changed (160)

perception the way a person selects, organizes, and interprets sensory information (50)

perceptual adaptation a process in which a person adjusts to changes in the environment by adjusting sensory input (63)

perceptual load the processing difficulty or complexity of a task (191)

perceptual set a mental disposition based on previous experiences and expectations that influences the way a person perceives things (60)

perceptual speed the time it takes a person to perceive and compare stimuli (186)

peripheral nervous system (PNS) the part of the nervous system that serves the limbs and organs (34)

peripheral route a path to persuasion that involves evaluating an argument based on tangential cues rather than on the argument's merits (208)

perpetuating cause a consequence of a disorder that helps keep it going once it has manifested (235)

perseverance effect a phenomenon in which it is difficult for people to shake their initial impressions (208)

personal control a person's sense of controlling his or her environment rather than feeling helpless (224)

personality the style in which a person interacts with the world, particularly with other people (218)

personality disorder a rigid, maladaptive pattern of behaviour that makes it difficult for individuals to have normal social relationships (242)

Personality inventory a long, scientifically rigorous questionnaire that asks questions about many different behaviours and assesses several traits at once (220)

person-centred therapy a type of humanistic therapy in which the therapeutic process focuses squarely on the client's abilities and insights rather than the therapist's thoughts and skills (256)

person-situation controversy the question of whether people's behaviours are more influenced by situational factors than by personality traits (221)

persuasion a deliberate effort to change an attitude or behaviour (208)

phenomenology the study of individual consciousness that addresses subjective experience (136)

phenotype the observable property that comes from a genotype (69)

pheromone a chemical substance released by an animal to trigger sexual arousal, aggression, or territorial behaviour in other members of that species (57)

phobia a persistent, irrational fear of a specific object, activity, or situation (236)

phonemes elementary vowel and consonant sounds that combine to form morphemes (90)

phonology how phonemes may be arranged to produce morphemes (90)

phylogeny the development of a species (75)

physical drug dependence compulsive drug use that leads to the development of tolerance and withdrawal symptoms (146)

physiological arousal a heightened bodily reaction to a stimulus (122)

physiological need a need that affects a person's physiology, such as hunger and thirst (130)

pituitary gland a gland that secretes human growth hormone and influences all other hormone-secreting glands (41)

placebo a substance or procedure that resembles medical therapy but has no intrinsic therapeutic value (29)

placebo effect a phenomenon in which participants taking a placebo react as if they were receiving treatment, simply because they believe they are actually receiving treatment (29)

planning function *see* **executive control function** (138)

plasticity a flexible ability to grow and change (37, 186)

pleasure principle a principle that states that a person should seek immediate gratification and pay no attention to societal expectations or constraints (221)

polygenic coming from the interaction of several genes (71)

pons a part of the brain that is involved in sleep, dreaming, left-right body coordination, and arousal (39)

pop-out stimulus a stimulus that is important or interesting to a person (59)

positive reinforcer something that strengthens a response by presenting a pleasurable consequence (157)

positive symptom a symptom that reflects an excess or distortion of normal functions, such as delusions and hallucinations (240)

posterior cingulate cortex part of the cingulate cortex; it is primarily involved in personal orientation (41)

post-hypnotic suggestion a suggestion made during hypnosis that is executed by the participant when he or she is no longer hypnotized (145)

post-synaptic neuron a neuron that receives a signal from a synapse (37)

post-traumatic stress disorder an anxiety disorder caused by experiencing or witnessing out-of-control events with feelings of helplessness and fear (239)

practical intelligence the ability to find many solutions to complicated or poorly defined problems and use those solutions in practical, everyday situations (185)

practical reasoning a type of reasoning in which a person considers what to do or how to act (188)

preattentive processing a complex processing of information that occurs without a person's conscious awareness (59)

precipitating cause an event in a person's day-to-day life that brings on a particular disorder (235)

preconscious information information that is usually outside a person's awareness but is able to be brought into consciousness on demand (136)

predictive validity a type of criterion validity in which you can use the results of a test to predict a person's score or performance in another area (28)

predisposing cause an existing underlying factor that makes an individual particularly susceptible to a certain disorder (235)

pre-existing schema a set of ideas or beliefs about others that leads a person to perceive others in a way that conforms with that person's expectations (201)

prefrontal cortex the very front of the brain and part of the neocortex; it is responsible for the executive functions, such as mediating conflicting thoughts and making choices between right and wrong; it is essential for the cognitive experience of emotion (39, 124)

prefrontal lobotomy a type of surgery in which the prefrontal area of the brain is disabled, causing people to feel less intense emotions but also leaving them unable to plan or manage their lives (124)

Premack principle a principle that states that a preferred activity can be used to reinforce a non-preferred task (158)

preservation and protection theory a theory that explains sleep as a mechanism evolved to preserve energy and provide protection during the night (141)

pre-synaptic neuron a neuron that delivers a signal to a synapse (37)

primacy effect the ability to recall information given first when given a list of things to remember (171)

primary appraisal a person's initial evaluation of the seriousness of a stressor and the extent of the demands it will put on that person (272)

primary auditory cortex a part of the brain involved in auditory processing (42)

primary cortex a part of the cerebral cortex that serves basic sensory and motor functions; one exists in each lobe of the cerebral cortex (42)

primary motor cortex a part of the brain that is responsible for generating the neural impulses that control the execution of movements (43)

primary reinforcer something that satisfies a basic biological need (157)

primary sex characteristics sexual organs present at birth and directly involved in human reproduction (84, 110)

primary somatosensory cortex a part of the brain that receives and interprets information about bodily sensations; it is located in the parietal lobe (43)

primary visual cortex a part of the brain that receives input from the eyes and translates that input into what people see (42)

priming the process of activating associations in memory just before starting a certain task (173)

principlism a desire to engage in prosocial behaviour out of principle (213)

proactive interference a phenomenon in which previously learned information interferes with a person's ability to recall new information (176)

problem of other minds the observation that because the nature of consciousness is internal, a person can't possibly determine how similar or different another person's perceptions are to his or her own (136)

problem solving the act of combining current information with information stored in memory to find a solution to a task (187)

problem-focused coping a coping strategy that involves a person's attempting to alleviate stress directly, either by eliminating the source of a stressor or by changing the way he or she behaves in stressful situations (272)

procedural memory a type of implicit memory consisting of habits and skills people perform (173)

prognosis a prediction of the typical course of a disease and the likelihood of recovery (233)

projector a person who actually sees letters as being certain colours, even though he or she knows what colour the type actually is (63)

proprioceptor a specialized nerve ending that provides a constant stream of information from a person's muscles through the spinal cord and on to the cortex of the parietal lobe (58)

prosocial positive and helpful (160)

prosocial behaviour behaviour carried out with the goal of helping others (213)

prosopagnosia a condition caused by damage to the ventral region of the temporal lobe in which a person is unable to recognize faces (203)

prospect theory a theory that states that people will more likely avoid risk in situations where they stand to gain but will seek risk when they stand to lose something (190)

prospective memory remembering to perform a specific action (90)

prototype a mental image or typical example that exhibits all the features associated with a concept (186)

proximal stimulus a pattern of physical energy created by the distal stimulus that stimulates a person's receptors (62)

proximity the tendency to perceive objects that are close to one another as part of the same group (61)

proximodistal rule the tendency for motor skills to emerge in sequence from inside to outside (84)

pseudoforgetting a type of encoding interference in which information is never actually stored because of some kind of attention interference (173)

psychic determinism the concept that unconscious processes underlie all conscious thoughts and actions (221)

psychoactive medication a type of drug that alleviates symptoms of mental disorders by acting on the bodily processes that may cause those symptoms (252)

psychoactive substances drugs that alter our consciousness (146)

psychoanalysis a type of psychotherapy that relates closely to Freudian concepts like the influence of the unconscious; it requires patients to talk to a psychiatrist about their lives while the psychiatrist listens, analyzes, and interprets each word (221, 254)

psychoanalytic approach a method of analyzing a psychological disorder in which unconscious conflicts and other possible underlying psychological factors are examined (235)

psychodynamic approach an approach to psychology based on the belief that behaviours are motivated by internal factors unavailable to the conscious mind (6)

psychodynamic theory a personality theory that focuses on the interaction of mental forces (221)

psychodynamic therapy a type of therapy based on Freudian psychodynamics, the theory of which states that unconscious conflicts underlie mental disorders, and these conflicts make their way to the surface through a person's speech and behaviour (254)

psychological diagnosis a label for a person's mental disorder assigned by identifying and classifying patterns of behaviour (233)

psychological drug dependence the cravings for a drug's pleasurable effects; this type of dependence is harder to overcome and can lead to a relapse (146)

psychological refractory period the interval during which the brain is too busy processing a stimulus to comprehend a second stimulus (192)

psychology the scientific study of behaviour and mental processes (4)

psychoneuroimmunology the study of how psychology relates to events involving the nervous system and immune system (156)

psychopathology *see* **abnormal psychology** (233)

psychopharmacology the study of how drugs affect the mind and behaviour (252)

psychophysics the study of the relationship between physical characteristics of stimuli and the sensory experiences that accompany them (50)

psychophysiological ("mind-body") illness a symptom such as chronic fatigue or hypertension that is caused by psychological reactions to stress (270)

psychosurgery a treatment method in which parts of the brain are surgically altered to treat mental disorders (254)

psychotherapy the interaction between a therapist and someone suffering from a psychological problem, the goal of which is to provide support or relief from the problem (254)

puberty the period in which a person's body goes through the changes that allow him or her to reproduce (84)

punishment a penalty given in an attempt to decrease the occurrence of a certain behaviour (158)

putamen a part of the basal ganglia; it is involved in reinforcement learning (40)

Pygmalion effect the tendency for people to behave in accordance with others' expectations (201)

questionnaire a series of questions with a strict purpose that has been developed using careful controls such as precise wording, carefully constructed questions, and random sampling (24)

random assignment the process by which participants in an experiment are randomly placed into groups (22)

random sampling a technique in which the participants in a survey are chosen randomly so as to get a fair representation of a population (24)

range the difference between the highest and lowest values in a data set (25)

rapid cycling an incidence of a person with bipolar disorder experiencing more than four episodes of either mania or depression a year (239)

rapid eye movement (REM) sleep a recurring stage of sleep during which vivid dreams usually occur (138)

rational choice theory a theory that states that people make decisions by determining how likely each outcome of that decision is, as well as the positive or negative value of each outcome (190)

rational coping a coping strategy that involves facing a stressor directly and working to overcome it (272)

reality principle a principle that states that basic drives and survival instincts should be achieved through actions that will be pleasurable rather than painful (222)

reason the skill of organizing information and beliefs into a series of steps leading to a conclusion (89)

reasoning a cognitive process of organizing information or beliefs into a series of steps to reach conclusions (187)

recall the process of retrieving a stored memory in the absence of external stimuli (175)

recency effect the ability to recall information most recently stored when given a list of things to remember (171)

receptor cell a specialized cell that responds to a particular type of energy (51)

recessive being suppressed by the dominant gene in a pair of alleles (70)

reciprocal altruism a theory that suggests that people may carry out altruistic acts with the expectation of being the recipient of altruism at some point in the future or because they have been helped by altruism sometime in the past (213)

reciprocal determinism a theory that states that a person's behaviour is both influenced by and influences a person's personal factors (226)

recognition the process of matching an external stimulus to a stored memory (175)

recognition-by-components theory a theory that states that a person recognizes an unfamiliar object by piecing together the cylinder, cone, wedge, and brick shapes of which it is composed (62)

reference group those people to whom a person feels affiliated (206)

referred pain a negative feeling that occurs when sensory information from internal and external areas converges on the same nerve cells in the spinal cord (57)

reflexes rapid and automatic neuromuscular actions generated in response to a specific stimulus (39)

reframing a coping strategy that involves finding a new or creative way to think about a stressor that reduces its threat (272)

regulatory drives drives that seek to preserve homeostasis (128)

reinforcement an act that causes a response to be more likely to recur (129, 157)

reinforcer/punisher a positive or negative consequence caused by an operant response (157)

relational memory theory a theory that states that the hippocampus processes events by linking them into relational frameworks (162)

relative deprivation a person's comparison of himself or herself to others; when the person compares himself or herself to someone of higher social standing, he or she feels worse, and when the person compares himself or herself to someone of lower social standing, he or she feels better (128)

relaxation response reduced muscle tension, cortical activity, heart rate, breathing rate, and blood pressure (276)

relaxation therapy a therapeutic technique that involves alternately tensing and relaxing muscles in the body and practising breathing exercises in order to relieve tension (276)

reliability the degree to which a measurement yields similar results every time it is used with a particular subject under particular conditions (27)

REM sleep the stage of sleep characterized by rapid eye movements (138)

repressive coping a coping strategy that involves maintaining an artificially positive viewpoint and trying not to think about a stressor (272)

resistance a client's attempt to avoid doing therapeutic work (255)

resting potential a relatively negative state inside a neuron in which the neuron's fluid interior contains a surplus of negatively charged particles (37)

restrictive function an aspect of consciousness that allows people to exercise selective attention, or a conscious focus on one stimulus or perception at a given time (137)

reticular formation a part of the brain that controls arousal (219)

retina a multi-layered tissue at the back of the eye that is responsible for visual transduction (52)

retrieval the process by which previously stored information is moved from long-term memory to working memory (168)

retrieval cue a stimulus that helps a person retrieve information from memory (175)

retroactive interference a phenomenon in which new information interferes with a person's ability to recall previously learned information (176)

retrograde amnesia memory loss characterized by the loss of past memories (177)

retrosplenial cortex part of the cingulate cortex; it is primarily involved in memory formation and retrieval (41)

reuptake a process in which neurotransmitters are released back to a pre-synaptic neuron (37)

reversible figure an illusion in which staring at an image long enough causes the figure and ground to reverse (61)

reward contrast effect a sudden shift in the attractiveness of a reward (158)

reward neuron a neuron involved with experiencing the positive emotions associated with receiving a reward (129)

Ribot's law a law that states that memory loss following brain damage affects recent memories to a greater extent than remote memories (162)

rod a photoreceptor cell in the retina that responds to varying degrees of light and dark (52)

Rorschach inkblot test a test that presents a participant with a series of nebulous inkblots and asks him or her to say whatever comes to mind upon viewing the inkblots; interpretations of the inkblots supposedly are related to the viewer's unconscious thoughts (222)

rote (or maintenance) rehearsal the process of repeating information, either out loud or silently, with the intent of learning that information (171)

safety a feeling of being in a secure and safe environment (130)

saturation the intensity of a colour (54)

savings the ability to reacquire a learned behaviour in a shorter period of time than it took to learn originally (152)

Schachter and Singer two-factor theory a theory that states that cognitive evaluation happens alongside a person's physiological arousal to create the emotion he or she experiences (123)

Schachter's cognition-plus-feedback theory a theory that states that how a person perceives an environment feeds back into physiological arousal and influences what the person feels (123)

schemas concepts or frameworks around which people organize and interpret information (86)

schizoid personality disorder a mental disorder that causes people to show very little interest in others and have few personal relationships (242)

schizophrenia a mental disorder that causes a person to experience distorted perceptions, inappropriate emotions or reactions, and confusion (240)

schizotypal personality disorder a mental disorder characterized by peculiar or eccentric mannerisms and difficulty forming social relationships (242)

seasonal affective disorder (SAD) a mood disorder in which a person gets depressed only at certain times of the year (239)

secondary appraisal a person's reassessment of a stressor that focuses on the actions he or she needs to take and the resources that will help him or her overcome the stressor (272)

secondary reinforcer something that becomes satisfying or pleasurable through experience (157)

secondary sex characteristics sexual organs and traits that develop at puberty and are not directly involved in reproduction (84, 110)

second-order conditioning a type of classical conditioning in which the conditioned stimulus is paired with a neutral stimulus (154)

secure relationship an intimate relationship in which both partners provide each other with comfort and security (101)

selective breeding the process by which pairs of organisms of the same species with desirable characteristics are mated in order to select for those characteristics (71)

selective storage function an aspect of consciousness that allows people to selectively analyze, interpret, and act on stimuli (137)

self theory a personality theory that states that all people want to become their "real" selves; to do so, people need to live according to their own wishes rather than those of other people (222)

self-actualization a complete feeling of self-acceptance and an awareness of fulfilling one's unique potential (130)

self-concept a person's understanding of who he or she is (222)

self-conscious emotion an emotion that relates to a person's thoughts about himself or herself and about his or her own actions (209)

self-consciousness the most self-aware state of consciousness; it allows a person to focus on his or her individual self (136)

self-efficacy a person's expectations about his or her own ability to perform a certain task (226)

self-fulfilling prophecy a belief that causes itself to become true (201)

self-regulation the process of practising self-discipline (99)

self-report method a form of data collection in which people are asked to describe their own behaviour or mental state (24)

self-serving bias the tendency for a person to attribute his or her failures to external events and his or her successes to personal characteristics and skills (201)

semantic containing factual and conceptual information that is not directly linked to life events (173)

semantic encoding the process of encoding meaning (170)

semicircular canal a tube located in the inner ear that helps to monitor the body's position in space (58)

sensation the process through which we detect physical energy from the environment and code that energy as neural signals (50)

sensory adaptation a process in which sensory receptor cells become less responsive to an unchanging stimulus (51)

sensory buffer part of the perceptual system that holds information for a short time before it is accepted or rejected by a filter (192)

sensory cortex the part of the brain that mediates the human sense of touch by encoding sensual information (168)

sensory memory a type of memory lasting no more than a few seconds in which the impression of a sensory stimulus is stored (168)

sensory neuron a neuron that carries information from the sensory receptors to the brain as a coded signal (34, 51)

sensory registers the parts of the brain that make up sensory memory (168)

sensory system the part of the nervous system responsible for processing sensory information (50)

serial position effect the ability to recall (or not recall) information in a list depending on that information's position in the list (171)

set of operations the steps that a person needs to take to get from the initial state to the goal state (187)

sex a person's biological classification as either male or female based on the sex chromosomes contained in his or her DNA (110)

sexism prejudice and unfair treatment against men or women based on gender stereotypes (114)

sexual orientation enduring sexual attraction toward members of our own sex, the other sex, or both (117)

sexual selection the process by which a mate is chosen (71)

shaping a process in which reinforcers are used to guide an organism's actions toward a desired behaviour (159)

shared identity a person's feeling that he or she is similar to other people in thought, feeling, and behaviour (206)

signal detection theory a theory that predicts how and when we detect the presence of a faint stimulus amid background stimulation (50)

similarity the tendency to perceive objects that are the same shape, size, or colour as part of a pattern (61)

simple cell a feature detector that only responds to a single feature of a stimulus (52)

simultaneous conditioning a type of classical conditioning in which the conditioned stimulus and unconditioned stimulus are presented at the same time (154)

situational attribution an attribution based on a person's situation or environment (200)

Situational Attribution Training a new technique designed to reduce our attribution biases by teaching us to focus on situational rather than dispositional explanations for the behaviours of others (200)

situational force an external factor involved in motivation (128)

skewed distribution a graphical representation of an unevenly distributed data set in which scores cluster together on one end rather than in the middle (27)

skin sense the sense relating to pressure, touch, and pain (57)

sleep a natural loss of consciousness (138)

sleep apnea a sleep disorder in which people intermittently stop breathing during sleep, which in turn causes the level of oxygen in the blood to plummet (142)

sleep spindle a burst of fast, sharply pointed brainwaves (138)

sleeper effect a phenomenon that occurs when a person forgets the unreliable source of a piece of information but remembers the information itself and believes that it's trustworthy (209)

social age a person's maturity level based on his or her life experiences (101)

social cognition underlying processes, such as attention and memory, that make social behaviour possible (203)

social cognitive theory a type of personality theory that places emphasis on the beliefs and habits of thought, both conscious and automatic, that a person forms through interactions with society (226)

social Darwinism a theory that states that society and culture evolved toward higher forms through the process of individuals adapting to hardship by either adapting and surviving or falling by the wayside (77)

social influence behavioural control (203)

social intuitionist account of morality a theory that states that a person has an instant gut reaction to moral situations that precedes moral reasoning (105)

social intelligence the ability to negotiate new social environments (185)

social learning theory a theory that emphasizes the role of cognition in motivation and the importance of expectations in shaping behaviour (113, 128)

social learning therapy a type of therapy designed to modify clients' problematic behaviour patterns through observation and behaviour reinforcement (260)

social loafing a phenomenon that occurs when people believe that their individual efforts don't matter or that they are not personally responsible because they are only one member of a group, so they tend to put less effort into a task (209)

social pain the pain of rejection or loss brought on by losing a close personal relationship or membership in a group (209)

social perception the process through which a person understands and categorizes the behaviour of others (200)

social phobia an irrational fear of being publicly humiliated or embarrassed (236)

social pressure real or imagined psychological forces that people exert over others through their example, judgments, and demands (203)

social psychologist a psychologist who studies how the thoughts, emotions, and behaviour of individuals influence and are influenced by interactions between people (200)

social trap a situation in which conflicting parties all try to win a conflict by engaging in mutually destructive behaviours, resulting in no one winning (213)

socialization   the process through which a person shapes his or her behavioural patterns according to the society he or she lives in (96)

socioemotional selectivity theory of aging   a theory that states that as people grow older and realize that the time they have left is limited, they focus on enjoying the present rather than looking to the future (105)

soma   the cell body of a neuron (34)

somatic nervous system   the part of the peripheral nervous system that picks up stimuli from the outside world, coordinates movements, and performs other consciously controlled tasks (34)

somatization disorder   a somatoform disorder characterized by vague, unverifiable symptoms such as dizziness and nausea (244)

somatoform disorder   a disorder characterized by physical symptoms that do not have an identifiable cause (244)

sound shadow   an area of reduced sound intensity around the ear farther away from where a sound originates (55)

sound wave   a change in air pressure caused by molecules of air or fluid colliding and moving apart (54)

source amnesia   a phenomenon in which a person remembers information but forgets or misremembers where that information came from (168)

species-typical behaviours   instinctive or characteristic ways of behaving particular to a certain species (75)

spermarche   a boy's first ejaculation (84)

spinal cord   a cord that connects the spinal nerves to the brain and organizes simple reflexes and rhythmic movements (39)

spontaneous recovery   a reoccurrence of a learned behaviour after extinction (152)

spoonerism   a common execution error in which a person exchanges the initial sounds of two or more words in a phrase (195)

standard deviation   a measure of the dispersion of a set of values using information from each individual score (25)

state   a person's transient disposition to behave in a certain way (218)

state-dependent memory   a stored memory that is more easily retrieved when a person is in the same state as they were when the information was first encoded (176)

statistical significance   an indication that the difference between the average scores from two reliable samples is not simply due to chance (27)

stereotype   a general belief about a group of people (210)

stereotype threat   a stereotyped group's knowledge that they must work against a negative stereotype (210)

stimulus discrimination   a process in which a learner is trained to distinguish between similar but distinct stimuli (152)

stimulus enhancement   a person's tendency to pay attention to a particular place or object in which someone else has shown interest (160)

stimulus-driven capture   a type of attention that is motivated by external factors (191)

storage   the process by which encoded information is placed into memory (168)

storage decay   a phenomenon in which many of a person's memories fade over time (176)

stranger anxiety   fear of strangers (96)

stress   a physical and mental response to threatening or challenging events (266)

stress inoculation   *see* **stress inoculation training (SIT)**   (272)

stress inoculation training (SIT)   a therapeutic technique in which clients are taught how to evaluate and cope with various stressors and are then exposed to increasingly stressful situations in a controlled environment to strengthen these coping mechanisms (258, 000)

stressor   an event that a person perceives as threatening or challenging (266)

structural ambiguity   confusion that occurs when syntax causes a sentence to have multiple meanings (195)

structuralism   a school of psychology concerned with the individual elements of consciousness and showing how they can be combined and integrated (4)

style shifting   the habit of a person to adapt his or her style of speaking in accordance with the person he or she is talking to, either to express solidarity or to maintain distance (193)

subconscious motivation   motivation that is not in a person's awareness but can be easily accessed (128)

subject-expectancy effect   an occurrence where participants in a study expect to behave in a certain way as a result of their treatment, causing them to adjust their behaviour (29)

subjective well-being   a person's self-perceived satisfaction with life (127)

successive approximations   behaviours that are incrementally closer to the overall desired action (159)

suggestibility   a person's susceptibility to the opinions of others (204)

sulci   grooves in the cerebral cortex (42)

superego   the part of the psyche that forces the ego to consider societal constraints and acceptable forms of behaviour (222)

suprachiasmatic nucleus   the part of the hypothalamus that controls the circadian clock (138)

survey   a series of questions about people's behaviour or opinions, in the form of a questionnaire or interview (24)

syllogism   a deductive pattern of logic in which a conclusion is made based on two or more premises (188)

syllogistic reasoning   a type of reasoning in which a person decides whether a conclusion logically follows from two or more statements that the person assumes to be true (188)

symmetry   the tendency to perceive two unconnected but symmetrical shapes as one object (61)

sympathetic division   *see* **sympathetic nervous system**   (124)

sympathetic nervous system   the part of the autonomic nervous system that is always active and acts as an accelerator for organs (34)

symptom   a characteristic of thought or behaviour that indicates a potential mental disorder (233)

synaesthesia   a condition in which signals from the sensory organs are processed in the wrong cortical areas of the brain (63)

synapse   the area between neurons across which nerve impulses travel (37, 175)

synaptic cleft   a narrow space between a transmitting neuron's terminal buttons and a receiving neuron's dendrites (37)

synaptic consolidation   memory consolidation that takes place within a few hours after learning (162)

syndrome   a combination of interrelated symptoms observed in an individual (233)

syntax   how words may be arranged to produce phrases and sentences (90)

system consolidation   gradual memory consolidation that takes weeks or months and involves the reorganization of the brain regions that support memory (162)

systematic desensitization   a variation of exposure treatment in which people, within a therapeutic environment, learn to pair states of deep relaxation with thoughts of anxiety-provoking situations, with the goal of replacing the anxiety felt during these situations with relaxation (259)

taste bud   a structure on the tongue that contains the receptor cells for taste (57)

taste-aversion learning   a form of conditioned learning in which exposure to a flavour paired with sickness will produce a consistent aversion to that flavour (153)

temporal lobe   a part of the brain involved in auditory processing (42)

teratogens   toxic substances that cross the placenta and may cause birth defects (83)

terminal buttons   structures at the ends of the branches that extend from axons (34)

testing   a type of observational method in which participants are provided with stimuli or problems to respond to and researchers collect data about how the participants perform a certain task (25)

testosterone   an androgen that is the principal male hormone (111)

thalamus   a part of the brain located just above the brainstem that receives sensory information, processes it, and sends it to the cerebral cortex; it helps to regulate the states of arousal, sleep and wakefulness, and consciousness (40, 103)

Thematic Apperception Test (TAT)   a test that presents a participant with a series of random, unfamiliar images and asks him or her to tell stories about them; these stories supposedly reflect the person's inner hopes, fears, and desires (222)

theoretical reasoning   a type of reasoning directed toward arriving at a belief or conclusion rather than at a practical decision (188)

theory   an idea that helps explain an existing fact (21)

theta wave   a type of brainwave that characterizes the first stage of sleep (138)

three-term contingency   a three-part process in which organisms learn that in the presence of certain stimuli, their behaviour is likely to have a particular effect on the environment; the three parts are the discriminative stimulus, the operant response, and the reinforcer/punisher (157)

threshold   the number of positive inputs a neuron must receive before it transmits information (37)

timbre   the quality and purity of the tone of a sound (54)

time-space synaesthesia   a condition in which a person experiences time units as occupying specific spatial locations (63)

token economy   a term for an operant-conditioning procedure in which individuals earn tokens when they exhibit desirable behaviour; later, people who've earned tokens can redeem them for privileges or treats (158, 260)

tolerance   occurs when an increasing amount of a drug is needed to produce intoxication (146)

tonotopic   pertaining to the way in which the primary auditory cortex is organized so that neurons that respond to particular frequencies are grouped together (55)

top-down processing   our use of beliefs, experiences, expectations, and other concepts to shape our view of the world (59)

total situation   a situation in which people are isolated from alternative viewpoints and given strict rewards and punishments from leaders (206)

trace conditioning   a type of classical conditioning in which the conditioned stimulus is discontinued before the unconditioned stimulus is presented (154)

trait   a person's relatively stable disposition to behave in a certain way (218)

trait theory   a theory that states that a set of meaningful and distinct personality dimensions can be used to describe how people differ from one another (219)

transduction   a process through which physical energy such as light or sound is converted into an electrical charge (51)

transference   an instance in which a client's unconscious feelings about a significant person in his or her life are instead directed toward the therapist (255)

transsexual   a person who has had sex reassignment surgery (112)

Type A   a personality type characterized by a competitive, impatient, verbally aggressive, easily angered nature (270)

Type B   a personality type characterized by an easygoing, relaxed nature (270)

unconditional positive regard   valuing a person despite his or her problems and weaknesses (224)

unconditioned response (UR)   a reflex action elicited by an unconditioned stimulus (154)

unconditioned stimulus (US)   an original, unlearned stimulus that elicits a certain reflex action (154)

unconscious encoding   a process of encoding that does not involve any deliberate thought or action (170)

unconscious inference   a phenomenon in which a person's visual systems use sensory information to draw conclusions about what he or she sees (60)

unconscious information   experiences, ideas, and motives that are so threatening or unacceptable that a person has permanently removed them from his or her consciousness (137)

unconscious motivation   a motivation that operates without a person's awareness (128)

underextended   referring to the relatively narrow use of common nouns (90)

universality hypothesis   a hypothesis that states that facial expressions are understood across all cultures (122)

valence   a positive or negative value along a continuum (127)

validity   the degree to which a measurement measures what it is intended to measure (28)

variability   the degree to which the numbers in a set of data differ from one another and the mean (25)

variable   a characteristic that can vary, such as age, weight, or height (21)

ventromedial prefrontal cortex   an area of the brain that serves as an executive control system that helps a person adhere to social and behavioural rules; it also plays a role in allowing a person to link his or her behaviour to its potential consequences (191)

vestibular sac   a group of cells that connect the semicircular canals to the cochlea (58)

vestibular sense   the sense relating to movement and body position (57)

view-dependent   pertaining to the idea that previously seen objects are stored as a template that is compared to a viewed shape in the retinal image (61)

view-independent   pertaining to the idea that the visual system recognizes objects as a combination of their visual parts (61)

visual accommodation   a process in which the lens adjusts in shape from thick to thin to enable a person to focus on objects that are close by or far away (52)

visual cortex   a part of the brain that mediates the human sense of sight by encoding visual information (168)

visual encoding   the process of encoding images (170)

wanting   a desire to achieve a particular goal in order to receive a reward (129)

wanting system   a system involved with achieving a goal to receive pleasure; it depends heavily on dopamine (129)

Weber's law   a law that states that regardless of size, two stimuli must differ by a constant proportion for the difference to be noticeable (51)

white matter   myelinated axons that form the connections within the brain (42)

withdrawal symptoms   symptoms that occur when we stop taking a drug for which we have developed a tolerance (146)

within-subject experiment   a study in which each participant is exposed to all the independent variables in an experiment (21)

Wolffian system   the precursor of male sex organs (110)

working memory   a type of memory in which information for short-term use is stored (168)

X chromosomes   sex chromosomes that exist as a matched pair in females and part of an unmatched pair in males (the other part being a Y chromosome) (110)

Y chromosomes   sex chromosomes that exist in males as part of an unmatched pair (the other part being an X chromosome) (110)

Yerkes-Dodson law   a law that states that, in general, performance peaks with a moderate level of arousal (129, 177)

zone of proximal development   the difference between what a child can do alone and what a child can do together with a more competent person (89)

zygote   a cell formed from the combination of a sperm and an egg (70)

REFERENCES

ABRAMSON, L. Y., METALSKY, G. I., & ALLOY, L. B. (1989). Hopelessness depression: A theory-based subtype. *Psychological Review, 96,* 358-372.

ACKERMAN, P. L., & BEIER, M. E. (2005). Knowledge and intelligence. In O. Wilhelm & R. W. Engle (Eds.), *Handbook of understanding and measuring intelligence.* Thousand Oaks, CA: Sage.

ADER, R., & COHEN, N. (1985). CNS-immune system interactions: Conditioning phenomena. *Behavioral and Brain Sciences, 8,* 379-394.

ADOLPHS, R., GOSSELIN, F., BUCHANAN, T., TRANEL, D., SCHYNS, P., & DAMASIO, A. (2005). A mechanism for impaired fear recognition after amygdala damage. *Nature, 433,* 68-72.

AFFLECK, G., TENNEN, H., URROWS, S., & HIGGINS, P. (1994). Person and contextual features of daily stress reactivity: Individual differences in relations of undesirable daily events with mood disturbance and chronic pain intensity. *Journal of Personality and Social Psychology, 66,* 329-340.

AIKEN, L. R., & GROTH-MARNAT, G. (2005). *Psychological testing and assessment* (12th ed.). Boston, MA: Allyn & Bacon.

AINSWORTH, M. D. S. (1979). Infant-mother attachment. *American Psychologist, 34,* 932-937.

AIZPURUA, A., & KOUTSTAAL, W. (2010). Aging and flexible remembering: Contributions of conceptual span, fluid intelligence, and frontal functioning. *Psychology and Aging, 25,* 193-207.

ALBEE, G. W. (1986). Toward a just society: Lessons from observations on the primary prevention of psychopathology. *American Psychologist, 41,* 891-898.

ALESSADRI, S. M., SULLIVAN, M. W., & LEWIS, M. (1990). Violation of expectancy and frustration in early infancy. *Developmental Psychology, 26,* 738-744.

ALEXANDER, G., & HINES, M. (2002). Sex differences in response to children's toys in nonhuman primates (Cercopithecus aethiops sabaeus). *Evolution and Human Behavior, 23*(6), 467-479.

AL-KANDARI, Y. Y. (2011). Relationship of strength of social support and frequency of social contact with hypertension and general health status among older adults in the mobile care unit in Kuwait. *Journal of Cross-Cultural Gerontology, 26,* 175-187.

AL-KRENAWI, A., & GRAHAM, J. R. (2006). A comparison of family functioning, life and marital satisfaction, and mental health of women in polygamous and monogamous marriages. *International Journal of Social Psychiatry, 52*(1), 5-17.

AL-KRENAWI, A., & SLONIM-NEVO, V. (2008). Psycho-social and familial functioning of children from polygynous and monogamous families. *Journal of Social Psychology, 148*(6), 745-764.

ALLAN, R., & FISHER, J. (2011). *Heart and mind: The practice of cardiac psychology* (2nd ed.). Washington, DC: American Psychological Association.

ALLEN, L. S., & GORSKI, R. A. (1992). Sexual orientation and the size of the anterior commissure in the human brain. *Proceedings of the National Academy of Sciences of the United States of America, 89*(15), 7199-7202.

ALLPORT, G. W. (1954). *The nature of prejudice.* Cambridge, MA: Addison-Wesley.

ALLPORT, G. W., & ODBERT, H. S. (1936). Trait names: A psycholexical study. *Psychological Monographs, 47*(1, Whole No. 211).

AMERICAN PSYCHIATRIC ASSOCIATION. (2000). *Diagnostic and statistical manual of mental disorders* text revision (DSMIV-TR) (4th ed.). Washington, DC: American Psychiatric Association.

AMERICAN PSYCHOLOGICAL ASSOCIATION. (2012). Retrieved from http://www.apa.org/

ANDERSON, C. A., & ANDERSON, D. C. (1984). Ambient temperature and violent crime: Tests of the linear and curvilinear hypothesis. *Journal of Personality and Social Psychology, 46,* 91-97.

ANDERSON, C. A., & BUSHMAN, B. J. (2001). Effects of violent video games on aggressive behavior, aggressive cognition, aggressive affect, physiological arousal and prosocial behavior: A meta-analytic review of the scientific literature. *Psychological Science, 12,* 353-359.

ANDERSON, I. M. (2000). Selective serotonin reuptake inhibitors versus tricyclic antidepressants: A meta-analysis of efficacy and tolerability. *Journal of Affective Disorders, 58,* 19-36.

ARCURI, L., CASTELLI, L., GALDI, S., ZOGMAISTER, C., & AMADORI, A. (2008). Predicting the vote: Implicit attitudes as predictors of the future behavior of decided and undecided voters. *Political Psychology, 29,* 369-387.

ARIES, E. (1987). Gender and communication. In P. Shaver & C. Hendrick (Eds.), *Review of Personality and Social Psychology, 7,* 149-176.

ARISTOTLE. (1908). *Nicomachean ethics.* Translated by W. D. Ross. Oxford, UK: Clarendon Press. (Original work published in 350 BCE)

ARNETT, J. J. (2000). Emerging adulthood: A theory of development from the late teens through the twenties. *American Psychologist, 55,* 469-480.

ARONSON, E., & GONZALEZ, A. (1988). Desegregation, jigsaw, and the Mexican-American experience. In P. A. Katz & D. A. Taylor (Eds.), *Eliminating racism: Profiles in controversy.* New York, NY: Plenum Press.

ASCH, S. E. (1940). Studies in the principles of judgment and attitudes: 2. Determination of judgments by group and ego standards. *Journal of Social Psychology,* S.P.S.S.I. Bulletin 12, 433-465.

ASCH, S. E. (1956). Studies of independence and conformity: A minority of one against a unanimous majority. *Psychological Monographs, 70* (9, Whole no. 416).

ASERINSKY, E. (1988, January 17). Personal communication.

ASERINSKY, E., & KLEITMAN, N. (1953). Regularly occurring periods of eye motility, and concomitant phenomena, during sleep. *Science, 118,* 273-274.

ASHA INTERNATIONAL. (2007). Retrieved from http://www.myasha.org

ASHBY, F. G. (1992). Multidimensional models of categorization. In F. G. Ashby (Ed.), *Multidimensional models of perception and cognition* (pp. 449-483). Hillsdale, NJ: Erlbaum.

ATKINSON, R. C., & SHIFFRIN, R. M. (1968). Human memory: A control system and its control processes. In K. Spence (Ed.), *The psychology of learning and motivation* (Vol. 2). New York, NY: Academic Press.

AXELROD, V., & YOVEL, G. (2011). Nonpreferred stimuli modify the representation of faces in the fusiform face area. *Journal of Cognitive Neuroscience, 23,* 746-756.

BACCUS, J. R., BALDWIN, M. W., & PACKER, D. J. (2004). Increasing implicit self-esteem through classical conditioning. *Psychological Science, 15,* 498-502.

BAHRKE, M. S., & MORGAN, W. P. (1978). Anxiety reduction following exercise and meditation. *Cognitive Therapy and Research, 2*(4), 323-333.

BAILEY, J. M., & BELL, A. P. (1993). Familiality of female and male homosexuality. *Behavior Genetics, 23*(4), 313-322.

BAILEY, J. M., DUNNE, M. P., & MARTIN, N. G. (2000). Genetic and environmental influences on sexual orientation and its correlates in an Australian twin sample. *Journal of Personality and Social Psychology, 78*(3), 524-536.

BAILLARGEON, R. (1995). A model of physical reasoning in infancy. In C. Rovee-Collier & L. P. Lipsitt (Eds.), *Advances in infancy research* (Vol. 9). Stamford, CT: Ablex.

BAILLARGEON, R. (1998). Infants' understanding of the physical world. In M. Sabourin, F. I. M. Craik, & M. Roberts (Eds.), *Advances in psychological science: Vol. 2. Biological and cognitive aspects.* Hove, England: Psychology Press.

BAILLARGEON, R. (2004). Infants' physical world. *Current Directions in Psychological Science, 13,* 89-94.

BAIRD, A. A., & FUGELSANG, J. A. (2004). The emergence of consequential thought: Evidence from neuroscience. *Proceedings of the Royal Society, B, Biological Sciences, 359,* 1797-1804. Reprinted in O. Goodenough and S. Zeki (Eds.), (2006), *Law and the Brain* (pp. 245-259). Oxford, UK: Oxford University Press.

BALABAN, M. T., & WAXMAN, S. R. (1997). Do words facilitate object categorization in 9-month-old infants? *Journal of Experimental Child Psychology, 64,* 3-26.

BANAJI, M. R., & GREENWALD, A. G. (1995). Implicit gender stereotyping in judgments of fame. *Journal of Personality and Social Psychology, 68,* 181-198.

BANDURA, A. (2003). Observational learning. In J. H. Byrne (Ed.), *Encyclopedia of learning and memory* (2nd ed., pp. 482-484). New York, NY: Macmillan.

BANDURA, A., BLANCHARD, E. B., & RITTER, B. (1969). Relative efficacy of desensitization and modeling approaches for inducing behavioral, affective, and attitudinal changes. *Journal of Personality and Social Psychology, 13,* 173-199.

BANDURA, A., ROSS, D., & ROSS, S. A. (1961). Transmission of aggression through imitation of aggressive models. *Journal of Abnormal and Social Psychology, 63,* 575-582.

BANERJEE, S. (2008, June 8). Pregnant man Thomas Beatie may have more children. *Telegraph.* Retrieved from http://www.telegraph.co.uk/news/newstopics/howaboutthat/2093580/Pregnant-man-Thomas-Beatie-may-have-more-children.html

BARELDS, D. P. H., DIJKSTRA, P., KOUDENBURG, N., & SWAMI, V. (2011). An assessment of positive illusions of the physical attractiveness of romantic partners. *Journal of Social and Personal Relationships, 28,* 706-719.

BARINAGA, M. (1991). How long is the human life span? *Science, 254,* 936-938.

BARNIER, A. J., & MCCONKEY, K. M. (2004). Defining and identifying the highly hypnotizable person. In M. Heap, R. J. Brown, & D. A. Oakley (Eds.), *High hypnotisability: Theoretical, experimental and clinical issues.* London, UK: Brunner-Routledge.

BAR-ON, R., TRANEL, D., DENBURG, N. L., & BECHARA, A. (2003). Exploring the neurological substrate of emotional and social intelligence. *Brain, 126*(Pt 8), 1790-1800.

BARON-COHEN, S. (2002). The extreme male brain theory of autism. *Trends in Cognitive Sciences, 6*(6), 248-254.

BARRATT, M. S., NEGAYAMA, K., & MINAMI, T. (1993). The social environments of early infancy in Japan and the United States. *Early Development and Parenting, 2,* 51-64.

BARTOSHUK, L. M. (1993). *The wisdom of the body: Using case studies to teach sensation and perception.* Paper presented to the National Institute on the Teaching of Psychology, St. Petersburg Beach, FL.

BATSON, C. D. (1994). Why act for the public good? Four answers. *Personality and Social Psychology Bulletin, 20,* 603-610.

BAUER, P. J. (2002). Long-term recall memory: Behavioral and neuron developmental changes in the first 2 years of life. *Current Directions in Psychology, 11,* 137-141.

BAUMEISTER, R. F. (2000). Gender differences in erotic plasticity: The female sex drive as socially flexible and responsive. *Psychological Bulletin, 126,* 347-374.

BAXENDALE, S. (2004). Memories aren't made of this: Amnesia at the movies. *British Medical Journal, 329,* 1480-1483.

BEARDSLEY, T. (1996, July). Waking up. *Scientific American, 14,* 18.

BECK, A. T. (1967). *Depression: Clinical, experimental, and theoretical aspects.* New York, NY: Hoeber Medical Division, Harper & Row.

BECK, A. T., RUSH, A. J., SHAW, B. F., & EMERY, G. (1979). *Cognitive therapy of depression.* New York, NY: Guilford Press.

BECKMAN, H., REGIER, N., & YOUNG, J. L. (2007). Effect of workplace laughter groups on personal efficacy beliefs. *Journal of Primary Prevention, 28,* 167-182.

BEITMAN, B. D., GOLDFRIED, M. R., & NORCROSS, J. C. (1989). The movement toward integrating the psychotherapies: An overview. *American Journal of Psychiatry, 146,* 138-147.

BELKIN, L. (2008, June 15). When mom and dad share it all. *The New York Times.* Retrieved from http://www.nytimes.com/2008/06/15/magazine/15parenting-t.html

BELL, A. (1984). Language style as audience design. *Language in Society, 13*(2), 145-204.

BELLEVILLE, G. (2010, September). Mortality hazard associated with anxiolytic and hypnotic drug use in the national population health survey. *Canadian Journal of Psychiatry, 55,* 558-567.

BELSKY, J., LANG, M., & HUSTON, T. L. (1986). Sex typing and division of labor as determinants of marital change across the transition to parenthood. *Journal of Personality and Social Psychology, 50,* 517-522.

BEM, D. J. (1996). Exotic becomes erotic: A developmental theory of sexual orientation. *Psychological Review, 103,* 320-335. doi:10.1037/0033-295X.103.2.320

BEM, S. L. (1975). Sex role adaptability: The consequence of psychological androgyny. *Journal of Personality and Social Psychology, 31,* 634-643.

BEM, S. L. (1981). Gender schema theory: A cognitive account of sex typing. *Psychological Review, 88,* 354-364.

BEM, S. L. (1993). *The lenses of gender: Transforming the debate on sexual inequality.* New Haven, CT: Yale University Press.

BENEDICT, H. (1979). Early lexical development: Comprehension and production. *Journal of Child Language, 6,* 183-200.

BENNET, M. P., ZELLER, J. M., ROSENBERG, L., & MCCANN, J. (2003). The effect of mirthful laughter on stress and natural killer cell activity. *Alternative Therapies in Health and Medicine, 9*(2), 38-45.

BENNETT, C. M., & BAIRD, A. A. (2006). Anatomical changes in the emerging adult brain: A Voxel-based morphometry study. *Human Brain Mapping, 27* (9), 766-777.

BERENBAUM, S. A., & SNYDER, E. (1995). Early hormonal influences on childhood sex-typed activity and playmate preferences: Implications for the development of sexual orientation. *Developmental Psychology, 31,* 31-42.

BERGSHLOM, P., LARSEN, J. L., ROSENDAHL, K., & HOLSTEN, F. (1989). Electroconvulsive therapy and cerebral computed tomography. *Acta Psychiatrica Scandinavia, 80,* 566-572.

BERKOWITZ, L. (1983). Aversively-stimulated aggression: Some parallels and differences in research with animals and humans. *American Psychologist, 38,* 1135-1144.

BERKOWITZ, L. (1989). Frustration-aggression hypothesis: Examination and reformulation. *Psychological Bulletin, 106,* 59-73.

BERKOWITZ, S. J. (2003). Children exposed to community violence: The rationale for early intervention. *Clinical Child and Family Psychology Review, 6,* 293-302.

BERNSTEIN, D. M., ERDFELDER, E., MELTZOFF, A. N., PERIA, W., & LOFTUS, G. R. (2011). Hindsight bias from 3 to 95 years of age. *Journal of Experimental Psychology: Learning, Memory, and Cognition, 37,* 378-391.

BETTENCOURT, A. B., & KERNAHAN, C. (1997). A meta-analysis of aggression in the presence of violent cues: Effects of gender differences and aversive provocation. *Aggressive Behavior, 23*(6), 447-456.

BHAR, S. S., THOMBS, B. D., PIGNOTTI, M., BASSEL, M., JEWETT, L., COYNE, J., & BECK, A. (2010). Is longer-term psychodynamic psychotherapy more effective than shorter-term therapies? Review and critique of the evidence. *Psychotherapy and Psychosomatics, 79,* 208-216.

BIALYSTOK, E., CRAIK, F. I. M., KLEIN, R., & VISWANATHAN, M. (2004). Bilingualism, aging, and cognitive control: Evidence from the Simon task. *Psychology and Aging, 19,* 290-303.

BIALYSTOK, E., & MARTIN, M. (2004). Attention and inhibition in bilingual children: Evidence from the dimensional change card sort task. *Developmental Science, 7,* 325-339.

BIEDERMAN, I. (1987). Recognition-by-components: A theory of human image understanding. *Psychological Review, 94,* 115-147.

BILLETER, J. C., ATALLAH, J., KRUPP, J. J., MILLAR, J. G., & LEVINE, J. D. (2009). Specialized cells tag sexual and species identity in Drosophila melanogaster. *Nature, 461,* 987-992. doi:10.1038/nature08495

BJÖRKQVIST, K., LAGERSPETZ, K. M. J., & KAUKIAINEN, A. (1992). Do girls manipulate and boys fight? Developmental trends in regard to direct and indirect aggression. *Aggressive Behavior, 18,* 117-127.

BLACK, K. A., & SCHUTTE, E. D. (2006). Recollections of being loved: Implications of childhood experiences with parents for young adults' romantic relationships. *Journal of Family Issues, 27*(10), 1459-1480.

BLANCHARD, R. (1997). Birth order and sibling sex ration in homosexual versus heterosexual males and females. *Annual Review of Sex Research, 8,* 27-67.

BLANCHARD, R. (2001). Fraternal birth order and the maternal immune hypothesis of male homosexuality. *Hormones and Behavior, 40,* 105-114.

BLANCHARD, R., ZUCKER, K. J., SIEGELMAN, M., DICKEY, R., & KLASSEN, P. (1998). The relation of birth order to sexual orientation in men and women. *Journal of Biosocial Science, 30,* 511-519.

BLATT, S. J., SANISLOW, C. A., III, ZUROFF, D. C., & PILKONIS, P. (1996). Characteristics of effective therapists: Further analyses of data from the National Institute of Mental Health Treatment of Depression Collaborative Research Program. *Journal of Consulting and Clinical Psychology, 64,* 1276-1284.

BLEIDORN, W., KANDLER, C., HÜLSHEGER, U. R., RIEMANN, R., ANGLEITNER, A., & SPINATH, F. M. 2010. Nature and nurture of the interplay between personality traits and major life goals. *Journal of Personality and Social Psychology, 99,* 366-379.

BOKSA, P. (2012). Abnormal synaptic pruning in schizophrenia: Urban myth or reality? *Journal of Psychiatry and Neuroscience, 37,* 75-77.

BOLGER, N., DELONGIS, A., KESSLER, R. C., & SCHILLING, E. A. (1989). Effects of daily stress on negative mood. *Journal of Personality and Social Psychology, 57,* 808-818.

BONE, J. (2008, March 26). Thomas Beatie, a married man who used to be a woman, is pregnant with a baby girl. *The Times.* Retrieved from http://www.timesonline.co.uk/tol/news/world/us_and_americas/article3628860.ece

BOSCARINO, J. A. (1997). Diseases among men 20 years after exposure to severe stress: Implications for clinical research and medical care. *Psychosomatic Medicine, 59,* 605-614.

BOSNIA WAR CRIME SUSPECT KARADZIC ARRESTED. (2008, July 21). CNN. Retrieved from http://www.cnn.com/2008/WORLD/europe/07/21/serb.arrest

BOWER, G. H., CLARK, M. C., LESGOLD, A. M., & WINZENZ, D. (1969). Hierarchical retrieval schemes in recall of categorized word lists. *Journal of Verbal Learning and Verbal Behavior, 8,* 323-343.

BOWLBY, J. (1969). *Attachment and Loss: Vol. 1. Attachment.* London, UK: Hogarth.

BOYCE, P., & BARRIBALL, E. (2010). Circadian rhythms and depression. *Australian Family Physician, 39,* 307-310.

BRAUN, S. (1996). New experiments underscore warnings on maternal drinking. *Science, 273,* 738-739.

BRAUN, S., PEUS, C., & FREY, D. (2012). Is beauty beastly? Gender-specific effects of leader attractiveness and leadership style on followers' trust and loyalty. *Zeitschrift für Psychologie/Journal of Psychology, 220,* 98-108. doi:10.1027/2151-2604/a000101

BRAY, O., KENNELLY, J. J., & GUARINO, J. L. (1975). Fertility of eggs produced on territories of vasectomized red-winged blackbirds. *The Wilson Bulletin, 87,* 187-195.

BRELAND, K., & BRELAND, M. (1951). A field of applied animal psychology. *American Psychologist, 6,* 202-204.

BRELAND, K., & BRELAND, M. (1961). The misbehavior of organisms. *American Psychologist, 16,* 681-684.

BRENNAN, D. S., & SPENCER, A. J. (2012). Social support and optimism in relation to the oral health of young adults. *International Journal of Behavioral Medicine, 19,* 56-64.

BRICKMAN, P., COATES, D, & JANOFF-BULMAN, R. J. (1978). Lottery winners and accident victims: Is happiness relative? *Journal of Personality and Social Psychology, 36,* 917-927.

BRIM, O. (1999). *The McArthur Foundation study of midlife development.* Vero Beach, FL: The McArthur Foundation.

BROADBENT, D. E. (1958). *Perception and communication.* Oxford, UK: Pergamon.

BRODY, J. E. Male hormone tied to aggressive acts. (1981, March 7). *The New York Times.* Retrieved from http://query.nytimes.com/gst/fullpage.html?res=9F0DE6DD1539F934A35750C0A967948260&sec=health&spon=

BROWN, A. J., & PALINSCAR, A. (1986). Guided cooperative learning and individual knowledge acquisition. In L. B. Resnik (Ed.), *Knowing, learning, and instruction* (pp. 393-451). Hillsdale, NJ: Erlbaum.

BROWN, A. S., SCHAEFER, C. A., WYATT, R. J., GOETZ, R., BEGG, M. D., GORMAN, J. M., & SUSSER, E. S. (2000). Maternal exposure to respiratory infections and adult schizophrenia spectrum disorders: A prospective birth cohort study. *Schizophrenia Bulletin, 26,* 287-295.

BROWN, S. C., & CRAIK, F. I. M. (2000). Encoding and retrieval of information. In E. Tulving & F. I. M. Craik (Eds.), *The Oxford handbook of memory* (pp. 93-108). New York, NY: Oxford University Press.

BURNS, S. M., & MAHALIK, J. R. (2011). Suicide and dominant masculinity norms among current and former United States military servicemen. *Professional Psychology: Research and Practice, 42,* 347-353. doi:10.1037/a0025163

BURNSTEIN, E., CRANDALL, C., & KITAYAMA, S. (1994). Some neo-Darwinian decision rules for altruism: Weighing clues for inclusive fitness as a function of the biological importance of the decision. *Journal of Personality and Social Psychology, 67,* 773-789.

BUSHMAN, B. J., & ANDERSON, C. J. (2002). Violent video games and hostile expectations: A test of the general aggression model. *Personality and Social Psychology Bulletin, 28,* 1679-1686.

BUSHMAN, B. J., BAUMEISTER, R. F., & STACK, A. D. (1999). Catharsis, aggression, and persuasive influence: Self-fulfilling or self-defeating prophecies? *Journal of Personality and Social Psychology, 76,* 367-376.

CABELLO, M., MELLOR-MARSA, B., SABARIEGO, C., CIEZA, A., BICKENBACH, J., & AYUSO-MATEOS, J. L. (2012). Psychosocial features of depression: A systematic literature review. *Journal of Affective Disorders, 141,* 22-33.

CALDERA, Y. M., HUSTON, A. C., & O'BRIEN, M. (1989). Social interactions and play patterns of parents and toddlers with feminine, masculine, and neutral toys. *Child Development, 60*(1), 70-76.

CAMPBELL, D. T. (1975). On the conflicts between biological and social evolution and between psychology and moral tradition. *American Psychologist, 30,* 1103-1126.

CAMPBELL, D. T., & SPECHT, J. (1985). Altruism: Biology, culture, and religion. *Journal of Social and Clinical Psychology, 3,* 33-42.

CAMPBELL, J. (1992). Male answer syndrome: Why men always have opinions, even on subjects they know nothing about. *Utne Reader, 49,* 107-108.

CAMPERIO-CIANI, A., CORNA, F., & CAPILUPPI, C. (2004). Evidence for maternally inherited factors favouring male homosexuality and promoting female fecundity. *Proceedings of the Royal Society: Biological Sciences, 271*(1554), 2217-2221.

CAMPOS, J. J., BERTENTHAL, B. I., & KERMOIAN, R. (1992). Early experience and emotional development: The emergence of wariness and heights. *Psychological Science, 3,* 61-64.

CANADIAN COUNCIL ON LEARNING. (2008). *Lessons in learning. The advantages of bilingualism in Canada.* Retrieved from http://www.ccl-cca.ca/pdfs/LessonsInLearning/Oct-16-08-The-advantages-of-bilingualism.pdf

CANADIAN GAMBLING ASSOCIATION. (2010). *Gambling.* Retrieved from http://www.canadiangaming.ca/english/home/index.cfm

CANADIAN INSTITUTES OF HEALTH RESEARCH. (2012). *Amydala: Two pathways of fear.* Retrieved from http://thebrain.mcgill.ca/flash/d/d_04/d_04_cr/d_04_cr_peu/d_04_cr_peu.html

CANADIAN MENTAL HEALTH ASSOCIATION. (2009). Retrieved from http://www.cmha.ca/bins/content_page.asp?cid=6-20-23

CANADIAN PSYCHOLOGICAL ASSOCIATION. (2010). The Canadian Psychological Association website. Retrieved from http://www.cpa.ca

CANNON, W. B. (1915). *Bodily changes in pain, hunger, fear, and rage: An account of recent researches into the function of emotional excitement.* New York, NY: Appleton.

CANNON, W. B. (1927). The James-Lange theory of emotion: A critical examination and an alternative theory. *American Journal of Psychology, 39,* 10-124.

CANNON, W. B., & WASHBURN, A. (1912). An explanation of hunger. *American Journal of Physiology, 29,* 441-454.

CANTOR, N., & KIHLSTROM, J. R. (1987). *Personality and social intelligence.* Englewood Cliffs, NJ: Prentice Hall.

CARDO, A. G., & GOTTESMAN, I. I. (2000). Twin studies of schizophrenia: From bow-and-arrow concordances to star wars Mx and functional genomics. *American Journal of Medical Genetics, 97*(1), 12-17.

CARLSON, S. M., & MELTZOFF, A. N. (2008). Bilingual experience and executive functioning in young children. *Developmental Science, 11,* 282-298.

CARLSSON, R., & BJÖRKLUND, F. (2010). Implicit stereotype content: Mixed stereotypes can be measured with the Implicit Association Test. *Social Psychology, 41,* 213-222.

CARPENTER, P. A., JUST, M. A., & SHELL, P. (1990). What one intelligence test measures: A theoretical account of the processing in the Raven Progressive Matrices test. *Psychological Review, 97*(3), 404-431.

CARRINGTON, P. (1998). *The book of meditation: The complete guide to modern meditation* (revised ed.). New York, NY: Element Books.

CARROLL, M. E., & OVERMIER, J. B. (2001). *Animal research and human health: Advancing human welfare through behavioral science.* Washington, DC: American Psychological Association.

CARRUTHERS, M. (2001). A multifactorial approach to understanding andropause. *Journal of Sexual and Reproductive Medicine, 1,* 69-74.

CARSTENSEN, L. L. (1991). Selectivity theory: Social activity in life-span context. *Annual Review of Gerontology and Geriatrics, 11,* 195-217.

CARTER, N. (2008). Stephen Harper, Canadian: A personality at a distance profile of Stephen Harper. *Inroads: The Journal of Canadian Opinion, 23,* 26-29.

CASTILLO, R. J. (1997). Eating disorders. In R. J. Castillo (Ed.), *Culture and mental illness: A client-centered approach* (p. 152). Pacific Grove, CA: Brooks/Cole Publishing.

CASTONGUAY, L. G., & GOLDFRIED, M. R. (1994). Psychotherapy integration: An idea whose time has come. *Applied & Preventive Psychology, 3,* 159-172.

CATALANO, R., NOVACO, R. W., & MCCONNELL, W. (1997). A model of the net effect of job loss on violence. *Journal of Personality and Social Psychology, 72,* 1440-1447.

CATALANO, R., NOVACO, R. W., & MCCONNELL, W. (2002). Layoffs and violence revisited. *Aggressive Behavior, 28,* 233-247.

CATTELL, R. B. (1963). Theory of fluid and crystallized intelligence: A critical experiment. *Journal of Educational Psychology, 54,* 1-22.

CATTELL, R. B. (1965). *The scientific analysis of personality.* Baltimore, MD: Penguin.

CBC NEWS. (2010, May). *DIRE STRAITS: Post-traumatic stress disorder. Soldiers with severe PTSD have trouble finding help.* Retrieved from http://www.cbc.ca/canada/story/2010/05/25/post-traumatic-stress-military.html

CENTERS FOR DISEASE CONTROL AND PREVENTION, NATIONAL CENTER FOR INJURY PREVENTION AND CONTROL. (2005). *Suicide: facts at a glance.* Web-based Injury Statistics Query and Reporting System (WISQARS). Retrieved from http://www.cdc.gov/ncipc/dvp/Suicide/suicide_data_sheet.pdf

CHAMBLESS, D. L., BAKER, M. J., BAUCOM, D. H., BEUTLER, L. E., CALHOUN, K. S., CRITS-CHRISTOPH, P., . . . WOODY, S. R. (1997). Update on empirically validated therapies, II. *The Clinical Psychologist, 51*(1), 3-16.

CHANG, M. (1996, October 4). Joined for life: Co-joined six-year-old Hensel twins share many body parts. *Science World*. Retrieved from http://wwww.findarticles.com

CHARTRAND, T. L., & BARGH, J. A. (1999). The chameleon effect: The perception-behavior link and social interaction. *Journal of Personality and Social Psychology, 76*(6), 893-910.

CHERRY, E. C. (1953). Some experiments on the recognition of speech, with one and two ears. *Journal of the Acoustical Society of America, 25,* 975-979.

CHIANG, Y. L., KLAININ-YOBAS, P., & IGNACIO, J. (2011). The impact of antipsychotic side effect on attitudes toward medication in patients with schizophrenia: A systematic review. *Joanna Briggs Institute Systematic Review Library, 9*(22).

CHOMSKY, N. (1957). *Syntactic structures.* The Hague, Netherlands: Mouton.

CHOW, P., & WOOD, W. (2001). *Comparing cognitive dissonance test scores of college students in Canada with those in the United Sates.* Education. Available at http://findarticles.com/p/articles/mi_qa3673/is_1_122/ai_n28879479/

CHRISTIE, W., & MOORE, C. (2005). The impact of humor on patients with cancer. *Clinical Journal of Oncological Nursing, 9*(2), 211-218.

CHU, J. A., FREY, L. M., GANZEL, B. L., & MATTHEWS, J. A. (1999). Memories of childhood abuse: Dissociation, amnesia, and corroboration. *American Journal of Psychiatry, 156,* 749-755.

CIANCIOLO, A. T., & STERNBERG, R. J. (2004). *Intelligence: A brief history.* Malden, MA: Blackwell Publishing.

CLANCY, S. A., MCNALLY, R. J., SCHACTER, D. L., LENZENWEGER, M. F., & PITMAN, R. K. (2002). Memory distortion in people reporting abduction by aliens. *Journal of Abnormal Psychology 111*(3), 455-461.

CLARK, C. (2008, July 23). The former pregnant man debuts his baby. *People.* Retrieved from http://www.people.com/people/article/0,,20214360,00.html

CLARK, H., & MARSHALL, C. (1981). Definite reference and mutual knowledge. In A. K. Joshi, B. L. Webber, & I. A. Sag (Eds.), *Elements of discourse understanding* (pp. 10-63). New York, NY: Cambridge University Press.

CLARK, K. B., & CLARK, M. P. (1947). Racial self-identification and preference in negro children. In T. M. Newcomb & E. L. Hartley (Eds.), *Readings in social psychology* (pp. 169-178). New York, NY: Henry Holt.

CLEARWATER, E., & HARVEY, C. (2007) Correlates of marital satisfaction in a Manitoba low income sample. *Journal of Consumer Studies.* doi:10.1111/j.1470-6431.1988.tb00476.x

CLONINGER, C. R., BOHMAN, M., & SIGVARDSSON, S. (1981). Inheritance of alcohol abuse: Cross-fostering analysis of adopted men. *Archives of General Psychiatry, 36,* 861-868.

CLOUD, J. (2007). Yep, they're gay. *Time.* Retrieved from http://www.time.com/time/magazine/article/0,9171,1582336,00.html

COATS, E. J., & FELDMAN, R. S. (1996). Gender differences in nonverbal correlates of social status. *Personality and Social Psychology Bulletin, 22*(10) 1014-1022.

COFFEY, C. E. (Ed.). (1993). *Clinical science of electroconvulsive therapy.* Washington, DC: American Psychiatric Press.

COHEN, N. J., & EICHENBAUM, H. (1993). *Memory, amnesia, and the hippocampal system.* Cambridge, MA: MIT.

COHEN, S., DOYLE, W. J., TURNER, R., ALPER, C. M., & SKONER, D. P. (2003). Sociability and susceptibility to the common cold. *Psychological Science, 14,* 389-395.

COLAPINTO, J. (1997, December 11). The true story of John/Joan. *Rolling Stone,* 54-97.

COLAPINTO, J. (2000). *As nature made him: The boy who was raised as a girl.* New York, NY: HarperCollins.

COLARELLI, S. M., SPRANGER, J. L., & HECHANOVA, M. R. (2006). Women, power, and sex composition in small groups: An evolutionary perspective. *Journal of Organizational Behavior, 27*(2), 163-184.

COLEY, R. L., & CHASE-LANSDALE, L. (1998). Adolescent pregnancy and parenthood: Recent evidence and future directions. *American Psychologist, 53,* 152-166.

COMSTOCK, G., & LINDSEY, G. (1975). *Television and human behavior: The research horizon, future and present.* Santa Monica, CA: Rand.

CONNELLY, B. S., & ONES, D. S. (2010). Another perspective on personality: Meta-analytic integration of observers' accuracy and predictive validity *Psychological Bulletin, 136,* 1092-1122.

CONSENSUS CONFERENCE. (1985). Electroconvulsive therapy. *Journal of the American Medical Association, 254,* 2103-2108.

CORBETTA, M., & SCHULMAN G. L. (2002). Control of goal-directed and stimulus-driven attention in the brain. *Nature Reviews Neuroscience, 3,* 201-215.

COREN, S. (1996). *Sleep thieves: An eye-opening exploration into the science and mysteries of sleep.* New York, NY: The Free Press.

CORKUM, V., & MOORE, C. (1998). The origins of joint visual attention in infants. *Developmental Psychology, 34,* 28-38.

COSTA JR., P. T., ZONDERMAN, A. B., MCCRAE, R. R., CORNONI-HUNTLEY, J., LOCKE, B. Z., & BARBANO, H. E. (1987). Longitudinal analyses of psychological well-being in a national sample: Stability of mean levels. *Journal of Gerontology, 42,* 50-55.

COULL, G., & MORRIS, P. G. (2011). The clinical effectiveness of CBT-based guided self-help interventions for anxiety and depressive disorders: A systematic review. *Psychological Medicine, 41,* 2239-2252.

CRESPI, L. (1942). Quantitative variation of incentive and performance in the white rat. *American Journal Psychology, 55,* 467-517.

CRESPI, L. (1944). Amount of reinforcement and level of performance. *Psychology Review, 51,* 341-357.

CRIMINAL JUSTICE: NEW TECHNOLOGIES AND THE CONSTITUTION. (1988, May). Retrieved from http://books.google.com/books?id=W40kUdI8bGoC&pg=PA41&lpg=PA41&dq=Male+sexual+offenders+given+Depo-Provera&source=web&ots=SfAUAFOPf&sig=ES1IuOM8VzeUg427QoAzKN6E2qk&hl=en&sa=X&oi=book_result&resnum=3&ct=result#PPA41,M1

CRUZ, C. A., HALL, L. C., LEHMAN, E. B., RENKEY, M. E., & SROKOWSKI, S. A. (2003). Directed forgetting of related words: evidence for the inefficient inhibition hypothesis. *The Journal of General Psychology, 130,* 380-398.

CSIKSZENTMIHALYI, M. (1990). *Flow: The psychology of optimal experience.* New York, NY: Harper & Row.

CSIKSZENTMIHALYI, M. (1999). If we are so rich, why aren't we happy? *American Psychologist, 54,* 821-827.

CUIJPERS, P., VAN STRATEN, A., HOLLON, S. D., & ANDERSSON, G. (2010). The contribution of active medication to combined treatments of psychotherapy and pharmacotherapy for adult depression: A meta-analysis. *Acta Psychiatrica Scandinavica, 121,* 415-423. doi:10.1111/j.1600-0447.2009.01513.x

CUMMING, E., & HENRY, W. E. (1961). *Growing old: The process of disengagement.* New York, NY: Basic Books.

CUTUMISU, N., & SPENCE, J. (2012). Sport fields as potential catalysts for physical activity in the neighbourhood. *International Journal of Environmental Research and Public Health, 9,* 294-314. doi:10.3390/ijerph9010294

DALTON, A. N., CHARTRAND, T. L., & FINKEL, E. J. (2010). The schema-driven chameleon: How mimicry affects executive and self-regulatory resources. *Journal of Personality and Social Psychology, 98,* 605-617.

DALTON, D., & ORTEGREN, M. (2011). Gender differences in ethics research: The importance of controlling for the social desirability response bias. *Journal of Business Ethics, 103,* 73-93.

DALTON, P., DOOLITTLE, N., & BRESLIN, P. A. S. (2002). Gender-specific induction of enhanced sensitivity to odors. *Nature Neuroscience, 5,* 199-202.

DAMASIO, A. R. (1994). *Descartes error: Emotion, reason, and the human brain.* New York, NY: Grossett/Putnam & Sons.

DAMASIO, H., GRABOWSKI, T., FRANK, R., GALABURDA, A. M., & DAMASIO, A. R. (1994). The return of Phineas Gage: Clues about the brain from the skull of a famous patient. *Science, 264,* 1102-1105.

DAMIANAKIS, T., & MARZIALI, E. (2011). Community-dwelling older adults' contextual experiencing of humour. *Ageing and Society, 31,* 110-124. doi:10.1017/S0144686X10000759

DANA FOUNDATION. (2003). *The Dana sourcebook of brain science* (3rd ed.). New York, NY: Dana Press.

DARLEY, J. M., & LATANÉ, B. (1968). Bystander intervention in emergencies: Diffusion of responsibility. *Journal of Personality and Social Psychology, 8,* 377-383.

DARWIN, C. (1872). *The expression of the emotions in man and animals.* London: John Murray.

DARWIN, C. (1872/1965). *The expression of the emotions in man and animals.* Chicago, IL: University of Chicago Press.

DARWIN, C. (1964). *On the origin of species.* Cambridge, MA: Harvard University Press. (Original work published 1859)

DASHIFF, C., DIMICCO, W., MYERS, B., & SHEPPARD, K. (2009). Poverty and adolescent mental health. *Journal of Child and Adolescent Psychiatric Nursing, 22,* 23-32. doi:10.1111/j.1744-6171.2008.00166.x

DAVIDSON, R. J., KABAT-ZINN, J., SCHUMACHER, J., ROSENKRANZ, M., MULLER, D., SANTORELLI, S. F., . . . SHERIDAN, J. F. (2003). Alterations in brain and immune function produced by mindfulness meditation. *Psychosomatic Medicine, 65*(4), 564-570.

DAVIS, K. C., SCHRAUFNAGEL, T. J., JACQUES-TIURA, A. J., NORRIS, J. G., WILLIAM H., ET AL. (2012). Childhood sexual abuse and acute alcohol effects on men's sexual aggression intentions. *Psychology of Violence, 2,* 179-193.

DAVIS, M. (1992). The role of the amygdala in conditioned fear. In J. P. Aggleton (Ed.), *The amygdala: Neurobiological aspects of emotion, memory, and mental dysfunction* (pp. 255–306). New York, NY: Wiley-Liss.

DAVIS, M., & MARSHALL, E. A. (2009). *A short history of mental health*. Retrieved from www.historyofmadness.ca

DAWKINS, K. (2012). Refinements in ECT techniques. *Psychiatric Times, Category 1*, 41–46.

DAWOOD, K., PILLARD, R. C., HORVATH, C., REVELLE, W., & BAILEY, J. M. (2000). Familial aspects of male homosexuality. *Archives of Sexual Behavior, 29*(2), 155–163.

DE BOER, H., BOSKER, R. J., & VAN DER WERF, M. P. C. (2010). Sustainability of teacher expectation bias effects on long-term student performance. *Journal of Educational Psychology, 102*, 168–179.

DE KONINCK, J. (2000). Waking experiences and dreaming. In M. Kryger, T. Roth, & W. Dement (Eds.), *Principles and practice of sleep medicine* (3rd ed.). Philadelphia, PA: Saunders.

DE WAAL, F. B. M. (1995, March). Bonobo sex and society: The behavior of a close relative challenges assumptions about male supremacy in human evolution. *Scientific American, 272*(3), 82–88.

DEL CASALE, A., KOTZALIDIS, G. D., RAPINESI, C., SERATA, D., AMBROSI, E., SIMONETTI, A., POMPILI, M., FERRACUTI, S., TATARELLI, R., & GIRARDI, P. (2011). Functional neuroimaging in obsessive-compulsive disorder. *Neuropsychobiology 64*, 61–85. doi:10.1159/000325223

DEARY, I. J. (2001). Human intelligence differences: Towards a combined experimental-differential approach. *Trends in Cognitive Sciences, 5*, 164–170.

DECI, E. L., KOESTNER, R., & RYAN, R. M. (1999, November). A meta-analytic review of experiments examining the effects of extrinsic rewards on intrinsic motivation. *Psychological Bulletin, 125*(6), 627–668.

DEMENT, W. C. (1978). *Some must watch while some must sleep*. New York, NY: Norton.

DEMENT, W. C. (1997). *What all undergraduates should know about how their sleeping lives affect their waking lives*. Retrieved from http://www.stanford.edu/~dement/sleepless.html

DEMENT, W. C. (1999). *The promise of sleep: A pioneer in sleep medicine explores the vital connection between health, happiness, and a good night's sleep*. New York, NY: Delacorte.

DEMENT, W. C., & WOLPERT, E. A. (1958, June). The relation of eye movements, body motility, and external stimuli to dream content. *Journal of Experimental Psychology, 55*(6), 543–553.

DENOLLET, J. (2011). Type D or not type D: That's the question. *The European Health Psychologist, 14*, 58–63.

DEREGOWSKI, J. B. (1969). Perception of the two-pronged trident by two- and three-dimensional perceivers. *Journal of Experimental Psychology, 82*, 9–13.

DEVINE, M. A., & DAWSON, S. (2010). The effect of a residential camp experience on self esteem and social acceptance of youth with craniofacial differences. *Therapeutic Recreation Journal, North America, 44*. Retrieved from http://js.sagamorepub.com/trj/article/view/886

DEW, M. A., HOCH, C. C., BUYSSE, D. J., MONK, H., BEGLEY, A. E., HOUCK, P. R., . . . REYNOLDS, C. F., III (2003). Healthy older adults' sleep predicts all-cause mortality at 4 to 19 years of follow-up. *Psychosomatic Medicine, 65*, 63–73.

DIENER, E., & BISWAS-DIENER, R. (2002). Will money increase subjective well-being? A literature review and guide to needed research. *Social Indicators Research, 57*,119–169.

DIENER, E., OISHI, S., & LUCAS, R. E. (2003). Personality, culture, and subjective well-being: emotional and cognitive evaluations of life. *Annual Review of Psychology, 54*, 403–425.

DIMBERG, U., THUNBERG, M., & ELMEHED, K. (2000). Unconscious facial reactions to emotional facial expressions. *Psychological Science, 11*, 86–89.

DOLLARD, J., DOOB, L. W., MILLER, N. E., MOWRER, O. H., & SEARS, R. R. (1939). *Frustration and aggression*. New Haven, CT: Yale University Press.

DOMHOFF, G. W. (1996). *Finding meaning in dreams: A quantitative approach*. New York, NY: Plenum Publishing.

DOMHOFF, G. W. (2002). Using content analysis to study dreams: Applications and implications for the humanities. In K. Bulkeley (Ed.), *Dreams: A reader on the religious, cultural, and psychological dimensions of dreaming* (pp. 307–319). New York, NY: Palgrave.

DOMHOFF, G. W. (2003). *The scientific study of dreams: Neural networks, cognitive development, and content analysis*. Washington, DC: APA Books.

DORUS, S., VALLENDER, E., EVANS, P., ANDERSON, J., GILBERT, S., MAHOWALD, M., . . . LAHN, B. T. (2004). Accelerated evolution of nervous system genes in the origin of Homo sapiens. *Cell, 119*(7), 1027–1040.

DOTY, R. L. (2001). Olfaction. *Annual Review of Psychology, 52*, 423–452.

DOVIDIO, J. F., GAERTNER, S. L., & KAWAKAMI, K. (2003). Intergroup contact: The past, present and the future. *Group Processes & Intergroup Relations, 6*, 5–21.

DRUCKMAN, D., & BJORK, R. A. (1991). *In the mind's eye: Enhancing human performance*. Washington, DC: National Academy Press.

DUCKWORTH, K. L., BARGH, J. A., GARCIA, M., & CHAIKEN, S. (2002). The automatic evaluation of novel stimuli. *Psychological Science, 13*(6) 513–519.

DUKE, A. A., GIANCOLA, P. R., MORRIS, D. H., HOLT, J. C., & GUNN, R. L. (2011). Alcohol dose and aggression: Another reason why drinking more is a bad idea. *Journal of Studies on Alcohol and Drugs, 72*, 34–43.

DUNCAN, J., & OWEN, A. M. (2000). Common regions of the human frontal lobe recruited by diverse cognitive demands. *Trends in Neurosciences, 23*, 475–483.

DUNN, E. W., GILBERT, D. T., AND WILSON, T. (2011). If money doesn't make you happy then you probably aren't spending it right. *Journal of Consumer Psychology, 21*(2), 115–125.

DUNN, M., THOMAS, J. O., SWIFT, W., & BURNS, L. (2011). Elite athletes' estimates of the prevalence of illicit drug use: Evidence for the false consensus effect. *Drug Alcohol Review, 31*, 27–32. doi:10.1111/j.1465-3362.2011.00307.x

DUNPHY, D. C. (1963, June). The social structure of urban adolescent peer groups. *Sociometry, 26*, 230–246.

DUNSON, D. B., COLOMBO, B., & BAIRD, D. D. (2002). Changes with age in the level and duration of fertility in the menstrual cycle. *Human Reproduction, 17*, 1399–1403.

DURSTON, S., HILLEKE, E., HULSHOFF, P., CASEY, B. J., GIEDD, J. N., BUITELAAR, J. K., & VAN ENGELAND, H. (2001). Anatomical MRI of the developing human brain: What have we learned? *Journal of the American Academy of Child and Adolescent Psychiatry, 40*, 1012–1020.

EAGLY, A. H., & JOHNSON, B. T. (1990). Gender and leadership style: A meta-analysis. *Psychological Bulletin, 108*(2), 233–256.

EAGLY, A. H., ASHMORE, R. D., MAKHIJANI, M., & KENNEDY, L. C. (1991). What is beautiful is good, but…: A meta-analytic review of research on the physical attractiveness stereotype. *Psychological Bulletin, 110*, 109–128.

EASTWICK, P. W., EAGLY, A. H., FINKEL, E. J., & JOHNSON, S. E. (2011). Implicit and explicit preferences for physical attractiveness in a romantic partner: A double dissociation in predictive validity. *Journal of Personality and Social Psychology, 101*, 993–1011.

EBBINGHAUS, H. (1885/1913). *Memory: A contribution to experimental psychology* (tr. by H. A. Ruger & C. E. Bussenius). New York, NY: Teachers College, Columbia University.

ECKERSLEY, R. (2000). The mixed blessings of material progress: Diminishing returns in the pursuit of happiness. *Journal of Happiness Studies, 1*, 267–292.

ECKLUND-FLORES, L. (1992). *The infant as a model for the teaching on introductory psychology*. Paper presented to the American Psychological Association annual convention.

EHRLICH, P. R., DOBKIN, D. S., & WHEYE, D. (1988). *Polyandry*. Retrieved from Stanford University, Birds of Stanford Web site: http://www.stanford.edu/group/stanfordbirds/text/essays/Polyandry.html

EISENBERGER, N. I., & LIEBERMAN, M. D. (2004). Why rejection hurts: A common neural alarm system for physical and social pain. *Trends in Cognitive Sciences, 8*, 294–300.

EISENBERGER, N. I., LIEBERMAN, M. D., & WILLIAMS, K. D. (2003). Does rejection hurt? An fMRI study of social exclusion. *Science, 302*, 290–292.

EISENMAN, D. P., GLIK, D., ONG, M., ZHOU, Q., TSENG, C. H., LONG, A., FIELDING, J., & ASCH, S. (2009). Terrorism-related fear and avoidance behavior in a multiethnic urban population. *American Journal of Public Health, 99*, 168–174. doi:10.2105/AJPH.2007.124206

EKMAN, P. (1982). *Emotion in the human face*. New York, NY: Cambridge University Press.

EKMAN, P. (1994). Strong evidence for universals in facial expressions: A reply to Russell's mistaken critique. *Psychological Bulletin, 115*, 268–287.

EKMAN, P., & FRIESEN, W.V. (1975). *Unmasking the face*. Englewood Cliffs, NJ: Prentice-Hall.

EKMAN, P., FRIESEN, W. V., O'SULLIVAN, M., CHAN, A., DIACOYANNI-TARLATZIS, I., HEIDER, K., . . . TZAVARAS, A. (1987). Universals and cultural differences in the judgments of facial expressions of emotion. *Journal of Personality and Social Psychology, 53*, 712–717.

ELFENBEIN, H. A., & AMBADY, N. (2002). On the universality and cultural specificity of emotion recognition: A meta-analysis. *Psychological Bulletin, 128*, 203–235.

ELFENBEIN, H. A., & AMBADY, N. (2003). When familiarity breed accuracy: Cultural exposure and facial emotion recognition. *Journal of Personality and Social Psychology, 85,* 276-290.

ELIAS, C. L., & BERK, L. E. (2002). Self-regulation in young children: Is there a role for sociodramatic play? *Early Childhood Research Quarterly, 17*(2), 216-238.

ELLIOTT, M. E. (1996). Impact of work, family, and welfare receipt on women's self-esteem in young adulthood. *Social Psychology Quarterly, 59,* 80-95.

ELLIOTT, R., & DOLAN, R. J. (1998). Neural response during preference and memory judgments for subliminally presented stimuli: A functional neuroimaging study. *The Journal of Neuroscience, 18*(12), 4697-4704.

ELLIOTT, R., RUBINSZTEIN, J. S., SAHAKIAN, B. J., & DOLAN, R. J. (2002). The neural basis of mood-congruent processing biases in depression. *Archives of General Psychiatry, 59,* 597-604.

ELLIS, L., & BLANCHARD, R. (2001). Birth order, sibling sex ratio, and maternal miscarriages in homosexual and heterosexual men and women. *Personality and Individual Differences, 30,* 543-552.

ERICKSON, K., DREVETS, W. C., CLARK, L., CANNON, D. M., BAIN, E. E., ZARATE, C. A. JR., . . . SAHAKIAN, B. J. (2005). Mood-congruent bias in affective go/no-go performance of unmedicated patients with major depressive disorder. *American Journal of Psychiatry, 162,* 2171-2173.

ERIKSON, E. H. (1963). *Childhood and society.* New York, NY: Norton.

ERON, L. D. (1987). The development of aggressive behavior from the perspective of a developing behaviorism. *American Psychologist, 42,* 435-442.

ERRERA, P. (1972). Statement based on interview with forty "worst cases" in the Milgram obedience experiments. In J. Katz (Ed.), *Experimentation with human beings* (p. 400). New York, NY: Russell Sage Foundation.

ESSES, V., & WEBSTER, C. (2006). Physical attractiveness, dangerousness, and the Canadian Criminal Code. *Journal of Applied Social Psychology.* doi:10.1111/j.1559-1816.1988.tb01190.x

EVANS, P. D., GILBERT, S. L., MEKEL-BOBROV, N., VALLENDER, E. J., ANDERSON, J. R., VAEZ-AZIZI, L. M., . . . LAHN, B. T. (2005, September 9). Microcephalin, a gene regulating brain size, continues to evolve adaptively in humans. *Science, 309*(5741), 1717-1720.

EXPERT: L.A.'S 5.4 QUAKE 'SMALL SAMPLE' OF ONE TO COME. (2008, July 30). CNN. Retrieved from http://www.cnn.com/2008/US/07/29/earthquake.ca/

EYSENCK, H. J. (1967). *The biological basis of personality.* Springfield, IL: Thomas.

EZEQUIEL, M. (2011). Consciousness and the brain: The nuts and bolts underlying human action. *Psychology Today.* Retrieved from http://www.psychologytoday.com/blog/consciousness-and-the-brain/201106/do-we-use-only-10-percent-our-brain

FABBRI-DESTRO, M., & RIZZOLATTI, G. (2008). Mirror neurons and mirror systems in monkeys and humans. *Physiology, 23,* 171-179.

FANTZ, R. L. (1961, May). The origin of form perception. *Scientific American, 204,* 66-72.

FAZIO, R. H., JACKSON, J. R., DUNTON, B. C., & WILLIAMS, C. J. (1995). Variability in automatic activation as an unobtrusive measure of racial attitudes: A bona fide pipeline? *Journal of Personality and Social Psychology, 69,* 1013-1027.

FBI. (2004). Crime in the United States 2003, Five-Year Arrest Trends by Sex, 1999-2003. Table 35.

FEDEROFF, I. C., & MACFARLANE, T. (1998). Cultural aspects of eating disorders. In S. S. Kazarian & D. R. Evans (Eds.), *Cultural clinical psychology: Theory, research and practice* (pp. 152-176). New York, NY: Oxford University Press.

FEINGOLD, A. (1992). Good-looking people are not what we think. *Psychological Bulletin, 111,* 304-341.

FERGUSON, C. J. (2010). A meta-analysis of normal and disordered personality across the life span. *Journal of Personality and Social Psychology, 98,* 659-667.

FERRARI, J. R., & PYCHYL, T. A. (2012). "If I wait, my partner will do it:" The role of conscientiousness as a mediator in the relation of academic procrastination and perceived social loafing. *North American Journal of Psychology, 14,* 13-24.

FERRARI, P. F., ROZZI, S., & FOGASSI, L. (2005). Mirror neurons responding to observation of actions made with tools in monkey ventral premotor cortex. *Journal of Cognitive Neuroscience, 17,* 212-226.

FESTINGER, L. (1957). *A theory of cognitive dissonance.* Stanford, CA: Stanford University Press.

FESTINGER, L., & CARLSMITH, J. M. (1959). Cognitive consequences of forced compliance. *Journal of Abnormal and Social Psychology, 58,* 203-210.

FINK, A., SLAMAR-HALBEDL, M., UNTERRAINER, H.-F., & WEISS, E. M. (2012). Creativity: Genius, madness or a combination of both? *Psychology of Aesthetics, Creativity, and the Arts, 6,* 11-18.

FLAXMAN, P., & BOND, F. (2010). A randomised worksite comparison of ACT and stress inoculation training. *Behaviour Research & Therapy, 48,* 816-820.

FORD, M. R., & WIDIGER, T. A. (1989). Sex bias in the diagnosis of histrionic and antisocial personality disorders. *Journal of Consulting and Clinical Psychology, 57*(2), 301-305.

FORNITO, A., ZALESKY, A., PANTELIS, C., & BULLMORE, E. T. (2012). Schizophrenia, neuroimaging and connectomics. *NeuroImage, 62,* 2296-2314.

FOSTER, H., HAGAN, J., & BROOKS-GUNN, J. (2008). Growing up fast: Stress exposure and subjective "weathering" in emerging adulthood. *Journal of Health and Social Behavior, 49,* 162-177.

FOULKES, D. (1982). *Children's dreams.* New York, NY: Wiley.

FOULKES, D. (1999). *Children's dreaming and the development of consciousness.* Cambridge, MA: Harvard University Press.

FOX, E., LESTER, V., RUSSO, R., BOWLES, R. J., PICHLER, A., & DUTTON, K. (2000). Facial expressions of emotion: Are angry faces detected more efficiently? *Cognition and Emotion, 14*(1), 61-92.

FRANK, S. J. (1982). Therapeutic components shared by all psychotherapies. In J. H. Harvey & M. M. Parks (Eds.), *The Master Lecture Series: Vol. 1. Psychotherapy research and behavior change.* Washington, DC: American Psychological Association.

FREDRICKSON, B. L. (2000). Why positive emotions matter in organizations: Lessons from the broaden-and-build theory. *The Psychologist-Manager Journal, 4,* 131-142.

FREEDMAN, J. L. (1978). *Happy people.* San Diego, CA: Harcourt Brace Jovanovich.

FREQUENTLY ASKED QUESTIONS ABOUT LOBOTOMIES. (2005, November 16). NPR. Retrieved from http://www.npr.org/templates/story/story.php?storyId=5014565

FREUD, S. (1900). *The interpretation of dreams.* Translated by A. A. Brill. (1913). New York by Macmillan.

FREUD, S. (1960). *A general introduction to psychoanalysis.* New York, NY: Washington Square Press. (Original work published 1935)

FREUD, S., & GAY, P. (1977). *Inhibitions, symptoms, and anxiety. Standard edition of the complete works of Sigmund Freud.* New York, NY: W. W. Norton.

FRIEDMAN, M., ROSENMAN, R. H., CARROLL, V., & TAT, R. J. (1958). Changes in the serum cholesterol and blood clotting time in men subjected to cyclic variation of occupational stress. *Circulation, 17,* 852.

FRY, D. (2006). *The human potential for peace: An anthropological challenge to assumptions about war and violence.* New York and Oxford: Oxford University Press.

FRY, D. (2007). *Beyond war: The human potential for peace.* New York, NY: Oxford University Press.

FRY, D. P. (1992, Sept.). Respect for the rights of others is peace: Learning aggression versus nonaggression among the Zapotec. *American Anthropologist, 94*(3), 621-636.

FURMARK, T., TILLFSFORS, M., MARTEINSBOTTIR, I., PISSIOTA, A., LÅNGSTRÖM, B., & FREDRIKSON, M. (2002). Common changes in cerebral blood flow in patients with social phobia treated with citalopram or cognitive-behavioral therapy. *Archives of General Psychiatry, 59,* 425-433.

GABRIELI, J. D. E. (1998). Cognitive neuroscience of human memory. *Annual Review of Psychology, 49,* 87-115.

GALANTER, E. (1962). Contemporary psychophysics. In R. Brown, E. Galanter, E. H. Hess, & G. Mandler (Eds.), *New directions in psychology.* New York, NY: Holt, Rinehart, & Winston.

GALANTER, M., HAYDEN, F., CASTANEDA, R., & FRANCO, H. (2005). Group therapy, self-help groups, and network therapy. In R. J. Frances, S. I. Miller, & A. H. Mack (Eds.), *Clinical textbook of addictive disorders* (3rd ed., pp. 502-527). New York, NY: Guilford.

GALEF, B. G., & WIGMORE, S. W. (1983). Transfer of information concerning distant foods: A laboratory investigation of the "information-center" hypothesis. *Animal Behavior, 31,* 748-758.

GALLATE, J., WONG, C., ELLWOOD, S., CHI, R., & SNYDER, A. (2011). Noninvasive brain stimulation reduces prejudice scores on an Implicit Association Test. *Neuropsychology, 25,* 185-192.

GARCIA, J., & KOELLING, R. A. (1966). Relation of cue to consequence in avoidance learning. *Psychonomic Science, 4,* 123.

GARDNER, H. (1983). *Frames of mind: Multiple intelligences.* New York, NY: Basic Books, xi.

GARLAND, E. J., & SMITH, D. H. (1991). Case study: Simultaneous prepubertal onset of panic disorder, night terrors, and somnambulism. *Journal of the American Academy of Child & Adolescent Psychiatry, 30,* 553-555.

GAZZANIGA, M. S. (1967). The split-brain in man. *Scientific American, 217*(2), 24-29.

GEITHNER, C., & MCKENNEY, D. (2010). Strategies for aging well. *Strength and Conditioning Journal, 32,* 36-50.

GELDARD, F. A. (1972). *The human senses* (2nd ed.). New York, NY: Wiley.

GENESEE, F., & JARED, D. (2008). Literacy development in early French immersion programs. *Canadian Psychology, 49,* 140-147.

GENOME CANADA. (2012). *Cracking the mystery of autism.* Retrieved from http://www.genomecanada.ca/en/info/human/autism.aspx

GERIN, W., CHAPLIN, W., SCHWARTZ, J. E., HOLLAND, J., ALTER, R., WHEELER, R., . . . PICKERING, T. G. (2005). Sustained blood pressure increase after an acute stressor: The effects of the 11 September 2001 attack on the New York City World Trade Center. *Journal of Hypertension, 23,* 279-281.

GHAHRAMANI SENO, M. M., HU, P., GWADRY, F. G., PINTO, D., MARSHALL, C. R., CASALLO, G., & SCHERER, S. W. (2010). Gene and miRNA expression profiles in autism spectrum disorders. *Brain Research, 1380,* 85-97. doi:10.1016/j.brainres.2010.09.046

GIBSON, H. B. (1995, April). Recovered memories. *The Psychologist,* 153-154.

GILES, D. E., DAHL, R. E., & COBLE, P. A. (1994). Childbearing, developmental, and familial aspects of sleep. In J. M. Oldham & M. B. Riba (Eds.), *Review of Psychiatry, (Vol. 13).* Washington, DC: American Psychiatric Press.

GILLIGAN, C. (1982). *In a different voice: Psychological theory and women's development.* Cambridge, MA: Harvard University Press.

GILLIGAN, C., LYONS, N. P., & HAMMER, T. J. (1990). (Eds.). (1990). *Making connections: The relational worlds of adolescent girls at Emma Willard School.* Cambridge, MA: Harvard University Press.

GILOVICH, T. (1991). *How we know what isn't so: The fallibility of human reason in everyday life.* New York, NY: The Free Press.

GINZBURG, K., SOLOMON, Z., KOIFMAN, B., KEREN, G., ROTH, A., KRIWISKY, M., . . . BLEICH, A. (2003). Trajectories of post-traumatic stress disorder following myocardial infarction: A prospective study. *Journal of Clinical Psychiatry, 64*(10), 1217-1223.

GLASS, R. M. (2001). Electroconvulsive therapy: Time to bring it out of the shadows. *Journal of the American Medical Association, 285,* 1346-1348.

GLATER, J. D. (2001, March 26). Women are close to being majority of law students. *The New York Times.* Retrieved from http://query.nytimes.com/gst/fullpage.html?res=9806E3D8103CF935 A15750C0A9679C8B63

GLICK, P., & FISKE, S. T. (2001). An ambivalent alliance: Hostile and benevolent sexism as complementary justifications for gender inequality. *American Psychologist, 56*(2), 109-18.

GODDARD, A. W., MASON, G. F., ROTHMAN, D. L., BEHAR, K. L., PETROFF, O. A. C., & KRYSTAL, J. H. (2004). Family psychopathology and magnitude of reductions in occipital cortex GABA levels in panic disorder. *Neuropsychopharmacology, 29,* 639-640.

GOLDFRIED, M. R., & PADAWER, W. (1982). Current status and future directions in psychotherapy. In M. R. Goldfried (Ed.), *Converging themes in psychotherapy: Trends in psychodynamic, humanistic, and behavioral practice.* New York, NY: Springer.

GOLDMAN, R. (2008, April 3). *It's my right to have a kid, pregnant man tells Oprah.* ABC News. Retrieved from http://abcnews.go.com/Health/story? id=4581943&page=1

GOLDSTEIN, I., LUE, T. F., PADMA-NATHAN, H., ROSEN, R. C., STEERS, W. D., & WICKER, P. A. (1998). Oral sildenafil in the treatment of erectile dysfunction. *New England Journal of Medicine, 338,* 1397-1404.

GOODE, E. (1999, February 16). Tales of midlife crisis found greatly exaggerated. *The New York Times.* Retrieved from http://www.nytimes.com

GOODE, E. (2000, July 18). Once again, Prozac takes center stage, in furor. *The New York Times.* Retrieved from http://www.nytimes.com/library/national/science/health/071800hth-behavior-prozac.html

GOODE, E. (2003, January 28). Even in the age of Prozac, some still prefer the couch. *The New York Times.* Retrieved from http://www.nytimes.com

GOODNOUGH, A. (2002, May 2). Post 9/11 pain found to linger in young minds. *The New York Times.* Retrieved from http://query.nytimes.com/gst/fullpage.html?res=9E07EFDC1231F931A35756C0A9649C8B63

GORDON, S. K., & CLARK, W. C. (1974a). Adult age differences in word and nonsense syllable recognition memory and response criterion. *Journal of Gerontology, 29,* 659-665.

GORDON, S. K., & CLARK, W. C. (1974b). Application of signal detection theory in prose recall and recognition in elderly and young adults. *Journal of Gerontology, 29,* 64-72.

GORDON, S., & GILGUN, J. F. (1987). Adolescent sexuality. In V. B. Van Hasselt & M. Hersen (Eds.), *Handbook of adolescent psychology.* New York, NY: Pergamon Press.

GORE, A., JR. (1992) *Earth in the balance: Ecology and the human spirit.* Boston, MA: Houghton-Mifflin.

GOSLING, S. D., & JOHN, O. P. (1999). Personality dimensions in nonhuman animals: A cross-species review. *Current Directions in Psychological Science, 8,* 69-75.

GOSSELIN, F., PERETZ, I., JOHNSEN, E., & ADOLPHS, R. (2007). Amygdala damage impairs emotion recognition from music. *Neuropsychologia, 45,* 236-244.

GOTTESMAN, I. I. (1991). *Schizophrenia genesis: The origins of madness.* New York, NY: Freeman.

GRAF, P., & SCHACTER, D. L. (1985). Implicit and explicit memory for new associations in normal and amnesic subjects. *Journal of Experimental Psychology: Learning, Memory, and Cognition, 11,* 501-518.

GRANT, P. R., & GRANT, B. R. (2002). Unpredictable evolution in a 30-year study of Darwin's finches. *Science, 296,* 707-711.

GRAVES, L. A., HELLER, E. A., PACK, A. I., & ABEL, T. (2003). Sleep deprivation selectively impairs memory consolidation for contextual fear conditioning. *Learning & Memory, 10,* 168-176.

GRAY, J. A. (1972). The psychophysiological basis of introversion-extraversion: A modification of Eysenck's theory. In V. D. Nebylitsyn & J. A. Gray (Eds.), *The biological basis of individual behavior.* New York, NY: Academic.

GREENBERG, M. T., WEISSBERG, R. P., O'BRIEN, M. U., ZINS, J. E., FREDERICKS, L., RESNIK, H., & ELIAS, M. (2003). Enhancing school-based prevention and youth development through coordinated social, emotional, and academic learning. *American Psychologist, 58,* 466-474.

GREENFELD, L. A. (1998). *Alcohol and crime: An analysis of national data on the prevalence of alcohol involvement in crime.* Washington, DC: Document NCJ-168632, Bureau of Justice Statistics. Retrieved from http://www.ojp.usdoj.gov/bjs

GREENWALD, A. G., BANAJI, M. R., RUDMAN, L. A., FARNHAM, S. D., NOSEK, B. A., & MELLOTT, D. S. (2002). A unified theory of implicit attitudes, stereotypes, self-esteem, and self-concept. *Psychological Review, 109,* 3-25.

GREENWALD, A. G., MCGHEE, D. E., & SCHWARTZ, J. K. L. (1998). Measuring individual differences in implicit cognition: The Implicit Association Test. *Journal of Personality and Social Psychology, 74,* 1464-1480.

GREENWALD, A. G., OAKES, M. A., & HOFFMAN, H. (2003). Targets of discrimination: Effects of race on responses to weapons holders. *Journal of Experimental Social Psychology, 39,* 399-405.

GRICE, H. P. (1975). Logic and conversation. In P. Cole & J. Morgan (Eds.), *Syntax and Semantics: Vol. 3,* Academic Press, pp. 41-58.

GROSS, C. G., & SERGENT, J. (1992). Face recognition. *Current Opinion in Neurobiology, 2,* 156-161.

GRUZELIER, J. H. (1998). A working model of the neurophysiology of hypnosis: A review of evidence. *Contemporary Hypnosis, 15,* 3-21.

GUERIN, B. (1986). Mere presence effects in humans: A review. *Journal of Personality and Social Psychology, 22,* 38-77.

GUERRERO, L., & ROTHSTEIN, M. G. (2012). Antecedents of underemployment: Job search of skilled immigrants in Canada. *Applied Psychology: An International Review, 61,* 323-346.

GUR, R. C., TURETSKY, B. I., MATSUI, M., YAN, M., BILKER, W., HUGHETT, P., & GUR, R. E. (1999). Sex differences in brain gray and white matter in healthy young adults: Correlations with cognitive performance. *The Journal of Neuroscience, 19*(10), 4065-4072.

GUTTMACHER INSTITUTE. (2006). *U.S. teenage pregnancy statistics: National and state trends and trends by race and ethnicity.* Retrieved from http://www.guttmacher.org/pubs/2006/09/11/USTPstats.pdf

GUZMAN-MARIN, R., SUNTSOVA, N., METHIPPARA, M. GREIFFENSTEIN, R., SZYMUSIAK, R., & MCGINTY, D. (2005). Sleep deprivation suppresses neurogenesis in the adult hippocampus of rats. *European Journal of Neuroscience, 22,* 2111-2116.

GUZMAN-MARIN, R., SUNTSOVA, N., STEWART, D., GONG, H., SZYMUSIAK, R., MCGINTY, D. (2003). Sleep deprivation reduces proliferation of cells in the dentate gyrus of the hippocampus in rats. *Journal Physiology, 549,* 563-571.

HA, T., OVERBEEK, G., & ENGELS, R. C. (2010). Effects of attractiveness and social status on dating desire in heterosexual adolescents: An experimental study. *Archives of Sexual Behavior, 39,* 1063-1071.

HAFNER, A., & STOCK, A. (2010). Time management training and perceived control of time at work. *The Journal of Psychology, 144,* 429-447.

HAIDT, J. (2001). The emotional dog and its rational tail: A social intuitionist approach to moral judgment. *Psychological Review, 108,* 814-834.

HALL, G. S., & LINDZEY, G. (1978). *Theories of personality*. New York, NY: Wiley.

HALL, J. A. (1984). *Nonverbal sex differences: Communication accuracy and expressive style*. Baltimore, MD: Johns Hopkins University Press.

HALL, J. A. (1987). On explaining gender differences: The case of nonverbal communication. In P. Shaver & C. Hencrick (Eds.), *Review of Personality and Social Psychology, 7,* 177-200.

HALL, R. E., & PIZARRO, J. M. (2010). Unemployment as conduit of black self-hate: Pathogenic rates of black male homicide via legacy of the antebellum. *Journal of Black Studies, 40,* 653-665.

HAMER, D. H., HU, S., MAGNUSON, V. L., HU, N., & PATTATUCCI, A. M. (1993). A linkage between DNA markers on the X chromosome and male sexual orientation. *Science, 261*(5119), 321-327.

HAMILTON, S. P., SLAGER, S. L., DE LEON, A. B., HEIMAN, G. A., KLEIN, D. F., HODGE, S. E., . . . KNOWLES, J. A. (2004). Evidence for genetic linkage between a polymorphism in the Adenosine 2A receptor and panic disorder. *Neuropsychopharmacology, 29,* 558-565.

HANSEN, C. H., & HANSEN, R. D. (1988). Finding the face in the crowd: An anger superiority effect. *Journal of Personality and Social Psychology, 54*(6), 917-924.

HARKINS, S. G., & SZYMANSKI, K. (1989). Social loafing and group evaluation. *Journal of Personality and Social Psychology, 56,* 934-941.

HARLOW, H. (1958). The nature of love. *American Psychologist, 13,* 573-685.

HARLOW, H. F., DODSWORTH, R. O., & HARLOW, M. K. (1965). Total social isolation in monkeys. *Proceedings of the National Academy of Sciences of the United States of America, 54,* 90-97.

HARRIS, K. (2010, October 27). Sleepless children more likely to suffer from heart disease: Study. *The Montreal Gazette*. Retrieved from http://www.canada.com/health/Sleepless+children+more+likely+suffer+from+heart+disease+Study/3733419/story.html

HART, D., & FEGLEY, S. (1995). Altruism and caring in adolescence: Relations to self-understanding and social judgment. *Child Development, 66,* 1346-1359.

HARVEY, S. M. (1987). Female sexual behavior: Fluctuations during the menstrual cycle. *Journal of Psychosomatic Research, 31,* 100-110.

HASSED, C. (2001). How humour keeps you well. *Australian Family Physician, 30*(1), 25-28.

HATFIELD, E., & SPRECHER, S. (1986). *Mirror, mirror . . . the importance of looks in everyday life*. Albany, NY: State University of New York Press.

HAVINGHURST, R. J. (1957). The leisure activities of the middle-aged. *American Journal of Sociology, 63,* 152-162.

HAYDEN, A., BHATT, R. S., ZIEBER, N., & KANGAS, A. (2009). Race-based perceptual asymmetries underlying face processing in infancy. *Psychonomic Bulletin and Review, 16,* 270-275.

HAZEL, M. T. (2005). Visualization and systematic desensitization: Intervention for habituating and sensitizing patterns of public speaking anxiety. *Dissertation Abstracts International Section A: Humanities and Social Sciences, 66,* 30.

HEAD, D., SINGH, T., & BUGG, J. M. (2012). The moderating role of exercise on stress-related effects on the hippocampus and memory in later adulthood. *Neuropsychology, 26,* 133-143. doi:10.1037/a0027108

HEALTH CANADA. (2012). *Pan-Canadian Fetal Alcohol Spectrum Disorder (FASD) Initiative*. Retrieved from http://www.hc-sc.gc.ca/hc-ps/alc/index-eng.php

HEBB, D. O. (1949). *The organization of behavior*. New York, NY: Wiley.

HEGADOREN, K. M., LASIUK, G. C., & COUPLAND, N. (2006). Posttraumatic stress disorder part III: Health effects of interpersonal trauma among women. *Perspectives in Psychiatric Care, 42,* 163-173.

HEIDER, F. (1958). *The psychology of interpersonal relationships*. New York, NY: Wiley.

HEILMAN, M. E., & STOPECK, M. H. (1985). Attractiveness and corporate success: Different causal attributions for males and females. *Journal of Applied Psychology, 70,* 379-388.

HELLIWELL, J., LAYARD, R., & SACHS, J. (EDS.). (2012). *World happiness report*. The Earth Institute, Columbia University. Retrieved from http://www.bhutan-research.org/articles/2012/john-helliwell-richard-layard-and-jeffrey-sachs-2012-world-happiness-report

HENLEY, N. M. (1989). Molehill or mountain? What we know and don't know about sex bias in language. In M. Crawford & M. Gentry (Eds.), *Gender and thought: Psychological perspectives*. New York, NY: Springer-Verlag.

HENNINGER, P. (1992). Conditional handedness: Handedness changes in multiple personality disordered subject reflect shift in hemispheric dominance. *Consciousness and Cognition, 1,* 265-287.

HERZ, R. S (2001). Ah sweet skunk! Why we like or dislike what we smell. *Cerebrum, 3*(4) 31-47.

HERZOG, H., LELE, V. R., KUWERT, T., LANGEN, K. J., KOPS, E. R., & FEINENDEGEN, L. E. (1990/1991). Changed pattern of regional glucose metabolism during yoga meditative relaxation. *Neuropsychobiology, 23,* 182-187.

HESS, R., JR., (1965). Sleep and sleep related disturbances in the electroencephalogram. In K. A. Kert, C. Bally, & J. P. Shade (Eds.), *Sleep mechanisms* (pp. 127-139). Amsterdam, Netherlands: Elsevier.

HIGGINS, N. C., & BHATT, G. (2001). Culture moderates the self-serving bias: Etic and Emic features of causal attributions in India and in Canada. *Social Behavior and Personality, 29,* 49-62.

HILGARD, J. R., & LEBARON, S. (1984). *Hypnotherapy of pain in children with cancer*. Los Altos, CA: Kaufman.

HILL, C. E., & NAKAYAMA, E. Y. (2000). Client-centered therapy: Where has it been and where is it going? A comment on Hathaway. *Journal of Clinical Psychology, 56,* 875-961.

HILLIER, L. W., FULTON, R. S., FULTON, L. A., GRAVES, T. A., PEPIN, K. H., WAGNER-MCPHERSON, C., . . . WILSON, R. K. (2003). The DNA sequence of human chromosome 7. *Nature, 424,* 157-164.

HIRSCHFELD, R. M. A. (2011). Deep brain stimulation for treatment-resistant depression. *American Journal of Psychiatry, 168,* 455-456. doi:10.1176/appi.ajp.2011.11020231

HMHL. (2002, January). Disaster and trauma. *Harvard Mental Health Letter,* 1-5.

HO, B-C., ANDREASEN, N. C., ZIEBELL, S., PIERSON, R., & MAGNOTTA, V. (2011). Long-term antipsychotic treatment and brain volumes: A longitudinal study of first-episode schizophrenia. *Archives of General Psychiatry, 68,* 128-137.

HOFFMAN, D. D. (1998). *Visual intelligence: How we create what we see*. New York, NY: W. W. Norton.

HOLDEN, C. (1993). Wake-up call for sleep research. *Science, 259,* 305.

HOLMES, B. M., & JOHNSON, K. R. (2009). Adult attachment and romantic partner preference: A review. *Journal of Social and Personal Relationships, 26,* 833.

HOOD, S., CASSIDY, P., COSSETTE, M-P., WEIGL, Y., VERWEY, M., ROBINSON, B., . . . AMIR, S. (2010). Endogenous dopamine regulates the rhythm of expression of the clock protein PER2 in the rat dorsal striatum via daily activation of D2 dopamine receptors. *The Journal of Neuroscience, 30,* 14046-14058. doi:10.1523/JNEUROSCI.2128-10.2010

HORN, J. L. (1982). The aging of human abilities. In J. Wolman (Ed.), *Handbook of developmental psychology* (p. 128). Englewood Cliffs, NJ: Prentice-Hall.

HOROWITZ, T. S., CADE, B. E., WOLFE, J. M., & CZEISLER, C. A. (2003). Searching night and day: A dissociation of effect of circadian phase and time awake on visual selective attention and vigilance. *Psychological Science, 14,* 549-557.

HORVATH, K. J., DANILENKO, G. P., WILLIAMS, M. L., SIMONI, J., AMICO, K. R., OAKES, J. M., & ROSSER, B. R. S. (2012). Technology use and reasons to participate in online social networking websites for people living with HIV in the US. AIDS and Behavior, 16, 900-910.

HOWES, O. D., & KAPUR, S. (2009). The dopamine hypothesis of schizophrenia: Version III—The final common pathway. *Schizophrenia Bulletin, 35,* 549-562.

HU, S., PATTATUCCI, A. M. L., PATTERSON, C., LI, L., FULKER, D. W., CHERNY, S. S., . . . HAMER, D. H. (1995). Linkage between sexual orientation and chromosome Xq28 in males but not in females. *Nature Genetics, 11,* 248-256.

HUBEL, D. H., & WIESEL, T. N. (1979, September). Brain mechanisms of vision. *Scientific American,* 150-162.

HUGHES, T. A. (2007). The advantages of single-sex education. *National Forum of Educational Administration and Supervision Journal, 23*(2), 5-14.

HUGHES, V. (2010). Science in court: Head case. *Nature, 464,* 340-342.

HUIJBREGTS, S. C. J., SÉGUIN, J. R., ZOCCOLILLO, M., BOIVIN, M., & TREMBLAY, R. E. (2008). Maternal prenatal smoking, parental antisocial behavior, and early childhood physical aggression. *Development and Psychopathology, 20,* 437-453. doi:10.1017/S0954579408000217

HULL, C. L. (1943). *Principles of behavior: An introduction to behavior theory*. New York, NY: Appleton-Century-Crofts.

HULL, C. L. (1952). *A behavior system: An introduction to behavior theory concerning the individual organism*. New Haven, CT: Yale University Press.

HUNG, Y., SMITH, M. L., & TAYLOR, M. J. (2012). Development of ACC-amygdala activations in processing unattended fear. *Neuroimage, 60,* 545-552.

HUPRICH, S. K., & KEASCHUK, R. A. (2006). Psychodynamic psychotherapy. In F. Andrasik, (Ed.), *Comprehensive handbook of personality and psychopathology: Adult psychopathology* (Vol. 2, pp. 469-486). Hoboken, NJ: Wiley.

Hutchinson, A. (2012). *Bat man. Reader's Digest.* Reader's Digest Magazines Canada Limited.

Ikonomidou, C., Bittigau, P., IShimaru, M. J., Wozniak, D. F., Koch, C., GEnz, K., . . . Olney, J. W. (2000). Ethanol-induced apoptotic neurodegeneration and fetal alcohol syndrome. *Science, 287,* 1056-1060.

Inamori, T., Farhad, A., & Kakabadse, N. (2012). Can perceptual differences account for managerial success?: The case of Japanese aid workers. *Management Research Review, 35,* 32-51.

Indrupati, J., & Henari, T. (2012). Entrepreneurial success, using online social networking: Evaluation. *Education, Business and Society: Contemporary Middle Eastern Issues, 5,* 47-62.

Injeyan, M. C., Shuman, C., Shugar, A., Chitayat, D., Atenafu, E. G., & Kaiser A. (2011). Personality traits associated with genetic counselor compassion fatigue: The roles of dispositional optimism and locus of control. *Journal of Genetic Counseling, 20,* 526-540.

Inzlicht, M., & Kang, S. K. (2010). Stereotype threat spillover: How coping with threats to social identity affects, aggression, eating, decision-making, and attention. *Journal of Personality and Social Psychology, 99,* 467-481.

Irwin, M., Mascovich, A., Gillin, J. C., Willoughby, R., Pike, J., & Smith, T. L. (1994). Partial sleep deprivation reduces natural killer cell activity in humans. *Psychosomatic Medicine, 56,* 493-498.

Isacsson, G., Rich, C. L., Jureidini, J., & Raven, M. (2010). The increased use of antidepressants has contributed to the worldwide reduction in suicide rates. *British Journal of Psychiatry, 196,* 429-433.

Ito, M. (2000). Mood-congruent effect in self-relevant information processing. A study using an autobiographical memory recall task. *Japanese Journal of Psychology, 71,* 281-288.

Jackson, J. M., & Williams, K. D. (1988). *Social loafing: A review and theoretical analysis.* Unpublished manuscript. Fordham University.

James, William (1890/1950). *Principles of psychology.* New York, NY: Dover.

Jamison, K. R. (1995). *An unquiet mind.* New York, NY: Vintage.

Jarick, M., Dixon, M. J., Maxwell, E. C., Nicholls, M. E., & Smilek, D. (2009a). The ups and downs (and lefts and rights) of synaesthetic number-forms: Validation from spatial-cueing and SNARC-type tasks. *Cortex: Special Section on Spatial Forms and Synaesthesia, 45,* 1190-1199.

Jarick, M., Dixon, M. J., Stewart, M. T., Maxwell, E. C., & Smilek, D. (2009b). A different outlook on time: Visual and auditory month names elicit different mental vantage points for a time-space synaesthete. *Cortex: Special Section on Spatial Forms and Synaesthesia, 45,* 1217-1228.

Jasper, H., & Penfield, W. (1954). *Epilepsy and the functional anatomy of the human brain* (2nd ed.). Boston, MA: Little, Brown and Co.

Jensen-Campbell, L., Graziano, W. G., & West, S. G. (1995). Dominance, prosocial orientation, and female preferences: Do nice guys really finish last? *Journal of Personality & Social Psychology, 68,* 427-440.

Johansson, G. (1973). Visual perception of biological motion and a model for its analysis. *Perception and Psychophysics, 14,* 195-204.

Johansson, P., Hall, Sikström, S., & Olsson, A. (2005). Failure to detect mismatches between intention and outcome in a simple decision task. *Science, 310,* 116-119.

Johnson, J. S, & Newport, E. L. (1991). Critical period effects on universal properties of language: The status of subjacency in the acquisition of a second language. *Cognition, 39,* 215-258.

Johnson, M. E., & Hauck, C. (1999). Beliefs and opinions about hypnosis held by the general public: A systematic evaluation. *American Journal of Clinical Hypnosis, 42,* 10-20.

Johnston, T. D., & Edwards, L. (2002). Genes, interactions, and the development of behavior. *Psychological Review, 109,* 26-34.

Judge, T. A., Hurst, C., & Simon, L. S. (2009). Does it pay to be smart, attractive, or confident (or all three)? Relationships among general mental ability, physical attractiveness, core self-evaluations, and income. *Journal of Applied Psychology, 94,* 742-755.

Jung-Beeman, M., Bowden, E. M., Haberman, J., Frymiare, J. L., Arambel-Liu, S., Greenblatt, R., . . . Kounios, J. (2004). Neural activity when people solve verbal problems with insight. *Public Library of Science Biology, 2,* e97.

Jureidini, J. (2009). How do we safely treat depression in children, adolescents and young adults? *Drug Safety, 32,* 275-282.

Kabat-Zinn, J., Massion, A. O., Kristellar, J., Peterson, L. G., Fletcher, K. E., Pbert, L., . . . Santorelli, S. F. (1992). Effectiveness of a meditation-based stress reduction program in the treatment of anxiety disorders. *American Journal of Psychiatry, 149*(7), 936-943.

Kahneman, D., & Tversky, A. (1979). Prospect theory: An analysis of decision under risk. *Econometrica, 47,* 263-291.

Kanwisher, N. G., Mcdermott, J., & Chun, M. M. (1997). The fusiform face area: A module in human extrastriate cortex specialized for face perception. *Journal of Neuroscience, 17,* 4302-4311.

Kaplan, H. I., & Saddock, B. J. (Eds.). (1989). *Comprehensive textbook of psychiatry, V.* Baltimore, MD: Williams and Wilkins.

Kappenberg, E., & Halpern, D. (2006). Kinship Center attachment questionnaire. Development of a caregiver-completed attachment measure for children younger than 6 years. *Educational and Psychological Measurement, 66,* 852-873.

Kasser, T. (2002). *The high price of materialism.* Cambridge, MA: MIT Press.

Keller, M. C., & Nesse, R. M. (2005). Is low mood an adaptation? Evidence for subtypes with symptoms that match precipitants. *Journal of Affective Disorders, 86,* 27-35.

Kelley, H. H. (1967). Attribution theory in social psychology. In D. Levine (Ed.), *Nebraska symposium on motivation* (Vol. 15). Lincoln, NE: University of Nebraska Press.

Keltner, D., & Anderson, C. (2000). Saving face for Darwin: The functions and uses of embarrassment. *Current Directions in Psychological Science, 9,* 187-192.

Kendall-Tackett, K. A. (2000). Physiological correlates of childhood abuse: Chronic hyperarousal in PTSD, depression, and irritable bowel syndrome. *Child Abuse and Neglect, 24*(6), 799-810.

Kendler, K., & Schaffner, K. (2011). The dopamine hypothesis of schizophrenia: An historical and philosophical analysis. *Philosophy, Psychiatry, & Psychology, 18,* 41-63.

Kennedy, E., Majnemer, A., Farmer, J-P., Barr, R., & Platt, R. (2009). Motor development of infants with positional plagiocephaly. *Physical & Occupational Therapy in Pediatrics, 29.* Available at http://www.informaworld.com/POTP

Kerr, N. L., & Bruun, S. E. (1983). Dispensability of member effort and group motivation losses: Free-rider effects. *Journal of Personality and Social Psychology, 44,* 7-94.

Kessler, R. C., Berglund, P., Demler, O., Jin, R., Merikangas, K. R., & Walters, E. E. (2005). Lifetime prevalence and age-of-onset distributions of DSM-IV disorders in the National Comorbidity Survey Replication. *Archives of General Psychiatry, 62,* 593-602.

Kiecolt-Glaser, J. K., Belury, M. A., Porter, K., Beversdorf, D. Q., Lemeshow, S., & Glaser, R. (2007). Depressive symptoms, omega-6:omega-3 fatty acids, and inflammation in older adults. *Psychosomatic Medicine, 69,* 217-224.

Kiehl, K. A., Smith, A. M., Mendrek, A., Forster, B. B., Hare, R. D., & Liddle, P. F. (2004). Temporal lobe abnormalities in semantic processing by criminal psychopaths as revealed by functional magnetic resonance imaging. *Psychiatry Research: Neuroimaging, 130,* 297-312.

Kim, J. J., Rison, R. A., & Fanselow, M. S. (1993). Effects of amygdala, hippocampus, and periaqueductal gray lesions on short- and long-term contextual fear. *Behavioral Neuroscience, 107*(6), 1093-1098.

Kirby, M. M., & DiPaola, M. F. (2011). Academic optimism and community engagement in urban elementary schools. *Journal of Educational Administration, 49,* 542-562.

Kisilevsky, B., Hains, S., Lee, K., Xie, X., Huang, H., Ye, H., . . . Wang, Z. (2003). Effects of experience on fetal voice recognition. *Psychological Science, 14,* 220-224.

Kohlberg, L. (1969). Stage and sequence: The cognitive-developmental approach to socialization. In D. A. Goslin (Ed.), *Handbook of socialization theory and research.* Chicago, IL: Rand McNally.

Kohlberg, L. (1981). *Essays on moral development: Vol. 1.The philosophy of moral development.* San Francisco, CA: Harper & Row.

Kohlberg, L. (1984). *Essays on moral development: Vol. 2. The psychology of moral development.* San Francisco, CA: Harper & Row.

Kohn, M. (1977). *Class and conformity: A study in values* (2nd ed.). Chicago, IL: University of Chicago Press.

Kopta, S. M., Lueger, R. J., Saunders, S. M., & Howard, K. I. (1999). Individual psychotherapy outcome and process research: Challenges leading to greater turmoil or positive transition? *Annual Review of Psychology, 30,* 441-469.

Kounios, J., & Holcomb, P. J. (1994). Concreteness effects in semantic processing: ERP evidence supporting dual-coding theory. *Journal of Experimental Psychology: Learning Memory and Cognition, 20,* 804-823.

Kourtis, N., & Tavernarakis, N. (2011). Cellular stress response pathways and ageing: Intricate molecular relationships. *EMBO Journal, 30,* 2520-2531.

Kroes, M. C., Rugg, M. D., Whalley, M. G., & Brewin, C. R. (2011). Structural brain abnormalities common to posttraumatic stress disorder and depression. *Journal of Psychiatry & Neuroscience, 36,* 256-265.

KROHN, M., LISTING, M., TJAHJONO, G., REISSHAUER, A., PETERS, E., KLAPP, B., & RAUCHFUSS, M. (2011). Depression, mood, stress, and Th1/Th2 immune balance in primary breast cancer patients undergoing classical massage therapy. *Supportive Care in Cancer, 19,* 1303-1311. doi:10.1007/s00520-010-0946-2

KRUGER, A. C. (1992). The effect of peer and adult-child transactive discussions on moral reasoning. *Merrill-Palmer Quarterly, 38,* 191-211.

KUBZANSKY, L. D., SPARROW, D., VOKONAS, P., & KAWACHI, I. (2001). Is the glass half empty or half full? A prospective study of optimism and coronary heart disease in the normative aging study. *Psychosomatic Medicine, 63,* 910-916.

KULIK, J. A., & MAHLER, H. I. M. (1993). Social support and recovery from surgery. *Health Psychology, 8,* 221-238.

KURAMOTO, A. M. (2006). Therapeutic benefits of Tai Chi exercise: Research review. *Official Publication of the State Medical Society of Wisconsin, 105,* 42-46.

KURTZ, L. D. (2004). Support and self-help groups. In C. D. Garvin, L. M. Gutierrez, & M. J. Galinsky (Eds.), *Handbook of social work with groups* (pp. 139-159). New York, NY: Guilford.

KUTAS, M. (1990). Event-related brain potential (ERP) studies of cognition during sleep: Is it more than a dream? In R. R. Bootzin, J. F. Kihlstrom, & D. Schacter (Eds.), *Sleep and cognition.* Washington, DC: American Psychological Association.

KYLLONEN P. C., & CHRISTAL, R. E. (1990). Reasoning ability is (little more than) working memory capacity? *Intelligence, 14,* 389-433.

LACHMAN, M. E., & WEAVER, S. L. (1998). The sense of control as a moderator of social class differences in health and well-being. *Journal of Personality and Social Psychology* 74(3), 763-773.

LAMBERT, W. E., GENESEE, F., HOLOBOW, N., & CHARTRAND, L. (1993). Bilingual education for majority English speaking children. *European Journal of Psychology of Education, 8,* 3-22.

LANGE, C. (1887). Ueber Gemuthsbewgungen, 3, 8.

LARSEN, R. J., KASIMATIS, M., & FREY, K. (1992). Facilitating the furrowed brow: An unobtrusive test of the facial feedback hypothesis applied to unpleasant affect. *Cognition and Emotion, 6,* 321-328.

LATANÉ, B. (1981). The psychology of social impact. *American Psychologist, 36,* 343-356.

LAVENEX, P., STEELE, M. A., & JACOBS, L. F. (2000). The seasonal pattern of cell proliferation and neuron number in the dentate gyrus of wild adult eastern grey squirrels. *European Journal of Neuroscience, 12,* 643-648.

LAXTON, A., TANG-WAI, D. F., MCANDREWS, M. P., ZUMSTEG, D., WENNBERG, R., KEREN, R., WHERRETT, J., NAGLIE, G., HAMANI, C., SMITH, G. S., & LOZANO, A. M. (2010). A Phase I trial of deep brain stimulation of memory circuits for Alzheimer s disease. *Annals of Neurology, 68,* 521-534.

LAZAR, S. W., BUSH, G., GOLLUB, R. L., FRICCHIONE, G. L., KHALSA, G., & BENSON, H. (2000, May 15). Functional brain mapping of the relaxation response and meditation. *Neuroreport, 11*(7), 1581-1585.

LAZARUS, R. S. (1991). Cognition and motivation in emotion. *American Psychologist, 46,* 352-357.

LAZARUS, R. S. (1998). *Fifty years of the research and theory of R. S. Lazarus. An analysis of historical and perennial issues.* Mahwah, NJ: Erlbaum.

LEDOUX, J. E. (1994). Emotion, memory and the brain. *Scientific American, 270,* 32-39.

LEFCOURT, H. M. (1982). *Locus of control: Current trends in the theory and research.* New Jersey, NY: Erlbaum.

LEHMAN, A. F., STEINWACHS, D. M., DIXON, L. B., GOLDMAN, H. H., OSHER, F., POSTRADO, L., . . . ZITO, J. (1998). Translating research into practice: The schizophrenic patient outcomes research team (PORT) treatment recommendations. *Schizophrenia Bulletin, 24,* 1-10.

LEMING, J. S. (1993). In search of effective character education. *Educational Leadership, 51,* 63-71.

LENNEBERG, E. (1967). *Biological foundations of language.* New York, NY: Wiley.

LENZENWEGER, M. F., DWORKIN, R. H., & WETHINGTON, E. (1989). Models of positive and negative symptoms in schizophrenia: An empirical evaluation of latent structures. *Journal of Abnormal Psychology, 98,* 62-70.

LEPROULT, R., COPINSKI, G., BUXTON, O., & VAN CAUTER, E. (1997). Sleepiness, performance, and neuroendocrine function during sleep deprivation: Effects of exposure to bright lights or exercise. *Journal of Biological Rhythms, 12,* 245-258.

LESHAN, L. (1942). The breaking of habit by suggestion during sleep. *Abnormal Social Psychology, 37,* 406-408.

LEVAY, S. (1991). A difference in hypothalamic structure between heterosexual and homosexual men. *Science, 253*(5023), 1034-1037.

LEVIN, I. P., & GAETH, G. J. (1988). Framing of attribute information before and after consuming the product. *Journal of Consumer Research, 15,* 374-378.

LEVINSON, C. A., GIANCOLA, P. R., & PARROTT, D. J. (2011). Beliefs about aggression moderate alcohol's effects on aggression. *Experimental and Clinical Psychopharmacology, 19,* 64-74.

LEWIS, D. O., PINCUS, J. H., FELDMAN, M., JACKSON, L., & BARD, B. (1986). Psychiatric, neurological, and psychoeducational characteristics of 15 death row inmates in the United States. *American Journal of Psychiatry, 143,* 838-845.

LEWIS, M., ALESSANDRI, S. M., & SULLIVAN, M. W. (1990). Violation of expectancy, loss of control, and anger in young infants. *Developmental Psychology, 26,* 745-751.

LI, Y. J., JOHNSON, K., COHEN, A. B., WILLIAMS, M., KNOWLES, E. D., & CHEN, Z. (2012). Fundamental(ist) attribution error: Protestants are dispositionally focused. *Journal of Personality and Social Psychology, 102,* 281-290. doi:10.1037/a0026294

LIBBY, R., & RENNEKAMP, K. (2012). Self-serving attribution bias, overconfidence, and the issuance of voluntary disclosures. *Journal of Accounting Research, 50,* 197-231.

LILIENFELD, S., & ARKOWITZ, H. (2008, February/March). Uncovering "brain-scams": In which the authors debunk myths concerning the three-pound organ inside our head. *Scientific American Mind,* 80-81.

LILIENFELD, S. O., LYNN, S. J., RUSCIO, J., & BEYERSTEIN, B. L. (2010). *50 great myths of popular psychology.* United Kingdom: Wiley-Blackwell.

LIVESLEY, W. J. (2012). Integrated treatment: A conceptual framework for an evidence-based approach to the treatment of personality disorder. *Journal of Personality Disorders, 26,* 17-42.

LIVINGSTONE, M., & HUBEL, D. (1988). Segregation of form, color, movement, and depth: Anatomy, physiology, and perception. *Science, 240,* 740-749.

LOFTUS, E. F., & PALMER, J. C. (1974). Reconstruction of automobile destruction: An example of the interaction between language and memory. *Journal of Verbal Learning & Verbal Behavior, 13,* 585-589.

LOPES DA SILVA, R. (2012). Humor and music to reduce the stress and pain related to invasive diagnostic and therapeutical procedures in patients with hematological malignancies. *Annals of Hematology, 91,* 133-134.

LORENZ, K. (1937). The companion in the bird's world. *Auk, 54,* 245-273.

LOUIE, K., & WILSON, M. (2001). Temporally structured replay of awake hippocampal ensemble activity during rapid eye movement sleep. *Neuron, 29,* 145-156.

LOVAAS, O. I. (1987). Behavioral treatment and normal educational and intellectual functioning in young autistic children. *Journal of Consulting and Clinical Psychology, 55,* 3-9.

LUDEKE, R. J., & HARTUP, W. W. (1983) Teaching behavior of 9- and 11 year-old girls in mixed-age and same-age dyads. *Journal of Educational Psychology, 75*(6), 908-914.

LUDWIG, S., & NAFZIGER, J. (2011). Beliefs about overconfidence. *Theory and Decision, 70,* 475-500.

LUMSDEN, C. J., & WILSON, E. O. (1983). *Promethean fire: Reflections on the origin of mind.* Cambridge, MA: Harvard University Press.

LUO, L. (2010). Social networking websites: An exploratory study of student peer socializing in an online LIS program. *Journal of Education for Library and Information Science, 51,* 86-102.

LUPIEN, S. J. (2009). Brains under stress. *Canadian Journal of Psychiatry-Revue Canadienne De Psychiatrie, 54,* 4-5.

LUPIEN, S. J., FIOCCO, A., WAN, N., MAHEU, F., LORD, C., SCHRAMEK, T., & TU, M. T. (2005). Stress hormones and human memory function across the lifespan. *Psychoneuroendocrinology, 30,* 225-242.

LUU, P., SILL, O. C., GAO, L., BECKER, S., WOJTOWICZ, J. M., & SMITH, D. M. (2012). The role of adult hippocampal neurogenesis in reducing interference. *Behavioral Neuroscience, 126,* 381-391. doi:10.1037/a0028252

LYDECKER, K. P., TATE, S. R., CUMMINS, K. M., MCQUAID, J., GRANHOLM, E., & BROWN, S. A. (2010). Clinical outcomes of an integrated treatment for depression and substance use disorders. *Psychology of Addictive Behaviors, 24,* 453-465.

LYKKEN, D. T., & TELLEGEN, A. (1996). Happiness is a stochastic phenomenon. *Psychological Science, 7*(3), 186-189.

LYKKEN, D. T., TELLEGEN, A., BOUCHARD, T. J., JR., WILCOX, K., SEGAL, N., & RICH, S. (1988). Personality similarity in twins reared apart and together. *Journal of Personality and Social Psychology, 54,* 1031-1039.

LYNCH, G., & STAUBLI, U. (1991). Possible contributions of long-term potentiation to the encoding and organization of memory. *Brain Research Reviews, 16,* 204-206.

MAAS, J. B. (1999). *Power sleep. The revolutionary program that prepares your mind for peak performance.* New York, NY: HarperCollins.

MACCOBY, E. E. (1998). *The two sexes: Growing up apart, coming together.* Cambridge, MA: Harvard University Press.

MACFARLANE, A. (1978, February). What a baby knows. *Human Nature,* 74-81.

MACLEAN, P. (1990). *The triune brain in evolution: Role in paleocerebral functions.* New York, NY: Springer.

MACPHERSON, H., ELLIS, K. A., SALI, A., & PIPINGAS, A. (2012). Memory improvements in elderly women following 16-weeks treatment with a combined multivitamin, mineral and herbal supplement—A randomized controlled trial. *Psychopharmacology 220,* 351-365.

MACWHINNEY, B. (1998). Models of the emergence of language. *Annual Review of Psychology, 49,* 1999-2227.

MAGUIRE, E. A., SPIERS, H. J., GOOD, C. D., HARTLEY, T., FRACKOWIAK, R. S., & BURGESS, N. (2003). Navigation expertise and the human hippocampus: A structural brain imaging analysis. *Hippocampus, 13*(2), 250-259.

MAIA, T. V., COONEY, R. E., & PETERSON, B. S. (2008). The neural bases of obsessive-compulsive disorder in children and adults. *Development and Psychopathology, 20,* 1251-1283.

MAIER, N. R. F. (1931). Reasoning in humans II. The solution of a problem and its appearance in consciousness. *Journal of Comparative Psychology, 12,* 181-194.

MAIN, M., & HESSE, E. (1990). Parents' unresolved traumatic experiences are related to infant disorganized attachment status: Is frightened and/or frightening parental behavior the linking mechanism? In M. T. Greenberg, D. Cicchetti, & E. M. Cummings (Eds.), *Attachment in the preschool years: Theory, research, and intervention* (pp. 161-182). Chicago, IL: University of Chicago Press.

MAJOR, B., SCHMIDLIN, A. M., & WILLIAMS, L. (1990). Gender patterns in social touch: The impact of setting and age. *Journal of Personality and Social Psychology Bulletin, 10,* 634-643.

MAK, G. K., ENWERE, E. K., GREGG, C., PAKARAINEN, T., POUTANEN, M., HUHTANIEMI, I., & WEISS, S. (2007). Male pheromone–stimulated neurogenesis in the adult female brain: Possible role in mating behavior. *Nature Neuroscience 10,* 1003-1011.

MALNIC, B., HIRONO, J., SATO, T., & BUCK, L.B. (1999). Combinational receptor codes for odors. *Cell, 96,* 713-723.

MANDEL, S. E., HANSER, S. B., & RYAN, L. (2010). Effects on a music-assisted relaxation and imagery compact disc recording on health-related outcomes in cardiac rehabilitation. *Music Therapy Perspectives, 28,* 11-21.

MANN, H., KORZENKO, J., CARRIERE, J. S., & DIXON, M. J. (2009). Time-space synaesthesia—a cognitive advantage? *Consciousness & Cognition, 18,* 619-627.

MANSOUR, E. (2012). The role of social networking sites (SNSs) in the January 25th Revolution in Egypt. *Library Review, 61,* 128-159.

MAQUET, P. (2001). The role of sleep in learning and memory. *Science, 294,* 1048-1052.

MAQUET, P., & FRANCK, G. (1996). Functional neuroanatomy of human rapid eye movement sleep and dreaming. *Nature, 383,* 163-166.

MAQUET, P., PETERS, J-M., AERTS, J., DELFIORE, G., DEGUILDRE, C., LUXEN, A., & FRANCK, G. (1996). Functional neuroanatomy of human rapid-eye-movement sleep and dreaming. *Nature, 383,* 163-166.

MARGOOB, M. A., ALI, Z., & ANDRADE, C. (2010). Efficacy of ECT in chronic, severe, antidepressant- and CBT-refractory PTSD: An open, prospective study. *Brain Stimulation, 3,* 28-35.

MARIAN, V., SHILDKROT, Y., BLUMENFELD, H. K., KAUSHANSKAYA, M., FAROQI-SHAH, Y., & HIRSCH, J. (2007). Cortical activation during word processing in late bilinguals: Similarities and differences as revealed by fMRI. *Journal of Clinical and Experimental Neuropsychology, 29*(3): 247-265.

MARICH, J. (2010). EMDR in addiction continuing care: A phenomenological study of women in recovery. *Psychology of Addictive Behaviors, 24,* 498-507.

MARKUS, H., & KITAYAMA, S. (1991). Culture and the self: Implications for cognition, emotion, and motivation. *Psychological Review, 98,* 224-253.

MARLOWE, F. (1999). Male care and mating effort among Hadza foragers. *Behavioural Ecology and Sociobiology, 46,* 57-64.

MARLOWE, F. (2000). Paternal investment and the human mating system. *Behavioural Processes, 51,* 45-61.

MARTIN, C. L., RUBLE, D. N., & SZKRYBALO, J. (2002). Cognitive theories of early gender development. *Psychological Bulletin, 128,* 903-933.

MARTINO, T. A., OUDIT, G. Y., HERZENBERG, A. M., TATA, N., KOLETAR, M. M., KABIR, G. M., . . . SOLE, M. J. (2008, February 13). Circadian rhythm disorganization produces profound cardiovascular and renal disease in hamsters. *American Journal of Physiology—Regulatory, Integrative and Comparative Physiology.* doi:10.1152/ajpregu.00829.2007

MARTINS, R. A., VERÍSSIMO, M. T., COELHO, E., SILVA, M. J., CUMMING, S. P., & TEIXEIRA, A. M. (2010). Effects of aerobic and strength-based training on metabolic health indicators in older adults. *Lipids in Health and Disease, 9,* 76.

MASLOW, A. (1954). *Motivation and personality.* New York, NY: Harper.

MASLOW, A. H. (1970). *Motivation and personality.* New York, NY: Harper & Row.

MASLOW, A. H. (1971). *The farther reaches of human nature.* New York, NY: Viking.

MATHER, M., CANLI, T., ENGLISH, T., WHITFIELD, S. L., WAIS, P., OCHSNER, K. N., . . . CARSTENSEN, L. L. (2004). Amygdala responses to emotionally valenced stimuli in older and younger adults. *Psychological Science, 15,* 259-263.

MATSUMOTO, D. (1994). *People: Psychology from a cultural perspective.* Pacific Grove, CA: Brooks/Cole.

MAURER, D., & MAURER, C. (1988). *The world of the newborn.* New York, NY: Basic Books.

MCCANN, I. L., & HOLMES, D. S. (1984). Influence of aerobic exercise on depression. *Journal of Personality and Social Psychology, 46,* 1142-1147.

MCCARTHY, A., & LEE, K. (2009). Children's knowledge of deceptive gaze cues and its relation to their actual lying behavior. *Journal of Experimental Child Psychology, 103,* 117-134.

MCCARTHY, A., LEE, K., ITAKURA, S., & MUIR, D. (2006). Cultural display rules drive eye gaze during thinking. *Journal of Cross-Cultural Psychology, 37,* 717-722.

MCCARTHY, A., LEE, K., ITAKURA, S., & MUIR, D. (2008). Gaze display when thinking depends on culture and context. *Journal of Cross-Cultural Psychology, 39,* 716-729.

MCCONKEY, K. M. (1995). Hypnosis, memory, and the ethics of uncertainty. *Australian Psychologist, 30,* 1-10.

MCCRAE, R. R., & COSTA, P., JR. (1994). The stability of personality: Observations and evaluations. *Current Directions in Psychological Science, 3,* 173-175.

MCCRAE, R. R., TERRACCIANO, A., & 79 MEMBERS OF THE PERSONALITY PROFILES OF CULTURES PROJECT. (2005). Personality profiles of cultures: Aggregate personality traits. *Journal of Personality and Social Psychology, 89,* 407-425.

MCCRINDLE, B. (2010, October 27). Sleepless children more likely to suffer from heart disease: Study. *The Montreal Gazette.* Retrieved from http://www.canada.com/health/Sleepless+children+more+likely+suffer+from+heart+disease+Study/3733419/story.html

MCCUTCHEON, L. E., APPERSON, J. M., HANSON, E., & WYNN, V. (1992). Relationships among critical thinking skills, academic achievement, and misconceptions about psychology. *Psychological Reports, 71,* 635-639.

MCGUE, M., BOUCHARD, T. J., JR., IACONO, W. G., & LYKKEN, D. T. (1993). Behavioral genetics of cognitive ability: A life-span perspective. In R. Plomin & G. E. McClearn (Eds.), *Nature, nurture and psychology* (pp. 442-443). Washington, DC: American Psychological Association.

MCHUGH, P. R. (1995). Witches, multiple personalities, and other psychiatric artifacts. *Nature Medicine, 1*(2), 110-114.

MCKELLAR, J., STEWART, E., & HUMPHREYS, K. (2003). Alcoholics Anonymous involvement and positive alcohol-related outcomes: Cause, consequence, or just a correlate? A prospective 2-year study of 2,319 alcohol-dependent men. *Journal of Consulting and Clinical Psychology, 71,* 302-308.

MCMURRAY, C. (2004, January 13). *U.S., Canada, Britain: Who's getting in shape?* Gallup Poll Tuesday Briefing. Retrieved from http://www.gallup.com/poll/10312/US-Canada-Britain-Whos-Getting-Shape.aspx

MCNEIL, D. W., & ZVOLENSKY, M. J. (2000). Systematic desensitization. In A. E. Kazdin (Ed.), *Encyclopedia of psychology* (Vol. 7, pp. 533-535). Washington, DC: American Psychological Association.

MEICHENBAUM, D. (1977). *Cognitive-behavior modification: An integrative approach.* New York, NY: Plenum Press.

MEICHENBAUM, D. (1985). *Stress inoculation training.* New York, NY: Pergamon.

MEKEL-BOBROV, N., GILBERT, S. L., EVANS, P. D., VALLENDER, E. J., ANDERSON, J. R., HUDSON, R. R., . . . LAHN, B. T. (2005, September 9). Ongoing adaptive evolution of ASPM, a brain size determinant in Homo sapiens. *Science, 309*(5741), 1720-1722.

MELZACK, R. (1980). Psychological aspects of pain. In J. J. Bonica (Ed.), *Pain.* New York, NY: Raven Press.

MELZACK, R. (1992, April). Phantom limbs. *Scientific American,* 27-33.

MELZACK, R., & KATZ, J. (2004). The gate control theory: Reaching for the brain. In T. Hadjistavropoulos & K. Craig (Eds.), *Pain: Psychological perspectives* (pp. 13-34). Mahwah, NJ: Erlbaum.

MERCIER, H., & SPERBER, D. (2011). Why do humans reason? Arguments for an argumentative theory. *Behavioral and Brain Sciences, 34,* 57-74.

MESMER-MAGNUS, J., GLEW, D., & VISWESVARAN, C. (2012). A meta-analysis of positive humor in the workplace. *Journal of Managerial Psychology, 27,* 155-190.

MESSINA, C. R., LANE, D. S., GLANZ, K., WEST, D. S., TAYLOR, V., FRISHMAN, W., & POWELL, L. (2004). Relationship of social support and social burden to repeated breast cancer screening in the Women's Health Initiative. *Health Psychology, 23*(6), 582–594.

MESTON, C. M., & FROHLICH, P. F. (2000). The neurobiology of sexual function. *Archives of General Psychiatry, 57,* 1012–1030.

MEUWISSEN, I., & OVER, R. (1992). Sexual arousal across phases of the humans menstrual cycle. *Archives of Sexual Behavior, 21,* 101–119.

MICHAEL, R. T., GAGNON, J. H., LAUMANN, E. O., & KOLATA, G. (1994). *Sex in America: A definitive survey.* Boston, MA: Little, Brown and Company.

MILES, D. R., & CAREY, G. (1997). Genetic and environmental architecture of human aggression. *Journal of Personality and Social Psychology, 72,* 207–217.

MILGRAM, S. (1963). Behavioral study of obedience. *Journal of Abnormal and Social Psychology, 67,* 371–378.

MILGRAM, S. (1964). Issues in the study of obedience: A reply to Baumrind. *American Psychologist, 19,* 848–852.

MILGRAM, S. (1974). *Obedience to authority: An experimental view.* New York, NY: Harper & Row.

MILLER, G. A. (1956). The magical number seven, plus or minus two: Some limits on our capacity for processing information. *Psychological Review, 63,* 81–97.

MILLER, G. A. (2003). The cognitive revolution: A historical perspective. *Trends in Cognitive Sciences, 7*(3), 141–144.

MILLER, G. E., CHEN, E., & PARKER, K. J. (2011). Psychological stress in childhood and susceptibility to the chronic diseases of aging: Moving toward a model of behavioral and biological mechanisms. *Psychological Bulletin, 137,* 959–997. doi:10.1037/a0024768

MILLER, M. E., & BOWERS, K. S. (1993). Hypnotic analgesia: Dissociated experience or dissociated control? *Journal of Abnormal Psychology, 102,* 29–38.

MILLER, S. D., BLACKBURN, T., SCHOLES, G., WHITE, G. L., & MAMALIS, N. (1991). Optical differences in multiple personality disorder: A second look. *Journal of Nervous and Mental Disease, 179,* 132–135.

MILNE, A. M., MACQUEEN, G. M., & HALL, G. B. (2012). Abnormal hippocampal activation in patients with extensive history of major depression: An fMRI study. *Journal of Psychiatry and Neuroscience, 37,* 28–36.

MILLS, M., & MELHUISH, E. (1974). Recognition of mother's voice in early infancy. *Nature, 252,* 123–124.

MIMICA, N., STIPE, D., & PRESECKI, P. (2009). Involuntary emotional expression disorder in Alzheimer's disease—Psychopharmacotherapy aspects. *Psychiatria Danubina, 21,* 425–428.

MISCHEL, W. (1968). *Personality and assessment.* New York, NY: Wiley.

MISCHEL, W. (1984). Converges and challenges in the search for consistency. *American Psychologist, 39,* 351–364.

MISCHEL, W. (2004). Toward an integrative science of the person (Prefatory Chapter). *Annual Review of Psychology, 55,* 1–22.

MIYAKE, K., CHEN, S., & CAMPOS, J. J. (1985). Infant temperament, mother's mode of interaction and attachment in Japan: An interim report. In I. Bretherton & E. Waters (Eds.), *Growing points of attachment theory and research. Monographs of the Society for Research in Child Development, 50*(1–2 Serial No. 109), 276–297.

MOGIL, J. (2006). New pain research shows mice capable of empathy. *ScienceDaily.* Retrieved from http://www.sciencedaily.com/releases/2006/06/060630100140.htm

MOHR, P., RODRIGUEZ, M., SLAVÍČKOVÁ, A., & HANKA, J. (2011). The application of vagus nerve stimulation and deep brain stimulation in depression. *Neuropsychobiology, 64,* 170–81. doi:10.1159/000325225

MOLL, T., JORDET, G., & PEPPING, G-J. (2010). Emotional contagion in soccer penalty shootouts: Celebration of individual success is associated with ultimate team success. *Journal of Sports Sciences, 28,* 983–92. doi:10.1080/02640414.2010.484068

MONEY, J., & MATTHEWS, D. (1982). Prenatal exposure to virilizing progestins: An adult follow-up study of 12 women. *Archives of Sexual Behavior, 11*(1), 73–83.

MONEY, J., & NORMAN, B. F. (1987). Gender identity and gender transposition: Longitudinal outcome study of 24 male hermaphrodites assigned as boys. *Journal of Sex and Marriage Therapy, 13,* 75–79.

MONSON, C. M., FREDMAN, S. J., & DEKEL, R. (2010). Posttraumatic stress disorder in an interpersonal context. In J. G. Beck (Ed.), *Interpersonal processes in the anxiety disorders: Implications for understanding psychopathology and treatment* (pp. 179–208). Washington, DC: American Psychological Association.

MOOD DISORDERS SOCIETY OF CANADA. (2009). Quick facts on mental illness and addictions in Canada (3rd ed.). Retrieved from http://www.mooddisorderscanada.ca/page/quick-facts

MOOD DISORDERS SOCIETY OF CANADA. (2009). Retrieved from http://www.mooddisorderscanada.ca

MOODY, R., & PERRY, P. (1993). *Reunions: Visionary encounters with departed loved ones.* London, UK: Little, Brown and Company.

MOORE, D. W. (2004, December 17). *Sweet dreams go with a good night's sleep.* Gallup News Service.

MOORE, P. (1985). *Disguised: A true story.* Texas: Word Books.

MORA-RIPOLL, R. (2010). The therapeutic value of laughter in medicine. *Alternative Therapies in Health and Medicine, 16,* 56–64.

MORRY, M. M., KITO, M., & ORTIZ, L. (2011). Tests of the attraction-similarity model in dating couples: Projection, perceived similarity, and psychological benefits. *Personal Relationships, 18,* 125–143.

MOUCHETANT-ROSTAING, Y., & GIARD, M. H. (2003). Electrophysiological correlates of age and gender perception on human faces. *Journal of Cognitive Neuroscience, 15,* 900–910.

MROCZEK, D. K. (2001). Age and emotion in adulthood. *Current Directions in Psychological Science, 10,* 87–90.

MULLER-OERLINGHAUSEN, B., BERGHOFER, A., & BAUER, M. (2002). Bipolar disorder. *Lancet, 359,* 241–247.

MULROW, C. D. (1999, March). *Treatment of depression—Newer pharmacotherapies, summary.* Evidence Report/Technology Assessment, 7. Agency for Health Care Policy and Research, Rockville, MD. Retrieved from http://www.ahrq.gov/clinic/epcsums/deprsumm.htm

MULTIPLE SCLEROSIS SOCIETY OF CANADA. (2012). *Managing MS symptoms: Inappropriate affect.* Retrieved from http://mssociety.ca/en/information/symptoms_mng_inapproaff.htm

MUND, M., & MITTE, K. (2012). The costs of repression: A meta-analysis on the relation between repressive coping and somatic diseases. *Health Psychology, 31,* 640–649.

MUNRO, G. D., & DITTO, P. H. (1997). Biased assimilation, attitude polarization, and affect in reactions to stereotype-relevant scientific information. *Personality and Social Psychology Bulletin, 23,* 636–653.

MUNSEY, C. (2007, February). Accentuating the positive—why older people are happier. *Monitor on Psychology, 38*(2), 17.

MURPHY, S. T., MONAHAN, J. L., & ZAJONC, R. B. (1995). Additivity of nonconscious affect: Combined effects of priming and exposure. *Journal of Personality and Social Psychology, 69,* 589–602.

MYERS, D. G. (2000). *The American paradox: Spiritual hunger in an age of plenty.* New Haven, CT: Yale University Press.

NAKHAIE, R., & ARNOLD, R. (2010). A four year (1996–2000) analysis of social capital and health status of Canadians: The difference that love makes. *Social Science & Medicine, 71,* 1037–1044.

NAPOLITAN, D. A., & GOETHALS, G. R. (1979). The attribution of friendliness. *Journal of Experimental Social Psychology, 15,* 105–113.

NASH, M. R. (2001, July). The truth and the hype of hypnosis. *Scientific American,* 47–55.

NATHAN, P. E., & GORMAN, J. M. (2002). Efficacy, effectiveness and the clinical utility of psychotherapy research. In P. E. Nathan and J. M. Gorman (Eds.), *A guide to treatments that work* (2nd ed.). New York, NY: Oxford University Press.

NELSON, K. J., LANEY, C., FOWLER, N. B., KNOWLES, E. D., DAVIS, D., & LOFTUS, E. F. (2011). Change blindness can cause mistaken eyewitness identification. *Legal and Criminological Psychology, 16,* 62–74. doi:10.1348/135532509X482625

NESTLER, E. J., & MALENKA R. C. (2004). The addicted brain. *Scientific American.* Retrieved from http://www.wireheading.com/article/addiction.html

NEUBURGER, S., JANSEN, P., HEIL, M., & QUAISER-POHL, C. (2011). Gender differences in pre-adolescents' mental-rotation performance: Do they depend on grade and stimulus type? *Personality and Individual Differences, 50,* 1238–1242.

NEUGARTEN, D. A. (Ed.). (1996). *The meanings of age: Selected papers of Bernice L. Neugarten.* Chicago, IL: University of Chicago Press.

NEWBERG, A. B., ALAVI, A., BAIME, M., POURDEHNAD, M., SANTANNA, J., & D'AQUILI, E. (2001). The measurement of regional cerebral blood flow during the complex cognitive task of meditation: A preliminary SPECT study. *Psychiatric Research in Neuroimaging, 106,* 113–122.

NEWCOMBE, N. S., DRUMMEY, A. B., FOX, N. A., LIE, E., & OTTINGER-ALBERTS, W. (2000). Remembering early childhood: How much, how, and why (or why not). *Current Directions in Psychological Science, 9,* 55–58.

NEWELL, A., & SIMON, H. A. (1972). *Human problem solving.* Englewood Cliffs, NJ: Prentice-Hall.

NICKERSON, R. S., & ADAMS, M. J. (1979). Long-term memory for a common object. *Cognitive Psychology, 11,* 287-307.

NIKULINA, V., WIDOM, C. S., & CZAJA, S. (2011). The role of childhood neglect and childhood poverty in predicting mental health, academic achievement and crime in adulthood. *American Journal of Community Psychology, 48,* 309-321. doi:10.1007/s10464-010-9385-y

NISBETT, R. E., & NORENZAYAN, A. (2002). Culture and cognition. In H. Pashler & D. Medin (Eds.), *Steven's handbook of experimental psychology: Vol 2. Memory and cognitive processes* (3rd ed., pp. 561-597). New York, NY: Wiley.

NOBEL FOUNDATION. (1986). *Elie Wiesel.* Retrieved from http://nobelprize.org/nobel_prizes/peace/laureates/1986/wiesel-bio.html

NOCENTINI, A., MENESINI, E., PASTORELLI, C., CONNOLLY, J., PEPLER, D., ET AL. (2011). Physical dating aggression in adolescence: Cultural and gender invariance. *European Psychologist, 16,* 278-287.

NOEL, J. G., FORSYTH, D. R., & KELLEY, K. N. (1987). Improving the performance of failing students by overcoming their self-serving attributional biases. *Basic and Applied Social Psychology, 8,* 151-162.

NORCROSS, J. C. (2002). *Psychotherapeutic relationships that work.* New York, NY: Oxford University Press.

NORDGREN, L. F., BANAS, K., & MACDONALD, G. (2011). Empathy gaps for social pain: Why people underestimate the pain of social suffering. *Journal of Personality and Social Psychology, 100,* 120-128.

NURULLAH, A. S. (2009). Social influence in impaired driving: An exploration in Alberta, Canada. *International Journal of Interdisciplinary Social Sciences, 5,* 447-464.

O'DONNELL, R. (2001). *How Rosie O'Donnell beat depression.* ABC News. Retrieved from http://abcnews.go.com/GMA/Depression/Story?id=126783&page=2.

O'KEEFE, J., & NADEL, L. (1978). *The hippocampus as a cognitive map.* Oxford University Press.

O'NEILL, J., SENIOR, T., & CSICSVARI, J. (2006). Place-selective firing of CA1 pyramidal cells during sharp wave/ripple network patterns in exploratory behavior. *Neuron, 49,* 143-155.

O'RAND, A. M. (2004). Women in science: Career processes and outcomes. *Social Forces, 82*(4), 1669-1671.

OBERLE, E., SCHONERT-REICHL, K. A., & THOMSON, K. (2010). Understanding the link between social and emotional well-being and peer relations in early adolescence: Gender-specific predictors of peer acceptance. *Journal of Youth and Adolescence, 39,* 1330-1342.

OLFSON, M., MARCUS, S. C., & SHAFFER, D. (2006). Antidepressant drug therapy and suicide in severely depressed children and adults. *Archives of General Psychiatry, 63,* 865-872.

OLSON, I. R., PLOTZKER, A., & EZZYAT, Y. (2007). The enigmatic temporal pole: A review of findings on social and emotional processing. *Brain: A Journal of Neurology, 130*(7), 1718-1731.

OREN, D. A., & TERMAN, M. (1998). Tweaking the human circadian clock with light. *Science, 279,* 333-334.

ORNE, M. T., & HOLLAND, C. H. (1968). On the ecological validity of laboratory deceptions. *International Journal of Psychiatry, 6,* 282-293.

OUIMETTE, P., HUMPHREYS, K., MOOS, R. H., FINNEY, J. W., CRONKITE, R., & FEDERMAN, B. (2001). Self-help group participation among substance use disorder patients with posttraumatic stress disorder. *Journal of Substance Abuse Treatment, 20,* 25-32.

OWENS, G. P., WALTER, K. H., CHARD, K. M., & DAVIS, P. A. (2012). Changes in mindfulness skills and treatment response among veterans in residential PTSD treatment. *Psychological Trauma: Theory, Research, Practice, and Policy, 4,* 221-228. doi:10.1037/a0024251.

PACKER, C., & PUSEY, A. E. (1983). Adaptations of female lions to infanticide by incoming males. *The American Naturalist, 121*(5), 716-728.

PAFFENBARGER, R. S., HYDE, R. T., WING, A. L., LEE, I., JUNG, D. L., & KAMPERT, J. B. (1993, February 25). The association of changes in physical-activity level and other lifestyle characteristics with mortality among men. *New England Journal of Medicine, 328,* 538-545.

PAGE, S. (1977). Effects of the mental illness label in attempts to obtain accommodation. *Canadian Journal of Behavioral Science, 9,* 84-90.

PAIVIO, A. (1986). *Mental representations: A dual coding approach.* New York, NY: Oxford University Press.

PAN, D., HUEY, S. J., & HERNANDEZ, D. (2011). Culturally adapted versus standard exposure treatment for phobic Asian Americans: Treatment efficacy, moderators, and predictors. *Cultural Diversity and Ethnic Minority Psychology, 17,* 11-22.

PARKER, G., ROY, K., HADZI, P. D., & PEDIC, F. (1992). Psychotic (delusional) depression: A meta-analysis of physical treatments. *Journal of Affective Disorders, 24,* 17-24.

PARTONEN, T., & LONNQVIST, J. (1998). Seasonal affective disorder. *Lancet, 352*(9137), 1369-1374.

PATRY, M. W. (2008). Attractive but guilty: Deliberation and the physical attractiveness bias. *Psychological Reports, 102,* 727-733.

PAULEY, J. (2004). *Interview with Matt Lauer, Today show.* Retrieved from http://www.msnbc.msn.com/id/5860105

PAVLOV, I. P. (1927). *Conditioned reflexes* (G. V. Anrep, Trans.). London, UK: Oxford University Press.

PAYNE, V. G., & ISAACS, L. D. (1987). *Human motor development: A lifespan approach.* Mayfield, CA: Mountainview.

PEDERSEN, N. L., PLOMIN, R., MCLEARN, G. E., & FRIBERG, L. (1988). Neuroticism, extraversion, and related traits in adult twins reared apart and reared together. *Journal of Personality and Social Psychology, 55,* 950-957.

PENG, K., & NISBETT, R. E. (1999). Culture, dialectics, and reasoning about contradiction. *American Psychologist, 54,* 741-754.

PENNEBAKER, J. W., & O'HEERON, R. C. (1984). Confiding in others and illness rate among spouses of suicide and accidental-death victims. *Journal of Abnormal Psychology, 93*(4), 473-476.

PENNEBAKER, J. W., BARGER, S. D., & TIEBOUT, J. (1989). Disclosure of traumas and health among Holocaust survivors. *Psychosomatic Medicine, 51*(5), 577-589.

PEPLAU, L. A., GARNETS, L. D., SPALDING, L. R., CONLEY, T. D., & VENIEGAS, R. C. (1998). A critique of Bem's "Exotic Becomes Erotic" theory of sexual orientation. *Psychological Review, 105*(2), 387-394.

PERKINS, H. W. (1991). Religious commitment, Yuppie values, and well-being in post-collegiate life. *Review of Religious Research, 32,* 244-251.

PERLS, F. (1969). *Gestalt psychotherapy verbatim.* Lafayette, CA: Real People Press.

PERRY, B. L. (2011). The labeling paradox: Stigma, the sick role, and social networks in mental illness. *Journal of Health and Social Behavior, 53,* 1-17.

PETERS, M. (1995). Race differences in brain size. *American Psychologist, 50,* 947-948.

PETERS, M. (1996). Does brain size matter? A reply to Rushton and Ankney. *Canadian Journal of Experimental Psychology, 49,* 748-750.

PETERS, T. J., & WATERMAN, R. H., JR. (1982). *In search of excellence: Lessons from America's best-run companies.* New York, NY: Harper & Row.

PETERSON, C., & BARRETT, L. C. (1987). Explanatory style and academic performance among university freshmen. *Journal of Personality and Social Psychology, 53*(3), 603-607.

PETERSON, C., SEMMEL, A., VON BAEYER, C., ABRAMSON, L., METALSKY, G. I., & SELIGMAN, M. E. P. (1982). The attributional style questionnaire. *Cognitive Therapy and Research, 6,* 287-300.

PETITTO, L. A., & MARENTETTE, P. F. (1991). Babbling in the manual mode: Evidence for the ontogeny of language. *Science, 251,* 1493-1493.

PETRACCA, G. M., JORGE, R. E., ACIÓN, L., WEINTRAUB, D., & ROBINSON, R. G. (2009). Frequency and correlates of involuntary emotional expression disorder in Parkinson's disease. *The Journal of Neuropsychiatry and Clinical Neurosciences, 21,* 406-412.

PETTEGREW, J. W., KESHAVAN, K. S., & MINSHEW, N. J. (1993). 31P nuclear magnetic resonance spectroscopy: Neurodevelopment and schizophrenia. *Schizophrenia Bulletin, 19,* 35-53.

PETTIGREW, T. F., & TROPP, L. R. (2006). A meta-analytic test of intergroup contact theory. *Journal of Personality and Social Psychology, 90,* 751-783.

PETTY, R. E., & CACIOPPO, J. T. (1986). The elaboration likelihood model of persuasion. In L. Berkowitz (Ed.), *Advances in experimental social psychology, 19,* 123-205. New York, NY: Academic Press.

PFUNGST, O. (2000). *Clever Hans: The horse of Mr. von Osten.* (R. H. Wozniak, Ed.). Bristol, UK: Thoemmes Press. (Original work published 1911)

PHELPS, E. A., O'CONNOR, K. J., CUNNINGHAM, W. A., FUNAYAMA, E. S., GATENBY, J. C., GORE, J. C., & BANAJI, M. (2000). Performance on indirect measures of race evaluation predicts amygdala activation. *Journal of Cognitive Neuroscience 12*(5), 729-738.

PHILLIPS, P. E. M., STUBER, G. D., HEIEN, M. L. A. V., WIGHTMAN, R. M., & CARELLI, R. M. (2003). Subsecond dopamine release promotes cocaine seeking. *Nature, 422*(6932), 614-618.

PHUTANE, V. H., THIRTHALLI, J., KESAVAN, M., KUMAR, N. C., & GANGADHAR, B. N. (2011). Why do we prescribe ECT to schizophrenia patients? *Indian Journal of Psychiatry, 53,* 149-151.

PIAGET, J. (1932). *The moral judgment of the child.* New York, NY: Harcourt, Brace & World.

PICKAR, D., LABARCA, R., LINNOILA, M., ROY, A., HOMMER, D., EVERETT, D., & PAYL, S. M. (1984). Neuroleptic-induced decrease in plasma homovanillic acid and antipsychotic activity in schizophrenic patients. *Science, 225,* 954-957.

PIKO, B. F., KOVACS, E., & FITZPATRICK, K. M. (2009). What makes a difference? Understanding the role of protective factors in Hungarian adolescents' depressive symptomatology. *European Child and Adolescent Psychiatry, 18,* 617-624.

PLUTCHIK, R. (1980). *Emotion: A psychoevolutionary synthesis.* New York, NY: Harper & Row.

POLESHUCK, E., GAMBLE, S., CORT, N., HOFFMAN-KING, D., CERRITO, B., ROSARIO-MCCABE, L., & GILES, D. (2010). Interpersonal psychotherapy for co-occurring depression and chronic pain. *Professional Psychology: Research and Practice, 41,* 312-318.

POPULATION DIVISION OF THE DEPARTMENT OF ECONOMIC AND SOCIAL AFFAIRS OF THE UNITED NATIONS SECRETARIAT, WORLD POPULATION PROSPECTS. (2006). Executive summary.

POST, J. M., & PANIS, L. K. (2011). Crimes of obedience: "Groupthink" at Abu Ghraib. *International Journal of Group Psychotherapy 61,* 48-66.

PRESSMAN, S. D., COHEN, S., MILLER, G. E., BARKIN, A., RABIN, B. S., & TREANOR, J. J. (2005). Loneliness, social network size, and immune response to influenza vaccination in college freshman. *Health Psychology, 24*(3), 297-306.

PRESSON, P. K., & BENASSI, V. A. (1996). Illusion of control: A meta-analytic review. *Journal of Social Behavior and Personality, 11*(3), 493-510.

PUJOL, J., HARRISON, B. J., ORTIZ, H., DEUS, J., SORIANO-MAS, C., LOPEZ-SOLA, M., YUCEL, M., PERICH, X., & CARDONER, N. (2009). Influence of the fusiform gyrus on amygdala response to emotional faces in the non-clinical range of social anxiety. *Psychological Medicine, 39,* 1177-1187.

PUKALL, C., KANDYBA, K., AMSEL, R., KHALIFÉ, S., & BINIK, Y. (2007). Sexual pain disorders: Effectiveness of hypnosis for the treatment of vulvar vestibulitis syndrome: A preliminary investigation. *The Journal of Sexual Medicine, 4,* 417-425. doi:10.1111/j.1743-6109.2006.00425.x

QUINN, P. C., BHATT, R. S., BRUSH, D., GRIMES, A., & SHARPNACK, H. (2002). Development of form similarity as a Gestalt grouping principle in infancy. *Psychological Science, 13,* 320-328.

RAINE, A. (1999). Murderous minds: Can we see the mark of Cain? *Cerebrum: The Dana Forum on Brain Science, 1*(1), 15-29.

RAINE, A., LENCZ, T., BIHRLE, S., LACASSE, L., & COLLETTI, P. (2000). Reduced prefrontal gray matter volume and reduced autonomic activity in antisocial personality disorder. *Archives of General Psychiatry, 57,* 119-127.

RAINVILLE, P., DUNCAN, G. H., PRICE, D. D., CARRIER, B., & BUSHNELL, M. C. (1997). Pain affect encoded in human anterior cingulated but not somatosensory cortex. *Science, 277,* 968-971.

RAMACHANDRAN, V. S. (2000, June). Mirror neurons and imitation learning as the driving force behind "the great leap forward" in human evolution. *Edge, 69.*

RAUCH, S. L., & JENIKE, M. A. (1993). Neurobiological models of obsessive-compulsive disorder. *Psychomatics, 34,* 20-32.

RAZRAN, G. (1949). Semantic and phonetographic generalizations of salivary conditioning to verbal stimuli. *Journal of Experimental Psychology, 39,* 642-652.

RECANZONE, G. H., JENKINS, W. M., HRADEK, G. T., & MERZENICH, M. M. (1992). Progressive improvement in discriminative abilities in adult owl monkeys performing a tactile frequency discrimination task. *Journal of Neurophysiology, 67*(5), 1015-1030.

RECHTSCHAFFEN, A., & BERGMAN, B. M. (1965). Sleep deprivation in the rat by the disk-over-water method. *Behavioral Brain Research, 69,* 55-63.

REEVES, J. L., REDD, W. H., STORM, F. K., & MINOGAWA, R. V. (1983). Hypnosis in the control of pain during hyperthermia treatment of cancer. In J. J. Bonica, V. Lindblom, & A. Iago (Eds.), *Advances in pain research and therapy.* New York, NY: Raven.

REICHMAN, J. (1998). *I'm not in the mood: What every woman should know about improving her libido.* New York, NY: Morrow.

REINER, W. G., & GEARHART, J. P. (2004). Discordant sexual identity in some genetic males with cloacal exstrophy assigned to female sex at birth. *New England Journal of Medicine, 350,* 333-341.

REIO, T. G. JR. (2011). Supervisor and coworker incivility: Testing the work frustration aggression model. *Advances in Developing Human Resources, 13,* 54-65. doi:10.1177/1523422311410648

REISS, A. L., ABRAMS, M. T., SINGER, H. S., ROSS, J. L., & DENCKLA, M. B. (1996). Brain development, gender and IQ in children. A volumetric imaging study. *Brain, 119,* 1763-1774.

REYES, H. L. M., FOSHEE, V. A., BAUER, D. J., & ENNETT, S. T. (2011) Developmental associations between adolescent alcohol use and dating violence perpetration. *Journal of Research on Adolescence, 48,* 344-350.

RICHESON, J. A., BAIRD, A. A., GORDON, H. L., HEATHERTON, T. F., WYLAND, C. L., TRAWALTER, S., & SHELTON, J. N. (2003). An fMRI investigation of the impact of interracial contact on executive function. *Nature Neuroscience, 6,* 1323-1328.

RICHTER, C. P., (1936). Increased salt appetite in adrenalectomized rats. *American Journal of Physiology, 115,* 155-161.

RICHTER, C. P., & ECKERT, J. F. (1937). Increased calcium appetite of parathyroidectomized rats. *Endocrinology, 21,* 50-54.

RINI, C. K., DUNKEL-SCHETTER, C., WADHWA, P. D., & SANDMAN, C. A. (1999). Psychological adaptation and birth outcomes: The role of personal resources, stress, and sociocultural context in pregnancy. *Health Psychology, 18,* 333-345.

RISSMAN, J., GAZZALEY, A., & D'ESPOSITO, M. (2008). Dynamic adjustments in prefrontal, hippocampal, and inferior temporal interactions with increasing visual working memory load. *Cerebral Cortex, 18*(7), 1618-1629.

ROBERTS, L. W., CLIFTON, R. A., FERGUSON, B., KAMPEN, K., & LANGOIS, S. (Eds.). (2005). *Recent social trends in Canada, 1960-2000.* Montreal, QC-Kingston, ON: McGill-Queen's University Press.

ROENNEBERG, T., KUEHNLE, T., PRAMSTALLER, P. P., RICKEN, J., HAVEL, M., GUTH, A., & MERROW, M. (2004). A marker for the end of adolescence. *Current Biology, 14,* R1038-9.

ROGERS, C. (1980). *A way of being.* Boston, MA: Houghton Mifflin.

ROGERS, C. R. (1961). *On becoming a person: A therapist's view of psychotherapy.* Boston, MA: Houghton Mifflin.

ROGOVIK, A. L., & GOLDMAN, R. D. (2007). Hypnosis for treatment of pain in children. *Canadian Family Physician, 53,* 823-825.

ROHNER, J. C., & RASMUSSEN, A. (2012). Recognition bias and the physical attractiveness stereotype. *Scandinavian Journal of Psychology, 53,* 239-246. doi:10.1111/j.1467-9450.2012.00939.x

ROSCH, E. (1978). Principles of categorization. In E. Rosch & B. L. Lloyd (Eds.), *Cognition and categorization.* Hillsdale, NJ: Earlbaum.

ROSE, J. S., CHASSIN, L., PRESSON, C. C., & SHERMAN, S. J. (1999). Peer influences on adolescent cigarette smoking: A prospective sibling analysis. *Merrill-Palmer Quarterly, 45,* 62-84.

ROSEN, W. D., ADAMSON, L. B., & BAKEMAN, R. (1992). An experimental investigation of infant social referencing: Mothers' messages and gender differences. *Developmental Psychology, 28,* 1172-1178.

ROSENHAN, D. L. (1973). On being sane in insane places. *Science, 179,* 250-258.

ROSENMAN, R. H., BRAND, R. I., JENKINS, C. D., FRIEDMAN, M., STRAUS, R., & WURM, M. (1975). Coronary heart disease in the Western Collaborative Group Study, final follow-up experience of 81/2 years. *Journal of the American Medical Association, 233,* 812-817.

ROSENTHAL, R. (1974). *On the social psychology of the self-fulfilling prophecy: Further evidence for Pygmalion effects and their mediating mechanisms.* New York, NY: MSS Modular Publications.

ROSENZWEIG, M. R., BENNETT, E. L., DIAMOND, M. C. (1972). Brain changes in response to experience. *Scientific American, 226*(2), 22-29.

ROSS, L. (1977). The intuitive psychologist and his shortcomings. In L. Berkowitz (Ed.), *Advances in experimental social psychology* (Vol. 10, pp. 173-220). New York, NY: Academic Press.

ROSS, L., GREENE, D., & HOUSE, P. (1977). The false consensus effect: An egocentric bias in social perception and attribution processes. *Journal of Experimental Social Psychology, 13,* 279-301.

ROTTER, J. B. (1954). *Social learning and clinical psychology.* Englewood Cliffs, NJ: Prentice-Hall.

ROTTER, J. B. (1966). Generalized expectancies for internal versus external control of reinforcement. *Psychological Monographs, 80*(Whole No. 609).

ROWE, D. C., ALMEIDA, D. M., & JACOBSON, K. C. (1999). School context and genetic influences on aggression in adolescence. *Psychological Science, 10,* 277-280.

ROZZET, J. H., HAGE, S., & CHOW, H. (2011). Academic dishonesty in the Canadian classroom: Behaviours of a sample of university students. *Canadian Journal of Higher Education, 41,* 35-57.

RUSHTON, J. P. (1991). Mongoloid-Caucasoid differences in brain size from military samples. *Intelligence, 15,* 351-359.

RUSHTON, J. P. (1992). Cranial capacity related to sex, rank, and race in a stratified random sample of 6,325 U.S. military personnel. *Intelligence, 16,* 401-413.

RUSHTON, J. P. (1997). Cranial size and IQ in Asian Americans from birth to age seven. *Intelligence, 25,* 7-20.

SACHDEV, P., & SACHDEV, J. (1997). Sixty years of psychosurgery: Its present status and its future. *Australian and New Zealand Journal of Psychiatry, 31,* 457-464.

SADKER, D. (2000). Gender equity: Still knocking at the classroom door. *Equity & Excellence in Education, 33*(1), 80-83.

SAKURAI, T., AMEMIYA, A., ISHII, M., MATSUZAKI, I., CHEMELLI, R. M., TANAKA, H., . . . YANAGISAWA, M. (1998). Orexins and orexin receptors: A family of hypothalamic neuropeptides and G-protein coupled receptors that regulate feeding behaviour. *Cell, 92*, 573-585.

SALLEH, A. (2003, August 18). Brain shrinkage: Early sign of schizophrenia? *ABC Science Online.* Retrieved from http://www.abc.net.au/science/news/stories/s925547.htm

SALZINGER, S., NG-MAK, D. S., FELDMAN, R. S., KAM, C. M., & ROSARIO, M. (2006). Exposure to community violence: Processes that increase the risk for inner-city middle-school children. *Journal of Early Adolescence, 26*, 232-266.

SANDERSON, A. R. (2012). Beauty pays: Why attractive people are more successful. *Choice, 49*, 1113-1114.

SANFORD, A. J., FRAY, N., STEWART, A., & MOXLEY, L. (2002). Perspective in statements of quality, with implications for consumer psychology. *Psychological Science, 13*, 130-134.

SARRIS, J., MISCHOULON, D., & SCHWEITZER, I. (2012). Omega-3 for bipolar disorder: Meta-analyses of use in mania and bipolar depression. *Journal of Clinical Psychiatry, 73*, 81-86.

SAVIC, I., BERGLUND, H., & LINDSTRÖM, P. (2005). Brain response to putative pheromones in homosexual men. *Proceedings of the National Academy of Sciences of the United States of America, 102*(20), 7356-7361.

SAYKIN, J. A., GUR, R. C., GUR, R. E. ET AL. (1991). Neuropsychological function in schizophrenia: Selective impairment in memory and learning. *Archives of General Psychiatry, 48*, 618-624.

SCHACHTER, S., & SINGER, J. E. (1962). Cognitive, social, and physiological determinants of emotional state. *Psychological Review, 69*, 379-399.

SCHACTER, D. L. (1996). *Searching for memory: The brain, the mind, and the past.* New York, NY: Basic Books.

SCHACTER, D. L. (1999). The seven sins of memory: Insights from psychology and cognitive neuroscience. *American Psychologist, 54*, 182-201.

SCHANBERG, S., & FIELD, T. (1988). Maternal deprivation and supplemental stimulation. In T. Field, P. McCabe, & N. Schneiderman (Eds.), *Stress and coping across development.* Hillsdale, NJ: Erlbaum.

SCHEIER, M. F., & CARVER, C. S. (1992). Effects of optimism on psychological and physical well-being: Theoretical overview and empirical update. *Cognitive Therapy and Research, 16*(2), 201-228.

SCHERMER, J. A., JOHNSON, A. M., VERNON, P. A., & JANG, K. L. (2011). The relationship between personality and self-report abilities: A behavior-genetic analysis. *Journal of Individual Differences, 32*, 47-53.

SCHERMER, V. L. (2010). Mirror neurons: Their implications for group psychotherapy. *International Journal of Group Psychotherapy, 60*, 486-513.

SCHIENLE, A., HETTEMA, J., CÁCEDA, R., & NEMEROFF, C. (2011). Neurobiology and genetics of generalized anxiety disorder. *Psychiatric Annals, 41*, 113-123.

SCHNYDER, U., MÜLLER, J., MAERCKER, A., & WITTMANN, L. (2011). Brief eclectic psychotherapy for PTSD: A randomized controlled trial. *Journal of Clinical Psychiatry, 72*, 564-566.

SCHMITT, D. P., ALLIK, J., MCCRAE, R. R., BENET-MARTINEZ, V., ALCALAY, L., AULT, L., . . . POELS, K. (2007). The geographic distribution of Big Five personality traits: Patterns and profiles of human self-description across 56 nations. *Journal of Cross-Cultural Psychology, 38*, 173-212.

SCHNEIDER INSTITUTE FOR HEALTH POLICY, BRANDEIS UNIVERSITY. (2001). *Substance abuse: The nation's number one health problem.* Princeton, NJ: Robert Wood Johnson Foundation. Retrieved from http://www.rwjf.org/files/publications/other/SubstanceAbuseChartbook.pdf

SCHONFIELD, D., & ROBERTSON, B. A. (1966). Memory storage and aging. *Canadian Journal of Psychology, 20*, 228-236.

SCHUR, C. (2010). *Sleep disorders.* Retrieved from http://www.associatedsleepservices.com/main/

SCHWARTZ, P. (1994, November 17). Some people with multiple roles are blessedly stressed. *The New York Times.*

SCHWARTZ, R. C., LENT, J., & GEIHSLER, J. (2011). Gender and diagnosis of mental disorders: Implications for mental health counseling. *Journal of Mental Health Counseling, 33*, 347-358.

SEEMAN, P., GUAN, H-C., & VAN TOL, H. H. M. (1993). Dopamine D4 receptors elevated in schizophrenia. *Nature, 365*, 441-445.

SEI, H., SAITOH, D., YAMAMOTO, K., MORITA, K., & MORITA, Y. (2000). Differential effect of short-term REM sleep deprivation on NGF and BDNF protein levels in the rat brain. *Brain Research, 877*(2) 387-390.

SEIFERT, A. E., POLUSNY, M. A., & MURDOCH, M. (2011). The association between childhood physical and sexual abuse and functioning and psychiatric symptoms in a sample of U.S. Army soldiers. *Military Medicine, 176*, 176-181.

SEKIYAMA, K., MIYAUCHI, S., IMARUOKA, T., EGUSA, H., & TASHIRO, T. (2000). Body image as a visuomotor transformation device revealed in adaptation to reversed vision. *Nature, 407*, 374-377.

SELIGMAN, M. E. P. (1968). Chronic fear produced by unpredictable electric shock. *Journal of Comparative and Physiological Psychology, 66*, 402-411.

SELIGMAN, M. E. P. (1971). Phobias and preparedness. *Behavior Therapy, 2*, 307-320.

SELIGMAN, M. E. P., & YELLEN, A. (1987). What is a dream? *Behavior Research and Therapy, 25*, 1-24.

SEMIN, G. R., & MANSTEAD, A. S. R. (1982). The social implications of embarrassment displays and restitution behavior. *European Journal of Social Psychology, 12*, 367-377.

SHADISH, W. R., MATT, G. E., NAVARRO, A. M., & PHILLIPS, G. (2000). The effects of psychological therapies under clinically representative conditions: A meta-analysis. *Psychological Bulletin, 126*, 512-529.

SHAHANI-DENNING, C., DUDHAT, P., TEVET, R., & ANDREOLI, N. (2010). Effect of physical attractiveness on selection decisions in India and the United States. *International Journal of Management, 27*, 37-51.

SHAMDASANI, P., & JUNG, K. (2011). Relationship quality between in-groups and out-groups. *The International Business & Economics Research Journal, 10*, 33-51.

SHANE, S., NICOLAOU, N., CHERKAS, L., & SPECTOR, T. D. (2010). Genetics, the Big Five, and the tendency to be self-employed. *Journal of Applied Psychology, 95*, 1154-1162.

SHAPIRO, F. (1989). Efficacy of the eye movement desensitization procedure in the treatment of traumatic memories. *Journal of Traumatic Stress, 2*, 199-223.

SHAPIRO, F. (2002). *EMDR as an integrative psychotherapy approach: Experts of diverse orientations explore the paradigm prism.* Washington, DC: APA Books.

SHARMA, T. (2003). Characterisation of cognitive impairment in schizophrenia. *Lancet Neurology, 2*, 10.

SHAW, P., GREENSTEIN, D., LERCH, J., CLASEN, L., LENROOT, R., GOGTAY, N., ET AL. (2006). Intellectual ability and cortical development in children and adolescents. *Nature, 440*, 676-679.

SHEDLER, J. (2010). The efficacy of psychodynamic psychotherapy. *American Psychologist, 65*, 98-109.

SHERGILL, S. S., BRAMMER, M. J., WILLIAMS, S. C. R., MURRAY, R. M., MCGUIRE, P. K. (2000). Mapping auditory hallucinations in schizophrenia using functional magnetic resonance imaging. *Archives of General Psychiatry, 57*, 1033-1038.

SHERRY, D., & VACCARINO, A. L. (1989). Hippocampus and memory for food caches in black-capped chickadees. *Behavioral Neuroscience, 103*, 308-318.

SHIELDS, B. (2005). *Down came the rain: My journey through post-partum depression.* New York, NY: Christa Incorporated.

SIECCAN. (2010). *The Sex Information and Education Council of Canada.* Retrieved from http://www.sieccan.org

SIEGEL, S., HINSON, R. E., KRANK, M. D, & MCCULLY, J. (1982, April 23). Heroin "overdose" death: Contribution of drug-associated environmental cues. *Science, 216*(4544), 436-437.

SIERRA CLUB. (2008). *Global population and environment: Population, consumption, & our ecological footprint.* Retrieved from http://www.sierraclub.org/population/consumption

SILVA, C. E., & KIRSCH, I. (1992). Interpretive sets, expectancy, fantasy proneness, and dissociation as predictors of hypnotic response. *Journal of Personality and Social Psychology, 63*, 847-856.

SILVERSTEIN, S. M., ALL, S. D., KASI, R., BERTEN, S., ESSEX, B., LATHROP, K., & LITTLE, D. M. (2010). Increased fusiform area activation in schizophrenia during processing of spatial frequency-degraded faces, as revealed by fMRI. *Psychological Medicine, 40*, 1159-1169.

SILVIA, P. J., & KIMBREL, N. A. (2010). A dimensional analysis of creativity and mental illness: Do anxiety and depression symptoms predict creative cognition, creative accomplishments, and creative self-concepts? *Psychology of Aesthetics, Creativity, and the Arts, 4*, 2-10.

SIMEK, T. C., & O'BRIEN, R. M. (1981). *Total golf: A behavioral approach to lowering your score and getting more out of your game.* New York, NY: Doubleday.

SIMEK, T. C., & O'BRIEN, R. M. (1988). A chaining-mastery discrimination training program to teach Little Leaguers to hit a baseball. *Human Performance, 1*, 73-84.

SIMONS, D. J., & LEVIN, D. T. (1998). Failure to detect changes to people during a real-world interaction. *Psychonomic Bulletin and Review, 5*, 644-649.

References

SIMONS, R. L., LEI, M. K., BEACH, S. R., BRODY, G. H., PHILIBERT, R. A., & GIBBONS F. X. (2011). Social environmental variation, plasticity genes, and aggression: Evidence for the differential susceptibility hypothesis. *American Sociological Review, 76,* 833-912. doi:10.1177/0003122411427580

SKINNER, B. F. (1948). *Science and human behavior.* New York, NY: Macmillan.

SKINNER, B. F. (1957). *Verbal behavior.* Englewood Cliffs, NJ: Prentice Hall.

SKLAR, L. S., & ANISMAN, H. (1981). Stress and cancer. *Psychological Bulletin, 89,* 396-406.

SKRE, I., ONSTAD, S., TORGERSEN, S., LYGREN, S., & KRINGLEN, E. (1993). A twin study of DSM-III-R anxiety disorders. *Acta Psychiatrica Scandinavica, 88,* 85-92

SLEEP WELL CANADA. (2010). Retrieved from http://sleepwellcanada.com/sleep-apnea

SLINING M., ADAIR, L. S., GOLDMAN, B. D., BORJA, J. B., & BENTLEY, M. (2010). Infant overweight is associated with delayed motor development. *The Journal of Pediatrics, 157,* 20-25.

SLOANE, R. B., STAPLES, F. R., CRISTOL, A. H., YORKSON, N. J., & WHIPPLE, K. (1975). *Psychotherapy versus behavior therapy.* Cambridge, MA: Harvard University Press.

SMILEK, D., CARRIERE, J., & CHEYNE, J. A. (2010). Out of mind, out of sight: Eye blinking as indicator and embodiment of mind wandering. *Psychological Science, 21,* 786-789. doi:10.1177/0956797610368063

SMITH, J. C., & CURRY, S. C. (2011). Prolonged toxicity after amitriptyline overdose in a patient deficient in CYP2D6 activity. *Journal of Medical Toxicology, 7,* 220-223.

SMITH, M. L., GLASS, G. V., & MILLER, R. L. (1980). *The benefits of psychotherapy.* Baltimore, MD: Johns Hopkins Press.

SMITH, N. A., & TRAINOR, L. J. (2008). Infant-directed speech is modulated by infantfeedback.*Infancy,13*(4),410-420.doi:10.1080/15250000802188719

SNYDER, C. R., SYMPSON, S. C., YBASCO, F. C., BORDERS, T. F., BABYAK, M. A., & HIGGINS, R. L. (1996). Development and validation of the State Hope Scale. *Journal of Personality and Social Psychology 70,* 321-335

SNYDER, M. (1984). When beliefs create reality. In L. Berkowitz (Ed.), *Advances in experimental social psychology* (Vol. 18, pp. 247-305). New York, NY: Academic Press.

So, K. T., & ORME-JOHNSON, D. W. (2001). Three randomized experiments of the longitudinal effects of the Transcendental Meditation technique on cognition. *Intelligence, 29*(5), 419-440.

SOLOMON, D. A., KEITNER, G. I., MILLER, I. W., SHEA, M. T., & KELLER, M. B. (1995). Course of illness and maintenance treatments for patients with bipolar disorder. *Journal of Clinical Psychiatry, 56,* 5-13.

SOLOMON, J. (1996, May 20). Breaking the silence. *Newsweek,* pp. 20-22.

SOLOMON, K., & ANNIS, H. M. (2006). Outcome and efficacy expectancy in the prediction of post-treatment drinking behaviour. *Addiction.* doi:10.1111/j.1360-0443.1990.tb03528.x

SPECIAL SENATE COMMITTEE ON AGING. (2009). *Special Senate Committee on Aging Final Report. Canada's Aging Population: Seizing the Opportunity.* Retrieved from http://www.parl.gc.ca/40/2/parlbus/commbus/senate/com-e/agei-e/rep-e/AgingFinalReport-e.pdf

SPENCE, I., YU, J. J., FENG, J., & MARSHMAN, J. (2009). Females match males when learning a spatial skill. *Journal of Experimental Psychology: Learning, Memory, & Cognition, 35,* 1097-1103.

SPERLING, G. (1960). The information available in brief visual presentations. *Psychological Monographs, 74,* 1-29.

SPIEGEL, K., LEPROUL, R., & VAN CAUTER, E. (1999). Impact of sleep debt on metabolic and endocrine function. *Lancet, 345,* 1435-1439.

ST. ONGE, J. R., & FLORESCO, S. B. (2008, July 30). Dopaminergic modulation of risk-based decision making. *Neuropsychopharmacology.* [Epub ahead of print]

STANFORD UNIVERSITY CENTER FOR NARCOLEPSY. (2002). *Narcolepsy is a serious medical disorder and a key to understanding other sleep disorders.* Retrieved from http://www.med.stanford.edu/school/Psychiatry/narcolepsy

STATISTICS CANADA. (2006). *Survey of earned degrees.* Retrieved from http://www.statcan.gc.ca/cgibin/imdb/p2SV.pl?Function=getSurvey&SDDS=3126&lang=en&db=imdb&adm=8&dis=2

STATISTICS CANADA. (2007). *Families and households, 2006 Census.* Retrieved from http://www.statcan.gc.ca/bsolc/olc-cel/olc-cel?catno=97-553-XIE&lang=eng

STATISTICS CANADA. (2007). *Marriages. The Daily.* Retrieved from http://www.statcan.gc.ca/daily-quotidien/070117/dq070117a-eng.htm

STATISTICS CANADA. (2009). *Canadian community health survey.* Retrieved from http://www.statcan.gc.ca/daily-quotidien/090625/dq090625b-eng.htm

STATISTICS CANADA. (2009). *University degrees, diplomas and certificates awarded.* Retrieved from http://www.statcan.gc.ca/daily-quotidien/090713/dq090713b-eng.htm

STATISTICS CANADA. (2010). *Gambling.* Retrieved from http://www.statcan.gc.ca/pub/75-001-x/topics-sujets/gambling-jeuxdehasard/gambling-jeuxdehasard-2009-eng.htm

STATISTICS CANADA. (2011). *General Social Survey, 2010. Overview of the time use of Canadians.* Retrieved from http://www5.statcan.gc.ca/bsolc/olc-cel/olc-cel?catno=89-647-X&lang=eng

STATISTICS CANADA. (2012). *Health.* Retrieved from http://www5.statcan.gc.ca/subject-sujet/theme-theme.action?pid=2966&lang=eng&more=0

STATISTICS CANADA. (2012). *Household, family and personal income.* Retrieved from http://www5.statcan.gc.ca/subject-sujet/subtheme-soustheme.action?pid=3868&id=2812&lang=eng&more=0

STATISTICS CANADA ETHNIC DIVERSITY SURVEY. (2007). Retrieved from http://www.statcan.gc.ca/rdc-cdr/proj-eng.htm#projects

STEELE, C. M., & ARONSON, J. (1995). Stereotype threat and the intellectual test performance of African-Americans. *Journal of Personality and Social Psychology, 69,* 797-811.

STEIN, EDWARD. (1999). *The mismeasure of desire: Science, theory, and the ethics of sexual orientation.* New York, NY: Oxford University Press.

STEPHANOPOULOS, G. (1999). *All too human: A political education.* New York, NY: Little Brown.

STERNBERG, R. J. (1985). *Beyond IQ: A triarchic theory of human intelligence.* New York, NY: Cambridge University Press.

STERNBERG, R. J., & KAUFMAN, J. C. (1998). Human abilities. *Annual Review of Psychology, 49,* 479-502.

STETTER, F., & KUPPER, S. (2002). Autogenic training: A meta-analysis of clinical outcome studies. *Applied Psychophysiology and Biofeedback, 27,* 45-98.

STEWART, T. L., LATU, I. M., KAWAKAMI, K., & MYERS, A. C. (2010). Consider the situation: Reducing automatic stereotyping through situational attribution training. *Journal of Experimental Social Psychology, 46,* 221-225.

STICKGOLD, R., HOBSON, J. A., FOSSE, R., & FOSSE, M. (2001, November 2). Sleep, learning, and dreams: Off-line memory reprocessing. *Science, 294*(5544), 1052-1057.

STITH, S. M., ROSEN, K. H., MIDDLETON, K. A., BUSCH, A. L., LUNDEBERG, K., & CARLTON, R. P. (2000). The intergenerational transmission of spouse abuse: A meta-analysis. *Journal of Marriage and the Family, 62,* 640-654.

STONE, A. A., & NEALE, J. M. (1984). Effects of severe daily events on mood. *Journal of Personality and Social Psychology, 46,* 137-144.

STRACK, F., MARTIN, L., & STEPPER, S. (1988). Inhibiting and facilitating conditions of the human smile: A nonobtrusive test of the facial feedback hypothesis. *Journal of Personality and Social Psychology, 54,* 768-777.

STRATHEARN, L., Li, J., FONAGY, P., & MONTAGUE, P. R. (2008, July). What's in a smile? Maternal brain responses to infant facial cues. *Pediatrics, 122,* 40-51.

STRAYER, D. L., & JOHNSTON, W. A. (2001). Driven to distraction: Dual-task studies of simulated driving and conversing on a cellular telephone. *Psychological Science, 12,* 462-466.

STRUPP, H. H. (1986). Psychotherapy: Research, practice, and public policy (How to avoid dead ends). *American Psychologist, 41,* 120-130.

SULLIVAN, HARRY STACK. (2008). In Encyclopædia Britannica Online. Retrieved from http://www.search.eb.com/eb/article-9070262

SULLIVAN, P. F., NEALE, M. C., & KENDLER, K. S. (2000). Genetic epidemiology of major depression: Review and meta-analysis. *American Journal of Psychiatry, 157,* 1552-1562.

SURTEES, P. G., WAINWRIGHT, N. W., LUBEN, R. N., KHAW, K. T., & BINGHAM, S. A. (2010). No evidence that social stress is associated with breast cancer incidence. *Breast Cancer Research and Treatment, 120,* 169-174.

SUSAC, A., ILMONIEMI, R. J., RANKEN, D., & SUPEK, S. (2011). Face activated neurodynamic cortical networks. *Medical and Biological Engineering and Computing, 49,* 531-543.

SWARTZ, H. A., LEVENSON, J. C., & FRANK, E. (2012). Psychotherapy for bipolar II disorder: The role of interpersonal and social rhythm therapy. *Professional Psychology: Research and Practice, 43,* 145-153. doi:10.1037/a0027671

SWERDLOW, N. R., & KOOB, G. F. (1987). Dopamine, schizophrenia, mania, and depression: Toward a unified hypothesis of cortico-statio-pallido-thalamic function (with commentary). *Behavioral and Brain Sciences, 10,* 197-246.

SZASZ, T. (1960). The myth of mental illness. *American Psychologist, 15,* 113-118.

SZATMARI, P., OFFORD, D. R., & BOYLE, M. H. (1989). Ontario child health study: Prevalence of attention deficit disorder with hyperactivity. *Journal of Child Psychology and Psychiatry, 30*(2), 219-223.

TAHERI, S. (2004). The genetics of sleep disorders. *Minerva Medica, 95,* 203-212.

TAJFEL, H. (Ed.). (1982). *Social identity and intergroup relations.* New York, NY: Cambridge University Press.

TAKAHASHI, A., QUADROS, I., DE ALMEIDA, R., & MICZEK, K. (2011) Brain serotonin receptors and transporters: Initiation vs. termination of escalated aggression. *Psychopharmacology, 213,* 183-212.

TAMIS-LEMONDA, C. S., BORNSTEIN, M. H., CYPHERS, L., TODA, S., & OGINO, M. (1992). Language and play at one year: A comparison of toddlers and mothers in the United States and Japan. *International Journal of Behavioral Development, 15*(1), 19-42.

TAMRES, L. K., JANICKI, D., & HELGESON, V. S. (2002). Sex differences in coping behavior: A meta-analytic review and an examination of relative coping. *Personality and Social Psychology Review, 6*(1), 2-30.

TANGNEY, J. P. (1999). The self-conscious emotions: Shame, guilt, embarrassment and pride. In T. Dalgleish & M. J. Power (Eds.), *Handbook of cognition and emotion* (pp. 541-568). Chichester, England: Wiley.

TANNEN, D. (1990). *You just don't understand: Women and men in conversation.* New York, NY: William Morrow.

TAUBES, G. (1994). Will new dopamine receptors offer a key to schizophrenia? *Science, 265,* 1034-1035.

TAYLOR, S. E. (2002). *The tending instinct: Women, men, and the biology of our relationships.* New York, NY: Holt.

TAYLOR, S. E., SEEMAN, T. E., EISENBERGER, N. I., KOZANIAN, T. A., MOORE, A. N., & MOONS, W. G. (2010). Effects of a supportive or an unsupportive audience on biological and psychological responses to stress. *Journal of Personality and Social Psychology, 98,* 47-56.

TAYLOR, S. L., STANEK, L. M., RESSLER, K. J., & HUHMAN, K. L. (2011). Differential brain-derived neurotrophic factor expression in limbic brain regions following social defeat or territorial aggression. *Behavioral Neuroscience, 125,* 911-920.

THASE, M. E. (2011). Antidepressant combinations: Widely used, but far from empirically validated. *Canadian Journal of Psychiatry, 56,* 317-323.

THOITS, P. A. (2011). Perceived social support and the voluntary, mixed, or pressured use of mental health services. *Society and Mental Health, 1,* 4-19.

THORNDIKE, E. L. (1898). Animal intelligence. *Psychological Review Monograph, 2*(4, Whole No. 8).

TOLMAN, E. C., & HONZIK, C. H. (1930). Introduction and removal of reward, and maze learning in rats. *University of California Publications in Psychology, 4,* 257-275.

TORGERSEN, S., KRINGLEN, E., & CRAMER, V. (2001). The prevalence of personality disorders in a community sample. *Archives of General Psychiatry, 58,* 590-596.

TORREY, E. F. (1986). *Witchdoctors and psychiatrists.* New York, NY: Harper & Row.

TOWN, J., ABBASS, A., & HARDY, G. (2011). Short-term psychodynamic psychotherapy for personality disorders: A critical review of randomized controlled trials. *Journal of Personality Disorders, 25,* 723-740.

TREISMAN, A. (1987). Properties, parts, and objects. In K. R. Boff, L. Kaufman, & J. P. Thomas (Eds.), *Handbook of perception and human performance.* New York, NY: Wiley.

TREISMAN, A. M., & GELADE, G. (1980). A feature-interpretation theory of attention. *Cognitive Psychology, 12,* 97-136.

TRISCARI, M. T., FARACI, P., D'ANGELO, V., URSO, V., & CATALISANO, D. (2011). Two treatments for fear of flying compared: Cognitive behavioral therapy combined with systematic desensitization or eye movement desensitization and reprocessing (EMDR). *Aviation Psychology and Applied Human Factors, 1,* 9-14.

TRIVERS, R. L. (1971). The evolution of reciprocal altruism. *Quarterly Review of Biology, 46,* 35-57.

TRIVERS, R. L. (1972). Parental investment and sexual selection. In B. Campbell (Ed.), *Sexual selection and the descent of man.* New York, NY: Aldine de Gruyter.

TRUT, L. N. (1999). Early canid domestication: The farm-fox experiment. *New Scientist, 87,* 160-169.

TRYON, R. C. (1940). Studies in individual differences in maze ability VII: The specific components of maze ability and a general theory of psychological components. *Journal of Comparative Psychology, 30,* 283-338.

TSIEN, J. Z. (2000, April). Building a brainier mouse. *Scientific American,* 62-68.

TURNER, W. J. (1995). Homosexuality, type 1: An Xq28 phenomenon. *Archives of Sexual Behavior, 24*(2), 109-134.

TUULIO-HENRIKSSON, A., PARTONEN, T., SUVISAARI, J., HAUKKA, J., & LÖNNQVIST, J. (2004). Age at onset and cognitive functioning in schizophrenia. *The British Journal of Psychiatry, 185,* 215-219.

TWENGE, J. M., BAUMEISTER, R. F., TICE, D. M., & STUCKE, T. S. (2001). If you can't join them, beat them: Effects of social exclusion on aggressive behavior. *Journal of Personality and Social Psychology, 81,* 1058-1069.

TWENGE, J. M., CATANESE, K. R., & BAUMEISTER, R. F. (2002). Social exclusion causes self-defeating behavior. *Journal of Personality and Social Psychology, 83,* 606-615.

UHLMANN, E. L., & NOSEK, B. A. (2012). My culture made me do it: Lay theories of responsibility for automatic prejudice. *Social Psychology, 43,* 108-113. doi:10.1027/1864-9335/a000089

UNDERWOOD, B. (2008). *About Ben.* Retrieved from http://www.benunderwood.com/aboutme.html

UNITED NATIONS STATISTICS DIVISION. (2005). *World and regional trends. Millennium Indicators Database.* Retrieved from http://millenniumindicators.un.org/unsd/mdg

UNITED STATES OLYMPIC COMMITTEE. (2008). *Julie Ertel.* Retrieved from http://www.usatriathlon.org/athlete/athlete/990

VAN DE CASTLE, R. (1994). *Our dreaming mind.* New York, NY: Ballantine Books.

VAN DEN BERG, D. P., & VAN DER GAAG, M. (2012). Treating trauma in psychosis with EMDR: A pilot study. *Journal of Behavior Therapy and Experimental Psychiatry, 43,* 664-671. doi:10.1016/j.btep.2011.09.011

VAN ENGEN, M. L., & WILLEMSEN, T. M. (2004). Sex and leadership styles: A meta-analysis of research published in the 1990s. *Psychological Reports, 94*(1), 3-18.

VAN INGEN, D. J., & NOVICKI, D. J. (2009). An effectiveness study of group therapy for anxiety disorders. *International Journal of Group Psychotherapy, 59,* 243-251.

VARVOGLI, L., & DARVIRI, C. (2011). Stress management techniques: Evidence-based procedures that reduce stress and promote health. *Health Science Journal, 5,* 74-89.

VEMER, E., COLEMAN, M., GANANG, L. H., & COOPER, H. (1989). Marital satisfaction in remarriage: A meta-analysis. *Journal of Marriage and the Family, 51,* 713-725.

VERNON, P. A., VILLANI, V. C., SCHERMER, J. A., KIRILOVIC, S., MARTIN, R. A., PETRIDES, K. V., . . . SPECTOR, T. D. (2009). Genetic and environmental correlations between trait emotional intelligence and humor styles. *Journal of Individual Differences, 30,* 130-137.

VERONA, E., SADEH, N., & CURTIN, J. J. (2009). Stress-induced asymmetric frontal brain activity and aggression risk. *Journal of Abnormal Psychology, 118,* 131-145.

VOGELEY, K., BUSSFELD, P., NEWEN, A., HERRMANN, S., HAPPE, F., FALKAI, P., . . . ZILLES, K. (2001). Mind reading: neural mechanisms of theory of mind and self-perspective. *Neuroimage, 14,* 170-181.

VOGT, B. A., VOGT, L., FARBER, N. B., & BUSH, G. (2005). Architecture and neurocytology of monkey cingulate gyrus. *Journal of Comparative Neurology, 485,* 218-239.

VOLTERRA, A., & STEINHÄUSER, C. (2004). Glial modulation of synaptic transmission in the hippocampus. *Glia 47*(3), 249-257.

VON DER HEYDT, R., PETERHANS, E., & BAUMGARTNER, G. (1984). Illusory contours and cortical neuron responses. *Science, 224,* 1260-1262.

VON SENDEN, M. (1932/1960). *Space and sight: The perception of space and shape in the congenitally blind before and after operation* (P. Heath, Trans.). Glencoe, IL: Free Press.

VYAZOVSKIY, V. V., CIRELLI, C., PFISTER-GENSKOW, M., FARAGUNA, U., & TONONI, G. (2008). Molecular and electrophysiological evidence for net synaptic potentiation in wake and depression in sleep. *Nature Neuroscience, 11*(2), 200-208.

VYGOTSKY, L. (1978). The role of play in development. In M. Cole (Trans.) *Mind in society.* Cambridge, MA: Harvard University Press.

WADSWORTH, M. E., SANTIAGO, C. D., EINHORN, L., MORAN, E. G., RIENKS, S., & MARKMAN, H. J. (2011). Preliminary efficacy of an intervention to reduce psychosocial stress and improve coping in low-income families. *American Journal of Community Psychology, 48,* 257-271.

WAGER, K. D. (2011). Children and pets: A winning combination. *Psychiatric Times, 28*(11).

WALDRON, B., BENSON, C., O'CONNELL, A., BYRNE, P., DOOLEY, B., & BURKE, T. (2010). Health locus of control and attributions of cause and blame in adjustment to spinal cord injury. *Spinal Cord, 48,* 598-602.

WALKER, J. (2004). *The death of David Reimer: A tale of sex, science, and abuse. Reason Online.* Retrieved from http://reason.com/links/links052404.shtml

WALLACE, R. K., & BENSON, H. (1972). The physiology of meditation. *Scientific American, 226*(2), 84-90.

WALLACH, M. A., & WALLACH, L. (1983). *Psychology's sanction for selfishness: The error of egoism in theory and therapy.* New York, NY: Freeman.

WALLIS, C. (1996, March 25). The most intimate bond. *Time.* Retrieved from http://www.time.com

WALUM, H., WESTBERG, L., HENNINGSSON, S., NEIDERHISER, J. M., REISS, D., IGL, W., . . . , & LICHTENSTEIN, P. (2008). Genetic variation in the vasopressin receptor 1a gene (AVPR1A) associates with pair-bonding behavior in humans. *Proceedings of the National Academy of Sciences, 105*(37), 14153–14156.

WAMPOLD, B. E. (2001). *The great psychology debate: Models, methods, and findings.* Mahwah, NJ: Erlbaum.

WANG, C., & CHEN, W. (2000). The efficacy of behavior therapy in 9 patients with phobia. *Chinese Mental Health Journal, 14,* 351–352.

WANNEMUELLER, A., JOEHREN, P., HAUG, S., HATTING, M., ELSESSER, K., & SARTORY, G. (2011). A practice-based comparison of brief cognitive behavioural treatment, two kinds of hypnosis and general anaesthesia in dental phobia. *Psychotherapy and Psychosomatics, 80,* 159–165.

WARE, M. A., WANG, T., SHAPIRO, S., ROBINSON, A., DUCRUET, T., ET AL. (2010). Smoked cannabis for chronic neuropathic pain: A randomized controlled trial. *Canadian Medical Association Journal, 182,* E694–701.

WATSON, J. B., & RAYNER, R. (1920). Conditioned emotional reactions. *Journal of Experimental Psychology, 3,* 1–14.

WATSON, J. S., & RAMEY, C. T. (1972). Reactions to response-contingent stimulation in early infancy. *Merrill-Palmer Quarterly, 18,* 219–227.

WAYMENT, H. A., & PEPLAU, L. A. (1995). Social support and well-being among lesbian and heterosexual women: A structural modeling approach. *Personality and Social Psychology Bulletin, 21,* 1189–1199.

WEATHERS, H. (2006, December 31). *Abigail and Brittany Hensel: An extraordinary bond. Mail Online.* Retrieved from http://www.dailymail.co.uk

WEBB, W. B., & CAMPBELL, S. S. (1983, October). Relationships in sleep characteristics of identical and fraternal twins. *Archives of General Psychiatry, 40*(10), 1093–1095.

WECHSLER, D. (1975). *The collected papers of David Wechsler.* New York, NY: Academic Press.

WEISBERG, R. W. (1994). Genius and madness? A quasi-experimental test of the hypothesis that manic-depression increases creativity. *Psychological Science, 5,* 361–367.

WEISSMAN, M. M. (1999). Interpersonal psychotherapy and the health care scene. In D. S. Janowsky (Ed.), *Psychotherapy indications and outcomes.* Washington, DC: American Psychiatric Press.

WELLMAN, H. M., & GELMAN, S. A. (1992). Cognitive development: Foundational theories of core domains. *Annual Review of Psychology, 43,* 337–375.

WERKER, J. F. (1989). Becoming a native listener: A developmental perspective on human speech perception. *American Scientist, 77*(1), 54–59. [Republished in 1991: J. S. DeLoache (Ed.), *Current readings in child development* (pp. 99–106). Boston: Allyn & Bacon. Also republished in 1993: R. H. Wozniak (Ed.), *Worlds of childhood reader* (pp. 166–172). New York, NY: Harper Collins College Publishers. Also republished in 1994: J. S. DeLoache (Ed.), *Current readings in child development* (2nd ed., pp. 88–95). Boston: Allyn & Bacon.]

WESTEN, D. (1998). Unconscious thought, feeling and motivation: The end of a century-long debate. In R. F. Bornstein & J. M. Masling (Eds.), *Empirical perspectives on the psychoanalytic unconscious* (pp. 1–43). Washington, DC: American Psychological Association.

WHORF, B. L. (1956). Science and linguistics. In J. B. Carroll (Ed.). *Language, thought, and reality: Selected writings of Benjamin Lee Whorf.* Cambridge, MA: MIT Press.

WIEBE, J., MUN, P., & KAUFFMAN, N. (2006). *Gambling and Problem Gambling in Ontario 2005. Toronto: Responsible Gambling Council.* Retrieved from www.gamblingresearch.org/funding/fundingdetail .php?cid=2643&aid=111

WIENS, A. N., & MENUSTIK, C. E. (1983). Treatment outcomes and patient characteristics in an aversion therapy program for alcoholism. *American Psychologist, 38,* 1089–1096.

WILDER, D. A. (1981). Perceiving persons as a group: Categorization and intergroup relations. In D. L. Hamilton (Ed.), *Cognitive processes in stereotyping and intergroup behavior.* Hillsdale, NJ: Erlbaum.

WILKINSON, P., KELVIN, R., ROBERTS, C., DUBICKA, B., & GOODYER, I. (2011). Clinical and psychosocial predictors of suicide attempts and nonsuicidal self-injury in the Adolescent Depression Antidepressants and Psychotherapy Trial (ADAPT). *The American Journal of Psychiatry, 168,* 495–501.

WILLIAMS, J. E., PATON, C. C., SIEGLER, I. C., EIGENBRODT, M. L., NIETO, F. J., & TYROLER, H. A. (2000). Anger proneness predicts coronary heart disease risk: Prospective analysis from the atherosclerosis risk in communities (ARIC) study. *Circulation, 101,* 2034.

WILLIAMS, K. D., CHEUNG, C. K. T., & CHOI, W. (2000). Cyberostracism: Effects of being ignored over the Internet. *Journal of Personality and Social Psychology, 79*(5), 748–762.

WILSON, T. D. (2002). *Strangers to ourselves: Discovering the adaptive unconscious.* Cambridge, MA: Harvard University Press.

WINSTON, A.S. (1996). The context of correctness: A comment on Rushton. *Journal of Social Distress and the Homeless, 5,* 231–250.

WINSTON, A. S. (2003). The funding of scientific racism: Wickliffe Draper and the Pioneer Fund (review). *Journal of the History of Medicine and Allied Sciences, 58,* 391–392.

WINSTON, A. S. (Ed.) (2004). *Defining difference: Race and racism in the history of psychology.* Washington, DC: American Psychological Association.

WISE, R. A. (1978). Catecholamine theories of reward: A critical review. *Brain Research 152,* 215–247.

WITTGENSTEIN, L. (1953). *Philosophical investigations.* Oxford, UK: Blackwell.

WOJCIESZAK, M., & PRICE, V. (2009). What underlies the false consensus effect? How personal opinion and disagreement affect perception of public opinion. *International Journal of Public Opinion Research, 21,* 25–46.

WOLFF, E. (2007, September 23). Dual lives of twins separated at birth. *New York Post.* Retrieved from http://www.nypost.com/seven/09232007/ news/regionalnews/dual_lives_of_twins_separated_.htm?page=0

WOLPE, J. (1958). *Psychotherapy by reciprocal inhibition.* Stanford, CA: Stanford University Press.

WOLPE, J., & PLAUD, J. J. (1997). Pavlov's contributions to behavior therapy: The obvious and the not so obvious. *American Psychologist, 52,* 966–972.

WONPAT-BORJA, A. J., YANG, L. H., LINK, B. G., & PHELAN, J. C. (2012). Eugenics, genetics, and mental illness stigma in Chinese Americans. *Social Psychiatry and Psychiatric Epidemiology, 47,* 145–156.

WOOD, W. (1987). Meta-analytic review of sex differences in group performance. *Psychological Bulletin, 102,* 53–71.

WOODMAN, T., ROBERTS, R., HARDY, L., CALLOW, N., & ROGERS, C. H. (2011). There is an "I" in TEAM: Narcissism and social loafing. *Research Quarterly for Exercise and Sport, 82,* 285–290.

WORLD HEALTH ORGANIZATION. (2011). Global summary of the HIV/AIDS epidemic, December 2011. Retrieved from http://www.who.int/hiv/data/en/

WRIGHT, L. (1997). *Twins: And what they tell us about who we are.* New York, NY: Wiley.

WYNN, K. (1992). Addition and subtraction by human infants. *Nature, 358,* 749–759.

WYNN, K. (2000). Findings of addition and subtraction in infants are robust and consistent: Reply to Wakeley, Rivera, and Langer. *Child Development, 71,* 1535–1536.

WYON, D. P. (2000). Individual control at each workplace: The means and the potential benefits. In D. J. Croome & D. Clements-Croome (Eds.), *Creating the productive workplace.* New York, NY: Routledge.

YERKES. R. M., & DODSON, J. D. (1908). The relation of strength of stimulus to rapidity of habit formation. *Journal of Comparative Neurology and Psychology, 18,* 459–482.

YODER, M., TUERK, P. W., PRICE, M., GRUBAUGH, A. L., STRACHAN, M., MYRICK, H., & ACIERNO, R. (2012). Prolonged exposure therapy for combat-related posttraumatic stress disorder: Comparing outcomes for veterans of different wars. *Psychological Services, 9,* 16–25.

YOO, S., HU, P. T., GUJAR, N., JOLESZ, F. A., & WALKER, M. P. (2007, February). A deficit in the ability to form new human memories without sleep. *Nature Neuroscience, 10,* 385–392.

YOSHIKAWA, H., ABER, J. L., & BEARDSLEE, W. R. (2012). The effects of poverty on the mental, emotional, and behavioral health of children and youth: Implications for prevention. *American Psychologist, 67,* 272–284. doi:10.1037/a0028015

ZAHN-WAXLER, C., FRIEDMAN, R. J., COLE, P. M., MIZUTA, I., & HIRUMA, N. (1996). Japanese and United States preschool children's responses to conflict and distress. *Child Development, 67,* 2462–2477.

ZAJONC, R. B. (1965). Social facilitation. *Science, 149,* 269–274.

ZAJONC, R. B. (1968). Attitudinal effects of mere exposure. *Journal of Personality and Social Psychology, Monograph Supplement, 9*(2, Part 2), 1–27.

ZAJONC, R. B. (1980). Feeling and thinking. Preferences need no inferences. *American Psychologist, 35,* 151–175.

ZAJONC, R. B. (1984). On the primacy of affect. *American Psychologist, 39,* 117–123.

ZAVOS, H. M. S., GREGORY, A. M., & ELEY, T. C. (2012). Longitudinal genetic analysis of anxiety sensitivity. *Developmental Psychology, 48,* 204–212.

ZIMBARDO, P. (1971). The pathology of imprisonment. *Society, 9*(6), 4–8.

ZISSELMAN, M. H., & JAFFE, R. L. (2010). ECT in the treatment of a patient with catatonia: Consent and complications. *American Journal of Psychiatry, 167,* 127–132.

CREDITS

PHOTO CREDITS

CHAPTER 1 PAGE 2: Roger Viollet/Getty Images; **4:** Courtesy of the Psychology Department, University of Toronto; **7:** © kickers/iStockphoto.com; **8:** © pandapaw/Shutterstock; **9:** Sean Kilpatrick/The Canadian Press; **10:** © Adam Gregor/Shutterstock; **11:** Marc Pokempner/Getty Images; **14:** © Sepah News/Handout/Document Iran/Corbis.

CHAPTER 2 PAGE 16: © vario images GmbH & Co.KG/Alamy; **18 (top):** ABACAPRESS.COM/The Canadian Press; **(bottom):** © Fabrice/Fotolia; **19:** Chris Stowers © Dorling Kindersley; **20 (diagram, clockwise from top left):** Margo Harrison/Shutterstock; Yuri Arcurs/Shutterstock; © Vasko Miokovic Photography/iStockPhoto; Jupiter Images; © Pierre Perrin/Sygma/Corbis; **(bottom):** The Granger Collection, New York; **23:** © pjcross/Shutterstock; **24:** John M. Harlow, "Recovery from the passage of an iron bar through the head," Publications of the Massachusetts Medical Society, v. 2 (1868): 327–347. Courtesy of the Warren Anatomical Museum, Countway Library of Medicine, Harvard Medical School; **25:** Image Source/Images.com, IPSNStock Royalty Free; **28:** © Michael Keller/Corbis.

CHAPTER 3 PAGE 32: Laguna Design/Getty Images; **34:** © Yuri Arcurs/Shutterstock; **36 (top):** © EPA/Frank May/Corbis RF; **37:** © Franck Seguin/TempSport/Corbis; **39 (from top):** © Tomasz Trojanowski/Shutterstock; © Eric Isselée/Shutterstock; © Patrizia Tilly/Shutterstock; © Michael Monahan/Shutterstock; Jonathan Hayward/The Canadian Press; **42 (bottom):** © Dorling Kindersley; **43 (left):** © Booka/Shutterstock; **43 (right):** © Ruslan Semichev/Shutterstock; **44 (from left):** Peter Baxter/Shutterstock; Anatomical Design/Shutterstock; © Shutterstock; © Kurt Kormann/Corbis; **45 (from left):** © Roger Ressmeye/Corbis; Mark Herreid/Shutterstock; Volker Steger/Peter Arnold/Getty Images; Courtesy of Holland Bloorview Kids Rehabilitation Hospital; Magneto encephalography Brain Imaging Laboratory, http://archive.nrc-cnrc.gc.ca/eng/facilities/ibd/meg-lab.html, 2011. Reproduced with the permission of the Minister of Public Works and Government Services Canada, 2012.

CHAPTER 4 PAGE 51: Photo by: Cpl Tina Gillies, Canadian Forces Combat Camera, photo WT2010-0136-08 URL: http://www.combatcamera.forces.gc.ca/netpub/server.np?find&catalog=photos&template=detail_eng.np&field=item id&op=matches&value=22537&site=combatcamera. Department of National Defence, 2010. Reproduced with the permission of the Minister of Public Works and Government Services Canada, 2012; **52 (clockwise from top):** Patrick Watson/Pearson Education/PH; © Jacob Wackerhausen/iStockphoto.com; © Lou Dematteis/Reuters/Corbis; **54 (from left):** Maksym Bondarchuk/Shutterstock; Justin Maresch/Shutterstock; LoopAll/Shutterstock; An Nguyen/Shutterstock; **55 (top):** © Oleg Prikhodko/iStockPhoto; **(c):** Photo Researchers/Getty Images; **(bottom):** Mauro Fermariello/Photo Researchers; **62 (top):** Howard Shooter © Dorling Kindersley; **(bottom):** © Jared Milgrim/Corbis.

CHAPTER 5 PAGE 66: © Comstock/Thinkstock; **70:** © Fotolia; **71:** Hans Neleman/Getty Images; **72:** © Ace Stock Limited/Alamy; **74:** Paul Ekman, Ph.D./Paul Ekman Group, LLC; **76:** D. J. Peters/AP Images.

CHAPTER 6 PAGE 80: Abby and Brittany Hensel; **82 (from left):** © Shutterstock; Dr. G. Moscoso/Science Source/Photo Researchers; James Stevenson/Science Source/Photo Researchers; **83:** Courtesy of Robin Hanbury; **84:** David Mager/Pearson Learning Photo Studio; **86:** Barry Austin/Digital Vision/Thinkstock; **87 (top):** © Dorling Kindersley; **(bottom):** Forrest E. Baird, Ph.D.; **88:** Bruno De Hogues/Getty Images; **89:** Ellen B. Senisi; **91:** © Christina Kennedy/PhotoEdit.

CHAPTER 7 PAGE 94: © Lena S/Shutterstock; **96:** Thomas McAvoy/Time Life Images/Getty Images; **97:** © Hemera/Thinkstock; **98:** (clockwise from the top right): George Dodson/Pearson Education/PH College; © Cultura/Corbis RF; Vanessa Davies © Dorling Kindersley; © Dorling Kindersley; **99:** Ethel Wolvovitz/The Image Works; **101:** © Stephen Coburn/Sutterstock; **102:** © Jamie Grill/Corbis; **104 (top):** Silver Burdett Ginn; **(bottom):** © Anna Peisl/Corbis.

CHAPTER 8 PAGE 108: Chris Young/The Canadian Press; **111 (top):** © SW Productions/Brand X/Corbis-Brand X Pictures; **(bottom):** © Will Binns/Gaz Shirley Pacificcoastnews.com; **112:** Katelyn Metzger/Merrill Education; **113:** © Corbis Premium RF/Alamy; **114:** © Liao Yujie/Xinhua Press/Corbis; **(bottom):** © iStockphoto/Thinkstock; **117:** © Dorling Kindersley.

CHAPTER 9 PAGE 120: Andrew Vaughan/The Canadian Press; **122:** Erik Dreyer/Getty Images; **125 (from top):** Jurgen Vogt/Image Bank/Getty Images; © 2happy/Shutterstock; Muntz/Image Bank/Getty Images; **125 (bottom):** ©

Gregg Segal/Corbis Outline; **126:** J.P. Moczulski/Reuters/Landov; **128:** Dave King © Dorling Kindersley; **129:** Alan Keohane © Dorling Kindersley; **131 (top):** © Shutterstock; **(bottom):** © auremar/Fotolia.

CHAPTER 10 PAGE 134: China Photos/Getty Images; **136:** © Spencer Grand/PhotoEdit; **137:** © Moodboard/Corbis RF; **139:** © Fred Goldstein/Shutterstock; **140:** *Dream Caused by the Flight of a Bee Around a Pomegranate One Second Before Waking Up,* 1944 (oil on panel), Dali, Salvador (1904–89)/Thyssen-Bornemisza Collection, Madrid, Spain/Giraudon/The Bridgeman Art Library/Salvador Dali, Gala-Salvadro Dali Foundation/SODRAC (2012); **143:** Matthias Clamer/Getty Images; **144:** Chip Simons/Getty Images; **146:** © Yuri Arcurs/Shutterstock.

CHAPTER 11 PAGE 150: Photographer: Denis-Carl Robidoux; **152:** © Dorling Kindersley; **153:** © Dianna Sarto/Corbis; **154:** Steve Gorton © Dorling Kindersley; **155 (bell):** Courtesy of Madison Museum of Early Trades and Crafts; **(Jack Russell):** Tim Ridley © Dorling Kindersley; **(bowl of dog food):** Tracy Morgan © Dorling Kindersley; **(Parson Jack Russell Terrier):** Tracy Morgan © Dorling Kindersley; **156:** © Anton Gvozdikov/Fotolia; **158 (clockwise from top left):** © Stockbyte/Thinkstock; © James Shaffer/PhotoEdit; Sean Murphy/Getty Images; © Myrleen Pearson/PhotoEdit; **159:** © Jultta Klee/Corbis; **161:** © Richard Hutchings/PhotoEdit.

CHAPTER 12 PAGE166: © tovovan/Fotolia; **168:** Photodisc/Getty Images; **171:** © Corbis; **172:** © Dorling Kindersley; **173:** Photodsic/Getty Images; **174 (from left):** © Orjan F. Ellingvag/Corbis; Logan Mock-Bunting/Getty Images; © NASA/Corbis; © Corbis; © Ryan Pyle/Corbis; Dave Chidley/The Canadian Press; Paul Darrow/Reuters/Landov; The Canadian Press; The Canadian Press; The Canadian Press; The Canadian Press; **176:** © MedicalFR.com/Corbis.

CHAPTER 13 PAGE 180: China Photos/Stringer/Getty Images; **182 (clockwise from top left):** © Pokaz/Shutterstock; **(Chomsky):** © Christopher Felver/Corbis; **(Von Neuman):** Bettmann/Corbis; © argus/Shutterstock; © Yannis Ntousiopoulos/Shutterstock; **(Simon and Newell):** Bill Pierce/Time Life Pictures/Getty Images; © Lukiyanova Natalia/frenta/Shutterstock; **(Donders):** Hulton Archive/Getty Images; © Matka Wariatka/Shutterstock; © Valentin Mosichev/Shutterstock; © Anna Sedneva/Shutterstock; © Lev Dolgachov/Shutterstock; **(Piaget):** Hulton Archive/Getty Images; **183:** © Steve Cukrov/Shutterstock; **184 (clockwise from top):** Bill Burlingham/Prentice Hall School Division; © Dorling Kindersley; Laima Druskis/Pearson Education/PH College; David Mager/Pearson Learning Photo Studio; Andy Crawford © Dorling Kindersley; Pearson Education/PH College; Michael Heron/Pearson Education/PH College; EMG Education Management Group; **186:** Photo courtesy Aron K. Barbey; **189:** © Thomas Northcut/Digital Vision/Thinkstock; **190:** © STANCA SANDA/Alamy; **191:** © YinYang/iStockPhoto; **192:** Pearson Scott Foresman; Ian OíLeary © Dorling Kindersley; © Wolfgang Flamisch/Zefa/Corbis; Jay Penni/Prentice Hall School Division; **192 (left to right):** Pearson Scott Foresman; Ian O'Leary © Dorling Kindersley; © Wolfgang Flamisch/Zefa/Corbis; Jay Penni/Prentice Hall School Division; **193:** © Monart Design/Fotolia; **195:** Chad Ehlers/Stock Connection.

CHAPTER 14 PAGE 198: © Vinod Kurien/Alamy; **200 (from left):** © BananaStock/Thinkstock; © Yuri Arcurs/Shutterstock; © vgstudio/Shutterstock; **202:** Photodisc/SW Productions/Getty Images; **203:** © Andresr/Shutterstock; **204:** © Andresr/Shutterstock; **206:** © stockphoto.com; **208 (clockwise from top left):** © Julio Etchart/Alamy; © ZUMA Wire Service/Alamy; © ZUMA Wire Service/Alamy; Adrian Wyld/The Canadian Press; Sean Kilpatrick/The Canadian Press; **210:** © Somos Images/Corbis; **211 (woman):** © Yuri Arcurs/Shutterstock; **(monitor):** © Carla Donofrio/Shutterstock; **212:** Carolyn Kaster/AP/The Canadian Press.

CHAPTER 15 PAGE 216: Chris Jackson/Getty Images; **218:** AJPhoto/Science Source/Photo Researchers; **220:** AP Photo/Charles Dharapak; **222:** © Uguntina/Shutterstock; © Ralph A. Clevenger/Corbis; © Zhuda/Shutterstock; **223:** Irene Springer/Pearson Education/PH College; **224: (from left):** Andy Crawford © Dorling Kindersley; © David Arky/Corbis RF; © AVAVA/Shutterstock; Sven Hoppe/Shutterstock; © Julian Rovagnati/Shutterstock; **225 (top):** Steve McAlister/Image Bank/Getty Images; **(bottom):** © Polka Dot/Jupiter Images; **226:** UPI/Christine Chew/Landov.

CHAPTER 16 PAGE 230: © Studio_G/Shutterstock; **232:** Ray Kachatorian/Getty Images; **233:** © Shutterstock; **234:** Chris Pizzello/AP/The Canadian Press; **236:** Justin Slide © Dorling Kindersley; © Dorling Kindersley; **237 (top):** Frank

Greenaway © Dorling Kindersley; **(bottom):** © Dorling Kindersley; **238:** Georgia Kokolis/Getty Images; **241:** © Llin Sergey/Shutterstock; © image 100/Corbis RF; © Graeme Dawes/Shutterstock; **243:** Betsie Van der Meer/Stone/Getty Images.

CHAPTER 17 PAGE 248: Frank Gunn/The Canadian Press; **250:** Elisabetta A. Villa/Getty Images; **251 (from top):** © iStockPhoto; © Chris Schmidt/iStockPhoto; © Andresr/Shutterstock; © Pinkcandy/Shutterstock; © Francisco Romero/ iStockPhoto; © Leslie Banks/iStockPhoto; © Sophia Tsibikaki/iStockPhoto; © Carlos E. Santa Maria/Shutterstock; © Richard Lord/PhotoEdit; **251 Health care worker cards (top left to right):** © Chris Schmidt/iStockPhoto; © Andresr/ Shutterstock; © Pinkcandy/Shutterstock; **(middle left to right):** ©Francisco Romero/iStockPhoto; ©Leslie Banks/iStockPhoto; © Ladida/iStockPhoto; **(bottom):** ©Carlos E. Santa Maria/Shutterstock; **251 (bottom):** © Richard Lord/ PhotoEdit; **253:** © Jonathan Nourok/PhotoEdit; **255:** © Bill Aron/PhotoEdit; **257:** © Dana Bartekoske/iStockPhoto; © Arvid Emtegren/iStockPhoto; **258:** Clinton/Photodisc/Getty Images; **259:** AP Photo/Ric Feld.

CHAPTER 18 PAGE 264: © Yuri Arcurs/Shutterstock; **267:** Louie Palu/ The Canadian Press; **268:** © JGI/Blend Images/Corbis RF; **269:** © Elnur/ Shutterstock; **271:** © Bettmann/Corbis; **272:** © Randy Faris/Corbis RF; **273:** © YinYang/iStockPhoto; **274:** Trish Gant © Dorling Kindersley; **275 (clockwise from top left):** © Monkey Business Images/Shutterstock; © Zsoit Nyulazi/ Shutterstock; © Tatjana Strelkova/Shutterstock; © Stockbyte/Thinkstock; © Galina Barskaya/Shutterstock; © WavebreakmediaMicro; © Tips Images/Tips Italia Srl a socio unico/Alamy; © Monkey Business Images/Shutterstock; **276:** ananaimages/Corbis RF.

READINGS PAGE R1-1: © Skip Odonnell/www.iStockphoto.com; **R1-2, R1-4:** Galushko Sergey/Shutterstock **R2-1:** © Gina Sanders/Fotolia; **R3-1–R3-6:** © fotoblin/Fotolia; **R4-1–R4-2:** © Ana Blazic Pavlovic/Fotolia; **R5-1–R5-2:** © WoodyStock/Alamy; **R6-1–R6-2:** © xpixel/Shutterstock; **R6-3:** © doomu/ Fotolia; **R7-1–R7-2:** © shotsstudio/Fotolia; **R8-1–R8-2:** Comstock/Thinkstock; **R9-1 to R9-4:** David Lichtneker/Alamy Images Royalty Free; **R10-1–R10-2:** Jochen Schoenfeld/Shutterstock.

TEXT, TABLE, AND FIGURE CREDITS

CHAPTER 2 PAGE 26: Statistics Canada: Labour Force Survey, April 2012.

CHAPTER 5 PAGE 67: Genome Canada.

CHAPTER 7 PAGE 100: From Avenue Q. Copyrighted and reprinted here by permission of Avenue Q LLC.

CHAPTER 8 PAGE 115: Statistics Canada 2012.

CHAPTER 9 PAGE 123: Robert Plutchik, EMOTION: PSYCHOEVOLUTIONARY SYNTHESIS, Fig. "Plutchik's Emotion Wheel", © 1979 Individual Dynamics Inc. Reproduced by permission of Pearson Education, Inc.

CHAPTER 12 PAGE 170: Source: Official Voting Results, 39th General Election 2006, Table 7, Distribution of seats by political affiliation and sex, Elections Canada, 2006 and Official Voting Results, 41st General Election 2011, Table 7, Distribution of seats by political affiliation and sex, Elections Canada, 2011. This is an adaptation of the version available at www.elections.ca. Data reproduced with the permission of Elections Canada, but adaptation rests with the author.

CHAPTER 15 PAGE 224: From *Motivation and Personality*, 3rd by Maslow, ed. By Robert D. Frager and James Fadiman. © 1987. Reprinted and electronically reproduced by Pearson.

CHAPTER 16 PAGE 236: Mood Disorders Society of Canada. Adapted from the Statistics Canada CANSIM database http://cansim2.statcan.gc.ca, 105-1100, December 31, 2010.

CHAPTER 17 PAGE 261: OECD (2010), "Suicides," Health: Key Tables from OECD, No. 15. doi: 10.1787/20758480-2010-table10.

CHAPTER 18 PAGE 269: Adapted from Statistics Canada, Leading causes of death, by sex, numbers, 2007; Accessed at http://www40.statcan.gc.ca/l01/ cst01/hlth36a-eng.htm.

CHAPTER 18 PAGE 275: Canada (2011). General Social Survey—2010. Overview of the time use of Canadians.

READINGS PAGE R1-1: Mitja D. Back, Stefan C. Schmukle & Boris Egloff, *Psychological Science* (volume 19, issue 5), p. 2, copyright © 2008 by Sage Publications. Reprinted by Permission of SAGE Publications. **R2-1:** *Your Creative Brain: 7 Steps to Maximize Imagination, Creativity, and Innovation* by Shelley Carson, Boston, MA: Harvard Health Publications, 2010, 384 pp. ISBN: 978-0-470-54763-2. **R3-1:** "The Normative Implications of Biological Research" by Peter K. Hatemi and Rose McDermott, *PS: Political Science & Politics*, Volume 44, Issue 02 (April 2011), pp. 325–329. Copyright © 2011 American Political Science Association. **R4-1:** "Emotion" © 2012 American Psychological Association 2012, Vol. 12, No. 3, 437–441. **R5-1:** Hausmann, M. & Schober, B. (2012). *Sex and Gender Differences: New Perspectives and New Findings Within a Psychobiosocial Approach.Zeitschrift fur Psychologie*, 220, 56–60. © 2012 Hogrefe Publishing. All Rights Reserved. **R6-1:***Experimental and Clinical Psychopharmacology,* 2012, Vol. 20, No 1, 71–75. **R7-1:** "Emotion" © 2010 American Psychological Association 2010, Vol. 10, No. 5, 717–721. **R8-1:** "Decades Later, Still Asking: Would I Pull that Switch?" by Benedict Carey, *The New York Times,* July 1, 2008. **R9-1:** "Facebook Profiles Reflect Actual Personality, Not Self-Idealization" by Mitja D. Back, Juliane M. Stopfer, Simine Vazire, Sam Gaddis, Stefan C. Schmukle, Boris Egloff and Samuel D. Gosling, March 2010; vol. 21, 3: pp. 372–374, first published on January 29, 2010. Reprinted by permission of SAGE Publications. **R10-1:** "Psychology of Addictive Behaviors" © 2011 American Psychological Association 2012, Vol. 26, No. 1, 171–177.

INDEX

320